THE UNABRIDGED
JAMES DEAN
HIS LIFE AND LEGACY FROM A TO Z

THE UNABRIDGED
JAMES DEAN
HIS LIFE AND LEGACY FROM A TO Z

RANDALL RIESE

WINGS BOOKS
New York • Avenel, New Jersey

Copyright © 1991 by Randall Riese and RGA Publishing Group, Inc.

All rights reserved.

This 1994 edition is published by Wings Books,
distributed by Random House Value Publishing, Inc.,
40 Engelhard Avenue, Avenel, New Jersey 07001,
by arrangement with Contemporary Books, Inc.

Random House
New York • Toronto • London • Sydney • Auckland

Printed and bound in the United States of America

Library of Congress Cataloging-in-Publication Data

Riese, Randall.
    The unabridged James Dean : his life and legacy from A to Z /
Randall Riese.
        p.   cm.
    Originally published: Chicago : Contemporary Books, ©1991.
    Includes bibliographical references and index.
    ISBN 0-517-10081-9
    1. Dean, James, 1931-1955.   2. Motion picture actors and
actresses—United States—Biography.   I. Title.
PN2287.D33R54   1994
791.43'028'092—dc20
    [B]   94-6989
                                                                     CIP

8 7 6 5 4 3 2 1

ACKNOWLEDGMENT OF PERMISSIONS

Some of the material in this book was culled from the Warner Brothers Archives at
the University of Southern California. The material is copyrighted by Warner Brothers
and is reprinted herein with permission. Memorandums from George Stevens
reprinted with permission from George Stevens, Jr., and the George Stevens
Collection at the Academy of Motion Picture Arts and Sciences. Excerpts from
"Soliloquy on James Dean's 45th Birthday" by Derek Marlowe reprinted with the
permission of *New York* magazine, copyright © 1990 News America Publishing
Incorporated. Excerpts from *James Dean* by William Bast reprinted with permission
of Ballantine Books, a Division of Random House, Inc., copyright © 1956. Excerpts
from *The Whole Truth and Nothing But* by Hedda Hopper reprinted with permission
of Doubleday, a division of Bantam. Doubleday, Dell Publishing Group, Inc., copyright
© 1963. Material from *The Hollywood Reporter* reprinted with permission. Excerpts
from *See the Jaguar*, copyright © 1953 by N. Richard Nash. Copyright © renewed
1981. Caution: *See the Jaguar*, being duly copyrighted, is subject to a royalty. The
amateur performance rights are controlled exclusively by the Dramatists Play Service,
Inc., 440 Park Avenue South, New York, NY 10016. No amateur production of the play
may be given without obtaining, in advance, the written permission of the Dramatists
Play Service, Inc., and paying the requisite fee. Inquiries regarding all other rights
should be addressed to Bill Craver, Writers and Artists Agency, 19 West 44th Street,
Suite 1000, New York, NY 10036. The *Rolling Stone* cover reprinted with permission
from Straight Arrow Publishers, Inc., copyright © 1980. All rights reserved.

To Mark Goins and the little Toaster:
thanks for the good memorabilia.

CONTENTS

"Life is in color . . .
but black and white
is more realistic."
— Wim Wenders

ACKNOWLEDGMENTS

I would like to thank the following:

☆ Christopher Esposito, Neal Hitchens, and Linda Laucella for their warm and nurturing efforts to keep me healthy during the lengthy development of this work

☆ Jack Artenstein and Nancy Crossman for the opportunity

☆ Sylvia Bongiovanni for her encouragement and her selfless contributions to this work

☆ Howard H. Prouty, archivist of the Academy of Motion Picture Arts and Sciences, for his seemingly infinite knowledge of television history—and his willingness to share it

☆ And, for their varying contributions, the following:

The Academy of Motion Picture Arts and Sciences
The Academy of Television Arts and Sciences
Amy Adams, The Actors Studio
Leith Adams, University of Southern California, Warner Brothers Archivist
Corey Allen
Steve Allen
Michael Antonello
Nancy Artenstein
Carroll Baker
Christine Benton
Sherry Blackmon, the *Chronicle-Tribune*
Gilbert and Bernicia Carreira
Maxwell Caulfield
Hugh Caughell
Carol Christiansen, Doubleday Books
Collectors Book Store
Curtis Management
Bill Dakota
Matt DeHaven
The Directors Guild
The Fairmount Historical Museum
Irene Gilbert, Stella Adler Conservatory of Acting
Gigi Grajdura
Grant County Convention and Visitors Bureau
Michael Greaves, Random House
Maggie Hall, Santa Monica College
Diane Hanville
Julie Harris
Robert Headrick, Jr.
George Roy Hill
Don Hines, Chief Deputy Coroner, San Luis Obispo County

Gerilee Hundt
Angela Hynes
Bradley G. Kalos, Dramatists Play Service
Joy Kashiwagi
Aaron Kass
Kenneth Kendall
Gia Kourlas, *New York* magazine
Ed Lane
David Loehr
Beverly Long
Lillian Love, Santa Monica/Malibu Unified School District
Chaz MacRina, The Actors Studio
The Margaret Herrick Library
Joseph Messina
Yuji Mitani
Adeline Mart Nall
The National Academy of Recording Arts and Sciences
Patricia Neal
Judith Noack, Warner Brothers
Seita Ohnishi
Betsy Palmer
Bob Pulley
Lee Raskin
Cherry Rees
Bob Rees
Pam Richardson
Beulah Roth
Georgene Sainati
Carrie Schadle, *Rolling Stone* magazine
The Screen Actors Guild
The Screenwriters Guild
James Sheldon
Amy Shuster
Steffi Sidney
Ron Silverman, *The Hollywood Reporter*
Eleanor Speert, Dramatists Play Service
George Stevens, Jr.
Susan Tracy, Grant County Convention and Visitors Bureau
Jeannine Tudor
The University of Southern California, School of Cinema-
   Television
We Remember Dean International fan club
Kathy Willhoite
Lise Wood
Jeremy Williams, Warner Brothers

THE UNABRIDGED

JAMES DEAN

HIS LIFE AND LEGACY FROM A TO Z

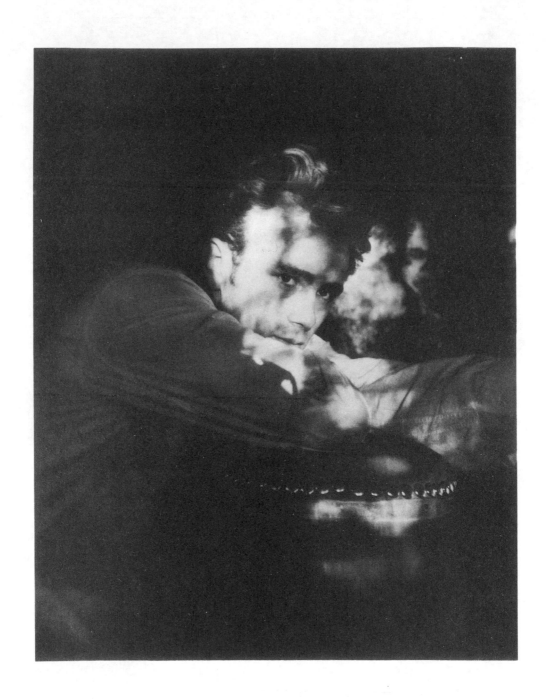

INTRODUCTION

The death of James Dean spawned a national epidemic of hysterical necrophilia, the extent of which had never before been seen in America. The mass mourning was packaged and marketed by enterprising businessmen who made up in acumen what they decidedly lacked in taste. They aimed their ghoulish products, all of which in some way offered a piece of the dear departed Dean, primarily at the teenage market. Faithful fans were encouraged to console themselves by purchasing Dean memorabilia such as buttons, badges, busts, medallions, and, perhaps most morbid, lifelike masks of Jimmy's face manufactured with a creepy concoction called Miracleflesh that were churned out and peddled at $30 a face. The macabre mentality was such that the masks could have been marketed with the slogan "It's so real you can touch it, kiss it, stick a cigarette in its mouth," and no one would have cried "Foul!" Fans were further prodded to mail in 50¢ and a self-addressed stamped envelope to receive a photograph of "Jimmy's resting place." And, when the wreckage of his Porsche was sent on a national tour, fans lined up to pay another 50¢—to sit behind the wheel of the crushed car.

Contrary, however, to the claims of cynics who denounced the Dean legend (or the Monroe or Presley legends, for that matter) as a fabrication of American capitalism, it wasn't the business community that created the hysteria (although, once started, the media, Warner Brothers included, helped to stir and spur it on). Rather it was a generation of young people who saw in James Dean a mirror image of themselves—or of what they most wanted to be. James Dean gave body, face, and voice to their pain, and they reciprocated with collective appreciation and adulation. The likes of Dean had never before been seen on a screen, and it was a revelation to many— male and female—to see a grown man cry with such open emotion, such naked *need*. And it wasn't the need for money, sex, or even the love of a good woman, but rather the simple need of a grown man who longed for the love of a man he could call his father. Critics of the period saw the name Kazan on the screen and insisted that Dean was another Brando. But the image of Marlon Brando grasping for father love is about as farfetched as that of James Dean "Stella"-ing his way through *A Streetcar Named Desire*. Brando busted out of his T-shirt, while Dean withdrew inside of his; Brando clenched his fist, while Dean clenched his face; Brando busted up the opposition, and so did Dean—but only when provoked, and he was always sorry for it afterward.

James Dean was also androgynous, probably the first movie actor with such an appeal. His body was slight, his facial features delicate, almost pretty, and he emoted feelings that were thought at the time to be feminine, but he did so with such powerhouse force that no one cast aspersions on his masculinity. James Dean's appeal had none of the limitations usually found in other actors. Men (straight and gay alike) and women wanted either to be like him or to be *with* him or a combination of the two.

On screen he was unobtainable, almost asexual. In *East of Eden* his primary object of affection wasn't Julie Harris; it was Raymond Massey. In *Rebel Without a Cause* he was in love with Sal Mineo just as much as with Natalie Wood, and he didn't make love to either of them. And in *Giant* he didn't want Elizabeth Taylor to go to bed with him as much as he wanted her to mother him and redeem him and tell him that he'd been a good boy. In real life he was unattached. As a lover he belonged to no one and everyone. And because he died young, he didn't live to disappoint.

> They wore what he wore. They walked as he walked. They played
> the parts they saw him play. They searched for answers they thought
> he was searching for. Some found a kinship they had never known
> before. Youth mourned itself in the passing of James Dean.
> Stewart Stern, *The James Dean Story*, 1957

Within a year after his death James Dean had arisen, Christlike, to become the biggest movie star in America, perhaps the world. But it wasn't really Dean. It was a distorted, adolescent vision of Dean, who had been killed not by a mere car crash but by the big-city pressures and fast living of Hollywood; by a mother who had died on him and a father who had deserted him; by a world of insensitive adults who couldn't hear no matter how loudly he shouted what had since become a teenage anthem: *"You're tearing me apart!"* This wasn't Dean. It was a James Dean impersonator.

He was a dead man overwhelmed by his legend. Under siege Warner Brothers (which still had *Giant* to release) proudly reported that it was receiving 5,000 to 8,000 fan letters a week. The letters, many of them addressed to Dean, contained common themes. They begged for the rerelease of *East of Eden* and *Rebel Without a Cause*. They demanded the release of *Giant* and threatened retaliation if a single frame of their hero was edited from the picture. They pleaded for photographs and, when bold, a lock of his hair or anything that he had personally owned or touched. People who had known Dean, even superficially, were bombarded with similar requests and were treated with respect and reverence. The legend spread with astounding alacrity, and its impact was felt in varying degrees in every community in the country. Teenage boys wore their James Dean smolder on their faces and their James Dean attitude in their jeans, and if they didn't have any angst of their own they adopted his; teenage girls fluttered and swooned over a corpse.

In 1956 a teenage girl wrote to columnist Dorothy Dix with a common dilemma of the period:

> I am 15 and in love. The problem is that I love the late James Dean.
> I don't know what to do.

Dix quipped in response, "Time heals all wounds."

In the meantime the legend continued to spread like an infectious disease. As more was learned about Dean, particularly regarding his maca-

bre obsession with death, rumors began to circulate that his death had been
a suicide. Columnist Dick Williams wrote at the time:

> The James Dean popularity boom continues to roll on and there is
> no indication that it has reached its crest. Interest in the late actor is
> greater now than it has ever been. By now the Dean delirium has
> moved into the controversial field, with many of his friends and
> former associates condemning the hubbub as being in the worst
> possible taste.

Not only did America's youth continue to mourn; the mourning degen-
erated from innocent idolatry to psychological affliction. Columnist Erskine
Johnson reported:

> Teenagers from coast to coast are trading the inside gossip that
> Jimmy Dean isn't dead. Their story insists that he escaped fatal
> injuries in that automobile crash, but is so horribly disfigured that
> he has secluded himself from the world. The story is in the same
> league with other Hollywood falsehoods that once insisted that
> Shirley Temple was a midget.

The publishing business, which had already exhausted its available
information on James Dean, eagerly exploited the new angle. Magazines
went as far as offering a reward for information leading to his whereabouts
and printing such propaganda as:

> James Dean was never killed! Informed sources, whose names we
> cannot disclose, say that Jimmy was horribly mangled by that "fatal"
> accident last year. He is said to be afraid for the world to see his
> now-marred face. So to you, Jimmy, we write this open letter: Come
> out of hiding. Your fans love you—will always love you, no matter
> what you look like! Remember, the face doesn't make the man.
> Besides, today plastic surgery is easy and simple and relatively
> painless. . . .

By mid-1957 the James Dean pandemonium had settled down into some
semblance of sanity. America's parents heaved a sigh of relief as the nails
were finally hammered into the coffin. Dorothy Dix had been partially right.
Time did heal this particular wound, but it was not time alone. It had been
nearly two years since Dean's death. His fans had grown older and had gotten
around to the business of living and loving and loving the living. Dean's last
film, *Giant,* had been released toward the end of 1956 and had played itself
out. As long as Dean was appearing, larger than life, on a movie screen in
Rebel Without a Cause and *Giant*—both of which were released after his
death—it had been difficult for many to accept his death, but now there were
no new Dean film appearances to anticipate. Finally the attention of America's youth had transferred in mass exodus to a hip-swiveling, lip-quivering
singer from the South by the name of Elvis Presley.

That should have been it. But it wasn't. The James Dean presence was
somehow always there, in spirit if not in form, quiet and steady perhaps, but
ingrained into the consciousness of a nation. No, a world. In September 1964

two teenage girls from northern Germany took their own lives. In their suicide note to their parents they wrote, "This was the anniversary of the day Jimmy died . . . ," and that, even though they had been too young to be impacted at the time of his death nine years before, their lives were now unbearable without him. The most tragic aspect of the James Dean legend is the untold number of suicides that have been committed in its name.

By 1974 the world had changed drastically since Dean's death. Elvis had been crowned king and had gotten fat from the consumption of his wealth; Marilyn had glowed with luminosity (and real talent) before she burned herself out; the Beatles had united a generation with music and then broken up; two Kennedys and a King had raised the hopes of a nation and then died; and Nixon—well, Nixon had lied.

James Dean seemed to recall simpler times, purer minds. He was a constant when nothing else seemed to be. He was always there with his half smirk, half smolder. He didn't get fat, his hairline didn't recede, and he still wore straight-legged blue jeans while the rest of the country had gone off on an ill-advised fashion tangent known as bell-bottoms.

Nineteen years had passed since his death, and those who had been James Dean's teenage fans in the 1950s had become adults with decision-making power at their fingertips, purchasing power in their pockets, and young children of their own in their homes. The publishing business shrewdly realized that the timing was right for a Dean revival aimed at this specialized market, and between 1974 and 1975 *six* new books about James Dean were published. The entertainment industry, trend sensers that they are, followed with a James Dean motion picture documentary, a television special, a British stage musical, and a song recorded by the Eagles, "James Dean," all produced between 1974 and 1977.

Today the demand for Dean memorabilia is higher (as is the price) than it has been in over 30 years. Peddled are replicas of the jacket he wore in *Rebel*, the Stetson he wore in *Giant*, copies of sunglasses he wore, and a litany of items bearing his usually brooding image: T-shirts, greeting cards, posters, buttons, satin pillows, puzzles, calendars, watches, porcelain plates, pins, shower curtains, clocks, and checkbook covers. Also marketed are purported patches of his blue jeans ("Now *you* can get into James Dean's jeans!") and strands of his hair.

The James Dean legend has grown to such enormous and complicated proportions that the memory of the man has metamorphosed into something that he himself would undoubtedly fail to recognize. Not only has his image been used repeatedly in movies and television shows to evoke immediate sentiments of nostalgia, rebellion, alienation, and/or cool (take your pick); it has also been plastered on billboards and print advertisements throughout the world to sell everything from spark plugs to tennis shoes. It is ironic, and somewhat fitting, that it was in the era of Ronald Reagan, his former co-star, that James Dean became a symbol to sell corporate America. It is interesting to speculate that, years from now, when memories of Reagan are largely relegated to stately presidential libraries and historical retrospectives, the image of James Dean will be perennially contemporary and the legend of James Dean will be perennially passed from generation to generation.

One final thing. James Dean, the legend, the icon, was also an actor—a simple fact but one that has somehow been forgotten or dismissed. Just take another look at *East of Eden*. Dean's work in that film offers one of the most astonishing performances in motion picture history. And *that* may be the biggest revelation of all.

James Dean, circa 1951–1952, by Joseph Abeles.

A

JOSEPH ABELES
Some of the first professional photographs ever taken of James Dean were shot by Joseph Abeles. The photos were taken in New York City circa late 1951 and early 1952.

"ABRAHAM LINCOLN"
Episode of the CBS television series "Studio One," in which Jimmy had a brief part as William Scott, a soldier from Vermont who is court-martialed after being caught asleep on guard. He is subsequently pardoned by his commanding officer, Abraham Lincoln. The program aired on May 26, 1952, was written by John Drinkwater, and starred Robert Pastene as Lincoln.

Dean aficionados frequently refer to this program as "Asleep on Guard."

MORT ABRAHAMS
Mort Abrahams, born in 1916, was the producer of "The Evil Within," a 1953 episode of the ABC television series "Tales of Tomorrow" in which Jimmy was featured. Abrahams later produced "I'm a Fool," a 1954 episode of the CBS series "General Electric Theater" in which Jimmy had a starring role.

He also was the executive producer of the television programs "Producer's Showcase" (1956) and "Suspicion" (1958) as well as "Target: The Corruptors" (1961) and "Route 66" (1962).

GERALD ABRAMS
Gerald Abrams was the co-executive producer of "James Dean," a 1976 made-for-television movie.

THE ACADEMY AWARDS
See THE OSCARS.

THE ACADEMY OF MOTION PICTURE ARTS AND SCIENCES
On January 24, 1983, the Academy of Motion Picture Arts and Sciences produced "A Tribute to James Dean," an evening of discussion, film clips, and a screening of *Rebel Without a Cause*. The tribute was held at the academy's Samuel Goldwyn Theater in Beverly Hills. Participating speakers included Martin Landau, Leonard Rosenman, Stewart Stern, Bill Bast, Beulah Roth, and Jim Backus. The event was coordinated by Doug Edwards.

The academy also houses the Margaret Herrick Library, an incomparable repository of information pertaining to the movies in general and movie personalities in particular (including Dean). The library is closed on Wednesdays (address: 333 South La Cienega Boulevard, Beverly Hills, CA 90212).

ACTING

> If anyone was ever dedicated to the art of acting, it was Jimmy. He had the greatest power of concentration I have ever encountered. He prepared himself so well in advance for any scene he was playing, that the lines were not simply something he had memorized—they were actually a very real part of him.
>
> Jim Backus, *Rocks on the Roof*

As an actor James Dean had several strengths, including his eyes, which expressed volumes of unspoken hurt and alienation; his power and intensity of concentration; his ingenuity at improvisation (Who could forget his use of the toy monkey and the milk bottle in *Rebel* or the piece of rope in *Giant*?); and his individual and unconventional technique. A typical Deanism, for example, involved his infamous preparation for a scene. Prior to shooting, Jimmy would frequently prepare himself by engaging in arduous physical exercise such as running and jumping up and down, much to the chagrin of the rest of the cast and crew, who waited on the set, tapping their feet and exercising their patience. This workout served to cast out Jimmy's inhibitions while simultaneously raising his energy level to perilous heights.

Hollywood is abound with specific tales of Jimmy's scene preparations. For the chickie-run sequence in *Rebel Without a Cause*, which concludes with Jimmy looking over a cliff at his dead rival (played by Corey Allen), Jimmy had the prop man paint the bitten part of an apple red, which Jimmy then tossed over the cliff as some sort of sacrificial stand-in to prepare himself emotionally for the tragedy. Also during *Rebel*, Jimmy refused to permit the standard use of tape on the floor to block a scene. He also prohibited the use of the directorial terms "roll 'em," "action," "quiet on the set," etc.—all for the sake of realism. While others were making a movie, Dean was re-creating life.

Another tale took place on the open set of *Giant* in Marfa, Texas. Intimidated prior to the shooting of his initial scene with Elizabeth Taylor, Jimmy shuffled away, stopped, unzipped his fly, and, in front of thousands of spectators, watered the dry Marfa soil with his *personal* garden hose. Apparently Jimmy thought that if he could expose himself to an aghast crowd of strangers he could certainly appear in a scene opposite Elizabeth Taylor!

Perhaps more than any of his other qualities, though, what James Dean possessed as an actor was the absolute poetic expressiveness of his body. Just take another look at the opening scene in *East of Eden*, in which he seemingly gets lost in the big city sidewalk, or the opening scene in *Rebel Without a Cause*, in which he lies in the fetal position in the middle of a neighborhood street, cradling that toy monkey. Arguably no actor in the history of motion pictures has used his body to better effect than James Dean.

THE ACTORS STUDIO

> I have made great strides in my craft. After months of auditioning, I am very proud to announce that I am a member of the Actors Studio. The greatest school of the theater. It houses great people like Marlon Brando, Julie Harris, Arthur Kennedy, Elia Kazan, Mildred Dunnock, Kevin McCarthy, Monty Clift, June Havoc, and on and on and on. Very few get into it, and it is absolutely free. It is the best thing that can happen to an actor. I am one of the youngest to belong. If I can keep this up and nothing interferes with my progress, one of these days I might be able to contribute something to the world.
>
> James Dean in a letter to his family in Fairmount, Indiana, 1952

In the 1950s the Actors Studio was *the* premier acting school in the United States. Helmed by Lee Strasberg, the studio gained prominence for its revolutionary teaching of "The Method" style of acting and worldwide notoriety for its star-studded list of alumni.

In the summer of 1952, along with his scene partner, Christine White, Jimmy auditioned for Strasberg and the Actors Studio. They performed a scene from an original play penned by White entitled "Ripping Off Layers to Find Roots." Approximately 150 aspiring young New York actors competed in this particular audition. Fifteen were eventually bestowed entrée. James Dean and Christine White were among the selected elite. Strasberg commented on the audition: "It seemed simple, easy, believable. [It had a] wonderful quality. Very much what we would like to see from people when they come to us." At that time Jimmy, age 21, became the youngest member in the history of the Actors Studio.

For Jimmy acceptance was a thrilling experience, the pinnacle of his young career. He was mostly out of work and starving, or a meal or two away from it, but at last he had something consequential to sink his teeth into.

The security, however, was short-lived. While at the studio Jimmy appeared in in-house productions of *End as a Man*, *The Sea Gull*, and *Aria da Capo*. He also read a scene from *Matador*, after which Strasberg critically and publicly lambasted Jimmy's performance. Shattered, Jimmy withdrew, and for a while he refused to attend further classes at the studio. When he did return, he audited classes and did not participate. He sat in his chair, slumped and sunken in his seat, absorbing everything, emitting nothing. As described by Elia Kazan, "[Dean sat] in a sort of poutish mess in the front row and scowled." As quoted in *A Player's Place* by David Garfield, Strasberg elaborated on Dean's acting:

> "It was my feeling that he didn't go far enough. It seemed . . . that he was not using enough of himself. He continued on the same level. . . . The work continued, [but] it did not make any progress that I remember or was aware of."
>
> Lee Strasberg, *A Player's Place* by David Garfield

Nevertheless the Actors Studio remains an important phase in the career of James Dean, as it was through the studio that *East of Eden* director Elia Kazan first became aware of him.

In the 1960s and through the 1980s the Actors Studio lost much of its original prestige. Actors like Marlon Brando, Montgomery Clift, and James Dean seemed to *belong* to the 1950s. And Lee Strasberg passed away in 1982, which ended an era.

During James Dean's membership the Actors Studio was housed in two locations: the top floor of the Anta Theatre, 245 West 52nd Street, from September 1952 to August 1954; and at Malin Studios, 1545 Broadway at West 46th Street, Room 610, from October 1954 to June 1955. Contrary to previously published reports, Jimmy did *not* attend the Actors Studio at its present location, 432 West 44th Street. The studio did not have its first session at that location until October 14, 1955, two weeks after Jimmy's death.

Star Alumni of the Actors Studio

Beatrice Arthur	Elia Kazan	Sydney Pollak
Carroll Baker	Martin Landau	Martin Ritt
Anne Bancroft	Cloris Leachman	Cliff Robertson
Marlon Brando	Sidney Lumet	Eva Marie Saint
Ellen Burstyn	Karl Malden	Kim Stanley
Jill Clayburgh	Walter Matthau	Maureen Stapleton
Montgomery Clift	Steve McQueen	Rod Steiger
Robert De Niro	Marilyn Monroe*	Joan Van Ark
Sandy Dennis	Patricia Neal	Jo Van Fleet
Bruce Dern	Paul Newman	Christopher Walken
Robert Duvall	Jack Nicholson	Eli Wallach
Sally Field	Carroll O'Connor	David Wayne
Jane Fonda	Al Pacino**	James Whitmore
John Forsythe	Arthur Penn	Gene Wilder
Julie Harris	Anthony Perkins	Shelley Winters
Dustin Hoffman	Sidney Poitier	Joanne Woodward

*Monroe was an honorary member of the studio.
**Pacino was rejected the first time he auditioned for the studio. He was accepted the second time.

Stars Rejected by the Actors Studio
George C. Scott
Barbra Streisand

ACTORS WHO HAVE PORTRAYED JAMES DEAN OR DEAN-BASED CHARACTERS

Surprisingly only a small number of actors have thus far attempted to portray James Dean or a Dean-based character. Far more, however, have strived to emulate Dean in a variety of other roles: Martin Sheen as a Charlie Starkweather–like killer in *Badlands*, Dennis Hopper in *The Last Movie*, Michael Parks in *Bus Riley's Back in Town* and almost anything else, Christopher Jones, Sean Penn, and many others in various roles. Among the actors who have attempted direct portrayals of Dean or a Dean-based character:

Stephen Brannan: *James Dean: A Dress Rehearsal* (play, 1984)
Paul Carr: "To Climb Steep Hills" (television, 1962)

Glenn Conway: *Dean* (British stage musical, 1977)
Stephen McHattie: "James Dean" (made-for-television movie, 1976)
Mark Patton: *Come Back to the Five and Dime, Jimmy Dean, Jimmy Dean* (stage play and movie, 1982)

NICK ADAMS

The biggest controversy in actor Nick Adams's short life seems to have been whether or not he was a friend of James Dean's. One camp in this not-so-great debate maintains that Adams was a gold digger, an ambitious actor who systematically befriended at least two stars—Jimmy and, later, Elvis Presley—in an effort to capitalize on their popularity. Nick Adams, this faction claims, was no friend to James Dean. The other camp says that Jimmy and Nick were not only friends but best friends—perhaps even *intimate* friends—and, for a period, roommates.

Representing the first camp is Beverly Long, an actress who appeared with Jimmy and Nick in *Rebel Without a Cause* and who had known both men since 1950. "Nick would have done anything to be a star," said Long. "Anything. Nothing would have stopped him. Nick would have given his life; he would have given anything to have been a friend of Jimmy Dean's. He tried *very* hard to be a friend of Jimmy's. [But] I always had the feeling that Jimmy knew that Nick was sucking it up. He knew that Nick was trying to hang on to him. It seemed so obvious to me, obvious to everyone else."

Beverly qualified her statement somewhat with the admission that she wasn't terribly fond of Nick Adams. "He was the only boy I ever had a fistfight with in my life. Nick was so horrid so many times. I remember punching him on the way to a location one time on the bus. Did Steffi [Sidney] tell you about the time he punched her in the ribs and said her line? Steffi had this one line [in *Rebel*]: 'Watch out, Buzz, he's got a chain!' [Steffi, by the way, got the line back.] He used to do really terrible things like that. He was impossible!"

The other camp is represented by Bill Dakota, a friend and former employee of Nick Adams's. "Nick Adams was Jimmy's closest friend. *Everybody* said he was riding on Jimmy's publicity, which was bullshit. Nick didn't like that riding on the publicity stuff. He was such a friend. Really great. He'd do anything for you. They were very tight. They built a car together!"

James Dean first met Nick Adams in 1950, when they both appeared in a television commercial for Pepsi-Cola. According to some reports, albeit unsubstantiated, Jimmy and Nick became friends and decided to pool their struggling actor resources by sharing an apartment in Hollywood. If true, the living situation was a brief one. Jimmy moved to New York in 1951, and when he returned to Hollywood in 1954 it was to star in *East of Eden*.

The next glimpse of the Jimmy/Nick "friendship" is gleaned from a scarcely seen wardrobe test prior to the shooting of *Rebel Without a Cause*. Their repartee is certainly improvised, certainly friendly, and forever enshrined on film. The joke was an inside one that involved studio honcho Jack Warner and a line from *Rebel*.

NICK: (wisecracking) Good-looking shirt.
JIMMY: (cautiously) Thanks.
NICK: Have it cleaned and burned.
JIMMY: (pause) Nice-looking hat . . .

The routine ended with both men breaking down in laughter. It seems that during preproduction preparations for the film, Jimmy ran into Warner who was engaged in giving a visiting VIP a walking tour of the lot. Jimmy halted before his boss and surveyed him up and down, taking particular interest in Warner's apparel. Then to Warner's astonishment, Jimmy delivered a line out of the *Rebel* script and walked away. The line? "Have it cleaned and burned."

On the set of *Rebel* Jimmy and Nick frequently entertained themselves and others by exchanging their impressions of Hollywood stars like Marlon Brando and Charlie Chaplin. Their skills were so adept, in fact, that they entertained the idea of taking their act on the road and into nightclubs.

What has incensed many people who knew James Dean is the flagrant manner in which Nick Adams acted *after* Jimmy's death. He penned several

Giving it a stab—two of the first Dean disciples, Nick Adams and Dennis Hopper.

fan magazine articles like "The James Dean I Knew" and "Hollywood's Mixed-Up Blabbermouths" for *Screen Star*, "Jimmy's Happiest Moments" for *Modern Screen*, and the most blatantly titled "Jimmy Dean, Why We Loved Him" for *Movie Life*. He was touted by the media as "the next James Dean" while the public was still mourning the loss of the genuine article. He dated Natalie Wood, shrewdly aware that the liaison would bolster his image and further link him to Dean. He made a personal appearance in Jimmy's birthplace of Marion, Indiana, for the world premiere of *The James Dean Story* (1957). He starred in the exploitively titled television series "The Rebel" (1959–1961). And when *Giant* director George Stevens needed someone to loop Jimmy's drunken Jett Rink banquet speech due to technical sound problems, Nick stuffed his cheeks with wads of gum to produce his best James Dean slur. Even Nick's friend and supporter Bill Dakota has admitted, "Nick *did* like to get attention."

Attention he got. Stardom, alas, he did not get. Nick Adams may have been able to put words into James Dean's mouth, but he was never quite able to fill his shoes. In 1968, after a career of mostly B-movies in which he played a litany of neurotic characters, Adams was found dead in his Beverly Hills home (address: 2126 El Roble Lane) from a drug overdose. He was 37 years old.

Nick Adams was born Nicholas Adamschock in 1931. He made his film debut in a mediocre Betty Hutton musical, *Somebody Loves Me* (1952). His other films include *Rebel Without a Cause* (in which he played gang member Cookie, 1955), *Mister Roberts* (1955), *No Time for Sergeants* (1958), *Pillow Talk* (1959), *Hell Is for Heroes* (1962), *The Hook* (1963), *Twilight of Honor* (Best Supporting Actor Oscar nomination, 1963), *Young Dillinger* (1965), *Monster of Terror* (England, 1966), *Frankenstein Conquers the World* (Japan, 1966), and *Fever Heat* (1967).

LEITH ADAMS
Archivist of the Warner Brothers Collection at the University of Southern California and co-author of *James Dean: Behind the Scene*, a book published by Birch Lane Press in 1990.

JUSTUS ADDISS
Justus Addiss was the director of "The Unlighted Road," a 1955 episode of the CBS television series "Schlitz Playhouse of Stars" that starred James Dean.

ADMINISTRATORS
Following James Dean's death in 1955, his father, Winton Dean, hired two Beverly Hills businessmen, Carl Coulter and William Gray, as the administrators of the James Dean estate. For their efforts Coulter and Gray were paid the sum of $3,039.28.

ADVERTISEMENTS

Since his death James Dean's image has been used in numerous print advertisements, in the United States and throughout the world, to promote such companies as:

Champion Spark Plugs
Chevron
Classic Potato Chips (South Africa)
Converse Shoes
Coors Beer
Daiwa Bank (Japan)
Dean's Men's Stores of South Africa
Krizia Uomo Cologne by Sanofi Beauty
    Products

Levi's (Japan)
Levi's (U.S.A.)
Maxell Tapes
National Westminster Bank of England
Patriot Banks of Boston
Rebel Cologne
Sportswear International (Italy)

THE AGENTS

The following is a chronological list of the agents and agencies James Dean was represented by:

Isabelle Draesemer, the Isabelle Draesemer Agency
Jane Deacy, the Louis Schurr Agency and the Jane Deacy Agency
Dick Clayton, Famous Artists Corporation

AIRPLANES

James Dean had a fear of flying. His first flight took place on March 8, 1954, when, at the age of 23, he was flown by Warner Brothers from New York City to Los Angeles to star in *East of Eden*. His belongings were wrapped in paper, tied with string.

EDDIE ALBERT

Eddie Albert co-starred in "I'm a Fool," a 1954 episode of the CBS television series "General Electric Theater." In that program James Dean portrayed Albert's character, the narrator, as a young man.

Eddie Albert Heimberger was born in 1908 and has been acting in motion pictures since his 1938 debut in *Brother Rat*. His some 75 films include *Roman Holiday* (Best Supporting Actor Oscar nomination, 1953), *Oklahoma!* (1955), *The Heartbreak Kid* (Best Supporting Actor Oscar nomination, 1972), and *The Concorde—Airport '79* (1979). Nevertheless he is probably most beloved for his role as Oliver Douglas in the successful television series "Green Acres" (1965–1971).

BEN ALCOCK

In 1950 Ben Alcock was an advertising executive at Pepsi-Cola who hired a struggling young actor to appear in a television commercial to be shot in Hollywood. The actor was James Dean, and it was his first professional acting job.

THE ALGONQUIN HOTEL

One of New York's designated historic landmarks, the Algonquin (address: 59 West 44th Street) is a turn-of-the-century hotel legendary for its Algonquin round table. In the 1920s some of New York's elite (Irving Berlin, George S. Kaufman, Harpo Marx, Dorothy Parker, Alexander Woollcott, et al.) used to congregate at the table to sharpen their tongues in marathon rounds of witty repartee. Over the years the hotel has continued to be popular among the distinguished movie (Sir Laurence Olivier, Sir John Gielgud) and literary crowd. Circa 1952–1953, James Dean frequently loitered in the Algonquin lobby, in a noble, albeit transparent, effort to refine his Hoosier roots.

"ALIAS JANE DOE"

CBS radio program that Jimmy had a bit part on during his struggling Hollywood period in 1951. The advertising agency that handled "Alias Jane Doe" was Foote, Cone and Belding, a company that was instrumental in Jimmy's early career.

COREY ALLEN

> I got cast in *Rebel* [and] I wanted to see what I was working with. And I was so awed by what I saw in *Eden*. I got to the set and I was scared, [but] I thought I'd take the bull by the horns and go introduce myself to Jimmy. He was sitting there and there were a bunch of kids around him and they were fawning over him. And I just walked over and said, 'I'm Corey Allen, we're gonna be working together.' And Jimmy said [without looking up] 'Yeah, hi.' And he refused to do more than that.
>
> Corey Allen

In the hearts and minds of millions Corey Allen was cast forever as Buzz Gunderson, James Dean's teenage adversary in *Rebel Without a Cause*. He got the part after director Nick Ray saw him in a Los Angeles stage play, *The Pick-Up Girl*. At the time, Allen was barely 20 years old and something of a Marlon Brando look-alike.

Born in 1934, Corey Allen did not attain much success as an actor, although he appeared in several films, including *The Mad Magician* (1954), *The Night of the Hunter* (1955), *Shadow on the Window* (1957), *Party Girl* (1958), *Private Property* (1960), *Sweet Bird of Youth* (1962), and *The Chapman Report* (1962). He has had far more success as a director, particularly as a television director. Allen's feature films include *Thunder and Lightning* (1977) and *Avalanche* (1978). His television credits include episodes of "Hill Street Blues" (for which he won a Best Director Emmy award), "Star Trek: The Next Generation," "J. J. Starbuck," "Murder, She Wrote," "Hunter," and the television movie "The Ann Jillian Story" (1988).

Corey Allen was interviewed about Jimmy in the documentaries *James Dean: The First American Teenager* (1976), *Hollywood: The Rebel James Dean*, and "Forever James Dean" (1988) and on episodes of the television programs "Entertainment Tonight" and "Show Biz Today" (both in 1985).

GLEN ALLEN

An honorary member of the We Remember Dean International fan club, Glen Allen was regarded as "the walking chamber of commerce" of Marion, Indiana, and "Mr. Marion" because of his contributions to the community. It was Glen Allen who, in 1980, was most instrumental in having an honorary star placed in Marion to commemorate the birth site of its most famous son, James Dean. Glen Allen died in 1983 at the age of 59.

STEVE ALLEN

> I discovered him by mistake. I was watching television one night in the early fifties. He was so *real*. My attention was *riveted*. He was speaking the language [of the hipster] so authentically, I couldn't believe he was an actor. I remember saying to my wife, Jayne, "I must find out who this director is because he's done a brilliant thing. He's hired some real street kid and made him learn those lines!" I couldn't believe he was an actor! The result was electrifying. [A few years later] as soon as I began to see his pictures in magazines, I said "That's the kid I saw. . . ."
>
> Steve Allen, 1991

Comedian, musician, singer, composer, and writer Steve Allen became engaged in a public feud involving James Dean in October 1956. Allen's nemesis in the battle was Ed Sullivan. At the time, Allen hosted NBC's "The Steve Allen Show" on Sundays at 8:00 P.M.; Sullivan hosted CBS's "The Ed Sullivan Show" in the same time slot. Just as the two television hosts battled to get Elvis Presley to appear on their shows (a battle won by Allen in June 1956), they battled to be the first to telecast a posthumous tribute to James Dean.

Competition between rival television shows was nothing new in the race for ratings. What *was* unusual was the way that the two hosts waged their war in the press. Allen contended that the idea of doing a Dean tribute show was *his*, a show that he planned to air on October 21, 1956. According to Allen, Ed Sullivan, or someone in his organization, pilfered the idea and scheduled a Dean tribute to air on October 14. Another aspect of the feud concerned which show would be allowed to televise preview clips of the then-unreleased and much anticipated film *Giant*. Yet another point of contention concerned Jimmy's aunt and uncle from Fairmount, Indiana, Ortense and Marcus Winslow, and which program they would appear on as special guests. Allen recently recalled, "We heard that the people in Fairmount had also been grabbed from under our noses. I suppose from Ed's viewpoint, that of the newspaperman, such a clearly unethical act was simply a matter of scooping the competition. We naturally didn't see it that way; I complained, loudly, and, I now realize, somewhat naively."

Allen subsequently bumped up his program to October 14, which pitted it head to head against the Sullivan show. Sullivan ended up getting the *Giant* clips and the Winslows, but Allen, a huge Dean fan, was not to be outdone. He recorded a tribute album, *The James Dean Story*, which was released on Coral Records in 1956. Years later he was interviewed about

Jimmy in the ABC documentary "James Dean Remembered" (1974).

In addition to "The Steve Allen Show" (1956–1961) on NBC, Allen, born in 1921, hosted "The Steve Allen Show" (CBS, 1950–1952), "Songs for Sale" (CBS, 1951–1952), "Talent Patrol" (ABC, 1953), "Tonight" (NBC, 1954–1956), "I've Got a Secret" (CBS, 1964–1967), and "The Steve Allen Comedy Hour" (CBS, 1967). He was also a panelist on the quiz show "What's My Line?" (CBS, 1953–1954).

ROBERT ALTMAN

In 1957, at the genesis of his prolific career, Robert Altman co-produced, co-directed, and co-edited *The James Dean Story*, which was billed by Warner Brothers as a documentary "tribute" to its dead star. Twenty-five years later Altman returned to the subject of James Dean with his stage and film productions of *Come Back to the Five and Dime, Jimmy Dean, Jimmy Dean* (1982).

Robert Altman's other films include *The Delinquents* (1957), *Nightmare in Chicago* (1964), *Countdown* (1968), *That Cold Day in the Park* (1969), *M*A*S*H* (Best Director Oscar nomination, 1970), *Brewster McCloud* (1970), *McCabe and Mrs. Miller* (1971), *Images* (1972), *The Long Goodbye* (1973), *Thieves Like Us* (1974), *California Split* (1974), *Nashville* (Best Director Oscar nomination, 1975), *Buffalo Bill and the Indians, or Sitting Bull's History Lesson* (1976), *3 Women* (1977), *A Wedding* (1978), *Quintet* (1979), *A Perfect Couple* (1979), *H.E.A.L.T.H.* (1980), *Popeye* (1980), *Streamers* (1983), *Secret Honor* (1984), *Fool for Love* (1985), *Beyond Therapy* (1987), *O.C. & Stiggs* (1987), *Aria* (1988), for which he was one of several contributing directors, and *Vincent & Theo* (1990). Recently Altman has directed several television movies, including "The Laundry Mat" (1985), "The Dumb Waiter" (1987), "The Room" (1987), and "The Caine Mutiny Court Martial" (1988).

AMBULANCE

The ambulance that rushed James Dean's body from the scene of the accident to the Paso Robles hospital on September 30, 1955, was a two-tone Buick driven by Cholame, California, businessman Paul Moreno. It was the only ambulance in Cholame. The cost of transportation? $56.14.

"AMERICAN REBEL"

"American Rebel" is the theme song of the Cinemax cable documentary "Forever James Dean" (1988). It was written by George Elworthy and sung by Chris Busone.

JAMES AMICK

James Amick was an Indiana doctor after whom Winton and Mildred Dean named their son, James.

STEVE AMM

In 1989 a singer by the name of Steve Amm was being hyped as "the James

Dean of country music." Unfortunately, however, no one at the National Academy of Recording Arts and Sciences or at the Academy of Country Music has ever heard of him—or his music.

ERNIE ANDERSON
Ernie Anderson was the narrator of "James Dean: An American Original," a half-hour tribute that aired on the television series "Hollywood Close-Up" in 1983.

PHILIP W. ANDERSON
Phil Anderson was one of the assistant editors of George Stevens's massive production, *Giant*, for which he received a 1956 Oscar nomination. Anderson was again nominated for a Best Editing Oscar the following year for his work on *Sayonara* and in 1961 for *The Parent Trap*.

SHERWOOD ANDERSON
"I'm a Fool," a 1954 episode of the CBS television series "General Electric Theater," which starred James Dean and Natalie Wood, was based on a short story by Sherwood Anderson.

URSULA ANDRESS
> Jimmy Dean is studying German so that he can fight with Ursula Andress in two languages. Jimmy says he likes Ursula because she talks back.
>
> *The Hollywood Reporter*, August 12, 1955

Swiss-born Ursula Andress's penchant for talking back was not the only characteristic that attracted James Dean to her. There was her directness, her leanings toward existentialist philosophy, and, obviously, her looks. In 1955 Ursula Andress was blond, buxom, and blossoming with beauty, youth, and promise.

In 1955 Ursula Andress was also 19 years old and freshly imported by Paramount from Rome after appearing in an Italian picture, *The Loves of Casanova*. Almost immediately upon arrival in Los Angeles she was dubbed by some clever press agent or columnist as "the female Marlon Brando." And with her short-cropped hair and full, pouting lips, she did resemble Brando, who was, at the time, the biggest name in Hollywood. This resemblance, of course, did not go unnoticed by Jimmy, who had an obsession with Brando for years.

Further, Ursula provided Jimmy with a challenge. As Beulah Roth, a friend of Jimmy's, recently recalled, "One day Jimmy came to me and said, 'I was with Ursula Andress last night, and she kept talking about existentialism. What is it?' I said, 'Jimmy, I can't explain in a paragraph what it is.' I knew that Ursula had been in Paris. I used to see her with Jean-Paul Sartre and that whole crowd. Anyway, I tried to explain to him what it was." And, according to Bill Bast, another friend of Jimmy's, it was in Ursula Andress that Jimmy met his intellectual match.

Ursula Andress, "the female Brando," attended a Westwood screening of *Rebel Without a Cause* with James Dean—the week of his death. They are pictured here together at another function.

Composer Leonard Rosenman attributed Dean's attraction to Andress to another factor: "[When] I was introduced to her they were swimming at a friend's pool, and she looked like Jimmy. I felt she was kind of a female Jimmy. I thought, 'My gosh, he's going with a mirror image.' "

So while she took lessons in English, and Hollywood twiddled its collective thumbs and pondered over what to do with her, Ursula made the

nightlife rounds of the Villa Capri, Don the Beachcombers, and other spots
with Jimmy Dean. It was a volatile, futile relationship. At the time, Ursula
confided to writer Joe Hyams:

> "Jimmy . . . come by my house one hour late. He come in room like
> animal in cage. Walk around and sniff of things. . . . We go hear
> jazz music and he leave table. Say he going to play drums. He . . . no
> come back. I don't like to be alone. He come by here later with
> motorsickle. Say he sorry and ask if I want see motorsickle. We sit on
> walk in front of motorsickle and talk until five. He nice but only
> boy."

In early September 1955 Ursula terminated the relationship with the
"boy" star five years her senior. The last time she saw Jimmy was a few days
before his death. He drove over to her house to show off his new toy, a
Porsche. Then, a few nights later, the news arrived. Ursula rushed over to the
home of Sanford and Beulah Roth. Said Beulah, "She was very devastated.
My husband didn't come home until the next morning. And Ursula stayed in
the other twin bed. She just wanted to be with somebody who was close to
Jimmy." One Hollywood trade paper reported: "No one mourned his death
more than his ex-sweetheart Ursula Andress, who wept hysterically and
blamed herself for the actor's death, declaring that she wished she hadn't
broken off their romance a few weeks ago. She cried, 'I tried to understand
him, but I just couldn't make it work.' " She also lamented that Jimmy
longed for "somebody to understand him" and that he was "always asking for
advice." The press wasn't entirely sympathetic toward Andress. One fan
magazine, *Hush, Hush*, proposed shamelessly, "His [Jimmy's] rejection that
September afternoon by Ursula led him to an act that was inevitable—
suicide!"

Shortly after Jimmy's death Ursula married actor John Derek, a union
that lasted for seven years. (Derek, of course, subsequently became involved
with Linda Evans, and later, Bo Derek.) Ursula then had an eight-year affair
with actor Jean-Paul Belmondo, followed by a shorter pairing with actor
Harry Hamlin, with whom she had a son.

The film career of Ursula Andress has been colorful, though hardly on
a par with that of Brando, her one-time male counterpart: *Dr. No* (1962),
Four for Texas (1963), *Fun in Acapulco* (1963), *She* (1965), *Nightmare in the
Sun* (1965), *What's New, Pussycat?* (1965), *Up to His Ears* (1965), *The Tenth
Victim* (1965), *Once Before I Die* (1965), *The Blue Max* (1966), *Casino Royale*
(1967), *The Southern Star* (1969), *Perfect Friday* (1970), *Red Sun* (1972), *Five
Against Capricorn* (1972), *The Life and Times of Scaramouche* (1976), *The
Loaded Guns* (1976), *The Sensuous Nurse* (1976), *The Fifth Musketeer* (1979),
and *Clash of the Titans* (1981).

Over the years Andress has been relatively quiet about her relationship
with James Dean, but she did appear for an interview in a 1983 episode of
"Hollywood Close-Up" called "James Dean: An American Original."

PIER ANGELI

While Ursula Andress was strong, aggressive, outspoken, and practical, her predecessor, Pier Angeli, was fragile, prim, shy, and romantic. But there *was* a common denominator in the women that Hoosier farm boy James Dean found most attractive: they were foreign-bred and -born. Women who typified Hollywood's standard of beauty at the time, all-American dream queens like Betty Grable, Marilyn Monroe, Terry Moore, and others, did little for him. Like Brando, Jimmy was intrigued by dark corners and exotic women.

Pier Angeli was born Anna Maria Pierangeli on June 19, 1932. After some success in Italian films like *Tomorrow Is Too Late* (1950) and *Tomorrow Is Another Day* (1951), Pier Angeli was discovered by writer Stewart Stern and flown to Hollywood to star in *Teresa* (1951). The film was a success, and a flurry of films followed. In 1954 Pier was cast by Warner Brothers opposite Paul Newman in *The Silver Chalice*. At the same time, on the same lot, relatively unknown actor James Dean was making his official film debut in *East of Eden*. One day, during a break from shooting, Jimmy wandered over to the set of *Chalice* to meet with Newman, his old friendly foe from New York. It was then that he met Pier Angeli.

There was speculation at the time, and over the years, that the James Dean/Pier Angeli romance was strictly publicity propagated by Warner Brothers. The evidence, however, suggests otherwise.

> I could hear what went on in his quarters—through the walls. What went on was Pier Angeli. But clearly that didn't go well for Dean either. I could hear them *boffing*, but more often arguing through the walls.
>
> director Elia Kazan, who roomed next to Dean
> during the filming of *East of Eden*

Likely what they were arguing about most often was Pier's mother, Mrs. Luigi Pierangeli, and her staunch disapproval of Jimmy. Jimmy moaned to reporters that while Pier was indeed a rare and genuine person, she was also a confused one with an unfortunate penchant for listening to too many advisors. Still, for a while, Jimmy and Pier sneaked out on dates to the beach, to the Hollywood hills, to a movie screening. Years later Pier sold the story of Jimmy's Romeo and her Juliet to the *National Enquirer*, although it is difficult to discern how much of it had been colored by nostalgia:

> "We used to go to the California coast and stay there secretly in a cottage on a beach far away from all prying eyes. We'd spend much of our time on the beach, sitting there or fooling around just like college kids. We would talk about ourselves and our problems, about the movies and acting, about life and life after death. We had complete understanding of each other. Sometimes on the beach we loved each other so much we just wanted to walk together into the sea holding hands because we knew then that we would always be together. We didn't need to be in the gossip columns or be seen at the big Hollywood parties. We were like kids together and that's the way

Angeli: "James Dean is a fine
young man, a sensitive
artist, and a person of fine
intellect."

we both liked it. Sometimes we would just drive along and stop at a hamburger stand for a meal or go to a drive-in movie. It was all so innocent and so emphatic."

Nevertheless, Mrs. Pierangeli prevailed, and suddenly, without warning, on October 4, 1954, Pier announced her engagement to singer Vic Damone. As Hedda Hopper mused at the time, "Another surprised party was actor James Dean who as recently as last Wednesday escorted Pier to the premiere of *A Star Is Born* and had been her constant companion since they met a few months ago." As for Damone, he had been dating Joan Benny, comedian Jack Benny's daughter. Among those who attended the lavish storybook wedding, which took place on November 24, 1954, were Debbie Reynolds (Angeli's closest friend), Ann Miller, and Dean Martin. *The Hollywood Reporter* also noted that "Jim Dean, who used to date Pier, watched the Angeli-Damone wedding a-straddle his motorcycle across from St. Timothy's [Church]." Over the years legend has added fuel to the proverbial fire that when the newlyweds exited the church Jimmy gunned the engine of his motorcycle in a cry of anguish. At the time, however, Jimmy was decidedly flippant when he remarked to reporters:

"I figure that when I went back to New York after finishing *East of Eden*, her family and friends got her ear and changed her mind about me. I won't try to pretend I'm not sorry. Pier's still okay with me. She broke the news to me the night before she announced her engagement but she wouldn't tell me who the guy was. I was floored when I learned it was Vic Damone. Oh, well, maybe she likes his singing."

It has never been detailed exactly why Pier suddenly disposed of Jimmy and married Damone. Speculation, however, has abounded. Writer Joe Hyams claimed in his 1973 book *Mislaid in Hollywood* that he saw Pier at Jimmy's house in September 1955 and that Jimmy blurted out to him that Pier was going to have a baby. According to Hyams, Jimmy then started to cry, so he took and held Jimmy in his arms. Two days later, according to Hyams, Jimmy was dead. Perhaps time, however, had confused Hyams's account. Pier's baby had been born two months before Jimmy's death. What *is* curious is that the baby, Perry Rocco Luigi Damone, was born on July 21, 1955—only eight months after Pier's sudden and unexpected marriage to Vic Damone. It's also interesting to note that Pier had still been seeing Jimmy as late as two weeks before her marriage.

In January 1956, according to press reports, Pier tumbled down the stairs of her Bel Air home and broke her ankle. In December 1956 she suffered a miscarriage. In August 1957 she separated from Damone, and in November 1958 she filed for divorce, charging "great mental anguish" and insane jealousy. The divorce was granted. In April 1959 Dean's old nemesis, Mrs. Pierangeli, launched a bitter and public attack on Damone. She charged that he had beaten Pier and had threatened to kill her. "On the night of February 15, 1959," she told reporters, "he struck and choked my daughter. He ambushed her that night. He hid in the dark outside her house and when she came home he dragged her out of the car and beat her." Damone, in turn, denied the charges and denounced his former mother-in-law: "All I can say is she's sick." In late October 1959 Damone sent police rushing to Pier's home "to prevent her from injuring herself." According to Damone, Pier had threatened to slash her wrists. When the police arrived, however, they found no suicide attempt.

For the next six years Damone and Angeli were in and out of court, fighting over the custody of their son, Perry. Angeli once carried Perry off to Europe, defying a court order; Damone was once charged with kidnapping. The charges and countercharges were endless. It was an ugly struggle. In court in 1965 Pier retracted previous statements that Damone had beaten her after their divorce. Eventually she was awarded custody.

In 1962 Angeli married bandleader Armando Trotajoli, whom she subsequently divorced in 1966. Later Pier lamented to the press:

"Jimmy is the only man I ever loved deeply as a woman should love a man. I never loved either of my husbands the way I loved Jimmy. . . . I would lie awake in the same bed with my husband, think of my love for Jimmy and wish it was Jimmy and not my husband who was next to me. I had to separate from my husbands because I don't think one can be in love with one man—even if he is dead—and live with another."

Interestingly, Angeli, nicknamed "Miss Pizza," was up for the part of Juana, Dennis Hopper's wife in *Giant*. She also ended up starring in *Somebody Up There Likes Me*, the 1956 Rocky Graziano biopic that Dean was slated to star in.

After such a promising start the film career of Pier Angeli declined quietly into mediocrity. Her other films include *The Light Touch* (1951), *The Devil Makes Three* (1952), *The Story of Three Loves* (1953), *Sombrero* (1953), *The Flame and the Flesh* (1954), *Santerella* (Italy, 1954), *Somebody Up There Likes Me* (1956), *Port Afrique* (England, 1956), *The Vintage* (1957), *Merry Andrew* (1958), *S.O.S. Pacific* (1960), *The Angry Silence* (England, 1960), *Musketeers of the Sea* (Italy, 1960), *White Slave Ship* (Italy, 1962), *Sodom and Gomorrah* (Italy, 1963), *Battle of the Bulge* (1965), *Spy in Your Eye* (Italy, 1966), *Missione Morte* (Italy, 1966), *Per Mille Dollari al Giorno* (Italy, 1966), *Shadow of Evil* (1966), *Red Roses for the Feuhrer* (Italy, 1967), *One Step to Hell* (1967), *Vive America* (Spain, 1968), *Les Enemoniades* (Spain, 1970), *Every Bastard a King* (Israel, 1970), *Nelle Pieghe della Carne* (1971), and *Octaman* (1971).

In 1971, after making an X-rated picture in Italy called *Addio, Alexandra* (*Love Me, Love My Wife*), Pier returned to Hollywood with the hope of landing a comeback role in Paramount's *The Godfather* (1972). However, Pier did not get the part, and, a short time later, in September 1971, she died from an overdose of barbiturates at her apartment in Los Angeles (address: 355 South McCarty Drive). She was 39 years old.

KENNETH ANGER

Born in 1929, Kenneth Anger is an independent filmmaker and author who has attained fame with his classic tales of Hollywood debauchery, *Hollywood Babylon* and its sequel, *Hollywood Babylon II*. Anger incited the wrath of Dean fans with the latter, in which he contended, among other things, that Jimmy was a masochist with a preference for cigarette burns, gay bars, beatings, boots, belts, and bondage scenes.

MICHAEL ANSARA

Actor Michael Ansara was the co-star of "Hill Number One," a 1951 presentation of "Family Theatre" that featured unknown actor James Dean.

Born in 1922, Ansara appeared in several films, including *Action in Arabia* (1944), *The Robe* (1953), *The Ten Commandments* (1956), and *Guns of the Magnificent Seven* (1969). He has also starred in the television programs "Broken Arrow" (1956–1960) and "Law of the Plainsman" (1959–1962).

JOSEPH ANTHONY

Joseph Anthony was an Actors Studio member who appeared with James Dean in a studio production of Chekhov's *The Sea Gull*.

Anthony, born in 1912, appeared onstage in several plays, including *The Country Girl* (1951), *Camino Real* (1953), and *Anastasia* (1954).

One of the most prolific directors in the history of the theater, Anthony was nominated for Tony awards for *The Lark* (1956), *A Clearing in the Woods* (1957), *The Most Happy Fella* (1957), *The Best Man* (1960), *Rhinoceros* (1961), and *110 in the Shade* (1964). He also directed several films and later worked as a professor of theater arts at New York State University.

THE ANTOINETTE PERRY AWARD

See THE TONY AWARDS.

KIRA APPEL

Kira Appel was a French journalist who met Jimmy on the set of *Giant* in 1955. Kira described their initial encounter to *Movieland* writer Vi Swisher:

> "He was standing apart from the rest of the actors. . . . Immediately I sensed a oneness with him, as if his thoughts and feelings were my own. Soon I noticed a Mexican actress go up and exchange a few words with him. . . . I approached her and asked her to present me to James Dean. She . . . took me to him and said very simply, 'Madame Appel is French. She would like to know you.' . . . James turned and looked directly into my eyes. Without acknowledging the introduction, he exploded a question that hit me like a bolt from the blue. 'Did you ever know Harry Baur?' he demanded. I was stunned. The late Harry Baur had been one of France's greatest actors, a superb artist. But that was twenty years ago. Never had I so much as heard his name mentioned in Hollywood."

The two became friends, and Jimmy was a frequent guest at the home Kira shared with her husband, Robert. To Jimmy, Kira became something of a tutor, coaching him in the social graces, introducing him to artists and musicians of importance. On her former apprentice, Appel told Swisher:

> "He had no small talk to use as protective 'verbal drapery' to clothe a hypersensitive nature. In his soul he had a deep respect, a reverence for truth and honesty. His simple honesty tore the truth out of him, often shocked people and even made him appear rude—to some."

JOE ARCHER
Joe Archer is the Indiana native who penned the fictional article "Here Is the Real Story of My Life by James Dean As I Might Have Told It to Joe Archer," which is on file at the Marion, Indiana, Public Library.

ARTHUR ARENT
Arthur Arent wrote the teleplay of "The Thief," a 1955 episode of the ABC television program "The U.S. Steel Hour," which co-starred James Dean. Arent based his script on a play by Henri Bernstein.

ARIA DA CAPO
James Dean appeared in an Actors Studio production of Edna St. Vincent Millay's *Aria da Capo*. The play was directed by Fred Stewart. Jimmy portrayed the role of Pierrot.

ARMED SERVICES
After turning 18 in 1949, Jimmy registered for the draft in Fairmount, Indiana. Reportedly, due to religious objections and a physical handicap (nearsightedness), Jimmy was exempted from military duty. Years later, though, he told friends that he had dodged the draft by telling the local recruiters "You can't draft me, I'm homosexual!" In 1976 Jimmy's friend Bill Bast told *The Advocate*, the national gay newspaper: "When Jim got his draft notice, he, like any other intelligent human being, would have done anything to get out of going into the service. So, he wrote a letter saying that he was a homosexual, and he was deferred." Jimmy's explanation to another friend: "I kissed the doctor."

"ARMSTRONG CIRCLE THEATRE"
"Armstrong Circle Theatre" was a television drama series that ran on Tuesday nights on NBC from 1950 to 1957 and on Wednesday nights on CBS from 1957 to 1963. It was sponsored by the Armstrong Cork Company. Jimmy appeared in an episode entitled "The Bells of Cockaigne." It aired on November 17, 1953.

ART
James Dean was a talented amateur artist. Growing up, encouraged first by his mother, and then by his aunt Ortense, Jimmy drew and painted numer-

ous farm animals and landscapes of Fairmount. He was also adept with watercolors and at cartoon caricatures and works of sculpture. His works include a faceless sculpture he dubbed *Self*, an oil painting entitled *Man in Woman's Womb*, a sketch depicting a man as a human ashtray, and a sketch entitled *The Composer*. Jimmy frequently gifted his friends with his works of art, including a painted orchid he presented to his high school teacher, Adeline Nall.

ARTISTS WHO HAVE INTERPRETED THE DEAN IMAGE

Over the years hundreds of artists have used the James Dean image as a subject for their work. The following is a selective list of some of the best:

David Bull	Kenneth Kendall	Mike Shaw
Michael Faure	Ed Lane	Dante Volpe
Steve Gulbis	Yasuo Mizui	Andy Warhol
Mark Heckman	William Moore	Scott Wilson
Gottfried Helnwein	Ocampo	

El Torero Muerto: a fantasy on the death of James Dean by Kenneth Kendall.

The Torn Poster by Kenneth Kendall.

Untitled Dean by Ed Lane.   Untitled Dean by Ed Lane.

TED ASHTON
Ted Ashton was the Warner Brothers studio publicist on *East of Eden* and
Giant.

"ASLEEP ON GUARD"
See "ABRAHAM LINCOLN."

MARY ASTOR
Mary Astor co-starred in "The Thief," a 1955 episode of the ABC television
series "The U.S. Steel Hour," which co-starred James Dean. One of Hollywood's all-time leading ladies, Astor was not used to being upstaged and later
wrote in her autobiography, "Jimmy Dean, in his quiet, thoughtful, mumbling way, got the notices. Paul [Lukas] and I were 'also in the cast.' "
    Mary Astor, born Lucile Langhanke in 1906, has made a plethora of
motion pictures, including such silent films as *The Beggar Maid* (1921), *Beau
Brummel* (1924), *Don Q Son of Zorro* (1925), and *Don Juan* (1926); her sound
films include *Ladies Love Brutes* (1930), *Red Dust* (1932), *Dodsworth* (1936),
The Prisoner of Zenda (1937), *The Hurricane* (1937), *The Great Lie* (Best
Supporting Actress Oscar, 1941), *The Maltese Falcon* (1941), *The Palm Beach*

Story (1942), *Meet Me in St. Louis* (1944), *Little Women* (1949), *Return to Peyton Place* (1961), *Hush . . . Hush, Sweet Charlotte* (1964), and many others.

Still, she is perhaps best known for her infamous extramarital affair with playwright George S. Kaufman circa 1935. The relationship was detailed extravagantly in Astor's diary, which was leaked to the press. On Kaufman, Astor wrote, "Was any woman happier? It seems that George is just *hard* all the time. I don't see how he does it, he is perfect!"

ASTOR THEATER

The Astor Theater was the New York movie theater where *East of Eden* premiered on March 9, 1955, in a celebrity benefit for the Actors Studio. Marilyn Monroe, Milton Berle, Sammy Davis, Jr., Elia Kazan, John Steinbeck, Jack Warner, and others were in attendance. James Dean was not. The following day *Eden* opened at the Astor to the general public.

Several months later, on October 26, 1955, *Rebel Without a Cause* premiered at the Astor—just four weeks after Jimmy's death. The Astor, no longer in existence, was located at 45th Street and Broadway.

ASTROLOGY

James Dean's astrological sign was Aquarius.

ATTORNEYS

L. Dean Petty was the Beverly Hills attorney who handled the administration of the James Dean estate. Petty was paid $3,029.28 for his work.

THE AUDIENCE AWARDS ELECTION

On December 6, 1955, the Audience Awards Election was held at the Beverly Hills Hotel in Los Angeles to honor the best movie performances of the year, as voted by the filmgoing public. An estimated 15 million ballots were cast in thousands of theaters all over the country. Sponsored by the Council of Motion Picture Organizations, the Audience Awards Election marked the first time that the public was given the opportunity, on a national basis, to vote on year-end movie preferences.

When the name James Dean was announced as the year's Best Actor (for his performance in *East of Eden*), the audience rose to its feet in posthumous tribute.

Other "Audie" winners that evening included Best Actress, Jennifer Jones (*Love Is a Many Splendored Thing*); Most Promising New Personalities, Tab Hunter (*Battle Cry* and *Track of the Cat*) and Peggy Lee (*Pete Kelly's Blues*); Best Picture, *Mister Roberts*. George Murphy hosted the festivities, and other participants included Walt Disney, Alec Guinness, William Holden, Rosalind Russell, and Grace Kelly. Jimmy's award was picked up by Natalie Wood, who accepted "in behalf of the thousands of fans who were touched by Jimmy's greatness."

AUNTS
Mildred Dean
Ortense Winslow
Mildred Wilson Dean's sister (name unknown)

AUTOPSY
No autopsy was conducted on the body of James Dean following his fatal car crash in 1955.

TED AVERY
For a short time in 1951 Jimmy, then working as a parking lot attendant, lived in the Hollywood home of Ted Avery, one of his co-workers. Avery, also a struggling actor at the time, taught Jimmy how to execute rope tricks—a skill Jimmy later employed in *Giant*.

THE AWARDS
For Dean
   School
☆ First place, National Forensic League, Indiana state contest, April 1949
☆ Sixth place, National Forensic League, national contest, April 1949
☆ Drama and athletic awards, Fairmount High School, May 1949
   Community
☆ Various awards for his dramatic readings, The Women's Christian Temperance Union
   Stage
☆ The Daniel Blum Theatre World Award, Most Promising Personalities, *The Immoralist*, 1954
   Movies
☆ Academy Award nomination, Best Actor, *East of Eden*, 1955
☆ *Film Daily* award, Best Performance by a Male Star, *East of Eden*, 1955
☆ *Film Daily* award, Finds of the Year, *East of Eden*, 1955
☆ Golden Globe award, Special Posthumous Award, 1955
☆ Motion Picture Exhibitors award, Stars of Tomorrow, 1955
☆ *Modern Screen* Silver Cup award, Special Achievement Award, 1955
☆ *Photoplay* Gold Medal award, Special Achievement, *East of Eden*, 1955
☆ *Picturegoer* award (England), Best Actor, *East of Eden*, 1955
☆ British Academy award, Best Actor, *East of Eden*, 1955
☆ The Crystal Star award (France), Best Foreign Actor, *East of Eden*, 1955
☆ Audience Awards Election, Best Actor, *East of Eden*, 1955
☆ National Association of Theatre Owners award, Best Actor, *Rebel Without a Cause*, 1955
☆ The Yokohama Movie Circle Council (Japan), Best Male Star, 1956
☆ The Million Pearl Award (Japan), Best Foreign Actor, *East of Eden*, 1956
☆ The Tokyo Movie Fan's Association, Top Foreign Actor, *Rebel Without a Cause*, 1956
☆ Academy Award nomination, Best Actor, *Giant*, 1956
☆ Golden Globe award, World Film Favorite, 1956
☆ *Film Daily* award, Best Performances by Supporting Actors, *Giant*, 1956
☆ New York Film Critics award, Best Actor runner-up, *Giant*, 1956
☆ Winged Victory Award (France), Best Actor, *Giant*, 1957

Dean fondling one of his many awards.

For the Television Shows
☆ "Omnibus" won an Emmy award as Best Variety program of 1953—the year that Jimmy appeared in "Glory in Flower," an episode written by William Inge.

For the Movies
    East of Eden
☆ Academy Award Nominations, 1955:

    Best Actor, James Dean
    Best Supporting Actress, Jo Van Fleet
    Best Director, Elia Kazan
    Best Screenplay, Paul Osborn

☆ Academy Award Winner: Best Supporting Actress, Jo Van Fleet
☆ Golden Globe award, Best Picture, Drama

☆ Directors Guild of America nominee, 1955: Best Director, Elia Kazan
☆ Cannes Film Festival, Best Dramatic Picture, 1955
☆ National Board of Review, Ten Best List, Second Best Picture, 1955
☆ *Film Daily* award, Ten Best List, Third Best Picture, 1955
☆ *Film Daily* award, Year's Outstanding Directors, Elia Kazan, 1955
☆ *Film Daily* award, Best Performances by Supporting Actresses, Jo Van Fleet, 1955
☆ *Film Daily* award, Best Performances by Juvenile Actresses, Lois Smith, 1955
☆ *Films in Review*, One of the Year's Ten Best, 1955
☆ *Look* magazine, Best Supporting Actress, Jo Van Fleet, 1955
☆ Blue Ribbon award (Japan), Best Foreign Film, 1955
☆ Vienna Film Critics Golden Pen award, Best Picture, 1955
☆ Danish Oscar, Bodil award, Best American Film, 1957

Rebel Without a Cause

☆ Academy Award Nominations, 1955:

> Best Supporting Actor, Sal Mineo
> Best Supporting Actress, Natalie Wood
> Best Story, Nicholas Ray

☆ *Film Daily* award, Best Performances by Juvenile Actors, Sal Mineo, 1955
☆ *Film Daily* award, Best Performances by Juvenile Actresses, Natalie Wood, 1955
☆ Best Picture (Spain), 1964

Giant

☆ Academy Award nominations, 1956:

> Best Picture
> Best Actor, James Dean
> Best Actor, Rock Hudson
> Best Supporting Actress, Mercedes McCambridge
> Best Director, George Stevens
> Best Screenplay, Adapted, Fred Guiol and Ivan Moffat
> Best Editing, William Hornbeck, Philip W. Anderson, and Fred Bohanan
> Best Art Direction, Boris Leven, art direction; Ralph S. Hurst, set decoration
> Best Costume Design, Moss Mabry and Marjorie Best
> Best Music Scoring, Dimitri Tiomkin

☆ Academy Award winner: Best Director, George Stevens
☆ Directors Guild of America award: Best Director, George Stevens
☆ New York Film Critics award, Best Picture runner-up, 1956
☆ New York Film Critics award, Best Director runner-up, 1956
☆ *New York Times*, One of the Best Films of the Year, 1956
☆ *Film Daily* award, Ten Best List, Second Best Picture, 1956
☆ *Film Daily* award, Year's Outstanding Directors, George Stevens, 1956
☆ *Film Daily* award, Best Screenplay
☆ *Film Daily* award, Finds of the Year, Carroll Baker, 1956
☆ *Film Daily* award, Best Performances by Juvenile Actresses, Carroll Baker, 1956
☆ *Redbook* magazine, One of the Best Films of the Year, 1956
☆ *Look* magazine, Best Actor, Rock Hudson, 1956
☆ *Look* magazine, Best Director, George Stevens, 1956
☆ *Photoplay*, Best Picture, 1956
☆ *Picturegoer* (England), Seal of Merit award, One of the Year's Best Films, 1956

LEMUEL AYERS

It was Rogers Brackett who introduced Jimmy to producer Lemuel Ayers, who gave him his first *important* acting job. It was 1952, and by August of that year Jimmy had finagled a position as crewman (inexperienced though he was) aboard the Ayers yacht on a 10-day cruise to Cape Cod. By November Jimmy had landed himself a choice role in the Broadway production of *See the Jaguar*, a play produced by Ayers, further exemplifying that old entertainment adage, "It's all *who* you know."

In addition to producing plays on Broadway, Ayers designed costumes. In fact he won a Tony award in 1949 for his costumes. For *See the Jaguar* Ayers designed not only the costumes but the sets as well.

AZTEC INDIANS

For a period, Jimmy had an intense interest in the culture of the Aztec Indians, and he reveled in the opportunity to discuss it. After Jimmy's death *Modern Screen* writer Jack Shafer recalled an interview that he had conducted with Jimmy:

> Several years ago, the press agent for the Broadway play *See the Jaguar* suggested I interview one of the show's young stars on a Sunday evening program I was handling for a New York radio station. "His name is Jimmy Dean," the press agent told me.
>
> Long after the program was over, I kept remembering the serious-minded, friendly, handsome, young [21-year-old] kid—and the one thing that had made a very deep impression on me: he had brought a book along with him about Aztec Indians. "I've always been fascinated by the Aztec Indians. They were very fatalistic people, and I sometimes share that feeling. They had such a weird sense of doom that when the war-like Spaniards arrived in Mexico, a lot of the Aztecs just gave up to an event they believed couldn't be avoided."

B

BACK CREEK FRIENDS CHURCH

The Back Creek Friends Church in Fairmount, Indiana, is the church that Jimmy Dean attended with his family while growing up. It is also the church where his funeral services were held on October 8, 1955.

JIM BACKUS

I've played fight scenes before, but nothing like this. Jim is so carried away. He works himself up into such a pitch of intensity. I thought he was going to kill me. No kiddin'! In one rehearsal he grabbed me by the lapels, half carried me down the stairs, fought me across the living room sofa. This kid is strong as a bull. In another rehearsal *he broke off parts of the stair railing*, but even though we grappled, he always held on to me so that I wouldn't get hurt.

Jim Backus, *Rocks on the Roof*

Jim Backus as Jim Stark's apron-stringed father in *Rebel*. Backus's real-life wife, Henny, was up for the role of Judy's mother in the same picture.

The role of Frank Stark, James Dean's wife-whipped, apron-stringed father in *Rebel Without a Cause*, was an unequivocal career stretch for Jim Backus. Up until that time Backus had been known primarily as a comic. In fact, just prior to the shooting of *Rebel* Backus finished a run on the television situation comedy "I Married Joan" (1952–1955).

Jim Backus first met James Dean on Thanksgiving Day in 1954 at a party at actor Keenan Wynn's house. By the time they started shooting *Rebel* in March 1955, the two men had developed a camaraderie. Said Backus, "I liked him. That wasn't a very popular attitude. You weren't supposed to like him." The first day on the set, Jimmy approached Backus with a plea: "Teach me one thing," he said. "How to do Magoo." Backus, at the time, was most famous as the voice of the television cartoon character Mr. Magoo. Three days later, according to Backus, "He did it better than I did." Jimmy's impression was subsequently incorporated into the film.

Born in 1913, Jim Backus will probably be most remembered as Thurston Howell III on the television series "Gilligan's Island" (1964–1967). In addition to *Rebel* his film credits include *The Great Lover* (1949), *Hollywood Story* (1951), *His Kind of Woman* (1951), *I Want You* (1951), *Pat and Mike* (1952), *Androcles and the Lion* (1953), *The Great Man* (1956), *Man of a Thousand Faces* (1957), *Macabre* (1958), *Ice Palace* (1960), *Boys' Night Out* (1962), *It's a Mad Mad Mad Mad World* (1963), *Advance to the Rear* (1964), *Billie* (1965), *Where Were You When the Lights Went Out?* (1968), *Now You See Him, Now You Don't* (1972), *Pete's Dragon* (1977), and *There Goes the*

Dean and Backus off the set of *Rebel*.

Bride (England, 1979). In addition to those previously mentioned, his television credits include "Hollywood House" (1949–1950), "Talent Scouts" (1962), "Continental Showcase" (1966), and "Blondie" (1968–1969).

In his 1958 autobiography, *Rocks on the Roof,* Backus wrote a chapter about his experiences with James Dean. He also participated in a 1983 tribute to Jimmy sponsored by the Academy of Motion Picture Arts and Sciences and was interviewed about him on 1985 episodes of "Entertainment Tonight" and "Show Biz Today."

On July 3, 1989, Jim Backus died following a bout with double pneumonia complicated by Parkinson's disease. He was 76 years old.

BADLANDS

Badlands, Terrence Malick's 1973 motion-picture blood ballet, was derived from the killing spree of Charlie Starkweather. Actor Martin Sheen reportedly modeled his portrayal of Kit, the Starkweather character, on James Dean. Curiously both Sheen and Starkweather are devout Dean fans.

DONATELLA BAGLIVO

Donatella Baglivo produced the excellent Italian documentary, *Hollywood: The Rebel James Dean.*

JEANNE BAIRD

Jeanne Baird was the queen of the March 1955 Palm Springs Road Race in which James Dean competed. In April Baird showed up on the set of *Rebel Without a Cause* to present Jimmy with his first- and second-prize trophies.

CARROLL BAKER

Former female magician Carroll Baker co-starred as Luz Benedict, the precocious love interest of James Dean in *Giant.* Contrary to previous reports, it was not her film debut. She had appeared in *Easy to Love* (1953), an Esther Williams water ballet picture, a few years before. After *Giant,* possibly because she was considered an intense and difficult member of the Actors Studio, Baker was hyped in the media, absurdly, as "the female James Dean." Probably this stemmed more from the fact that her next picture was directed by Elia Kazan, the man who directed Dean in *East of Eden.* For Baker the film was *Baby Doll.* It earned her a 1956 Best Actress Oscar nomination and made her a star.

After such an auspicious start the film career of talented Carroll Baker declined rapidly, due primarily to her arduous battles with Warner Brothers. Audaciously she walked away from Warners without signing a proposed seven-year contract, and in 1969 she fled Hollywood for Rome. Her films: *The Big Country* (1958), *The Miracle* (1959), *But Not for Me* (1959), *Something Wild* (1961), *Bridge to the Sun* (1961), *How the West Was Won* (1963), *The Carpetbaggers* (1964), *Station Six–Sahara* (England, 1964), *Cheyenne*

Autumn (1964), *The Greatest Story Ever Told* (1965), *Sylvia* (1965), *Mister Moses* (England, 1965), *Harlow* (1965), *Jack of Diamonds* (1967), *The Sweet Body of Deborah* (Italy and France, 1969), *Paranoia* (1968), *The Harem* (1968), *The Spider* (1970), *The Fourth Mrs. Anderson* (1971), *Captain Apache* (1971), *Bloody Mary* (1972), *Baba Yaga Devil Witch* (1974), *Andy Warhol's Bad* (1977), *The Devil Has Seven Faces* (1977), *The World Is Full of Married Men* (England, 1979), *The Watcher in the Woods* (1980), *Star 80* (1983), *Red Monarch* (1983), and *Ironweed* (1987).

Reportedly Warner Brothers offered Carroll, with Dean's approval, the Natalie Wood part in *Rebel Without a Cause,* a part Carroll claims to have turned down. When they did work together in *Giant,* apparently there were equal measures of camaraderie and competition between them. During the shooting of the bar scene in which Jett Rink proposes marriage to Luz, Jimmy slid one of his hands under the table and allegedly assaulted Carroll between her legs in a schoolboy fit of one-upmanship.

On the night of September 30, 1955, Carroll was in a Warner Brothers projection room with George Stevens, Elizabeth Taylor, and Rock Hudson. They were watching the rushes from *Giant* when a phone call informed them that Jimmy had been killed in a car crash.

Carroll Baker wrote about her experiences with James Dean in her fascinating 1983 autobiography, *Baby Doll* (surely one of the best celebrity autobiographies). She was also interviewed about him in the 1976 documentary *James Dean: The First American Teenager* and on a 1985 episode of "Entertainment Tonight."

CHET BAKER

Trumpet player Chet Baker was dubbed "the James Dean of jazz" in the 1950s. Baker, with his cool good looks, physically resembled Dean. He also recorded an album, *Theme Music from 'The James Dean Story,'* for World Pacific Records. From that album the single "Let Me Be Loved," with a flip side of "Jimmy Jimmy," was released.

Born in 1929, Chet Baker began his rise to prominence in jazz circles in 1952, when the legendary Charlie Parker chose him to be his sideman for a Los Angeles nightclub gig. At that time Parker reportedly warned his New York friends Miles Davis and Dizzy Gillespie, "You better watch out. There's a white cat on the West Coast who's gonna eat you up." For the next few years Baker was wildly successful. However, his career declined almost as rapidly with a deluge of narcotics, arrests, and critical backlash.

Baker died from a tragic fall in 1987, shortly after photographer/filmmaker Bruce Weber had completed the documentary film of Baker's life entitled *Let's Get Lost.*

BAKERSFIELD, CALIFORNIA

On May 1, 1955, Jimmy entered a car race at Minter Field in Bakersfield, California. He placed third.

BALDWIN HILLS, CALIFORNIA
One of the primary shooting locations for *Rebel Without a Cause* was Baldwin Hills, California. The area served in the film as the neighborhood in which Jim Stark, the character portrayed by James Dean, resided. One of the exteriors shot was the house located at 5975 Citrus Avenue.

MARGARET BARKER
Margaret Barker, born in 1908, was a cast member of *See the Jaguar* (1952).

JIM BARRINGTON
Over the years, various parts of the infamous 1955 Porsche Spyder in which James Dean was killed have been sold and parceled out. Jim Barrington of Piedmont, California, is the owner of Dean's transaxle.

GEORGE BARRIS
George Barris, who was customizing the Mercury that Jimmy was to drive in *Rebel Without a Cause*, met Dean on the set. The two men became friendly, and when Jimmy purchased a Porsche Spyder in September 1955 he asked Barris to customize it. Among other details, Barris painted the words "Little Bastard" across the tail end of the Porsche at his garage, which was then located at 3457 South LaBrea.

Nevertheless, Barris claims to have pleaded with Jimmy *not* to drive the Porsche to Salinas. As he told a reporter for the *Los Angeles Times*, "[The car] was much more powerful than anything he had before. To take off and go to Salinas just like that—we all had funny feelings about it. Ursula [Andress] said before he left, 'I feel something about it. Don't go!' [But] he had ants in his pants; he wanted to go race."

After the crash Barris purchased the wreckage from the James Dean estate for anywhere from $900 to $2,500, depending on the source. Barris subsequently resold parts of the car and sent the wreckage on a tour to discourage reckless driving.

George Barris has been customizing cars for 50 years. He created the "Batmobile" and the jalopy in "The Beverly Hillbillies" for television and Herbie in *The Love Bug* for the movies.

Barris was interviewed about Jimmy in the cable television documentary "Forever James Dean" (1988) and on a 1989 episode of "A Current Affair."

Other Celebrities for Whom George Barris Has Customized Cars:

Clark Gable	Liberace	Frank Sinatra
Zsa Zsa Gabor	Dean Martin	Sylvester Stallone
Bob Hope	Elvis Presley	

BARS
The following is a selective list of the bars that were frequented by James Dean:

Crescendo Club, Los Angeles
Jerry's Bar and Restaurant, New York City
Jimmy Ryan's, New York City
Louie's Tavern, New York City

Minetta Tavern, New York City
Tablehoppers, Los Angeles
Tony's Bar, New York City

BARS

In the seventh grade Jimmy competed in a speech competition sponsored by the Women's Christian Temperance Union of Fairmount, Indiana. For his presentation Jimmy performed a dramatic reading from a play entitled *Bars*. He did not win the contest, because he utilized a chair as a prop and props were strictly forbidden by the regulations. Even back then, at the age of 12, Jimmy Dean was breaking and making his own rules.

JAMES BARTON

Co-star of "The Foggy, Foggy Dew," a 1952 episode of the television program "Lux Video Theatre," which also featured James Dean.

BASEBALL

Jimmy was a member of his Fairmount High School baseball team.

JAMES BASEVI

James Basevi was one of the art directors on *East of Eden*. He was also a five-time Oscar nominee for his work on *Wuthering Heights* (1939), *The Westerner* (1940), *The Gang's All Here* (1943), and *Keys of the Kingdom* (1945); he won one for *The Song of Bernadette* (1943).

BASKETBALL

> "He wasn't too coachable. You had to be careful about not changing his style. And I learned not to embarrass him in front of the other boys."
>
> coach Paul Weaver

While he also participated in baseball during his school years, Jimmy was far more adept on the basketball court. He was a member of his elementary school team in 1942, and by his high school years, despite a lack of height, he had become a star player. He played guard and wore the number three. In his senior year he scored a last-second field goal to lead his team to a victory over archrival Gas City. The game was anything but a shoot-out, with Fairmount victorious 39–37. In another game Jimmy scored 15 of his team's 34 points. That year he was the Quakers' number one scorer. The 1949 Fairmount High yearbook noted, "Jim Dean, brilliant senior guard, was one of the main cogs in the Quaker line-up this season," and "Jim is our regular guy and when you're around him, time will fly."

When Jimmy moved to California after graduation and enrolled at Santa Monica City College, he promptly signed up as a member of the school basketball team. That year the team went on to set a school record for the most points scored in a season. In 24 games, the team scored 1,388 points or a less-than-astounding 57.83 points a game.

Because of his height, Jimmy never seriously considered a career as a basketball player. However, his father, Winton, encouraged him to forgo an acting career and become a physical education teacher and/or basketball coach.

Pretty boy Dean, top row center.

Jimmy's Teammates on the Fairmount Quakers Basketball Team

Rex Bright	Jim Grindle	David Jones
Bud Cox	Vic Hilton	Paul Smith
David Fox	Bob Howell	John Webster

WILLIAM BAST

"When I first met him, he was a bumpkin from the farm. He was a user of people, and I was being devoured. He was retiring and shy and very ill at ease."

Bill Bast on James Dean

Bill Bast is frequently regarded as James Dean's closest friend. The pair met in 1950 at the University of California, Los Angeles (UCLA), where both were studying acting. They subsequently became roommates not far from the school's Westwood campus. It was decidedly *not* a case of immediate affinity that prompted the move, but rather of financial necessity. In fact, Bast looked upon Dean with disdain, finding him moody and self-indulgent.

Eventually "Willie" and "Deaner," as they tagged one another, became friends bound together by a love of acting, a battle with hunger, and Jimmy's inexhaustible quest for ideas and information from everyone he admired. The two friends parted company on bitter terms with the arrival of a young actress who switched her affections from Bast to Dean.

Several months later, Jimmy moved to New York (without the girl), still in pursuit of an acting career. In May 1952 Bast also moved to New York, with his artistic pursuits redirected to writing. Once in the city, Bast looked up his old friend Jimmy. Shortly thereafter they once again took up residence together, this time in a one-room apartment at the Iroquois Hotel on West 44th Street.

In the summer and fall of 1952 Bill Bast, Jimmy Dean, and a third partner, a dancer named Elizabeth "Dizzy" Sheridan, were virtually inseparable. They played together (bullfighting was a favorite amusement, with Jimmy sashaying as the matador and Bill and Dizzy alternating as the bull), plotted together, read together, and lived together (at various apartments) decades before the latter was fashionable or even tolerated. They nurtured one another's ambitions, consoled one another for their failures, and combined their pocket change in order to eat. Then, when Jimmy decided to return home to Indiana in October for a pre-Thanksgiving feast, Bast and Sheridan tagged along. For a good home-cooked meal, the three of them hitchhiked across state lines.

However, with his personal success in *See the Jaguar* at the end of 1952, Jimmy's lifestyle changed and the Bohemian trio gradually disengaged. In December Jimmy moved back to the Iroquois—alone. Bast later moved into a room across from Jimmy, but by mid-1953 he had won a writing job at NBC television and moved back to California.

The two friends did not see each other again until March 1954, when Jimmy returned triumphantly to Hollywood to star in *East of Eden*. By then the nature of their relationship had changed dramatically. When they first met, Jimmy had been attracted to Bast's superior intellect. By the time he returned to Hollywood, however, it was obviously Jimmy who had the upper hand. Still they managed to resume a friendship and even contemplated working together, with Bast writing a script for Jimmy to star in.

After Jimmy's death Bast wrote the superb autobiographical book *James Dean*, which was published by Ballantine in 1956. He later wrote "The Movie Star," a television drama inspired by Dean that aired on "The DuPont Show of the Week" in 1962. And in 1976, 20 years after its publication, Bast adapted his book about Dean into a television movie entitled "James Dean." The televised portrait was intimate, revealing, and somewhat startling with its implication of a latent homosexual desire between the Bast and Dean characters.

He has also appeared in front of the camera in interviews about Dean: "James Dean: An American Original" (1983), "Entertainment Tonight"

(1985), *Hollywood: The Rebel James Dean*, and "Forever James Dean" (1988). In addition, he appeared on a panel in a 1983 Dean tribute sponsored by the Academy of Motion Picture Arts and Sciences.

Over the years Bill Bast has also had a great deal of success in non-Dean-related works. His television credits include episodes of "Ben Casey," "Combat," "Dr. Kildare," "The Outer Limits," "Perry Mason," "The Fugitive," "The Mod Squad," "It Takes a Thief," "The Waltons," "Hawaii Five-O," "Tucker's Witch" (which he created as well), "The Hamptons," and "The Colbys" (which he also produced). He also wrote the made-for-television movies "The Legend of Lizzie Borden" (1975), "The Man in the Iron Mask" (1977), "Mistress of Paradise" (1981), "The Star Maker" (1981), "The Scarlet Pimpernel" (1982), "The First Modern Olympics" (miniseries, 1984), and "Twist of Fate" (1988). Additionally Bast scripted the feature film *The Betsy* (1978).

Although they were certainly close friends, Bill Bast has, over the years, expressed ambivalent feelings about James Dean. Some would say that he has been bitter, even traitorous, to his old friend. Perhaps he has just been candid. To one reporter he said, "In real life, [Jimmy] was not an extraordinary person. If anything, he was rather bothersome." On "Entertainment Tonight" he said, "[Jimmy] was cocky and arrogant. And he was pushing his limits as much as he could. He was very, very shrewd. He knew what he was doing most of the time. But he was, at the same time, privately very mystified by what was going on and how this [sudden success] was happening." In perhaps his most telling interview, Bast offered the following to *The Advocate* in 1976:

> "The thing I resent most is that Jim was never honest with himself. He put down the games that one had to play in Hollywood in order to succeed. He felt that he was above having to kiss anyone's ass in order to get a part, and whenever he saw his friends in that situation, he put them down for it, said he lost respect for them. The truth, though, is that Dean kissed a lot of asses, and he hated this about himself."

Bill Bast's friendship with James Dean has forced an ironic dichotomy. On one hand, it has made him famous. He is sought after and revered by thousands as a link to Dean. On the other hand, no matter what he has achieved in his life and career, no matter how much talent he has displayed (and it has been considerable), he will stand in the shadow of his old friend. There is simply no getting around it. For in the hearts and minds of millions of fans around the world, James Dean will always be The Matador. And Bill Bast, alas, will always be The Bull.

ARTHUR BATANIDES
Cast member of *See the Jaguar* (1952).

KATHY BATES

Kathy Bates is an actress who was featured in *Come Back to the Five and Dime, Jimmy Dean, Jimmy Dean*, a 1982 Broadway play and its subsequent film adaptation.

In 1990 Bates won acclaim for her performance in the picture *Misery*.

BATTLE CRY

In 1953 Jimmy screen-tested for a part in the Warner Brothers war picture *Battle Cry*. He didn't get the part. Later, during a break from shooting *East of Eden*, Jimmy visited the *Battle Cry* set to see his old friend and mentor, James Whitmore. While on the set Jimmy met the young actor who won the *Battle Cry* part that he had tested for—Tab Hunter. *Battle Cry* was released in 1955, was directed by Raoul Walsh, and starred Van Heflin, Aldo Ray, Mona Freeman, Dorothy Malone, Raymond Massey, Nancy Olson, Whitmore, Hunter, and Anne Francis.

"THE BATTLER"

On October 18, 1955, Jimmy was scheduled to star in a television production of Ernest Hemingway's autobiographical story "The Battler." The program was to have aired live from New York on the NBC-TV series "Pontiac Presents Playwrights 56." Jimmy was to have played the role of the Hemingway character, Nick Adams. In fact, shortly before his death, Jimmy even filmed a promotional spot announcing his upcoming performance in "The Battler."

After Jimmy's death the part was awarded to Dewey Martin. The show was produced by Fred Coe and directed by Arthur Penn. The teleplay was adapted by A. E. Hotchner and Sidney Carroll. The rest of the cast included Paul Newman, Phyllis Kirk, and Frederick O'Neal. The program aired as scheduled on October 18, 1955.

GEORGE BAU

One of the makeup men on *Giant*.

GORDON BAU

Gordon Bau was the makeup supervisor at Warner Brothers during James Dean's tenure there.

BARBARA BAXLEY

Barbara Baxley was the actress who portrayed the malevolent nursemaid in *East of Eden*. Her other films include *The Badlanders* (1958), *No Way to Treat a Lady* (1968), *Nashville* (1975), and *Norma Rae* (1979).

Born in 1927, Baxley was a member of the Actors Studio and appeared in many plays, including *Period of Adjustment*, for which she was nominated for a Best Actress Tony in 1961.

NICKY BAZOOKA

Nicky Bazooka, an alias, is the James Dean mystery fan who annually guns his motorcycle into Fairmount, Indiana, and leads a memorial procession to the cemetery where Dean is buried. Little is known about the reticent Bazooka except that he is fortyish and has a penchant for dressing in black leather motorcycle regalia.

THE BEACH BOYS

The Beach Boys recorded a song, "A Young Man Is Gone," about James Dean. The song is included on the group's *Little Deuce Coupe* album.

THE BEAT GENERATION

Along with Charlie Parker, Jack Kerouac, and others, James Dean is generally regarded as one of the heroes of the Beat Generation that emerged in America in the 1950s. A beatnik, as defined by beat writer John Clellon Holmes in *Esquire* in 1958, was "The hipster and his preoccupation was with speed, sex, drugs, jazz and death."

"BEAT THE CLOCK"

"Beat the Clock" was a long-running (1950–1958) CBS television game show produced by Mark Goodson and Bill Todman and hosted by Bud Collyer. The show featured contestants who attempted to execute various stunts, devised by Frank Wayne and Bob Howard, within a given time frame. A typical stunt had a contestant don oversized underwear into which he or she would attempt to stuff 12 inflated balloons—without breaking any of them— in 45 seconds. In November 1951, struggling young actor James Dean was hired to pretest the stunts and warm up the studio audience.

WARREN NEWTON BEATH

Born in California in 1951, Warren Newton Beath is a Dean collector and fan who authored the book *The Death of James Dean*, which was published by Grove Press in 1986.

THE BEATLES

When "The Fab Four" initiated their group in Liverpool, England, there were *five* members in the band. A few weeks before the group recorded its first hit record, "Love Me Do," in 1962, fifth member Stewart Sutcliffe died from a brain tumor. He was 21 years old.

Years later John Lennon acknowledged, "[Stewart Sutcliffe] was really our leader, and he was really into the James Dean thing. He idolized him. Stewart died young before we made the big time, but I suppose you could say that without Jimmy Dean, The Beatles would never have existed."

BORIS BECKER

Boris Becker, the redheaded, freckle-faced, power-slamming tennis star from

West Germany, is a huge Dean fan and has even visited the Cholame, California, site where Jimmy was killed. Born in 1968, Becker has also expressed some belief that he is *the* rebel with a racket, the reincarnation of James Dean.

ED BEGLEY

Ed Begley was the star of "Harvest," an episode of the NBC television show "Robert Montgomery Presents the Johnson's Wax Program." Begley portrayed the father of the character portrayed by James Dean.

Begley (1901–1970) has also appeared in numerous films, including *Big Town* (1947), *Sorry, Wrong Number* (1948), *12 Angry Men* (1957), *Sweet Bird of Youth* (Best Supporting Actor Oscar winner, 1962), *Wild in the Streets* (1968), and *The Dunwich Horror* (1970). He also hosted a television series, "Roller Derby" (1951), and starred in another one, "Leave It to Larry" (1952).

JIMMY BELLAH

The son of novelist James Warner Bellah, Jimmy Bellah was a classmate of James Dean's at UCLA, circa 1950–1951. It was through Bellah that Jimmy was hired for a 1950 commercial for Pepsi-Cola.

"THE BELLS OF COCKAIGNE"

"The Bells of Cockaigne" was an episode of the NBC television series "Armstrong Circle Theatre" that starred Gene Lockhart, James Dean, Vaughn Taylor, Donalee Marans, and John Dennis. The program was directed by James Sheldon, produced by Hudson Faussett, and written by George Lowther. It aired on November 17, 1953.

Jimmy portrayed Joey Frazier, a blue-collar laborer struggling to support his wife and asthmatic child. However, the program is probably best remembered as the show in which James Dean was stripped to the waist. Director James Sheldon remembers it for a different reason: "I remember Jimmy on 'The Bells of Cockaigne' because we had a scheduled dress rehearsal and Jimmy was late. They had to run down and find him in the drugstore. And so . . . I went to talk to him and I said, 'You've really been acting up. You've been making a lot of enemies.' And he said, 'Oh, people *love* to work with me! Gene Lockhart *loves* to work with me!' He was completely unaware; he was insensitive to what was happening."

JEAN-PAUL BELMONDO

Jean-Paul Belmondo was one of several actors touted as "the James Dean of France" in the late 1950s and early 1960s. Born in 1933, Belmondo is a bona fide star in Europe but is less well known to American audiences. His films include *Dimanche . . . Nous Volerons* (France, 1956), *A Bout de Soufflé* (France, 1959), *Two Women* (Italy, 1961), *Un Singe en Hiver* (France, 1962), *That Man from Rio* (France, 1964), *Is Paris Burning?* (1966), *L'Animal* (France, 1977), *Le Marginal* (France, 1983), and many others.

JOHN BELUSHI
In the early morning of March 5, 1982, comedian John Belushi returned to his bungalow (number 2) at the Chateau Marmont Hotel. This is the same hotel suite where, in 1955, James Dean used to visit director Nick Ray to rehearse scenes for *Rebel Without a Cause*.

Later that morning Robin Williams, then Robert De Niro, stopped by to visit Belushi. A few hours later Belushi was found dead from an overdose of cocaine.

FRAN BENNETT
Blond San Antonio heiress who portrayed Judy Benedict in *Giant*. During the Marfa, Texas, location shooting of *Giant*, Fran Bennett and James Dean were frequent companions.

STEVEN BENTINCK
Steven Bentinck was the producer of *Dean*, a 1977 stage musical produced in London.

LEE BERGERE
Lee Bergere appeared in "The Little Woman," a 1954 episode of the CBS television series "Danger" that co-starred James Dean. Years later Bergere returned to television in the comedy series "Hot L Baltimore" (1975).

HARRY BERGMAN
Harry Bergman was a cast member in and a stage manager of *See the Jaguar* (1952).

IRVING BERMAN
Following Jimmy's death the James Dean estate paid the sum of $10 to Dr. Irving S. Berman for medical services rendered.

TOM BERNARD
Tom Bernard was one of the gang members in *Rebel Without a Cause*. A few years earlier he had appeared in the television series "The Ruggles" (1949-1952).

SARAH BERNHARDT
Sarah Bernhardt (1844-1923), born Henriette-Rosine Bernard, was the great French stage actress who won international acclaim for her performances in *Ruy Blas*, *Phèdre*, and *La Dame aux Camélias*. She also appeared in several early silent pictures, including *Queen Elizabeth* (1912). Although her leg was amputated in 1915, she continued to work in pictures. Her name and legend have endured over the years, and one of her biggest fans was James Dean. As recalled by Beulah Roth, "There was a hotel in Venice, California, where Sarah Bernhardt had stayed when she came here to perform. It was there when Jimmy was alive . . . we [she and her husband, Sandy] took him there

and we told him this was where Sarah Bernhardt had stayed. She had appeared on the Venice Pier in a theater.

"He was thrilled. He said, 'Let's go to the hotel.' So, we go in and it's a fleabag hotel, a transient's hotel, and no one there had ever heard of Sarah Bernhardt except for one old guy who said, 'Oh, yeah, I remember, that French actress.' And we said, 'Do you remember the room?' And he said, 'Yeah, I'll take you up there.' He took us up to this really horrible room. I guess in its day it was elegant. And Jimmy said, 'You go out of the room. I want to be here alone. I want Sarah Bernhardt to come to me.' And he said he lay on the bed where she had slept. And he really felt that he had made contact with Sarah Bernhardt."

Oddly, one of the things Sarah Bernhardt is most remembered for is her penchant for sleeping in a satin-lined coffin. She also was photographed in the coffin. Many years later, when James Dean posed in a coffin for photographer Dennis Stock, he was condemned as depraved. Others pointed it out as proof that he harbored a secret death wish. Perhaps, morbidity aside, he was just aping Sarah Bernhardt.

HENRI BERNSTEIN
Henri Bernstein wrote the play on which "The Thief," a 1955 episode of the ABC television series "The U.S. Steel Hour," was based. The episode co-starred James Dean.

MALCOLM BERT
Malcolm Bert was the art director of both *East of Eden* and *Rebel Without a Cause*. Bert also did the art direction for *A Star Is Born* (1954) and *Auntie Mame* (1958), both of which earned him Oscar nominations.

MARJORIE BEST
Marjorie Best designed the multitude of costumes for *Giant*, with the exception of those that were designed by Moss Mabry for Elizabeth Taylor. For her work on *Giant* Best received an Oscar nomination. She received additional nominations for *Sunrise at Campobello* (1960) and *The Greatest Story Ever Told* (1965) and won an Oscar for her work on *Adventures of Don Juan* (1948).

THE BEST OF JAMES DEAN IN THE SCANDAL MAGAZINES, 1955–1958
The Best of James Dean in the Scandal Magazines, 1955–1958, edited by Alan Betrock and published by Shake Books in 1988, is a surprisingly fascinating one-shot magazine that dredges up some of the ridiculously trashy pages from *Whisper, Rave, Personal Romances, Exposed,* etc.

BEVERAGES
In bars Jimmy generally drank beer. Sometimes he'd opt for whiskey or a scotch and soda. Occasionally he'd have a double scotch. His favorite brands

of beer were Guinness and Tuborg. Of nonalcoholic beverages, Jimmy drank milk and was a notoriously fanatical coffee consumer. His last drink? A Coke, which he drank at a rest stop en route to Salinas, California, in the afternoon of September 30, 1955.

RICHARD BEYMER

Richard Beymer, born in 1939, screen-tested with James Dean for the part of Plato in *Rebel Without a Cause*. The role was eventually awarded to Sal Mineo, and Beymer had to wait until 1961 to attain success in *West Side Story*. However, his career never fulfilled that early promise, although he appeared in several films and became a regular in two television series, "Paper Dolls" in 1984 and "Twin Peaks" in 1990.

"THE BIG STORY"

"The Big Story" was a successful television drama series based on actual news stories that aired on Friday nights on NBC from 1949 to 1957. Jimmy starred in the September 11, 1953, program, which was directed by Stuart Rosenberg and narrated by Bob Sloane. The episode featured reporter Rex Newman from the Joplin, Missouri, *Globe and News Herald*. The rest of the cast included John Kerr, Wendy Drew, Carl Frank, Donald McKee, Ken Walken, Bobby Nick, and Susan Harris.

EDWARD BINNS

Ed Binns appeared in "Glory in Flower," a 1953 episode of the CBS television series "Omnibus" that featured James Dean. Binns later co-starred in the police series "Brenner" (1959–1964), "The Nurses" (1962–1964), and "It Takes a Thief" (1969–1970). He also appeared in several feature films, including *Teresa* (1951), *12 Angry Men* (1957), *North by Northwest* (1959), *Judgment at Nuremberg* (1961), and *Patton* (1970).

THE BIOGRAPHIES ISSUED BY WARNER BROTHERS

The following is a cursory examination of the studio biographies that Warner Brothers issued on behalf of its star, James Dean. As with all studio biographies, some of the information was either exaggerated, incorrect, or purely the concoction of an imaginative, albeit well-intentioned, publicist.

The initial Warner Brothers Dean biography was issued on July 28, 1954, shortly before *East of Eden* completed shooting. It highlighted the Cinderella aspect of Dean's farm-to-fame story ("Only a few years ago James Dean was a farm boy in Fairmount . . . he was kept busy with the farm boy's usual chores of milking cows and feeding chickens . . .") and hailed his discovery as one of the most important acting finds in many years. To support this contention, the studio made much of the acclaim Dean had received earlier that year for his performance on Broadway in *The Immoralist*. "For this," the bio read, "he won the David Blum award as the most promising newcomer of the year." Little did it matter that, in fact, Dean was one of *12* performers presented that year with a *Daniel* Blum Theatre

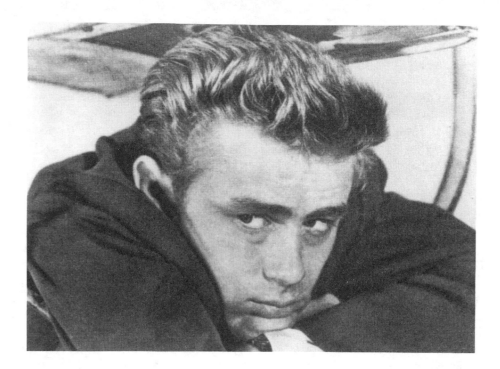

World award as the "Most Promising Personalities." The former claim, understandably, made better copy.

Dean's childhood years were retraced in a couple of sentences that mentioned that he had been raised on a farm by an aunt and uncle. The reason given for this was that "his mother died while he was still a baby." In fact, Dean's mother, Mildred, died when he was nine years old—hardly a baby by any standard. Apparently, the studio publicist felt that the loss of a mother would be perceived as being more tragic to a baby than to a boy about to enter the fourth grade. Interestingly, the bio made no mention of Dean's father, Winton.

Dean's high school achievements in art and athletics are acknowledged, as is his early talent in dramatics. Upon graduation, according to the biography, Dean headed west and enrolled at UCLA. In fact, Dean first attended the less prestigious Santa Monica City College and later transferred to UCLA, where he lasted only a few months, not the two years stated in the bio.

Dean's departure from Los Angeles and arrival in New York City are sparsely but accurately covered, although no mention is made of Rogers Brackett, Dean's benefactor and alleged homosexual lover during this period.

His successes on Broadway in *See the Jaguar* and *The Immoralist* are mentioned, as is his interest in literature ("He prefers to read five or six books at a time . . ."). His other interests at the time included horses, sailing, fencing, gymnastics, boxing, tennis, chess, and bullfighting. His goals included stepping into the arena as a matador, directing his own plays and movies, and portraying Hamlet.

The second Dean biography was released in early 1955, and contained virtually the same information (and misinformation) given in the initial one. However, by this time Dean's controversial character had been deemed good copy by the powers-that-be and was played up by the Warner Brothers publicity department. "He also is acquiring the reputation of being one of Hollywood's most offbeat and controversial characters," the bio gushed, giving the same emphasis to Dean's personality as to his "sensitive" performance in *East of Eden*. "To strangers," it continued, "he can be aloof and downright rude. He doesn't care what people say about his eccentricities." As for his unconventional wardrobe, "He favors old dungarees and shirts," the bio states, "and has been dubbed a member of the 'dirty shirt school of acting.' "

Interestingly, the way in which Dean was cast in *See the Jaguar* varies slightly between the first and second biographies. The first correctly stated that Jimmy took a job as a sailor, even though he knew nothing about seamanship, when he learned that the ship's owner had "theatrical connections." Actually, the ship's owner, Lem Ayers, was the producer of *Jaguar*, a fact Dean was well aware of. The second omitted any indication that Dean's stint as a sailor had been calculated. It just so happened, according to the second bio, that "the skipper had theatrical connections and arranged for an interview on *See the Jaguar*."

Also of interest, before the second bio was issued by the studio, a paragraph was deleted. It read in part: "He admits to being neurotic and claims he was an actor before he became an actor." It then quotes Dean: "A neurotic person has the necessity to express himself and my neuroticism manifests itself in the dramatic. Why do most actors act? To express the fantasies in which they have involved themselves."

Mentioned again is Dean's goal of directing his own plays and movies. Added, however, is his burgeoning interest in writing. "He has written several plays and a number of short stories," according to the bio, "but [he] declines to show them to anyone. He does not want to submit a manuscript until he has come of age as a writer."

Also expressed is Dean's interest in music ("He is awakened by music and goes to sleep with it") and photography ("[He] has spent a small fortune on equipment"), his comparison to Brando, the fact that he frequently took his girlfriends for a spin on the back of his motorcycle, and the fact that he was disorderly. "To step into his apartment," the biography warns, "is like arriving at the scene of a hurricane."

It also submits in Dean's defense, "Some persons think he is self-centered. It's not true. He is greatly interested in other people, their problems and ambitions."

After Dean's death, shortly before the release of *Giant*, Warners issued another Dean biography. The Dean legend was in its early stages and was clearly evident in the bio. "One of the most remarkable young actors ever to appear in motion pictures," it began, "James Dean, with just three screen roles, made a deeper impression on the world's film goers than any of his contemporaries. It is likely that his work will be remembered for many years."

The remainder of the bio was almost identical to the previous ones, except for mention of the upcoming *Giant* ("Perhaps the most compelling role of his career") and a reference to Winton Dean ("His father was a dental technician . . ."). Also, it correctly states that Dean's mother died when he was nine years old and not when he was a baby, as the previous bios had indicated.

In describing Dean's interests, an addition was made to the previous biographies. "After watching several road races in California, he developed a passionate interest in the sport and participated with notable success in several amateur events."

The biography concluded with a eulogy. "On September 30, 1955, a few days after completing his role in *Giant*, Dean was fatally injured in a highway crash while en route to Salinas, California, to compete in a racing event, bringing to a tragic close a brilliant career that had only begun to bloom."

A final Dean biography was issued by Warner Brothers upon the release of the 1957 documentary *The James Dean Story*. The bio was virtually identical to the previous ones, the exceptions being the mention of Dean's posthumous Oscar nominations and the production of *The James Dean Story*. The film, according to the bio, "is a motion picture biography in which every actor plays himself, including the late James Dean." What was meant, presumably, was that Dean appeared in the film via footage and still photographs.

BIRTH
James Byron Dean was born at home in Marion, Indiana, at 2:00 A.M. on February 8, 1931, to Winton and Mildred Dean.

RICHARD BISHOP
Actor who appeared in "The Foggy, Foggy Dew," a 1952 episode of the television program "Lux Video Theatre" that co-starred James Dean.

WARD BISHOP
Ward Bishop was a stage manager on *See the Jaguar*.

KAREN BLACK
Karen Black co-starred in *Come Back to the Five and Dime, Jimmy Dean, Jimmy Dean*, a 1982 Broadway play and its subsequent film adaptation.

Born Karen Ziegeler in 1942, Karen Black has appeared in numerous films, including *You're a Big Boy Now* (1966), *Easy Rider* (1969), *Five Easy Pieces* (1970), *Drive, He Said* (1972), *Cisco Pike* (1972), *Portnoy's Complaint*

(1972), *The Great Gatsby* (1974), *Airport 1975* (1975), *The Day of the Locust* (1975), *Nashville* (1975), *Family Plot* (1976), *Burnt Offerings* (1976), *In Praise of Older Women* (Canada, 1978), and *Can She Bake a Cherry Pie?* (1983). Black also starred in the television movie "Trilogy of Terror" (1975).

RALPH BLACK
Ralph Black was the production manager on *Giant*.

BLACKWELL'S CORNER
At approximately 5:00 P.M. on the afternoon of September 30, 1955, James Dean, en route to Salinas, California, parked his Porsche 550 Spyder at a grocery store/gas station/rest stop. Located at the corner of U.S. 466 and Highway 33 near Bakersfield, it was known locally as Blackwell's Corner. Jimmy and his companion, Rolf Wütherich, spent approximately 15 minutes at Blackwell's Corner before venturing back on the road. For James Dean it was his last stop.

Blackwell's Corner burned to the ground in 1967 and has since been rebuilt.

GERARD BLAIN
Gerard Blain, born in 1930, was another actor who was hyped as "the James Dean of France" in the 1950s. Blain's films as an actor include *Les Fruits Sauvages* (France, 1954), *The Hunchback of Notre Dame* (France, 1957), *Crime and Punishment* (France, 1958), *Le Beau Serge* (France, 1958), *Les Cousins* (France, 1959), and *The American Friend* (1977). Blain later wrote and directed such films as *Les Amis* (1971), *Le Pelican* (1973), *Utopia* (1978), and *Le Rebelle* (1980).

"THE BLIND RUN"
"The Blind Run" was the title of Nicholas Ray's short story about juvenile delinquency that was adapted for film and released by Warner Brothers under the name *Rebel Without a Cause*.

BLUE JEANS
Arguably James Dean has done more for the sales of blue jeans than any individual in history, with the possible exception of Bruce Springsteen. In *Rebel Without a Cause* and *Giant*, as well as in his personal life, Dean wore jeans. Perhaps he wore them for comfort. Perhaps he wore them as a symbol of rebellion. Whatever his purpose, he wore them *well*, and tens of thousands of teenage boys dropped their chinos and donned their denim in an effort to emulate him.

Subsequently, over the years blue jeans and James Dean have become somewhat synonymous. Decades after Dean's death, enterprising clothing manufacturers continue to market their jeans by capitalizing on the Dean image. Taking the connection to an extreme, one shrewd greeting card

company went so far as to produce a card onto which a patch of denim was attached. The accompanying copy read: "Now you can finally get into James Dean's jeans!"

SUSAN BLUTTMAN

Co-curator of the 1986 James Dean television retrospective produced by the Museum of Broadcasting in New York, Bluttman also penned the informative article "Rediscovering James Dean: The TV Legacy," published in the October 1990 issue of *Emmy* magazine.

HUMPHREY BOGART

> Dean never looked at Bogart. He said "Hello" and stared at the floor. For a minute and a half Bogart tried to carry on a gentleman's conversation; he paid Dean a great compliment by saying he admired the young man's technique. Dean said, "Yeah? That's okay by me." Suddenly, Bogey grabbed Dean by the lapels, nearly yanking him off the ground. "You little punk, when I talk to you, you look in my eyes, you understand? Who the hell do you think you are, you two-bit nothing!" Then Bogey shoved the stunned actor away and stormed off the set.
>
> Merv Griffin, *Merv*

What Merv Griffin left out about the meeting between Humphrey Bogart and James Dean on the set of *East of Eden* was that Jimmy, new to Hollywood, was a Bogart fan and was quite possibly more awestruck and awkward than intentionally rude.

Humphrey Bogart died of cancer in 1957 at the age of 57. He left behind a legacy of such classic films as *The Petrified Forest* (Note: It was Bogart's performance in this play that propelled him to stardom on Broadway; 1936), *Angels with Dirty Faces* (1938), *The Maltese Falcon* (1941), *Casablanca* (Best Actor Oscar nomination, 1943), *To Have and Have Not* (1944), *The Big Sleep* (1946), *The Treasure of the Sierra Madre* (1948), *Key Largo* (1948), *The African Queen* (Best Actor Oscar winner, 1951), *The Caine Mutiny* (Best Actor Oscar nomination, 1954), *Sabrina* (1954), and *The Barefoot Contessa* (1954).

FRED BOHANAN
Fred Bohanan received a 1956 Oscar nomination for his work as one of the assistant editors on *Giant*.

SUDIE BOND
Sudie Bond was featured in *Come Back to the Five and Dime, Jimmy Dean, Jimmy Dean*, the 1982 Broadway play and its subsequent film adaptation. Bond, born in 1928, had previously appeared on stage in several plays, including *Summer and Smoke* (1952), *Auntie Mame* (1958), and *Grease* (1972); her credits also include the film *A Thousand Clowns* (1965) and the television programs "Temperatures Rising" (1973–1974) and "Flo" (1980–1981).

SYLVIA BONGIOVANNI
Native New Yorker Sylvia Bongiovanni is the highly effectual president and co-founder of the We Remember Dean International fan club. She first

WRDI president Sylvia Bongiovanni, surrounded by Dean.

became aware of James Dean through his performances on live television in the early 1950s. Then, as she describes it today, "I saw *East of Eden*, and that's what did it. My girlfriend Cathy and I went to the RKO Castle Hill Theater in the Bronx and saw it every night for as long as it played."

Sylvia is still under the Dean spell. In addition to working full-time hours on her club duties, she works as a legal secretary in Fullerton, California. Her Dean collection, amassed over 35 years, includes 16 scrapbooks of photographs, postcards, and clippings; books; magazines; records; and a plethora of assorted memorabilia.

BONGO DRUMS

> "He would be at parties where the other actors were [and] never say a word to anyone. If we were listening to music, he would sit in a corner and play his bongo drums. And I don't think I ever remember him holding a conversation with anyone. Maybe a few words here and there."
>
> Carroll Baker

During his New York period in the early 1950s Jimmy became quite adept at playing the bongo drums. He was a common, if odd, sight strutting down the streets of Manhattan with his bongos strapped to his back or pounding out his own personal rhythms in a dark corner of some smoke-infested club. Later, when he moved back to Los Angeles, Jimmy was frequently found in impromptu jazz sessions in nightclubs along the Sunset strip.

THE BOOKS ABOUT JAMES DEAN

It's no surprise that more books have been written and published about Marilyn Monroe and Elvis Presley than any other show business personality. However, not far down the list are Greta Garbo and, of course, James Dean.

Nonfiction

The following is a chronological list of every nonfiction book ever published about James Dean. It does not include foreign-language titles or books in which Jimmy is only mentioned—there are too many to include here. It also does not include special-issue one-shot magazines. Naturally the quality (and accuracy) of the books listed varies greatly. For more information on each title, see individual entries.

TITLE	AUTHOR	YEAR
James Dean	William Bast	1956
The Rebel	Royston Ellis	1962
Continuity and Evolution in a Public Symbol: An Investigation into the Creation and Communication of the James Dean Image in Mid-Century America	Robert Wayne Tysl	1965
The Films of James Dean	Mark Whitman	1974
James Dean: A Short Life	Venable Herndon	1974
James Dean: The Mutant King	David Dalton	1974*
James Dean: A Biography	John Howlett	1975

The James Dean Story	Ronald Martinetti	1975
The Real James Dean	John Gilmore	1975
James Dean Revisited	Dennis Stock	1978**
James Dean: A Portrait	Roy Schatt	1982
James Dean	Beulah Roth (text) Sanford Roth (photos)	1983
James Dean: The Way It Was	Terry Cunningham	1983
James Dean Is Not Dead	Stephen Morrissey	1983
The Last James Dean Book	Dante Volpe	1984
Rebels United: The Enduring Reality of James Dean	Joel Brean	1984
James Dean: American Icon	David Dalton (text) Ron Cayen (photos)	1984
James Dean: Footsteps of a Giant	Wolfgang Fuchs	1986
The Death of James Dean	Warren Newton Beath	1986
James Dean on Location	Marceau Devillers	1987***
Wish You Were Here, Jimmy Dean	Martin Dawber	1989
James Dean: In His Own Words	Mick St. Michael	1989
James Dean: Shooting Star	Barney Hoskyns (text) David Loehr (photos)	1990
Jimmy Dean on Jimmy Dean	Joseph Humphreys	1990
James Dean: Behind the Scene	Leith Adams and Keith Burns	1990

*A revised edition was published by St. Martin's Press in 1983.
**Reprinted by Chronicle Books in 1987.
***Originally published in France in 1985.

Fiction
In addition to the multitude of nonfiction books about Dean, there have been several novels that have fictionalized his life story. They include:

TITLE	AUTHOR	YEAR
I, James Dean	T. T. Thomas	1957
The Immortal	Walter S. Ross	1958
Farewell My Slightly Tarnished Hero	Ed Corley	1971

BOOKS READ BY JAMES DEAN
"I think reading was probably a painful experience for him."
Leonard Rosenman

Over the years there has been speculation that James Dean had a reading problem. Some of those who knew him have even suggested that he was more of a scanner than a reader. Nevertheless he was known to tote books with impressive titles. Included in his personal home library were books by Kafka, Shakespeare, Garcia Lorca, and various others, including:

The Art of Etching, by E. S. Lumsden
The Burns Mantle Best Plays of 1947–1948
The Burns Mantle Best Plays of 1949–1950
The Best Plays of 1950–1951
The Bible
Charlotte's Web, by E. B. White
The Complete Works of James Whitcomb Riley
The Creation of the Universe, by George Gamow
Dance to the Piper, by Agnes De Mille
Death in the Afternoon, by Ernest Hemingway
Death in Venice, by Thomas Mann
De Profundis, by Oscar Wilde
Garcia Lorca, by Edwin Honig
A Goddess to a God, by John L. Balderston
How to Sail
I Go Pogo, by Walt Kelly
Learn Chess Fast
The Little Prince, by Antoine de Saint-Exupery
Los Toros, by Jose Cassio
Moulin Rouge, by Pierre La Mure
Pain, Sex, and Time, by Gerald Heard
The Seven Pillars of Wisdom, by T. E. Lawrence
Stanislavsky Directs, by Nikolai M. Gorchakov
To the Actor, by Michael Chekhov

Books That Jimmy Gave to Bill Bast
The Andre Maurois Reader
The Heart Is a Lonely Hunter, by Carson McCullers
The Little Prince, by Antoine de Saint-Exupery
Orlando, by Virginia Woolf

ERNEST BORGNINE
Ernest Borgnine won the 1955 Academy Award as Best Actor for his performance in Paddy Chayefsky's *Marty*. Borgnine won the award over fellow nominees:

James Cagney, *Love Me or Leave Me*
James Dean, *East of Eden*
Frank Sinatra, *The Man with the Golden Arm*
Spencer Tracy, *Bad Day at Black Rock*

For Ernest Borgnine, born Ermes Borgnino in 1915, the Oscar was the pinnacle of his career. His many other films include *China Corsair* (1951), *From Here to Eternity* (1953), *Johnny Guitar* (1954), *The Catered Affair* (1956), *The Best Things in Life Are Free* (1956), *The Vikings* (1958), *Pay or Die* (1960), *McHale's Navy* (1964), *The Dirty Dozen* (1967), *Ice Station Zebra* (1968), *The Wild Bunch* (1969), *The Poseidon Adventure* (1972), and *Escape from New York* (1981). He also starred in the television programs "McHale's Navy" (1962–1966) and "Future Cop" (1976).

JERRY BOS

Jerry Bos was the director of wardrobe for "The Unlighted Road," a 1955 episode of "Schlitz Playhouse of Stars" that starred James Dean.

ROBERT BOSSERT

Robert Bossert had the unenviable distinction of being the doctor who, on September 30, 1955, pronounced James Dean dead. Dr. Bossert diagnosed his famous patient as follows:

> He was dead and gross examination revealed fractured neck, multiple fractures of forearms, fractured leg and numerous cuts and bruises about the face and chest. I believe that he died of these injuries and that death came at the time, or shortly after the accident.

HAROLD BOSTWICK

Harold Bostwick was an actor who was excised out of the opening sequence of *Rebel Without a Cause*. In the original opening the character portrayed by Bostwick was victimized by "the gang." The scene was eventually cut because it was thought to be excessively violent.

HOYT BOWERS

Hoyt Bowers was the casting agent on *Giant*.

DAVID BOWIE

David Bowie, former glitter-glamour boy turned enduring rock star and actor, is a self-professed James Dean fan. Bowie paid homage to Dean in his song "Rebel Rebel."

BOX OFFICE

The figures that follow are approximations and do not account for television and video sales.

☆ *East of Eden*: $5 million
☆ *Rebel Without a Cause*: $8 million (one of the biggest-grossing films of 1956)
☆ *Giant*: $25 million (the second-biggest-grossing picture of all time [at that time], behind only *Gone with the Wind*; one of the biggest-grossing films of 1956 *and* 1957)

James Dean at the Box Office

Surprisingly James Dean was *not* one of the biggest box-office stars of 1955, or 1956. Who was?

1955

1. Jimmy Stewart
2. Grace Kelly
3. John Wayne
4. William Holden
5. Gary Cooper
6. Marlon Brando
7. Dean Martin and Jerry Lewis
8. Humphrey Bogart
9. June Allyson
10. Clark Gable

1956

1. William Holden
2. John Wayne
3. Jimmy Stewart
4. Burt Lancaster
5. Glenn Ford
6. Dean Martin and Jerry Lewis
7. Gary Cooper
8. Marilyn Monroe
9. Kim Novak
10. Frank Sinatra

JERRY BOXHORN

Costume designer for "The Bells of Cockaigne," a 1953 episode of the television series "Armstrong Circle Theatre" that co-starred James Dean.

WALDEN BOYLE

Dr. Walden Boyle directed the 1950 UCLA production of *Macbeth* in which sophomore James Dean was featured.

LEWIS BRACKER

Arizona-born Lew Bracker was Jimmy's insurance agent. The two men were introduced to one another in early 1955 by Leonard Rosenman. They became fast, close friends. It was Bracker who accompanied Jimmy when he pur-

Lew Bracker: "I know what I've lost in terms of a lifelong friendship."

chased the infamous Porsche 550 Spyder. And the week preceding September 30, 1955, it was Bracker who prophetically issued a life insurance policy on James Dean. At the time, Bracker's insurance company was located at 12040 Wilshire Boulevard in Sawtelle, California.

> "He said, 'We have to get married.' I said, 'To each other?' And he said, 'No. We both have to get married and have families. That's what we both want; that's what we both need.' He never talked to me like a man that was worried about cutting it short or having it cut short."

> Lew Bracker

On September 30 Bracker made plans to attend a football game. Jimmy wanted Bracker to accompany him to Salinas. "I can't talk you into it?" he cajoled. Bracker stood firm. "No, I'm going to the game." As Jimmy turned around to leave, he stated, as friends often do when refused, "Okay, it's your funeral!" Years later, Bracker recalled wistfully, "That's the last thing he ever said to me." On October 8, 1955, accident witness Sanford Roth dated a letter of testimony to the district attorney who was investigating the death of James Dean. Sadly, the letter was notarized by Lew Bracker.

The nature of Lew Bracker's friendship with Jimmy Dean will probably never be known. Over the years Bracker has been decidedly reticent about his old friend. In the interviews he *has* given (*The James Dean Story*, 1957; "A Current Affair," 1989), he has been rather brief and vague. Still, it is obvious that the feelings ran deep. When asked, some 35 years later, how he was impacted by Jimmy's death, Lew Bracker answered:

"I know what I've lost in terms of a lifelong friendship."

ROGERS BRACKETT

> "My primary interest in Jimmy was as an actor. His talent was so obvious. Secondarily, I loved him, and Jimmy loved me. If it was a father-son relationship, it was also somewhat incestuous."

> Rogers Brackett

In 1951 Rogers Brackett was a successful radio director affiliated with CBS and the powerful advertising agency Foote, Cone and Belding. Jimmy Dean, 15 years his junior, was a parking lot attendant at CBS. Their subsequent relationship was a West Hollywood rendering of the classic pairing between Professor Henry Higgins and Eliza Doolittle. But it was *not* about "the rain in Spain" that Brackett was teaching Dean.

Not only did Brackett help Jimmy, then 20 and barely out of his farm-boy overalls, get bit parts on radio programs and in feature films; he also introduced him to literature, fine art, and an entirely new world—the life of a Hollywood insider. Through Brackett Jimmy gained entrée into the movie-money milieu of pool parties, dinners at the Mocambo, after-dinner "screenings," and miscellaneous other Hollywood hobnobbing. Within a short period of time Jimmy moved into Brackett's home in the fashionable area of Sunset Plaza Drive.

"It was a question of marrying Joan Davis's daughter or going off to live with a studio director. In any case, the next thing they were living together. And it was with this man he went to Chicago and on to New York."

Isabelle Draesemer

Rogers Brackett's role as benefactor in the life and career of James Dean has never really been explored. Certainly he was instrumental in Jimmy's subsequent success, and he has never really been duly credited. First of all, it was Brackett, as much as anyone else, who prompted Jimmy to move to New York to seriously pursue an acting career. Further, he not only prompted the move but reportedly also financed it.

Then, when Brackett also moved to New York, Jimmy once again moved in with him. And once again Brackett began to open the proverbial show business doors to his young protégé—doors that otherwise would have likely remained closed. It was through Brackett that Jimmy met director James Sheldon, who later cast him in two television dramas and, more importantly, introduced him to agent Jane Deacy. Beyond that it was Brackett who instigated Jimmy's first major break—he opened the doors to the home of Lem Ayers, an introduction that resulted in *See the Jaguar*, Jimmy's first Broadway play—the play that launched his career.

Details of the breakup between Rogers Brackett and James Dean are unclear. In all likelihood, given the nature of their relationship, Jimmy dispensed with Brackett because he had no further use for him. The two men last saw one another in New York, in 1955, just prior to the release of *East of Eden*. Their parting was not amicable. Jimmy resented Brackett and anyone else who had a claim on him. He was also probably terribly insecure, and understandably so, that his relationship with Brackett would be made public. As a result, to the press and to his friends Jimmy adamantly but inaccurately contended that he had gotten where he had without the help of Brackett, without the help of anyone.

TOM BRADLEY
Los Angeles mayor Tom Bradley declared September 30, 1985, "James Dean Day" to commemorate the 30th anniversary of Dean's death.

THERESE BRANDES
Up until the time of her death in the early 1970s, Therese Brandes was the founder and longtime president of the James Dean Memory Club, one of the most successful of all the Dean clubs.

MARLON BRANDO
At times, he seemed obsessed with Brando. Occasionally, for no apparent reason, he would begin quoting from *A Streetcar Named Desire*. One time, during a discussion of Method acting, he took off his shirt and ripped his undershirt to shreds, yelling "Stella!" in imitation of Marlon Brando as Stanley Kowalski yelling for his wife.

Roy Schatt, *James Dean: A Portrait*

During his brief ascent to stardom James Dean was frequently compared to Marlon Brando. With the release of *East of Eden* in early 1955 many industry insiders snickered, fangs bared. "The Mickey Mouse Marlon Brando!" they proclaimed with spittle foaming from the side of their collective mouths. One critic went so far as to suggest that a public spanking was in order.

Granted, the similarities *were* obvious. Brando and Dean both balked at convention. They both had an affinity for mumbling and motorcycles. They both played the recorder and the bongo drums. They both belonged to the same unruly school of fashion. They both wore scowls on their faces, boots on their feet, and *attitude* in their jeans. They were offered the same types of roles. In fact Brando was offered the lead in *Rebel Without a Cause* in *1947*! He was also offered the lead in *East of Eden*. Thankfully for Dean fans, he declined both. Finally, and perhaps most significantly, they were both discovered by Elia Kazan. Some critics were more aware of the significance of this than others:

> He will inevitably be compared to Marlon Brando, for Kazan has stamped him with the same hesitant manner of speech, the same blind groping for love and security that he gave Brando in *On the Waterfront*. But if the performances are akin, so are the roles, and to complain about the similarities would be quibbling.
> William Zinsser, *New York Herald Tribune*, March 1955

Still, the Brando/Dean comparison did not begin with Elia Kazan. It began, in all likelihood, with director James Sheldon. When Jimmy arrived in New York in 1951, he read for Sheldon. At the time, Sheldon was an advertising executive who handled the television show "Mama," which was a successful adaptation of the stage play *I Remember Mama*. And it just so happened that the producers of the show were looking to recast the part of the young brother. In the play the part had been played by Marlon Brando. Recalled Sheldon, "The part was played by a very young, very blond Marlon Brando. And Jimmy reminded me of an even younger Marlon."

In part because of that resemblance, Sheldon attempted to have Jimmy cast in the part. Ultimately he was not hired, but he did leave a definite impression on Sheldon, who continued to aid him in his struggling career.

Jimmy was probably first aware of Marlon Brando in 1950, after seeing Brando's film debut in *The Men*. Their first meeting reportedly took place at the Actors Studio in New York in 1952. They met again in 1954 during the shooting of *East of Eden*. At the time, Brando was shooting *Desiree* at 20th Century-Fox. He visited the *Eden* set at the invitation of Kazan. Around the same time they met again at a party. It was the first and reportedly only time that the two men spent any substantial time together. As Brando later told writer Truman Capote:

> "When I finally met Dean [again, by several accounts, the two men had met a few years earlier at the Actors Studio] it was at a party where he was throwing himself around, acting the madman. So I spoke to him. I took him aside and asked him didn't he know he was

sick? I gave him the name of an analyst and he went. And at least his work improved. Towards the end I think he was beginning to find his own way as an actor."

Publicly Jimmy alternately accepted and rejected the comparison. As he told *Newsweek* in March 1955, "People were telling me I behaved like Brando before I knew who Brando was. I am not disturbed by the comparison, nor am I flattered. I have my own personal rebellion and I don't have to rely on Brando's." And, as recalled by Jimmy's friend, Roy Schatt, "He often said, each time as if I had never heard it, 'I had a motorbike before he [Brando] did!' "

Truthfully, however, there is little doubt that Jimmy idolized Brando and was despondent over Brando's apparent rejection of him.

Dean once told me he was convinced Brando hated him. Brando indicated [to me], however, such was not the case.
Bob Thomas, *Hollywood Citizen-News*

"[Jimmy] *was* fixated on Marlon for a while. I was gonna go to a get-together, and Marlon was supposed to be there . . . so, when I got back, Jimmy made me imitate everything that went on. What Marlon said, how he walked. . . ."
Christine White, *Jimmy Dean on Jimmy Dean* by Joseph Humphreys

Jimmy was so adoring [of Brando] that he seemed shrunken and twisted in misery.
Elia Kazan, *Kazan: A Life*

"[Jimmy] adored Marlon. One hears all sorts of stories about how Jimmy stalked him all over New York."
Stewart Stern, *Hollywood Speaks: An Oral History* by Mike Steen

"Dean was never a friend of mine. But he had an idée fixe about me. Whatever I did, he did. He was always trying to get close to me. He used to call me up. I'd listen to him talking to the answering service, asking for me, leaving messages. But I never spoke up. I never called him back."

Marlon Brando

[Jimmy] fell futilely in love with Marlon after viewing *The Wild One* and besieged him with phone calls.
Charles Higham, *Brando: The Unauthorized Biography*

In 1956 Brando, at the age of 32, was offered the starring role in a dramatized film biography of James Dean. Brando reportedly, and surprisingly, considered the role before dismissing it. He was then asked to narrate the Warner Brothers documentary tribute, *The James Dean Story*. Again Brando declined.

Nevertheless the link between Brando and Dean has extended well beyond the latter's death. Decades later, fans and film scholars are still debating over the talents and contributions of the two men. In his biography *Marlon Brando: The Only Contender*, author Gary Carey boldly ventures,

Brando: brood and brawn.

"[Dean] was the most flagrant and successful of the Brando imitators . . . and a surprising number of people who otherwise have good taste prefer Dean to Brando."

The question, of course, is *why* a choice had (or has) to be made at all. Despite their obvious similarities, Brando and Dean were distinctly different actors with different appeals. To categorize them both in the same ridiculous rebel straitjacket only diminishes their greatness—their mutual *individual* greatness.

The career of Marlon Brando has spanned more than 40 years and is typified by an astounding range of roles in films of vastly varying quality: *The Men* (1950), *A Streetcar Named Desire* (Best Actor Oscar nomination, 1951), *Viva Zapata!* (Best Actor Oscar nomination, 1952), *Julius Caesar* (Best Actor Oscar nomination, 1953), *The Wild One* (1954), *On the Waterfront* (Best Actor Oscar winner, 1954), *Desiree* (1954), *Guys and Dolls* (1955), *The Teahouse of the August Moon* (1956), *Sayonara* (Best Actor Oscar nomination, 1957), *The Young Lions* (1958), *The Fugitive Kind* (1960), *One-Eyed Jacks* (which he also directed, 1961), *Mutiny on the Bounty* (1962), *The Ugly American* (1963), *Bedtime Story* (1964), *The Saboteur* (1965), *The Chase* (1966), *The Appaloosa* (1966), *A Countess from Hong Kong* (1967), *Reflections in a Golden Eye* (1967), *Candy* (1968), *The Night of the Following Day* (1969), *Queimada* (Italy, France, 1969), *The Nightcomers* (England, 1972), *The Godfather* (Best Actor Oscar winner, 1972), *Last Tango in Paris* (Best Actor Oscar nomination, 1973), *The Missouri Breaks* (1976), *Superman* (1978), *Apocalypse Now* (1979), *The Formula* (1980), *A Dry White Season* (Best Supporting Actor Oscar nomination, 1989), and *The Freshman* (1990).

> "Acting has absolutely nothing to do with anything important. When you get paid enough to buy an island, sit on your ass and talk to *Playboy* magazine, there's nothing other than acting that allows for that."
>
> Marlon Brando

MICHAEL BRANDON
The actor who starred as Bill Bast in the 1976 television movie "James Dean."

Michael Brandon has also appeared in other films including *Lovers and Other Strangers* (1970) and *FM* (1978), the television movie "A Vacation in Hell" (1979), and the television programs "Emerald Point N.A.S." (1983–1984) and "Dempsey & Makepeace" (1985).

STEPHEN BRANNAN
Stephen Brannan portrayed James Dean in the play *James Dean: A Dress Rehearsal*, which was first produced in Denver, Colorado, in 1984.

ROBERT BRAUNT
After Jimmy's death his 1955 Ford station wagon was purchased by Robert F. Braunt for the sum of $2,200.

SUSAN BRAY

Perhaps indicating that he was showing signs of conforming to Hollywood standards, James Dean, toward the end of his life, hired a maid. Her name was Susan Bray. For the week ending September 24, 1955, Bray was paid $14.72 for cleaning up Jimmy's Sherman Oaks pad.

JOEL BREAN

Indiana native Joel Brean is the publisher and author of the book *Rebels United: The Enduring Reality of James Dean*, published in paperback in 1984 by Brean-Jones Publishing. In the book Brean contends that James Dean made a half-dozen visits to him from the afterlife because, as Brean quotes Jimmy, "The main reason that I came to see you, Joely, is that our vibrations are in harmony. Your vibrations, like mine, are the vibrations of the rebel."

One particularly strange passage in a very strange book has Jimmy cooing to Brean: "Joely, you ought to know by now that I can read your mind whenever I want to. I know what your desire is. You want to kiss my lips. . . ."

BRENTWOOD COUNTRY MART

In 1951 Jimmy attended an acting workshop directed by James Whitmore. The workshop was housed in a room above the Brentwood Country Mart in Brentwood, California. Today the building, built in 1948 and resembling a New England red barn, is still intact and functions as a shopping center (address: 26th Street at San Vicente Boulevard).

BRENTWOOD ELEMENTARY SCHOOL

From 1936 to 1938 Jimmy Dean was a student at Brentwood Elementary School in West Los Angeles, California. Today the building, which is 80 years old, still stands at 740 Gretna Green Way and is known as the Brentwood Unified Science Magnet School.

PAT BRESLIN

Pat Breslin was an actress who co-starred in "Prologue to Glory," a 1952 episode of "Kraft Television Theatre" in which James Dean appeared. Breslin later co-starred with Jackie Cooper in the television series "The People's Choice" (1955–1958).

JAMES BRIDGES

The September 30, 1955, death of James Dean had a profound effect on the then 27-year-old James Bridges of Conway, Arkansas. Upon hearing the news Bridges loaded up his beat-up convertible, quit school at the teacher's college where he was an undergraduate, and drove to Hollywood.

What resulted some 20 years later was the autobiographical, Dean-inspired motion picture *September 30, 1955* (1977). What also resulted was an impressive career as a writer and director for James Bridges. His films: *The Appaloosa* (as co-writer, 1966), *The Forbin Project* (as writer, 1970), *The Baby Maker* (1970), *The Paper Chase* (Best Screenplay Oscar nomination, 1973),

The China Syndrome (1979), *Urban Cowboy* (1980), *Mike's Murder* (1984), *Perfect* (1985), and *Bright Lights, Big City* (1988).

REX BRIGHT
Rex Bright was one of Jimmy's teammates on the Fairmount High Quakers basketball team. Six years after graduation Bright served as one of the pallbearers at Jimmy's funeral.

VIRGINIA BRISSAC
Virginia Brissac portrayed the grandmother of the character portrayed by James Dean in *Rebel Without a Cause*.

Brissac's other films include *A Tree Grows in Brooklyn* (1945), *Monsieur Verdoux* (1947), *The Snake Pit* (1948), and *Cheaper by the Dozen* (1950). She died in 1979 at the age of 85.

BROADWAY
The other shows playing on Broadway when *See the Jaguar* had its brief run in December 1952 were:

Guys and Dolls
The King and I, with Yul Brynner
The Millionairess, with Katharine Hepburn
The Seven Year Itch
South Pacific

When *The Immoralist* was on Broadway in February 1954, the other shows bidding for theatergoers' attention were:

Can-Can
Picnic
The Caine Mutiny Court Martial, with Henry Fonda and John Hodiak
Tea and Sympathy, directed by Elia Kazan, with Deborah Kerr

CHARLES BRONSON
Charles Bronson, the movies' grimacing gun-toting macho man of the 1970s, was up for the part of Pinky Snythe (which eventually went to Bob Nichols) in *Giant* (1956).

> "I have often thought, how lovely it would be to lean on a mantelpiece with a cocktail in my hand and let the dialogue do the acting."
>
> Charles Bronson

ADELINE BROOKSHIRE
See ADELINE NALL.

BROTHERS
None. James Dean was an only child. However, Jimmy's cousin, Marcus (Markie) Winslow, Jr., was sometimes regarded as his younger brother.

WALTER C. BROWN

Walter C. Brown wrote the teleplay for "The Unlighted Road," a 1955 episode of the CBS television series "Schlitz Playhouse of Stars" that starred James Dean.

Brown was also a frequent contributor to the television series "The Web" (1950–1957).

JACKSON BROWNE

Talented singer/songwriter who co-wrote the song "James Dean" recorded by the Eagles in 1974.

JOEL BRYKMAN

Co-producer of the 1982 stage play *Come Back to the Five and Dime, Jimmy Dean, Jimmy Dean.*

YUL BRYNNER

Yul Brynner won the 1956 Best Actor Oscar for his performance in *The King and I,* a role in which he was perennially cast. For the Oscar, Brynner defeated Kirk Douglas (*Lust for Life*), Rock Hudson (*Giant*), Sir Laurence Olivier (*Richard III*), and James Dean (*Giant*).

Brynner's other pictures include *Port of New York* (1949), *The Ten Commandments* (1956), *Anastasia* (1956), *The Brothers Karamazov* (1958), and *The Magnificent Seven* (1960). Brynner, born Taidje Khan in 1915, also starred in the television series "Anna and the King" (1972) and was a producer and director in the early years of television. He died of lung cancer in 1985.

HORST BUCHHOLZ

Actor who was hyped as "the James Dean of West Germany" in the 1950s. As one writer mused in the early 1960s, "He does have the same brooding intensity, the tousled hair, the sex appeal, the same high Slavic cheekbones, and he did wrap a car around a tree!"

Born in 1933, Buchholz appeared in films including *Marianne de Ma Jeunesse* (1954), *Tiger Bay* (England, 1959), *The Magnificent Seven* (1960), *Fanny* (1961), *One Two Three* (1961), *The Great Waltz* (1972), and *Avalanche Express* (1979). He also appeared in the television movie "Raid on Entebbe" (1977).

BULLFIGHTING

While growing up in Fairmount, Indiana, Jimmy was introduced to the art of bullfighting by the local town hero, Reverend James DeWeerd. As early as 1949 Jimmy wrote of his passion to a friend, Jim McCarthy. According to McCarthy, "He wrote . . . He loved the grace of the matadors, the way they made a kind of dance out of the sparring with the bull, how clean and beautiful it was, how much courage it took. . . ."

It was an interest that Jimmy retained throughout his young adult years in Hollywood and New York. He was frequently known to engage his friends in a few rounds of simulated action with Jimmy as the cape-swishing matador and a friend as the human bull. And when he couldn't find a willing participant, he improvised. Beulah Roth recalled: "He really loved bullfighting, admired bullfighters. Very often at dinner we would have French rolls, and Jimmy would stick toothpicks in them. He'd have imaginary bullfights."

His imaginary bullfights were not confined to the dinner table. A Warner Brothers publicity release, dated August 1954, read:

> The other day he walked off his set, sauntered over to the Warner Brothers wardrobe department and drew a full bullfighter's costume. Then he went to the backlot and for the better part of two hours he whirled and spun in veroninas and other classic passes of the bullfight. Watching adoringly was piquant Pier Angeli. Dean claims he'll be ready to step into the arena within two years. He first became interested in the sport while caring for the bulls on his uncle's farm.

At the time of his death Jimmy's estate included a pair of bull's horns and a matador's cape.

BURBANK, CALIFORNIA
During the shooting of *East of Eden* in the spring of 1954 Jimmy lived for a period in his dressing room at Warner Brothers Studios in Burbank, California. Prior to that he lived for a short time in Apartment 3, 3908 Olive Avenue, across the street from the studio.

BURIAL
James Dean is buried in the Winslow family plot at Park Cemetery in Fairmount, Indiana.

THE *BURLINGTON ZEPHYR*
The train (aka the *Denver Zephyr*) that Jimmy and his teacher, Adeline Nall, took from Chicago to Denver to compete in a national speech competition in 1949.

FRANK BURNS
Frank Burns is the television director who had the dubious distinction of having fired James Dean—before he became a star. The ill-fated production was a 1952 episode of the NBC television series "Martin Kane, Private Eye."

KEITH BURNS
Co-author of *James Dean: Behind the Scene*, a book published by Birch Lane Press in 1990. Burns also directed an award-winning documentary on the life of comedian Ernie Kovacs.

RAYMOND BURR

Raymond Burr co-starred in "Hill Number One," a special presentation of the television program "Family Theatre" that featured unknown actor James Dean.

Burr, born William Stacey Burr in 1917, is a longtime formidable presence in Hollywood, having appeared in films such as *Without Reservations* (1946), *Adventures of Don Juan* (1948), *A Place in the Sun* (1951), *Rear Window* (1954), and *Out of the Blue* (1982) and television programs such as "Perry Mason" (1957–1966; Best Actor Emmy winner, 1959), "Ironside" (1967–1975), "Kingston: Confidential" (1977), and "Centennial" (1978).

RICHARD BURTON

Born Richard Jenkins in 1925, actor Richard Burton was considered for the part of Jett Rink in *Giant* before it was eventually awarded to James Dean.

SCOTT BUSHNELL

Producer of the 1982 movie *Come Back to the Five and Dime, Jimmy Dean, Jimmy Dean.*

CHRIS BUSONE

Singer of "American Rebel," the theme song of the 1988 cable television documentary "Forever James Dean."

DAWS BUTLER

After Jimmy's death *Giant* director George Stevens hired actor Nick Adams and Daws Butler, the voice behind Elroy Jetson and many other cartoon characters, to imitate Jimmy's voice to dub into the Jett Rink banquet scene in the film. It is uncertain whether it is Adams's or Butler's voice in the final version of the film.

ROBERT BUTLER

Director of the 1976 made-for-television movie "James Dean."

Butler's film credits include *Guns in the Heather* (1969), *The Barefoot Executive* (1971), and *Now You See Him, Now You Don't* (1972). Butler also directed the television movie "Death Takes a Holiday" (1971).

BYE BYE JIMMY

Bye Bye Jimmy is a 1990 British documentary made directly for the video market. It was produced and directed by Nick Taylor and Paul Watson and narrated by Nick Clemente. Basically this hour-long movie retraces Jimmy's final, fatal drive, and is interspersed with various interviews.

C

CAHIERS DU CINÉMA

French film magazine that has published several articles about James Dean, including one written by director George Stevens that was published in the July 1956 issue.

JAMES CAIRES

James Caires is a multioffset printer from Randolph, Massachusetts. Caires is a member of the We Remember Dean International fan club and has been a Dean fan and collector since 1962. According to Caires, "All I can say is that, as I was growing up, James Dean was probably the single biggest influence in my life."

CALABASAS, CALIFORNIA

The chickie-run sequence of *Rebel Without a Cause* was shot at the Warner Ranch in Calabasas, California. On one particularly clear Calabasas evening during the spring of 1955 the cast and crew of *Rebel* gathered together and stared at the sky with collective awe at what they thought was an atomic bomb explosion. The following day cast member Steffi Sidney scoured the local newspapers for any mention of the explosion and found none.

Years later she learned that on that evening the United States government had secretly tested an atomic bomb outside of Las Vegas, Nevada.

CALENDARS

James Dean is a perennial calendar boy. Recent Dean calendars have been marketed by:

Danilo Promotions
3947 East Road
London, England N16AH

Pacific Press Service
CPO Box 2051
Tokyo, Japan

Landmark Calendars
51 Digital Drive
Novato, California 94949

Pomegranate Publications
975 Transport Way
Petaluma, California 94952

NMR Entertainment Group
7105 Trans Canada Highway
St. Laurent, Quebec, Canada H4T 1A2

Portal Publications, Ltd.
21 Tamal Vista Blvd.
Corte Madera, California 94925

ALBERT CALL

A Paso Robles, California, coroner's assistant who was one of the individuals who conducted the October 1955 investigation into the death of James Dean.

MUSHY CALLAHAN
Mushy Callahan, a former boxer, was employed by Elia Kazan to teach James Dean how to fight for *East of Eden*. Callahan tutored Jimmy's left jab, while Ace Hudkins, "The Nebraska Wildcat," gave him pointers on a right jab. Later Callahan helped to stage the knife-fight sequence between James Dean and Corey Allen in *Rebel Without a Cause*. Callahan also served as Jimmy's stand-in on both pictures.

Characteristic of Jimmy, if someone had something that he wanted or knew something that he wanted to know, he would befriend that person until he absorbed whatever he could. In the case of Mushy Callahan, Jimmy wanted to learn how to fight. After all, if he was going to portray a boxer in future projects (as he would later be signed to do), he wanted to know how to box with authority. So, in between takes of *Rebel Without a Cause*, Mushy Callahan sparred with James Dean.

VICTOR CAMERON
Victor V. Cameron was the Marion, Indiana, doctor who, on February 8, 1931, delivered James Dean into the world.

ROBERT CAMPBELL
Robert Campbell composed the score for *Dean*, a 1977 British stage musical.

"CAMPBELL SOUNDSTAGE"
"Campbell Soundstage" was a dramatic anthology series telecast by NBC on Friday nights from June 1952 to September 1954. It was produced live from New York and was originally titled "Campbell Playhouse." In June 1954 its title was changed to "Campbell Summer Soundstage."

James Dean appeared in the "Something for an Empty Briefcase" episode, which aired on July 17, 1953, and in the "Life Sentence" episode, which aired on October 16, 1953.

CANNES FILM FESTIVAL
The 1955 Cannes Film Festival took place from April 25 to May 11. That year *Marty* became the first American movie to capture the Golden Palm, the festival's grand prize. Another big winner that year was *East of Eden*, which was awarded the Best Dramatic Film prize—the first important award bestowed on a James Dean film. Dean did not attend the festivities.

ROGER CANNON
Roger Cannon is the founder of the James Dean Memorial Car Rally, held annually in California.

MARIETTA CANTY
Marietta Canty portrayed the maid and surrogate mother of the character portrayed by Sal Mineo in *Rebel Without a Cause*.

Canty has also appeared in the films *The Searching Wind* (1946), *Home Sweet Homicide* (1946), *Father of the Bride* (1950), *My Foolish Heart* (1950), and *The I Don't Care Girl* (1953), among others.

TRUMAN CAPOTE

> I am an alcoholic. I am a drug addict.
> I am a homosexual. I am a genius.
>
> Truman Capote

In Cold Blood author Truman Capote, born Truman Streckfus Persons in 1925, was most definitely *not* a Dean fan: to interviewer Lawrence Grobel, Capote lip-lashed:

> "I didn't think very much of him [Dean]. I knew him when he was in New York. He was a good friend of several friends of mine. And he did that Gide play. I don't think he was very good in the play, to put it mildly. I never thought anything about him as an actor. I didn't think he had any quality at all."

"THE CAPTURE OF JESSE JAMES"

February 8, 1953, episode of the television program "You Are There" in which Jimmy portrayed Bob Ford, the man who shot Jesse James. "The Capture of Jesse James" was directed by Sidney Lumet and aired on Jimmy's 22nd birthday. It was only the second episode of the series, which subsequently ran through 1957. Walter Cronkite hosted the show.

CAR RACING

> In those final days, racing was what he cared about most. If he had lived, he might have become a champion driver.
>
> Bill Hickman

> I remember him bringing photographs of his car racing to the set. His car racing was the most important thing in the world to him. I remember one time we were shooting [*Rebel Without a Cause*] at the [Griffith Park] Planetarium, and he said, "Ya wanna see some pictures?" You know I thought, "Oh, God," knowing Jimmy—he was always teasing me, always teasing—that they were probably horribly dirty pictures or something. So I was really nervous and said, "Well, I don't know." He takes them out, and they were just of him and his race car. . . . I just remember it was so bizarre that he went into this graphic detail of this race and he had all these eight by ten photos. . . . He was so excited by the race. He would get real animated about things like that.
>
> Beverly Long

> "Out on the track, I learn about people and myself."
>
> James Dean

James Dean was enamored of speed. Contrary to public perception it was not a sudden or passing interest. As a teenager in Fairmount, Indiana, Jimmy

Rebel racer: Jimmy accepting his trophies for the cameras.

used to hang out at the local motorcycle shop to absorb what he could about bikes, cars, and racing. He'd stage imaginary races in his head while gesticulating wildly and shouting out the standings with breathless abandon to an audience of none.

In Hollywood Jimmy was infamous for his solitary races through the hills of Mulholland. With the release of *East of Eden*, he purchased a white Porsche Speedster. In March 1955, he began to tire of his high-speed phantom chases. He needed new territory to challenge. And so, years before Paul Newman or Tom Cruise even contemplated pistons and pit stops, James Dean took his high-voltage act onto the racetrack.

The following is a chronological record of James Dean's racing career:

Race No. 1

March 26, 1955. Two-day event. Palm Springs Road Races. Jimmy won the preliminary race, qualifying him for the finals. In the finals Jimmy competed against such veterans as Ken Miles and Cy Yedor, both of whom were driving MG Specials. Jimmy finished the race in third place. But later Miles was disqualified on a technicality and Jimmy was bumped up to second place.

At the races.

Race No. 2
May 1, 1955. Minter Field, Bakersfield, California. Jimmy entered the 1,300–2,000cc production and 750–1,500cc modified race. He placed third behind Marion Playan in an MG Special and John Kunstle in a Panhard Devin.

Race No. 3
Memorial Day, May 28–29, 1955. Santa Barbara Road Races. Jimmy entered the under-1,500cc production event. He moved up to fourth place before his Porsche blew a piston.

Race No. 4
October 2, 1955. Salinas. This was the race in which Jimmy was going to debut his new silver Porsche 550 Spyder—the race that he never made it to.

At the time of his death James Dean's personal possessions included two gold cup trophies mounted on square wooden bases. The plaque on the bases read "Kern County SCC Bakersfield, National Sports Car Race 1955." The emblem on the cups read "Sports Car Club of America." Also included in the estate was one silver cup trophy mounted on a wooden base. The emblem on this cup was inscribed "Eighth Running Palm Springs Road Race."

Jimmy's Car Racing Numbers
Porsche Speedster: #75
Porsche Spyder: #130

TIMOTHY CAREY
Professional baseball pitcher who quit the sport to make movies, including *East of Eden*. Carey portrayed Kate's bouncer, Joe, to whom James Dean uttered his first line of dialogue in *Eden*: "You want me?"

Usually cast as a villain, Carey, born in 1925, has also appeared in *Hellgate* (1952), *Paths of Glory* (1957), and *The Conversation* (1974), among other films.

LESLIE CARON
Leslie Caron is an actress/dancer who once dated James Dean. She was so affected by the news of Jimmy's death, according to one fan magazine, that she vowed never to dance again. If true (get serious), the vow was short-lived. Years later Caron was interviewed in the 1976 documentary *James Dean: The First American Teenager*.

Born in 1931 and discovered by Gene Kelly, Leslie Caron has appeared in numerous films, including *An American in Paris* (1951), *Lili* (Best Actress Oscar nomination, 1953), *Daddy Longlegs* (1955), *Gigi* (1958), *Fanny* (1961), *The L-Shaped Room* (Best Actress Oscar nomination, 1963), *Father Goose* (1964), *Promise Her Anything* (1966), *Is Paris Burning?* (1966), and *Valentino* (1977). She also appeared in the television movie "QB VII" (1974).

PAUL CARR
Actor who portrayed a car-racing movie star in the Dean-inspired "To Climb Steep Hills," a 1962 episode of the television program "Straightaway."

JOHN CARRADINE
Starred in "Hound of Heaven," a 1953 episode of the daytime television program "The Kate Smith Show," in which James Dean co-starred.

Carradine, born in 1906 and father of the acting Carradine clan (David, Keith, and Robert), appeared in several other television programs including "My Friend Irma" (1953–1954). His many feature films include *Tol'able David* (1931), *Bride of Frankenstein* (1935), *Stagecoach* (1939), *The Grapes of Wrath* (1940), *The Ten Commandments* (1956), *The Man Who Shot Liberty Valance* (1962), and *The Scarecrow* (New Zealand, 1982).

JACK CARROLL
Jack Carroll recorded some of the music on the Unique Records tribute album *Music James Dean Lived By*, including "The Story of James Dean," which was also included on another album, *A Tribute to James Dean*.

THE CARS
"The James Dean Car" is a tag frequently attached to the 1949 Mercury Jimmy drove in *Rebel Without a Cause*. In fact the 1949, 1950, and 1951 Mercurys have become collector's items revered by car aficionados because of the Dean association.

Jimmy Dean learned how to drive on a tractor on his uncle's farm. Later he graduated to driving more sophisticated—and faster—vehicles.

The Winslow family Ford.

However, in life James Dean did not own a Mercury. In Fairmount, Indiana, circa 1949, he *did* drive around in his uncle Marcus's new Ford, but that's as far as it went.

What other cars did Jimmy drive? The following is a chronological list:

☆ Winton Dean purchased a used 1939 Chevy for his son in the summer of 1949.
☆ Upon returning to Hollywood in the spring of 1954 to make *East of Eden*, Jimmy rented a Ford convertible.
☆ In May 1954 Jimmy purchased a red 1953 MG.
☆ Jimmy later purchased a 1955 Ford station wagon. The car was white with wood paneling on the sides.
☆ In March 1955 Jimmy purchased a Porsche 356 Super Speedster.
☆ During the summer 1955 shooting of *Giant* in Marfa, Texas, Jimmy drove a rented Chevy. However, the producers of the film retrieved the car after learning that Jimmy had shot out its windows with a BB gun.
☆ On September 21, 1955, Jimmy purchased a silver Porsche 550 Spyder.
☆ Prior to his death, Jimmy had made plans to purchase a Lotus Mark 9 racing car. It was to have been delivered to him in October 1955.

ROBERT CARSON
Writer whose story "You Gotta Stay Happy" was adapted into "Ten Thousand Horses Singing," a 1952 episode of the CBS television program "Studio One" in which James Dean had a bit part.

LYNNE CARTER
> He spoke as I watched him remove his make-up and strip off the garb he wore as an Arab boy. He didn't seem a bit shy about appearing half-nude in front of me, so I attempted to conceal my uneasiness by constant chattering. It was the first time I noticed how well-built he was. . . ."
>
> Lynne Carter on James Dean, *Rave* magazine

Lynne Carter was a model when she met James Dean in Philadelphia during the early 1954 pre-Broadway tryout of *The Immoralist*. After Jimmy's death Carter penned an article for *Rave* magazine entitled "I Was a Friend of Jimmy Dean" in which she gushed, "What we had between us I consider beautiful and rare, and I am proud to put it into words." And put it into words she did. Words and photos, that is.

After their initial meeting, according to Carter, she traveled to New York City and ended up in Jimmy's apartment at 3:00 A.M. "Jimmy laid his head on my lap and asked me to massage his temples. While I did it, he recited Shakespeare. He tried to kiss me several times and told me that I knew nothing about art. He said he would teach me. . . ."

Of another intimate occasion she wrote, "He decided to take a shower, and reappeared with a towel around his waist and, as ever, wearing his boots."

Carter ended her article by concluding "Knowing Jimmy Dean was one of the most vibrating experiences of my life." Presumably she didn't intend the line to be amusing.

It is impossible to discern how much of her story was true, how much was every girl's fantasy, and how much was blatant self-promotion. One thing is certain: it is difficult to take Lynne Carter seriously after glancing at the photographs that accompanied the article. In one shot Carter posed in an unbuttoned blouse; in another she wore a tiger-print bikini; and in yet another she wore nothing but an oversized scarf. In all of them she wore a Marilyn Monroe–esque pout and smolder.

The success of Lynne Carter's article prompted another one. In this one, titled "I Learned About Love From Jimmy Dean," she appeared wrapped only in a towel in one photograph. At least she spared us the boots.

MARY CARTER
Mary Carter was a Fairmount, Indiana, landscape painter who gave Jimmy art lessons when he was a child.

CARTER MOTORS
At the age of 15 Jimmy Dean was presented with his first motorcycle. It had been purchased from Carter Motors, a motorcycle shop in Fairmount, Indiana. For the next few years Jimmy was a frequent visitor at Carter Motors, attempting to learn as much as he could about motorcycles.

Carter Motors owner Marvin Carter was interviewed in the 1957 documentary *The James Dean Story*.

ETHEL CASE
See ETHEL DEAN.

"THE CASE OF THE SAWED-OFF SHOTGUN"
Episode of the television program "Treasury Men in Action" in which James Dean was featured. It aired on NBC on April 16, 1953.

"THE CASE OF THE WATCHFUL DOG"
Episode of the television program "Treasury Men in Action" in which James Dean was featured. It aired on NBC on January 29, 1953.

DON CASH
Don Cash was the make-up artist on "The Unlighted Road," a 1955 episode of the "Schlitz Playhouse of Stars" that starred James Dean.

CASTAIC JUNCTION
One of Jimmy's first stops en route to Salinas, California, on September 30, 1955, was at Tip's Diner in Castaic Junction, aka Castaic Landing.

GEORGE CATES
George Cates recorded some of the songs on the Coral Records tribute album *The James Dean Story*.

HUGH CAUGHELL

Hugh Caughell was Jimmy's biology teacher at Fairmount High School. Jimmy attended Caughell's class, located in the basement, in his freshman year. Caughell was also the adviser of the school's 4-H Club, of which Jimmy was a member, and the co-sponsor of the class of 1949. Caughell described his former, famous student as having been "quiet and cooperative" in the classroom and "fun-loving" outside of the classroom.

MAXWELL CAULFIELD

Maxwell Caulfield is an actor and devout Dean fan. Caulfield named his cat Marcus, as Jimmy had done. He also visited Jimmy's hometown of Fairmount, Indiana, in August 1988 and attended the unveiling of the Dean monument at the Griffith Park Observatory in November 1988.

Maxwell Caulfield: rebel without a good movie role.

Born in 1959, Caulfield burst on the scene in the off-Broadway production of Joe Orton's *Entertaining Mr. Sloane* in which he was hailed by some as "the next James Dean." However, his well-muscled physique seems to have elicited more critical favor over the years than his chosen screen projects. Caulfield's films include *Grease 2* (1982) and *The Boys Next Door* (1986). He also co-starred in the television series "The Colbys."

Perhaps representing many young actors who have been similarly inspired, Maxwell Caulfield composed an original poem in homage to James Dean. It is reprinted below:

U.S. FRIEND

Hey Jimmy!
Tied to the land
You yearned to soar

Red hot
Blue cool,
Young God
Lil' Bastard
Genius actor
Thanx man
Big time!

BUTCH CAVELL
Actor who was featured in "Prologue to Glory," a 1952 episode of the NBC television program "Kraft Television Theatre" in which James Dean appeared.

RON CAYEN
Ron Cayen is a consultant in the acquisition of fine art and photography. He also served as photo editor of the book *James Dean: American Icon* by David Dalton (St. Martin's Press, 1984). Cayen also published *The James Dean Portfolio*, a collection of photographs by Dennis Stock.

CBS RADIO
Circa 1951, Jimmy worked as a part-time usher and parking lot attendant at CBS Radio Studios in Hollywood (address: 6121 Sunset Boulevard).

"CBS RADIO WORKSHOP"
Numerous publications have reported that, before stardom, James Dean had a bit part on the "CBS Radio Workshop" program in 1951. In fact, Jimmy did appear on several radio shows, but "CBS Radio Workshop" was *not* one of them. It did not premiere until January 27, 1956, several months after Jimmy's death. "CBS Radio Workshop" had a short life of its own; it was canceled on September 22, 1957.

CENSORSHIP
Two scenes were cut out of *East of Eden* because they were thought to be too suggestively erotic. The first scene featured Cal (James Dean) climbing through a bedroom window and fondling a slipper owned by Abra (Julie Harris).

The second was a bedroom scene between the two brothers, Cal and Aron (Richard Davalos). The scene opened with Cal in shadow and Aron in bed. The dialogue itself was hardly provocative; however, some of the powers-that-be at Warner Brothers apparently perceived homoeroticism in the way that Cal wrapped his lips around the recorder and in the way he seemed to caress Aron with his words. The scene, written by Paul Osborn, is reprinted below.

> CAL: You're the one that Dad loves. He doesn't love me and never has. [Imitating his father] This is my son, *Aron*, that is. Thinks I got a great idea here. This is my other son, Cal [no longer imitating his father], who saved his money when we were kids and bought him a beautiful jackknife. And you got him a lousy, mangy little dog you picked up somewhere. Well, he loved that dog, Aron. He didn't even say 'thank-you' for my jackknife. Didn't say nothing.

[Cal starts to cry. Then, he picks up his recorder and starts to play. Aron gets up, approaches Cal's bed.]

ARON: What have you ever done to deserve Dad's love? What I mean is—who used to be decent to him and try to make things half-way pleasant?

CAL: You did.

ARON: And what have you done? Ever since I can remember, you've growled at him and snapped at him. You can't win anybody's love by fighting them every minute, Cal. You've got to fight with them. You've got to show them that you're on their side. Cal, why don't you give Dad a chance? Why don't you show him that you love him?

CAL: [Pleading] How?

ARON: It's so easy. Just tell him. Show him. Why don't you do something for him? It's so easy. You'll see. It's the simplest thing in the world.

CAL: I know it. I know it is, Aron.

Prior to shooting, *Eden* had considerable problems with the censors. The Breen Office, the film industry censor, insisted that no scenes be shot in Kate's brothel, so a saloon was established instead; they also demanded that "no actual prostitutes" be shown and that the term *madam* be excised from the script. The Breen Office also objected to a scene in which Anne (Lois Smith) "entertained" Cal.

The entire opening scene of *Rebel Without a Cause* was excised from the final version of the film due to what was regarded as excessive violence. The scene depicted the gang boot-stomping an apparently nice, middle-class gentleman—for kicks. The man was carrying an Easter basket that held a stuffed toy monkey. As recalled by gang member Steffi Sidney, "We sort of tease him and stomp him because we're not very nice kids. Well, we're nice kids, but we've got nothing better to do. Nick Ray, I think, was very big on feet shots or shoe shots, because I know we all had to get our feet in there and kick him. And he stumbles away.

"But what eventually happens, of course, is that the basket he's holding breaks open and the monkey tumbles out. And then Jimmy Dean comes wandering up the street, and he finds the monkey.

"Well, they cut that all out, and now the picture just opens where he's coming up the street and he finds the monkey and he cuddles up with it, you know. And, of course that business with the monkey was all improvised."

Additional cuts were made in the British version of *Rebel*. The knife-fight sequence between Jim (Dean) and Buzz (Corey Allen) was cut to a minimum because it was thought that it might encourage impressionable teenage boys to engage in blade fights. Also, the police station scene in which Jim pounds his fist into a desk was cut because, according to the censors, it displayed "excessive emotion." In addition, the following exchange of dialogue in the chickie-run sequence was cut, presumably because the censors feared that it would provoke British teenagers to drive off cliffs in droves:

BUZZ: You know, I like you.

JIM: Why do we do this, then?

BUZZ: You've go to do something, now don't you?

Rebel Without a Cause was also banned in Mexico and Spain, reportedly because James Dean as Jim Stark was considered to be too weak a role model for young Latin men. It was also banned outright in Memphis, Tennessee, for some reason or another.

Despite its homogenized, family nature, even *Giant* had censorship problems. During preproduction a letter from the censor, dated December 13, 1954, was issued to Warner Brothers. In it the censor disapproved of several sequences in the script and included the following notations:

☆ "The expression 'Good Lord' is unacceptable."
☆ "Jett's use of the word 'damn' is unacceptable."
☆ "The fight sequence, as well as other scenes of physical conflict, must be handled with great care in order that there be no excessive brutality or gruesomeness. Of late, our industry has received severe criticism from many quarters for what has been termed our 'sadistic love of brutality for its own sake.' "

CENTRAL PARK
In preparation for their 1952 audition for the Actors Studio James Dean and Christine White spent countless rehearsal hours in Central Park, one of Dean's favorite New York hangouts.

APRIL CHANNING
New York showgirl whom Dean dated. A 1955 press item read: "All those letters James Dean has been writing on the set of *Rebel Without a Cause* go to April Channing whom Dean met on his last trip to the East."

JACK CHAPLAIN
In the early 1960s Jack Chaplain was a Dean look-alike and a protégé of Nick Adams. In an effort to launch his career Chaplain was hyped as "the next James Dean"—a label he did little to fulfill.

LONNY CHAPMAN
Lonny Chapman was a member of the Actors Studio during the same period as Jimmy. The two men became friendly and discussed plans to make a western movie together. Chapman also had a small part in *East of Eden*.

He also appeared in several other pictures, including *Young at Heart* (1954), *Baby Doll* (1956), *The Birds* (1963), *The Reivers* (1969), *The Cowboys* (1972), *Where the Red Fern Grows* (1974), *Moving Violation* (1976), and *Norma Rae* (1979). His television credits include "The Investigator" (1958) and "For the People" (1965).

CHATEAU MARMONT HOTEL
Landmark West Hollywood hostelry (address: 8221 Sunset Boulevard), popular among movie and music personages and infamous as the hotel in which comedian John Belushi died from a drug overdose.

In late 1954 and early 1955 Jimmy was a frequent visitor at Bungalow 2 of the Chateau Marmont Hotel, where director Nick Ray resided. In fact the entire cast of *Rebel Without a Cause* met there in January 1955 to put the script on audiotape, and some of the subsequent rehearsals for *Rebel* were conducted there. In addition, Ray hosted afternoon tea parties in his bungalow every Sunday. It was in the Nick Ray bungalow where John Belushi died on March 5, 1982.

Jimmy was also a frequent visitor at the Marmont's pool, as were other members of the *Rebel* cast.

In September 1955 Jimmy's agent, Jane Deacy, flew to Los Angeles from New York and took up temporary residence at the Chateau Marmont. On Sunday, September 25, Jane held a party in her suite to celebrate Jimmy's new Warner Brothers contract and the near completion of *Giant*. Five days later Jimmy was dead.

ARA CHEKMAYAN

Writer, producer, and director of the 1988 cable television documentary, "Forever James Dean."

CHER

Cher co-starred in the 1982 Broadway play *Come Back to the Five and Dime, Jimmy Dean, Jimmy Dean*. Her performance in that play and its subsequent film adaptation rescued her slumping career from the barren wastelands of television reruns. Further, it gave her respect and credibility as an actress.

Cherilyn Sarkesian was born in 1946. In 1971, after a successful recording and live performance career, Cher and her husband, the future mayor of Palm Springs, Sonny Bono, starred in a musical variety series on CBS entitled "The Sonny and Cher Comedy Hour." The show was a hit and ran until 1974, when the couple divorced. At that point Cher starred in a solo series, "Cher" (1975–1976), before reteaming with Sonny for a resumption of "The Sonny and Cher Comedy Hour," which ran until 1977.

Her other films: *Good Times* (1967), *Silkwood* (Best Supporting Actress Oscar nomination, 1983), *Mask* (1985), *The Witches of Eastwick* (1987), *Suspect* (1987), *Moonstruck* (Best Actress Oscar winner, 1987), and *Mermaids* (1990).

> "I've been a joke all my career life. I've been one of the most popular women in America—and a joke."
>
> Cher, 1982

> "I never liked myself. I always thought I was a second-rater—a second-rate singer, a second-rate television performer. At first, all I wanted was to be famous. Then I realized that fame had nothing to do with talent. So then I wanted to be good."
>
> Cher, 1985

CHERRY LANE THEATRE
An off-Broadway theater where Jimmy appeared in a stage play, *Women of Trachis*, in early 1954. The theater still exists and is located at 38 Commerce Street.

CHEVRON
The Chevron oil company featured an image of James Dean in one of its 1988 print advertisements. The ad copy read, in part, "There are legends. And there are legends."

CHICAGO, ILLINOIS
En route to Longmont, Colorado, in April 1949, Jimmy, accompanied by his coach and chaperon, Adeline Nall, had a three-hour layover in Chicago. Two-and-a-half years later Jimmy visited Chicago briefly before moving to New York City.

CHICAGO TRIBUNE
Chicago newspaper that has published several articles about James Dean, including:

☆ "The Last Hour of James Dean," February 5, 1956 (*Chicago Tribune Magazine*)
☆ "The Truth About James Dean," September 9, 1956 (*Chicago Tribune Magazine*)
☆ "Stevens Gives His Opinion of Jim Dean," October 14, 1956
☆ "Hoosier Home Towns Re-live James Dean's Story," September 29, 1957 (*Chicago Tribune Magazine*)
☆ "Head Missing from Bust of James Dean," April 1, 1959
☆ "James Dean Foundation Goes Broke," October 16, 1960
☆ "Dean Disgusts Hedda, Then Charms Her," March 5, 1963
☆ "Giant Legacy, The Hero That James Dean Created Still Lives," September 15, 1985

CHILDREN OF THE DARK
Children of the Dark was a novel by Irving Shulman that was based on the movie *Rebel Without a Cause*. The book was published by Holt Books in 1956.

CHOLAME, CALIFORNIA
Small California town (pronounced "show-lamb") located near the site of the 1955 car crash in which James Dean was killed. In 1977 a memorial to Dean was erected outside the Cholame post office. Today Dean fans throughout the world continue to make the pilgrimage to Cholame, population 25, to follow the route that Jimmy took the day of his death and to observe the memorial.

CHRISTIE'S
In 1987 the Christie's auction house of New York auctioned off a Lotus racing car that was touted, incorrectly, as having been delivered to James Dean a week before his death. Jimmy never received or drove the car, although he

did have it on order. The car, a Lotus Mark 9, was valued at $25,500. It sold for a reported sum of $46,750 to an unidentified California bidder.

CIGARETTES

Jimmy was an incessant smoker. He was also notorious for using a cigarette as a prop in photographs and on screen. His favorite brands? Winstons and Chesterfields. In Japan one enterprising tobacco company marketed a brand of cigarettes called "Dean."

In his classic scandal chronicle, *Hollywood Babylon*, writer Kenneth Anger contended that Jimmy was a "human ashtray" who enjoyed the masochistic torture of having others extinguish their cigarettes on his flesh. The report, however, has never been substantiated.

CINEMA BOOKS

Seattle-based store (address: 4753 Roosevelt Way N.E., Seattle, Washington) that features "the largest selection of books and magazines on film in the Northwest." More to the point, Cinema Books features a large collection of Dean memorabilia, including a few dozen posters, many still photographs and postcards, calendars, checkbook covers, gift bags, books, and more.

CINEMATOGRAPHERS JIMMY WORKED WITH

Ernest Haller: *Rebel Without a Cause*
Ted McCord: *East of Eden*
William Mellor: *Giant*

CINEMONDE MAGAZINE

French film publication that named James Dean the Best Foreign Actor of 1955. For four straight years after Jimmy's death *Cinemonde* continued to fan the flames by devoting its September issues to his memory.

CIPOLLA THE GREAT

After the release of *East of Eden* Jimmy made tentative plans to direct *Cipolla the Great*, a one-act opera written by Leonard Rosenman, at the Tanglewood Summer Music Festival in Massachusetts. However, the proposed collaboration never came to fruition.

JOSEPH CLAPSADDLE

Co-producer of *Come Back to the Five and Dime, Jimmy Dean, Jimmy Dean*, a 1982 Broadway play.

DAVID CLARKE

Cast member of *See the Jaguar*, which co-starred James Dean.

CLASSIC POTATO CHIPS

South African potato chip company that used the Dean image to promote its product in 1988. One of its typical advertisements read: "There are actors and actors . . . but few classics. There are chip and chips . . . but only one Classic."

DICK CLAYTON

Dick Clayton, of the Famous Artists Corporation, was Jimmy's agent in Hollywood in 1954–1955. Jimmy's primary agent, Jane Deacy, was based in New York.

Upon hearing the news of Jimmy's death in the early evening of September 30, 1955, Clayton, along with Deacy (who was in Hollywood on business), drove to Jimmy's father's house in Santa Monica to break the news to him.

GEORGE T. CLEMENS

George Clemens was the director of photography of "The Unlighted Road," a 1955 episode of the CBS program "Schlitz Playhouse of Stars" that starred James Dean.

NICK CLEMENTE

Narrated the British documentary *Bye Bye Jimmy*.

MONTGOMERY CLIFT

Reportedly Montgomery Clift had wanted the part of Cal Trask in *East of Eden* but was instead offered the role of Aron, opposite Marlon Brando's Cal.

Just as he was compared to Brando when he arrived on the scene in 1954,

Before there was Brando or Dean there was **Montgomery Clift.**

James Dean was also compared to Clift. Like Brando, Clift was also a subject of James Dean's idolization:

> "He's a punk and a helluva talent. He likes racing cars, waitresses—and waiters. He says you're his idol."
>
> Elia Kazan to Monty Clift

> "Jimmy used to call Monty Clift when he was in New York and say, 'I'm a great actor and you're my idol and I need to see you because I need to communicate.' And Clift would change his phone number. Then after Jimmy was dead, Monty saw all three of his films, and every time he'd get drunk and cry and cry about the fact he'd denied this young man the opportunity of seeing him and talking to him."
>
> Dennis Hopper

In May 1956, eight months after James Dean's death, Montgomery Clift was seriously injured and disfigured in an automobile accident. He died 10 years later, at the age of 46, following a battle with alcoholism, depression, and a lifelong sexual attraction to men.

Montgomery Clift's stage credits include *The Skin of Our Teeth* (1942), *Our Town* (1944), *The Searching Wind* (1944), and *The Sea Gull* (1954). His prolific film work: *The Search* (Best Actor Oscar nomination, 1948), *Red River* (1948), *The Heiress* (1949), *The Big Lift* (1950), *A Place in the Sun* (Best Actor Oscar nomination, 1951), *I Confess* (1953), *From Here to Eternity* (Best Actor Oscar nomination, 1953), *Indiscretion of an American Wife* (1954), *Raintree County* (1957), *The Young Lions* (1958), *Lonelyhearts* (1959), *Suddenly Last Summer* (1959), *Wild River* (1960), *The Misfits* (1961), *Judgment at Nuremberg* (Best Supporting Actor Oscar nomination, 1961), *Freud* (1962), and *The Defector* (1966).

CLUBS, GUILDS, AND ORGANIZATIONS JAMES DEAN JOINED

☆ Actors Equity
☆ American Federation of Television and Radio Artists (AFTRA)
☆ Band, Fairmount High School
☆ Baseball Team, Fairmount High School
☆ Basketball Team, Fairmount High School
☆ Basketball Team, Santa Monica City College
☆ Debate Team, Fairmount High School
☆ Drama Club, Santa Monica City College
☆ 4-H Club, Fairmount High School
☆ Jazz Appreciation Club, Santa Monica City College
☆ Miller Playhouse Theater Guild
☆ Opheleos Men's Honor Service Organization, Santa Monica City College
☆ Screen Actors Guild (SAG)
☆ Sigma Nu Fraternity, UCLA
☆ Sports Car Club of America
☆ Thespians Club, Fairmount High School
☆ Track Team, Fairmount High School

COACHES
See TEACHERS.

THE COBWEB

The Cobweb was a 1955 MGM movie in which director Vincente Minnelli and producer John Houseman wanted James Dean to star as a young patient in a mental clinic. However, Warner Brothers, the studio Jimmy was contracted to, blocked the deal, and John Kerr was cast in the part instead.

The Cobweb was written by John Paxton from a novel by William Gibson. In addition to Kerr, the cast included Richard Widmark, Lauren Bacall, Charles Boyer, Lillian Gish, Gloria Grahame, Susan Strasberg, Oscar Levant, Tommy Rettig, Paul Stewart, and Adele Jergens. Leonard Rosenman composed the music.

FRED COE

Shortly before his death James Dean had been hired by producer Fred Coe to star in a television adaptation of Ernest Hemingway's "The Battler." The show was to have aired in October 1955.

Fred Coe, born in Alligator, Mississippi, was a prominent producer/director in the early years of television. He is also considered to be at least partially responsible for drafting such talents as Paddy Chayefsky, Rod Serling, and Horton Foote into the medium.

JAMES R. COGAN

James Dean's eye doctor. Following Jimmy's death the James Dean estate paid the sum of $25 to Dr. Cogan for unspecified services rendered. In 1955 Cogan's offices were located at 414 North Camden Drive in Beverly Hills.

LARRY COLEMAN

Larry Coleman wrote the song "James Dean (Just a Boy from Indiana)," which was recorded on the Coral Records tribute album *The James Dean Story.*

VIVIAN COLEMAN

In July 1956 the now-defunct James Dean Memorial Foundation was incorporated in Jimmy's hometown of Fairmount, Indiana, with the purpose, according to Vivian Coleman, the foundation's coordinating director at the time, of aiding "in every way, talented persons in all fields of artistic endeavors."

THOMAS COLEY

Actor who starred in "Prologue to Glory," a 1952 episode of the NBC television program "Kraft Television Theatre" in which James Dean appeared.

"THE COLGATE VARIETY HOUR"

Modern Screen magazine bestowed a posthumous "special achievement" award on James Dean on the November 27, 1955, episode of the NBC television program "The Colgate Variety Hour," which had formerly been known as "The Colgate Comedy Hour." The program was hosted by Robert Paige.

COLLECTORS BOOK STORE
One of the finest stores of its kind in the world, Collectors Book Store (address: 1708 North Vine Street) in Hollywood houses a vast collection of motion picture photographs, posters, and books, including an impressive catalog of James Dean material.

COLLIERS MAGAZINE
On September 30, 1955, photographer Sanford Roth followed James Dean en route to a car race in Salinas, California, to cover the event for *Colliers* magazine. Jimmy, of course, never made it to the race, but that did not stop *Colliers* from publishing "The Late James Dean" by Sanford Roth in its November 25, 1955, issue.

JOAN COLLINS
"My theory is never stand when you can sit and never sit when you can lie down . . ."

Joan Collins

"Intense, moody, incredible charisma. He was short, myopic, not good-looking in life, really. You know who he was like? A young, better-looking Woody Allen, in a way. He has those same qualities of shyness, uncertainty and insecurity."

Joan Collins on James Dean

Television's bewigged, bejeweled (and still reigning) goddess of bitch once had a brush with the Dean mystique. Joan Collins described the encounter in her autobiography, *Past Imperfect* (Simon and Schuster, 1984):

It was during the filming of *Giant* that I first met him. It was a brief meeting at a small dinner party in the [San Fernando] Valley. I was particularly mesmerized by his eyes, which were a deep, piercing blue and could change instantly from a look of sullen brooding to an expression of extreme mischievousness. He was quite short for a film actor and had longish, blond wavy hair. He seemed terribly shy and clutched the hand of his girlfriend, a gorgeous Swiss starlet under contract to Paramount called Ursula Andress. She had a fabulous body and the shortest haircut I had ever seen. They made a striking couple, both wearing white T-shirts and Levi's.

"COME BACK JIMMY DEAN, JIMMY DEAN"
Song recorded by Bette Midler on her *No Frills* album.

COME BACK TO THE FIVE AND DIME, JIMMY DEAN, JIMMY DEAN
The Play
Come Back to the Five and Dime, Jimmy Dean, Jimmy Dean, inspired by the

Dean legend, was written by Ed Graczyk and opened on Broadway at the Martin Beck Theatre on February 18, 1982. The production was directed by Robert Altman and produced by Dan Fisher, Joseph Clapsaddle, Joel Brykman, and Jack Lawrence. It starred Sandy Dennis, Cher, Karen Black, Sudie Bond, Gena Ramsel, Kathy Bates, Marta Heflin, and Mark Patton as "Joe," the Dean figure.

Come Back to the Five and Dime dramatizes the influence James Dean had and continues to have on a group of small-town Texas women, the secrets they harbor, and the lies they perpetrate. The primary focal point is Mona, the character portrayed by Sandy Dennis, who clings to the claim that James Dean fathered her child while he was in Marfa shooting *Giant*. As evidence of the conception she strokes a chunk of the Reata mansion that she scavenged from the *Giant* set, and she calls out after her son, whom she named Jimmy Dean.

It was in this play that Cher made her legitimate acting debut. At the time it was considered a brazen (some thought foolish) casting move on the part of Altman, who had originally intended the role to be Shelley Duvall's.

The Film
With an $800,000 budget, 16mm film, and *19 days*, Robert Altman shot a filmed version, released theatrically in 1982, of the Ed Graczyk play. Altman directed and co-edited, the latter with Jason Rosenfield. The film was produced by Scott Bushnell. The cast remained the same.

The picture is remarkable in many ways. Particularly outstanding is Altman's use of his set. Rarely has *so little* been shot to better effect. And although the performances are sometimes overplayed (have there ever been two actresses more mannered than Sandy Dennis and Karen Black in the same film?), they are consistently entertaining.

COMEDY
James Dean was serious about comedy—so serious, in fact, that he had aspirations to perform as a stand-up comic. In June 1955 Warner Brothers issued the following official release:

KEEP 'EM LAUGHING
James Dean Wants to Switch from
Dramatic Scenes to Comedy Routines

BURBANK, Calif.—When James Dean said he wanted to do a comedy nightclub act, he couldn't understand the raised eyebrows.

"There's nothing astonishing about my desire to do comedy," Dean says. "After I finish *Rebel Without a Cause* at Warner Bros., I go into *Giant*. Counting *East of Eden*, that will make three pictures in which I've played emotional dramatic roles.

"I think no actor should tie himself to one particular brand of acting," he adds.

Dean says he is also toying with the notion of doing a Shakespearean comedy in 1956.

"I'm positive," Dean says, "after I do a comedy I shall be able to return to serious roles with added verve and vivacity. I think the change will do me good."

Dean didn't give comedy any consideration until the day he started clowning around on the set of *Rebel Without a Cause* with Nick Adams, [a] Jersey City lad who has a featured role in the youth drama.

Adams imitated Marlon Brando and Dean took the part of Elia Kazan, who directed *East of Eden*.

Within a few minutes Dean and Adams had the cast and crew of *Rebel* laughing uproariously. The reaction was so good, the two actors decided then and there that someday they would do a nightclub comedy act.

"I shall be busy for the rest of 1955," Dean says, "and Nick will be doing film work for the next six months.

"Come 1956, however, I wouldn't be surprised to find myself with Adams doing a two-a-night nightclub routine—or acting in a comedy by William Shakespeare."

And just how adept at comedy was Dean? According to Jim Backus, his *Rebel* co-star, Jimmy "had a collection of the worst jokes. Henny Youngman rejects."

COMMERCIALS

In 1950, while still struggling as an actor, Jimmy *sang* in a Pepsi-Cola television commercial. Coincidentally Nick Adams and Beverly Long, both of whom later appeared in *Rebel Without a Cause*, were also cast as singing teenagers in this commercial.

A few years later, on September 17, 1955, Jimmy taped a public service television commercial for the National Safety Council (of all things!) with actor Gig Young. The commercial played as follows:

> GIG: Have you ever been in a drag race?
> JIMMY: Are you kidding me?
> GIG: How fast will your car go?
> JIMMY: Oh, clocked, about 106 [m.p.h.], 107.
> GIG: You've won a few races, haven't you?
> JIMMY: Oh, one or two.
> GIG: Where?
> JIMMY: Well, I showed pretty good at Palm Springs. Bakersfield.
> GIG: Jimmy, we probably have a great many young people watching our show tonight and for their benefit, I'd like your opinion about fast driving on the highway.
> JIMMY: I used to fly around, but, you know, I took a lot of unnecessary chances on the highway. Then I started racing and, uh, now when I drive on the highways I'm, uh, extra cautious. No one knows what they're doing half the time. You don't know what this one's gonna do or that one. . . . I find myself being very, very cautious on the highway. I don't have the urge to speed on the highway. People think racing is dangerous. But I'll take my chances on the track any day than on a highway.

[Jimmy turns to leave.]

GIG: Wait a minute, Jimmy. One more question. Do you have any special advice for the young people who drive?

[Jimmy turns back around.]

JIMMY: Take it easy driving. *The life you might save might be mine.*

Jimmy, of course, did not realize the sad irony of his words. Less than two weeks later he was killed in a car accident on a California highway.

COMPETITION MOTORS

On the last morning of his life James Dean visited Johnny von Neumann's Competition Motors in Hollywood for last-minute preparations of his new Porsche Spyder. Jimmy had been a frequent visitor at the garage since September 21, when he walked into the shop and traded in his white Porsche Speedster (along with $3,000), for a silver Porsche 550 Spyder. Jimmy enjoyed loitering around the garage, talking to the mechanics. He also enjoyed listening to and learning from the seasoned speed demons who invariably hung out at the shop.

In 1955 Competition Motors was located at 1219 North Vine Street. Today it is no longer in existence, and its former location is occupied by Vine Auto Center.

Competition Motors Mechanics, 1955:
Tony Bucher
Horst Rieschel
Rolf Wutherich

"THE COMPLETE MAN"

James Dean saved the following newspaper clipping from a publication called *The Religious Weekly*:

THE COMPLETE MAN

These Are His Needs:

☆ The need for love and security.
☆ The need for creative expression.
☆ The need for recognition and self-esteem.

E. P. CONKLE

Writer of "Prologue to Glory," a 1952 episode of "Kraft Television Theatre" in which James Dean appeared.

JOHN CONNELL

John Connell had a small part in "Harvest," a 1953 episode of the television program "Robert Montgomery Presents the Johnson's Wax Program" that co-starred James Dean.

MIKE CONNOLLY
Hollywood fan magazine writer who penned an article, "This Was My Friend Jimmy Dean," for *Modern Screen*, December 1955.

RAY CONNOLLY
Ray Connolly wrote and directed the excellent 1976 documentary *James Dean: The First American Teenager.*

ROBERT CONRAD
Actor Robert Conrad, born Conrad Robert Falk in 1935, was reportedly considered to portray James Dean in a movie biography, which was eventually filmed as a documentary, *The James Dean Story* (1957). Nevertheless the movie was instrumental in launching Conrad's career. At the time, Conrad was 22 years old and a James Dean fan. So much of a fan, in fact, that he

Robert Conrad "had a face that stopped traffic."

introduced himself to Jimmy's family, the Winslows. Then, when Nick Adams made a personal appearance in Marion, Indiana, for the premiere of *The James Dean Story*, the Winslows introduced Adams to Conrad. According to Bill Dakota, who worked for Adams: "Nick brought Conrad out here [to Hollywood]. Conrad was so handsome. He had a face that stopped traffic. And Nick talked him into coming out here. He said he'd get him started in pictures."

So, indirectly and because he bore something of a resemblance to James Dean, Robert Conrad ventured out to Hollywood. Two years later he was starring in a television series, "Hawaiian Eye" (1959–1963). Other shows like "The Wild, Wild West" (1965–1970) and "Baa Baa Black Sheep" (1976–1978) followed, as did a slew of mostly mediocre made-for-television movies. Conrad's motion picture career includes *Palm Springs Weekend* (1963), *Young Dillinger* (1965), and *Wrong Is Right* (1982).

CONTINUITY AND EVOLUTION IN A PUBLIC SYMBOL: AN INVESTIGATION INTO THE CREATION AND COMMUNICATION OF THE JAMES DEAN IMAGE IN MID-CENTURY AMERICA

Author: Robert Wayne Tysl
Publisher: Michigan State University
Year: 1965

The title might be long-winded and perhaps a bit aggrandizing, but this work is a well-researched thesis. Partially as a result of this 670-page work, Tysl received his doctor of philosophy degree from Michigan State University's Department of Speech. It is a finely detailed book that examines the emergence and growth of the James Dean legend. Although it was never released by a commercial publisher, it remains one of the most ambitious and worthwhile projects ever attempted about Dean.

CONVERSE SHOES

A 1987–1988 print advertisement for Converse Shoes featured a photograph of Jimmy and a rather cryptic caption that read, "Cool dogs. Cool cat. Not fade away." According to Michael George, marketing director of Converse, sales of the Jack Purcells shoe, actually worn by Dean in the fifties and modeled by him in the ad, rose between 30 and 50 percent. The reason? According to George, "The image projected in the photograph is very hip and nostalgic."

GLENN CONWAY

Actor who portrayed James Dean in the 1977 British stage musical *Dean*.

ALISTAIR COOKE

James Dean appeared in "Glory in Flower," a 1953 episode of the CBS television series "Omnibus" (1953–1957), which was hosted by Alistair Cooke.

GARY COOPER

> "[Dean's] death caused a loss in the movie world that our industry could ill afford. Had he lived long enough, I feel he would have made some incredible films. He had sensitivity and a capacity to express emotion."
>
> Gary Cooper

Gary Cooper was considered for the role of James Dean's father in *East of Eden*. The role eventually went to Raymond Massey. Nonetheless, Cooper reportedly was one of the few Hollywood establishment stars to welcome young James Dean to the scene. The affinity was certainly reciprocated. Among the few actors Jimmy idolized much has been made over his link to Brando and Clift. But little has been said about Gary Cooper, and in some ways James Dean identified more with Cooper than with any other actor in Hollywood.

After seeing a screening of *East of Eden*, Gary Cooper became an instant Dean fan and requested that officials at Warner Brothers introduce them. Elia Kazan had wanted Coop for the Ray Massey part in *Eden*.

Like Jimmy, Cooper had a background in art. Also like Jimmy, he specialized in cartoon sketches. Jimmy grew up on a large farm; Cooper on a ranch. They both had a passion for horses. They both had a difficult time expressing themselves verbally. And they used the same technique with women. Director Howard Hawks once said about Cooper, "If I ever saw him with a good-looking girl and he was kind of dragging his feet over the ground and being very shy and looking down, I'd say, 'Oh-oh, the snake's gonna strike again.' He found that the little bashful boy approach was very successful." Hawks could just as easily have been talking about Dean.

In her autobiography, *The Quality of Mercy*, Mercedes McCambridge related a story about Jimmy. As part of her *Giant* costume McCambridge wore a Stetson hat that somehow looked more authentic than the hats worn by the other actors in the film. When Jimmy found out that the hat had previously been owned and worn by Gary Cooper, he repeatedly attempted to steal it from McCambridge. He was, much to his chagrin, unsuccessful.

James Dean was not alone in his admiration of Gary Cooper. During the 1930s and 40s, Cooper, born Frank James Cooper in 1901, had the world in his hands and, seemingly, half the women of Hollywood in his pants. Clara Bow (his earliest admirer), Helen Hayes, Marlene Dietrich, Lupe Velez, Patricia Neal, and Carole Lombard were just a few of the women who raved that, despite his image, there was *nothing* "Average Joe" about him.

Cooper died in 1961 of spinal cancer, leaving a legendary legacy that included such films as *The Thundering Herd* (1925), *It* (1927), *Wings* (1927), *A Farewell to Arms* (1932), *Mr. Deeds Goes to Town* (Best Actor Oscar nomination, 1936), *The Plainsman* (1937), *Beau Geste* (1939), *The Westerner* (1940), *Meet John Doe* (1941), *Sergeant York* (Best Actor Oscar winner, 1941), *The Pride of the Yankees* (Best Actor Oscar nomination, 1942), *For Whom the Bell Tolls* (Best Actor Oscar nomination, 1943), *The Fountainhead* (1949), *High Noon* (Best Actor Oscar winner, 1952), *Vera Cruz* (1954), *Friendly Persuasion* (1956), *Love in the Afternoon* (1957), *Ten North Frederick* (1958), and *The Naked Edge* (1961). Cooper was also awarded an honorary Oscar for lifelong achievement in 1960.

IRVING COOPER
Company manager of *The Immoralist* (1954).

COORS BEER
A 1987 marketing campaign for Coors Beer featured a photograph of Jimmy in one of its television commercials. The tie-in according to Coors? Coors and Jimmy were both "originals."

EDWIN CORLEY
Ed Corley penned *Farewell My Slightly Tarnished Hero* (Dodd, Mead & Co., 1971), a fictionalized biography of James Dean.

"THE CORN IS GREEN"
Shortly before James Dean's death his agent, Jane Deacy, successfully negotiated for him to star in a "Hallmark Hall of Fame" television presentation of "The Corn Is Green" for NBC. The special was to have co-starred Judith Anderson.

The program was broadcast as scheduled on January 18, 1956, but with John Kerr and Eva La Gallienne as the stars. The show was produced by Maurice Evans, directed by George Schaefer, and written by Arthur Arent.

CORONER
The Paso Robles, California, coroner who conducted an investigation into the death of James Dean was Paul Merrick. The assistant coroner was Albert Call.

CORONER'S INQUEST
On October 11, 1955, a coroner's inquest regarding the death of James Dean was held at the San Luis Obispo Civic Center in Paso Robles, California.

State of California

County of __San Luis Obispo__   } ss.

In the matter of the Inquisition upon the Body of   Before

__James DEAN__   Paul E. Merrick

Deceased.   Coroner.

We, the undersigned, jurors summoned to appear before _____

__Paul E. Merrick__   Coroner of the County of

__San Luis Obispo__, at __The Civic Center, 10th
and Park Streets, __ council chambers, City
Hall, Paso Robles,

on the __11th__ day of __October__ 19__55__, to inquire into the cause of the death of
__James DEAN__

having been sworn and charged according to law, and having made such inquisition, after

hearing the testimony adduced, upon our oaths. each and all do say:

That we find the deceased was named __James DEAN__

and that __he came to __ __his__ death on the __30th__ day of __September__,
19__55__, at __Cholame__

in the County of __San Luis Obispo__, State of California, by
injuries received in an accident at the intersection of Highways 41
& 466 according to evidence presented, in a two car collision. We find
no indication that James Dean met death through any criminal act
of another and that he died of a fractured neck and other injuries received.

All of which we certify by this inquisition, in writing, by us signed, this
__11th__ day of __October__ 19__55__.

DH Orcutt _____ Foreman
Dorothy Schwartz
Enid L Eddy
Mrs Glen A. Daley
Keith D Harris
Charles H. Carleton
Ray J Stamp
Cliff O Bickel
J F Hanson
Mac Margarini
J P Brush
L C Dauth

Cowdery's Form No. 614—INQUISITION BY JURY, CORONER'S. (Gov. C. Sec. 27504.)

The witnesses who testified were Donald Turnupseed, Paul Moreno, Ernie Tripke, Tom Frederick, O. V. Hunter, Clifford Hord, Ron Nelson, and Don Dooley. Jimmy's passenger in the Porsche, Rolf Wütherich, had previously given his deposition at the hospital. The deposition of Dr. Robert Bossert was also admitted as evidence. Also present were Turnupseed's parents; his attorney, Peter Andre; the district attorney, Herbert Grundell; the assistant district attorney, Harry Murphy; the coroner, Paul Merrick; and the court reporter, Judith Rooney.

After hearing all the testimony, the 12 jurors deliberated for 20 minutes before they issued their verdict:

> We find the deceased was named James Dean and that he came to his death on the 30th day of September, 1955, at Cholame in the County of San Luis Obispo, State of California by injuries received in an accident at the intersection of highways 41 and 466, according to the evidence presented, in a two car collision. We find no indication that James Dean met death through any criminal act of another, and that he died of a fractured neck and other injuries received.

The consensus of the jury seemed to be that James Dean had been speeding, and that, added to other circumstances such as the make and color of his car (low-slung and silver), the time of day (sunset), etc., was the probable cause of the accident. No charges were pressed.

The Jurors Who Investigated the Death of James Dean

D. H. Orcutt, Foreman	Kenneth G. Harris	J. G. Hanson
Dorothy Schwartz	Charles H. Ashton	Mac Marzirini
Enid S. Eddy	Ray J. Damp	J. P. Brush
Mrs. Alan A. Dale	Cliff O. Bickell	L. C. Dauth

CORONET MAGAZINE

Coronet magazine published several articles about James Dean, including:

☆ June 1955 "Young Men of Hollywood" by Hedda Hopper
☆ July 1955 "Young Men of Hollywood" by Hedda Hopper
☆ Nov. 1956 "The Strange James Dean Death Cult"

FRANK CORSARO

> Jimmy fell completely under Frank's influence. . . . [He was] a slight little man with a bundle of nervous energy that keeps him active twenty-four hours a day.
>
> Bill Bast

In 1953, when he befriended James Dean, Frank Corsaro was a 28-year-old actor and stage director at the Actors Studio in New York. Jimmy appeared in Corsaro's off-Broadway production of *The Scarecrow* in June 1953. And when Jimmy stalked out of the Actors Studio after being publicly reprimanded by Lee Strasberg, it was Frank Corsaro who lured him back. Like Rogers Brackett before him, Corsaro educated Jimmy in literature (Huxley) and music (Schönberg).

In 1956 Corsaro won acclaim for his direction of *A Hatful of Rain* on Broadway. He directed several other plays, including *Night of the Iguana* (1961), before concentrating his directorial efforts on the New York City Opera Company. In 1968 Corsaro returned to acting in Paul Newman and Stewart Stern's motion picture *Rachel, Rachel*.

THE CORT THEATRE
Broadway theater where *See the Jaguar* opened on December 3, 1952, and closed on December 6, 1952. The Cort Theatre is still in existence and is located at 138 West 48th Street.

COSMOPOLITAN MAGAZINE
Cosmopolitan has published several articles about James Dean, including one of the earliest to recognize his stardom:

☆ March 1955 "James Dean: New Face with a Future" by Louella Parsons

CO-STARS
The following is a selective, alphabetized list of the actors and actresses who co-starred in television programs, stage plays, and movies in which James Dean appeared:

Eddie Albert	Hume Cronyn	Walter Hampden
Corey Allen	Dick Davalos	Pat Hardy
Michael Ansara	Albert Dekker	Julie Harris
Mary Astor	Ann Doran	Dennis Hopper
Jim Backus	Mildred Dunnock	Rock Hudson
Carroll Baker	Constance Ford	Ruth Hussey
Ed Begley	John Forsythe	Burl Ives
Raymond Burr	Ben Gazzara	Anne Jackson
John Carradine	Dorothy Gish	Louis Jourdan

Arthur Kennedy	Patricia Neal	Rod Steiger
Cloris Leachman	Geraldine Page	Jessica Tandy
Gene Lockhart	Betsy Palmer	Elizabeth Taylor
Paul Lukas	Edward Platt	Vaughn Taylor
E. G. Marshall	Cameron Prud'homme	Jo Van Fleet
Raymond Massey	Ronald Reagan	Eli Wallach
Mercedes McCambridge	Lydia Reed	Jane Withers
Roddy McDowall	Jack Simmons	Natalie Wood
Sal Mineo	Edgar Stehli	Gig Young

JAMES K. COSSMAN

In 1950 James Cossman served as one of the advisers of the Opheleos Men's Honor Service Organization at Santa Monica City College, of which James Dean was a member.

COSTUME DESIGNERS

The following is a list of some of the designers who fashioned costumes worn by James Dean in various television, stage, and film productions:

Lemuel Ayers: *See the Jaguar* (1952)
Marjorie Best: *Giant* (1956)
Jerry Bos: "The Unlighted Road" (1955)
Jerry Boxhorn: "The Bells of Cockaigne" (1953)
Gunther Jaeckel: "Harvest" (1953)
Anna Hill Johnstone: *East of Eden* (1955)
Moss Mabry: *Rebel Without a Cause* (1955)
Motley: *The Immoralist* (1954)

THE COSTUMES

East of Eden: The Cal Trask Costumes

Note: Anna Hill Johnstone's wardrobe for Cal Trask is odd in the sense that most of it is a variation of a single outfit: white shirt, bone-colored trousers with a built-in belt, and a pocket watch and chain.*

☆ Salinas opening: off-white short-sleeved shirt, tan sweater (also worn tied around the waist and wrapped around his face), bone-colored trousers with belt, pocket watch and chain, light shoes
☆ In field with Abra: light checked shirt with sleeves rolled up, blue overalls, shoes
☆ Lettuce scene: white short-sleeved shirt with striped collar and pocket, bone-colored trousers with belt, pocket watch and chain, light shoes
☆ Money from Kate scene: same outfit as above with a light V-necked sweater
☆ Carnival scene: brown jacket, white shirt, brown trousers with belt, pocket watch and chain, shoes
☆ Birthday party scene: dark three-piece suit with white dress shirt, red tie, worn with and without jacket, dark shoes

---

*Collector David Loehr owns one of the light-colored shirts and a pair of the trousers with the built-in belt worn by Dean in *East of Eden*. It is on display at Loehr's James Dean Gallery in Fairmount, Indiana. The outfit was reportedly purchased at a Sotheby's auction for $2,500. Actor Martin Sheen also owned one of the light-colored shirts worn by Dean. Sheen wore the shirt in one of his television movies, "Blind Ambition." He later donated it to the Fairmount Historical Museum, where it is on display.

Wardrobe test, *East of Eden*. Dean's outfit was rejected.

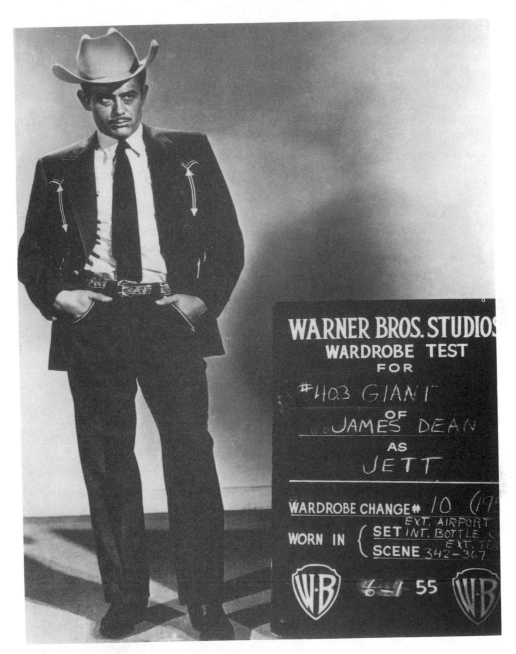

Wardrobe test, *Giant*.

Rebel Without a Cause: The Jim Stark Costumes

☆ Opening scene: dark blazer, long-sleeved white shirt, brown knit tie, dark trousers, brown belt, dark shoes. At police station, the jacket is taken off.

☆ First day of school: blazer, white dress shirt, T-shirt underneath, dark tie, brown wool trousers*, brown belt, brown penny loafers, white socks. Upon leaving home, Jim removes the tie.

☆ Knife-fight scene: same as above, but Jim also takes off his jacket. Later at home, Jim removes both shirts.
☆ Chickie-run scene: red nylon jacket, white T-shirt, blue jeans**, no belt, boots. Scenes later, Jim takes the jacket off and gives it to Plato. At the film's end Jim wears his father's blazer.

---

*Today Dean collector David Loehr owns the brown trousers, which he bought at a Sotheby's auction for a reported $2,000. They are on display at Loehr's James Dean Gallery in Fairmount, Indiana.
**When *Rebel* was abruptly converted from black and white to Warnercolor, a problem materialized. According to Steffi Sidney: "We got out to the location, and it seems that in Warnercolor the boys' jeans ran; the color ran on film. So they had to be specially dipped, which delayed the shooting tremendously."

Giant: The Jett Rink Costumes

☆ Opening/Leslie's arrival: cowboy hat, light long-sleeved shirt*, dark vest, blue jeans, belt, boots
☆ Driving Miss Leslie: same as above, but wearing a pair of brown gloves
☆ Luz's funeral/offer to Jett Rink: hat (which he later takes off), dark blazer, light shirt, dark tie, jeans, boots
☆ Leslie's visit: brown jacket with furlike collar (which he takes off), unbuttoned short-sleeved shirt (torn at sleeve), blue jeans, belt, boots
☆ The oil scene: dark shirt with sleeves rolled up, jeans with red bandanna in back pocket, belt, boots
☆ More oil/transition scene: tan long-sleeved shirt (seen only from waist up)
☆ More oil: sunglasses, dark suit, white shirt, striped tie (loosened), dark shoes and socks
☆ Fender-bender fight: dark tuxedo, white shirt, dark tie, dark cummerbund**, dark shoes
☆ Jett revisits Reata/Christmas: dark hat (which he takes off), blue overcoat with black collar, white shirt, dark tie, one glove on and the other off, dark pants, dark shoes
☆ Parade: cowboy hat, brown sunglasses, brown blazer with white detailing, light shirt, dark tie, dark trousers
☆ Bar scene: tuxedo with dark jacket, white vest, white shirt, cuff links, white bow tie, white carnation, dark slacks, dress shoes***

---

*Jimmy wore the same shirt in several scenes. He also wore it off camera and, for the sake of character and realism, refused to have it cleaned—much to the chagrin of some of the other cast members.
**Today artist Kenneth Kendall owns this cummerbund. He also owns a stand-up collar worn by Dean in this picture.
***During rehearsals of this scene Jimmy wore suspenders with the outfit. However, presumably because he felt constricted, the scene was shot sans suspenders.

CARL COULTER

Carl Coulter was one of the administrators of the James Dean estate, as appointed by Winton Dean. In 1955 Coulter's office was located on Brighton Way in Beverly Hills.

COUNCIL OF MOTION PICTURE ORGANIZATIONS

On December 6, 1955, the Council of Motion Picture Organizations held the first (and only) Audience Awards Election, which was designed to honor the public's favorite movie performers. That night James Dean was awarded posthumously as Best Actor for his performance in *East of Eden*.

COUSINS

Betsy Jane Dean	Gerrell Reece Peacock	Joan [Winslow] Peacock
David Dean	Jane Ann Peacock	Marcus (Markie) Winslow, Jr.
Joseph Dean		

CHERYL CRAWFORD

Cheryl Crawford was one of the founders of the Actors Studio. She was not particularly fond of one of its members. About Jimmy Dean, Crawford was quoted as saying, "As a human being he was too sick."

A formidable presence in the theater, Crawford, born in 1902, was one of the founders of the Group Theatre in 1931. She also produced such plays as *Porgy and Bess* (1941), *The Rose Tattoo* (1951), *Paint Your Wagon* (1951), *Camino Real* (1953), and *Sweet Bird of Youth* (1959).

ROBERT J. CREAN

"The Movie Star," a 1962 Dean-inspired episode of the television program "The DuPont Show of the Week," was adapted by Robert J. Crean from an original teleplay by Bill Bast.

LEWIS CRIST

Lewis Crist was president of the short-lived James Dean Memorial Foundation, which was incorporated in Fairmount, Indiana, after Jimmy's death.

CROMWELL'S PHARMACY

New York version of Schwab's coffee shop and pharmacy in Hollywood. In the 1950s the struggling young actors and actresses of New York City gravitated to Cromwell's for coffee, conversation, and companionship. Jimmy Dean was one such aspiring (and hungry) thespian. Today Cromwell's, which was located at 30 Rockefeller Plaza, no longer exists.

WALTER CRONKITE

Walter Cronkite hosted the television series "You Are There" (1953–1957), which re-created dramatic events from history. In February 1953 relatively unknown actor James Dean appeared in an episode entitled "The Capture of Jesse James."

HUME CRONYN

Hume Cronyn co-starred in "Glory in Flower," a 1953 presentation of the television program "Omnibus" that featured James Dean.

Born Hume Blake in 1911, Cronyn has appeared in numerous films, plays, and television programs. His films include *Shadow of a Doubt* (1943), *Sunrise at Campobello* (1960), *Cocoon* (1985), and *Cocoon: The Return* (1988). On stage, Cronyn won a 1964 Tony award as Best Supporting Actor for his work in *Hamlet*. He has also made several guest appearances on television.

SANGER CRUMPACKER

"Jimmy Dean, he was a good boy, but a little moody. A little nearsighted, too. He never did want to wear his glasses when he played [basketball]. I guess he was a little proud about letting people know he couldn't see too well."

Sanger Crumpacker

Sanger Crumpacker has attained something resembling fame for having coached Dustin Hoffman in tennis and James Dean in basketball during his tenure at Santa Monica City College from 1935 to 1964.

Identified incorrectly in previous reports as *Samuel* Crumpacker, the coach taught Jimmy circa 1949–1950.

THE CRYSTAL STAR AWARD

In 1956 the French Film Academy posthumously bestowed its prestigious Crystal Star award to James Dean as Best Foreign Actor for his performance in *East of Eden*.

TERRY CUNNINGHAM

Author of *James Dean: The Way It Was*, published in England in 1983 by Electric Reader.

"A CURRENT AFFAIR"

Fox television program that aired a rather bleak segment about James Dean on May 10, 1989. The segment dealt primarily with Jimmy's alleged death wish and the jinx that he purportedly bequeathed to those associated with him or his Porsche. Among those interviewed were George Barris, Lew Bracker, Maila Nurmi, and Leonard Rosenman. The show was hosted by Maury Povich.

"A Current Affair" also produced another Dean segment on its September 27, 1989, program. It showed clips from some of Jimmy's television appearances that had been seen, albeit only on occasion, before.

TONY CURTIS

After Dean's death Tony Curtis campaigned unsuccessfully to get the role of Rocky Graziano, a role in which Dean had been cast, in MGM's *Somebody Up There Likes Me* (1956).

CURTIS MANAGEMENT GROUP

Curtis Management Group is the Indianapolis marketing firm that owns the rights to license the James Dean image. The group also represents the estates of Elvis Presley, Charlie Chaplin, Fred Astaire, Judy Garland, Humphrey Bogart, Mark Twain, Will Rogers, Abbott and Costello, Hank Williams, Sr., Babe Ruth, Lou Gehrig, Ty Cobb, Casey Stengel, Roberto Clemente, and Vince Lombardi.

In the increasingly lucrative field of movie star licensing Marilyn Monroe, Elvis Presley, and James Dean stand alone at the top. According to Mark Roesler, president of the group, "Internationally, James Dean is the biggest. Domestically, Elvis Presley is number one."

The Curtis Management Group can be contacted at 1000 Waterway Boulevard, Indianapolis, Indiana 46202.

ZBYGNIEW CYBULSKI
Actor who was hyped as "the James Dean of Poland" in the 1950s. His films include *A Generation* (1954), *Ashes and Diamonds* (1958), and *He, She or It* (1962). In 1967 he died accidentally at the age of 40.

D

DAIWA BANK
In 1989 the Daiwa Bank of Japan mounted a massive advertising campaign featuring the Dean image on television, billboards, posters, etc. One of the bank's marketing slogans is *"Dekkai* Dream *wa Daiwa kara"*—"Big Dreams Come from Daiwa Bank."

THE DAKIN COMPANY
San Francisco company that marketed the James Dean Doll in 1986.

WILLIAM DAKOTA

> I was a doorman at a theater back in Michigan. Guess I was 16 years old. *Rebel Without a Cause* was booked at the theater where I worked, and Jimmy had died two weeks [Actually, *Rebel* was not released until a month after Jimmy's death] before we played the picture. I was so fascinated with that film. I would get off work, go home, pack a lunch, and come back and sit and watch the movie.
>
> William Dakota

Bill Dakota's fascination with James Dean lured him to Hollywood in 1956. Within a short time he befriended Nick Adams, whom he went to work for as an assistant. Primarily he answered fan mail.

Years later Dakota founded the controversial James Dean Memorial Foundation in Hollywood. The ultimate purpose of the foundation was to have a monument dedicated to Dean at the Hollywood Memorial Park Cemetery. Dakota spent years on this effort and managed to enlist the support of Los Angeles mayor Tom Bradley, Steve Allen, Eartha Kitt, and others but was not able to raise the estimated $200,000 price tag.

Dakota ran into further trouble when he started selling James Dean memorabilia and videotapes of some of Dean's television performances. According to Dakota, "I went to NBC and to different private collectors and got the masters, bought the masters and probably put $20,000 into changing them from Kinescope to tape." However, Curtis Management Group of Indianapolis, which owns the James Dean licensing rights, was unimpressed by Dakota's efforts. In 1988, due to legal (as of this writing, Dakota and Curtis were embroiled in pretrial preparations) and financial difficulties, Dakota shut down the James Dean Memorial Foundation and opened a fast-food hot dog operation on Hollywood Boulevard, not far from James Dean's star on the Hollywood Walk of Fame.

DAVID DALTON

David Dalton is the author of two books about James Dean: *James Dean: The Mutant King*, published by Straight Arrow Books in 1974, and the superlative *James Dean: American Icon*, published by St. Martin's Press in 1984. Dalton also penned the article "How James Dean Came of Age on T.V." for the March 4, 1986, edition of *Village Voice* and served as a consultant for the 1988 cable television documentary "Forever James Dean."

In addition to his Dean-related works, David Dalton, born in 1944, was a contributing editor for *Rolling Stone* (1968-1975). His other books include *The Rolling Stones: The First Twenty Years* and *Piece of My Heart: The Life, Times and Legend of Janis Joplin*.

DAMN YANKEES

Shortly before Jimmy's death there was speculation in Hollywood that he would star in the Warner Brothers film version of the hit Broadway musical *Damn Yankees*. The film was eventually made in 1958 with Tab Hunter, Gwen Verdon, and Ray Walston.

VIC DAMONE

Singer Vic Damone has the distinction of being the man whom Pier Angeli left James Dean to marry. Damone was divorced from Pier Angeli in 1959 and today is married to singer/actress Diahann Carroll.

Born Vito Farinola in 1929, Damone was at one time considered to be Frank Sinatra's most serious rival. In 1956-1957, he starred in his own variety series "The Vic Damone Show." He starred in other television variety shows, and in films including *Rich, Young and Pretty* (1951), *The Strip* (1951), *Kismet* (1955), and *Hell to Eternity* (1960).

PATSY D'AMORE

Patsy D'Amore was the owner of the Villa Capri restaurant in Hollywood, one of Jimmy's favorite hangouts. At the time of Jimmy's death he owed D'Amore the sum of $299.95, presumably the result of unpaid restaurant bills.

DANCE

At the age of five Jimmy was taking tap and ballet lessons and appeared in a recital with the Marion College of Dance and Theater Arts. Years later he continued his dance lessons with instructor Katherine Dunham in New York.

JOE D'ANGELO

Joe D'Angelo was Jimmy's stand-in on *Giant*.

"DANGER"

"Danger" was a dramatic series broadcast by CBS on Tuesday nights from

September 1950 until May 1955. The program was hosted and narrated by Richard Stark. Directors of the show included Yul Brynner, Sidney Lumet, and John Frankenheimer.

James Dean appeared in the following episodes of "Danger":

☆ "No Room": April 14, 1953
☆ "Death Is My Neighbor": August 25, 1953
☆ "The Little Woman": March 30, 1954
☆ "Padlocks": November 9, 1954

THE DANIEL BLUM THEATRE WORLD AWARD

In 1954 James Dean was one of several young stage performers to be presented with the prestigious Daniel Blum Theatre World Award as Most Promising Personality for his performance in *The Immoralist*. The other performers cited that year were, in no particular order:

Carol Haney	Harry Belafonte	Elizabeth Montgomery
Leo Penn (Sean's father)	Kay Medford	Jonathan Lucas
Orson Bean	Joan Diener	Scott Merrill
Eva Marie Saint	Ben Gazzara	

"THE DARK, DARK HOUR"

"The Dark, Dark Hour"—aka "Out of the Night" and "The Dark, Dark Hours"—was an episode of the CBS television series "General Electric Theater." It was directed by Don Medford and written by Arthur Steuer. The star of the show was none other than Ronald Reagan. It co-starred James Dean, Constance Ford, and Jack Simmons.

The plot of "The Dark, Dark Hour" revolved around a small-town doctor (Reagan) and his wife (Ford) who are held prisoner in their own home by a pistol-armed delinquent (Dean). One particularly intriguing scene involved Jimmy forcing Reagan to administer to his wounded friend (Simmons). To ward off anxiety over his friend's fate, Jimmy dances around the room while waving his gun at the future president of the United States. "The Dark, Dark Hour" aired on December 12, 1954.

THE DARK OF THE MOON

The Dark of the Moon was a UCLA stage production that Jimmy auditioned for in 1951. He did not get the part.

DATES

In the 1950s Hollywood studios were infamous for scheduling "studio dates" in which studio-owned actors would squire studio-owned actresses to various industry functions. The purpose of this commonly practiced public relations prostitution was, of course, to capitalize on photo opportunities and bolster the couple's individual careers.

So who were James Dean's female dates, staged and otherwise? The following is a selective list:

Ursula Andress	Katy Jurado	Lori Nelson
Pier Angeli	Lilli Kardell	Maila Nurmi
Fran Bennett	Claire Kelly	Betsy Palmer
Leslie Caron	Jeanetta Lewis	Arlene Sachs
April Channing	Ella Logan	Dizzy Sheridan
Connie Dugovich	Tasha Martel	Christine White
Eileen Forham	Jeanette Mille	Beverly Wills
Barbara Glenn	Terry Moore	Natalie Wood
Pat Hardy	Marilyn Morrison	Diane Wynters

DATES: THE JAMES DEAN CHRONOLOGY

2-08-31	Birth
7-14-40	Mother, Mildred Dean, dies
7-16-40	Jimmy returns to Fairmount, Indiana, from California
10-16-46	Warner Brothers purchases *Rebel Without a Cause*
4-09-49	Jimmy wins first place in the Indiana State Speech Tournament
4-29-49	Jimmy travels to Colorado for the National Forensic League Finals and places sixth
5-16-49	High school graduation
6-14-49	Jimmy moves to Los Angeles
9-06-49	Jimmy enters Santa Monica City College
9-05-50	Jimmy enters UCLA
11-29-50	Appears in *Macbeth* at UCLA
12-50	Gets his first agent
12-13-50	Pepsi commercial
3-51	Attends James Whitmore's acting workshop
3-25-51	Appears in "Hill Number One"
10-51	Returns to Fairmount for visit
10-51	Moves to New York City
2-20-52	Appears in "Sleeping Dogs"
3-52	Moves in with Rogers Brackett in New York
3-03-52	Appears in "Ten Thousand Horses Singing"
3-17-52	Appears in "The Foggy, Foggy Dew"
5-52	Moves to the Iroquois Hotel with Bill Bast
5-21-52	Appears in "Prologue to Glory"
5-26-52	Appears in "Abraham Lincoln"
6-02-52	Appears in "Forgotten Children"
7-52	Meets Christine White
8-52	Dramatic reading of *The Metamorphosis*
8-52	Audition and acceptance, the Actors Studio
8-52	Last week of August, cruise with Lem Ayers
9-52	Moves to 46th Street, then to 13 West 89th Street
10-52	Hitchhikes to Fairmount
11-13-52 to 11-15-52	Out-of-town tryouts, *See the Jaguar*
12-03-52	*See the Jaguar* opens on Broadway
12-06-52	*See the Jaguar* closes on Broadway
12-52	Moves back into the Iroquois Hotel
1-15-53	Appears in "Hound of Heaven"
1-29-53	Appears in "The Case of the Watchful Dog"
2-08-53	Appears in "The Capture of Jesse James"

4-14-53	Appears in "No Room"
4-16-53	Appears in "The Case of the Sawed-Off Shotgun"
5-01-53	Appears in "The Evil Within"
Spring '53	Moves to 19 West 68th Street
5-06-53	Appears in *End as a Man* at Actors Studio
6-16-53	Appears in *The Scarecrow*
6-21-53	*The Scarecrow* closes
7-17-53	Appears in "Something for an Empty Briefcase"
8-17-53	Appears in "Sentence of Death"
8-25-53	Appears in "Death Is My Neighbor"
9-11-53	Appears in "The Big Story"
10-04-53	Appears in "Glory in Flower"
10-14-53	Appears in "Keep Our Honor Bright"
10-16-53	Appears in "Life Sentence"
11-11-53	Appears in "A Long Time Till Dawn"
11-17-53	Appears in "The Bells of Cockaigne"
11-23-53	Appears in "Harvest"
12-18-53	Rehearsals of *The Immoralist*
12-53	To Fairmount for Christmas
12-31-53	Rehearsals of *The Immoralist* resume
1-09-54	To Philadelphia for out-of-town tryouts of *The Immoralist*
2-01-54	*The Immoralist* opens in previews on Broadway
2-08-54	*The Immoralist* opens on Broadway
2-05-54	Kazan informs Warners that he has found "new boy" for *East of Eden*
2-54	Appears in *Women of Trachis* off Broadway
2-16-54	Tests for *East of Eden* in New York
2-22-54	Kazan screens Dean's test
2-23-54	Gives his final performance in *The Immoralist*
3-05-54	Warner Brothers announces that Dean is cast in *East of Eden*
3-08-54	To Hollywood
3-30-54	Appears in "The Little Woman" back in New York
4-54	Moves, temporarily, to father's home back in Los Angeles
4-07-54	Signs Warner Brothers *Eden* contract
5-54	Moves into apartment across street from Warner Brothers; *East of Eden* screen and photographic tests
5-17-54	Final *Eden* script is completed
5-20-54	Appears in *Eden* wardrobe tests
5-27-54	*Eden* begins shooting in Mendocino (until 6-02)
6-04-54	*Eden* shoots in Salinas (until 6-11)
6-54	Begins dating Pier Angeli on Warner Brothers lot
7-06-54	Gets California driver's license
7-54	Moves into Warner Brothers dressing room
8-09-54	*Eden* finishes shooting
8-54	Moves back to New York apartment on 68th Street
9-05-54	Appears in "Run Like a Thief"
10-07-54	Six-month Warner Brothers contract expires and is extended
11-09-54	Appears in "Padlocks"
11-54	Back to Hollywood
11-14-54	Appears in "I'm a Fool" in Hollywood
11-24-54	Pier Angeli marries Vic Damone
12-06-54	*East of Eden* screens at Huntington Park Theater

12-12-54	Appears in "The Dark, Dark Hour" in Hollywood
12-18-54	Back to New York
12-29-54	Shoots "Torn Sweater" session for Roy Schatt
1-04-55	Appears in "The Thief" in New York
1-04-55	Warner Brothers announces that Dean is cast in *Rebel Without a Cause*
1-18-55	Moves back to Hollywood; moves into Sunset Plaza Drive apartment
1-55	*Rebel* cast reading at the Chateau Marmont
2-55	Fairmount visit with photographer Dennis Stock
2-14-55	Attends Fairmount High Sweethearts Ball
2-55	To New York with Dennis Stock
3-06-55	Back to Hollywood
3-07-55	*Life* magazine hails "Moody New Star" with photos by Dennis Stock
3-09-55	Benefit premiere of *Eden* in New York; Dean doesn't attend
3-10-55	*Eden* officially opens in selected markets; television interview preceding "The Life of Emile Zola"
3-55	Celebrates *Eden* success—buys a Porsche
3-13-55	"Another Dean Hits the Big League" interview is published in the *New York Times*
3-16-55	*Eden* officially opens in Los Angeles
3-21-55	*Time* magazine rave of *Eden*
3-23-55	Appears in *Rebel* wardrobe test
3-26-55	Enters Palm Springs car race
3-27-55	Hedda Hopper raves about *Eden*
3-28-55	*Rebel Without a Cause* begins shooting
4-02-55	Warner Brothers contract again expires and again is extended
4-09-55	*East of Eden* opens nationally
4-14-55	Warner Brothers announces Dean is cast in MGM's *Somebody Up There Likes Me*
4-25-55	*Eden* enters the Cannes Film Festival
5-01-55	Enters car race in Bakersfield
5-06-55	Appears in "The Unlighted Road"
5-18-55	Attends *Giant* preproduction party
5-23-55	*Giant* begins shooting at Warner Brothers without Dean
5-26-55	*Rebel* finishes shooting
5-28-55	Enters car race in Santa Barbara
5-31-55	Cast and crew of *Giant* to Marfa, Texas
6-03-55	Joins cast and crew of *Giant* in Marfa
7-10-55	Cast and crew back to Hollywood
7-55	Dates Ursula Andress
7-23-55	Moves into Sherman Oaks home
8-16-55	Attends Villa Capri party for Frank Sinatra
9-17-55	Tapes National Safety Council commercial
9-19-55	Test-drives Porsche Spyder at Competition Motors
9-21-55	Buys Porsche Spyder
9-22-55	Finishes shooting *Giant*
9-25-55	Attends a party in his honor at Chateau Marmont
9-27-55	Attends a preview of *Rebel Without a Cause*
9-29-55	Dinner at the Villa Capri; attends party
9-30-55	En route to car race in Salinas, James Dean is killed in a two-car highway collision
10-04-55	Body is returned to Fairmount

10-08-55	Funeral in Fairmount
10-11-55	Coroner's inquest in San Luis Obispo
10-26-55	*Rebel Without a Cause* premieres in New York
10-29-55	*Rebel* premieres in Los Angeles
11-27-55	"The Colgate Variety Hour" presentation
12-06-55	Posthumously awarded Best Actor at the Audience Awards Election
2-18-56	Nominated for Best Actor Oscar for *Eden*
3-21-56	The Academy Awards
10-10-56	*Giant* premieres in New York
10-14-56	Dean tributes on "The Steve Allen Show" and "The Ed Sullivan Show"
10-17-56	*Giant* premieres in Los Angeles
11-24-56	*Giant* opens nationally to public
2-18-57	Nominated for Best Actor Oscar for *Giant*
3-27-57	The Academy Awards
8-13-57	*The James Dean Story* premieres in Indiana
9-30-85	James Dean Day in Los Angeles
9-22-88	Opening of David Loehr's James Dean Gallery
11-01-88	Unveiling of Griffith Park monument

DICK DAVALOS

"We literally became these characters. I was Mr. Goody-two-shoes, and while we were doing the film we lived together across the street from the studio, and he'd just leave the place in a mess, and of course I was going around and tidying up, à la Aron, and he was very heavy into being Cal."

Dick Davalos, CNN

Shortly before he was cast in *East of Eden*, Dick Davalos worked as an usher at the Trans-Lux Theater in New York City. Originally Warner Brothers brought him to Hollywood to test for the role of Cal. However, upon reading the script, according to Davalos, he campaigned for the role of Cal's twin brother, Aron. Eventually the competition was pared down to two actors, Dick Davalos and Paul Newman. After a series of screen and photographic tests the part was awarded to Davalos.

During the early shooting of *East of Eden* Dean and Davalos shared a one-room apartment across the street from Warner Brothers. And although their personal relationship inherited some of the adversarial qualities of their characters, they became, for a period, quite close. Certainly their scenes together in *Eden* suggested at least a touch of latent homosexuality, a factor which only served to ignite Jimmy's androgynous appeal.

As for Dick Davalos, his acting career never fulfilled the promise obviously evident in *East of Eden*. In 1961 he co-starred in a television series, "The Americans."

COLLIER DAVIDSON
One of the ambulance attendants who carted Jimmy's mangled body off to the Paso Robles, California, hospital on September 30, 1955.

SAMMY DAVIS, JR.

> My own deep regret is that when Dean was hanging around town, I
> didn't take more notice of him. He would sit alone in the corner at
> some Hollywood party, looking depressed and sulky. If someone
> approached him, he would look up and say "I want to act," and then
> slump back into his own world. Hollywood hardly touched him as a
> person. It is to our eternal shame as a community that we passed
> him off as a bit of a slob. He *was* difficult to talk to, but we should
> have tried harder.
>
> Sammy Davis, Jr., *Hollywood in a Suitcase*

Entertainer Sammy Davis, Jr., born in 1925, had a friendly acquaintance
with James Dean. Relatively unknown at the time, he performed at the *East
of Eden* postscreening benefit gala in New York on March 9, 1955. Years later
he was interviewed in the ABC documentary "James Dean Remembered"
(1974) and in the documentary feature *James Dean: The First American
Teenager* (1976).

In the 1960s and 1970s, Davis was a familiar presence as one of Hollywood's "Rat Pack," and on television in such programs as "The Hollywood
Palace" (1964–1970), "The Sammy Davis Jr. Show" (1966), and "NBC Fol-
lies" (1973). He also appeared on stage in *Golden Boy*, for which he was
nominated for a 1965 Best Actor Tony, and appeared in several films including *Anna Lucasta* (1958), *Porgy and Bess* (1959), *Ocean's Eleven* (1960), *A
Raisin in the Sun* (1961), *Robin and the Seven Hoods* (1964), *Sweet Charity*
(1968), and *Cannonball Run* (1981).

Davis, dubbed by some as "Mr. Entertainment," died at his Beverly Hills
home in May 1990 following a lengthy battle with throat cancer.

MARTIN DAWBER

Author of *Wish You Were Here, Jimmy Dean*, a biography published in
England in 1988.

LOUIS DE LISO

Jimmy's favorite waiter at Jerry's Bar and Restaurant in New York City.

JANE DEACY

> Jane Deacy was a great force in his life. She had taken charge of it.
> She believed in him. And, of course, she was right.
>
> Betsy Palmer

In 1952 Jane Deacy was an agent with the Louis Schurr Agency in New York
City. One of Jane's clients and friends was James Sheldon. And it was
through Sheldon that she was introduced to unknown actor James Dean,
whom she signed promptly. As recalled by Sheldon years later, "They had a
love relationship immediately. They just really hit it off." So, when Jane
Deacy left Louis Schurr to form her own agency (address: 60 East 42nd Street)
later that year, James Dean was one of the clients she took with her.

Jane Deacy's clients, Jimmy included, called her "Mom." She had a close relationship with the actors she represented, and, just as importantly, she had a good eye for talent. It was largely due to Jane Deacy that James Dean became a star. She gave him the opportunity. He capitalized on it. For although she was hired as his agent, she functioned unofficially as his manager. She was also his friend.

During the last week of September 1955 Jane Deacy flew out to Hollywood to negotiate Jimmy's new contract at Warner Brothers. She also finalized some of his future commitments. On Sunday, September 25, Deacy threw a party at the Chateau Marmont in honor of her newly famous client. Together they had conquered Broadway and then Hollywood. Together there was no limit to what could be achieved. Such was the promise that the party symbolized. Five days later, however, James Dean was dead.

According to James Sheldon, "For years after, she would always have Jimmy's picture on her desk with a rose that was changed every day. And one day one of her clients, George C. Scott, said he was leaving her. She said, 'Why?' And he said it was because he couldn't stand that picture. 'You put that away or I'm leaving,' he said. So the picture was put away, and George became her only client. She managed him, and she was wrapped up in George's life and career when he was having a great, big time."

Today Jane Deacy is retired. For over 35 years she has opted not to talk publicly about her former client, James Dean.

Jane Deacy's Other Clients Included:
Larry Hagman
Pat Hingle
Martin Landau

DEADLINE U.S.A.
Over the years there has been speculation that James Dean had a bit part in this 1952 20th Century-Fox film. The speculation, however, has never been substantiated. *Deadline U.S.A.* was written and directed by Richard Brooks and starred Humphrey Bogart, Kim Hunter, Ethel Barrymore, Ed Begley, Paul Stewart, Warren Stevens, Martin Gabel, and Jim Backus.

DEAN
Stage musical about the life of James Dean that opened in London in August 1977. The script was written by Dean biographer John Howlett, with musical numbers by Robert Campbell. The production was directed by Robert Livingston, produced by Steven Bentinck, and starred Glenn Conway and Anna Nicholas.

A typical review for *Dean* read:

"Conway is remarkably similar to Dean in physical appearance and has captured Dean's slouch and physical mannerisms, but lacks the intensity, power, and charisma of Dean, leaving the show empty at the core."

The show was an unequivocal flop. After only one week at the Casino Theatre it was canceled.

CAL DEAN
Jimmy's great-grandfather. Winton Dean's grandfather. A farmer turned auctioneer.

CHARLES DEAN
Jimmy's grandfather. Winton Dean and Ortense Winslow's father. Lifelong farmer. Died in 1961.

When Jimmy returned to Fairmount, Indiana, with photographer Dennis Stock in February 1955, he went to visit his grandparents, Charlie and Emma Dean. Unbeknownst to them, Jimmy tape-recorded their conversation. It is transcribed, in part, below:

> JIMMY: Grandma, I played a character in the movie *East of Eden*, his name is Cal. What I wanted to ask you is, I went by the cemetery and there's a name out there, you know, great-granddaddy, named Cal Dean. And it's so funny, uh, I played the character Cal, and Cal is your father. What was he like? Did he have any interest in the arts or anything? Was he an arty kind of guy? What kind of guy was he?
>
> EMMA: He was an auctioneer. One of the best ever was.
>
> CHARLIE: He was one of the best auctioneers ever I heard. And I heard hundreds of 'em.
>
> JIMMY: Well, what's it take to be a good auctioneer?
>
> CHARLIE: You gotta be a good judge of stock. You gotta be a good judge of human nature. You gotta have a talent of it.

(Jimmy then coerces his grandfather into demonstrating a bit of rapid-tongue auctioneering. It ends with all of them breaking down in laughter.)

> CHARLIE: I'll tell you what kills auctioneers. He'll eventually get too much confidence in himself. . . . He'll pull a lot of stuff. . . . soon as the people find out that you are doing it, they'll quit you. That's what kills all of 'em.
>
> JIMMY: That's what kills an actor, too. Same thing. You gotta be an honest man along with it.

CHARLIE NOLAN DEAN
Jimmy's uncle. Winton's brother. In September 1955 Charlie Nolan Dean traveled to California to visit with his brother, Winton, and his movie star nephew, James Dean. On September 30, before he commenced his trip to Salinas, Jimmy had a quick lunch with his uncle Charlie and his father. He also showed them his brand-new toy. It was a Porsche 550 Spyder.

EMMA DEAN
Jimmy's grandmother. Winton Dean and Ortense Winslow's mother. Charlie Dean's wife. When Jimmy's mother, Mildred, became fatally ill in 1940,

Emma Dean took a train from Indiana to California to help run the household.

After Jimmy's death Emma told her story to *Photoplay* magazine under the title "James Dean—The Boy I Loved." She also traveled to California with her husband, Charlie, to accept *Photoplay*'s 1955 award honoring Jimmy for special achievement. Emma and Charlie also appeared in the 1957 Warner Brothers documentary *The James Dean Story*. Like Charlie, Emma Dean died in 1961.

> "We're not rich, but we're not poor, either. So long as I live, I'll always have a porch to sit on, a rocking chair to rock in, and a clock that strikes."
>
> Emma Dean, *Photoplay*, March 1956

ETHEL DEAN

Jimmy's father, Winton Dean, remarried circa 1944–1945. Her name was Ethel Case. Jimmy never developed much of a relationship with his stepmother, and the relationship that they did have was not a close one.

JAMES DEAN: AN ORAL BIOGRAPHY

"Jimmy was a cute little boy. He wasn't afraid of anybody or anything. He was a pretty boy. I've heard people say he was too pretty to be a boy. He was fair-skinned, rosy cheeks, lips, and his mother dressed him cute."

Ortense Winslow, aunt

"I'd say that James Dean did do dumb stunts more than the average boy. I remember a high school dance when he was swinging across the barn rafters. At that time, no one else was doing it. All in all, [though,] I'd say James Dean was pretty normal."

Jerry Garner, classmate

"He was nobody's tragic hero. James Dean was quiet and shy. He didn't chase around. He didn't have a hundred girls. He wasn't reckless."

Adeline Nall, high school teacher

"He had a lot of pep. And he just always was doing things. And when he got so he could give readings and be in plays, he just seemed to like that."

Ortense Winslow

"There was a genius quality about that boy."

Adeline Nall

"I never knew him to be a complex and difficult personality. Jimmy was not moody, temperamental, unpredictable, or rude. These terms did not describe the Jimmy Dean I knew. When I read some of the stories about Jimmy, it is almost as though I were reading about another person entirely. I do not understand why so many write about him as though he were a sort of juvenile delinquent. He was never that. I never knew him to be untidy or rebellious. He was always polite and thoughtful. His enthusiasm for everything that pertained to the theater was boundless."

Gene Owen, college teacher

"He was real upset. He told me these four Hollywood executives had put him into a glass room and had given him a script to read. Well, I guess that script was too tough for him because he said he broke down and cried right while he was trying to read it. He said he cried like a baby."

Sanger Crumpacker, college basketball coach

"I thought he was pretty much of a creep until we got to the picnic and then all of a sudden he came to life."

Beverly Wills, girlfriend

"He sapped the minds of his friends as a bloodsucker saps the strength of an unsuspecting man."

Bill Bast, friend and biographer

"He looked hungry, he looked lonely, he looked like he needed a friend. Actually, years later, I found out that he always looked that way."

Dizzy Sheridan, girlfriend

"We didn't write Jimmy money—we wired it! If Jim asked for funds, we knew he had already missed several meals."

Marcus Winslow, uncle

"I was typing in an office and this funny little boy was leaning on a door frame with glasses on, and he was really annoying me, and then he came over and looked at what I was working on. And he said, 'What are you doing?' And I said, 'I'm writing a play.' And he said, 'Oh, can I read a scene?' And I said, 'Are you an actor?' And he said, 'I hope so.' "

Christine White, girlfriend

"All I know is that Jimmy was a very moody person who had a great smile and charm and loved to work. That was his whole life. And he really cared about what he did. And he did it in his own way, which didn't always conform to other people's way of doing things. And that kind of quality was an original quality. It was his. [Sometimes] he would just sit there. Wouldn't say a thing. And one moment he'd be smiling and sparkling. And then he'd be like that [aloof]. I don't think he was being rude. I think he was being wrapped up with what he was doing."

James Sheldon, director

"He was so unhappy and I was, too, and we made a date to meet in Columbus Circle under the pigeons and we were going to a movie. We were both so miserable about being poor and not getting anywhere. It was one of the best dates that I had with Jimmy."

Dizzy Sheridan

"He could look in a delicatessen window and suddenly start waving at a bowl of prunes like they were alive. He was childish in a charming way."

Christine White

"He was a boy that was hard to understand."

Louis de Liso, waiter

"He was a sad-faced, introverted oddball. Jimmy'd sit alone in a corner by himself even when we'd all gather together. None of us thought the others were peculiar because we all were. My hair was in a bun. I was dreary and desperately trying to be intellectual. Rod Steiger would always greet you with a French or German or Jewish accent. Rod was always practicing accents. So Jimmy was no weirder than the rest of us."

Carroll Baker

"His existence seemed so pointless and haphazard, and no matter how I questioned him, I couldn't get a straight answer. He was obviously very beautiful and a gifted actor, but he didn't seem to want anything. In some weird way he reminded me of Peter Pan, but without the joy, as if he had sprung from never-never land and would disappear back into it."

Shelley Winters

"James Dean, who originated the role of the young Arab servant in the Broadway offering, *The Immoralist*, has been signed by Elia Kazan for the male lead in the forthcoming Warner Brothers version of John Steinbeck's novel, *East of Eden*. The announcement was made yesterday by the local offices of Mr. Kazan, who will produce and direct the Cinemascope project through the film company."

New York Times, March 6, 1954

"He didn't comb his hair. He had a safety-pin holding his pants together. He was introspective and very shy. When he landed at L.A., Jimmy looked like a dead-beat straight from the Bronx, completed with parcel tied with string under his arm containing all his belongings."

Elia Kazan

"He was very beguiling. There was something very sweet about him even though he was sort of a bad boy. He liked being a bad boy."

Julie Harris

"The latest genius sauntered in dressed like a bum and slouched down in silence a table away from mine. He hooked another chair with his toe, dragged it close enough to put his feet up, while he watched me from the corner of his eye. Then he stood up to inspect the framed photographs of Warner's stars that covered the wall by his head. He chose one of them, spat in its eye, wiped off his spittle with a handkerchief, then, like a ravenous hyena, started to gulp the food that had been served to him."

Hedda Hopper, columnist

"Jim knew how to *play* people. He could work me around his little finger! He was very observing of people and he also knew how to get their attention. 'It's better to be noticed than ignored,' he'd tell me. That's how he got all that publicity in Hollywood, you see. He knew he had to move fast."

Adeline Nall

"He just reminded me from the very beginning of Tom Sawyer . . . a guy who would always get you to paint the fence."

Julie Harris

"He was so twisted and sick. People said he was like Brando. [He was] nothing like Brando at all. He had very little pliability. He had sort of one hurt, a very hurt person."

Elia Kazan

"He would be bothered when someone would say he was mean and disrespectful. Because, actually, he wasn't. They took silence to mean he cared little or nothing for them. They didn't have the insight, or didn't care to exercise their insight, in knowing that he was a shy boy that just didn't know how to approach them. Instead of making an attempt to approach him, they just, well, they just wrote him off."

Lew Bracker, friend

"When I worked with him on TV I found him to be an intelligent young actor who seemed to live only for his work. He was completely dedicated, and, although a shy person, he could hold a good conversation on many wide-ranging subjects."

Ronald Reagan

"Sneak preview audience of *East of Eden* went crazy over James Dean."
The Hollywood Reporter

"Quality film based on the Steinbeck novel. Excellent production, acting and direction. Introducing James Dean Who May Be a Hypo at the Box-Office."
The Hollywood Reporter

"The picture is a brilliant entertainment and more than that, it announced a new star, James Dean, whose prospects look as bright as any young actor's since Marlon Brando. Dean, a young man from Indiana, is unquestionably the biggest news Hollywood has made in 1955."
Time

"I have a great respect for his talent. However, in *East of Eden*, Mr. Dean appears to be wearing my last year's wardrobe and using my last year's talent. [He's] just a lost boy trying to find himself."
Marlon Brando

"Ever since he flew in from New York last Sunday morning, Jimmy Dean has been holed up in his Sunset Plaza apartment ignoring his telephone and the beseeching fan-mag writers. He's trying to 'get things set in his own mind.' Dean isn't purposely pulling the hermit routine just to show Hollywood he's different. He may be the intense, brooding young man that the magazines have delightedly discovered, but he's also pretty cagey when it comes to his career."
Kendis Rochlen, columnist, *Los Angeles Mirror-News*, March 11, 1955

"This boy's pretty smart. Of course he's pleased with all the praise and attention he's getting as the result of *East of Eden*, but he knows it means he must be doubly careful of the next picture he does before going into *Giant*."
Dick Clayton, agent

"I was walking down the hallway with my agent in Warner Brothers one day and, uh, this guy walked by who wasn't shaven, had his head down, very thick glasses, hair was a mess. He had on a turtleneck sweater. He just looked really strange and I just saw this weird guy and was wondering what he was doing in the studio. And he walked by. And my agent said, 'That's Jimmy Dean.'"
Dennis Hopper

"The day that we got the part [in *Rebel*] Jack Grinnage and I went to see *East of Eden*, which was playing up on Hollywood Boulevard at the Egyptian Theater. We thought, 'Oh, we'll go and see Jimmy's picture.' So, we went to see the picture, and after the movie I was just totally blown away. I kept saying, 'Oh my God!' I had no idea he was that talented. I had no idea. What a shock. You know, to sit there, watching this movie, and know that next Monday you're gonna start working with him was really amazing because he was, I thought, just brilliant."
Beverly Long

"There were mornings when he really was awful to people in that he totally disregarded them, would never say anything to them or to me personally. Of course, I felt rejected. What did I do wrong? If he didn't say 'good morning' to me, I was a wreck the whole day. But when he did, and if he put his arm around me, that was fabulous, because then I knew he meant it. But I always felt he was testing people, testing to see how far he could push someone. And if someone stood up to him, he dug it, he respected that."

Sal Mineo

"He would come in sometimes in the morning and look like he hadn't slept a wink. His hair had that cowlick in the back and it'd be standing straight up and everybody would be putting tons of hairspray on it to make it lay down."

Beverly Long

"He was so inspiring, always so patient and kind. He was very critical of himself, never satisfied with his work. He was so great when he played a scene, he had the ability to make everyone else look great too."

Natalie Wood

"Jimmy rode a motorcycle. There were days when he did not shave. He dressed casually, untidily, which was invariably interpreted as a gesture of revolt. Not entirely true . . . it saved time, and Jim detested waste."

Nicholas Ray

"The most exciting young talent I've worked with in my 30 motion pictures. He seemed so introspective and brooding, but within a couple of weeks his shell of reserve disappeared."

Jim Backus

"I used to tell people that John Barrymore impressed me more than any other actor. Now I have to add the name of James Dean."

Ann Doran, actress

"I've directed eight pictures. I've worked with a lot of young people. I've never met anyone with the ability of Dean. He cannot be compared with any actor, present or past. I'm sure he'll bring performances to the screen the likes of which haven't yet been thought of."

Nick Ray

"I was terrified of him. I was afraid of him. And I really didn't know him at all. And gradually it [their relationship] grew as it did in the film. The thing that I loved about him and the thing that I wanted to be one day was the way he dealt with people in a higher position. He would never take anything from anybody. He didn't take any nonsense from anybody. And he would stand up to them no matter what the situation was."

Sal Mineo

"He was being really snotty to me. He was teasing me. I'll never forget it. I was the butt of the joke. He said to me, he was holding the tire iron at that point. He picks up the tire iron and he says to me, 'Here, hold this.' And I said, 'Oh, okay.' So I was holding the tire iron and he says, 'Did you ever feel anything *so hard* in your life?' Well, then everybody just started laughing. And I went, 'Oh, no!' And I dropped it. I was just mortified. He loved it. He loved it. That was the kind of thing he'd do."

Beverly Long

"He didn't show you very much. He'd challenge you to find him. Then when you'd found him, he'd still make you guess. It was an endless game with him. The thing people missed about

Jimmy was his mischievousness. He was the most constantly mischievous person I think I've ever met. Full of tricks, full of magic, full of outrageousness."

Stewart Stern, screenwriter

"I think that he really was not a rebel in the sense that he was not rejecting parents. He wasn't sort of saying 'Leave me alone. I don't want to have anything to do with you. I'm going to do my own thing.' He was really saying 'Listen to me.' You know, 'Hear me, love me.' "

Natalie Wood

"He's hard to figure out. Some people [reporters] he'll see and others he won't. He's one kid you can't figure. The only concessions he will make are to his own conscience. He is determined to live his life in his own way—not according to the rules of a young actor's conduct as prescribed by Hollywood."

a Warner Brothers publicist

"He was mercurial, quixotic, moody. He would go from really black, noncommunicative moods to being hyper. He was enigmatic, extremely creative. A kind of lost soul. He was like a little boy. An extremely complicated, multifaceted, talented little boy. And he was very hard to get to know. He had a lot of walls up."

Beverly Long

"I hadn't seen the rushes and frankly, from what I'd seen, I didn't know what the fuss was about. I didn't think he was very good. Then I saw the screening, and he was great. He was sitting just behind me in the cinema and half a dozen times, when he was really terrific, I turned around to look at him. He was giving that grin of his, and almost blushing, looking down at the floor between his legs."

Sal Mineo

"Jimmy had, in my estimation, a severe identity problem. He really didn't know who he was. Now I think very often [that] people, with the same kind of identity crisis, identified with Jimmy. And the irony was that—and I knew Jimmy, I think better than anybody—I felt very strongly that the irony was that all these people identified with an aspect of Jimmy that Jimmy himself hated in himself and wanted to change."

Leonard Rosenman

"He would all of a sudden just leave and go away and move over to some buddy of his and start talking about cars or something like that and be gone for half an hour. And he was very moody. He could one minute be very deep in thought about something and then snap out of it, and the next minute he would be up on the floor dancing and making some joke of some kind. And it was just no use getting mad at him for that kind of thing because that just didn't do any good. You just had to understand that that was the way he was."

Lilli Kardell, girlfriend

"George Stevens, master editor, director, had a lot of problems with Jimmy. Everybody seemed to have a lot of problems with Jimmy. Nobody had more problems with Jimmy than Jimmy had."

Mercedes McCambridge, actress

"Dean wanted success badly and he had a concrete plan to achieve it. He has been described as reluctant, presswise. Don't believe it. He worked hard to get publicity and always had a photographer with him. He had a fine concept of how Jimmy Dean could be made popular and he and his personally attached cameraman would roam around looking for the right people to be photographed with."

George Stevens

"He wasn't easy to know. But the weeks I spent trying to record the subtleties of his personality convinced me that, while he was intense and shy (he sometimes sat for hours in his car outside a friend's house waiting for other visitors to leave), he was at the same time dedicated to his career."

Sanford Roth, photographer and friend

"He had the enthusiasm of a young boy and the sense and intellectual and reasoning powers of a natural philosopher."

Beulah Roth, friend

"James Dean, who has wound up his starring role in *Giant*, George Stevens' production for Warner Brothers, leaves for New York on October 4. He'll do a TV drama, 'The Battler,' for Pontiac."

Ted Ashton, WB publicist, September 29, 1955

"James Dean kept his promise to George Stevens of no automobile racing during the filming of *Giant* at Warner Brothers studios but it didn't take him long to enter his first car race after completing the role of Jett Rink a few days ago. Dean is entering the races at Salinas this weekend in the Porsche Spyder he purchased last week."

Ted Ashton, September 29, 1955

"A Warner Brothers studio executive who used to watch James Dean zoom out of the studio in his fast foreign racing car often shook his head and declared: 'That crazy kid is going to kill himself!' Last night his prophecy came true as one of the most brilliant newcomers I've discovered on the Hollywood scene was killed in his white [sic] Porsche in a highway accident near Paso Robles. I don't think you'd find anyone, whether business associates, girlfriend or buddy, who wouldn't agree that James Dean was a strange, moody, sensitive boy. He was unpredictable and eccentric in his social behavior. He was tough to understand, this one. But likable, too."

Dick Williams, *Los Angeles Mirror-News*, October 1, 1955

"Nice career move, boy."

Unidentified Hollywood producer on Jimmy's death

"He died at just the right time. If he had lived, he'd never have been able to live up to his publicity."

Humphrey Bogart

"Jimmy's car in twilight, on that country road, was invisible. And who expected to see a silver Porsche on that road?"

Beulah Roth

"He seemed to come into this world like a phantom—doing a job and leaving it."

Henry Ginsberg, producer

"There is no part of Jimmy I don't like, no part of him that hasn't always the attraction that goes with complete naturalness. Maybe it is the way he sidles next to someone, chin hugging his chest, then squints up out of the corner of his eye, mumbling a greeting. Or maybe the way he can run a boyish giggle right through his words. . . ."

George Stevens, while cutting *Giant*

"James Dean's death had a profound effect on me. The instant I heard about it, I vomited. I don't know why."

Montgomery Clift

"One felt that he was a boy one had to take care of, but even that was probably his joke. I don't think he needed anybody or anything—except his acting."

Elizabeth Taylor

"I always felt that he would burn himself out. He was really riding on a very, very hot sort of line."

Betsy Palmer, actress

"I liken it to a kind of star or comet that fell through the sky and everybody still talks about it. They say 'Ah, remember the night when you saw that shooting star?' "

Julie Harris

"James Dean was great in two respects. He had great timing and great hair. Essentially that is what made him a hero of youth culture. I suspect he was also a good actor—but that is another matter altogether."

Ray Connolly, writer and director

"He was the loneliest man in the world. He wanted a wife and children, and he used to talk about how important it is to be married to a woman who is understanding. He could be a lonely man in a room full of people."

Lew Bracker

"Who is the most popular star in Hollywood? An actor who does not live there or anywhere else. He is Jimmy Dean, who was killed a year ago."

Life, September 24, 1956

"People were robbed of him. Whenever you're robbed of something, it lingers with you. When Garbo left the screen at the height of her career, she remained a legend. When Valentino died at an early age, he remained a legend."

Martin Landau

"Dean was withdrawn, compulsively promiscuous, but friendless, suspicious, moody, uncooperative, boorish and rude. He could, on occasion, be charming; on most occasions he was annoyingly nuts. He betrayed a psychopathic personality with fits of despondency that alternated with fits of wild jubilation. A classic manic-depressive. Mr. Nice Guy he wasn't. But his tormented screen persona hit a nerve with men, women, the young and the not-so-young."

Kenneth Anger, author

"[James Dean was] the damaged but beautiful soul of our time."

Andy Warhol

"James Dean was more than a phenomenon or even a legend. He was far more than a cinematic genius who could act his balls off. He was simply the greatest screen experience of all time. The fact that he was cut off in his prime is unfortunate but irrelevant. The three films he left us with stand as their own monument. He remains indestructible. He accomplished only three roles, but he ruined the careers of a hundred other aspiring actors who tried to follow him."

Sammy Davis, Jr.

"His film career was one of the most brilliant and one of the most spectacularly brief in history. He was more like a comet than a star."

Academy of Motion Picture Arts and Sciences

"We cannot speak of cinema without mentioning the name of James Dean, the freshly plucked fleur du mal, James Dean, who *is* the cinema, in the same sense as Lillian Gish, Chaplin, Ingrid Bergman, etc."

Francois Truffaut, film critic and director

"All of us were touched by Jimmy and he was touched by greatness."

Natalie Wood

"We are as caught up by James Dean as [was] the first generation, experiencing that tender, romantic, marvelously masochistic identification with the boy who does everything wrong because he cares so much. And because Dean died young and hard, he is not just another actor who outlived his myth and became ordinary in stale roles. He is the symbol of misunderstood youth."

Pauline Kael, film critic

"He seemed to capture that moment of youth, that moment where we're all desperately seeking to find ourselves."

Dennis Hopper

"Jimmy Dean started the entire youth movement."

Sal Mineo

"I'll be damned if I know why."

Elia Kazan on the endurance of the Dean legend, September 30, 1985

"I wish everybody could have been with us in Indiana. The way he treated the animals. The way he treated even the dirt around the farm. Sort of the love he had for nature and everything showed me how completely simple he was."

Dizzy Sheridan

"You would have thought that a boy being gone all these years would leave us in peace, but on Jimmy's birthday last year I looked out the window and counted over a dozen cars parked outside the gate, people just looking at the house."

Marcus Winslow

"I've often wondered what Jimmy would think if he knew all these people were coming to our house from all over the country to ask about him. I expect he'd laugh. I don't know. I just don't know."

Ortense Winslow

"Oh, God, he's having a good giggle, isn't he?"

Bill Bast

JOANNA DEAN
No relation. Joanna Dean recorded the song "He's My Jim" for Kent Records.

MILDRED DEAN
Jimmy's aunt. Charlie Nolan Dean's wife.

MILDRED DEAN
The most mysterious figure in the life of James Dean. Very little is known about Jimmy's mother, Mildred Dean. She was born Mildred Marie on September 15, 1910, in Grant County, Indiana, to John and Minnie Wilson. In 1929, while still a teenager, she married Winton Dean. Two years later she

gave birth to her only child. She was dark, fairly pretty, and, if vintage photos are any indication, slightly plump. She recited poetry in church. She instilled her creative ambitions and energies into her young son. She encouraged his drawings. She sent him out for professional dance lessons in a land where young boys did *not* dance. She created a miniature puppet theater constructed of cardboard in which she and her son staged their own in-house productions. And she died when she was 29. Her son was nine.

The Dean family was in California when Mildred became sick in September 1939. Her foremost concern, of course, was for Jimmy. Her sister-in-law, Ortense Winslow, whom she had become quite close to, recently recalled, "I heard her say different times she wanted to live to raise Jimmy. She never wanted to die and leave Jimmy." Previous reports have erroneously stated that Mildred died on April 14, 1940, from either lung or breast cancer. But the cause of her death was carcinoma of the uterus, and the date was July 14, 1940.

On July 16 Jimmy accompanied his mother's body on the train back to Fairmount, Indiana. Legend has it that he clipped a lock of her hair while she was in her coffin and placed it under his pillow. But Mildred Dean left her son much more than a lock of hair. She left him a legacy of creative wonder, of separateness, and of pain.

Mildred Dean with her husband, Winton, and her baby, Jimmy.

WINTON DEAN

More might be known about Jimmy's father than his mother, but if anything, he is *less* understood. For many Winton Dean will always be regarded as the man who gave up his only son.

The first Deans came from Lexington, Kentucky, and settled in Grant County, Indiana, in 1815. Born in 1907, Winton married at the age of 21. Two years later he was a father. While Jimmy was an infant, Winton got a job as a dental technician at the Marion, Indiana, Veterans Administration

Happy in the heartland: Winton Dean, Jimmy, and friends.

Hospital. Five years later Winton moved his young family to California after being transferred to the Sawtelle Veterans Administration Hospital. Four years later he was a widower.

Two days after he lost his wife, Winton Dean also lost his son. Perhaps he thought he was being selfless, sacrificing his personal desire for what he thought were the best interests of his child. Perhaps the illness of his wife left him financially and/or emotionally incapable of being a parent. Perhaps he thought the separation from his son would be only temporary. *Whatever* he thought, however he was provoked, what Winton Dean did was to put his nine-year-old son on a train to be raised by relatives in Indiana. This unofficial adoption was to leave an indelible scar on the self-esteem of James Dean. Not only was his mother inexplicably taken from him, but he was voluntarily abandoned by his father.

If Winton Dean had planned to reclaim his son, it was a plan unful-filled. In 1943 he was drafted into the Army Medical Corps. A few years later he remarried, further forging a wedge between father and son. After gradu-ation from high school in 1949 Jimmy returned to Los Angeles. Father, son, and stepmother attempted to portray some semblance of family. It was not a particularly happy reunion. Too much time had passed; too few words had been exchanged. To further compound the strain, Winton wanted his son to become a lawyer, a physical education instructor, or a basketball coach. His son wanted to become an actor.

About a year later Jimmy moved out of his father's house, intent on stardom—stardom fueled by an ambition to show the father who deserted him and the mother who died on him just what he could accomplish without either of them.

Over the next five years Winton Dean's relationship with his son is seen only in passages:

☆ In October 1952 Winton traveled from California to see Jimmy (then a New Yorker) in Indiana.
☆ When Jimmy returned to Hollywood in March 1954, the first thing he wanted to do was flaunt his success at his father. Straight from the airport, with Elia Kazan at his side, Jimmy marched into the Sawtelle VA Hospital where Winton still worked. According to Kazan, "Obviously, there was a strong tension between the two, and it was not friendly. I sensed the father disliked the son."
☆ Still in March 1954 Jimmy reportedly moved back into his father's house. Again, the stay was a short one.
☆ In the summer of 1955 Winton traveled to Marfa, Texas, to visit Jimmy on the set of *Giant*. During a break from shooting they threw horseshoes together.
☆ On September 30, 1955, Winton, along with his brother, Charlie, visited Jimmy in Hollywood. They had a quick lunch before Jimmy set out for Salinas.
☆ On September 31, 1955, Winton went to the Paso Robles funeral home to see his son one last time. He selected his son's casket and the suit he was to be buried in. A few days later Winton accompanied his son's body back to Fairmount, Indiana, via plane.
☆ Back in Hollywood Winton began collecting the scattered pieces of Jimmy's life. He went to the home of Jimmy's friends, Sandy and Beulah Roth, to retrieve a self-portrait in clay sculpted by Jimmy shortly before his death. Beulah Roth recalled: "Mr. Dean came over, and I said, 'You should have this.' And he took it away, and I don't know what he did with it. I didn't like him. He was kind of a grim man. He wasn't at all—he didn't seem perturbed by this [Jimmy's death]. He was cold, just cold. I didn't like his whole attitude. It was as though [he thought] I intended to keep this [sculpture]. I couldn't wait to get it out. I had to keep Turkish towels on it for weeks to keep it from drying out!"

What has angered many of James Dean's friends and fans is the manner in which Winton Dean handled his son's estate. Just prior to his death Jimmy took out a life insurance policy, the bulk of which he reportedly intended to go to the aunt and uncle in Fairmount, Indiana, who raised him. However, because he did not issue an official will, the entire estate, life insurance policy included, was awarded to the nearest living relative, his father, Winton Dean. Legally it did not matter that Winton had been for the most part an absentee father.

Over the years Winton Dean has shied away from the press and from his son's fans and friends. For many years he lived in Florida. Recently he returned to Indiana, but he has remained reticent on the subject of his son.

Winton Dean, pictured with his son, Jimmy. That's Mildred on the left.

In the past 35 years Winton Dean expressed himself publicly just once. That occasion came shortly after the release of *East of Eden*, when Jimmy was still alive. Winton gave writer Richard Moore an interview, which is reprinted in part below. Its candor is stunning. It suggests an almost poetic quality and could be entitled "The Saga of a Father and a Son."

> "My Jim is a tough boy to understand. At least he is for me. But maybe that's because I don't understand actors, and he's always wanted to become one. Another reason is that we were separated for a long period of time. From when he was nine until he was eighteen. Those are important, formative years when a boy and his father usually become close friends. Jim and I—well, we've never had that closeness. It's nobody's fault, really. Just circumstances. . . .
>
> "I didn't know what to do. How do you tell an eight-year-old boy his mother's going to die? I tried. In my own stumbling way I tried to prepare Jim for it.
>
> "Nowadays, he lives in a world we don't understand too well, the actor's world. We don't see too much of him. But he's a good boy, my Jim. A good boy, and I'm very proud of him. Not easy to understand, no sir. He's not easy to understand. But he's all man, and he'll make his mark. Mind you, my boy will make his mark."
>
> *Modern Screen*, August 1955

THE DEANERS

A Los Angeles–area rock band that was founded in the early 1980s as a tribute to James Dean. Said a spokesman for the group, "If James Dean had been a rock star, his band would have been named 'The Deaners.' " The same spokesman also proclaimed "James Dean lives!"

DEAN'S MEN'S STORES

Dean's Men's Stores is a line of clothing stores in South Africa, of all places, named after James Dean. The company operates under the slogan banner "His spirit of independence is imbued in Dean's Men's Stores everywhere."

DEATH

Also see THE LAST DAY: SEPTEMBER 30, 1955

James Dean died shortly before 6:00 P.M. on September 30, 1955, as the result of injuries sustained in a two-car collision on a highway approximately 28 miles northeast of Paso Robles, California. The official cause of death was a fractured neck.

At the time of his death Dean had completed work on three films: *East of Eden, Rebel Without a Cause,* and *Giant.* However, only *Eden* had been released, and his celebrity had just begun. For James Dean true stardom came posthumously.

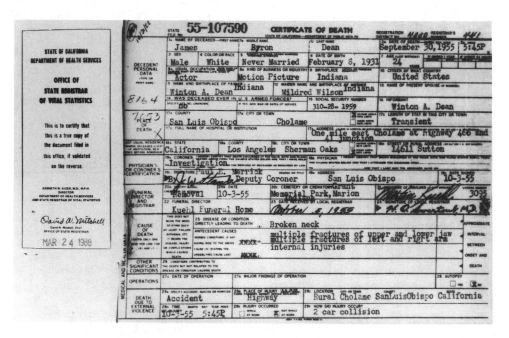

Other Stars Who Died Before Their Final Movie Was Released (a Selective List)

Jean Harlow, *Saratoga* (1937)
Carol Lombard, *To Be or Not To Be* (1942)
Walter Huston, *The Furies* (1950)

Robert Walker, *My Son John* (1952)
John Hodiak, *On the Threshold of Space* (1956)
Clark Gable, *The Misfits* (1961)

Natalie Wood, *Brainstorm* (1983)
Richard Burton, *1984* (England, 1984)
Laurence Olivier, *War Requiem* (1990)

"DEATH IS MY NEIGHBOR"

"Death Is My Neighbor" is an August 25, 1953, episode of the CBS television program "Danger" that co-starred James Dean. The episode was directed by John Peyser, produced by Franklin Heller, and written by Frank Gregory. Walter Hampden and Betsy Palmer also starred.

The plot featured Jimmy as a psychotic janitor who attempts to murder the character portrayed by Betsy Palmer. It is incorrectly referred to elsewhere as "Death Is My Neighborhood." During the shooting, Dean was characteristically temperamental. Producer Heller related the following to researcher Susan Bluttman:

> "At the first read-through, Jimmy suddenly threw his script on the floor and said, 'This is shit!' I stopped the rehearsal and took him out in the hall.
>
> Finally I threatened to fire him. At that point Mr. Hampden took *me* out in the hall and said, 'I've seen this young man on television and I think he's very talented. As a matter of fact, I think he's going to be a big star.' "

Emmy, October 1990

THE DEATH OF JAMES DEAN
Author: Warren Newton Beath
Publisher: Grove Press
Year: 1986

Warren Newton Beath is a James Dean fan who became obsessed by Dean's death. Beath's belief was that the accident that killed James Dean was the fault of the other driver, Donald Turnupseed, and that the local officials had propagated a cover-up to protect him. *The Death of James Dean* is the result of Beath's investigation and obsession. The following is a typical passage:

> All conjecture was improper. The facts were that Jimmy had been in his proper lane, there was no evidence that his speed was a factor in the crash, and the other driver had crossed over into Jimmy's right of way possibly thirty yards before the intersection with no signal or warning.
>
> The other driver had been a local boy, even though he was from Tulare. Like many of the local kids, he was a student at Cal Poly. Dean was an outsider from Hollywood. The other driver was a navy veteran. On the other hand, Dean was a movie actor. He had been on his way to a sports car race, a rich kid's sport, in a car which had cost more money than many of the local farmers would scratch from the soil that whole year.

Ultimately *The Death of James Dean* is compelling but unconvincing. It is all but ruined by text devoted to Beath's obsession with television's Vampira, Maila Nurmi, and his feud with another, unidentified James Dean fan.

THE DEATH OF JAMES DEAN
German stage recitation (*Der Tod des James Dean*) that opened in February 1981 at the Bliss Theatre in Munich. The performance featured actors Hanni Stadler and Gunther Geiermann.

DEATH WISH?
Almost immediately after the death of James Dean came a rash of reports that he had secretly harbored a death wish. Thirty-five years later the reports continue. Proponents of this belief point out the following:

☆ He had a hangman's noose hanging in his apartment.
☆ He told more than one friend, "I'm not going to live past 30."
☆ He raced cars and motorcycles at frenetic speeds.
☆ He was obsessed with bullfighting.
☆ In his copy of Ernest Hemingway's *Death in the Afternoon* Jimmy underlined the passage "The only place where you could see life and death, i.e. violent death now that the wars were over, was in the bullring."
☆ In the same book Dean inscribed the following: "God gave James Dean so many gifts to share with the world, has he the right to throw them away in the bull ring?"
☆ In the same book he underlined other passages in various colors to signify death, disability, disfigurement, or degradation.
☆ He posed for a photograph in a coffin.
☆ According to photographer Frank Worth, he made a series of audiotapes shortly before his death. The tapes featured Jimmy contemplating a common theme: death.
☆ According to Maila Nurmi, she once asked Jimmy why he wanted to die. Said Nurmi, "He had to think of it awhile. I said, 'Is it because you wanna be close to your mother?' He said, 'That's not it.' He said it's because 'That's the only way I'll ever know any peace.' "
☆ According to Leonard Rosenman, "I think he saw death as a challenge."
☆ Car customizer George Barris put it another way: "He had a death cloud hanging over him."

THE DEBATE CLUB
In his senior year at Fairmount High School Jimmy was a starring member of the Debate Club. The club was advised by Adeline Nall. Other club members that year were:

Shirley Hill	Barbara Leach	Betty Todd
Sue Hill	Janet Roth	Earl Vetor
Dean Hurlock	Paul Smith	

ALBERT DEKKER
Albert Dekker portrayed Will in *East of Eden*. Born in 1905, Albert Dekker was a reputable stage and screen actor. His films include *Great Garrick* (1937), *Dr. Cyclops* (1940), *Strange Cargo* (1940), *The Killers* (1946), *Gentleman's Agreement* (1947), *The Silver Chalice* (1954), *Suddenly Last Summer* (1959), and *The Wild Bunch* (1969).

In 1968 Dekker committed suicide by hanging. He was found wearing women's lingerie and a pair of handcuffs.

ROBERT DeKOLBE

Writer who penned an article for *True Strange* magazine entitled "James Dean Speaks from the Grave." The basis for the article was an interview DeKolbe purportedly conducted with James Dean—who was channeled from the beyond by psychic Anna Van Deuseun. The article read, in part:

> Last night I actually talked with Jimmy Dean . . . and his message was not to me but to all of his present-day mourners. "Tell them," he said, "to stop mourning for me. I am very happy where I am. Here, there is no confusion, no unhappiness, no cold, no hunger . . . and I have my mother with me, whom I lost when I was only seven years old."

DeKolbe concluded his article with "The above dialogue I have written verbatim. . . ."

Really? Jimmy was *nine*, not seven, when his mother died, and it is unlikely that he would have provided a reporter with this erroneous information. Further, elsewhere in the article DeKolbe has Jimmy talking about his birthplace of "Marion, Ohio." Jimmy was, of course, born in Marion, Indiana. Apparently this was not only a bad case of ESP but a bad case of reporting as well.

DEL MAR MOTEL AND APARTMENTS

On May 28–29, 1955, James Dean visited Santa Barbara, California, to compete in a car racing event. While there he stayed at the Del Mar Motel and Apartments, which was located at 231 West Mason Street in downtown Santa Barbara.

ALAIN DELON

Alain Delon was known as "the James Dean of France" during a period in the 1960s. Delon, born in 1935, eventually became one of France's leading men. His films include *Plein Soleil* (France, 1959), *The Leopard* (France, Italy, 1963), *Once a Thief* (1965), *Is Paris Burning?* (1966), *Scorpio* (1973), *Mr. Klein* (1977), and *The Concorde—Airport 79* (1979).

JACQUES DeMONTROSTY

James Dean's number one fan in France, deMontrosty is an active member of the California-based We Remember Dean International fan club. He has devoted a lot of his time to promoting the Dean name throughout Europe.

JOHN DENNIS

John Dennis appeared in two 1953 television productions that co-starred James Dean: "The Bells of Cockaigne," an episode of "Armstrong Circle Theatre," and "Harvest," an episode of "Robert Montgomery Presents the Johnson's Wax Program." Dennis has also appeared in the films *From Here to Eternity* (1953) and *Earthquake* (1974) among others.

NICK DENNIS
Actor who appeared in *East of Eden*. Nick Dennis's other films include *A Streetcar Named Desire* (1951), *Spartacus* (1960), and *Birdman of Alcatraz* (1961).

SANDY DENNIS
Sandy Dennis co-starred in *Come Back to the Five and Dime, Jimmy Dean, Jimmy Dean*, a 1982 Broadway play and its subsequent film adaptation. Dennis, easily identified by her quirky mannerisms and speech patterns, was born in 1937 and has appeared in numerous films including *Splendor in the Grass* (1961), *Who's Afraid of Virginia Woolf?* (Best Supporting Actress Oscar winner, 1966), *Up the Down Staircase* (1967), *That Cold Day in the Park* (1969), *The Out-of-Towners* (1970), and *The Four Seasons* (1981).

DENVER, COLORADO
In April 1949, en route to the national speech finals in Longmont, Colorado, Jimmy traveled via train from Indiana to Chicago and transferred to another train that took him to Denver. In Denver he had a layover of a few hours before transferring to another train bound for Longmont. On the way back to Indiana after losing the competition Jimmy, with chaperon Adeline Nall, stopped off in Denver for a little consolatory sight-seeing.

JOHN DEREK
Pier Angeli left James Dean for Vic Damone. Ursula Andress replaced him with John Derek.

Born Derek Harris in 1926, John Derek somewhat resembled James Dean in appearance and was discovered by Nicholas Ray for *Knock on Any Door* in 1949. Previously Derek had appeared in one picture, *I'll Be Seeing You* (1945). His subsequent films include *All the King's Men* (1949), *Rogues of Sherwood Forest* (1950), *The Prince of Players* (1955), *The Ten Commandments* (1956), and *Exodus* (1960). He also co-starred in the television series "Frontier Circus" (1961–1962).

In recent years, however, John Derek has gained more notoriety for his female companionship. Following Andress were Linda Evans and Bo Derek. With the latter as his star Derek has attempted a second career as the director of such films as *Tarzan and the Ape Man* (1981) and *Bolero* (1984).

DESIREE
James Dean reportedly visited Marlon Brando on the 20th Century–Fox set of *Desiree*, a 1954 costume drama in which Brando portrayed Napoléon.

MARCEAU DEVILLERS
Author of the book *James Dean on Location*, which was originally published in France in 1985. It was subsequently published in Great Britain by Sidgwick & Jackson.

JAMES DeWEERD

Reverend James DeWeerd was the Fairmount, Indiana, town hero, the pastor of the Fairmount Wesleyan Church, and undoubtedly one of the biggest influences in the life of James Dean.

Born in 1916, DeWeerd was literate and well educated. He did his postgraduate studies at Cambridge University and served as a chaplain in the U.S. Army in France circa 1943–1945 before becoming a minister in Fairmount. To young Jimmy Dean DeWeerd represented the outside world and the potential adventures and challenges that awaited him.

> "Jimmy was usually happiest stretched out on my library floor, reading Shakespeare or other books of his choosing. He loved good music playing softly in the background. Tchaikovsky was his favorite."
>
> Reverend James DeWeerd, the *Chicago Tribune*,
> September 9, 1956

In addition to literature and classical music, DeWeerd introduced his young protégé to fine art, philosophy, bullfighting, and car racing. It was DeWeerd who took Jimmy to see the races at Indianapolis. Reportedly it was also DeWeerd who taught Jimmy how to drive.

For Jimmy's funeral James DeWeerd was flown from Cincinnati, where he hosted a religious television program, to the Marion, Indiana, airport. He was then escorted to the Back Creek Friends Church in Fairmount, where he co-conducted the services.

DeWeerd died on March 28, 1972, and is buried at Park Cemetery in Fairmount.

JOE DiANGELO

James Dean's double on *Giant*.

MARLENE DIETRICH

When asked by celebrity conduit Hedda Hopper if he wanted to meet Marlene Dietrich, Jimmy replied:

> "I don't know. She's such a figment of my imagination. I go whoop in the stomach when you just ask me if I'd like to meet her. *Too much woman.* You look at her and think, I'd like to have that."
> *The Whole Truth and Nothing But* by Hedda Hopper

At that time Dietrich, born Maria Magdalene Dietrich in 1901, was 54 years old. Her legendary career included such pictures as *The Blue Angel* (1930), *Morocco* (Best Actress Oscar nomination, 1930–31), *Blonde Venus* (1932), *Destry Rides Again* (1939), *Around the World in 80 Days* (1956), *Witness for the Prosecution* (1957), *Touch of Evil* (1958), *Judgment at Nuremberg* (1961), and *Just a Gigolo* (1978).

DIG MAGAZINE

Fan magazine that published several articles about James Dean, including:

☆ April 1957   "James Dean"
☆ November 1957   "The Life of James Dean"
☆ August 1962   "The Miracle of James Dean"
☆ August 1962   "The James Dean Story, A Legend Revisited"

VARETTA DILLARD

Recorded the song "I Miss You Jimmy" for Groove Records.

BRADFORD DILLMAN

Actor who was featured in the 1953 off-Broadway production of *The Scarecrow* in which James Dean had a bit part. Dillman, born in 1930, has appeared in several films including *Compulsion* (1959), *The Way We Were* (1973), and *Sudden Impact* (1983). He has also co-starred in the television programs "Court-Martial" (1966) and "King's Crossing" (1981).

CHARLES DINGLE

Charles Dingle appeared as Bocage in the 1954 Broadway play *The Immoralist*, which featured James Dean. Born in 1887 in Wabash, Indiana, Dingle was best known for his performance on Broadway in *The Little Foxes*, a role he re-created in the film version (1941). His many other film credits include *The Song of Bernadette* (1943), *Duel in the Sun* (1946), *Call Me Madam* (1953), and *The Court-Martial of Billy Mitchell* (1955). Charles Dingle died in 1956.

DIRECTING

James Dean wanted to become a stage and film director. He craved the creative challenge and control extended to directors. Many of those who knew him believe that, had he lived, Dean would have certainly become a film director and that his directorial skills would have eventually eclipsed his performing abilities.

Directors Who Directed TV Shows in Which Dean Appeared

Justus Addiss	"The Unlighted Road"	1955
Vincent J. Donehue	"The Thief"	1955
Dick Dunlap	"A Long Time Till Dawn"	1953
John Frankenheimer	"Padlocks"	1954
Richard Goode	"The Foggy, Foggy Dew"	1952
Jeffrey Hayden	"Run Like a Thief"	1954
Maury Holland	"Keep Our Honor Bright"	1953
Sidney Lumet	"The Capture of Jesse James"	1953
Andrew McCullough	"Glory in Flower"	1953
Andrew McCullough	"The Little Woman"	1954
Don Medford	"Something for an Empty Briefcase"	1953
Don Medford	"The Evil Within"	1953
Don Medford	"I'm a Fool"	1954
Don Medford	"The Dark, Dark Hour"	1954

Dean "directing" *East of Eden*. "Someday, I would like to follow in the footsteps of my great idol, Elia Kazan," said Dean.

Paul Nickell	"Ten Thousand Horses Singing"	1952
Paul Nickell	"Sentence of Death"	1953
John Peyser	"Death Is My Neighbor"	1953
Arthur Pierson	"Hill Number One"	1951
Stuart Rosenberg	"The Big Story"	1953
James Sheldon	"The Bells of Cockaigne"	1953
James Sheldon	"Harvest"	1953
Lela Swift	"The Web"	1952

Directors Who Directed Plays in Which Dean Appeared

Frank Corsaro	*The Scarecrow*	1953
Michael Gordon	*See the Jaguar*	1952
Daniel Mann	*The Immoralist*	1954
Howard Sackler	*Women of Trachis*	1954
Herman Shumlin	*The Immoralist*	1954

Directors Who Directed Movies in Which Dean Starred

Elia Kazan	*East of Eden*	1955
Nicholas Ray	*Rebel Without a Cause*	1955
George Stevens	*Giant*	1956

Directors Who Directed Television Movies/Specials About Dean

Robert Butler	"James Dean"	1976

Ara Chekmayan	"Forever James Dean"	1988
Craig Haffner	"James Dean: An American Original"	1983
Jack Haley, Jr.	"James Dean Remembered"	1974

Directors Who Directed Plays About or Inspired by Dean
Robert Altman	*Come Back to the Five and Dime, Jimmy Dean, Jimmy Dean*	1982
Patricia Leone	*James Dean: A Dress Rehearsal*	1984
Robert Livingston	*Dean*	1977

Directors Who Directed Movies About or Inspired by Dean
Robert Altman	*The James Dean Story*	1957
Robert Altman	*Come Back to the Five and Dime, Jimmy Dean, Jimmy Dean*	1982
James Bridges	*September 30, 1955*	1977
Ray Connolly	*James Dean: The First American Teenager*	1976
George W. George	*The James Dean Story*	1957
Claudio Masenza	*Hollywood: The Rebel James Dean*	*
Nick Taylor	*Bye Bye Jimmy*	*
Paul Watson	*Bye Bye Jimmy*	*

*Made for the video market. No theatrical release date.

DISCOGRAPHY
See THE RECORD ALBUMS ABOUT JAMES DEAN.
See THE SONGS ABOUT JAMES DEAN.

DOCTORS
The following is a selective list of the doctors who administered to James Dean:

| Dr. Irving S. Berman | Dr. Victor V. Cameron | Dr. Ronald E. Sattler |
| Dr. Robert Bossert | Dr. James R. Cogan | |

DOLLS
The official James Dean Doll was produced in 1986 by the Dakin Company. The doll was 18 inches high, constructed of vinyl, and dressed in the prerequuisite red jacket, white T-shirt, blue jeans, and black motorcycle boots. The doll was equipped with a cigarette prop much to the horror of the American Cancer Society. Something less than a national controversy erupted over the smoking doll, and Dakin responded by distributing a smokeless Dean doll for the sum of $99.95. Today neither version of the doll is available.

THE DONALDSON AWARD
It has been repeatedly published that James Dean won the Donaldson award for his performance in *The Immoralist*. However, the 1953–1954 Donaldson, like almost every other Best Supporting Actor theater prize that year, went to John Kerr for his performance in *Tea and Sympathy*.

VINCENT J. DONEHUE

Vincent J. Donehue directed "The Thief," a 1955 episode of the ABC television program "The U.S. Steel Hour" that co-starred James Dean. Donehue (1916–1966) was primarily a stage director who won a Tony Award in 1958 for *The Sunrise at Campobello*. He also directed *The Sound of Music* (1960) on Broadway, for which he received a Tony nomination. Donehue's screen credits include *Lonelyhearts* (1958) and the film version of *Sunrise at Campobello* (1960).

DON DOOLEY

Shandon, California, resident who was a witness to the September 30, 1955, accident that killed James Dean. Dooley testified at the subsequent coroner's inquest.

ANN DORAN

Actress who portrayed Jim Stark's nagging mother in *Rebel Without a Cause*. During the shooting Doran and Dean developed a friendly acquaintance. Jimmy once coerced her to take a ride on his motorcycle through the Warner Brothers lot. It was a hellish ride that Jimmy frequently tormented his passengers with. Another typical Dean scenario also involved Ann Doran. As described in the book *Hollywood Anecdotes* by Paul Boller, Jr., and Ronald Davis:

> After the movie was finished Doran was awakened at her home one morning around three o'clock by someone in her front yard yelling, "Mom! Mom!" The actress stuck her head out a window and asked, "Who is it? You're going to wake the neighbors." From out in the yard she heard a drunken voice say, "It's your son, Jimmy." Doran invited Dean in and took him to the kitchen. She brewed some coffee, and the two of them sat on the kitchen floor while the young actor poured out his loneliness. They talked until dawn, and it was the first of several such visits.

Born in 1914, Ann Doran has appeared in many films including *Penitentiary* (1938), *Blondie* (1938), *The More the Merrier* (1943), *The Snake Pit* (1948), *Rosie* (1967), and *First Monday in October* (1981). She has also co-starred in the television programs "National Velvet" (1960–1962) and "Longstreet" (1971–1972).

MARION DOUGHERTY

Marion Dougherty was the NBC casting director who cast Jimmy in "A Long Time Till Dawn," a 1953 episode of the television series "Kraft Television Theatre."

SUSAN DOUGLAS

Co-star of "Something for an Empty Briefcase," a 1953 episode of the NBC television series "Campbell Soundstage" that co-starred James Dean.

HARRISON DOWD
Cast member, *See the Jaguar* (1952).

WILLIAM DOZIER
Executive producer of "Death Is My Neighbor," a 1953 episode of the CBS television program "Danger" that co-starred James Dean.

DR. JEKYLL AND MR. HYDE
Reportedly, shortly before his death Jimmy had been working on a film script, a remake of the horror classic *Dr. Jekyll and Mr. Hyde,* which he hoped to star in and direct. The role had previously been played by John Barrymore (1920 silent), Fredric March (1932), and Spencer Tracy (1941).

ISABELLE DRAESEMER
James Dean's first agent. Isabelle Draesemer (incorrectly spelled Isabel Draesmer in other reports) signed Jimmy to a contract after seeing his performance in a UCLA production of *Macbeth* in late 1950. Her office, at the time, was located in Hollywood at 8272 Sunset Boulevard.

WENDY DREW
Appeared in the September 11, 1953, episode of the NBC television program "The Big Story," which starred James Dean. Drew also appeared in the television program "School House" (1949) and "Jimmy Hughes, Rookie Cop" (1953).

JOHN DRINKWATER
John Drinkwater (1882–1937) wrote the teleplay for "Abraham Lincoln," a 1952 episode of the CBS television program "Studio One" in which James Dean had a small part.

DRIVER'S LICENSE
Jimmy's California driver's license number: B854267. Restriction: Corrective lenses required.

ARTHUR DROOKER
Producer of "James Dean: An American Original," a 1983 episode of the syndicated television program "Hollywood Close-Up."

DRUGS
With his penchant for experimentation in all directions, it should come as no surprise that James Dean was not a stranger to drugs. One of his most frequent partners in crime was Dennis Hopper.

> Dennis would go to Jimmy's house in the San Fernando Valley, a then-rural suburb of Los Angeles. They would get several six-packs of beer, some pot, and spend an afternoon and evening getting high.

The sweet smell of pot hung in the air of Dean's little house like a blanket of fog.
>*Dennis Hopper: A Madness to His Method* by Elena Rodriguez

"We smoked a lot of grass. At that period of time, I guess [Robert] Mitchum smoked grass, but I don't think any of the others were into it. Yeah, we smoked grass. We'd [also] take a few uppers, occasionally."
>Dennis Hopper, *James Dean: The First American Teenager*

DRUMS
Contrary to what skeptics thought at the time, James Dean's interest in the drums was not newfound during his New York period in the early 1950s. Actually, Jimmy received his first drum at the age of nine, when he was in the fourth grade. It was a present from his aunt Ortense and uncle Marcus Winslow.

MILDRED DUAVOD
Co-star of "The Little Woman," a 1954 episode of the CBS television program "Danger" that also starred James Dean.

ROLAND DUBOIS
In 1948 Roland Dubois was the principal at Fairmount High School, where Jimmy Dean was a student.

GORDON DUFF
Producer of "Run Like a Thief," a 1954 episode of the NBC television program "Philco TV Playhouse" that co-starred James Dean.

DUMONT BARBER SHOP
The New York City barbershop where James Dean used to have his hair cut. Located next door to the Iroquois Hotel at 49 West 44th Street, the Dumont Barber Shop is, remarkably, still in existence.

KATHERINE DUNHAM
During his New York period Jimmy attended dance classes given by well-known dancer/choreographer Katherine Dunham. In 1989, at the age of 79, Dunham was the recipient of a National Medal of Arts award presented by President George Bush.

DICK DUNLAP
Dick Dunlap produced and directed "A Long Time Till Dawn," a 1953 episode of the television program "Kraft Television Theatre" that starred James Dean.

Born in 1923, Dunlap also directed, among other programs, "Lux Video Theatre" and "The Patti Page Show."

RALPH DUNN
Actor who co-starred in "Sentence of Death," a 1953 episode of "Studio One Summer Theatre" that featured James Dean. Dunn's feature films include *Laura* (1944) and *The Pajama Game* (1957).

MILDRED DUNNOCK
Actress who co-starred with James Dean in "Padlocks," a 1954 episode of the CBS television program "Danger."

Mildred Dunnock, born in 1900, has appeared in numerous plays including *Death of a Salesman* (1949) and *Cat on a Hot Tin Roof* (1955); and films including *The Corn Is Green* (1945), *Death of a Salesman* (Best Supporting Actress Oscar nomination, 1951), *Baby Doll* (Best Supporting Actress Oscar nomination, 1956), *The Nun's Story* (1959), *Sweet Bird of Youth* (1962), and *The Spiral Staircase* (1975).

"THE DUPONT SHOW OF THE WEEK"
NBC television program (1961–1964) that presented a 1962 episode entitled "The Movie Star," which was based on the death of James Dean.

BOB DYLAN
Legendary singer/songwriter whose songs of social protest made him a symbol of the 1960s. Born Robert Zimmerman in 1941, Dylan is also an unabashed James Dean fan who made the star trek to Jimmy's hometown of Fairmount, Indiana, in July 1988.

E

THE EAGLES
Country rock band of the 1970s ("Take It Easy," "Best of My Love," "Take It to the Limit," "Hotel California," etc.) that recorded a song entitled "James Dean" in 1974. The song is included on their *On the Border* album, recorded on Asylum Records. It was written by Jackson Browne, Glenn Frey, Don Henley, and J. D. Souther. Dean aficionados generally consider this to be the finest song recorded in tribute to James Dean. The Eagles disbanded in 1982.

EARTH GIRLS ARE EASY
Nineteen eighty-nine movie starring Geena Davis, Jeff Goldblum, and the clever Julie Brown about a trio of aliens with active libidos. In one scene the aliens are watching television and the "You're tearing me apart" scene from *Rebel Without a Cause* flashes on. Later in the film one of the aliens, Jim Carrey, does a manic comic impersonation of James Dean from the same scene.

EAST OF EDEN
Novel by John Steinbeck, a portion of which was adapted into the 1954 Warner Brothers movie of the same title. *East of Eden* was published by Viking Press in 1952.

EAST OF EDEN ★★★★
1954   115 minutes   WarnerColor   CinemaScope
Warner Brothers
Directed by: Elia Kazan
Produced by: Elia Kazan
Screenplay by: Paul Osborn, from the novel by John Steinbeck
Photographed by: Ted McCord
Edited by: Owen Marks
Music by: Leonard Rosenman
Cast: Julie Harris, James Dean, Raymond Massey, Burl Ives, Dick Davalos, Jo Van Fleet, Albert Dekker, Lois Smith, Harold Gordon, Nick Dennis, Richard Garrick, Timothy Carey, Lonny Chapman, Barbara Baxley, Bette Treadville, Tex Mooney, Harry Cording, Loretta Rush, Bill Phillips, Mario Siletti, Jonathan Haze, Jack Carr, Roger Creed, Effie Laird, Wheaton Chambers, Ed Clark, Al Ferguson, Franklyn Farnum, Rose Plummer, John George, C. Ramsay Hill, Edward McNally, Earl Hodgins

The first time we see James Dean in *East of Eden*, he is sitting on a

---

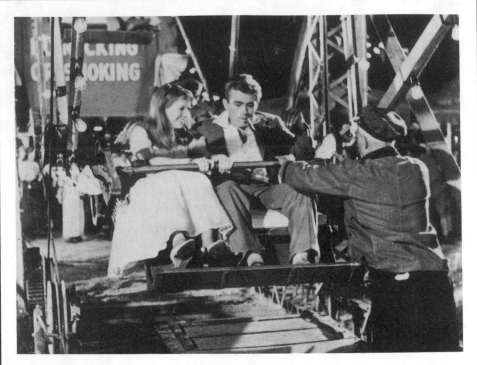

Kazan instructed composer Leonard Rosenman to score the love scene between James Dean and Julie Harris as if it were "the birth of the angels."

curb, slouched, almost ingrained into the sidewalk. He waits, watches, like a scared and hungry cat, uncertain whether to advance or retreat, as the woman he suspects is his mother, Jo Van Fleet, walks past him without a trace of recognition. He follows her, tentatively, then angrily and, unable to articulate his conflicting emotions, he hurls a rock at her house of ill repute. Such was the auspicious, startling, and yet strangely familiar introduction of moviegoing audiences to a little-known actor by the name of James Dean back in 1955. Audiences not only recognized a new star in Dean, as the film progressed they recognized something greater, something lasting; in his fumbling search for the affection of a parent, they recognized *themselves.*

East of Eden was purchased by Warner Brothers in November 1952. John Steinbeck, who was also initially slated to write the screenplay, was paid the then-considerable sum of $125,000 plus 25 percent of the film's net profits. When the film went into preproduction in 1953, Elia Kazan had a fairly specific idea of how he wanted to cast his leading role. In a letter to Jack Warner dated July 27, 1953, Kazan wrote that Cal Trask "needs someone like Marlon Brando or Monty Clift (except that they should be nineteen years old)."

Cal Trask, with Abra, waiting to be sentenced.

At the time Kazan had, at the very least, knowledge of 22-year-old Jimmy Dean through his work at the Actors Studio. Over the years Kazan's own story of how Dean was cast in *Eden* has fluctuated greatly. Only recently has he acknowledged that the film's screenwriter, Paul Osborn, persuaded him to see Dean's performance in *The Immoralist* on Broadway in February 1954. Later Kazan invited Dean to meet with him at Warner Brothers' New York office. Following their meeting Dean gave Kazan an initiation rite: a motorcycle ride through the city. Kazan then escorted Dean to meet John Steinbeck, who issued the dictum "He *is* Cal!"

Warner Brothers officially announced Dean's casting on March 6, 1954. At about the same time that the studio was making the news public, Kazan scrawled a letter to Jack Warner from New York. "About casting," he wrote, "I think Dean is o.k. Impress on him or have someone impress on him again when he arrives out there, the great importance of living an outdoor life, sunshine, exercise, food. . . . Just all the healthy things, and lots of sleep. He's an odd kid and I think we should make him as handsome as possible."

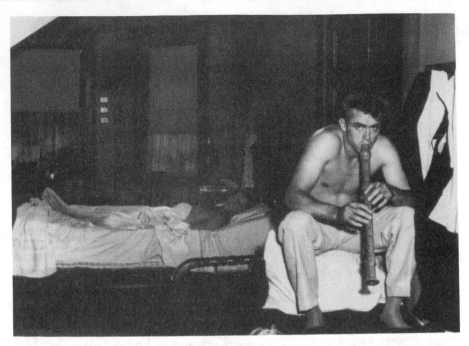

Undertones of brotherly incest and latent homosexuality.

Ray Massey (right) didn't care much for James Dean, his on-screen son.

Kazan decided to "impress on" Dean himself. On March 8 Elia Kazan escorted James Dean on an airplane ride from New York to Hollywood. On March 10 Jack Warner responded tellingly to Kazan's letter: "You said he is an odd kid. I hope he isn't too odd, as it is getting to the point now that when we make pictures with odd people, the whole machine is thrown out of order. You know it only takes one odd spark plug to make the motor miss. I, too, am fed up with people who are too odd."

The final script, based on the last fourth of Steinbeck's novel, was completed on May 17. Wardrobe tests were conducted three days later. One of the production's earliest debates concerned the use of Cinema-Scope. Jack Warner wanted it; Kazan didn't. Warner won out, and *Eden* was later hailed by some nonfans of 20th Century–Fox's *The Robe* as the first "distinguished" production to be shot in CinemaScope. Another early debate concerned the hiring of the cinematographer. Kazan wanted, in order of preference, Harry Stradling, Russell Metty, or Jim Wong Howe. He settled for Ted McCord. Another particularly vexatious problem concerned the censors, who were relentlessly wary of the characterization of Kate, Cal and Aron Trask's madam of a mother. For the most part, however, Kazan was given free creative rein in the proceedings. He had, after all, directed *A Streetcar Named Desire* for Warners and the then-unreleased but much admired *On the Waterfront* for Columbia. The latter went on to win the 1954 Best Picture and Best Director Oscars.

Shooting began in Mendocino, which served in the film as Monterey, on May 27, 1954. Kazan, to the resentment of some, coddled Dean unabashedly and spent a good deal of his time huddled in conversation with him. Eventually Kazan concocted a system that allowed Jimmy to wander off by himself to prepare for a scene while the other actors were left waiting, stranded in filmmaking limbo. When Dean was ready for a take, he'd blow a whistle that Kazan had given him, and Kazan would then give the signal to his cast and crew that shooting was ready to resume. To the other actors (who not only had to wait but had to wait *in character*) it was an understandably disconcerting technique.

Early into the Mendocino shooting both Dick Davalos and James Dean contracted poison oak and were laid up briefly. Jimmy also complained that the sound of passing automobiles penetrated his hotel room and kept him awake all night. Subsequently he shunned his bed and found sleep in a Southern Pacific freight car used in the film. Meanwhile Julie Harris tried to stay in shape by spurning the company limousine. Instead she walked the three miles from the hotel to the set every morning.

On June 4 the company moved to neighboring Salinas, where the

lettuce refrigeration scene and the scene of Cal nursing his bean crop, among others, were filmed. Kazan synchronized the shooting of the latter with a local farmer so that the crops would measure three inches in height. He also collaborated with another local farmer while shooting the lettuce crop sequence. After the film's successful release the farmer contacted Warner Brothers and asked if he could market his produce as "lettuce from *East of Eden*." His request was denied.

Back in Burbank on June 12, set designers James Basevi and Malcolm Bert, along with the studio construction unit, had built a replica of Salinas, circa 1917, on the Warner Brothers back lot. Also erected was a full-scale amusement park for the carnival scene. For night sequences, such as the carnival scene, the company spent weeks shooting from 8:30 P.M. to 5:00 A.M. On July 13 a visitor showed up on the set and stayed until 4:00 A.M. It was Marlon Brando.

During shooting of the Ferris wheel love scene (if the peck Dean gives Julie Harris constitutes a love scene), however, no guests were allowed on the set. In fact Harris's extreme modesty prompted Kazan to order the cast and crew to turn their heads, with the obvious exception, of course, of cameraman Ted McCord. Harris apologized at the time: "I hope in the future I'll get over this silly nervousness." After watching a rehearsal of the scene, Kazan turned to Burl Ives and marveled, "I've *never* been able to get what I wanted in a love scene so quickly!" Shooting the scene, however, took longer. In fact the actors and extras on the Ferris wheel spent so much time up in the air that the doctor on the set had to administer sickness and movement pills.

The icehouse sequence posed other problems. Foremost was the temperature, which soared to the low hundreds. The scene called for Jimmy to vent his anger and frustration with his father by hurling several heavy blocks of ice down to their crashing demise. After rehearsing the scene, Jimmy left the set, as was typical, to prepare, leaving Ray Massey and Burl Ives, also in the scene, to wait and melt under the sweltering sun. To make matters worse, the scene was a difficult one for Dean, and he took more preparation time than usual. Ives, through a stream of sweat, turned to Massey and quipped, "Jimmy's got to get to *hate* the ice. It takes time." Then, when he *was* ready for a take, Jimmy couldn't lift the exceptionally heavy blocks of ice. Forever the master motivator, Kazan made a particularly derogatory remark—not about Dean's lack of strength but about his acting ability. The tactic worked. Jimmy picked up the block of ice and hurled it to the ground below.

The member of the *Eden* cast with whom Dean clashed most severely was Ray Massey, who portrayed his stoic, Bible-quoting father in the film. According to Kazan, "[Ray] simply couldn't stand the sight of the kid, dreaded every day he worked with him. 'You never know what he's going to say or do!' Ray said. 'Make him read the lines the way they're written.' Jimmy knew that Ray was scornful of him, and he responded with a sullenness he didn't cover. This was an antagonism I didn't try to heal; I aggravated it."

One scene in which Kazan's aggravation worked to the picture's benefit was the scene in which Massey orders Dean to read from the Bible. When Jimmy's disrespectful reading failed to provoke the reaction Kazan wanted from Massey, Kazan called a break and huddled with Dean. When shooting resumed, Jimmy improvised the scene and peppered his Bible-reading with four-letter obscenities. Massey, for the first and only time during the production, exploded in rage and threatened to walk out of the picture. It was the shot of that reaction that Kazan incorporated into the film.

As filming continued, word spread through the movie industry

about Kazan's talented new protégé. Jimmy Dean had become something of a celebrity—Hollywood's flavor of the month. As Kazan later
related, "We began to suspect something outstanding was going to
happen with him about three-quarters through the picture. You could
just see that he was so good. I've never seen anything like it in the
movies in my whole life, including Marlon Brando. [But] he got kind of
spoiled, abusing, throwing his weight around."

He began staying out at all hours of the night, hanging out at

Googie's coffee shop, going on midnight motorcycle cruises down Sunset Boulevard. He also started disobeying his mentor, Kazan. At the time Dean was also falling in love with Pier Angeli, and his rebellion against Kazan was not unlike the rebellion of a teenager in love against a parent.

He also started showing up late on the set. Once, when he was supposed to be shooting, Jimmy was loitering on another Warner soundstage, watching Judy Garland shoot a dance sequence for *A Star Is Born*. There is something ironic in the image of James Dean watching Judy Garland shoot *A Star Is Born*. At that time, *at that moment*, on that lot, it was Dean's star that was being born.

Even months before *East of Eden* premiered in New York on March 9, 1955, various industry screenings generated a considerable rumble in Hollywood. In a town of hype *the real thing* was a revelation. And from the moment he slouched onto that sidewalk and hurled a rock at his mother's house, from the moment he wailed at his father "I gotta know what I am, I gotta know what I'm like!" and from the moment he struggled to embrace his father and present him with the money that he had earned to win his love, James Dean was the real thing.

East of Eden is unquestionably his finest picture. It is also one of the finest portraits of alienated youth ever filmed. Dean's Cal Trask with his slinking gait and strangled speech is the classic depiction of the good boy who is bad because he feels too much and is loved too little, the boy for whom everything goes wrong because he tries too hard. It is a performance and a film that millions of men have watched with a lump in their throats and a look of bittersweet recognition on their faces.

"EAST OF EDEN"

Another version of the Steinbeck novel that was presented as an eight-hour miniseries on ABC television in February 1981. Unlike the 1955 motion picture, this adaptation encompassed the entire novel, thereby changing the focus from the character of Cal Trask to the character of Kate, his prostitute mother.

"East of Eden" starred Jane Seymour as Kate, Timothy Bottoms as Adam, Bruce Boxleitner as Charles (Adam's brother), Lloyd Bridges as Sam Hamilton, and Sam Bottoms as Cal, the character James Dean had portrayed over 25 years before. Also in the cast were Hart Bochner, Anne Baxter, and Karen Allen.

"THE ED SULLIVAN SHOW"

"The Ed Sullivan Show" aired a tribute to James Dean on its October 14, 1956, program, which was tied into the release of *Giant*. The show provoked a feud with a rival program "The Steve Allen Show," which had also produced a Dean tribute. The October 4 edition of the *New York Times* read:

> Steve Allen fired another blast yesterday at his television competitor, Ed Sullivan, as a drama titled "Battle by Press Release" moved into the second act. Mr. Allen's second formal handout within twenty-four hours seemed to reiterate his earlier charge that Mr. Sullivan had pirated a program idea that the comedian planned to use.
>
> The idea pertained to a tribute to James Dean, late film actor, that Mr. Allen had planned to present on his National Broadcasting Company on October 21. The comedian charged that Mr. Sullivan "or someone in his organization" pilfered the idea and scheduled a tribute to Mr. Dean for October 14 over the Columbia Broadcasting Network.
>
> Mr. Sullivan did not retaliate with a press release, but over the telephone said: "Everything Allen has charged is a complete lie. I won't take his word for anything any more."

The feud was resolved when Steve Allen bumped his Dean tribute to October 14, which put it head to head against the Sullivan show tribute.

"The Ed Sullivan Show," one of the most successful programs in television history, aired on Sunday nights from 1948 until 1971.

EDITORS
The following is a list of the film editors who spent countless hours in darkened Hollywood editing rooms cutting the image of James Dean.

Phil Anderson: *Giant*
Fred Bohanan: *Giant*
William Hornbeck: *Giant*
Owen Marks: *East of Eden*
William Ziegler: *Rebel Without a Cause*

DOUG EDWARDS
Host of the Academy of Motion Picture Arts and Science's 1983 tribute to James Dean.

MORRY EFRON
Company manager, *See the Jaguar* (1952).

THE EGYPTIAN
When Marlon Brando strutted out of *The Egyptian*, a 1954 film adaptation of the bestselling novel by Mika Waltair, 20th Century-Fox offered the role to James Dean, who likewise turned it down. The film was subsequently made anyway with Edmund Purdom, Victor Mature, Peter Ustinov, Bella Darvi, Gene Tierney, Michael Wilding, and Jean Simmons. It was directed by Michael Curtiz (*Casablanca*) but was a failure nonetheless.

THE EGYPTIAN THEATER

Famed Hollywood movie theater where *East of Eden* premiered in Los Angeles in March 1955. Columnist Sidney Skolsky wrote:

> I saw Jimmy Dean in a black leather jacket, wearing his customary eye-glasses, standing unrecognized outside of the Egyptian Theater watching the people standing in line to buy tickets for *East of Eden*.

The Egyptian Theater was also the site of Hollywood's very first movie premiere. The movie was *Robin Hood*, and it starred Douglas Fairbanks, Sr., and Wallace Beery. The year was 1921. Today the Egyptian is still in existence at 6708 Hollywood Boulevard.

DWIGHT EISENHOWER

Legend has it that on the day of James Dean's death, September 30, 1955, the president of the United States, Dwight David Eisenhower (1890–1969) suffered a heart attack. In this case, however, legend exaggerated truth. Actually Eisenhower suffered a heart attack in the early morning hours of September 24, 1955, after having devoured a meal of roast lamb a few hours before. A few days later, on September 26, the stock market crashed by over 30 points, a loss of some $12 billion. On November 11 the president was released from the hospital. The following year he waged a successful campaign and was reelected to a second term.

JOE ELLIOT

Jimmy lost the lead in the Fairmount High School senior play to fellow Quaker Joe Elliot.

GUY ELLIS

Guy Ellis is the Fairmount, Indiana, resident who found James Dean's stolen gravestone in May 1983. Ellis had been driving home from work when he spotted the stone sitting atop a tree stump. The good Samaritan stopped, wrapped the stone in a quilt, and took it to the Fairmount Police Department. The police subsequently returned the gravestone to Jimmy's cousin, Marcus Winslow, Jr.

ROYSTON ELLIS

Author of *Rebel*, a biography about James Dean published by Consul Books in Great Britain in 1962. Ellis, born in Middlesex, England, in 1941, is also a former landscape gardener, ferryboat engineer, and music columnist. His other books include *Driftin' with Cliff*, a biography of Cliff Richard (1959), *The Shadows by Themselves* (1961), and *Myself for Fame* (a novel, 1964).

ELVIS AND JIMMY

Nineteen fifty-six one-shot cover-to-cover magazine that exploited the James Dean/Elvis Presley connection. While other publications were issuing monthly proclamations lauding Elvis as "the next Dean," this one promised "How It Feels to Be Elvis" and "The Tragedy and Triumph of Jimmy Dean."

GEORGE ELWORTHY

Writer of "American Rebel," the theme song of the 1988 cable television documentary "Forever James Dean."

LEON EMBRY

In July 1957 aspiring actor Leon Embry, a native of Kentucky, was announced as the co-winner of the first James Dean Theatre School Scholarship. The scholarship had been designed to encourage outstanding young talent.

END AS A MAN

James Dean appeared in an in-house Actors Studio production of Calder Willingham's *End as a Man*. The presentation starred Ben Gazzara, Albert Salmi, Pat Hingle, Arthur Storch, Paul Richards, and William Smithers. Jimmy appeared in the small part of Starkson. The production was directed by Jack Garfein and was presented to studio members in three performances during May and June 1953.

The enormous success of these performances prompted an off-Broadway staging at the Theatre De Lys in Greenwich Village. However, by the opening night of September 15, 1953, Jimmy had bowed out of the cast. His reason, most likely, was that by the latter half of 1953 he was working, seemingly without interruption, on television. He just didn't have the time.

A month after the subsequent off-Broadway success of *End as a Man*, and after a few more cast revisions, it was promoted to the big time: Broadway.

For James Dean that was not the end of *End as a Man*. In February 1954 the play's cast members, including its star, Ben Gazzara, went on strike, demanding more money. At the time Jimmy was having problems of his own with his employers on *The Immoralist*. Shrewdly, he approached director Garfein and offered to take over the starring role in *End as a Man*. However, the strike was resolved promptly, and Jimmy had to content himself with *The Immoralist*—temporarily.

"ENTERTAINMENT TONIGHT"

Syndicated entertainment series that aired a multipart tribute to James Dean in 1985 to commemorate the 30th anniversary of his death. The segments included footage and stills of Dean and interviews with Ortense Winslow, Marcus Winslow, Jr., Bill Bast, Jim Backus, Elizabeth Taylor, Dennis Hopper, Burl Ives, Martin Landau, Corey Allen, Carroll Baker, Ernie Tripke, and Adeline Nall. The tribute was hosted by Mary Hart and was entitled "The Legend That Won't Die."

LEIF ERICKSON

Co-star of "Hill Number One," a 1951 television Easter special in which James Dean had a small part.

Leif Erickson, born William Anderson in 1911, also starred as Big John Cannon in the television western series "High Chaparral" (1967–1970) in addition to making numerous appearances on other programs. Erickson's film credits include *Sorry, Wrong Number* (1948), *On the Waterfront* (1954), *Tea and Sympathy* (1957), and *The Carpetbaggers* (1964).

WILLIAM ESCHRICH

Burbank, California, surgeon and racing enthusiast who acquired the undamaged engine of James Dean's Porsche after the 1955 crash. Eschrich reportedly paid $1,000 to George Barris for the engine. At the time Eschrich denied that his purchase had anything to do with its former owner: "I bought it for the engine and it was worth it."

Interestingly, Dr. Eschrich had previously competed against Jimmy in the May 1, 1955, race at Bakersfield. In that race he had been in a virtual tie for first place before a mishap occurred and he crashed into the hay. Then, in an October 1956 race at the Pomona Fairgrounds, Eschrich was involved in yet another accident. In this one his car was powered with the engine from Dean's Porsche, fueling a rash of reports of "the James Dean jinx."

ESQUIRE MAGAZINE

Esquire has published several articles about James Dean, including:

☆ "The Death of James Dean," October 1958, reprinted in October 1973
☆ "Rebel Without a Cause," October 1982

THE ESTATE

At the time of Dean's death the James Dean estate consisted of the following items:

☆ One pair of silver cuff links
☆ One traveling clock, inscribed "James Byron Dean," in a leather case
☆ One round, black-faced wristwatch with a gold dial and a missing strap
☆ One silver perfume flask
☆ One pair of square, ribbed gold cuff links
☆ One silver ID bracelet with a heavy silver chain
☆ Two gold cup racing trophies
☆ One silver cup racing trophy
☆ One Marlin 22-inch rifle
☆ One set of three bongo drums
☆ One red leather suitcase monogrammed LBR (probably Leonard Rosenman)
☆ A pair of bull's horns and a matador's cape

By 1957, with the eventual sale of his cars, motorcycle, and other personal items, along with collection of his $100,000 life insurance policy, the

James Dean estate was valued at $124,507.95. The administrators of the estate were Carl Coulter and William Gray. The beneficiary was Winton Dean.

THE EULOGY

On October 8, 1955, Reverend Xen Harvey delivered the eulogy at the James Dean funeral in Fairmount, Indiana. It was titled "The Life of James Dean: A Drama in Three Acts," and it concluded, rather melodramatically, with "The career of James Dean has not ended. It has just begun. And remember, *God himself is directing the production.*"

At a memorial service in 1980 to commemorate the 25th year of his passing, Jimmy's former high school teacher, Adeline Nall, presented her version of the same eulogy.

RAY EVANS

Co-writer of the Dean-inspired song "Let Me Be Loved," which was incorporated as the theme song of the 1957 Warner Brothers documentary *The James Dean Story.*

Along with his composer partner, Jay Livingston, lyricist Evans wrote many popular songs for the movies including "Que Sera Sera" from *The Man Who Knew Too Much*, for which he won a 1956 Best Song Oscar, "Buttons and Bows" from *The Paleface* (1948), and the title song from *Tammy* (1957). Ray Evans also co-wrote the theme from "Bonanza" and the Broadway production of *Oh Captain!*, which was nominated for a Tony as the Best Musical of 1958.

TED EVANS

Following his death James Dean's 1955 Triumph motorcycle was purchased by Ted Evans of Culver City, California, for the sum of $475.

"THE EVIL WITHIN"

It was not discovered until 1985 that Jimmy had appeared, over 30 years before, in an episode of the science fiction television series "Tales of Tomorrow." The episode was entitled "The Evil Within," and it starred Rod Steiger as a scientist whose wife (Margaret Phillips) accidentally consumes a dose of her husband's evil-inducing serum. Jimmy was featured in a brief part as Steiger's lab assistant. "The Evil Within" aired on ABC on May 1, 1953. It was produced by Mort Abrahams, directed by Don Medford, and written by Manya Starr.

As was typical of him, Dean drove his director to distress with his unconventional approach to acting. Still, Medford later acknowledged, "the fact he had no discipline was part of the charm of his work. If we'd gone too far with the discipline, we'd probably have ruined him."

ROBERT EWING

The makeup man on *East of Eden*.

THE EYES

His eyes were blue; his vision was nearsighted. He could see virtually nothing without his eyeglasses.

> "He wore these thick glasses and his uncle had to get him a new pair every week 'cause he would break them. I still see him with that string around his neck for the glasses."
>
> Adeline Nall

> "[Off screen] he had these pale, rather unexpectedly pale, eyes and a very small nose. And he wore glasses because he had very weak eyes. They didn't seem to have any power of penetration at all."
>
> Ivan Moffat

> What I remember most about him was the little boy quality shining forth at you from behind those thick glasses of his, tearing at your heart.
>
> Louella Parsons

Today it is not a line of prescription eyeglasses but rather a line of designer sunglasses that bears the James Dean name. It is marketed by Shady Character Unlimited of New York City. Another, Japanese, line is marketed by Japan Optical USA, based in Carson, California.

F

THE FACE

"His face is so desolate and lonely and strange. And there are
moments when you say 'Oh, God, he's so handsome. What's being
lost here! What goodness is being lost here!' "

Elia Kazan, *New York*, November 8, 1976

JERRY FAIRBANKS

Jerry Fairbanks was the producer of the 1950 Pepsi commercial in which
James Dean made his professional acting debut. A few months later, Fairbanks, as executive producer, hired Jimmy for "Hill Number One," an Easter
presentation of the religious television program "Family Theatre." Fairbanks's production office at the time was located at 6052 Sunset Boulevard.

FAIRMOUNT HIGH SCHOOL

"Whatever abilities I may have crystallized there in high school,
when I was trying to prove something to myself. That I could do *it*, I
suppose."

James Dean, *New York Times*, March 13, 1955

From September 1943 until May 1949 Jimmy Dean attended seventh through
12th grade at Fairmount High School. Academically he was not particularly
adroit. In fact, with the exception of art, speech, and drama, at which he
excelled, and Spanish, which he nearly flunked, he was basically a C student.
One of his 11th-grade report cards read, in part:

English . . . . .D
U.S. History C
Geometry . . . . .C+
Art . . . . .A
Safety Driving . . . . .C+

What he lacked in classroom brilliance, however, he compensated for
with extracurricular effort and enthusiasm. Hardly the loner or rebel that he
would later be tagged, Jimmy participated in band, baseball, basketball, and
track (excelling in the latter two). He was also a member of the 4-H Club and
was an eager participant in its various excursions. He also participated in
functions such as class trips, proms, etc. And, of course, he was a star
member of the school's speech, debate, and drama associations. He was
repeatedly cast in Fairmount High's theatrical productions, and he represented his school and state in the 1949 National Forensic League speech
competition. In fact the only mar on Jim Dean's high school record was his

The FHS graduating class of 1949.

participation during his senior year in a fistfight with another student. He was suspended for three days.

On May 16, 1949, James Dean graduated along with a class of 49 students.

In 1969 Fairmount High School was converted into a junior high school, then a middle school. It was permanently shut down in 1987 and as of this writing was in the process of being torn down. However, the demolition has been stalled by a community group of citizens and Dean fans who want to see the building restored and preserved. Several "Save the Old School" benefits have been staged to aid the campaign. Of particular concern to many is the

Quaker commencement: May 16, 1949.

Fairmount High School: still standing.

theater's stage, on which James Dean developed his craft. Today there is a plaque on the wall beside the stage that reads: "James Dean first exhibited his extraordinary talent publicly in this hall in the spring of 1946."

Fairmount High School is a 92-year-old red brick building. It is located, at least for now, at the corner of South Vine and Adams streets.

THE FAIRMOUNT HISTORICAL MUSEUM

Founded in 1975 by the residents of Fairmount, Indiana, to pay homage to its citizens, the Fairmount Historical Museum of course includes a tribute to the town's most famous son, James Dean. The James Dean Room is largely derived from the private collection of Jimmy's family. Included are such personal items as Jimmy's matador cape, athletic trophies, artworks, school yearbooks, and clothing, in addition to various commercialized artifacts and memorabilia. The Fairmount Historical Museum is located at 203 East Washington Street.

FAIRMOUNT, INDIANA

MY TOWN

My town likes industrial impotence
My town's small, loves its diffidence
My town thrives on dangerous bigotry
My town's big in the sense of idolatry
My town believes in God and his crew
My town hates the Catholic and Jew
My town's innocent, selfistic caper
My town's diligent, reads the newspaper
My town's sweet, I was born bare
My town is not what I am, I am here
by James Dean

(James Dean wrote his poem "My Town" in his copy of Edwin Honig's *Garcia Lorca. Here* in the last line refers to New York, where the poem was written.)

The church that
Jimmy Dean attended.

Carter Motors, one of
Jimmy's childhood
hangouts.

"After all the years of seeing Jimmy alone and without a family, it
was a wonderful thing to watch him touch again the gentle roots of
his early years. He was back in his element again, and he loved it."
     Bill Bast, on his 1952 trip to Fairmount with James Dean

James Dean loved the simplicity of his hometown of Fairmount. He
loved the animals, the trees, the open fields. He hated, however, the confines
of its collective closed minds. Like other small-town boys with big-city ideas,
Jimmy grew up bursting the seams of his britches with unbridled energy.
While other local boys were driven by their hormones, Jimmy Dean was
driven by ambition. He wasn't looking to get lucky behind the school
bleachers; he was looking to get *out*. It wasn't just the lack of opportunity in
Fairmount that Jimmy bemoaned; it was also the lack of expression. When
he went to Longmont, Colorado, in 1949, he confided to a friend, Jim
McCarthy, "Man, the minute I get out of school I'm heading west. California."

And so, in June 1949, the young man went west. It was not the first time that he had moved out of the Fairmount/Marion area. In 1936, along with his parents, Jimmy moved to Santa Monica, California. He returned to Fairmount four years later, after his mother's death.

In the six years between his high school graduation and his own death Jimmy made several return visits to Fairmount. They are recalled in the following glimpses:

☆ The summer of 1950. Of this visit Marcus Winslow related a telling story to British writer Terry Cunningham:

> "Jimmy told none of his friends he was back in town. He just worked from sun-up to sun-set with me. Never said much, drove his bike up to the cemetery and tended his mother's grave and took one trip into Marion to see a movie. He arrived back in Fairmount with less than thirty dollars and he would not accept any money from us."

☆ Late 1951. After visiting Chicago and before moving to New York, Jimmy stopped off in Fairmount for a brief visit.
☆ October 1952. Jimmy, accompanied by friends Bill Bast and Dizzy Sheridan, hitchhiked from New Jersey to Fairmount for an early Thanksgiving feast. Jimmy took his friends to his grandparents' house and to his old high school, where he lectured the drama class. He took his friends horseback riding and out shooting. He stayed a week before receiving a phone call informing him he had been cast in *See the Jaguar*. Jimmy and his friends hitchhiked back to New York.
☆ December 1953. Between rehearsals of *The Immoralist* Jimmy returned to Fairmount for Christmas.
☆ February 1955. After the completion of *East of Eden*, but before its release, Jimmy returned to Fairmount with photographer Dennis Stock to shoot a photo essay for *Life* magazine.

Fairmount is a town of tree-lined streets, bean and corn fields, and some 3,000 people with Quaker ideals. It's a quiet town that takes quiet pride in itself. Its people don't believe in calling attention to themselves. And yet they've been forced into an unflickering and, at times, unflattering spotlight by a world wanting a piece of James Dean.

The town seems to have ambivalent feelings about its most famous son. Locals cringe upon hearing stories of Jimmy's bicoastal escapades, his infamous crudeness, his bisexuality. They prefer to remember only the boy who played basketball and hid behind a thick pair of eyeglasses. Jimmy, they say, was just a normal boy, no better or worse than or different from Bud Cox, Rex Bright, or any of the other normal Fairmount boys. But some residents harbor an undeniable bitterness toward Jimmy's memory. As one local explained, "They figured Dean was a draft dodger. He didn't go in the army, you know. Star or no star, that didn't go over with some people around here." Said another, "I don't know why he is a legend. I don't really care. I'm tired of all the flimflam about him."

Adeline Nall, Fairmount's resident celebrity drama teacher, explained it to writer David Dalton in his book *James Dean: American Icon*:

The home Jimmy was raised in.

> "It's a catty little town. People still don't want to give Jim the credit due him. At the twenty-fifth reunion of his high school, Jim was the only deceased member of his class, and can you imagine they wouldn't let in a reporter who wanted to do a little piece on Jim's classmates? They said it was *their* reunion. There is still a lot of jealousy about Jim in town, but he's now accepted as an artist and their greatest native son."

Fairmount would probably prefer to claim Alan Ladd or Gary Cooper or John Wayne as one of its own. Still, to its credit, over the past 35 years Fairmount *has* welcomed the infiltration of the Dean faithful—perhaps not with open arms, but at least with an outstretched hand.

Today, Jimmy's biggest fans continue to make the pilgrimage to Fairmount, Indiana. The following is a list of some of the Fairmount locations related to James Dean.

James Dean's Fairmount: A Tour Guide

Back Creek Friends Church
Carter Motors
Fairmount Family Restaurant
Fairmount High School
Fairmount Historical Museum
Home: 322 East Washington Street
Home: 414 West First Street

Home: 1001 Wheeling Pike (Jonesboro)
Grandparents' Home: 802 East Washington Street
The James Dean Gallery
Park Cemetery
The Wesleyan Tabernacle
The Winslow farmstead (Jonesboro)

Outside of Fairmount
Birth site: 320 East Fourth Street, Marion
Home: 3750 South Adams Street, Marion
Marion Veterans Administration Hospital

> "Jimmy Dean loved the feel of Indiana soil under his feet and I think that was the source of much of his strength."
> Adeline Nall, *Los Angeles Times*, July 22, 1973

THE FAIRMOUNT MUSEUM DAYS FESTIVAL

For three days on the last weekend of every September the Fairmount Historical Museum sponsors the Fairmount Museum Days Festival. The event pays homage to such Fairmount native sons as Jim Davis, creator of the cartoon strip "Garfield"; Phil Jones, CBS correspondent; James Huston, World War II historian under President Harry Truman; and, of course, James Dean.

The festival typically consists of such activities as the James Dean Memorial 10-K Run, the James Dean Rock Lasso Contest, the James Dean Look-alike Contest, the James Dean Bicycle Tour, the James Dean Memorial Rod Run, the James Dean Memorial Service, and a screening of a James Dean movie. Obviously the event attracts people interested in James Dean, so it is not at all uncommon to see tourists from all over the world at the Festival. Approximately 20,000 people attend annually.

THE *FAIRMOUNT NEWS*

James Dean made the front page of a publication for the first time in the April 14, 1949, edition of the *Fairmount News*. Jimmy was lauded by the hometown press after winning first place in the Indiana State Speech Tournament. The headlines read: "F.H.S. Students Win State Meet" and "James Dean First Place Winner in Dramatic Speaking."

Later that year, when Jimmy moved to Los Angeles, the town of Fairmount threw a farewell party for him. The *Fairmount News* covered the event and reported in its June 15, 1949, edition:

> James Dean was honored at a farewell party Monday night. A farewell party was held Monday night in honor of James Dean who left Tuesday for Santa Monica, Calif., where he will enter the University of California at Los Angeles, planning to take a course in dramatics and fine arts.

A few months later the *News* issued this follow-up:

> "Mr. and Mrs. Charles Dean received a letter last week from their grandson, Jimmy Dean, who recently went to Santa Monica, Calif., to make his home with his father, Winton Dean. He stated in his letter that he was enjoying his vacation bowling and playing golf with his father . . ."

Less than six years later, on April 7, 1955, the *News* heralded its local boy who had made good:

> Even if Jimmy Dean weren't a hometown boy, *East of Eden* still would be one of the most powerful productions ever released by Warner Brothers and it would be worth the effort and money of everyone.
> Hometown folks will be going to see Dean. And, they won't be disappointed if they are looking to find a splendid performance and magnificent interpretation by Jimmy.
> Packed houses have seen *East of Eden* every place it has played and in our opinion this will be true from Fairmount to Timbuktu.

IN MEMORY OF JAMES DEAN

THE FAIRMOUNT NEWS

Volume LXXX · Fairmount, Grant County, Indiana · SPECIAL EDITION

James Dean Killed As Result Of California Car Accident

FAIRMOUNT IS STUNNED TO LEARN OF TRAGEDY WHICH CLAIMED NATIVE SON; HEADON COLLISION NEAR INTERSECTION CAUSES FATALITY FRIDAY

JAMES DEAN'S "EDEN" PROVES HIGH TALENT OF FAIRMOUNT ACTOR

... a Student at U.C.L.A.

James Dean

Last Rites Will Be Held Here Saturday

Dr. James A. DeWeerd, Rev. Xen Harvey To Conduct

Basketball Star

DEATH OF JAMES DEAN, FAIRMOUNT HIGH ALUMNI CASTS A PALL OF SADNESS OVER STUDENT BODY

$105,000 ESTATE LEFT BY ACTOR JIMMY DEAN

After Jimmy's death the *Fairmount News* issued a special edition, "In Memory of James Dean." The tribute read, in part:

James Dean, a native son who startled the nation with a brilliant flash of genius was brought back home this week for funeral rites. His brief career was as bright as a meteor which flows like a golden tear down the dark cheeks of night.

Later *News* articles about James Dean include:

☆ October 9, 1980   "For Fairmount's James Dean, 25th Memorial Services"
☆ March 19, 1986   "Dean Lasso Contest Held in England"
☆ February 4, 1987   "Dean Committee to Meet Sunday"
☆ February 11, 1987   "Madison-Grant Sells Old Fairmount High School with a Couple of
                         Strings"
☆ February 11, 1987   "100 See Film, Tour Museum Dean's Day"

FAIRMOUNT WEST WARD

After Jimmy returned to Fairmount following his mother's death in 1940, he
was enrolled in the fourth grade at Fairmount West Ward. The school, later
known as Fairmount Elementary, is no longer in existence.

After the death of his mother: Jimmy Dean (front row, third from right), with a
bandaged finger, at Fairmount West Ward elementary school.

"FAMILY THEATRE"

Aka "Father Peyton's TV Theatre" and "Father Peyton's Family Theatre,"
"Family Theatre" was a series of specials produced for television by Patrick
Peyton. Unknown actor James Dean appeared in an Easter presentation of
"Family Theatre" entitled "Hill Number One." The one-hour special ran on
Easter Sunday, March 25, 1951.

FAMOUS ARTISTS CORPORATION

In 1954, with the promise of stardom for her client, James Dean, New Yorker
Jane Deacy hired the Famous Artists Corporation to represent him on the

West Coast. Jimmy's agent at Famous Artists was Dick Clayton. The agency, then a Hollywood powerhouse, was located at 9441 Wilshire Boulevard in Beverly Hills.

FAMOUS LINES

"Make believe I'm carrying your books home from school, and you're hysterical with joy because my name is right and my money is right, and I belong to a good fraternity!"

as Hank Bradon, "Life Sentence"

"Talk to me, Father! I gotta know who I am. I gotta know what I'm like!"

as Cal Trask, *East of Eden*

"You're tearing me apart!"

as Jim Stark to his parents, *Rebel Without a Cause*

"If I had one day when I didn't have to be all confused and I didn't have to feel that I was ashamed of everything. If I felt that I belonged someplace, you know?"

Rebel Without a Cause

THE FAN CLUBS

After "Hill Number One" aired on television in 1951, the female students at Immaculate Heart High School in Los Angeles formed the first of what was to be many James Dean fan clubs. It was called the Immaculate Heart James Dean Appreciation Society. Some of the other early Dean clubs included the James Dean Memory Ring Around the World (President, Therese Brandes), the James Dean Fan Club (Bea Johnson), the James Dean Fan Club (Laura Dale), Dedicated Deans, Dean's Teens, the James Dean Memorial Club, Lest We Forget, the James Dean World Wide Club, and the James Dean Widows Club.

Listed below is contact information for the current major Dean fan club:

We Remember Dean International
PO Box 5025
Fullerton, California 92635
President: Sylvia Bongiovanni

THE FANS

I get letters to this day from eleven-year-old girls from Australia. You know, if Jimmy knew this he would laugh. He would chuckle. He never knew that he had *anything*. Half of them [the fans], if they met Jimmy, he would hate them. And maybe they would hate him too if they knew him personally.

Beulah Roth, Los Angeles, 1989

I plan on going to Fairmount in two days for my third visit. My seven-year-old son can tell you all about Jimmy's wreck, the date, the car, etc., and my three-year-old daughter can point out Jimmy in any store. My son keeps telling me if I get any more items I'll have my own museum!

Jeannine Tudor, Joliet, Illinois, 1989

Celebrity Fans

For whatever reason, James Dean has, over the years, attracted a large and diverse following of celebrity fans. The star-studded list includes the following:

Steve Allen	Teri Garr	Al Pacino
Brigitte Bardot	Jerry Glanville	Sean Penn
Boris Becker	Richard Grieco	Elvis Presley
David Bowie	Corey Haim	Alan Rachins
James Bridges	Jon-Erik Hexum	Rob Reiner
Nicolas Cage	Buddy Holly	John Ritter
Maxwell Caulfield	Paul le Mat	Axl Rose
Bruce Dern	Little Richard	Jean Seberg
Sammy Davis, Jr.	Madonna	Martin Sheen
Bob Dylan	John Cougar Mellencamp	Bruce Springsteen
The Everly Brothers	Eleanor Mondale	Francois Truffaut
Adam Faith	Stephen Morrissey	Henry Winkler

ROY FANT

Co-star of *See the Jaguar*, the 1952 stage play that featured James Dean. Fant portrayed Gramfa Ricks.

FAREWELL MY SLIGHTLY TARNISHED HERO

Fictionalized biography of James Dean by Edwin Corley. It was published by Dodd, Mead and Company in 1971.

FARM BUREAU INSURANCE COMPANY

Indiana insurance company that used the Dean name and image in one of its 1987 television commercials. The ad proclaimed, "Movie star James Dean . . . another Indiana legend."

FARMER'S MARKET

Over the years there has been something resembling a minor controversy over where James Dean had lunch on September 30, 1955. Some reports have indicated that Jimmy lunched with his father and uncle at the Hollywood Ranch Market in Hollywood. This makes logistical sense because it is known that Jimmy spent the morning at Competition Motors, which was located near the Hollywood Ranch Market (neither of which exists today).

However, it was *not* at the Hollywood Ranch Market where James Dean had his final lunch—it was at the Farmer's Market in West Hollywood. More specifically it was at Patsey's Pizza, which, in 1955, was located in the Farmer's Market. Patsey's Pizza was owned by Patsy D'Amore, who also owned the Villa Capri restaurant in Hollywood. Patsey's Pizza no longer exists, but the Farmer's Market remains a Los Angeles landmark (address: Fairfax Avenue and Third Street) and is a popular tourist site.

FARMING

While growing up in Fairmount, Indiana, Jimmy Dean's chores revolved around the maintenance of his uncle's farm. He was never particularly fond of farming, as he once related to Hedda Hopper:

> "I used to go out for the cows on the motorcycle. Scared the hell out of them. They'd get to running and their udders would start swinging, and they'd lose a quart of milk.
>
> "This was a real farm and I worked like crazy as long as someone was watching me. Forty acres of oats made a huge stage and when the audience left I took a nap and nothing got plowed or harrowed. Then I met a friend who lived over in Marion and he taught me how to wrestle, and kill cats, and [do] other things boys do behind barns . . . and I began to live."

FASHIONS

James Dean's unconventional fashion sense was getting him in trouble as early as 1949, at the National Forensic League speech championships in Longmont, Colorado. Instead of wearing the prerequisite suit and tie, Jimmy

A typical Dean outfit: dressed for a day at the office.

had his own ideas. As Jim McCarthy, his friend and fellow competitor, recalled in *Modern Screen*:

> "I kept trying to talk him into changing clothes. I'd brought my best suit. . . . So had everyone else, because we'd had it hammered into our heads that appearance counted for a lot. . . . Jim was wearing an open shirt and jeans when I met him, and that's the way he went into the tryouts every time. . . . [F]inally he admitted, 'Look, this bit I'm doing is a wild one and I've got to go crazy in it. How the heck can I go crazy in a shirt and tie?' "

Throughout his life Dean's personal wardrobe consisted primarily of blue jeans, T-shirts, work shirts, and turtlenecked sweaters. Toward the end of his life he also favored a leather jacket, motorcycle boots, and a cigarette dangling from the corner of his mouth.

On his last day Jimmy wore a typical outfit: white T-shirt, red jacket (which he wore on and off during the day), and dark sunglasses. Contrary to popular misconception, however, he was not wearing blue jeans. Instead he was wearing light blue trousers.

Today Dean collector David Loehr owns a couple of items from Jimmy's personal wardrobe: a 1942 basketball jersey and a brown motorcycle jacket with a fur collar. They are on display at the James Dean Gallery in Fairmount.

A western suede jacket with fringe owned by Jimmy is on display at the Fairmount Historical Museum.

FATHER
Natural father: Winton Dean
Foster father: Marcus Winslow

HUDSON FAUSSETT
Producer of "The Bells of Cockaigne," a 1953 episode of the NBC television program "Armstrong Circle Theatre" that co-starred James Dean.

FAVORITES OF DEAN
Favorite Actors
Marlon Brando   Gary Cooper   Gregory Peck
Montgomery Clift   John Garfield   Robert Walker

Favorite Actress
Jennifer Jones

Favorite Book
The Little Prince by Antoine de Saint-Exupery

Favorite Composers
Bela Bartok
Arnold Schonberg

Favorite Poet
James Whitcomb Riley

Favorite Quote
"What is essential is invisible to the eye." Antoine de Saint-Exupery, *The Little Prince*

Favorite Record Album
The Miraculous Mandarin by Bela Bartok

Favorite Singers
Frank Sinatra
Renata Tebaldi

Favorite Writers

Jean Genet	Gerald Heard	Oscar Wilde
Andre Gide	Curzio Malaparte	

Least Favorites

Flying	Haircuts	Pyotr Tchaikovsky
Formal parties	Victor Herbert	Waking up early

FEAR STRIKES OUT

Movie about a father who wants his son to become a professional baseball player. The son consequently suffers a nervous breakdown. At the time of his death Paramount was negotiating with Warner Brothers to borrow James Dean to star in *Fear Strikes Out*.

The film was eventually made in 1957 with Anthony Perkins in the role of the son. Karl Malden also starred. The film was directed by Robert Mulligan and produced by Alan J. Pakula.

FEBRUARY 8, 1931

James Dean's birth date.

Other Celebrities Born on February 8

Jules Verne (1828)	Ray Middleton (1907)	Jack Lemmon (1925)
Dame Edith Evans (1888)	Lana Turner (1920)	John Williams (1932)
King Vidor (1894)		

ABE FEDER

Lighting director, *The Immoralist* (1954).

RUBY FELKNER

One of the hairdressers on *Giant* (1956).

On the set of *Giant*, Edna Ferber holds court with a crown fashioned from a coconut.

EDNA FERBER

Author of the bestselling novel *Giant*, which was subsequently adapted into the 1956 movie of the same name. Because of her supreme confidence in the book, Edna Ferber balked tradition and opted *not* to sell the film rights to her story. Instead, Warner Brothers made her a one-third partner in the film (along with George Stevens and Henry Ginsberg), entitling her to receive a percentage of the film's profits, which proved to be considerable.

Despite its potentially enormous box-office success, Edna Ferber was not particularly pleased with the early development of the project, and she was quite vocal about her discontent. She was particularly incensed by the script and by the writers, Fred Guiol and Ivan Moffat, who adapted it. In a letter dated April 25, 1955, Ferber wrote to director George Stevens that the dialogue as scripted was wooden, inept, and uncharacteristic. Forever the writer, she also winced that some of it was ungrammatical.

Nevertheless, just prior to shooting, her aspirations for the film ran high. On May 17, 1955, she wired a telegram to "Henry and George and All

You Boys and Girls gathered today at Warner Studio." In her cable Ferber expressed that her interest in the motion picture presentation of *Giant* far exceeded that of the screen adaptations of her previous works. The reason for this, she suggested, was that the plot of *Giant* was imbued with purpose and meaning. She concluded her note by wishing the company the best of luck, with the postscript that luck was just slang for hard work.

Ferber's high hopes for the film ran to such an extent that, for the first time in her career, she visited the set to watch one of her stories unfold before the cameras. Upon seeing footage that had been shot, however, those hopes quickly dissipated. In a letter to Henry Ginsberg, Ferber wrote of her disapproval, particularly of the early Virginia (Maryland) sequences. She complained that Elizabeth Taylor's Leslie was "simpering," that the character of Dr. Lynnton had become dull, and that the Lynnton dining room looked like an apartment-house dinette and did not at all resemble the elegance that she had envisioned and expected.

Months later, as the film was prepared for release, Ferber became enraged after reading a Sidney Skolsky column that was headed, "Edna Ferber After Seeing *Giant* Told George Stevens: 'Thanks, That's the Story I Wanted to Write.'" She was so incensed by the fabricated story and suggested slur that she threatened legal action if a retraction wasn't published. Further, Ferber again wrote to Ginsberg, warning him that she would retaliate against the picture if the publicity at her expense continued.

Two months later *Giant* was released across the country and proved to be a mammoth critical and box-office success, pleasing nearly everyone, with the possible exception of its originator, Edna Ferber. Nevertheless, her qualms about the film (which, upon reviewing the film today, were valid) were kept quiet as they would have worked against the picture's success.

Just prior to his death James Dean was working on a sculpture of Edna Ferber, derived from photographs of her that he had taken on the set of *Giant*. The two artists had gotten along well during their brief visits together, and just a few days before his death Jimmy reportedly received a letter from Ferber that read, in part:

> Your profile is startlingly like John Barrymore's, but then I know your motorcycle racing or one thing or another will fix that.

Years later she wrote in her autobiography, *A Kind of Magic*:

> [James Dean] was spectacularly talented, handsome in a fragile sort of way and absolutely outrageous. He was an original. Impish, compelling, magnetic, utterly winning one moment, obnoxious the next. Definitely gifted. Frequently maddening.

Other motion pictures based on works by Ferber include *Show Boat* (1929, 1936, and 1951), *Cimarron* (1931 and 1960), *Dinner at Eight* (1933), *Come and Get It* (1936), *Stage Door* (1937), and *Saratoga Trunk* (1945).

Edna Ferber died in 1968 at the age of 81.

BETTY FIELD
One of Elia Kazan's initial choices to play the role of James Dean's mother in *East of Eden.* The role eventually went to and won an Oscar for Jo Van Fleet.

HENRY FIELD
One of the wardrobe men on *Rebel Without a Cause.*

THE FILM DAILY
Hollywood trade publication that, in 1955, cited James Dean as having given one of the "Best Performances by Male Stars" for his work in *East of Eden. The Film Daily* also named *Eden* one of the best pictures of the year and James Dean as one of the "Finds of the Year." The following year *The Film Daily* named *Giant* one of the best pictures of the year and James Dean as having given one of the "Best Performances by *Supporting* Actors."

The Film Daily **Awards, 1955**
    Best Picture

1. *Mister Roberts*
2. *Marty*
3. *East of Eden*
4. *The Blackboard Jungle*
5. *Bad Day at Black Rock*
6. *A Man Called Peter*
7. *Trial*
8. *Love Me or Leave Me*
9. *Summertime*
10. *Love Is a Many Splendored Thing*

   Best Male Performances
Ernest Borgnine, *Marty*
James Cagney, *Love Me or Leave Me*
James Dean, *East of Eden*
Henry Fonda, *Mister Roberts*
Spencer Tracy, *Bad Day at Black Rock*

   Finds of the Year
James Dean, *East of Eden*
Ernest Borgnine, *Marty*
Fess Parker, *Davy Crockett, King of the Wild Frontier*
Julie Harris, *I Am a Camera*
Dana Wynter, *The View from Pompey's Head*

The Film Daily **Awards, 1956**
   Best Picture

1. *The King and I*
2. *Giant*
3. *War and Peace*
4. *Friendly Persuasion*
5. *Anastasia*
6. *Moby Dick*
7. *Picnic* [actually released in 1955]
8. *The Ten Commandments*
9. *Tea and Sympathy*
10. *The Rose Tattoo* [actually released in 1955]

   Best Performances by Supporting Actors
Anthony Perkins, *Friendly Persuasion*
Oscar Homolka, *War and Peace*
James Dean, *Giant*
Arthur O'Connell, *Picnic*
Rod Steiger, *The Court-Martial of Billy Mitchell*

FILM THREAT: SEPTEMBER 30, 1955, NEVER HAPPENED
Cover-to-cover one-shot magazine about James Dean by Christian Gore. Published in 1988.

THE FILMS
See THE MOVIES.

FILMS AND FILMING MAGAZINE
Film industry magazine that has published several articles about James Dean, including:

☆ January 1957   "The Dean Myth"
☆ October 1965   "Dean, Ten Years After"
☆ September 1985   "James Dean: The Rebel Saint 30 Years On"

FILMS IN REVIEW MAGAZINE
Film industry magazine that named *East of Eden* one of the best pictures of 1955.

THE FILMS OF JAMES DEAN
Author: Mark Whitman
Publisher: BCW Publishing, Limited, Great Britain; Greenhaven Press, U.S.
Year: 1974 (Great Britain) and 1978 (U.S.)

Mediocre book containing recycled and occasionally inaccurate material. Further, given that Dean only starred in three pictures, a book devoted to "the films of" seems superfluous, and author Mark Whitman offers nothing to dispel that notion.

FIRSTS: THE 10 JAMES DEAN FIRSTS
First school: Brentwood Elementary School (1936)
First car: 1939 Chevy (1949)
First love: Santa Monica City College coed, known only as "Diane" (1949)
First professional acting job: Pepsi commercial (1950)
First agent: Isabelle Draesemer (1951)
First television drama: "Hill Number One" (1951)
First fan club: The Immaculate Heart James Dean Appreciation Society (1951)
First movie in which he had a line that was not cut: *Has Anybody Seen My Gal?* (1952)
First Broadway play: *See the Jaguar* (1952)
First line in *East of Eden*: "You want me?"

DAN FISHER
Co-producer of the 1982 stage play *Come Back to the Five and Dime, Jimmy Dean, Jimmy Dean.*

FIXED BAYONETS
Nineteen fifty-one 20th Century–Fox movie about the Korean War that starred Richard Basehart, Gene Evans, Michael O'Shea, Richard Hylton, and

Craig Hill. It was written and directed by Samuel Fuller.

Fixed Bayonets featured unknown actor James Dean in a bit part. Jimmy had a single line—"It's a rear guard coming back"—that was eventually cut out of the picture.

LARRY FLETCHER

Larry Fletcher was an actor who appeared in "Keep Our Honor Bright," a 1953 episode of the NBC television program "Kraft Television Theatre" that co-starred James Dean.

"THE FOGGY, FOGGY DEW"

Until now, a forgotten episode of the CBS television program "Lux Video Theatre" that co-starred James Dean in one of his earliest roles. "The Foggy, Foggy Dew" was produced by Cal Kuhl, directed by Richard Goode, and written by J. Albert Hirsch. The cast also included James Barton, Muriel Kirkland, and Richard Bishop. It aired on March 17, 1952.

GEORGE FOLEY, JR.

Executive producer of "The Evil Within," a 1953 episode of the ABC television program "Tales of Tomorrow" that co-starred James Dean.

JOSEPH FOLEY

Actor who had a small part in "Harvest," a 1953 episode of the NBC television series "Robert Montgomery Presents the Johnson's Wax Program" that co-starred James Dean.

Joseph Foley was also a regular on the television programs "The Aldrich Family" (1950–1953) and "Mr. Peepers" (1952–1953). He also appeared in the film *The Whistle at Eaton Falls* (1951). Foley died in 1955 at the age of 45.

LOUIS FONTANA

Jimmy's barber in New York City, circa 1952–1953.

FOOD

> "We ate Shredded Wheat. We bought a lot of sugar and a lot of milk and we ate Shredded Wheat, sugar and milk for dinner at my place lots of times. I had this little card table that we would set up with candlelight and make a big thing about our dinner of Shredded Wheat, sugar and milk."
>
> Dizzy Sheridan, *Photoplay*, October 1957

He didn't eat regularly, but when he did eat, it was something to see. In Texas, one disgustingly hot night during the filming of *Giant*, he and I ate a full jar of peanut butter, a box of crackers, and six Milky Ways, and drank twelve Coca-Colas!

Mercedes McCambridge, *The Quality of Mercy*

He would eat at our house all the time. I'd do the cooking. And very often he'd call me late at night and say, "How about a pizza?" I used to make little pizzas on English muffins with Jewish salami on top. *He loved them.* And he said, "I'll bring everything if you'll make them." So, at midnight, he'd come by with English muffins and mozzarella.

Beulah Roth

☆ What he ate at home when broke: in addition to the shredded wheat feast, Jimmy would combine dry oatmeal, mayonnaise, and jam.

☆ What he ordered in restaurants when broke: a bowl of chili.

☆ What he ordered in restaurants when he had money: steak.

☆ What he did with his food: Jimmy was notorious for playing with his food to entertain and/or repulse his companions. For Mercedes McCambridge he stuffed a pair of pecan rolls up his nostrils.

☆ His favorite food: spaghetti.

☆ His favorite confection: hot chocolate.

FOOTE, CONE AND BELDING

Advertising agency that directors (and Dean friends) Rogers Brackett and James Sheldon worked for. In the early 1950s Foote, Cone and Belding handled several radio programs, including "Alias Jane Doe," "Hallmark Playhouse," and "Stars over Hollywood"—all shows in which struggling actor James Dean landed parts.

In 1951–1952 Foote, Cone and Belding was located at 6233 Hollywood Boulevard in Hollywood and at 247 Park Avenue in New York City.

JOHN FORBES

Co-producer of "James Dean," a 1976 made-for-television movie.

CONSTANCE FORD

Constance Ford co-starred with James Dean twice. She portrayed Janna in the 1952 Broadway play *See the Jaguar* and Ronald Reagan's beleaguered wife in "The Dark, Dark Hour," a 1954 episode of the CBS television program "General Electric Theater."

Ford, born in 1929, has made numerous other television appearances. Her films include *The Last Hunt* (1956), *The Goddess* (1958), and *A Summer Place* (1959).

"FOREVER JAMES DEAN"

Average documentary film aired on cable television by Cinemax in 1988. "Forever James Dean" was written, directed, and produced by Ara Chekmayan. Others involved in the production include Jeff Lawenda and Michael Yudin, executive producers; Bob Gunton, narrator; David Loehr, archivist/researcher; Susan Bluttman, researcher; David Dalton, consultant. Those interviewed include Corey Allen, George Barris, Bill Bast, Rex Bright, Jack Grinnage, Julie Harris, Kenneth Kendall, Beverly Long, Frank Mazzola, Adeline Nall, Bob Pulley, Bob Roth, Steffi Sidney, and Frank Worth.

"FORGOTTEN CHILDREN"

A presentation of the "Hallmark Hall of Fame," this television drama starred Cloris Leachman, Don McHenry, Nancy Malone, and James Dean, the latter as a southern aristocrat. The program aired on NBC on June 2, 1952.

EILEEN FORHAM

Eileen Forham was a 1950s starlet who, in an article for *Motion Picture* fan magazine, claimed to have had an affair with James Dean. *Who didn't?*

THE FORREST THEATRE

Legitimate stage theater in Philadelphia (address: 1114 Walnut Street) where James Dean appeared during an out-of-town tryout of *The Immoralist* in early 1954. The Forrest Theatre has been in existence since the 1920s.

JOHN FORSYTHE

In 1952 John Forsythe starred in "Ten Thousand Horses Singing," an episode of the CBS television program "Studio One" in which James Dean had a bit part.

Forsythe, born John Freund in 1918, is best known as Blake Carrington on the television series "Dynasty" (1981–1988). His other credits include, on televison: "Bachelor Father" (1957–1962), "The John Forsythe Show" (1965–1966), "To Rome with Love" (1969–1971), and the voice of Charlie on "Charlie's Angels" (1976–1980); and in movies: *The Trouble with Harry* (1956), *In Cold Blood* (1967), and *And Justice for All* (1979).

ROBERT FOULK

Cast member, *Rebel Without a Cause*. Robert Foulk also appeared in the television programs "Father Knows Best" (1955–1959) and "Wichita Town" (1959–1960) and in feature films including *The Left-Handed Gun* (1958), *Tammy and the Doctor* (1963), and *Bunny O'Hare* (1971).

THE 4-H CLUB

While a student at Fairmount High School Jimmy Dean was an active member of that rebel-rousing hiker gang, the 4-H Club. His activities included raising chicks and growing a garden. He also raised a guernsey bull, which he entered in the county fair. Dean and his bull won the grand prize.

THE FOUR TUNES

Singing group that recorded the song "Ballad of James Dean" for Jubilee Records.

DAVID FOX

In 1949 David Fox was a junior at Fairmount High School while Jimmy Dean was a senior. On one occasion the two boys engaged in a fistfight, which resulted in Jimmy's suspension from school. It seems that Fox, by way of taunts and jeers, lambasted one of Jimmy's dramatic presentations for the class. Later, upon graduation, Jimmy bequeathed "my short temper to David Fox" in the high school yearbook.

FRANCE
Ever since his death James Dean has been an enormous star in France. *Variety* reported from Paris in July 1956:

IN DEATH, JAMES DEAN A HERO TO THE FRENCH
Name of the late James Dean is gaining marquee momentum in France on the strength of only two releases, *East of Eden* and *Rebel Without a Cause*. Apart from Marilyn Monroe, he has become the best-known U.S. star name in France since the war.

Newspapers here recently took up a story from a U.S. mag to the effect that Dean hadn't actually been killed in his auto accident, but marred, badly, was suffering from shock and was being kept out of public life by his family. Weird tale keeps getting printed and bruited about. Actually, the Dean name keeps getting more space in the press than most of his living colleagues. As he became a symbol of disoriented youth in the U.S. (at least in his screen roles), so he has become here an idol of the teenagers who still put him at the head of popularity polls.

ANTHONY FRANCIOSA
When James Dean dropped out of the cast of *End as a Man* before it made its off-Broadway debut in September 1953, he was replaced by Anthony Franciosa. At the time Franciosa had been working as a short-order cook. Franciosa later appeared on stage in *A Hatful of Rain*, for which he received a 1956 Tony nomination as Best Supporting Actor.

Born Anthony Papaleo in 1928, Franciosa appeared in films including *A Face in the Crowd* (1957), *A Hatful of Rain* (1957), and *Death Wish II* (1982). He has also starred in several television programs including "The Name of the Game" (1968–1971), "Search" (1972–1973), and "Finders of Lost Loves" (1984–1985).

ROBERT CHARLES FRANCIS
Robert Charles Francis was a 25-year-old actor who was killed in an airplane crash on July 31, 1955. Shortly before his death Francis appeared in the movies *The Caine Mutiny* and *The Long Gray Line*, and he looked to have a promising career in front of him. After his death the superstitious Hollywood press began to speculate as to who might be next. After all, it was written, "these things come in threes."

CARL FRANK
Actor who appeared in the September 11, 1953, episode of the NBC television program "The Big Story" that starred James Dean. Frank also appeared as a regular on the hit show "Mama" (1949–1956).

JOHN FRANKENHEIMER

John Frankenheimer directed James Dean in "Padlocks," a 1954 episode of the CBS television program "Danger."

By the time he turned 30, Frankenheimer, then the boy wonder of live television, had directed such programs as "Days of Wine and Roses" on "Playhouse 90," "Danger," "Mama," "You Are There," and "Studio One" and had earned five Emmy nominations. He went on to direct such motion pictures as *The Young Stranger* (1957), *The Manchurian Candidate* (1962), *Birdman of Alcatraz* (1962), *Seven Days in May* (1964), *The French Connection II* (1975), *52 Pick-Up* (1986), and *Dead Bang* (1989).

SIDNEY FRANKLIN

Sidney Franklin, well-known Brooklyn-born matador (1903–1976) and friend of Ernest Hemingway, presented James Dean with what became one of his most prized possessions: a matador's cape.

TOM FREDERICK

In the afternoon of September 30, 1955, Tom Frederick, a 28-year-old book-keeper from Shandon, California, was on Highway 466 en route to Bakersfield. Traveling about 55 miles per hour, Frederick was suddenly passed by a black and white Ford. Frederick saw the Ford slow down as it approached the intersection of Highway 41. Then, moments later, came the crash. Frederick parked his car and rushed to the site of the Porsche. He then directed another motorist to fetch an ambulance. At the subsequent hearing Frederick was called in to testify:

> DISTRICT ATTORNEY: Did you see the collision?
> FREDERICK: Yes sir, I did.
> DISTRICT ATTORNEY: Where were you when the collision occurred?
> FREDERICK: Well, I was approximately 50 yards behind the Ford.
> DISTRICT ATTORNEY: Did you see the Ford make a turn, or start to make a turn?
> FREDERICK: I did.
> DISTRICT ATTORNEY: Could you give us any estimate at all of the car's [the Ford's] speed at the time of the accident?
> FREDERICK: At the time we caught up to him, he must have not been going more than 40 miles an hour, or 45.
> DISTRICT ATTORNEY: What kind of car was it?
> FREDERICK: It was a Porsche; that's all I know.
> DISTRICT ATTORNEY: You say you saw it just before the accident. Did you see it just before or after the Ford began to make its turn?
> FREDERICK: After.
> DISTRICT ATTORNEY: You saw the Ford begin to make its turn. What did the Ford do then?

FREDERICK: Well, he started to make his turn and he acted like he saw the Porsche, and started to cut back to the right. He was coming in here, and he began making a turn back—he started to make a turn onto 41 and started to straighten up like he was going to try to dodge the Porsche or something.

Tom Frederick then caused havoc at the hearing by contending that *it had not been Jimmy (in a white T-shirt) behind the wheel of the Porsche, but rather his mechanic, Rolf Wütherich (in a red T-shirt).*

DISTRICT ATTORNEY: From seeing the two men after the accident, looking back, could you place the men in the car, on which side of the car they were?
FREDERICK: I could place one of them.
DISTRICT ATTORNEY: Which one of them?
FREDERICK: The one in the red T-shirt.
DISTRICT ATTORNEY: Which was he?
FREDERICK: He would be on the left side [the driver's side] of the Porsche. . . . The car was still in motion after the accident, and I could see the man in the red T-shirt on the left side of the car. That is after they hit.
DISTRICT ATTORNEY: The man in the T-shirt was in the driver's seat?
FREDERICK: They were both in T-shirts.
DISTRICT ATTORNEY: Did they both have on red T-shirts?
FREDERICK: No, Dean had a white one on—or the man that was still in the Porsche.
DISTRICT ATTORNEY: How do you remember that—what makes you remember the one with the red T-shirt being on the left?
FREDERICK: I seen him with his hands up in the air and seen he had a red T-shirt on.
DISTRICT ATTORNEY: When was that?
FREDERICK: Right after they had the accident.

Despite Tom Frederick's revelation that Rolf Wütherich might have been driving the Porsche, and not James Dean, nothing of consequence was made of his testimony and he was excused from the witness stand.

LEWIS FREEDMAN

Producer of "The Movie Star," a 1962 episode of the NBC television program "The DuPont Show of the Week" that was inspired by the death of James Dean.

Lewis Freedman won an Emmy award for producing "The Andersonville Trial," which was named the Most Outstanding Single Program of the 1970–1971 television season. He won another Emmy for "Benjamin Franklin," the Most Outstanding Limited Series of 1974–1975.

GLENN FREY
Singer/songwriter and former member of the Eagles recording group, Glenn Frey co-wrote the song "James Dean."

FRIENDS
If he was caught on a good day, at the right moment, it was relatively easy to initiate a friendship with James Dean. What was difficult, however, was to *maintain* that friendship. Jimmy's friendships typically did not run a very steady or lengthy course. He was extremely moody, at constant odds with himself—or someone or something—and prone to irrational behavior. He had a habit of arriving unannounced at the home of friends at 3:00 A.M. or waking them up in the middle of the night with the sound of an anxious and persistent ringing telephone. He was constantly pushing, constantly testing the tolerance of his friends, measuring their degree of affection for him.

And yet at other times he was virtually exploding with life, bouncing off walls, craving information and ideas with wild-eyed enthusiasm and idealism. For some he was exhilarating and intoxicating and infinitely unpredictable. For others he was lost and lonely and needed to be mothered or brothered and wrapped in a warm blanket and tucked into bed with a full stomach and a clear head. For still others he was something of a renegade genius. If they got close enough to him, perhaps some of that genius would rub off by association.

The consummate actor, James Dean was always changing, adapting himself to the situation or the person at hand. As a result he was many different things to many different people. He may have accumulated a long list of "friends" for such a short life, but very few among them got to see more of James Dean than James Dean wanted them to see, which wasn't much.

The following is a selective, alphabetized list of Jimmy's friends. Naturally these friendships varied greatly in intensity and duration.

Nick Adams	Bill Hickman	Whitey Rust
Kira Appel	Dennis Hopper	Howard Sackler
Bill Bast	Eartha Kitt	Roy Schatt
Johnny Bates	Glenn Kramer	James Sheldon
Lew Bracker	Martin Landau	Dizzy Sheridan
Rogers Brackett	Oscar Levant	Jack Simmons
Rex Bright	Maggie McNamara	Stewart Stern
Lonny Chapman	Stanley Meyer	Dennis Stock
Dick Clayton	Maila Nurmi	David Swift
Frank Corsaro	Geraldine Page	Elizabeth Taylor
Jane Deacy	Bob Pulley	Bill Tunstahl
James DeWeerd	Nick Ray	Christine White
Roger Donahue	Leonard Rosenman	Alec Wilder
Barbara Glenn	Bob Roth	Kent Williams
Bill Gunn	Sanford and Beulah Roth	Natalie Wood
Bob Heller	Steve Rowland	

WOLFGANG FUCHS
Author of the book *James Dean: Footsteps of a Giant*, published in West Germany by Taco in 1986.

SAMUEL FULLER
Director of *Fixed Bayonets* (1951) in which James Dean had a bit part.

Fuller, born in 1912, also directed *I Shot Jesse James* (1949), *The Naked Kiss* (1966), and *The Big Red One* (1980), among many others.

FUNERAL
Just as his mother's body was freighted back to Fairmount, Indiana, from California in 1940, so was James Dean's 15 years later. The funeral took place at the Back Creek Friends Church at 2:00 P.M. on Saturday, October 8, 1955. Services were co-conducted by Reverends James DeWeerd and Xen Harvey. The musical accompaniment was played on the organ and featured the song "Goin' Home." Approximately 3,000 people attended, a few hundred more than the total population of Fairmount. Among the mourners were, of course, his aunt and uncle, Ortense and Marcus Winslow, and Hollywood friends like Lew Bracker, Jack Simmons, and Dennis Stock. Henry Ginsberg, the producer of *Giant*, also attended. Elizabeth Taylor sent flowers.

Following the services, Jimmy's body was buried in the Winslow family plot in Fairmount's Park Cemetery.

Pallbearers at the James Dean Funeral

Rex Bright	Bob Middletown	Whitey Rust
James Fulkerson	Bob Pulley	Paul Smith

G

MARTIN GABEL

Actor who had been an acquaintance of Jimmy's in New York and later narrated the Warner Brothers documentary *The James Dean Story* (1957).

Martin Gabel (1912–1986) did most of his work on stage and won a 1961 Tony award as Best Supporting Actor for *Big Fish, Little Fish*. He also appeared in films including *Marnie* (1964), *Divorce American Style* (1967), and *The Front Page* (1975) and hosted the television game show "With This Ring" (1951).

JACK GARFEIN

"I loved Jimmy and we were very close to each other, but if I was in a restaurant with him and Hedda Hopper walked in, he would get up and walk over and say 'Hello' . . . and he would stay there with her for forty-five minutes and you're sitting at the table."

Jack Garfein, *Paul and Joanne* by Joe Morella and Edward Epstein

Jack Garfein directed James Dean in a 1953 Actors Studio production of *End as a Man*. Later, without Dean in the cast, Garfein directed *End as a Man* off Broadway and, after that triumph, *on* Broadway. The success of the play garnered Garfein official membership in the Actors Studio, where he became a close confidante of Lee Strasberg. It also took him to Hollywood, where he directed the film version of the play, which was released as *The Strange One* (1957).

Garfein, born Jacob Garfein in Czechoslovakia in 1930, was a World War II survivor of 11 concentration camps. He was liberated at Auschwitz on April 16, 1945. In 1955 Garfein, a sometime actor/writer as well as director, married actress Carroll Baker. He later had a falling out with Strasberg, divorced Baker, taught acting, and helmed the Actors' and Directors' Lab in New York.

JOHN GARFIELD

If James Dean borrowed attitude and style from Marlon Brando and Montgomery Clift, then they all owed a debt to John Garfield, the first of the film rebels.

Garfield, born Julius Garfinkle in 1913, appeared in the films *Four Daughters* (Best Supporting Actor Oscar nomination, 1938), *Juarez* (1939), *The Sea Wolf* (1941), *The Postman Always Rings Twice* (1946), *Humoresque* (1946), *Body and Soul* (Best Actor Oscar nomination, 1947), *Gentleman's*

Agreement (1947), *Force of Evil* (1948), *He Ran All the Way* (1951), and others. Garfield died of a heart attack in New York in May 1952.

TERI GARR

Actress Teri Garr, born in 1949, is an alumnus of "The Sonny and Cher Comedy Hour" (1973–1974) and the co-star of such films as *Oh, God!* (1977), *Close Encounters of the Third Kind* (1977), *One from the Heart* (1982), *Tootsie* (1982), and *Mr. Mom* (1983). She is a devout James Dean fan:

> "Ever since I can remember, I've been a James Dean freak. He lived in my aunt and uncle's house in Sherman Oaks just before he died. I used to go over and mow the lawn, hoping to catch a glimpse of him."

BEN GAZZARA

Ben Gazzara appeared in a 1953 Actors Studio production of *End as a Man* in which James Dean had a small part. At the time Gazzara was working as an elevator operator for the *New York Times*. The subsequent off-Broadway and Broadway productions of *End as a Man* made a star out of Gazzara.

End as a Man also made foes of Ben Gazzara and James Dean. When Gazzara left the production, asking for more money, Jimmy approached the play's producers and volunteered to take over the part. Further, when the play was being adapted into a film, Jimmy campaigned, albeit unsuccessfully, for the part. Gazzara, understandably, was not particularly pleased. Later, after Jimmy's death, Gazzara was one of the actors MGM honcho Dore Schary considered to replace Jimmy in *Somebody Up There Likes Me*.

Prior to *End as a Man* Gazzara appeared with James Dean in "The Case of the Sawed-Off Shotgun," a 1953 episode of the NBC television program "Treasury Men in Action."

Ben Gazzara, born in 1930, has appeared in the films *The Strange One* (movie adaptation of *End as a Man*, 1957), *Anatomy of a Murder* (1959), *Husbands* (1970), *They All Laughed* (1981), and *Inchon* (1981). He also appeared in the television programs "Arrest and Trial" (1963–1964) and "Run for Your Life" (1965–1968) and in numerous made-for-television movies including "QB VII" (1974) and "The Trial of Lee Harvey Oswald" (1977). In addition to *End as a Man*, Gazzara's stage credits include *Cat on a Hot Tin Roof* (as Brick, 1955), *A Hatful of Rain* (Best Actor Tony nomination, 1956), and a 1977 revival of *Who's Afraid of Virginia Woolf?* for which he was nominated for another Best Actor Tony.

RICHARD GEARIN

Richard Gearin (1927–1987) was a Fairmount maintenance man who was unofficially adopted by the Winslow family. According to some unsubstantiated reports, Gearin, for a short period, lived with Jimmy in New York City.

"GENERAL ELECTRIC THEATER"

"General Electric Theater" was a half-hour drama series that aired Sunday nights on CBS from February 1953 to September 1962. The program was broadcast from Hollywood and was hosted by and occasionally starred Ronald Reagan.

James Dean appeared in two episodes of "General Electric Theater." "I'm a Fool" aired on November 14, 1954, and "The Dark, Dark Hour" aired on December 12, 1954.

GEORGE W. GEORGE

Co-producer, co-director, and co-editor of the 1957 Warner Brothers documentary *The James Dean Story*.

George also produced *Dylan* (1964) and *Bedroom Farce* (1979) on Broadway, both of which earned him Tony nominations.

GARY GERHART

Author of *James Dean: Remembrance*, an unpublished biography copyrighted in 1987.

J. PAUL GETTY

The old mansion used as a location for *Rebel Without a Cause* was rented by Warner Brothers from its owner, oil billionaire J. Paul Getty.

STATHIS GIALLELIS

Nineteen sixty-three discovery of Elia Kazan whom Hedda Hopper, among others, touted as "the next James Dean." Giallelis, born in 1939, has appeared in films including *America, America* (1963), *Cast a Giant Shadow* (1966), and *The Eavesdropper* (1967).

GIANT

Bestselling novel by Edna Ferber, published in 1952 by Doubleday. By 1956 *Giant* had sold some 25 million copies.

GIANT ★★½
1956   198 minutes   WarnerColor
Warner Brothers
Directed by: George Stevens
Produced by: Henry Ginsberg, George Stevens
Screenplay by Fred Guiol, Ivan Moffat, adapted from the novel by Edna Ferber
Photographed by: William C. Mellor
Edited by: William Hornbeck, Fred Bohanan, Phil Anderson
Music by: Dimitri Tiomkin
Cast: Elizabeth Taylor, Rock Hudson, James Dean, Mercedes McCambridge, Chill
    Wills, Jane Withers, Robert Nichols, Dennis Hopper, Elsa Cardenas, Fran Bennett,

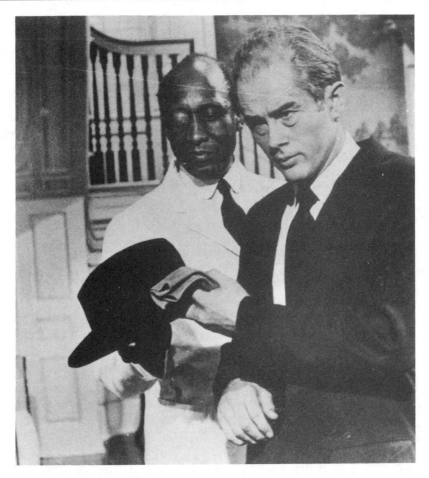

Makeup mishap?

Carroll Baker, Earl Holliman, Paul Fix, Judith Evelyn, Carolyn Craig, Rodney Taylor, Alexander Scourby, Sal Mineo, Monte Hale, Mary Ann Edwards, Napoleon Whiting, Charles Watts, Maurice Jara, Victor Millan, Pilar Del Ray, Felipe Turich, Sheb Wooley, Francisco Villalobos, Ray Whitley, Tina Menaro, Anna Maria Majalca, Mickey Simpson, Noreen Nash, Guy Teague, Natividad Vacio, Max Terhune, Ray Bennett, Barbara Barie, George Dunne, Slim Talbot, Tex Driscoll, Juney Ellis

"I can still remember the breathless excitement with which Jimmy came running into my office after he'd finished the screenplay of *Giant*. 'You know something, Mr. Stevens,' Jimmy told me, 'the part of Jett Rink, that's for me!'

George Stevens

Despite the relatively small size of the part, it's easy to understand James

Giant preproduction: explosive potential.

Dean's attraction to the role of Jett Rink, based, at least in part (though denied at the time by Warner Brothers), on the real-life exploits of rags-to-riches Texan Glenn McCarthy. Edna Ferber described Jett Rink as:

> . . . a muscular young fellow with a curiously powerful
> bullneck and shoulders. His big, sweat-stained hat was pushed
> back from his forehead and you saw his damp, dark curls. . . .
> Jett's all right when he behaves himself. When he drinks he
> goes kind of crazy. He's a kind of genius, Jett is. He's got a
> grudge against the world. He'll probably end up a billionaire—
> or in the electric chair. Put him in a car and he goes crazy.

Warner Brothers preproduction material described Jett as "a poor boy who makes a hundred million dollars. Tough, always angry, restless, bewildered and reckless, with animal charm and a tycoon's magnetism. He gets his way and loses his way with equal violence. Clever with his hands." Jett was also depicted as "a dangerous man possessing nothing but his anger and the knowledge that he was the world's equal

Method actor cowboy.

in everything but opportunity. Perhaps the term 'man' is wrong in describing Jett. The angry boy persisted throughout."

Giant went into preproduction in 1953, *three years* before its eventual release. While James Dean was in New York beginning to make a name for himself in live television, the powers at Warners gathered in Burbank to discuss the casting of *Giant*. The subsequent casting sheet, dated October 12, 1953, listed the following actors as the leading contenders for the role of Jett Rink: Marlon Brando, Robert Mitchum, Charlton Heston, Cornel Wilde, Tony Quinn, Richard Widmark, Richard Basehart, Monty Clift, John Hodiak, Robert Ryan, Jack Palance, Ralph Meeker, and Gordon MacRae. Later, names like Aldo Ray and Richard Burton joined the would-be Rinks. Other, bigger names like Clark Gable, Bill Holden, and Jimmy Stewart also expressed an interest in the part. Jett Rink may have been a relatively small role, but it was the most colorful role in a very big and status-filled picture.

Unlike *East of Eden* and *Rebel Without a Cause*, James Dean actively campaigned to be cast in *Giant*. Actually he had set his sights on the film after reading an early version of the script *before* he was even cast in *Eden*. After *Eden* he wielded whatever newfound power he had attained at the studio to secure the part in *Giant*. He loitered around the Warner Brothers lot like a politician lobbying for legislation, pleading his case to whoever would listen. He also hung out at the *Giant* production offices, flirting with the secretaries and, when given the opportunity, charming the director, George Stevens. He flattered and cajoled and flashed his hayseed smile and farm-boy dimples. He, of course, got the part.

As *Giant* finally went into production in May 1955, there was considerable cause for optimism. Like *East of Eden*, *Giant* was based on an important novel by a major author. Further, it was designed by Warner Brothers as a sprawling, Texan spectacular with lavish production values, an Oscar-winning director, and a cast top-lined by three of the biggest names in Hollywood. *Giant* was to have everything: lush landscapes, attractive faces, a titillating love triangle, and, for added prestige, a message of morality and social consciousness. Certainly, at the outset, James Dean was among the most optimistic (and gushing):

> "George Stevens, for my money, is the greatest director of them all—even greater than Kazan. This Stevens was born for the movies. He's so real, so unassuming, and he doesn't miss a thing. Also, we've got a wonderful script. You know, when it wants to, Hollywood can accomplish tremendous things. And this movie might be one of them. I sure hope so."

Giant started shooting at Warner Brothers in Burbank on May 23, 1955. The company then moved to its Virginia location to shoot the film's opening scenes with the Lynnton family and the introduction of Leslie Lynnton (Elizabeth Taylor) and Bick Benedict (Rock Hudson). The couple was based, again at least in part and despite the studio's denials, on real-life couple Bob and Helen Kleberg.

Meanwhile, back in Burbank, James Dean was completing work on *Rebel Without a Cause*. *Rebel*, which was behind schedule, finished shooting on Thursday, May 26. Dean was to be rushed immediately into production on *Giant*. Well, almost immediately. That weekend, probably unbeknown to his bosses, he scurried out of town to enter a car race in Santa Barbara. He signed up for the under-1500cc production event. He moved up to fourth place before his Porsche blew a piston. Talk about foreshadowing.

On Friday, June 3, Dean joined the *Giant* cast and crew in Marfa, Texas. Not only was he not in particularly good spirits; he was also tired and sick. *Rebel Without a Cause* was a creatively fulfilling experience for him, but it was also a physically debilitating one. He didn't function on *Rebel* like most actors work on most movies; he involved himself in virtually every facet of the production. Toward the latter stages of shooting *Rebel* he was given a complete physical and was subsequently placed on a high-protein diet. Nevertheless he was ushered directly into *Giant*, and he was, frankly, fatigued.

Soon after his arrival in Marfa, however, exhaustion gave way to exasperation. After working on the highly collaborative *Rebel*, in which his input had been encouraged, Dean was unaccustomed to, unprepared for, and thoroughly uncomfortable with being prodded like a piece of high-priced cattle, which was how he felt he was being treated by George Stevens. Worse, it quickly became apparent to Dean that his vision of the film differed from that of Stevens. Dean envisioned an intimate character study told on a vast landscape. Stevens, he felt, was taking the title of the picture all too literally, and Dean was openly vocal about his discontent. One of the friends he confided in was Eartha Kitt, who recalled years later, "He blamed everything on the director. He said the picture was going too big in an artificial way. He wanted the interpretation of him as an old man to be quite different from what it was turning out to be." Also according to Kitt, Dean confided to her, "I don't know how I can get through this film because I don't know how you can work with plastic people." To be fair, if he did indeed make the latter statement, it was probably made in anger and self-defense.

A major part of the problem certainly was that Dean had *not* previously starred in a purely Hollywood picture. *East of Eden* may have been filmed on the West Coast, but its mentality, its attitude, its soul, its director, and its actors were decidedly East Coast. On *Rebel Without a Cause* Nick Ray directed the production as he did all of his pictures—independently, as distanced from the Hollywood realm as he could possibly be. Although a substantial part of *Giant* was filmed in Texas, it is the quintessential Hollywood picture, and George Stevens is in many ways the ultimate Hollywood director. His approach to *Giant*, as was the case with much of his work, was to shoot every scene from virtually every angle and then conjure up some magic in the editing room. It is significant to note that out of all of Stevens's many pictures, two of which (*A Place in the Sun*, 1951; *Shane*, 1952) are considered by many to be among the finest American films ever made, *not one* of his leading actors or actresses ever won an Academy Award. Kazan had a tremendous talent for working with actors. Stevens, a visualist, was *not*

The original J.R.: striking it oil rich.

Dean with a couple of his rare *Giant* friends.

an actor's director. James Dean, on the other hand, was an actor's actor. Conflict was inevitable.

Naturally Stevens resented the young upstart's audacity to question his vision and began to suspect that Dean was trying to sabotage his direction. One week into shooting in the scorching heat of Marfa, Stevens harshly reprimanded Dean before the entire *Giant* company. Their relationship, and Dean's admiration for his director, never quite recovered. Virtually defenseless, Dean began to be regarded by much of the cast and crew as an outcast. Elizabeth Taylor and Mercedes McCambridge went to his aid; most of the others kept their distance.

And so he rebelled in the only way he knew how. He hid behind the brim of his Stetson hat, in the character of Jett Rink. After all, Jett Rink, like Dean, was the outcast of the picture—misguided, misunderstood, miserable. Much of the time he stayed in character even when he was off camera. It gave him an excuse for being surly and remote; it gave him something to protect himself with.

Like Jett, he exuded contemptuous disrespect for authority. He began to ignore his call times and, particularly after the Marfa shooting, frequently kept Stevens and the entire cast and crew waiting on the set.

During breaks in Marfa (not the most entertaining of towns), Jimmy spent much of his time with Bob Hinkle, the film's dialogue director. Hinkle taught him how to ride broncos, rope calves, and execute rope tricks with the expertise of a rodeo performer. Some nights the two of them went out hunting. Jimmy, who had toted his .22 rifle to Marfa, later reported proudly that he had bagged a mountain lion, a coyote, and 105 jackrabbits. Monte Hale, one of the actors in the cast, taught Dean how to play the guitar and sing country songs. Jimmy also learned how to roll a cigarette with one hand and how to hog-tie Elizabeth Taylor. Mornings, he'd wake up to the recordings of opera star Renata Tebaldi. He also, sporadically, studied German. His girlfriend back in Hollywood at the time was Ursula Andress and he wanted to impress her with prowess in the language. Occasionally he'd break out of his solitude and amaze those present with a burst of effervescence. Once, at the El Paisano Hotel, where the entire company dined, he entertained and impressed with his impersonation of Charlie Chaplin impersonating Marlon Brando. He also spent time boxing with Sheik Abdullah. It kept him in physical shape and, moreover, prepared him for what was scheduled to be his next picture, the Rocky Graziano biopic *Somebody Up There Likes Me*. Finally, as would any aspiring director, he spent as much time as he could *behind* the camera. As one Warner Brothers representative quipped at the time, "James Dean has practically become a fourth camera unit."

Most of the *Giant* company left Marfa by train on July 10, 1955. Dean stayed behind to shoot the oil sequences with the second camera unit directed by Fred Guiol. He left Marfa by plane on Tuesday, July 12.

Back at Warner Brothers, relations between James Dean and George Stevens grew more strained, aggravated in large part by the former's perpetual lateness. The conflict culminated on July 23. When he didn't show up for his early morning call, one of Stevens's assistants telephoned Dean at home. Dean answered the phone, said that he'd overslept and was tired but that he'd be right over. When hours passed and he still hadn't arrived, Stevens, furiously tapping his cowboy boot on the *Giant* soundstage, sent his assistant to retrieve Dean at his Sunset Plaza Drive home. But there was no sight of Dean there either. In an adolescent fit of punishment to his director, Dean had decided to take the day off—to move into his new rented house in the San Fernando Valley!

Not only did Stevens severely reprimand Dean; he privately commented that he would never work with him again. He also ordered his assistant to draft a report detailing Dean's infractions. The report was dated August 1, 1955, and cited the following shooting delays caused by the absences and/or tardiness of James Dean:

6-29-55	Wait for Dean 11:40 to 11:50
6-29-55	Wait for Taylor and Dean 2:50 to 3:17
6-29-55	Wait for Taylor and Dean 3:45 to 3:48
7-2-55	Wait for Dean 5:30 to 5:35
7-3-55	Wait for Dean 9:00 to 9:20
7-5-55	Wait for Dean to 9:45
7-5-55	Camera ready 10:05. Wait for Dean to 10:20
7-5-55	Wait for Dean 2:45 to 3:03
7-16-55	Wait for Dean to 9:30
7-16-55	Wait for Dean 1:40 to 1:55
7-18-55	Wait for Dean 10:30 to 10:55
7-19-55	Wait for Dean 9:10 to 9:41
7-23-55	Dean had 8:30 A.M. call—did not come in all day
7-29-55	Wait for Dean 9:00 to 9:30
7-29-55	Wait for Dean 2:00 to 2:28
8-1-55	Wait for Dean 8:30 to 9:30

Crippling the production even further was Elizabeth Taylor's rapidly deteriorating health and relationship with George Stevens. During July and August production was repeatedly shut down, delayed, or rerouted due to Taylor's illnesses and hospitalizations. Further, by this point Taylor and Dean had grown exceptionally close and often spent their evenings together. They also joined forces against their director and frequently showed up together on the set—late. If James Dean won

Home is where your hat is: Dean, the cowboy who read Kafka. In Marfa, 1955.

Tricks and treats on the Warner Brothers lot.

one major battle during the making of *Giant* (in addition to upstaging his co-stars), it was his recruitment of Elizabeth Taylor.

> I finally got around to visiting Jimmy Dean, Liz Taylor, Rock Hudson [note the billing], Jane Withers, Chill Wills and George Stevens and Henry Ginsberg and other pals on the *Giant* set. And a fine time we had, too. . . .
> I saw a reel of *Giant* and must say it lives up to George

Stevens' *Shane* and *Duel in the Sun* [sic—not a Stevens film]. This must be a biggie.

Jimmy Dean shaved his hair on both sides of his forehead to make him look old. I was surprised when I walked into his dressing room to find him reading *Elbert Hubbard's Notebook*. I said, 'Why, Jimmy, I thought you'd be reading Marcus Aurelius!' 'I've been finding a lot of good homey philosophy in this,' said he."

Hedda Hopper, *Los Angeles Times*, September 9, 1955

Back at home on his own turf, James Dean was, during the last few weeks of shooting *Giant*, in increasing high spirits. *Rebel Without a Cause* was about to be released, and advance word was highly favorable. The general consensus was that Dean had not only fulfilled the promise shown in *East of Eden* but had surpassed it. His agent, Jane Deacy, was successfully negotiating his new contract at Warner Brothers, which was to increase his salary from $1,500 a week (approximately $20,000–$30,000 a picture) to $100,000 a picture. He wasn't satisfied with *Giant* the way he had been with his previous films, but he already had a plethora of promising film projects lined up ahead of him and was in the process of establishing his own film production company. He also signed to do a couple of television specials and had several offers to return to Broadway. Personally he was in the process of dissolving his relationship with Ursula Andress, but it was a relationship that Dean recognized as futile. Besides, shortly after the completion of *Giant* he planned an enthusiastic return to New York, where he planned to live for as long as a year.

Dean's final day of work on *Giant* was Thursday, September 22. His final day of shooting had been September 17. On September 19 he test-drove the Porsche Spyder that he would buy two days later. Even with the accelerated pace of his life in those last weeks it was his purchase of the Porsche and the upcoming car race in Salinas about which James Dean was most excited.

On Friday, September 30, as Dean streaked down a stretch of California highway, *Giant* continued to lumber toward a finish line of its own. Shot that day were scenes with Rock Hudson and Elizabeth Taylor as Bick and Leslie Benedict, in the interior of their Reata mansion. One scene called for Bick to get out the Texas flag in a wave of patriotic sentiment. It was that kind of day. It was also that type of contrivance in *Giant* that James Dean had vehemently railed against. Meanwhile the real drama transpired at the corner of U.S. 466 and Highway 41. Later that night George Stevens, Taylor, Carroll Baker, and others were sitting in the studio projection room, watching the daily rushes, when the telephone rang with the news that Dean was dead.

On the set the following morning it was business as usual with the exception of Elizabeth Taylor, who literally got sick to her stomach. As noted in the film's daily progress report, the crew waited "for Liz Taylor who was too upset from the death of James Dean." Instead of reporting as scheduled at 8:15, Taylor arrived at 11:45. She kept Stevens waiting repeatedly during the day, and at 5:00 P.M. the crew was dismissed early because "Miss Taylor was unable to work."

Over the following week Elizabeth Taylor was hospitalized, reportedly due to an emotional breakdown, and production of *Giant* virtually shut down. James Dean, from the grave, was still giving George Stevens a difficult time. On October 12, 1955, after a colossal 115 shooting days, which marked one of the longest shooting schedules in Hollywood history, *Giant* officially completed production. It was 37 days behind schedule and cost an inflated (and at the time exorbitant) sum of $5.4 million.

In retrospect *Giant* in some ways was a giant exercise in waste. Judging by what made it into the final print, the Virginia location shooting was totally unnecessary. Virtually everything that was shot there could easily have been shot at the studio or thereabouts. Further puzzling was the casting of high-priced talent in what was tantamount to glorified bit parts; e.g., Paul Fix as Dr. Lynnton, who ended up on screen for seconds and was paid $1,500 a week—the same salary earned by James Dean.

Further, the film itself, despite its impressive star power and striking photography, is surprisingly dull. At three hours and 18 minutes, it is filled with extras, cattle, landscapes, costumes, and sets and is devoid of any real passion. It plays like a big-budgeted, multipart episode of "Dallas," with Rock Hudson as Bobby Ewing and James Dean as J.R., only Dean's Rink is far more deviant and pathetic and authentic than Larry Hagman's primetime caricature.

Jett Rink's introduction in *Giant* is classic James Dean: his body slinks and lumbers; when asked a question, he mumbles; a cigarette dangles from his mouth; his eyes smolder, barely seen beneath the brim of his Stetson hat. His physical language alone narrates that he is always alone, that he is unliked, perhaps most by himself. When he fusses about his little shack, struggling to prepare tea for Elizabeth Taylor's Leslie, he is the picture of a young man striving for something *more*. Later, after his well strikes oil, he is diseased and consumed by his own wealth and power. He is, in many ways, American capitalism at its ugliest. Given the plastic confines of the picture, it is a magnificent performance. It also seems as if, in an effort to combat the film's scope, Dean decided to incorporate every nuance, every attention to detail that he could possibly squeeze into each of the scenes in which he appeared. Later the film's cinematographer, William C. Mellor, was compelled to write:

> While we were making *Giant*, I think we all knew that young Jimmy Dean was giving a performance that not even the extreme adjectives of Hollywood could adequately sum up. It's not often a unit gets a feeling like that.
> *Picturegoer*, December 29, 1959

Still, repeated viewing reveals several problems with Dean's performance in *Giant*, all relative to his believability. First, his characterization, particularly in the early scenes, is so authentic it reeks of grit— this in a picture that practically gleams with high-priced Hollywood polish. Consequently Dean often appears to be acting in a different picture from the rest of the cast, a picture of his own design. Second, he, more than any of the other actors, was handicapped by the film's abrupt jump in time. In the script Jett Rink ages from 19 to 46 and is the only character who radically transforms, physically and otherwise, over that time period. To audiences the on-screen evolution of Jett Rink is startling, difficult to adjust to and accept. Finally, and perhaps most debilitating, was the unlikely, blatantly artificial makeup that Dean wore as the elder Rink. Because Dean had been rushed from *Rebel* into *Giant*, Gordon Bau, Warner's head of makeup, had virtually no time with him to experiment with the usual cosmetic tests, this in a film in which the makeup was of critical importance.

In a "wardrobe plot" written on December 30, 1954, Bau "was of the opinion that aging Jimmy Dean for the latter sequences presented his biggest makeup problem." Hence Bau requested additional time with Dean, time that was never allotted. Interestingly Bau also suggested that Dean be padded in the older scenes to give him a bloated appearance. George Stevens, however, rejected the idea.

In a memo dated April 21, 1955, about a month before *Giant* started shooting, Stevens understandably exerted pressure on the Warner Brothers front office to get Dean out of *Rebel Without a Cause* and into *Giant* as quickly as possible.

Stevens wrote:

> It is imperative that we get James Dean as early as possible for make up, wardrobe and photographic tests. It is our understanding at this time that Dean will be off on May 3 for a full day, part of a day on May 4, full days on May 17 and 18, and part of a day on May 24. We will take full advantage of these days for make up, wardrobe and photographic tests. However, I believe that every effort should be made on *Rebel Without a Cause* to finish with Dean as early as possible as we need every day that we can obtain for preparation of our picture.

However, *Rebel Without a Cause* fell behind schedule, and Dean's makeup and wardrobe tests for *Giant* did not take place until May 26, the day he completed *Rebel*, just *one week* before he joined the cast in Marfa. No one, not even Dean himself, realized how the rushed makeup job would hinder the impact of his performance. It was a fatal and unfortunate flaw in his final film.

For a year after Dean's death, as the director oversaw the editing of *Giant*, George Stevens's power struggle with Dean seemed to continue. Fans besieged Stevens and Warner Brothers with threatening letters, demanding that not a single frame of their beloved Jimmy be cut from the picture. While Stevens correctly maintained the stance that *Giant* was *his* picture, not Dean's, producer Henry Ginsberg lamented, "People simply cannot stop talking about him. For instance, we have a multi-million dollar movie, made by a great director from a best-selling novel with four stars. But *who* are we talking about?"

Giant premiered in New York on October 10, 1956, and in Los Angeles on October 17, to rave reviews and spectacular box office. Dean's performance was singled out as exemplary, although Rock Hudson also won plaudits for his acting for the first time, and Elizabeth Taylor continued to stake her claim as an actress of ability. The following February *Giant* garnered an impressive 10 Oscar nominations, including Best Actor nods to both Dean and Hudson. But it was George Stevens who went home with the Oscar. The Best Picture Oscar went to

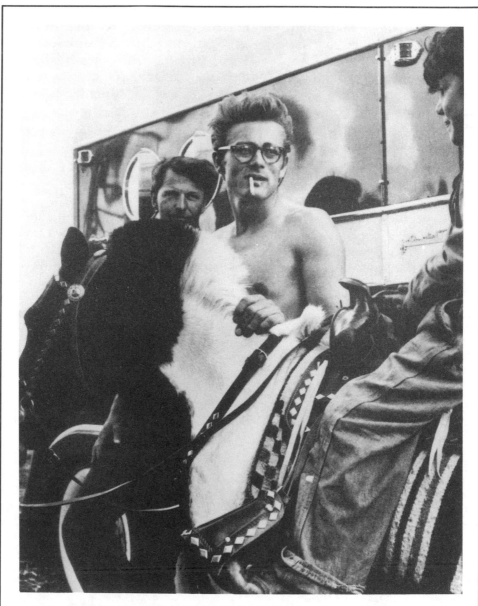

Jimmy with more of his *Giant* friends.

Mike Todd's *Around the World in 80 Days*, but the academy membership apparently felt that Stevens's 115 days made him the most deserving director. After all, not only did he make what was considered to be a monumental picture; he also made it in the face of innumerable obstacles, not the least of which was James Dean, the angry boy who persisted throughout.

GIANT, PART II: REATA

In the early 1980s the Hollywood trade papers announced that producer Gene Taft was slated to make a sequel to the hugely successful 1956 film *Giant*. It was to have been titled *Giant, Part II: Reata*. Reportedly Taft purchased the rights from the Edna Ferber estate. The project was to have been scripted by Robert Garland and was touted as including never-before-seen footage of Dean from *Giant*.

Not only did *Giant, Part II: Reata* never make it into the theaters; it never made it before the cameras.

ANDRE GIDE

André Gide, born Paul Guillaume in Paris in 1869, was the Nobel Prize–winning French novelist, essayist, and playwright whose semiautobiographical novel *The Immoralist* was adapted into a 1954 Broadway play costarring James Dean.

In 1947, Gide was awarded the Nobel Prize for literature. He died in 1951 at the age of 81.

WALTER GIESEKING

Concert pianist whom Jimmy admired and met at the Hollywood home of Kira and Robert Appel one evening in 1955. That night Gieseking and Dean played a piano duet.

Born in 1895, Gieseking was considered by some as the greatest interpreter of the French Impressionists, and won great acclaim for his performance of works by Debussy and Ravel. A child prodigy, he played all of the Beethoven piano sonatas in a series of recitals when he was 15.

He died in 1956, just before his 61st birthday.

GILA LAND COMPANY

Jimmy boarded his horse in stalls owned by the Gila Land Company. At the time of his death he owed Gila Land $80 for feed and stall.

MYRTLE GILBREATH

Myrtle Gilbreath was Jimmy's citizenship teacher during his freshman year at Fairmount High School.

JOHN GILMORE

John Gilmore is the author of the book *The Real James Dean*, published by Pyramid Books in 1975. According to Gilmore, he befriended Jimmy in New York in 1952. In his book he wrote: "Eventually I was to feel as though I were mother, brother, lover to him. . . ."

Gilmore's name also appeared in the byline of a rather crudely titled article, "I Had Sex with James Dean," published by *The Hollywood Star*, a 1980 gossip tabloid published by Bill Dakota. According to Dakota, "Gilmore told me, 'I wanna do the real story, the stuff I had left out of the book.' "

And just what was published in the article that had been left out of the book? The following is a salacious sample:

> Jimmy liked to cuddle in bed. He liked to be held and he liked to be kissed. . . . We kissed one another and it was strange because it was the first time I'd actually kissed—I mean, really kissed another male, another guy, and wasn't somehow trying to turn my face away. . . . We kissed and our teeth touched.

And the article quotes Jimmy asking Gilmore after a round of oral sex, "You want to do it again?"

Gilmore, a former child actor, was born in Los Angeles in 1935. His other writings include *Overpass Blues* (1967), *The Tucson Murders* (1970), *The Garbage People* (1971), and *Night Shark* (1975). His works of poetry won him a 1967 New York Circle award.

HENRY GINSBERG

The producer of *Giant*, for which he received a 1956 Best Picture Oscar nomination. Prior to that Henry Ginsberg had been a vice president in charge of production at Paramount Pictures.

Of his star James Dean, Ginsberg wrote prophetically to his son, John, in a letter dated October 6, 1955, less than a week after Jimmy's death:

> The passing of James Dean was indeed very tragic. He had a n.agnificent career ahead of him. He had completed his role in our picture two weeks before the accident, thus, hence there was nothing he was required to do for us. He gave a great performance in *Giant* and his aging from the early 20s to about 50 years is most realistic and convincing. The consensus of opinion—and I share this view— is that this boy was a rather unique personality and may develop into something of a legend. . . .

DOROTHY GISH

Dorothy Gish starred in the television drama "Harvest," a 1953 episode of the NBC series "Robert Montgomery Presents the Johnson's Wax Program" that co-starred James Dean. Gish portrayed the mother of the character portrayed by Dean.

Born Dorothy de Guiche, Dorothy Gish (1898–1968) was the younger of the legendary Gish sisters, both of whom starred in a series of silent pictures for D. W. Griffith. Gish's later "talkies" included *Our Hearts Were Young and Gay* (1944), *The Whistle at Eaton Falls* (1951), and *The Cardinal* (1963).

ZINA GLAD

In 1936 five-year-old Jimmy Dean was given dance lessons by Zina Glad at the Marion College of Dance and Theater Arts. In 1939 Glad visited the Dean family at their home in Santa Monica, California.

BARBARA GLENN

Barbara Glenn is something of a mystery woman in the life of James Dean. An actress, Glenn first met Jimmy at the end of 1952 at Cromwell's Pharmacy in New York City. They attended an acting workshop together and fell in love, seriously enough to contemplate marriage. Over the course of the next fourteen months they carried on a highly charged and dramatic affair full of subplots, breakups, and makeups.

Dean biographer David Dalton described Glenn in *The Mutant King*: "Tall, thin, hyperactive Barbara was as volatile as Jimmy, who once affectionately referred to her in a letter as 'my neurotic little shit.' " He also quotes her:

> "There's something so different about Jimmy. It's so hard to describe when you first meet him . . . the little boy quality. Insecure, uptight, but very involved. Trying very desperately to make conversation, badly. I found him utterly fascinating. . . . We had a lot of fights. I was very emotional. I cried and screamed a lot back then. But Jimmy never screamed back. The hardest thing for Jimmy to do was to be angry."

The relationship between the two unabashedly neurotic actors deteriorated after Jimmy went to Hollywood and fell in love with Pier Angeli. Just prior to that, though, Jimmy wrote to Barbara back in New York:

> I don't like it here, I don't like people here. I like it home (N.Y.) and I like you and I want to see you. . . . Wish you cooked. I'll be home soon. Write me please. I'm sad most of the time. Awful lonely too isn't it! (I hope you're dying) BECAUSE I AM.

After Jimmy's death the press referred to Barbara Glenn respectfully and with a semblance of finality:

> Friends prefer to leave "The Girl" anonymous, since she's now happily married and living in the Midwest.

ROY GLENN

Actor who appeared in "I'm a Fool," a 1954 episode of the CBS television program "General Electric Theater" that co-starred James Dean.

Glenn, who died in 1971, was also featured in films including *Carmen Jones* (1954), *A Raisin in the Sun* (1961), *Guess Who's Coming to Dinner?* (1967), and *The Great White Hope* (1970).

"GLORY IN FLOWER"

Identified elsewhere as "Glory in the Flower," this original play by William Inge was presented on October 4, 1953, on the CBS television program "Omnibus." It was directed by Andrew McCullough (not Bob Banner, as reported elsewhere) and produced by Fred Rickey. It starred Jessica Tandy, Hume Cronyn, Ed Binns, Frank McHugh, and James Dean. Jimmy portrayed (what else?) a troubled adolescent. It was Inge who suggested to

McCullough that Dean audition for the role. As McCullough later recalled, Dean made a memorable first impression:

> "He had a terrible attitude—very snotty, very arrogant. As he started to read for me, he put his feet on the table, pulled a knife from his boot and stuck it into the table."
>
> *Emmy,* October 1990

RUTH AND AUGUSTUS GOETZ

Ruth and Augustus Goetz wrote *The Immoralist*, the 1954 Broadway play that co-starred James Dean. The play was adapted from the novel by André Gide. Ruth Goetz described Jimmy to writer Venable Herndon: "The little son-of-a-bitch was one of the most unspeakably detestable fellows to work with I ever knew in my life." She was also interviewed about him in the Italian documentary *Hollywood: The Rebel James Dean*, in which she was not quite as sharp-tongued.

The husband and wife writing team of Augustus and Ruth Goetz also wrote the Broadway play *The Heiress* (1947), which they later adapted into a film (which did not, contrary to previous reports, win them a 1949 Oscar). Their other film collaborations include *Carrie* (1952).

THE GOLDEN GLOBE AWARDS

The Golden Globe awards annually honor the best in movies and television, as voted by members of the Hollywood Foreign Press Association. In 1955 James Dean was awarded a special posthumous Golden Globe. The following year he was awarded the most prestigious (and no longer given) Golden Globe as the male "World Film Favorite." That year Kim Novak was named the female "World Film Favorite" and Ronald Reagan was presented with a special "Hollywood Citizenship" award.

THE GOO GOO DOLLS

Singing group that recorded the song "James Dean" on its album *Jed.*

RICHARD GOODE

Director of "The Foggy, Foggy Dew," a 1952 episode of the CBS television program "Lux Video Theatre" that co-starred James Dean. Earlier, Goode directed and appeared in the NBC program "Dress Rehearsal" (1948).

MARK GOODSON

Producer of the television game show "Beat the Clock" (1950–1958) on which struggling actor James Dean was employed circa 1951–1952. Along with his partner Bill Todman, Goodson was also the executive producer of "Sleeping Dogs," a 1952 episode of the CBS television program "The Web" in which James Dean appeared.

Other Goodson-Todman productions have included "What's My Line?" (1950–1967), "The Name's the Same" (1951–1955), "I've Got a Secret"

(1952–1976), "To Tell the Truth" (1956–1967), and "The Price Is Right" (1957–1986).

GOOGIE'S
One of Jimmy Dean's favorite Hollywood hangouts. Like Schwab's, its more famous neighbor and counterpart, Googie's was usually counter-crowded with aspiring actors engaged in a daily cycle of sipping coffee and seeking employment.

Reportedly, upon hearing the news of Jimmy's death on the evening of September 30, 1955, a large group of mourners convened at Googie's for coffee and consolation. Googie's, no longer in existence, was located at 8100 Sunset Boulevard.

GOON WITH THE WIND
Goon with the Wind was a play presented by the Fairmount (Indiana) High drama department at the school's Halloween carnival on October 29, 1948. For the production Jimmy slapped on some macabre monster makeup and aped Frankenstein. Other Fairmount thespians in the cast included Joan Jones and David Nall.

HAROLD GORDON
Actor who was featured in *East of Eden* as the maligned German shopkeeper, Mr. Albrecht.

Gordon, who died in 1959 at the age of 39, also appeared in *Viva Zapata!* (1952) and *The Jazz Singer* (the unfortunate Danny Thomas version, 1953).

MICHAEL GORDON
Director of *See the Jaguar*, the 1952 Broadway play that, despite its failure, launched the career of James Dean.

Gordon's other credits include, on stage: *Anna Christie* (1952) and *The Male Animal* (1952); his film credits include *Boston Blackie Goes to Hollywood* (1942), *The Web* (1947), *Cyrano de Bergerac* (1950), *Pillow Talk* (1959), *Move Over Darling* (1963), and *How Do I Love Thee* (1970).

DAVE GOULD
James Dean's landlord at 1541 Sunset Plaza Drive, 1955.

GOWER PLAZA HOTEL
For a brief period during the summer of 1951 Jimmy lived at the Gower Plaza Hotel in Hollywood. The hotel was located at 1607 North Gower Street, right around the corner from CBS Radio, where Jimmy was employed as a parking lot attendant.

ED GRACZYK
Playwright of *Come Back to the Five and Dime, Jimmy Dean, Jimmy Dean*, a 1982 Broadway play that was adapted into a film later the same year.

SHEILAH GRAHAM
Hollywood columnist who reported on September 21, 1955:

> Jimmy's latest prank—racing around Warners in his new Porsche
> and chased by the cops who told him to drive slowly or get off the
> lot.

GRANDFATHERS
Charles Dean
John Wilson

GRANDMOTHERS
Emma Dean
Minnie Slaughter Wilson

LILY GRANT
Lily Grant is the postmaster of Cholame, California, and the honorary
custodian of the James Dean Memorial located there.

GRANT MEMORIAL PARK
Cemetery in Marion, Indiana, where Jimmy's mother, Mildred Dean, was
buried in 1940.

GRAUMAN'S CHINESE THEATER
Hollywood theater where *Giant* premiered on October 17, 1956. Legendary
for its famous forecourt of concrete handprints and footprints, Grauman's
Chinese Theater opened in 1927 for the premiere of Cecil B. DeMille's *The
King of Kings*. Today, with the name Mann's Chinese Theater, Grauman's is
a circuslike tourist attraction (address: 6925 Hollywood Boulevard).

He never made it into the cement at Grauman's Chinese Theater, but he was
immortalized nonetheless, in the cement of his uncle's barn.

WILLIAM GRAY
William Gray was one of the administrators of the James Dean estate, as appointed by Winton Dean. In 1955 Gray's office was located on Brighton Way in Beverly Hills.

BOB GRAYBO
Recorded some of the songs on the Unique Records tribute album *Music James Dean Lived By*.

RICHARD GRAYSON
Stage manager, *The Immoralist* (1954).

ROCKY GRAZIANO
Champion boxer whom Dean was scheduled to portray in *Somebody Up There Likes Me*. Graziano was to have served as Dean's technical adviser/coach on the film.

During his ring days Graziano was known to tell reporters "Somebody up there must like me." Hence, the subsequent book and movie of his life, with the slightly altered title, *Somebody Up There Likes Me*.

HARRY GREB
One-eyed boxer whose life story James Dean expressed an interest in portraying.

"GREEN BRIAR, BLUE FIRE"
Song written by Alec Wilder, sung by James Dean in the 1952 Broadway play *See the Jaguar*.

FRANK GREGORY
Telewriter of "Death Is My Neighbor," a 1953 episode of the CBS television program "Danger" that co-starred James Dean.

GRIFFITH PARK AND OBSERVATORY
Perhaps more than any other single location in the world, the Griffith Park and Observatory evokes images and memories of James Dean.

Dean's relationship to this Hollywood landmark dates back to December 1950, when, as a struggling actor and student at UCLA, he appeared in a television commercial for Pepsi that was filmed at Griffith Park.

The park is more famous, of course, for its observatory, where several key scenes of *Rebel Without a Cause* were shot in late March to mid-April 1955.

More than 30 years later, on November 1, 1988, artist Kenneth Kendall dedicated a bronze bust of Jimmy on the observatory's front lawn. Among those in attendance were Maxwell Caulfield, Ann Doran, Maila Nurmi, Phil Stern, members from the gang in *Rebel*, and members of the We Remember Dean International fan club.

JIM GRINDLE

Jim Grindle was Jimmy Dean's best friend and basketball teammate in high school. He later became an Indiana state trooper.

JACK GRINNAGE

Played one of the gang members in *Rebel Without a Cause*. Grinnage attended the 1988 Griffith Park monument ceremonies and was interviewed in the cable documentary "Forever James Dean" (1988).

Jack Grinnage was also a regular on the television programs "The Bob Newhart Show" (1961) and "Kolchak: The Night Stalker" (1974–1975).

GROOMING

People were generally shocked by the atrocious grooming habits of James Dean. In his personal life Jimmy was basically a slob. It wasn't so much that he was dirty; it was that he had a disregard for society's standards of appearance. His scalp flaked with dandruff, his hair was unkempt, his face unshaven, his wardrobe disheveled. While making a film, however, his groom-

ing habits improved somewhat, presumably to the agreement of his co-stars. On the set of *Rebel Without a Cause* he even employed the use of a Remington 60 electric razor.

"GROWING PAINS"

Popular ABC comedy series that, in one of its episodes, featured a takeoff of *Rebel Without a Cause*. The show included photographs of James Dean, dialogue about Dean, and clips from *Rebel*. "Growing Pains" stars Alan Thicke, Joanna Kerns, Kirk Cameron, and Tracey Gold.

HERBERT GRUNDELL

The Paso Robles, California, district attorney who conducted the October 11, 1955, investigation into the death of James Dean.

ALEC GUINNESS

On a September evening in 1955 James Dean ran into actor Alec Guinness at the Villa Capri restaurant in Hollywood. Jimmy, in one of his sprees of wild enthusiasm, had just purchased his Porsche and was eager to show it off. Guinness later recalled in his autobiography, *Blessings in Disguise*:

> The sports car looked sinister to me, although it had a large bunch
> of red carnations resting on the bonnet. . . . I heard myself saying in
> a voice I could hardly recognize as my own, "Please, never get in it."
> I looked at my watch. "It is now ten o'clock, Friday the 23rd of
> September, 1955. If you get in that car you will be found dead in it
> by this time next week."

Dean laughed at the prophet with the British accent. The two men then went into the restaurant, where Jimmy treated Guinness to a meal. A week later, Jimmy was dead.

Sir Alec Guinness, born in 1914, has had a phenomenal film career that includes *Kind Hearts and Coronets* (in which he portrayed eight roles, 1949), *The Lavender Hill Mob* (Best Actor Oscar nomination, 1952), *Bridge on the River Kwai* (Best Actor Oscar winner, 1957), *Lawrence of Arabia* (1962), *Dr. Zhivago* (1965), *Star Wars* (Best Supporting Actor Oscar nomination, 1977), *The Empire Strikes Back* (1980), *Return of the Jedi* (1984), *A Passage to India* (1984), *Little Dorrit* (Best Actor Oscar nomination, 1988), and many, many others. In 1964, he won a Best Actor Tony award for *Dylan*, and in 1979 he was honored with a special, second Oscar for lifetime achievement. Further, he received an additional Oscar nomination in 1958 for his adapted screenplay of *The Horse's Mouth*.

FRED GUIOL

Fred Guiol co-wrote the screenplay of *Giant*, which was adapted from the novel by Edna Ferber and for which he received a 1956 Oscar nomination.

Guiol (1898–1964) was basically a director who also worked as an assistant to *Giant* director George Stevens on many pictures. In fact, in addition to scripting *Giant*, Guiol also worked on the picture as a second-unit director. His films as a first-unit director include *Live and Learn* (1930), *The Nitwits* (1935), and *Here Comes Trouble* (1948). His films as a writer include *Gunga Din* (shared credit, 1939), *Vigil in the Night* (shared credit, 1940), and *Abroad with Two Yanks* (story credit, 1944).

GUN FOR A COWARD

Property that Warner Brothers purchased for James Dean to star in. After Jimmy's death the company dropped the option and the film was never made.

BILL GUNN

Bill Gunn was one of Jimmy's New York actor friends. He had met Jimmy in late 1953, after both of them had been cast in *The Immoralist*. In the play Gunn had a small part as Dolit. He also served as Jimmy's understudy, though he did not assume the role after Jimmy walked out.

Gunn later became the playwright of such works as *Black Picture Show*, *Ganja and Hess*, *Johannas*, and *Marcus in the Grass*. He died in April 1989 on the eve of the off-Broadway premiere of his final production, *The Forbidden City*. He was 59 years old.

Bill Gunn was interviewed in the Italian documentary *Hollywood: The Rebel James Dean*.

GUNS

In his dressing room at Warner Brothers, Jimmy kept a Colt .45. Reportedly, when the front office at Warners learned that its rebel employee was harboring a pistol, Jimmy was evicted from the dressing room in which he had been living.

Jimmy's estate, at the time of his death, included a 22-inch Marlin rifle, model 39A.

GUNS N' ROSES

"I always thought James Dean was kind of cool. . . . I got into Dean more on the level of how he thought and directed himself rather than the fact, 'Hey, I'm going to go out and get a red jacket and a white T-shirt and *be* him.' I was [intrigued] by a lot of the ways Dean went about his acting, his seriousness about his career. I took a lot of those things to heart."

Axl Rose, *Los Angeles Times*

With songs like "Sweet Child O'Mine" and "Welcome to the Jungle," Guns N' Roses became one of the most popular rock and roll bands of the 1980s. Unfortunately, amid charges of racism and homophobia, the band has also become one of the most controversial. It is somewhat ironic, then, that the band's lead singer, Axl Rose (real name Bill Bailey) is a James Dean fan. Dean, of course, was anything but racist and homophobic.

BOB GUNTON

Narrated the 1988 cable documentary "Forever James Dean." Previously, Gunton had been a regular on the short-lived CBS program "Comedy Zone" (1984).

WOODY GUTHRIE

Jimmy was a big fan of folk music legend Woody Guthrie. In fact Jimmy planned to utilize the guitar-playing skills he learned while making *Giant* and star in a proposed film biography of Guthrie. Twenty-one years after Jimmy's death Guthrie's life story was finally filmed under the title *Bound for Glory*. The film, directed by Hal Ashby and starring David Carradine, was hailed as a critical success and was honored with a Best Picture Oscar nomination in 1976.

GUYS AND DOLLS

In early 1955 Jimmy visited the MGM set of *Guys and Dolls*, which starred Frank Sinatra, Marlon Brando, Jean Simmons, Vivian Blaine, and Stubby Kaye. During his visit Jimmy posed for a series of now-famous stills for photographer Phil Stern.

H

CRAIG HAFFNER
Director of "James Dean: An American Original," a half-hour tribute that aired as a 1983 episode of the syndicated television program "Hollywood Close-Up."

COREY HAIM
Young actor who aspires to be "the next James Dean." His career has included such films as *First Born* (1984), *Murphy's Romance* (1985), *Secret Admirer* (1985), *Silver Bullet* (1985), *Lucas* (in which he was excellent, 1986), *The Lost Boys* (1987), *License to Drive* (1988), and *Dream a Little Dream* (1989).

Of his Dean-wannabe aspirations, teen throb Haim has said to the *Los Angeles Times*:

> "I know I can do it. Dean made only three movies and he's such a legend. People think he's so brilliant. He was so raw. He did such weird things. I mean the way he died in that little sports car. It's such a freaky thing to me. Maybe I don't have that total rebel image. I just want to be known like [Dean] was known. I just want people to think that I'm really, really good."

HAIR
James Dean's studio biographies listed his hair as "blond." Actually, though, it was closer to brown with blond highlights. Not one for elaborate grooming rituals, Jimmy frequently cut his own hair. He dubbed it "a Jim trim." After his death an international wave of teenage boys flocked to their barbers and asked for "the James Dean cut." Basically it was short on the sides, full and combed back on top. It was shown off to best advantage when worn with a red jacket, white T-shirt, blue jeans, and an affected pose.

HAIRSTYLISTS
Ruby Felkner, *Giant*
Tillie Starriet, *East of Eden*, *Rebel Without a Cause*
Patricia Westmore, *Giant*

MONTE HALE
Western singer/actor Monte Hale taught James Dean how to play the guitar during breaks from shooting *Giant*.

Hale, born in 1919, appeared in several westerns for Republic Pictures during the 1940s. His films include *Home on the Range* (1947), *South of Rio* (1948), *Rainbow Valley* (1949), *Giant* (1956), and *The Chase* (1966).

JACK HALEY, JR.

Director and executive producer of the television documentary "James Dean Remembered" (1974).

Jack Haley, Jr., is, of course, the son of Jack Haley who starred as the Tin Man in *The Wizard of Oz*. Aside from that, Haley Junior was president of 20th Century–Fox television in the 1970s, director of the films *Norwood* (1970) and *The Love Machine* (1971), and writer and director of the film *That's Entertainment!* (1974). Still, Haley, born in 1934, is probably best known to some as the former husband of Liza Minnelli and the director of Nancy Sinatra's 1967 television special.

SAM HALL

Telewriter of "Run Like a Thief," a 1954 episode of the NBC television program "Philco TV Playhouse" that co-starred James Dean.

ERNEST HALLER

Legendary cinematographer (1896–1970) who photographed *Rebel Without a Cause*.

Ernest Haller is best remembered as Bette Davis's favorite cinematographer and the man who shot *Gone with the Wind*, for which he won a 1939 Oscar. His other films include *Stella Dallas* (1925), *Dangerous* (1935), *Jezebel* (Oscar nomination, 1938), *Dark Victory* (1939), *All This and Heaven Too* (Oscar nomination, 1940), *Mr. Skeffington* (1944), *Mildred Pierce* (Oscar nomination, 1945), *Humoresque* (1946), *Whatever Happened to Baby Jane?* (Oscar nomination, 1962), *Lilies of the Field* (Oscar nomination, 1963), and *Dead Ringer* (1964).

"HALLMARK HALL OF FAME"

Periodically over the years Hallmark has presented television specials under the title "Hallmark Hall of Fame." At the time of his death James Dean was signed to appear in "The Corn Is Green," a Hallmark special. Earlier, he had appeared in a 1952 Hallmark presentation entitled "Forgotten Children."

"HALLMARK PLAYHOUSE"

Radio program that James Dean performed on circa 1951–1952. It was through the Foote, Cone and Belding advertising agency, which handled the "Hallmark Playhouse" account, that Jimmy got the job.

"HALLMARK SUMMER THEATRE"

Between July and August 1952 Jimmy worked as an off-screen assistant on this NBC television program sponsored by Hallmark cards.

HAMBURGER HAMLET

Chain of southern California hamburger-plus restaurants. In 1954–1955 James Dean was a frequent patron at the Hamburger Hamlet West Hollywood location at 8929 Sunset Boulevard. Today the location houses a foreign sports car dealer.

JACK HAMMER
Wrote the song "The Ballad of James Dean" from the Coral Records tribute album *The James Dean Story*.

EARL HAMNER, JR.
Wrote "Hound of Heaven," a 1953 episode of the daytime television program "The Kate Smith Show" in which James Dean appeared.

Earl Hamner, Jr., later gained fame and fortune as the creator and narrator of the television hit "The Waltons" (1972–1981).

WALTER HAMPDEN
Star of "Death Is My Neighbor," a 1953 episode of the CBS television program "Danger" in which James Dean co-starred.

Walter Hampden, born Walter Dougherty in 1879, was a stage, television, and film actor of considerable repute. His film credits include *Warfare of the Flesh* (1917), *The Hunchback of Notre Dame* (1939), *All This and Heaven Too* (1940), *All About Eve* (1950), *The Silver Chalice* (1954), *Sabrina* (1954), and *The Vagabond King* (1956). Hampden died in 1955.

DIANE HANVILLE
Diane Hanville is a Dean collector and member of the We Remember Dean International fan club. She works in the field of entertainment public relations and has been collecting material associated with James Dean for nearly 25 years.

Hanville's collection includes the books written about Dean, rare fan magazines from the 1950s, a work of original art painted by Jimmy in high school, and a chunk of the Reata set from *Giant*.

Of her attraction to Dean, Diane Hanville eloquently theorizes: "It has a lot to do with courage. To go for your dreams. Courage to do what you know is for you. And integrity. All sorts of things like that. When I read my diaries from when I was in high school, I kept talking about *needing*, wanting somebody to talk to, somebody who'd understand me. And he [Jimmy] came across in his movies as being that same kind of teenager. I've gone for years when I hardly looked at my collection, but then something will happen, something will click again, and I'll look at my pictures again, or look at the movies again. . . ."

HARDING MILITARY ACADEMY
Circa 1950–1951 Jimmy worked for a brief time as a camp counselor at the Harding Military Academy in Glendora, California.

PAT HARDY
Actress who co-starred in "The Unlighted Road," a 1955 episode of the CBS

television program "Schlitz Playhouse of Stars" that starred James Dean in his last television drama. Pat Hardy also dated Jimmy and, coincidentally, Vic Damone before his marriage to Pier Angeli.

JULIE HARRIS

With the possible exception of Geraldine Page, Julie Harris was unquestionably the finest actress to work opposite James Dean. *East of Eden* was *dominated* by the Dean image and presence, and it was reviewed accordingly upon its release in 1955. However, repeated viewing shows that Harris matches the brilliance executed by Dean and provides *Eden* with its emotional fulcrum. As Abra, she had the unenviable and difficult task of switching her affections from one brother to another without betraying the character's essential salubriousness. Further, she accomplished what would have been impossible for a lesser actress: she overcame a bad haircut (those bangs were *atrocious*).

During the course of shooting *Eden* James Dean and Julie Harris developed a mutual affinity of the brother and sister variety. Both were Actors Studio actors, stage actors, relatively unfamiliar with big-screen filmmaking. Yet Harris was secure and solid, at least outwardly so, and particularly nurturing to her young co-star. According to Elia Kazan, the film's director:

> The great one in that picture, the one who helped it come through behind the scenes, was Julie Harris, because she was so kind and tolerant to Dean. He was difficult and I had to be rough with him several times. But she was very kind to him and she supported him.

> I doubt that Jimmy would have ever got through *East of Eden* except for an angel on our set. Her name was Julie Harris.

The stage career of Julie Harris has been a phenomenal one, so much so that someone should start referring to her (and soon) as "The First Lady of the American Theater." Harris has won Tony awards as Best Actress for *I Am a Camera* (1952), *The Lark* (1956), *Forty Carats* (1969), *The Last of Mrs. Lincoln* (1973), and *The Belle of Amherst* (1977); she has received additional Tony nominations as Best Actress for *Marathon 33* (1964), *Skyscraper* (1966), and *The Au Pair Man* (1974).

She has also had a tremendous career on television. Her credits include "Little Moon of Alban," a presentation of the "Hallmark Hall of Fame" (Best Actress Emmy winner, 1958–1959), "Victoria Regina," another presentation of "Hallmark Hall of Fame" (another Best Actress Emmy winner, 1961–1962), "Thicker Than Water," a comedy series (1973), "The Family Holvak," a drama series (1975–1977), "Backstairs at the White House," a miniseries (1979), and "Knots Landing," a drama series (1981–1987).

Interestingly, despite a truly prodigious start, Julie Harris has had the least amount of success in motion pictures. She has appeared in the films *The Member of the Wedding* (Best Actress Oscar nomination, 1952), *I Am a Camera* (1955), *The Truth About Women* (1957), *Requiem for a Heavyweight* (1962), *The Haunting* (1963), *You're a Big Boy Now* (one of Francis Ford

Coppola's earliest films, 1966), *Reflections in a Golden Eye* (1967), *The People Next Door* (1970), *The Hiding Place* (1975), *Voyage of the Damned* (1976), *The Bell Jar* (1979), and *Gorillas in the Mist* (1988).

Harris, born in 1925, was interviewed in the Italian documentary *Hollywood: The Rebel James Dean* and the 1988 cable documentary "Forever James Dean." Of her famous former co-star, Julie Harris has said: "He was a very brilliant actor and a luminous young man. I can still see him, learning to play Bach on his recorder, looking like an angel on earth."

SUSAN HARRIS
Appeared in the September 11, 1953, episode of the NBC television program "The Big Story" that starred James Dean.

MARY HART
Leggy television hostess of the 1985 "Entertainment Tonight" James Dean tribute, "The Legend That Won't Die." Hart, who occasionally moonlights as a song and dance performer, has been hosting "Entertainment Tonight" since 1982.

HARTFORD, CONNECTICUT
James Dean visited Hartford, Connecticut, for the November 13–15, 1952, pre-Broadway tryout of *See the Jaguar*.

"HARVEST"
Thanksgiving episode of the NBC television series "Robert Montgomery Presents the Johnson's Wax Program." "Harvest" aired on November 23, 1953, and starred Ed Begley, Dorothy Gish, Vaughn Taylor, and James Dean. Also featured in the cast were Reba Tassell, John Connell, John Dennis, Joseph Foley, and Nancy Sheridan. "Harvest" was produced by Robert Montgomery, directed by James Sheldon, and written by Sandra Michael.

Jimmy portrayed Paul Zalenka, a farm boy who is jilted in love and so enlists, to the chagrin of his farmer father, in the navy. Uncharacteristic of his behavior on other television programs, Jimmy was pleasant to work with during the making of "Harvest." Recalled director James Sheldon: "On 'Harvest' he was lovely. He and Dorothy Gish got on very well. And Begley was good with him. And the girl, Reba Tassell, she and Jimmy got along very well."

XEN HARVEY
Fairmount, Indiana, pastor who read the eulogy and co-conducted the services at the October 8, 1955, funeral of James Dean.

HAS ANYBODY SEEN MY GAL?
Giant was not the only movie in which both Rock Hudson and James Dean appeared. During his struggling actor period in Hollywood Jimmy was cast in a bit part in *Has Anybody Seen My Gal?*, released in 1952. The film starred

Every little *bit* counts. That's Jimmy Dean (right), hamming it up on the set of *Has Anybody Seen My Gal?*

Charles Coburn, Piper Laurie, and Rock Hudson. The film was produced by Ted Richmond for Universal Pictures, directed by Douglas Sirk, and written by Joseph Hoffman. The plot revolved around a multimillionaire (Coburn) who feigns poverty to test the character of his distant relatives.

It was in *Has Anybody Seen My Gal?* that James Dean delivered his first line of movie dialogue that actually made it onto the screen. The line, hardly a profound introduction, was a little heavy on the sugar:

> Hey, Gramps, I'll have a choc malt, heavy on the choc, plenty of milk, four spoons of malt, two scoops of vanilla ice cream, one mixed with the rest and one floating.

HATS
The James Dean line of hats is marketed by Stetson, a New York–based company.

JEFFREY HAYDEN
Director of "Run Like a Thief," a 1954 episode of the NBC television series "Philco TV Playhouse" that co-starred James Dean. Hayden also directed episodes of "Omnibus," "Mannix," and "Ironside."

TERESE HAYDEN
During the summer of 1953 Terese Hayden produced four plays that ran consecutively at the Theatre De Lys in Greenwich Village. One of the plays was *The Scarecrow*, in which James Dean had a small part.

BILL HAYES
Recorded the song "Message from James Dean" for Cadence Records.

ROBERT HEADRICK, JR.
Bob Headrick is generally regarded as an expert on James Dean memorabilia. He has written numerous articles on the subject, has a book scheduled for publication in 1991, and has even taught a James Dean course at the University of Missouri.

THE HEARST CORPORATION
The Hearst Corporation donated the Cholame, California, land for the James Dean Memorial, which was erected in 1977. The memorial is located half a mile from the site of the accident in which Jimmy was killed.

"HEARTBREAK LOVE"
Music video by Johnny Rivers that re-created scenes from *Rebel Without a Cause*, employing James Dean and Natalie Wood look-alikes.

MARTA HEFLIN
Actress who was featured in *Come Back to the Five and Dime, Jimmy Dean, Jimmy Dean*, a 1982 Broadway play and subsequent film.

HEIGHT
> He was short. Self-consciously short. You know, in those days, movie stars were tall. But Jimmy acted with his whole body, you know? I mean, he just wasn't reading. So you weren't aware of his little size. Because he was big, you know? He was big.
>
> James Sheldon

No matter how you size it up, for a fully grown male, five feet, eight inches is short. *Off screen*, James Dean was short. People meeting Dean for the first time were always startled by his lack of stature because on screen he loomed so large.

Jimmy was, of course, self-conscious about his height, particularly in Hollywood, which generally judges primarily by shape and size. So he slouched, making his actual height hard to gauge, and he exaggerated his measurements by a couple of inches. According to his driver's license, James Dean was five feet, ten inches tall; his studio biography made the same claim; according to the measuring tape, however, he was five feet, eight inches. At best.

If he didn't lie about his height, he evaded the subject. To one curious reporter he quipped, "My feet just touch the ground. Abe Lincoln said that, too."

RAY HEINDORF

Backed by the Warner Brothers Orchestra, Ray Heindorf recorded the Columbia Records album *A Tribute to James Dean*. Heindorf also conducted (but did not compose) the scoring of *East of Eden*, *Rebel Without a Cause*, and *Giant*.

Heindorf (1908–1980) was the composer, arranger, conductor, and/or musical director of many movies, including *Yankee Doodle Dandy* (Best Musical Scoring Oscar, 1942), *This Is the Army* (Best Musical Scoring Oscar, 1943), *A Streetcar Named Desire* (1951), *A Star Is Born* (1954), *Pete Kelly's Blues* (1955), *Damn Yankees* (1958), and *The Music Man* (Best Adapted Musical Scoring Oscar, 1962).

JOHN HELDABRAND

John Heldabrand co-starred as Dr. Robert in the 1954 Broadway play *The Immoralist*.

Just prior to his work in *The Immoralist*, Heldabrand completed a role in the movie *On the Waterfront*, directed by Elia Kazan. His other film credits include *The Wrong Man* (1957).

FRANKLIN HELLER

Producer of "Sleeping Dogs," a 1952 episode of the CBS television program "The Web" in which James Dean appeared. Franklin Heller later hired Jimmy for his production of "Death Is My Neighbor," a 1953 episode of the CBS series "Danger."

ERNEST HEMINGWAY

At the time of his death James Dean was signed to appear in a television drama based on Ernest Hemingway's story "The Battler." Jimmy was to have portrayed the Hemingway-based character, Nick Adams.

Ernest Hemingway, the macho man of major American literature, and the figure whom Marilyn Monroe once dismissed as being too impressed with power, was born in 1899. His books, for which he won both Pulitzer and Nobel prizes, include *The Sun Also Rises*, *A Farewell to Arms*, *For Whom the Bell Tolls*, and *The Old Man and the Sea*. He died in 1961.

BILL HENDRICKS

Bill Hendricks was the director of publicity at Warner Brothers during James Dean's tenure there.

DON HENLEY

Singer/songwriter who co-wrote the song "James Dean" recorded by the Eagles in 1974.

TOM HENNESY

Tom Hennesy was the child welfare worker from the Los Angeles Board of Education who chaperoned minors Natalie Wood and Sal Mineo during the making of *Rebel Without a Cause*. It was Hennesy's job to see that Natalie and Sal were fed, schooled, and tucked into bed—on time and not at the discretion of Nick Ray and the Warner Brothers front office. While *Rebel* was in production, Hennesy and James Dean became friendly, and during a weekend break from shooting the two went to Catalina Island, where Hennesy taught Dean to skin-dive.

"HERE IS THE REAL STORY OF MY LIFE BY JAMES DEAN, AS I MIGHT HAVE TOLD IT TO JOE ARCHER"

Fictionalized article about James Dean, written in 1956 by Joe Archer and on file at the Marion, Indiana, Public Library.

VENABLE HERNDON

Author of the excellent biography *James Dean: A Short Life*, published by Doubleday in 1974.

Venable Herndon, born in 1927 and educated at Princeton and Harvard universities, has written several off-Broadway plays including *Until the Monkey Comes*, and several screen plays including *Alice's Restaurant* (shared credit, 1969).

Herndon was interviewed in the Italian documentary *Hollywood: The Rebel James Dean.*

BILL HICKMAN

"I'm sure I was his closest friend out here [Los Angeles], but I never really knew him that well. Sometimes I think I didn't know him at all. We had a running joke: He'd call me 'Big Bastard' and I'd call him 'Little Bastard.' I never stop thinking about those memories."
Bill Hickman, *Los Angeles Times*, July 22, 1973

On September 30, 1955, James Dean, his mechanic, and two of his friends, Sandy Roth and Bill Hickman, journeyed from Hollywood to Salinas. They took two cars—Jimmy and his mechanic in the Porsche, Roth and Hickman trailing behind in Jimmy's station wagon.

At the time Bill Hickman was 35 years old, over 10 years older than his young friend. Still, it is easy to understand their camaraderie. In addition to being an actor and stunt man Bill Hickman, like Dean, was a car enthusiast.

A few minutes after the crash Roth and Hickman arrived at the site. According to some reports it was Hickman who pulled Jimmy's body from the wreckage. He cradled Jimmy's head in his arms until the paramedics arrived. From there he went to the local hospital and then, the next day, to the funeral home.

In later years Bill Hickman developed a highly regarded reputation as the stunt driver in such famed action films as *Bullitt* (1968) and *The French Connection* (1971).

Nearly 20 years after it occurred, Bill Hickman recounted that fateful 1955 journey to Salinas to a reporter from the *Los Angeles Times*:

"We had just stopped for a Coke at a roadside stand. Jimmy took off, doing about 70. We were trying to get to Salinas by evening to get rested for a race he was entered in the next day. All I remember is an explosion and a great cloud of smoke and dust. He had collided at an intersection with another car.

"When I first got to him, I thought he was alive, because there seemed to be air coming from his nostrils; they told me later he had died instantly. His forehead was caved in and so was his chest."

MICHAEL HIGGINS

Actor who appeared in "Keep Our Honor Bright," a 1953 episode of the NBC television program "Kraft Television Theatre" in which James Dean co-starred.

Higgins also appeared on television in the nighttime soap opera "One Man's Family" (1949–1951) and in films including *The Arrangement* (1969) and *The Conversation* (1974).

GEORGE ROY HILL

Before he became the famous director of such films as *The World of Henry Orient* (1964), *Butch Cassidy and the Sundance Kid* (Best Director Oscar nomination, 1969), *The Sting* (Best Director Oscar winner, 1973), and *The World According to Garp* (1982), George Roy Hill was a television director and a sometime television actor and writer. In 1953 Hill wrote and appeared in "Keep Our Honor Bright," an episode of the NBC television program "Kraft Television Theatre" in which James Dean co-starred.

In addition to directing segments of "Kraft Television Theatre," George Roy Hill, born in 1921, directed episodes of "Playhouse 90" and "Studio One." He also directed plays on Broadway, including *Look Homeward, Angel*, for which he was nominated for a 1958 Tony award.

"HILL NUMBER ONE"

"Hill Number One" was a one-hour Easter television special presented on the religious program "Family Theatre" on March 25, 1951 (not April 1, 1951, as reported elsewhere). The program was produced by Father Patrick Peyton. Jerry Fairbanks was the executive producer. It was directed by Arthur Pierson and starred Ruth Hussey, Joan Leslie, Gene Lockhart, Jeanne Cagney, Leif Erickson, Regis Toomey, Henry Brandon, Nelson Leigh, Gordon Oliver, Roddy McDowall, Frank Wilcox, Everett Glass, Charles Meredith, and Michael Ansara.

Excluding an earlier commercial, it was in "Hill Number One" that James Dean made his television debut. He had a small role as John the Apostle. The plot revolved around an analogy between the events leading to the crucifixion and resurrection of Christ and a group of GIs fighting to recapture a hill in the Korean War. Dean had inane lines, which he delivered melodramatically; for example, "Rejoice! He has risen as He promised!"

PAT HINGLE
Actor who appeared in the 1953 Actors Studio production of *End as a Man* in which James Dean also appeared.

Pat Hingle's credits include, on stage: *The Dark at the Top of the Stairs* (Best Supporting Actor Tony nomination, 1958); on television: "Stone" (unsuccessful police series, 1980); and in films: *On the Waterfront* (1954), *The Strange One* (1957), *Splendor in the Grass* (1961), *The Ugly American* (1963), and *Norma Rae* (1979).

BOB HINKLE
"People said he was kind of stand-offish, so I stayed away from him. I thought, 'He's awful small to be playing a big mean Texan,' but he came to me and he was super nice—a completely different guy than he was around the press. He'd just cuss 'em out and he wouldn't give them the time of day. But to the ranchers and the people around there he was just as nice as he could be. Dean came to me and said, 'Bob, I want to be a Texan twenty-four hours a day. I'd like for you to work with me. I'll even pay you out of my pocket.' So I got him some clothes and boots and he starts talking like a Texan every day."

Bob Hinkle

When director George Stevens first approached Bob Hinkle, Hinkle hoped it was to cast him as Jett Rink in *Giant*. But, as Hinkle told a newspaper reporter, "The first thing he said was, 'Do you think you could teach Rock Hudson to talk like you do?' From that point on he hired me to teach his actors how to talk and act like Texans." For his new job as dialogue coach Hinkle audio-recorded all of the major roles in the film, with the exception of Elizabeth Taylor's (whose character was from the East Coast). The actors, including Dean, then listened to the recordings to perfect their Texan accents.

Bob Hinkle is a former cowboy from Brownfield, Texas. In the early 1950s he became a cowboy for hire on television. After *Giant*, Hinkle had a new profession as a dialogue coach to movie stars. His other films include *The Alamo* (1960) and *Hud* (for which he coached Paul Newman, 1963). As an actor, Hinkle appeared in the film *Stalag 17* (1953) and on television in the first episode of "Gunsmoke" (1955).

On the set of *Giant* in Texas, Hinkle and Dean became friendly. During evening breaks they occasionally went out on rabbit-hunting expeditions. During the day they passed time by executing rope tricks. After Jimmy's death Hinkle told his story to the one-shot magazine, *The Real James Dean*. The article was titled "My Friend, Jimmy."

J. ALBERT HIRSCH
Telewriter of "The Foggy, Foggy Dew," a 1952 episode of the CBS television program "Lux Video Theatre" that co-starred James Dean.

HOBBIES: THE DEAN LIST
Bullfighting (spectator and simulated)
Car racing
Dancing
Drawing
Gardening
Listening to and collecting records
Painting

Photography
Playing the bongo drums
Playing the recorder
Reading
Sculpting
Writing poetry

MAURY HOLLAND
Producer and director of "Keep Our Honor Bright," a 1953 episode of the NBC television program "Kraft Television Theatre" that co-starred James Dean. Holland was one of the regular producer/directors of "Kraft Television Theatre."

JEAN HOLLANDER
One of the producers of the television game show "Beat the Clock" (1950–1958), on which James Dean was employed.

HOLLYWOOD
> "Don't get me wrong. I'm not one of the wise ones who try to put Hollywood down. It just happens that I fit to cadence and pace better here [in New York] as far as living goes. New York is vital, and above all, fertile. They're a little harder to find, maybe, but out there in Hollywood, behind all that brick and mortar, there are human beings just as sensitive to fertility. The problem for this cat, myself, is not to get lost."
>
> James Dean, *New York Times*, March 13, 1955

Contrary to what he told the press, James Dean *was* one of the wise ones to put down Hollywood, which he regarded with equal measures of bitterness and disdain. Part of it, of course, was contrived. After all, Hollywood is a town that is contemptuous of itself. It is common practice in Hollywood to neglect its own and import on-screen talent from the New York stages and off-screen talent (executives, producers, writers, etc.) from Ivy League schools. It is also quite fashionable to bask poolside in the southern California sun while bemoaning the imagined superiority of the East Coast. The more one berates Hollywood, it seems, the more one is accepted in Hollywood. Perhaps it is just a variation on the concept of not wanting to belong to a club of which one is a member. Whatever it is, it's a silly game, but it goes with the territory, and James Dean had certainly learned the lesson well.

But part of the bitterness that James Dean felt for Hollywood, which he practically plastered across a billboard overlooking Sunset Boulevard, was sincere. At the fragile and impressionable age of 19, and for the next two years, Jimmy Dean pounded the proverbial Hollywood pavement, knocking on doors by day, going home to a shabby apartment and bandaging his wounds by night. It was *then* that he needed Hollywood's attention and

acceptance, but Hollywood not only rejected him, it barely noticed him. And so, like a boxer cornered in the ropes but not yet beaten, he changed tactics. He charmed and cajoled and allegedly little-boyed his way in and out of the bedsheets of the rich and well connected—all for a few free meals and the promise of a possible job—with his eyes wide open and one hand, fingers crossed, behind his back. But, for the most part, Hollywood ate him up and spit him out and dragged his remains across the Hollywood Walk of Fame.

He didn't, after all, *look* like a movie star. He was too short, too skinny, and too rumpled. Rock Hudson could walk into a room, flash one of those ear-to-ear smiles, turn on the voltage, and look like a movie star. James Dean didn't have voltage. Even later, after stardom, he didn't have voltage the way Rock Hudson or Marilyn Monroe had voltage. What he did have was energy, raw energy that he recycled into explosive, honest outbursts of emotion, the likes of which Hollywood had never before seen.

So, when Hollywood went to New York in search of Steinbeck's Cal Trask of *East of Eden* and beckoned in his direction, James Dean acquiesced, but he did so on his own terms. He was determined to demonstrate, in as flagrant a manner as possible, just how much he no longer needed Hollywood, that he had never really needed Hollywood, that all he had ever needed was himself and his art. Like the boxer, he had learned when to duck and when to jab and how not to end up sprawled out on the canvas. As Carroll Baker said he instructed her upon her arrival in Hollywood: "You've got to treat these guys like shit. It's the only thing they understand."

Today, more than 35 years after his death, James Dean is figuratively alive and well on Hollywood Boulevard, where his brooding image looms larger than life on nearly every street corner. In fact, with the exception of Marilyn Monroe, Dean appears to be the most revered star in the history of the movies. Amazing when one considers that he starred in only three movies, the first of which was released only six months before his death. Amazing when one considers that for two years the same James Dean walked the same streets of Hollywood trying to make an impression on all that brick and mortar, and barely managed to scrape up train fare out of town.

"HOLLYWOOD CLOSE-UP"
Entertainment/information television series that aired a half-hour tribute, "James Dean: An American Original," on September 30, 1983. The segment was produced by Arthur Drooker, directed by Craig Haffner, and narrated by Ernie Anderson. It included interviews with James Whitmore, Martin Landau, Ursula Andress, Bill Bast, and others.

HOLLYWOOD FOREIGN PRESS ASSOCIATION
See THE GOLDEN GLOBE AWARDS.

HOLLYWOOD RANCH MARKET
There has been speculation over the years that Jimmy had his last lunch at

the Hollywood Ranch Market on September 30, 1955. Located at 1248 Vine Street, the building that housed Hollywood Ranch Market was razed in 1982. *See* FARMER'S MARKET.

THE HOLLYWOOD REPORTER
Entertainment trade paper that has published innumerable items and several articles about James Dean. The articles include:

☆ March 1, 1956   "Princeton Honors Dean"
☆ August 9, 1968   "Some Unsentimental Memories of James Dean"
☆ February 11, 1986   "Museum Showing Dean's Work"

THE HOLLYWOOD STAR
Hollywood gossip paper published by Bill Dakota. Among its most infamous articles were "150 Bisexual Stars of Hollywood," a list that included James Dean, and "I Had Sex with James Dean" by John Gilmore. The final issue of *The Hollywood Star* featured the 1981 drowning death of Natalie Wood and the alleged cover-up that followed.

HOLLYWOOD STUDIO MAGAZINE
Hollywood fan publication, now known as *Hollywood Then & Now*, that has published several articles about James Dean, including:

☆ May 1982   "James Dean Tribute"
☆ August 1982   "James Dean, The Rebel Who Wouldn't Die"
☆ December 1985   "Jon-Erik Hexum: Another James Dean?"
☆ September 1986   "Sal Mineo and James Dean: Their Secret Friendship"
☆ March 1989   "The James Dean Dedication"

HOLLYWOOD: THE REBEL JAMES DEAN
Excellent Italian documentary written and directed by Claudio Masenza and produced by Donatella Baglivo. Those interviewed include Martin Landau, Venable Herndon, Ortense Winslow, Adeline Nall, Bill Bast, Dizzy Sheridan, Christine White, Ruth Goetz, Bill Gunn, Roy Schatt, Julie Harris, Leonard Rosenman, Stewart Stern, Dennis Hopper, Bob Thomas, Beulah Roth, and Corey Allen.

THE HOLLYWOOD WALK OF FAME
James Dean's star is located at 1717 Vine Street in Hollywood.

HOMES
He lived in many places, but the only real home that James Dean ever had was the one provided by the Winslow family outside of Fairmount, Indiana. It was there that he lived from 1940 to 1949 and where he returned thereafter for consolation and rejuvenation. Jimmy's apartment on West 68th Street in New York City had some semblance of home, but it was more of a cubbyhole or a locker than a home. Ironically, it was not until he rented his final home,

The Winslow farm home in which Jimmy was raised.

a log-cabin-like structure in Sherman Oaks, California, that he showed any penchant for settling down in domesticity. But he had barely unpacked his belongings before he was dead.

One of the most fascinating challenges in compiling the following chronology was to investigate, and sometimes disprove, previously published and sometimes erroneous information. Another interesting aspect was listening to the many individuals who contend, adamantly and with pride, that they presently live in a house in which James Dean once resided. At times it was difficult to discern what was fact and what was fabrication, because if these people are to be believed, then James Dean lived in a dozen different homes at the same time and with a different group of roommates at each home. It seems that any home in Hollywood that James Dean *set foot in*, he also resided in. It would be interesting to learn just how many homes have been sold by savvy real estate agents at least partly on the basis that James Dean had been a resident.

The following, then, is a chronological list, as well as can be determined, of James Dean's homes.

19 West 68th Street.
Jimmy's apartment
was on the fifth floor.

The Homes That James Dean Lived In

1.	320 E. Fourth St.	Marion, IN	1931
2.	1001 Wheeling Pike	Jonesboro, IN	1932
3.	414 W. First St.	Fairmount, IN	1932
4.	322 E. Washington St.	Fairmount, IN	1933–1934
5.	3750 S. Adams St.	Marion, IN	1935–1936
6.	1422 23rd St.	Santa Monica, CA	1936–July 1940
7.	7184 S. 150 E (the Winslow farmstead)	Jonesboro, IN	July 1940–June 1949
8.	814-B Sixth St.	Santa Monica, CA	June 1949–Sept. 1950
9.	601 Gayley Ave.	Westwood, CA	Sept. 1950–early 1951
10.	Comstock Avenue apt. with Bill Bast	Westwood, CA	early 1951–late summer 1951
11.	Gower Plaza Hotel, 1607 N. Gower St.	Hollywood, CA	Sept. 1951
12.	Ted Avery's apt.	Hollywood, CA	Sept. 1951
13.	Rogers Brackett's Sunset Plaza Drive Home	West Hollywood, CA	Sept. 1951–Oct. 1951
14.	Iroquois Hotel, 49 W. 44th St.	New York City	Oct. 1951–early 1952

15. YMCA, 5 W. 63rd St.	New York City	early 1952–March 1952
16. Rogers Brackett's apt. on W. 38th St.	New York City	March 1952–May 1952
17. Iroquois Hotel, 49 W. 44th St., Room #82, with Bill Bast	New York City	May 1952–Sept. 1952
18. W. 46th St. apt. with Bast, Dizzy Sheridan, others	New York City	Sept. 1952–Oct. 1952
19. 13 W. 89th St. apt. with Bast, Sheridan, others	New York City	Oct. 1952–Dec. 1952
20. Iroquois Hotel, 49 W. 44th St.	New York City	Dec. 1952–early 1953
21. W. 56th St. apt.	New York City	early 1953–spring 1953
22. 19 W. 68th St., fifth-floor apt.*	New York City	spring 1953–9/30/55
23. 1667 S. Bundy Dr. (Winton Dean's home)	Sawtelle, CA	April 1954–May 1954
24. 3908 W. Olive Ave., Apt. 3	Burbank, CA	May 1954–July 1954
25. 4000 W. Olive Ave. (Warner Brothers dressing room)	Burbank, CA	July 1954–Aug. 1954
26. 1541 Sunset Plaza Dr.	West Hollywood, CA	Jan. 1955–July 1955
27. the Jackson residence (rented house)	Marfa, TX	June 1955–July 1955
28. 14611 Sutton St. (rented house)	Sherman Oaks, CA	July 1955–9/30/55

*Since 1973, Russell Aaronson, a waiter/writer, has resided in this apartment. Occasionally, over the years, he has welcomed curious Dean fans into his home.

HOMOSEXUALITY

Ask almost any James Dean fan what the biggest misconception about him is, and the fan will mention without hesitation "that he was homosexual," which they insist he wasn't. And they're right. Dean didn't prefer to have sex with men; he preferred to have sex with whomever he was attracted to, man or woman. He was unequivocally bisexual, and to contend otherwise is to completely misunderstand James Dean and diminish his appeal. The point is not necessarily that he was bisexual but rather that he insisted on a life without limitations, without boundaries, and without prejudice. If he saw a wall, he knocked it down just to see what was on the other side. He was *not* a rebel in the sense that he held up liquor stores and terrorized neighbors; he was a rebel in the sense that he refused to conform to what society propagated as acceptable behavior. And *that* is what made him "cool," if he was, the cool of being true to himself—in and out of bed.

> [Bill] Bast won't say that [Dean] was gay, but he will say that Dean was definitely bisexual. He will go even further and say that he believes that Dean was basically heterosexually oriented [but] "he dabbled in everything."
>
> *The Advocate*, 1976

> Jimmy gay? Or bisexual? Well, maybe. His nuttiness and constant attempts at breaking from the humdrum could have led him into it.
> Roy Schatt, *James Dean: A Portrait*

Toward dawn, one of Jimmy's [gay] lovers put him "up against the wall" about his sexual identity and demanded that he "come out" once and for all and stop pretending to be sexually interested in women, except as his accuser put it scornfully, "for publicity purposes."

Venable Herndon, *James Dean: A Short Life*

Don't forget, in 1955 I had no idea. I didn't even know what a homosexual was. The world was a different place then. You didn't talk about stuff like that.

Beverly Long

"Well, I'm certainly not going through life with one hand tied behind my back."

James Dean on his sexuality

Growing up with homosexual inclinations (whatever their extent might be) in the ultra-conservative Quaker county of Fairmount, Indiana, would be particularly difficult for anyone, almost certain to inflict deep psychological scars and insecurities. It is ironic, and a bit sad, that an October 1980 edition of the *Fairmount News*, which paid tribute to Jimmy on the 25th anniversary of his death, also printed an editorial to its readers lambasting homosexuality. The article was headlined, incredibly, "Homo Power," and it read, in part:

The Justice Department is seeking from Congress legislation which would permit the immigration into the United States of admitted homosexuals. Worse, the department is winking at the present law which provides that any prospective entrant who admits being a homosexual must be barred from entering.

Thus the Carter Administration is playing politics on this front. In this connection, the recent Democratic Party platform included, for the first time, a plank on homo rights, signifying the growing political influence of homos in the United States.

DENNIS HOPPER

"I tried to get to know him. I started by saying 'hello.' No answer. He wouldn't talk to people on the set; he would be into himself, into his thing. He'd lock himself up into his dressing room. Finally, about halfway through the picture, in the chickie-run [scene], it was at night, and I grabbed him and literally threw him into a car and I said, 'Look, I really wanna be an actor, too. And I wanna know what you're doing, what your secret is.' "

Dennis Hopper, *James Dean: The First American Teenager*

Dennis Hopper is a graduate of the James Dean School of Acting. Intense, animated, and out of kilter, Hopper came to signify the late 1960s and early 1970s in much the same way that Dean represented the 1950s.

The making of *Rebel Without a Cause* was something of a revelation for Dennis Hopper, who portrayed Goon, one of the gang members in the film.

Barely 20, Hopper was being groomed for stardom by Warner Brothers at the time. Talented, good-looking in a fresh kind of way, and cocky-confident in a way only the young can be, Hopper was without peer—or so he thought. Suddenly he was confronted, *smash*, by another young actor who was obviously his acting superior. To his credit Hopper recovered quickly enough to study the other actor, James Dean, his methods and his motivations, and they developed a friendship built on something resembling hero worship and the priority of their art.

Like all growing experiences, it was a difficult one for Dennis Hopper, compounded by his increasingly strained relationship with Nick Ray, the film's director. Apparently, during the making of the picture, Hopper had fallen in love with Natalie Wood, who was seeing Ray. Then, on one particularly unfortunate night, Hopper entered Ray's bungalow at the Chateau Marmont unannounced and walked in on them in flagrante delicto. Steffi Sidney, another one of the film's gang members, recalled: "I had more of a crush on Dennis Hopper than on anybody else. He was a sweet, innocent kid. We were very friendly. He used me as a confidante. He told me about being in love with Natalie and what was he going to do [because] Nick hated him."

After *Rebel* Dennis Hopper was again slated in a picture with Dean. It was *Giant*, and it was Hopper's first important film role. Steffi Sidney continues: "Then he was going off to do *Giant*, which was a big thing for him, and he was really scared. I remember toward the end of the film Dennis came up to me and said, 'You know, I have this scene that I have to play in *Giant*, and I just don't know what to do. I'm just not a violent person. I don't know how to do it.' And I said, 'What's that?' And so he told me about the scene in which he comes in and smashes the mirror because they won't seat his wife. Anyway, he said, 'I just don't know how to do that.' I said, 'Well, just think of Nick Ray.' And he said, 'You're right!' "

(Note: Later in the film Hopper's character, Jordy Benedict, and Dean's character, Jett Rink, have a push-shove fight. After the scene was shot, the Hollywood columnists reported almost gleefully that Dennis Hopper was recovering from injuries sustained in a fight with James Dean.)

Despite having to overcome the scorn of Nick Ray on *Rebel* and a *wicked*, copper-colored hair dye on *Giant*, Dennis Hopper, born in 1935, has had an impressive, if sporadic, film career. He has also achieved one of the goals that James Dean most wanted to achieve: he became a director of note. He did not, however, fulfill Warner Brothers' hopes by becoming "the next James Dean."

The career of Dennis Hopper has included the films *I Died a Thousand Times* (1955), *The Story of Mankind* (1957), *Key Witness* (1960), *Night Tide* (1963), *The Sons of Katie Elder* (1965), *The Trip* (1967), *Cool Hand Luke* (1967), *Easy Rider* (which he also directed and co-wrote, Best Original Screenplay Oscar nomination, 1969), *The Last Movie* (which he also directed and wrote, 1971), *Kid Blue* (which he also directed, 1973), *Mad Dog Morgan*

Rebel gang members Steffi Sidney and Dennis Hopper. When James Dean temporarily backed out of *Rebel*, Hopper was the front-runner for the role of Jim Stark. After Dean's death Hopper was considered for *The Left-Handed Gun* and "The Battler."

(Australia, 1976), *The American Friend* (1977), *Tracks* (1977), *Apocalypse Now* (1979), *Out of the Blue*, (which he also directed, 1982), *The Osterman Weekend* (1983), *Hoosiers* (Best Supporting Actor Oscar nomination, 1986), *Blue Velvet* (in which he donned a gas mask as a sexual stimulant, 1986), and *Flashback* (1990).

Hopper was interviewed in the Italian documentary *Hollywood: The Rebel James Dean*, the 1976 feature documentary *James Dean: The First American Teenager*, and the 1985 television tributes on "Entertainment Tonight" and "Show Biz Today."

HEDDA HOPPER

> After watching him in operation with Hedda Hopper, whom I knew
> he didn't like, I accused him of being a phony.
>
> Joe Hyams, *Mislaid in Hollywood*

In the days when hatted female columnists stalked the land of Hollywood and issued dicta from the keys of their typewriters, no hat stood taller than the one worn by Elda Furry, aka Hedda Hopper (1890–1966). Virtually every studio executive, producer, and actor in Hollywood courted Queen Hedda's favor by smooching her royal (and substantial) rump. And James Dean, high-minded though he was, was no different. Granted, however, he was more successful.

Initially Hopper couldn't stomach the newcomer named Dean. She had witnessed his rebellious antics one afternoon at the Warners commissary and later proceeded to rage in her column:

They've brought out from New York another dirty-shirt-tail actor. If this is the kind of talent they're importing, they can send it right back so far as I'm concerned.

To her credit it was not coercion that caused Hedda Hopper to change her opinion of James Dean; it was talent. As she later wrote in her autobiography, *The Whole Truth and Nothing But*:

> When an invitation came to see the preview of *East of Eden*, nobody could have dragged me there. But I heard the next day from Clifton Webb, whose judgment I respect. [He said] "last night I saw one of the most extraordinary performances of my life. You'll be crazy about this boy Jimmy Dean." "I've seen him," I said coldly.
>   In the projection room I sat spellbound. I couldn't remember ever having seen a young man with such power, so many facets of expression, so much sheer invention as this actor. I telephoned Jack Warner. "I'd like to see your Mr. Dean."
>   A day or so later he [Dean] rang my doorbell, spic and span in black pants and black leather jacket, though his hair was tousled and he wore a pair of heavy boots that a deep-sea diver wouldn't have sneezed at. . . .

That day James Dean went to war, unleashed his charm like a lethal weapon, and wrapped the usually stalwart and unflappable Hedda around his littlest finger. Later he told friends, "She's my friend in court." She was, after all, a part of the Hollywood game that had to be played. If the movie business is indeed a war, which it has often been compared to, then the charming of Hedda Hopper, for any young actor, was an act of self-defense, nothing more. Still, those acquainted with James Dean were unsettled by his uncharacteristic deference to, of all people, a Hollywood gossip mogul. Carroll Baker was one such curious spectator:

> Hedda Hopper entered [the restaurant] from the street door and Jimmy leaped up to greet her. She swept in with a flourish, her flowered chiffon dress and enormous picture hat fluttering in the crosscurrent of the warm outside breeze and the cold of the air conditioning. It was a dramatic entrance that deserved recognition, but for a moment I was afraid that Jimmy was going to throw himself on his knees in front of her.
>
> *Baby Doll* by Carroll Baker

In return for his devotion Hopper frequently promoted Dean in her nationally syndicated column. For years after his death Hedda Hopper, perhaps more than anyone, championed the memory of James Dean. She worked to promote his place in history and even campaigned for an Oscar to be presented in his behalf.

Prior to finding her niche as a columnist, Hedda Hopper worked in Hollywood as an actress. She also made a few postcolumnist screen appearances. Her films include *Virtuous Wives* (1919), *Don Juan* (1926), *Wings* (1927), *Alice Adams* (1935), *Topper* (1937), *The Women* (1939), *Sunset Boulevard* (1950), and *The Oscar* (1966).

WILLIAM HOPPER

William Hopper, born William Furry (1915–1969), was Hedda Hopper's son. He was also the actor who portrayed the stoical father of Natalie Wood's character in *Rebel Without a Cause.*

Hopper's other films include *Footloose Heiress* (1937), *The High and the Mighty* (1954), and *The Bad Seed* (1956). He is best known, however, as Paul Drake in the television series "Perry Mason" (1957–1965).

CLIFFORD HORD

Paso Robles, California, farmer who testified at the October 1955 inquest that, at 5:30 P.M. on September 30, shortly before the fatal accident, he had been driven off the highway by James Dean's speeding Porsche. Hord, who had been en route to Bakersfield on Highway 466, testified:

> HORD: Well, this car—I was going up the highway, and there was another car coming down, and this car pulled out up here, this little car—I was beyond that intersection here, about four hundred yards, and this car come down, and I was going up, and this car came up above and just come all the way across; he come clear off the road on the side and pushed me clear off. . . ."
>
> DISTRICT ATTORNEY: Could you estimate the speed of that car that came over on your side of the road?
>
> HORD: It was terrific. I'd say it was well over a hundred miles an hour or better. It was very terrific.

Obviously Clifford Hord's testimony that day was damaging to any case that the blame for the accident belonged not to Dean but to the other driver involved in the crash.

WILLIAM HORNBECK

Colonel William Hornbeck (1901–1983) was one of the editors of *Giant*, for which he received an Oscar nomination. Hornbeck had also cut *A Place in the Sun* (Best Editing Oscar, 1951) and *Shane* (1953) for director George Stevens.

His other films include *A Small Town Idol* (1921), *The Extra Girl* (1923), *It's a Wonderful Life* (Best Editing Oscar nomination, 1946), *The Heiress* (1949), and *I Want to Live!* (1958).

In 1977 a poll of 100 of his peers named Hornbeck the best editor in the film industry. He was also hailed by Frank Capra as "the greatest film editor in the history of motion pictures."

MARTIN HORRELL

Producer of "Something for an Empty Briefcase," a 1953 episode of the NBC television series "Campbell Soundstage" in which James Dean appeared.

HORSES

As odd as it may seem to some, James Dean was a horseman. In fact he had been riding since the age of six. Years later, with his first substantial paycheck from Warner Brothers, it was not a sports car Dean purchased but a thoroughbred Palomino he dubbed Cisco the Kid. Jimmy kept the horse in a stable in Santa Barbara, reportedly owned by the family of his friend Lew Bracker.

After Jimmy's death Cisco the Kid was appraised at $125 and sold for $130.

BARNEY HOSKYNS

Author of the book *James Dean: Shooting Star*, published in England by Bloomsbury Publishing in 1989 and in the United States by Doubleday in 1990.

THE HOTELS WHERE DEAN STAYED

Del Mar Motel and Apartments, Santa Barbara, California
Gower Plaza Hotel, Hollywood, California
Hargrave Hotel, New York City
Iroquois Hotel, New York City
The Knickerbocker Hotel, Hollywood, California
Little River Inn, Mendocino, California
*El Paisano Hotel, Marfa, Texas
Royalton Hotel, New York City
St. James Hotel, Philadelphia, Pennsylvania

*Although Jimmy didn't stay there, El Paisano served as the location headquarters for the *Giant* company during the summer of 1955, and he spent a lot of time there.

HORACE HOUGH

One of the assistant directors on *East of Eden*.

"HOUND OF HEAVEN"

Episode of the daytime television program "The Kate Smith Show" that starred John Carradine, James Dean, Edgar Stehli, and a dog. The episode was written by Earl Hamner, Jr., and aired on January 15, 1953. Jimmy portrayed, of all things, an angel!

HOW MANY TIMES DID YOU SEE "EAST OF EDEN"?

Unproduced play written by James Bridges, inspired by James Dean, that was eventually adapted into Bridge's movie *September 30, 1955* (1977).

TREVOR HOWARD

After Dean's death his personally annotated copy of Ernest Hemingway's *Death in the Afternoon* was reportedly (and mysteriously) obtained by British actor Trevor Howard.

JOHN HOWLETT

Author of the book *James Dean: A Biography*, which was published in Great

Britain by Plexus Publishing, Ltd., in 1975. Howlett also scripted the 1977 London stage musical *Dean*.

GUSTI HUBER

Co-star of "Run Like a Thief," a 1954 episode of the NBC television program "Philco TV Playhouse" in which James Dean also co-starred.

Huber also appeared in the film *The Diary of Anne Frank* (1959).

PAUL HUBER

Paul Huber portrayed Dr. Garrin in *The Immoralist*, the 1954 stage play that co-starred James Dean.

Prior to *The Immoralist* Huber had been appearing on Broadway since 1920 in such plays as *Johnny Belinda* and *Point of No Return* (in which he portrayed Henry Fonda's father).

ROCHELLE HUDSON

Actress who portrayed the mother of Natalie Wood's character in *Rebel Without a Cause*.

Hudson (1914–1972) appeared in several films including *Imitation of Life* (1934), *Curly Top* (1935), *Meet Boston Blackie* (1941), and *Strait-Jacket* (1964). On television she co-starred in the series "That's My Boy" (1954–1959).

ROCK HUDSON

Rock Hudson personified everything that James Dean did not like in an actor: too handsome, too toothy, and too tall. Moreover, he wasn't particularly talented, at least not in Dean's view. Hudson was a *movie star*, not an actor, and for Dean the gap between the two was unbridgeable.

The relationship started out promisingly, though, when Hudson visited Dean on the set of *Rebel Without a Cause*. Jimmy told Rock about the picture they had previously made together, *Has Anybody Seen My Gal?*, in which Hudson had a co-starring role and Jimmy a bit part. They shared a laugh or two—Hudson, a hearty, robust, outdoorsy kind of laugh, Jimmy, that twisted little giggle. And, according to witnesses, each demonstrated for the other his Texan accent for *Giant*.

With the start of *Giant*, however, the relationship almost immediately began to resemble the one they had in the film—adversarial, distant, openly contemptuous. On location in Marfa the two actors were cleverly confined as roommates by director George Stevens. Hudson even used to host parties at the house he shared with Dean and not invite him! Further intensifying the situation, on camera and off, both men competed for the attention of Elizabeth Taylor, whose violet eyes and flashing wit seemed to have enraptured the entire *Giant* company. And while Dean privately mocked what he considered to be Hudson's plastic, rigid performance, Hudson had no patience for Dean's elaborate scene preparations, scene stealing, and, in his view, Method acting pretensions. Years later Hudson bemoaned to a reporter for *The Hollywood Reporter*:

> "[Dean] never smiled. He was sulky, and he had no manners—I'll take them where I find them—but Dean didn't have them. And he was rough to do a scene with for reasons that only an actor can appreciate. While doing a scene, in the giving and taking, he was just taking. He would take everything out and never give back."

Dean also publicized in the press his dislike for Hudson. To Hedda Hopper, his "friend in court," he groused:

> "I sat there for three days, made up and ready to work at nine o'clock every morning. By six o'clock I hadn't had a scene or a rehearsal. I sat there like a bump on a log watching that big, lumpy Rock Hudson making love to Liz Taylor."

The animosity between Hudson and Dean extended beyond the latter's death. In February 1957 both actors were nominated for Oscars in the same category (neither won), but it was Dean who got the notices and the press attention.

Years later Hudson continued to harbor a grudge. James Sheldon, who directed both men in television, recently recalled, "Twenty-five years later [actually, 20], I'm working with Rock Hudson, directing 'McMillan and Wife,' and I—trying to make conversation with the star—said, 'I used to be a friend of Jimmy Dean's.' To which Rock said, 'That *prick*!' As I got to know Rock—I did the show on and off for three years—I said, 'Why was he a prick?' And Rock said, 'He was so rude, so unprofessional.'

"Now, Rock was not the great talent that Jimmy was, but he certainly was a professional. He was always prepared, always on time. In my own mind, putting it together, Jimmy walked in his own sphere. Jimmy was an intellectual, emotional, methody sort of a person. Rock was a straight, come in, do it, don't make a big scene sort."

Obviously there was no male bonding between Rock Hudson and James Dean; it was more like male bitching. Part of it probably stemmed from the insecurity of sharing star billing with another male, which neither of them had been accustomed to. Perhaps there was also some degree of underlying sexual tension between them. More likely, though, it was due at least in part to the sexual *recognition* each man must have perceived in the other and the anxiety that recognition generated. For despite its rather liberal makeup the movie industry is a homophobic, repressed community, and in 1955 it was even more so.

Rock Hudson, born Roy Scherer (and later, Roy Fitzgerald) in 1925, appeared in numerous films, including *Fighter Squadron* (1948), *Magnificent Obsession* (which made him a star, 1954), *Written on the Wind* (1956), *Pillow Talk* (1959), *Lover Come Back* (1961), *Man's Favorite Sport?* (1964), *Send Me No Flowers* (1964), *Seconds* (1966), *Ice Station Zebra* (1968), *Darling Lili* (1970), *Pretty Maids All in a Row* (1971), *The Mirror Crack'd* (reunited with

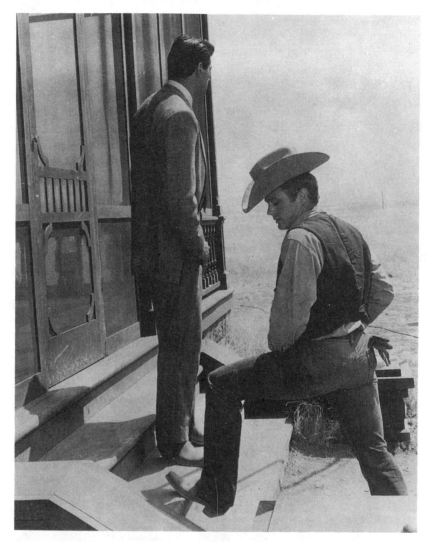

Rock Hudson and James Dean did not see eye to eye. Hudson's *Giant*
contract called for second billing, at least, to Elizabeth Taylor.

Elizabeth Taylor, England, 1980), and *The Ambassador* (1984). Hudson also
starred in the television programs "McMillan and Wife" (the title of which
was revised to "McMillan" in 1976, 1971–1977) and "The Devlin Connection" (1982). He also appeared in the hugely popular ABC series "Dynasty"
(which he privately referred to as "Die-Nasty," 1984–1985).

On October 2, 1985, after a career largely spent epitomizing the American male, Rock Hudson died from complications caused by AIDS. His death
provoked near-pandemonium and national awareness of his devastating
disease. Later, details of his sex life were publicized in court when his former
lover, Mark Christian, sued his estate (and won millions) for having not been
told that Hudson had contracted AIDS.

ED HUMMEL

Wrote the song "We'll Never Forget You," inspired by Dean, which was included on the Coral Records tribute album *The James Dean Story*.

JOSEPH HUMPHREYS

Author of the 1990 book *Jimmy Dean on Jimmy Dean*, published in Great Britain.

HUNT FUNERAL HOME

> "One day we walked into town, and I stopped by Wilbur Hunt's. Wilbur runs a kind of general store in Fairmount. He's also the town mortician, and in the back he's got a selection of caskets. 'Mind if we shoot some stuff in here?' I asked Wilbur. He's a wonderful guy. 'Help yourself,' he said. So we went into the back. There were these caskets. I got into one of them and lay down. 'Go ahead,' I said to Dennis. 'Start shooting.' He thought I was kidding, but I always wanted to see how I'd look in a casket."
>
> James Dean to writer Richard Moore, *Modern Screen*, August 1955

In February 1955 Jimmy startled photographer Dennis Stock by jumping into a coffin at the Hunt Funeral Home in Fairmount, Indiana, and demanding to be photographed. Several months later Jimmy made a return visit to the same funeral home—in a body bag.

On Tuesday, October 4, 1955, the body of James Dean was flown from Los Angeles to Indianapolis. Upon its arrival at 10:17 P.M. the body was met at the airport by a Hunt Funeral Home employee and carted via ambulance to the funeral home, where it remained until the funeral on Saturday, October 8.

MARSHA HUNT

It was Marsha Hunt, not Ann Doran, who was originally signed to portray the mother of James Dean's character in *Rebel Without a Cause*. She left the cast abruptly, for unspecified reasons. She was also one of the contenders for the role of Mrs. Lynnton in *Giant*.

Born in 1917, Marsha Hunt appeared in the films *Pride and Prejudice* (1940), *Blossoms in the Dust* (1941), *Blue Denim* (1959), and *Johnny Got His Gun* (1971). She also co-starred in the television series "Peck's Bad Girl" (1959–1960).

WILBUR HUNT

The owner of the Hunt Funeral Home and the mortician who handled James Dean's funeral arrangements. For his services Hunt was paid $415.

O. V. HUNTER

O. V. Hunter was the California highway patrolman who, at 3:30 P.M. on Friday, September 30, 1955, stopped and ticketed motorist James Dean for driving 65 mph instead of the allowed 55 mph. On the ticket he issued, Hunter misspelled Jimmy's name as James *Bryon* Dean. He also ticketed Sandy Roth and Bill Hickman, who were fast on Dean's trail.

TAB HUNTER

Actor who beat out James Dean for a role in Warner Brothers' production of Leon Uris's novel *Battle Cry* (1955). During the shooting of the picture Jimmy visited the set to see James Whitmore and met with Hunter, presumably to offer his congratulations. For his performance in the film Hunter won a 1955 Audience Awards Election poll as the most promising male movie newcomer. Later Hunter was up for two roles in *Giant*, Bob Dace and Jordy III, which went to Earl Holliman and Dennis Hopper respectively.

Tab Hunter, born Andrew Kelm in 1931, actually made his film debut in *The Lawless* (1950). Characterized primarily as a teen idol of the late 50s, early 60s, Hunter has appeared in films including *Damn Yankees* (1958), *The Life and Times of Judge Roy Bean* (1972), *Polyester* (1982), and *Grease II* (1982). He also starred in his own television show, "The Tab Hunter Show" (1960–1961) and later in "Mary Hartman, Mary Hartman" (1977–1978). In his career Hunter also had a number one hit record with "Young Love" in 1957.

When Jimmy temporarily backed out of *Rebel Without a Cause*, Tab Hunter was considered for the part.

RALPH S. HURST
Set decorator of *Giant*, for which he received an Oscar nomination.

RUTH HUSSEY
Star of "Hill Number One," a 1951 Easter television special in which James Dean made his dramatic debut on television. Also, like Marsha Hunt, Hussey was up for the part of Mrs. Lynnton in *Giant* (which eventually went to Judith Evelyn).

Hussey, born Ruth O'Rourke in 1914, appeared in many films including *The Women* (1939), *The Philadelphia Story* (Best Supporting Actress Oscar nomination, 1940), *The Great Gatsby* (1949), and *The Facts of Life* (1960).

BARBARA HUTTON
In *Poor Little Rich Girl*, his biography of Woolworth heiress Barbara Hutton (1912–1979), author C. David Heymann contends that James Dean met Hutton at Googie's coffee shop in West Hollywood and subsequently took her for a spin on the back of his motorcycle and then spent the night with her in her hotel room.

JOE HYAMS
Hollywood writer Joe Hyams was introduced to James Dean through a mutual friend, Lew Bracker. Hyams later wrote about his relationship with Jimmy in his 1973 book *Mislaid in Hollywood*. Hyams devoted an entire chapter to Jimmy ("James Dean: Rebel with a Cause").

> [*East of Eden*] was just another picture; after all, I saw dozens each month. But . . . [when] the film ended I was both drained and exhilarated. There was no doubt in my mind then that James Dean was going to be Hollywood's next big star.
>
> Joe Hyams, *Mislaid in Hollywood*

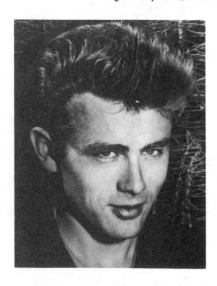

I

I, JAMES DEAN
Fictitious autobiography written by T. T. Thomas, published in paperback by Popular Library in 1957.

I REMEMBER THE DAY JAMES DEAN DIED
Book of short stories written by Albert Drake, published in 1983, that has absolutely *nothing* to do with James Dean.

ICE CREAM
Somehow the image of James Dean lapping up an ice cream cone is difficult to conjure and sustain. Nonetheless it was a common sight at Will Wright's ice cream parlor in West Hollywood. What was his favorite flavor? A combination of coffee and raspberry.

ILLNESSES
During the shooting of *East of Eden* Jimmy was stricken with a case of poison oak; during the shooting of *Rebel Without a Cause* he contracted malaria. In both cases he was laid up in bed, temporarily suspending the productions.

"I'M A FOOL"
Episode of the CBS television show "General Electric Theater" in which James Dean starred with Natalie Wood and Eddie Albert. "I'm a Fool" aired on November 14, 1954 (not December 17, 1954, as printed in previous reports), and was produced by Mort Abrahams, directed by Don Medford, and written by Arnold Schulman, from a story by Sherwood Anderson.

Dean made "I'm a Fool" in Hollywood, after he completed *East of Eden* but before its release. He portrayed a heartsick and foolish farm boy who assumes a false identity to impress a girl (Natalie Wood). The cast also included Roy Glenn, Eve March, Leon Taylor, Gloria Costillo, and Fiona Hale.

THE IMMACULATE HEART JAMES DEAN APPRECIATION SOCIETY
> I don't know if he ever saw any of those girls again, and I'm pretty sure he never had the time to attend another of their meetings, but I do know that he remembered that night vividly and mentioned it often until the day he died.
> Bill Bast, We Remember Dean International memorial tribute, 1985

After being smitten by James Dean's effective, albeit brief, performance in the 1951 "Hill Number One" episode of the television program "Family Theatre," a group of girls at Immaculate Heart High School in California founded the very first fan club in his honor. The girls dubbed themselves the Immaculate Heart James Dean Appreciation Society, and they invited their idol to attend one of the club's early meetings. He accepted, attended, gave a speech, signed some autographs, and basked in the adulation.

THE IMMORALIST
The Royale Theatre   February 8, 1954   104 performances
Written by: Ruth and Augustus Goetz, adapted from a novel by Andre Gide
Directed by: Daniel Mann
Produced by: Billy Rose
Settings by: George Jenkins
Lighting by: Abe Feder
Costumes by: Motley
Cast: Geraldine Page, Louis Jourdan, Charles Dingle, David J. Stewart, James Dean, John
    Heldabrand, Paul Huber, Adelaide Klein, Bill Gunn

The plight of the homosexual and of the woman he marries is at the center of *The Immoralist*. This is the play that made a Broadway name of James Dean and resulted, almost instantly, in his being cast in *East of Eden*. *The Immoralist* opened in previews at the Royale Theatre on February 1, 1954, and officially premiered a week later, on February 8, Dean's 23rd birthday. The three-act play was scripted by Ruth and Augustus Goetz, who adapted it from the 1902 novel by André Gide, who based it in part on his own marriage to his wife, Emmanuelle.

The immoralist referred to in the title is Michel (Louis Jourdan), tall, dark, and hopelessly homosexual. It seems that his sexual predilections first emerged when, at the age of 11, he was expelled from school for engaging in unspecified "misconduct" with another boy. More than a dozen years later he is still branded and ostracized, despite being a handsome, successful young archaeologist. However, as the play opens in Normandy, France, in 1900, Michel is proposed to by Marcelline (Geraldine Page), "the most respected girl in the village." He, of course, views the marriage with trepidation but accepts with the hope that it will provide him redemption, if not romance.

The honeymoon begins to unravel two months later in Biskra, North Africa, where Marcelline is confronted with the frustration of a husband who keeps his pants *on* and his hands to himself. Michel, meanwhile, is confronted with the lures and temptations that seem to permeate the village. Brave, admirable soldier that he is, though, he attempts to ward them off with chaste thoughts and crossed legs and the reminder that he is now married to a good and respectable woman.

James Dean, wearing his most seductive leer and all gussied up in a mask of brown makeup and a costume consisting of nothing more than a glorified bathrobe, portrays Bachir, the native homosexual houseboy with more than sweeping the floors on his devious mind. Entertaining thoughts

Wearing his most seductive leer and a costume consisting of a glorified bathrobe . . .

of blackmail, Bachir entraps Michel with his sensual charms, which include but are not limited to a homoerotic scissors dance. Bachir also taunts Michel into proving his masculinity by having, at long last, sex with his wife. Marcelline, who has taken a liking to a little wine before dinner, didn't know what hit her, so to speak.

The one-time encounter, however, leaves Michel despondent and Marcelline pregnant, and as the drama concludes they are back in Normandy, partners in desolation and doom and fatality, resigned to their tragedy of human nature. This ending resembled Gide's actual life (he stayed with his wife until her death in 1938) but strayed from the novel, in which Marcelline dies amid the squalor of the North African village.

Today the plot of *The Immoralist* reads like a dated "Donahue" subject, but back in 1954 it was considered highly controversial. In reviewing the play writers used ugly, odious terms like "the affliction" and "the abominable crime" in reference to homosexuality. Obviously, for the director, producer, writers, and actors, production of *The Immoralist* on the Broadway stage was a delicate proposition.

James Dean was cast in November 1953 after reading for Billy Rose, Herman Shumlin (who read opposite him), and the writers Goetz at Rose's office over the Ziegfeld Theatre. Years later Ruth Goetz recalled:

> "This extraordinary little sandy-haired, red-faced [actor] looked like
> a little Irishman, really. And he began to read and he was marvelous.
> He was instinctively, absolutely right. He had the quality of sweetness
> and charming attractiveness, and at the same time, a nasty
> undercurrent of suggestiveness and sexuality. And he was *smashing*."
> *Hollywood: The Rebel James Dean*

Rehearsals started December 18, 1953, at the Ziegfeld. The writers Goetz approached their subject with respect and, unfortunately, timidity, apparently uncertain whether or not to jump in and get their feet wet (and their hands dirty) or to quietly straddle the fence with as much dignity as they could retain. They decided, ultimately, to straddle.

In January the company moved to Philadelphia for a week of pre-Broadway tryouts. Director Herman Shumlin, however, did not pack for the trip. He was fired by Billy Rose, in conjunction with the Goetzes, reportedly for not treating the material with the desired degree of sensitivity. Dean, who had not gotten along particularly well with Shumlin, got along even less with his replacement, Daniel Mann. Dean treated Mann's direction with disdain, varying his own performance to suit his mood, or so it seemed (giving the impression to some who saw it that not only did he stand out from the rest of the cast but he sometimes appeared to be acting in another play; the same complaint was registered about Dean two years later in the movie *Giant*). Of his performance during rehearsals, Ruth Goetz later declared, "He was abominable." The battle brewed backstage and unfolded centerstage when Mann reprimanded Dean before the entire company. Jimmy stalked out of the theater but later returned with his pride tucked beneath his sulk.

Legend has it that it was opening night *on Broadway*, following the performance when James Dean turned in his resignation. Some sources claim that, legend aside, it was two nights later. No matter exactly when it was, he quit a Broadway show at the beginning of what looked to be a promising run—a show that, although not an unqualified hit, was treated with a fair measure of respect by the critics, a show in which his own performance was being uniformly praised (Dean's experimental tactics apparently worked, as many critics singled out his performance with lauda-tory adjectives). Billy Rose, Daniel Mann, Ruth and Augustus Goetz, and the theater community in general were astounded by his audacity. What they didn't know, however (and what Dean *did* know and had suppressed like the cat who had swallowed the family bird), was that starmaker supreme Elia Kazan had privately hand-picked him as the lead in a major motion picture of a major novel by a major author, *East of Eden*. He hadn't actually been given the part yet. He hadn't been tested and nothing had been signed, but he did have Kazan's verbal assurances.

It was still a risky proposition. James Dean left a sure thing, jeopardizing his reputation and future on the Broadway stage for a film that could have bombed, never been made, or, if made, never released. It was on Tuesday, February 23, 1954, that he gave his final performance in *The Immoralist*. Afterward he wiped off the brown muck of makeup, traded in his bathrobe for a pair of blue jeans, said good-bye to his friends in the cast—all two of them, Geraldine Page and Bill Gunn—strutted out the backstage exit, hopped atop his motorcycle, gunned the engine, sped away, and never looked back. He left behind him a trail of open mouths and upturned noses and the unmistakable smell of spoiled greasepaint. It was his final bow.

The Immoralist went on without him. Dean was replaced by Phillip Pine, and the play had a respectable run until May 1, 1954.

THE IMMORALIST
The Immoralist was revived at the Bouwerie Lane Theatre on November 7, 1963. It ran for 210 performances and closed on May 10, 1964. It was directed by George Keathley and produced by Bruce Becker. The revival starred Marcie Hubert and Frank Langella as the doomed couple, with Richard Manuel in the James Dean role of Bachir. The rest of the cast included Tom Klunis, Albert Ottenheimer, David Metcalf, Marian Carr, Cal Bellini, Paul Gennel, and Russell Stagg.

THE IMMORTAL
Fictional biography of James Dean by Walter S. Ross, published in 1958 by Simon and Schuster (which, of course, denied that the book was about Dean). Of his protagonist, dubbed Johnny Preston, Ross wrote, "His ability to convey emotion on a movie screen made him one of its (the Beat Generation) leading representatives. Only, adulation wasn't enough for Johnny. He had to move faster and live wilder than anyone else."

Metro-Goldwyn-Mayer subsequently bought the rights to *The Immortal* and announced plans to adapt it into a motion picture starring George Hamilton. The proposed film was to have been produced by Paul Gregory and written by Charles Kaufman. However, for whatever reason (perhaps Warner Brothers and/or the James Dean estate thought that MGM was infringing on its territory), the film was never produced.

THE INDIANAPOLIS 500
In 1949, just before his graduation from Fairmount (Indiana) High School, Jimmy attended the Indianapolis 500. That year Bill Holland was the winner, driving a Blue Crown Special; Johnny Parsons came in second.

Jimmy was reportedly taken to the races as a graduation present from his friend and mentor, Reverend James DeWeerd.

THE *INDIANAPOLIS NEWS*
Indiana newspaper that has published several articles about James Dean, including a 1957 piece entitled "James Dean Theater School Goes Broke. Shrine to New Star Now a Furniture Store."

Other *News* articles about Dean include:

☆ April 20, 1985   "No Idling for Idol's Car"
☆ August 29, 1985   "James Dean, Legendary Actor Lives On in Memory"

THE *INDIANAPOLIS STAR*
Indiana newspaper that has published several articles about James Dean, including:

☆ December 9, 1956   "A Living Memorial to James Dean"
☆ February 22, 1959   "James Dean, Fairmount Guard"
☆ September 22, 1985 "Dean Kin Grants Rare Interview"
☆ September 22, 1985 "Dean Tales, Fact or Fiction"
☆ September 22, 1985 "James Dean, Hoosier Legend"
☆ February 1, 1987   "Commercials Head for State Classrooms"
☆ March 15, 1987   "Rehabilitated Actor Recalls Idol James Dean"

WILLIAM INGE
Pulitzer Prize–winning playwright who penned "Glory in Flower," an original drama produced on a 1953 episode of the CBS television program "Omnibus" that co-starred James Dean.

William Inge (1913–1973) also wrote several plays that were subsequently adapted for the motion picture screen. They include *Come Back, Little Sheba* (1952), *Picnic* (1955), *Bus Stop* (1956), and *The Dark at the Top of the Stairs* (1960). Inge's original screenplays include *Splendor in the Grass*, for which he won a 1961 Best Screenplay Oscar. On stage, Inge's *Bus Stop* was nominated for a Tony as the Best Play of 1956, and *The Dark at the Top of the Stairs* won the 1958 Best Play Tony.

INJURIES
☆ As a child Jimmy broke his two front teeth. For the rest of his life he wore a bridge, which he publicly popped in and out, frequently at the most inopportune moments.
☆ During the shooting of *Rebel Without a Cause* Jimmy injured his hand while battering the desk at the police station. Fortunately, legend aside and despite Jim Backus's claim ("He played that scene so intensely that he broke two small bones in his hand . . ."), x-rays revealed no broken bones.
☆ Also while shooting *Rebel* Jimmy was nicked in the neck by Corey Allen during the knife-fight sequence. The injury wasn't serious, but shooting was halted while a first-aid attendant rushed over to Dean and applied a compress.

INSOMNIA
Like Marilyn Monroe, James Dean had serious insomnia. When unable to

sleep, he would frequently prowl the streets of New York City in the late night and early morning hours and seek refuge in dark, dingy jazz clubs or 24-hour coffeehouses. Later in Los Angeles he would take solitary drives to the beach or through the hills, or he'd hole up at the corner booth of an all-night eatery on the Sunset strip. Toward the latter part of shooting *East of Eden* the lack of sleep became evident on his face, much to the chagrin of his director and makeup man, in the form of dark bags below his eyes.

INSURANCE
Life insurance: Lloyds of London
Car insurance: Pacific Indemnity

The week of his death James Dean took out a $100,000 life insurance policy with Lloyds of London, issued to him by his friend and agent, Lew Bracker. Reportedly Jimmy wanted $85,000 to go to Marcus and Ortense Winslow, the aunt and uncle who had raised him, $10,000 to the education of Marcus Winslow, Jr., and the remaining $5,000 to his grandparents, Charlie and Emma Dean. However, because he did not live long enough to legalize his intentions, the entire sum subsequently went to his nearest living relative, his father, Winton Dean.

IROQUOIS HOTEL
When he first arrived in New York City in October 1951, James Dean, frightened by the big city combustion, sought solace in his room at the Iroquois Hotel (address: 49 West 44th Street, New York, NY 10036). In May

1952 Jimmy returned to the Iroquois with a roommate, Bill Bast. Together they shared room 82 (not #802 as published in previous reports), a single with two beds and a bath. It cost the struggling pair $90 a month. They left the Iroquois in September 1952, but Jimmy returned alone in December and stayed until early 1953.

Today James Dean fans from all over the world travel to New York City with hopes of staying in his old room at the Iroquois (not unlike a time many years ago, when Jimmy stayed in the hotel room of one of *his* idols, Sarah Bernhardt). To rent Jimmy's room at the Iroquois it would be prudent to make reservations well in advance in writing, and with an enclosed deposit.

GERALD ISENBERG

Co–executive producer of "James Dean," a 1976 made-for-television movie.

YUJIRO ISHIHARA

Actor Yujiro Ishihara was touted by *Time* magazine in 1963 as "Honshu's Jimmy Dean," the James Dean of Japan. *Life* magazine agreed and added, "With his brusque, devil-may-care manner, he is a symbol for Japan's rebellious youth."

BURL IVES

Big, burly Burl Ives co-starred as Sam in *East of Eden.* During the shooting of *Eden* Ives developed a camaraderie with James Dean, and during the breaks the two sometimes played duets with Jimmy on the recorder and Ives on the bagpipes.

Born Burl Ivanhoe in 1909, Burl Ives is an actor, singer, and former professional football player. His film credits include *Cat on a Hot Tin Roof* (as Big Daddy, 1958), *The Big Country* (Best Supporting Actor Oscar, 1958), *The Brass Bottle* (1964), and *Just You and Me, Kid* (1979). Ives's television credits include "The Lawyers" aka "The Bold Ones" (1969–1972) and "Roots" (the 1977 miniseries milestone).

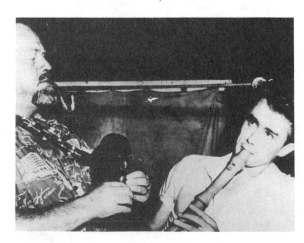

Off-the-set duet.

J

JACKETS
Contrary to popular belief, it was *not* a red leather jacket that James Dean wore and immortalized in *Rebel Without a Cause*—it was a red nylon windbreaker. Originally it was not the jacket that Jimmy was to have worn in the film. He was scheduled to wear a black leather jacket. However, an abrupt costume change was made after the film was upgraded from black and white

to color. Steffi Sidney, one of the film's gang members, recalled: "*I* had a red leather jacket, and I wanted to wear it for certain scenes. And they [the costumers] said, 'Fine.' I wore it in the scenes where we went to school and were changing cars, and I also wore it when we're walking up to school. I was gonna wear it to the chickie-run, too, but they changed the costumes [because of the conversion to color] and said, 'You cannot wear the red jacket because Jimmy is wearing a red jacket.' "

According to director Nick Ray the famous jacket had been borrowed spontaneously from a first-aid attendant on the set and was dipped in black dye to take off the sheen. According to other sources, however, the jacket had been purchased by the Warner Brothers wardrobe department at the now defunct Mattson's clothing store in Hollywood.

The jacket was reportedly owned for a while by entertainer Sammy Davis, Jr., who claimed that it had been presented to him by James Dean.

In real life Jimmy preferred black leather to red nylon. He also wore a black leather jacket (rather, a synthetic black leather jacket) in "The Unlighted Road," a 1955 episode of the CBS television program "Schlitz Playhouse of Stars."

A James Dean line of jackets is presently marketed by the Schott Brothers (address: 358 Lehigh Avenue, Perth Amboy, NJ 08861).

ANNE JACKSON

Actress who starred in "Sleeping Dogs," a 1952 episode of the CBS television program "The Web" in which James Dean appeared. Jackson also co-starred in *The Scarecrow*, a 1953 off-Broadway play in which Jimmy had a small part.

Anne Jackson, born in 1925, is married to actor Eli Wallach. Her other stage credits include *The Middle of the Night*, for which she was nominated for a 1958 Tony award as Best Supporting Actress. Her film credits include *So Young So Bad* (1950), *Tall Story* (which introduced Jane Fonda, 1960), *The Tiger Makes Out* (in which Jackson co-starred with her husband, 1967), and *The Shining* (1980). She also appeared in the very short-lived comedy television series "Everything's Relative" (1987).

CYRIL JACKSON

James Dean took bongo lessons from Cyril Jackson in New York City circa 1954–1955.

DICK JACOBS

Recorded some of the songs on the Coral Records tribute album *The James Dean Story*, including "The Ballad of James Dean," which was released as a single, and its B side, "A Boy Named Jimmy Dean."

Dick Jacobs, born in 1918, served as the music director of the television program "Your Hit Parade" (1957–1958). He also had a few minor hits of his own on the Coral label, including "Petticoats of Portugal" (1956) and "Fascination" (1957), both of which cracked the top 20 on *Billboard*'s charts.

TED JACQUES
Actor who had a small part as Meeker in *See the Jaguar* (1952).

JADE PRODUCTIONS
Jade Productions is a New York–based company (address: GPO 7961, New York, NY 10116-4635) that sells James Dean memorabilia and produces events related to Dean, such as birthday parties in his memory and screenings of his film and television performances. Jade Productions was founded by and is presided over by Dean archivist David Loehr, who derived the name of his company from the first two letters of James Dean's first and last names.

GUNTHER JAECKEL
Costume designer of "Harvest," a 1953 episode of the NBC television show "Robert Montgomery Presents the Johnson's Wax Program" in which James Dean co-starred.

JAMES DEAN
Author: William Bast
Publisher: Ballantine
Year: 1956

Also referred to as *James Dean: A Biography*, this is quite simply the first and finest biography ever written about James Dean. Bill Bast's autobiographical account of his fated relationship with the boy he called Deaner is intimate, exceedingly well written, and seemingly (and astonishingly) unbiased. For James Dean fans it has become, over the years, a bible of sorts. Still, it has never been given its critical due, dismissed by some as pulp biography scrawled by one friend capitalizing on another's fame and posthumous popularity. Nonsense. In a legend that has spawned more than its share of trash *James Dean* by William Bast is a classic.

"JAMES DEAN"
Television diminishes Bill Bast's autobiographical reflections (aka "James Dean: Portrait of a Friend") on his friendship with James Dean. Some of the scenes seem to be just going through the motions, while others seem contrived. One of the most startling aspects of Bast's 1956 book on the same subject was the candor with which he dealt with his own emotional turmoil over his friend and, particularly, his friend's success. TV, however, has never been particularly adept at portraying inner emotional turmoil, and this made-for-television movie is no exception. One attempt is the cheap and rather obvious device of putting the Bast character in therapy so that he can openly, verbally express his pain. Another equally obvious contrivance is the

use of dream sequences in which Dean comes back from the dead to lay a guilt trip on his old friend. In these and other sequences the intentions of the filmmakers are transparent, and the pain expressed rings hollow.

There are, on the other hand, remarkable revelations. When James Dean urges Bill Bast in earnest, "We owe it to our craft to experience everything we can. Don't knock it [homosexual relations] until you try it," and then insists that Bast experience a gay bar in New York, one gets the impression that television history is being made. Years before Rock Hudson's sexual escapades were made public, and years before the "outing" of celebrities became a media pastime, "James Dean" makes inferences to Dean's bisexuality and depicts him blatantly condoning homosexuality.

Also exceptional is the same unbiased tone that Bast employed in his book. In fact, if anything, Bill Bast is probably too hard on himself. As writer and producer of the film he depicts himself as a rather bland, passive character beside Dean's explosive one, and then he has the conviction to cast Michael Brandon, a rather bland-looking actor, instead of one of the hunks of the day, in the role. Further, the telefilm has Bast burdened with guilt over Dean's death, and the viewer is left with the urge to console him by saying, "Relax, it's okay; you were a good friend," which he was, at least as portrayed here.

Finally, there is Stephen McHattie's performance as James Dean. It was perfect casting. McHattie looks enough like Dean to suggest him, but not too much to be disarming or distracting. More importantly, his performance is never too posed, never too studied, and manages to evoke Dean without caricaturizing him. McHattie doesn't seem to have researched the role by analyzing and memorizing James Dean's still photographs in the way that, say, young actors like Johnny Depp and Richard Grieco seem to have done for their television shows, "21 Jump Street" and "Booker." McHattie's performance is a portrayal, not an attempted impersonation, and he is largely responsible for making this docudrama work to the extent that it does.

"James Dean" aired on NBC on February 19, 1976. Its credits include: Gerald Isenberg and Gerry Abrams, executive producers; John Forbes, co-producer; and Robert Butler, director. In addition to McHattie and Brandon, the cast featured Candy Clark, Amy Irving, Meg Foster, Brooke Adams, and Katherine Helmond.

"JAMES DEAN"
Song written by Jackson Browne, Glenn Frey, Don Henley, and J. D. Souther and recorded by the Eagles in 1974.

JAMES DEAN
Photographs: Sanford Roth
Text: Beulah Roth
Publisher: Pomegranate Books
Year: 1983

Sanford Roth's photographs of James Dean, impressively displayed and captioned in English, French, and Japanese.

JAMES DEAN
Nightclub/restaurant in Milan, Italy (address: Via Paolo Sarpi, 11 Milano).

JAMES DEAN: A BIOGRAPHY
Author: John Howlett
Publisher: Plexus Publishing, Ltd., Great Britain
Year: 1975

Above-average biography that provides a complete overview with minimal psychoanalyzing and interviews with Elia Kazan, Nicholas Ray, and Natalie Wood. Recommended.

JAMES DEAN: A DRESS REHEARSAL
Play about James Dean written and produced by Patricia Leone and staged initially in Denver, Colorado, in 1984. As of this writing Leone was attempting to restage the production, which features actor Stephen Brannan as James Dean, at an off-Broadway theater.

JAMES DEAN: A PORTRAIT
Author: Roy Schatt
Publisher: Delilah Books
Year: 1982

Roy Schatt's memoirs in photographs and text are also his homage to his old friend Jimmy Dean. Clearly *James Dean: A Portrait* provides one of the most revealing and invaluable glimpses of Dean in New York, a Dean still searching, still scratching, still experimenting with intangibles, but also a Dean definitely at the genesis of something very big. Recommended.

JAMES DEAN: A SHORT LIFE
Author: Venable Herndon
Publisher: Doubleday and Company
Year: 1974

While this biography is not as ambitious as *James Dean: The Mutant King* by David Dalton, which was published the same year, it is, in many ways, superior. *James Dean: A Short Life* is well written, informative, and forthright. A definitive work, highly recommended.

JAMES DEAN: A STORY IN WORDS AND PICTURES
One-shot cover-to-cover magazine published in 1985 by Anabas Books in England. Text by Roger St. Pierre.

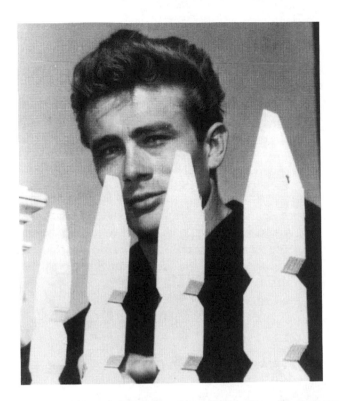

THE JAMES DEAN ALBUM
One-shot cover-to-cover magazine about James Dean that was published by Ideal in 1956.

JAMES DEAN: AMERICAN ICON
Text: David Dalton
Photo Editor: Ron Cayen
Archivist: David Loehr
Publisher: St. Martin's Press
Year: 1984

With Andy Warhol's neon rebel on its cover, *James Dean: American Icon* resembles its subject—exhaustively multidimensional, part biography, part scrapbook, and part coffee table photograph book. The text is provocative, the material, particularly the "Deanabilia" section, is entertaining, and the selection of photographs is easily the most comprehensive and illuminating of any book yet published on Dean. Highly recommended.

"JAMES DEAN: AN AMERICAN ORIGINAL"
See "HOLLYWOOD CLOSE-UP."

JAMES DEAN: BEHIND THE SCENE
Edited by: Leith Adams and Keith Burns
Publisher: Birch Lane Press
Year: 1990

Co-edited by Warner Brothers archivist Leith Adams, this book was culled primarily from the Warner files at the University of Southern California. Stunningly designed and produced by Birch Lane Press, *James Dean: Behind the Scene* offers a vast and impressive display of rare stills from *East of Eden*, *Rebel Without a Cause*, and *Giant*. The photos are interspersed with entertaining and informative interoffice correspondence from the desks of Jack Warner, Elia Kazan, Nick Ray, and various other Warner Brothers personnel. Easily one of the best books about James Dean. Highly recommended.

THE JAMES DEAN DRIVING EXPERIENCE
Rock band that has thus far failed to make much of an impact on radio or records. Among its releases is a single called "Dean's 11th Dream."

JAMES DEAN: FOOTSTEPS OF A GIANT
Author: Wolfgang Fuchs
Publisher: Taco, West Germany
Year: 1986

Mediocre trade paperback biography composed mainly of recycled material and riddled with inaccuracies. There are, however, some interesting photographs.

THE JAMES DEAN FOUNDATION
Indianapolis organization that oversees management of the James Dean estate, image, and name. Jimmy's cousin, Marcus Winslow, Jr., is a member.

THE JAMES DEAN GALLERY
Billed as "the world's largest collection of memorabilia and archives on James Dean," the James Dean Gallery (address: 425 North Main Street) opened its doors in Fairmount, Indiana, on September 22, 1988. The display, from the massive private collection of David Loehr, includes costumes from Dean's films, high school yearbooks, photographs, a Warner Brothers life mask, and literally thousands of other assorted items. The James Dean Gallery is housed in a 12-room Victorian-style house. It is open daily from 10:00 A.M. until 5:00 P.M.; admission is $2.

David Loehr's homage to his idol: the James Dean Gallery.

JAMES DEAN: IN HIS OWN WORDS
Compiled by: Mick St. Michael
Publisher: Omnibus Press, Great Britain
Year: 1989

Paperback book with photographs. Most of the quotes, which are generally unsourced, will be familiar to Dean's fans. Still, though it offers nothing particularly revelatory, the book serves its purpose.

JAMES DEAN IS NOT DEAD
Author: Stephen Morrissey
Publisher: Babylon Books, Great Britain
Year: 1983

James Dean may not be dead (perhaps he and Elvis Presley are having lunch and exchanging dialogue from *Rebel Without a Cause*), but this trade paperback biography by Stephen Morrissey, former lead singer of the British rock band the Smiths, is morose and lifeless. A front cover, a back cover, and a lot of wasted paper in between.

THE JAMES DEAN MEMORIAL

The stainless-steel memorial built in honor of James Dean was erected in Cholame, California, in 1977 by Dean mega-fan, Japanese businessman Seita Ohnishi. The memorial is located in front of the Cholame Post Office, about half a mile from the site where Dean was killed in 1955. Over the years the memorial has become a place of worship and meditation for Dean fans from all over the world.

THE JAMES DEAN MEMORIAL CAR RALLY

Modest California car "rally" (if five or fewer cars constitute a rally) that annually retraces the final route that James Dean traveled on September 30, 1955. The rally, which was initiated by Roger Cannon, starts at the Farmer's Market in West Hollywood and ends at the James Dean Memorial in Cholame.

THE JAMES DEAN MEMORIAL FOUNDATION

In July 1956 the James Dean Memorial Foundation was incorporated in Fairmount, Indiana, with the purpose of financially aiding aspiring young actors and actresses. The July 9, 1956, edition of *The Hollywood Reporter* announced that the corporation "aims to raise a fund of $1,000,000, with income to be used in aiding young actors and actresses. Kent Williams, friend of Dean and executive v.p. of the Foundation, planes to Hollywood late this week to see Henry Ginsberg [the producer of *Giant*] about the possibility of the Foundation sponsoring the premieres of *Giant*."

The James Dean Memorial Foundation's offices were located in Fairmount and New York City. Officers of the corporation included Vivian Coleman, coordinating director, and Lewis Crist, president. The foundation managed to produce one season of summer theater, a production of Thornton Wilder's *Our Town*. The play featured an aspiring young actor, Markie Winslow, Jr., Jimmy's cousin. However, shortly thereafter, the foundation was suspended permanently over a lack of funds and reported mishandling.

THE JAMES DEAN MEMORIAL FOUNDATION

> The reason I used the name is because they had started the James Dean Memorial Foundation in 1956 or 1957 back in Fairmount and it flopped. That left a bad taste in everybody's mouth. I was trying to clean up that name.
>
> Bill Dakota

Founded by Bill Dakota in 1984, the James Dean Memorial Foundation was established with the intention of raising funds to build in Los Angeles a life-size monument to James Dean. With that purpose in mind, according to Dakota, he opened shop in April 1987 at the corner of Hollywood and Vine, selling James Dean memorabilia.

A year later the foundation was shut down and the Dean toy store closed its doors. Dakota blames the termination on the intervention of Curtis Management, the Indianapolis firm that represents the James Dean estate and handles all licensing rights to the Dean image.

THE JAMES DEAN MEMORIAL FUND
In 1956 Dean friend Arthur Lowe, Jr., contributed $1,000 to establish the James Dean Memorial Fund at the Actors Studio in New York. As David Garfield wrote in *A Player's Place*, his exceptional study of life and lessons at the studio:

> In time others contributed to the fund, which lasted well over a decade and helped many members, providing minor loans and in one case, supporting a famous performer through a lengthy breakdown.

THE JAMES DEAN MEMORIAL ROD RUN
The James Dean Memorial Rod Run, not to be confused with the James Dean Memorial Run or the James Dean Memorial Car Rally, is an annual Fairmount, Indiana, car show (pre-1970 cars only). The event has been held in September, during the Fairmount Museum Days Festival, for the last 30 years. It was originated by and is still run by Fred Stocker (address: R.R. #1, Box 161, Albany, IN 47320) of Magic City Street Rods. There is a $15 registration fee.

THE JAMES DEAN MEMORIAL RUN
Initiated in 1978, the James Dean Memorial Run takes place in Los Angeles on the last weekend of September every year. The rally usually convenes in Van Nuys and proceeds to follow the route that James Dean undertook on the afternoon of his death. Typically the rally is composed of Dean fans with a penchant for vintage automobiles, and usually it draws 75 to 80 cars.

The James Dean Memorial Run, not to be confused with the smaller James Dean Memorial Car Rally, was founded by Will O'Neill and is presently produced by Joe Widmark and a group dubbed the South Bay Cruisers. To register, contact Widmark at 14509 Corday Avenue, Hawthorne, California 90250. For the $20 registration fee participants get a memorial T-shirt and dash plaque.

THE JAMES DEAN MEMORIAL SCHOLARSHIP TRUST
Founded by Adeline Nall, Jimmy's high school drama teacher, the James Dean Memorial Scholarship Trust was established to provide an award for "the most promising speech and/or drama student" each year at Madison-Grant High School in Fairmount, Indiana. According to Michael Miller, senior vice president and trust officer at Citizens Exchange Bank, "To my

knowledge it is the only perpetual, growing memorial to James Dean. Its purpose is to promote the education of other local high school students who share the love for the stage once displayed by James Dean." Further information can be obtained by writing to: James Dean Memorial Scholarship Trust, Citizens Exchange Bank, 102 South Main Street, Fairmount, Indiana 46928.

THE JAMES DEAN MEMORY CLUB

The James Dean Memory Club, presided over by Therese Brandes, was perhaps the most successful of all the early fan clubs devoted to Dean. In 1966 club members took out an ad in the entertainment trade paper *Variety*. It read, in part:

> The years are now eleven,
> Since you've been in heaven,
> There are some who say
> Your memory has faded away,
> Many more than some are saying today,
> Your memory is surely here to stay.

JAMES DEAN ON LOCATION

Author: Marceau Devillers
Publisher: Sidgwick & Jackson, Great Britain
Year: 1987

James Dean on Location was originally published in France in 1985. Despite some handsome black-and-white photographs, the book, in any language, is riddled with inaccuracies.

"JAMES DEAN REMEMBERED"

Pedestrian 1974 ABC documentary hosted by Peter Lawford, who slumps casually in a chair and interviews Sal Mineo, Sammy Davis, Jr., Steve Allen, Natalie Wood, and Leonard Rosenman, some of whom provide occasional insight. The program was directed by Jack Haley, Jr., written and produced by Al Ramrus, and co-produced by Ronald Lyon.

JAMES DEAN: REMEMBRANCE

Unpublished biography, copyrighted in 1987 by Gary Gerhart. Gerhart's primary thesis seems to be "You can't separate the man from the town" or "Understand the town, and you'll understand the man," so he proceeds to provide lengthy (and often extraneous) narrative about James Dean's hometown of Fairmount, Indiana.

What Gerhart does not acknowledge, however, is that Fairmount was only one phase of James Dean's development. He almost totally ignores Dean's years in Los Angeles and New York—tumultuous years of tremendous personal and professional growth, years that did as much, if not more, to shape the character of the man who became a legend.

Consequently Gerhart's remembrance is incomplete and ultimately unfulfilling. Nevertheless *James Dean: Remembrance* does provide more extensive information about Fairmount than any other Dean book and includes lengthy interviews with Jimmy's aunt, Ortense Winslow, and his teacher, Adeline Nall.

JAMES DEAN REVISITED
Author: Dennis Stock
Publishers: Viking Press (cloth)
                Penguin Books (paper)
Year: 1978

In February 1955, just before the release of *East of Eden*, young photographer Dennis Stock accompanied young star-to-be James Dean on his triumphant returns to Fairmount, Indiana, and New York City. The resulting photographs were published with a *Life* magazine article, "Moody New Star" (March 7, 1955), which heralded Dean's arrival.

The settings included everything from the farm to a coffin, Times Square, the Actors Studio, and Hollywood on the set of *Rebel Without a Cause*. Several classic black-and-white photographs emerged from the now-legendary sessions, including *Tintype with a Sow* and *Times Square*. All are included in *James Dean Revisited*, an intimate and revealing attempt to fuse the vastly different milieus of its multidimensional and unfailingly photogenic subject. Recommended.

JAMES DEAN: SHOOTING STAR
Text: Barney Hoskyns
Photo Editor: David Loehr
Publishers: Bloomsbury Publishing, Ltd., Great Britain
                Doubleday and Company, U.S.
Years: 1989, Great Britain
        1990, U.S.

Impressive selection of photographs from the David Loehr collection, some of which have never before been published. The text by Barney Hoskyns is provocative but familiar. Recommended.

THE JAMES DEAN STORY
Record album recorded by television personality Steve Allen in 1956. *See* THE RECORDS.

THE JAMES DEAN STORY
The James Dean Story was not Warner Brothers' tribute to James Dean, though it has been repeatedly touted as such. The feature documentary was produced by George Robert Productions, or, more specifically, by George W. George and Robert Altman, who also directed and edited. Reacting to Dean's burgeoning, posthumous personality, Warner Brothers acquired the rights to distribute the project, abandoning tentative plans to film a dramatized biography with an actor portraying Dean.

There is no actor portraying Dean in *The James Dean Story*. Instead, as the film was hyped at the time, James Dean "portrays" himself via film clips and photographs. Louis Clyde Stoumen, who is incorrectly referred to in other reports as the producer of the film, actually served as the production designer. Specifically, he shot the still photographs—a crucial task considering that *The James Dean Story* is a vigorous exercise in imaginative camera work. There are only so many ways to shoot a still photo, and this picture uses them all.

Also incorporated into the documentary are interviews with Dean's family, friends, and others who knew and worked with him, including Marcus and Ortense Winslow, Charlie and Emma Dean, Adeline Nall, Marvin Carter, Lew Bracker, and Lilli Kardell. Winton Dean is conspicuously absent, never seen or even mentioned in the production. Interoffice Warner Brothers memoranda issued at the time reveal that the producers attempted to enlist the aid of Jimmy's father and he refused to cooperate. Other members of Dean's family and some Fairmount, Indiana, residents agreed to participate in the project after the producers volunteered to donate 5 percent of the film's net profits to the James Dean Memorial Foundation.

The James Dean Story made its world premiere in Jimmy's birthplace of Marion, Indiana, on August 13, 1957. Despite optimistic forecasts by the filmmakers and distributor, it was a box-office flop, partly because by the time the film was released, nearly two years after Dean's death, the incredible surge in his posthumous popularity had already leveled out. If anything, it was beginning to wane. America's teenagers had stopped mourning and had transferred their attention to Elvis's pelvis and to other *living* idols of the moment.

Further, despite some interesting interviews and innovative camera techniques, *The James Dean Story* doesn't materialize as a celebration of anything. It's somber, sober, and gray, with a heavy-handed script and misguided attempts at poetry by Stewart Stern (who wrote *Rebel Without a Cause*). It is also doomed by Martin Gabel, who reads the narration as though he were at a funeral, with a voice that sounds like it came from the grave.

THE JAMES DEAN STORY
Author: Ronald Martinetti
Publisher: Pinnacle Books
Year: 1975 (paper)

Author Ron Martinetti was done a disservice by his publisher. His work, *The James Dean Story*, is one of the better biographies about James Dean. It includes some fresh information, a few invaluable interviews, is generally well presented, and deserved to be published in hardback and with some semblance of energy. Instead it went generally unnoticed and today is nowhere to be found in America's bookstores. Recommended.

JAMES DEAN: THE FIRST AMERICAN TEENAGER
Excellent documentary film about James Dean, written and directed by Ray

Connolly, that was released theatrically in 1976. It includes the prerequisite clips from Dean's three films and various television appearances as well as the expected slate of interviewees: Dennis Hopper, Sal Mineo, Leonard Rosenman, Natalie Wood, Corey Allen, Nick Ray, Christine White, Sammy Davis, Jr., and Maila Nurmi. A few surprises—Leslie Caron, Gene Owen (Jimmy's college drama instructor), actor Jack Larson, and artist Kenneth Kendall—are also included.

Still, despite its familiarity, *James Dean: The First American Teenager* is a highly evocative work that strikes and maintains a chord of authenticity. It also contains a great background score. The film was produced by David Puttnam and Sandy Lieberson and narrated by Stacy Keach.

JAMES DEAN: THE MAN AND THE LEGEND
One-shot cover-to-cover magazine published in Great Britain by SM Distribution in 1988.

JAMES DEAN: THE MUTANT KING
Author: David Dalton
Publisher: Straight Arrow Books
Year: 1974

David Dalton flexes his vocabulary in *James Dean: The Mutant King*, an ambitious, admirable biography that attempts a serious, analytical portrait of its subject. Unfortunately, however, *The Mutant King* is occasionally so overpowered by and impressed with its own psycho-babble that Jimmy Dean (just a human being, after all) is somehow lost in the translation. Dalton achieved more with less in his subsequent work *James Dean: American Icon*. Nevertheless, *The Mutant King* is for the most part well researched, substantive, and recommended.

JAMES DEAN: THE WAY IT WAS
Author: Terry Cunningham
Publisher: Electric Reader, Great Britain
Year: 1983

Mediocre trade paperback biography that, at its best, contains some original research; at its worst, numerous inaccuracies.

THE JAMES DEAN WALKING TOUR OF NEW YORK HANGOUTS
Annual tour organized and conducted by David Loehr. It takes place in June and involves exactly what its title implies. The tour has been produced every year since 1983 and generally lasts six hours. Participants, who travel from all over the country to attend, are encouraged to bring pocket money and comfortable shoes. For further information, send a SASE to David Loehr, GPO Box 7961, New York, New York 10116.

JAPAN
Dare wa Hollywood no ichiban movie star desu ka? Translation: "Who is the

number one Hollywood movie star?" In Japan it is none other than James Dean.

In 1956 Japanese movie critics bestowed *26* awards on *East of Eden.* Today clothing manufacturers and financial institutions pay money that goes all the way back to Fairmount, Indiana, to use the James Dean image in selling their products. One firm even uses a life-sized James Dean manne-quin to attract its clientele. Japanese companies also publish and print James Dean books, calendars, and postcards. And Dean's biggest fan in the world, Japanese businessman Seita Ohnishi, spends thousands of dollars erecting James Dean monuments all over the world.

Ever since his death James Dean has been inexplicably and arduously embraced by the people of Japan. Perhaps they love him in the same way they love Coca-Cola or baseball. Or perhaps they see in him American adolescence at its most attractive. Or perhaps it goes deeper. Perhaps they love James Dean so much because, on screen, he seemed to overcome a native inarticulateness and enormous suppression and somehow explode with emotion. The Japanese, on the other hand, are socialized at a very young age *not* to express excessive emotion; emotional outbursts, particularly in public, are discouraged. Perhaps James Dean, as he did for American teenagers in the 1950s, gives a voice (albeit a dubbed or subtitled one) to Japanese people of all ages.

GEORGE JENKINS
Set designer, *The Immoralist* (1954).

JERRY'S BAR AND RESTAURANT
Jerry's Bar and Restaurant, one of James Dean's favorite New York hangouts, was located at 1335 Sixth Avenue (now Avenue of the Americas) near West 54th Street. Jimmy spent the night of his 21st birthday there. His favorite meal was spaghetti; his favorite waiter, Louis de Liso. Jerry's Bar and Restaurant no longer exists.

JEWELRY
James Dean was not much of a jewelry wearer. He did wear a heavy silver identification bracelet and own a black-faced wristwatch and several pairs of cuff links. He also wore, for a period, a gold chain with a locket that reportedly held a lock of Pier Angeli's hair.

ROBERT JEWETT
One of James Dean's Sigma Nu fraternity brothers at UCLA, 1950–1951.

JIMMY
Another book of Sanford Roth's photographs of James Dean. This one was published exclusively in Japanese in 1983.

JIMMY DEAN ON JIMMY DEAN
Book written by Joseph Humphreys and published in Great Britain in 1990. At the time of this writing it was unavailable for review.

JIMMY DEAN RETURNS!
One-shot cover-to-cover magazine about Dean that was printed in 1956 by Rave Publishing. Its tacky subtitle: "Read His Own Words from the Beyond."

"JIMMY JIMMY"
Song about James Dean recorded by Madonna on her 1986 album *True Blue*.

JIMMY RYAN'S BAR
Another James Dean New York hangout, located then at 154 West 54th Street and no longer in existence.

JOBS
Before stardom James Dean held a curious variety of jobs, none of them for long:

☆ During the summer of 1950 Jimmy worked as an athletic instructor at a Los Angeles military academy.
☆ In early 1951 he worked, between classes, as an audio-video assistant and projectionist at UCLA.
☆ Circa May–June 1951 he worked as an usher at CBS Radio in Hollywood.
☆ Circa August–September 1951 he worked as a parking lot attendant at CBS Radio.
☆ In November 1951 he worked as an off-screen stunt tester on the New York–based television game show "Beat the Clock."
☆ In July–August 1952 he worked as an off-screen assistant on the television program "Hallmark Summer Theatre."
☆ In late August 1952 he worked as a crewman aboard a yacht.

DALE JOHNSON
Race car driver who won the May 28–29, 1955, event at Santa Barbara, California, in which James Dean was forced to forfeit because of engine problems.

ERSKINE JOHNSON
Hollywood columnist who, in early 1955, wrote:

> James Dean is making his film debut in *East of Eden*, already being hailed as a second Marlon Brando. A comparison he doesn't like. But they both come from farms, dress as they please, ride motorcycles, and were developed by Elia Kazan, the director. Dean matches Brando's indifference to the press and shares his dislike of small talk. People, he says, were telling him he behaved like Brando before he knew who Brando was.
>
> He's twenty-three years old and is under contract to Warner Brothers. It's our guess that you'll be hearing much about him. The screen can do with a couple of actors like Brando.

GEORGANN JOHNSON
Co-star of "Life Sentence," a 1953 episode of the NBC television program "Cambell Soundstage" that starred James Dean.

Georgann Johnson also appeared in the television programs "Mr. Peepers" (1952–1955), "Our Family Honor" (1985), and "The Colbys" (1986–1987).

RUSSELL JOHNSON
Famous as the professor on "Gilligan's Island" (1964–1967), Russell Johnson was one of the actors up for the part of Ray, the police officer who reprimands and befriends Jim Stark in *Rebel Without a Cause*. The part eventually went to Edward Platt. Johnson later appeared in the western series "Black Saddle" (1959–1960).

ANNA HILL JOHNSTONE
Costume designer, *East of Eden*.

Anna Hill Johnstone has been designing movie costumes for three decades. Her films include *The Godfather* (Oscar nomination, 1972) and *Ragtime* (Oscar nomination, 1981).

CHRISTOPHER JONES
"What did *you* think of Jimmy Dean? I thought he was a great actor. A fucking saint. That's why he had to die so young."
						Christopher Jones to his father-in-law, Lee Strasberg,
											Bittersweet by Susan Strasberg

Of all the would-be James Deans to smolder on a movie screen, Christopher Jones probably came closest to resembling Dean physically. Blond and blue-jeaned, Jones, like Dean, was slender and small yet strapping with fresh-faced farm-boy sexuality. For a while in the late 1960s Christopher Jones was being hailed as "the next James Dean," and he wore the rebel badge energetically, on and off the screen. Jones updated the role to include longer hairstyles and bell-bottoms and expanded it beyond Dean's seeming war against his parents to war against society and its evils, primordial and otherwise. He also befriended Dean's friends and married actress Susan Strasberg, who had a Dean connection or two herself.

But something didn't click. Jones made it to the threshold but not to the throne. What he *did* do that James Dean didn't was grow older. However, he reportedly suffered a nervous breakdown and, after a series of automobile accidents, became elusive and retired from public life. Today Christopher Jones, the man who would be Dean, remains something of an enigma. Take a look at *Wild in the Streets* (1968) on video. He was not James Dean (seriously, looks aside, he was not even close), but he did have *something*. He could have had, should have had, a far more successful career.

Christopher Jones was born either William Franks or William Frank Jones, depending on the source, in Jackson, Tennessee, in 1941. He had the title role in the television program "The Legend of Jesse James" (1965–1966) before embarking on a movie career that includes *Chubasco* (1968), *Three in the Attic* (1969), *The Looking Glass War* (England, 1970), and *Ryan's Daughter* (England, 1970).

L. Q. JONES

While shooting *Rebel Without a Cause*, James Dean befriended actor L. Q. Jones, who had just been signed to a Warners contract. Jones hailed from Texas, and Dean, preparing for *Giant*, spent as much time as he could with Jones in an effort to perfect his Texan accent. He also secured for his new friend a bit part in *Giant*.

L. Q. Jones was born Justice Ellis McQueen in 1927. He made his film debut in *Battle Cry* (1955), and subsequently appeared in films including *Love Me Tender* (with Elvis Presley, 1956) and *The Young Lions* (with Marlon Brando and Montgomery Clift, 1958). Jones also co-starred as a regular in the western television programs "Cheyenne" (1955–1956) and "The Virginian" (1964–1967). In addition he produced, directed, and wrote the 1975 film *A Boy and His Dog*, which starred Don Johnson and Jason Robards, Jr.

LOUIS JOURDAN

Louis Jourdan made his Broadway stage debut as the star of *The Immoralist* (1954) after having appeared in films including *Le Corsaire* (1939), *The Paradine Case* (for which he was discovered by David O. Selznick and brought to America, 1948), *Madame Bovary* (1949), and *Three Coins in the Fountain* (1954), which had not yet been released by the time *The Immoralist* opened.

In *The Immoralist* Jourdan portrayed Michel, a married man tormented by his suppressed homosexuality and by a conniving seductive houseboy played by James Dean. Offstage, the chemistry between the two actors was more vitriol than valentines. Dean dismissed Jourdan's performance as wooden (while others praised it as "restrained") and complained to Martin Landau, a friend, "Oh, Louis is great. He really loosened up. He raised both hands at the same time."

Jourdan reciprocated the ill will. According to Beulah Roth, "I was at a party one night, and Rock Hudson and Louis Jourdan were there. I said, 'Rock, what do you think of Jimmy?' He gave me *that look*, and Louis Jourdan said, '*Don't* mention his name.' " Director James Sheldon concurs, saying simply "Louis hated him."

For *The Immoralist*, Jourdan was given the Donaldson award for the Best Debut Performance of the year.

Born Louis Gendre in Marseilles, Louis Jourdan was underage for Army service at the time of the Nazi invasion of Paris. After the Allied liberation of Paris, Jourdan resumed an acting career and was eventually discovered by Selznick and transported to Hollywood. Jourdan's additional film credits include *Gigi* (1958), *Can-Can* (1960), *The V.I.P.'s* (England, 1963), *Made in Paris* (1966), and *Octopussy* (England, 1983).

KATY JURADO
Born Maria Jurado Garcia in 1927, Katy Jurado was one of Dean's Hollywood dates. Jurado has appeared in films including *The Bullfighter and the Lady* (1951), *High Noon* (1952), *Broken Lance* (Best Supporting Actress Oscar nomination, 1954), *Trapeze* (1956), *One-Eyed Jacks* (1961), and *Pat Garrett and Billy the Kid* (1973). She also appeared in the short-lived television series "A.K.A. Pablo" (1984).

K

JOHN KALIN

One of James Dean's Sigma Nu fraternity brothers at UCLA, 1950–1951.

LILLI KARDELL

> "Jimmy is a nice man. Some of those things he does, it is because he
> is youthful, and it takes time to handle fame. But he really is very
> polite, very kind. They tell me he does not smile enough. Not true.
> He smiles much. He has a good sense of humor."
>
> Lilli Kardell, *Modern Screen*, August 1955

Swedish-born actress Lilli Kardell was discovered at RKO's Stockholm office, where she had worked as a secretary. Upon her arrival in Hollywood in early 1955, when she was only 18 or 19 according to press reports, Lilli met and began to date James Dean.

According to her diary Kardell met Dean on February 19, 1955. She was still seeing him in April, when they were spotted together at the Villa Capri restaurant in Hollywood. It was love, at least for Kardell, who wrote in her diary on September 30, 1955:

> Jimmy Dean my only love died on his way to Salinas for the races.
> Auto crash. Please take care of him, God, and let him be happier
> now than before. I can only hope I will find my Jimmy in some
> other person. My thoughts will always be with you, Jimmy.
> Goodbye, forever. I love you and will never forget you and our
> memories.

Kardell's "other person" turned out to be an insurance executive whom she married in 1958 and, amid charges of cruelty, divorced a year later. In 1961 Kardell became seriously involved with actor Troy Donohue. They became engaged but didn't marry. Instead Kardell wound up in Cedars of Lebanon Hospital and alleged that fair Troy had beaten her up. Kardell filed a lawsuit, seeking $60,000, a case that was subsequently settled out of court.

Lilli Kardell's acting career consisted mainly of guest appearances on such television programs as "Our Miss Brooks," "Wagon Train," "Rawhide," "Route 66," and "The Tab Hunter Show."

BILLY KAREN

Part owner of the Villa Capri, James Dean's favorite Hollywood restaurant. Karen was interviewed in the documentary *The James Dean Story* (1957).

BORIS KARLOFF

Boris Karloff (1887–1969), born William Pratt, attained fame as Frankenstein's monster in 1931 and became a horror movie legend. Interestingly, Karloff was up for the part of Uncle Bawley in *Giant*, a part that eventually went to Chill Wills.

KURT KASZNAR
Co-star of "Run Like a Thief," a 1954 episode of the NBC television series "Philco TV Playhouse" that starred James Dean.

Kurt Kasznar (1913–1979), born in Austria, also appeared in films including *Lili* (1953), *The Last Time I Saw Paris* (1954), *My Sister Eileen* (1955), and *The Thrill of It All* (1963). He also appeared in the television series "Land of the Giants" (1968–1970).

"THE KATE SMITH SHOW"
Daytime television program that aired on NBC from 1950 to 1954. James Dean appeared in the January 15, 1953, episode entitled "Hound of Heaven."

ELIA KAZAN
> "The more success an actor has, the more he acquires the look of wax fruit."
>
> Elia Kazan, *James Dean: A Short Life* by Venable Herndon

Dwight Eisenhower may have been president of the United States in early 1954, but, as far as New York actors were concerned Elia Kazan was *God*, no less, and in Hollywood, where priorities have a tendency to become twisted, he was something even greater: a money-maker. Consequently beauteous bombshells like Marilyn Monroe dropped to their knees in awe and hung on his every word, dollar-hawking movie studios like Warner Brothers gave him carte blanche, and New York actors did somersaults to attract his attention and his favor.

Kazan had already directed the young Montgomery Clift and the young Marlon Brando on Broadway in *The Skin of Our Teeth* and *A Streetcar Named Desire*, respectively. He had also won Tony awards as Best Director for *All My Sons* (1947) and *Death of a Salesman* (1949), and he had won an Oscar for directing *Gentleman's Agreement* (1947) and was nominated for another one for the film version of *Streetcar* (1951).

In early 1954 Kazan was in New York, working on the production of Robert Anderson's stage play *Tea and Sympathy*. He was also working on his latest picture, *On the Waterfront*, and quietly preparing another one, an adaptation of the John Steinbeck novel *East of Eden*.

Kazan had probably been aware of James Dean since 1952, when Dean became a member of the Actors Studio, of which Kazan was a founding member. Some reports contend that Kazan had even been present at Dean's audition into the studio and had seen some of Dean's subsequent studio-related performances. For years, however, Kazan has denied this, claiming that he was unaware of James Dean until early 1954. Nevertheless Kazan also claimed for years that he did *not* see Dean's performance in *The Immoralist*, probably because he didn't want to give the impression (however true it may be) that he had lured Dean away from another producer's play. It has only been recently that Kazan has acknowledged that Paul Osborn, *Eden*'s screenwriter, had prompted him to see the young actor in *The Immoralist*.

After seeing the play, Kazan summoned Dean to a meeting at Warner Brothers' New York offices. Years later Kazan explained:

> "When he walked into the office, I knew immediately that he was right for the role. He was guarded, sullen, suspicious, and he seemed to me to have a great deal of concealed emotion. He looked and spoke like the character in *East of Eden*."
> *Los Angeles Times*, September 30, 1985

Kazan knew from the outset that to obtain the performance he desired from James Dean he would first have to comfort, cajole, pamper, provoke, indulge, and inspire him. Following their meeting, Jimmy offered to give Kazan a ride on his motorcycle, a test in guise of an offer that he frequently gave to prospective friends. Kazan hopped on, and then held on, through a madman's tour of New York City. Shortly afterward Kazan took Dean to John Steinbeck, who promptly announced, "He *is* Cal." As for Warner Brothers, if Kazan was God, his word was gold, and the studio executives, Jack Warner included, didn't require much persuasion to cast Dean, a virtual unknown, in a major motion picture. And so Kazan not only put his protégé on a plane to Hollywood; he also escorted him there.

Elia Kazan has often said he prefers to work with young, unknown actors because they tend to be less "spoiled," more human, less like "wax fruit." Of course this is probably partially true. It is also probably at least partially true that he preferred to direct young actors because they were more pliable, more susceptible to his tactics. There is no doubt that Kazan is among the most prolific directors of the American stage and screen. Part of his success, certainly, was that he was also a masterful manipulator of human nature and emotion. During *East of Eden* Kazan took aside each of his primary young actors, lowered his voice, softened his touch, wrapped his arms around their defenses, courted their affection and confidence, learned where they were most vulnerable, and, like an efficient clerk, filed the information away for future reference. When asked during the production of *Eden* how Elia Kazan was assisting his performance, James Dean answered thoughtfully:

> "Kazan asked me to relate any incidents in my life during which I had undergone severe physical or mental abuse. Then, just before a difficult scene, he would say, 'Now, Jim, remember when you got into that fight with a neighborhood kid, remember how angry you were, remember how you wanted to smash him again and again? Well, remember all this when you do the scene.' "

Dick Davalos, another young unknown who portrayed Dean's character's brother in the film, added, "By the time the picture was over, Kazan knew more about me than I did about myself."

Unarguably James Dean's relationship with his director started out promisingly. Actually it was a classic case of hero worship. Brando was Dean's idol; Kazan was the idolmaker. As Julie Harris, another of the film's young stars, related:

> Jimmy worshiped Mr. Kazan. They had sort of a father-son
> relationship. Gadge [Kazan] gave Jimmy one of his jackets and
> Jimmy wore it all the time.

At the time Kazan seemed to reciprocate. "Dean is a wonderful new boy," he lauded, "the best young actor to come along since Marlon Brando." Later Kazan would wince at comparisons between Brando and Dean and wonder how they ever got started in the first place.

As filming on *East of Eden* progressed, and as the buzz about his performance resonated throughout Hollywood, James Dean asserted himself and began to rebel against Kazan's tutelage. He began to resent being regarded as Kazan's new puppet. He started staying out until all hours of the night, prowling Sunset Boulevard, and then showing up late on the set. When he did show up, his face was fatigued and not at all "farm boy fresh," as Kazan had ordered. Perturbed by the transgressions and disloyalty of his young actor, Kazan pulled in the reins and relocated Dean's living quarters to a Warner Brothers dressing room—next to the one Kazan was living in. Once again Kazan's tactics worked, and he obtained the performance he desired from Dean. But when *East of Eden* completed shooting in August 1954, the director and his former protégé parted company and never saw one another again.

In the succeeding years Elia Kazan, like a scorned mentor, has expressed, at best, ambivalent feelings toward James Dean. *East of Eden* had been designed emphatically as "an Elia Kazan production," and there is little doubt that Dean's performance and emerging stardom overshadowed the rest of the film. It almost seemed that Kazan resented standing in Dean's shadow. In 1985 even Kazan finally had to acknowledge, "The film was a success, but he was even a greater success."

Kazan understood the success of *East of Eden* but not the enormous and enduring success of James Dean. Nor did he like him. To this day Kazan publicly refers to James Dean as "a young man I didn't like." He has also branded him in the past as "sick," "a cripple inside," and "easily castrated." Something obviously got strangled in their mentor-protégé relationship that resulted in mutual betrayal and vehement dislike.

Elia "Gadge" Kazan was born Elia Kazanjoglous in 1909. In addition to those film credits already mentioned, his phenomenal career has included *A Tree Grows in Brooklyn* (1945), *The Sea of Grass* (1947), *Boomerang* (1947), *Pinky* (1949), *Panic in the Streets* (1950), *Viva Zapata!* (1952), *Man on a Tightrope* (1953), *On the Waterfront* (Best Director Oscar, 1954) *Baby Doll* (1956), *A Face in the Crowd* (1957), *Wild River* (1960), *Splendor in the Grass* (1961), *America, America* (Best Director Oscar nomination, 1963), *The Arrangement* (which he also wrote, 1969), *The Visitors* (which he also wrote,

1972), and *The Last Tycoon* (1976).

In addition to being responsible for some excellent films, Kazan is responsible for the careers of some excellent actors.

Elia Kazan's Discoveries
Carroll Baker, *Baby Doll* (1956)
Warren Beatty, *Splendor in the Grass* (1961)
Marlon Brando, *A Streetcar Named Desire* (play, 1947)
James Dean, *East of Eden* (1955)
Sandy Dennis, *Splendor in the Grass* (1961)
Bruce Dern, *Wild River* (1960)
Andy Griffith, *A Face in the Crowd* (1957)
John Kerr, *Tea and Sympathy* (1954)
Jack Palance, *Panic in the Streets* (1950)
Lee Remick, *A Face in the Crowd* (1957)
Theresa Russell, *The Last Tycoon* (1976)
Eva Marie Saint, *On the Waterfront* (1954)
James Woods, *The Visitors* (1972)

STACY KEACH
Narrator of the 1976 documentary *James Dean: The First American Teenager*.

Born in 1941, Stacy Keach has appeared in several films including *The Heart Is a Lonely Hunter* (1968), *Brewster McCloud* (1970), and *That Championship Season* (1982). On television Keach appeared in "Get Smart" (as Carlson, 1966–1967), "Caribe" (1975), and "Mickey Spillane's Mike Hammer" (later titled "The New Mike Hammer," 1984–1987). The 1984–1985 season of the latter show was cut short due to Keach's six-month sentence in a British prison for cocaine possession.

"KEEP OUR HONOR BRIGHT"
James Dean appeared in "Keep Our Honor Bright," an episode of the NBC program "Kraft Television Theatre" that aired on October 14, 1953. The show was produced and directed by Maury Holland and written by George Roy Hill. The cast also featured Michael Higgins, Joan Potter, David White, George Roy Hill, Rusty Lane, Larry Fletcher, and Addison Richards.

The plot revolved around a college's student honor committee, which is confronted with a student cheating scandal. Jimmy portrayed a young man who attempts to commit suicide.

DOUGLAS M. KELLEY
The criminologist who served as a consultant on *Rebel Without a Cause*. For his expertise in delinquency Warner Brothers paid Kelley $350.

GRACE KELLY
"To me, she's the complete mother image, typifying perfect. Maybe she's the kind of person you'd like to have had for a mother."
James Dean on Grace Kelly, *The Whole Truth and Nothing But* by Hedda Hopper

At the Audience Awards Election ceremonies in December 1955 Grace Kelly presented the Best Actor trophy, which was awarded posthumously to James Dean for his work in *East of Eden*. The award was accepted by Natalie Wood.

Earlier that year Grace Kelly had been director George Stevens's first choice for the female lead in *Giant*. In fact Kelly had been suspended by her studio, MGM, for failing to report to the set of *Jeremy Rodock* with Spencer Tracy, reportedly because she wanted MGM to loan her out to Warner Brothers to make *Giant*. But among female stars in Hollywood Grace Kelly was second only to Marilyn Monroe, so MGM refused and instead offered Elizabeth Taylor. That year Kelly won the Best Actress Oscar for her performance in the 1954 drama *The Country Girl* (beating out Judy Garland's bravura comeback in *A Star Is Born*). Kelly's other pictures include *Fourteen Hours* (1951), *High Noon* (1952), *Mogambo* (1953), *Dial M For Murder* (1954), *Rear Window* (1954), *To Catch a Thief* (1955), and *High Society* (1956).

In April 1956 Kelly abdicated her position in Hollywood to become Princess of Monaco. In September 1982 her car crashed off a winding road and Grace, 52, was killed.

KELLY'S CLEANING CENTER
James Dean's cleaners. In September 1955 Jimmy owed Kelly's $12.41.

KENNETH KENDALL
In January 1955 James Dean, his face a chalky white, his lips unusually red, slouched and slumped and made a generally unimpressive entrance into artist Kenneth Kendall's studio at 8110 Melrose Avenue in West Hollywood. Jimmy, it seems, had seen Kendall's bust of (who else?) Marlon Brando and wanted (what else?) one sculpted of himself. Kendall was not particularly taken by the rather dowdy lump of an actor who dragged his feet on the ground and kept his head lowered, chin to chest. But when he turned to leave, James Dean metamorphosed. The white skin glowed, the blue eyes flashed, and the too-red mouth parted into a smile that Kenneth Kendall has never forgotten: "Suddenly he was beautiful. It was like being struck by lightning."

When Kendall heard the news on the night of Dean's death, he took out his clay almost instinctively and went to work on a bust of Dean because, as he recently explained, "It's what I could *do*." In May 1956 he presented the completed sculpture to Fairmount (Indiana) High School. A subsequent replica was presented in 1957 to Park Cemetery, where Dean is buried. It remained there for nine months before it was stolen. Today the Fairmount High bust is on display at the Fairmount Historical Museum.

What Kenneth Kendall has continued to do, over 35 years later, is devote his talent and life's work to the image and memory of James Dean. To date he has completed 100 oil paintings of Dean, which he exhibits to James Dean fans who travel from all over the world to Los Angeles to see his work. His most famous rendering, however, is his bronzed bust of Dean, which in November 1988 found a permanent home at Griffith Park (which served as

Kenneth Kendall, with the source and result of his inspiration.

one of the primary locations for *Rebel Without a Cause*), where it is enshrined in Hollywood history.

ARTHUR KENNEDY

Actors Studio member who starred as Dave Ricks in *See the Jaguar*, a 1952 Broadway play that featured the young unknown actor James Dean. During production of the play Kennedy and Dean got along exceptionally well. So well, in fact, that during rehearsals Kennedy frequently gave Dean advice—and Dean listened.

John Arthur Kennedy was born in Worcester, Massachusetts, in 1914. Discovered by James Cagney, Kennedy had a film career that started with *City of Conquest* (1940) in which Cagney starred. In 1949 he won a Tony award as Best Supporting Actor for *Death of a Salesman*. On screen Kennedy received *four* Oscar nominations as Best Supporting Actor: *Champion* (1949), *Trial* (1955), *Peyton Place* (1957), and *Some Came Running* (1959). He was also nominated for a Best Actor Oscar in 1951 for *Bright Victory*. His many other films include *The Glass Menagerie* (1950), *The Desperate Hours* (1955), *A Summer Place* (1959), and *Lawrence of Arabia* (England, 1962).

Kennedy's final films were *Signs of Life* (1989) and *Grandpa* (1990). He died of cancer in January 1990.

SANDY KENYON
Host of the 1985 James Dean tribute on CNN's "Show Biz Today."

JACK KEROUAC
"Jimmy and I were reading Kerouac; we were relating to that kind of breaking out. It was the only thing to read unless you went back to Fitzgerald or Hemingway. And we were busy getting rid of that Hemingway big-game hunting thing."
> Bill Gunn, *James Dean: The Mutant King* by David Dalton

"Kerouac would inspire such icons as Brando, Dean, Dylan, and more currently, Gere and Springsteen."
> Ken Kesey, *Esquire*, 1983

Despite the statements above, it is unlikely (though possible) that Jack Kerouac (1922–1969) had any influence on James Dean. If he did, the influence was minimal. Kerouac's *On the Road*, the novel that launched his career and a movement known as the Beat Generation, was not published by Viking until *1957*, two years after Dean's death.

Still, it is possible that Jimmy had gotten his hands on an excerpt of the novel that appeared as a short story in a literary publication circa 1954–1955. Nevertheless, if anything, James Dean, with his insistence on a life without boundaries, influenced the Beat Generation—not vice versa.

JOHN KERR
When the New York theater community bestowed its awards for best supporting actor in a play of 1954, it presented everything it could, including the prestigious Tony, to John Kerr for his performance in *Tea and Sympathy* as a schoolboy suspected of homosexuality. One of Kerr's primary competitors that year (although he failed to receive a Tony nomination) was James Dean for his brief performance in André Gide's *The Immoralist*.

Kerr and Dean certainly knew each other. In fact they had appeared together in a 1953 episode of the NBC television program "The Big Story." Two years later Kerr was up for the part of Jordy, one of Jett Rink's adversaries in *Giant*. The part was eventually given to Dennis Hopper. Around the same time, Warner Brothers refused to allow MGM to borrow James Dean for Vincente Minnelli's 1955 film *The Cobweb*, and John Kerr, making his film debut, was cast instead. After Dean's death, he was again replaced by Kerr, this time in the 1956 television production of "The Corn Is Green."

Despite his considerable early success, the career of John Kerr waned with age. His other pictures include *Gaby* (1956), *South Pacific* (1958), *The Pit and the Pendulum* (1961), and *Seven Women from Hell* (1962). Kerr also appeared in the television programs "Arrest and Trial" (1963–1964) and "Peyton Place" (1965–1966).

DOROTHY KILGALLEN
Hollywood columnist responsible for dishing the following item:

> James Dean and his landlady aren't seeing eye to eye over the actor's hobby of repairing his motorcycle. He does it in the bathroom.

ELINOR KILGALLEN
Casting director who was instrumental in hiring Jimmy for "Sleeping Dogs," a 1952 episode of the CBS television program "The Web," which provided him with his first television acting job in New York.

MARTIN KINGSLEY
Co-star of "No Room," a 1953 episode of the CBS television program "Danger" in which James Dean appeared.

MURIEL KIRKLAND
Co-star of "The Foggy, Foggy Dew," a 1952 episode of the CBS television program "Lux Video Theatre" that also co-starred unknown actor James Dean.

Muriel Kirkland (1903–1971) was primarily a stage actress. She appeared in a few minor films during the 1930s including *Fast Workers* (1933), *Hold Your Man* (1933), and *Nana* (1934).

HELEN KIRKPATRICK
Helen Kirkpatrick is a Fairmount, Indiana, resident and a longtime friend of the Dean and Winslow families. She is also a former secretary of the Fairmount Historical Museum and in 1978 was instrumental in founding the We Remember Dean International fan club, of which she remains an honorary member.

EARTHA KITT
> Jamie and I were like brother and sister. He told me in fact he thought of me as a sister. Our relationship was strictly platonic and spiritual.
>
> Eartha Kitt, *Alone with Me*

Before Ann-Margret scorched the screen in the 1960s as the kitten with a whip, Eartha Mae Kitt was the undisputed tigress with a growl. In 1951 she unleashed her act of song, sizzle, and bubbling brown sugar on Manhattan's supper club circuit. The following year she burned up Broadway in *New Faces of 1952*, which was adapted into a motion picture two years later.

It was at the tail end of this storm of activity that Eartha Kitt met and befriended James Dean. They were both young and talented and seemed to have a future of infinite possibilities. They were drawn together by all things musical—together they took dance class, played drums, listened to records—and by a mutual sense of alienation. They were both displaced personalities. Neither seemed to fit neatly into any of society's designated slots. It was a lonely, doomed quality, and they recognized it in each other. They also shared a friend who strengthened their bond in rebellion. Arthur Loew, Jr., was Dean's confidant and Kitt's lover. It was an interracial affair during a time when such things were not just frowned on but spat on. James Dean may have reveled in the daring of the relationship; nonetheless it was doomed.

In the 1960s Eartha Kitt's career collapsed. She has since suggested that she was blackballed by the White House after her infamous confrontation with First Lady Ladybird Johnson over America's involvement in the Vietnam War. The most notable job that Kitt obtained during this period was in the ABC television show "Batman." Kitt portrayed Catwoman with a prime-time purr that resounded with delicious vindictiveness. The performance has since become a camp classic.

In 1978 Eartha Kitt made a comeback on Broadway in *Timbuktu!*, for which she received a Tony nomination as the year's Best Actress in a Musical. She later attempted a foray into disco and registered a hit with "I Need a Man." Today Kitt is enjoying a revival of sorts. She performs, deep-throated growl still remarkably intact, in cabaret clubs around the world, including the legendary Cinegrill in Hollywood.

BOB AND HELEN KLEBERG
Despite Warner Brothers' contrary contentions at the time, Edna Ferber's Bick and Leslie Benedict of *Giant* (portrayed in the film by Rock Hudson and Elizabeth Taylor) were based on a real-life couple, Bob and Helen Kleberg. The Klebergs' homestead, King Ranch, was also the model for Ferber's Reata.

ADELAIDE KLEIN
Actress who appeared as Sidma in the 1954 Broadway play *The Immoralist*, which co-starred James Dean. Klein is best remembered on Broadway in *Uncle Harry* with Eva La Gallienne. On screen she appeared in films including *The Naked City* (1948) and *The Enforcer* (1951).

DANE KNELL
Actor who portrayed Jee Jee in the 1952 Broadway play *See the Jaguar*. Knell also served as Jimmy's stand-in during the production.

THE KNICKERBOCKER HOTEL
Hollywood hotel where Dean reportedly was a frequent guest. The Knickerbocker (address: 1714 North Ivar Street) is embedded in Hollywood legend.

It is where Marilyn Monroe dropped Joe DiMaggio off following their first date; where Frances Farmer was arrested by police, who carted her naked and flailing body through the lobby; and where famed Hollywood dress designer "Irene" leapt to her death from the top floor in 1962. The Knickerbocker was sold in 1972 and is currently an apartment building for senior citizens.

TONY KRABER
Cast member and stage manager, *See the Jaguar* (1952).

"KRAFT TELEVISION THEATRE"
Television drama series that aired on NBC on Wednesday nights from May 1947 to October 1958. The show was so popular that separate episodes ran concurrently on ABC on Thursday nights from October 1953 to January 1955. Ed Herlihy was the show's announcer from 1947 to 1955.

James Dean appeared in three episodes of "Kraft Television Theatre," all on NBC: "Prologue to Glory," May 21, 1952; "Keep Our Honor Bright," October 14, 1953; and "A Long Time Till Dawn," November 11, 1953.

TED KRING
Wardrobe man, *Giant*.

KRIZIA UOMO
Men's cologne manufactured by Sanofi Beauty Products that, in 1988, used James Dean's image in its advertising campaign. The print ads featured a black-and-white photograph of Dean with a cigarette protruding from the side of his mouth. The accompanying copy read: "Krizia Uomo. A touch of the maverick."

KUEHL FUNERAL HOME

Paso Robles, California, mortuary where, on the evening of September 30, 1955, the body of James Dean was taken.

MARTIN KUEHL

Owner of the Kuehl Funeral Home. Martin Kuehl's footnote in history (morbid though it may be) is that, on the evening of September 30, 1955, he served as James Dean's mortician. For his efforts Kuehl was paid $982.93.

CAL KUHL

Producer of "The Foggy, Foggy Dew," a 1952 episode of the CBS television program "Lux Video Theatre" that co-starred unknown actor James Dean.

RICHARD KULNEY

Clifton, New Jersey, actor who was the co-winner of the first James Dean Theater School Scholarship. The award was presented by the James Dean Memorial Foundation in July 1957.

JOHN KUNSTLE

John Kunstle was the winner of the October 2, 1955, race at Salinas, California, that James Dean had intended to participate in. Earlier, on May 1, 1955, Kunstle had finished second in a race at Bakersfield. In that race James Dean had placed third.

L

LA REINA THEATER

Movie theater (address: 14626 Ventura Boulevard) in Sherman Oaks, California, where Warner Brothers held one of its earliest sneak preview screenings of *East of Eden* at the end of 1954.

ALAN LADD

Hollywood's big little (five feet, five inches) guy of the 1940s and early 1950s, Alan Ladd was seriously considered for the role of Jett Rink in *Giant* before it was given to James Dean. It would have been interesting casting, to say the least. In 1955, when *Giant* was shot, Alan Ladd was 42 years old; Dean was 24.

LAKE OLIVER

During the summer of 1947 the Fairmount High 4-H Club, including member Jim Dean, went on a camping trip to Lake Oliver, located in the northeastern section of Indiana. The excursion was supervised by club adviser Hugh Caughell.

GARTH LAMBRECHT

James Dean's roommate at the Sigma Nu fraternity house, circa 1950–1951.

MARTIN LANDAU

Jimmy was a very close and good friend of mine. I have fond memories of Jim, the days we spent together in New York City as young actors—walking the streets and talking about the theater and wondering about our next job, reading books and discussing them; seeing plays, seeing films; working in acting workshops and being serious young fellows about the thing we loved most, which was acting in the theater and films.

Martin Landau, We Remember Dean International memorial tribute, 1985

New York actors Jimmy Dean and Marty Landau met at a cattle call audition at the Mansfield Theatre in 1952. According to Landau, "It was a fairly humiliating experience. We were both rejected that day . . . we ended up outside, sitting on the sidewalk." The two actors, despondent but acquainted with the feeling, were actually introduced to one another by a third actor, Tommy Tompkins. Dean and Landau sensed an immediate bond as hungry young people sometimes do and proceeded to take a walk. Years later Landau recalled the meeting in an interview for CNN that was never aired in its entirety:

> We took a walk that first day, and there was a building going up near Sixth Avenue, and we virtually became sidewalk superintendents by barking orders to people, playing the game of sidewalk superintendents. And we proceeded to go over to Rockefeller Center where there was a young girl skating, and we applauded her and she did her command performance.
>
> Our minds, our ability to fantasize, and our ability to communicate was kind of an instant thing. I had an amazingly instant rapport with him, and as a result we became friends immediately. He used to come out to my house, my parents' house in Queens, and my little nephews adored him. [We had] Christmases and Thanksgivings [together]. We were sort of a surrogate family.

Later Landau conducted an acting workshop that Jimmy, Barbara Glenn, Shelley Berman, Geraldine Page, and others attended. During the same period Jimmy was learning the art of photography and would constantly subject his friends, Landau included, to his camera lens.

For Martin Landau, born in 1933, fame came in 1966 by way of a television show, "Mission Impossible," which co-starred his wife, Barbara Bain. They stayed on the show for three years, and later returned to television in an epic-sized but unsuccessful science fiction series, "Space 1999" (1975–1977).

Despite appearances in several films, it has only been recently that the bushy-eyebrowed Landau has attained success as a movie actor, winning Best Supporting Actor nominations for both *Tucker* (1988) and *Crimes and Misdemeanors* (1989). His previous films include *North by Northwest* (1959), *Cleopatra* (1963), *Nevada Smith* (1966), *They Call Me Mr. Tibbs* (1970), *Meteor* (one of Natalie Wood's final films, 1979), *Without Warning* (1980), and *Alone in the Dark* (1982).

ED LANE
Soulsbyville, California, artist who has devoted much of his work to the memory of James Dean. Lane, a member of the We Remember Dean International fan club, has been a fan since the 1950s. Dean, he says, has had a profound impact on his life: "James Dean inspired me to do things I never thought I could do, such as learn to paint, take photographs, even do some set design for local church productions."

GEORGE LANE
One of the makeup men on *Giant*.

RUSTY LANE
Actor who appeared in "Keep Our Honor Bright," a 1953 episode of the NBC television program "Kraft Television Theatre" that co-starred James Dean.

Lane also starred as a regular in the television programs "Crime with Father" (1951), "Jimmy Hughes, Rookie Cop" (1953), and "Operation Neptune" (1953).

ARNIE LANGER
New York City cabdriver who was befriended by James Dean. Langer appeared in the 1957 documentary *The James Dean Story*.

ANGELA LANSBURY
Angela Lansbury was considered for two roles in *Giant*: Vashti Snythe, which went to Jane Withers, and Luz Benedict, which went to Mercedes McCambridge.

THE LAST DAY: SEPTEMBER 30, 1955
Despite being out late the night before, James Dean woke up early on Friday morning, September 30, 1955. It was to be an eventful day for Jimmy, and sleep was even more dispensable than usual. He threw on a pair of light blue slacks, a white T-shirt, a pair of shoes, a red windbreaker, and a pair of sunglasses. He then loaded his Ford station wagon with clothes, toiletries,

Untitled Dean
by Ed Lane.

and other items he would need for the trip, locked up his house in Sherman Oaks, and plowed his way through the early-morning rush hour traffic, north on the Hollywood Freeway to the Cahuenga exit. He then maneuvered his way down Vine Street, crossing Hollywood and Sunset boulevards through a maze of cars and signal lights, and finally arrived at Competition Motors, where he met his mechanic, Rolf Wütherich. It was 8:00 A.M. Wütherich was at work, making last-minute adjustments on Jimmy's new object of affection and, for the past few days, the primary source of his anxiety—a silver streak known as the Porsche 550 Spyder.

At around 10:00 A.M. Jimmy's companions-to-be, Bill Hickman and Sandy Roth, the latter equipped with a camera, met him at Competition Motors. At around noon Jimmy hopped into the Porsche and proudly paraded it through Hollywood and West Hollywood to the Farmer's Market, where he had lunch at Patsey's Pizza with his father, Winton Dean, and his uncle, Charlie Nolan Dean, visiting from out of town. After lunch Jimmy tried to cajole his uncle into accompanying him on the trip. His uncle declined. He looked at the car and shook his head. It didn't look like the cars they drove back in Indiana. It looked like danger with a dashboard.

Jimmy looked at the car and giggled his twisted giggle. A week before, actor Alec Guinness had told him the same thing, and had prophesied, with that distinguished British accent of his, that he would be killed by the demon Porsche. Jimmy had laughed then too.

Jimmy reunited with his companions. They had an adventure to embark on and, two days later, a race to win. Wütherich climbed into the Porsche beside Jimmy, along for the ride in case of any mechanical difficulties; Hickman and Roth got into Jimmy's station wagon. They stopped for gas. Roth took photos. And they were on their way. Salinas. Back to John Steinbeck country. Back to *East of Eden*. Back to the freeway.

The route: The Ventura Freeway to Sepulveda Boulevard to Route 99 (which is now known as Interstate 5); at Castaic Junction, the band of road racers stopped at Tip's Diner before venturing back on the road. At about 3:30 P.M. Jimmy was stopped by a California highway patrolman for speeding (65 mph in a 55 mph zone); hot on his trail, Hickman and Roth were also ticketed. Back on Route 99, Dean zipped through Bakersfield. In Wasco he got off Route 99 and onto Route 466 (now 46). At about 5:00 P.M. Jimmy pulled the Porsche into Blackwell's Corner ("population 9,002 . . . 9,000 squirrels, 2 humans"), a combination gas stop/café then known as "the world's largest parking lot" and located at the intersection of Route 466 and Highway 33. Inside he bought a Coke and guzzled it. He then went to the men's room.

Back in the parking lot Jimmy met and talked with Lance Reventlow, the 21-year-old son of heiress Barbara Hutton who was also en route to the Salinas races in a gray Mercedes.

Back in the Porsche and back on the road, James Dean looked ahead and liked what he saw: a large and looming sunset that graced with gold everything it touched and a naked stretch of highway that darted in and out of the

California hills. For Jimmy this was what it was all about. He may have had a passenger sitting beside him, but for at least a moment it was just him, the hum of the engine, the feel of the wheel in his hands, and the exuberance of the wind ripping through his hair and slapping his face. Then, suddenly, from over a hill and seemingly out of nowhere, a black-topped, white-hooded Ford sedan came lumbering toward him. The driver of the Ford, 23-year-old college student Donald Turnupseed, was returning home to Fresno for the weekend. It was after 5:30 P.M., closer to 6:00. At the intersection of U.S. 466 and Highway 41 Turnupseed proceeded to make what became a fatal left turn into history. Then, at the last second, he finally spotted the oncoming, obviously foreign sports car and attempted to straighten out. James Dean made a desperate swerve to the right and fulfilled a date with destiny, the reverberations of which are still, over 35 years later, being felt all over the world.

The two cars collided. It wasn't a fair fight. The Ford mauled the tiny Porsche, which crumpled like a wad of paper in a clenched fist. The Porsche didn't flip or spin or explode with flamboyance. It merely whimpered and hobbled ahead into a ditch. As for James Dean, the impact had thrown his head back, snapping his neck. His body had been tossed across to the right side of the car and lay slumped over the passenger door. His foot, however, was pinned in the wreckage, twisted around the clutch and brake. He was dying, almost dead.

Rolf Wütherich had been thrown from the Porsche and was sprawled out on the highway, seriously injured. Donald Turnupseed suffered only cuts and bruises but stumbled about the scene in a state of shock. Eyewitnesses, ambulance attendants, highway patrolmen, and Bill Hickman and Sandy Roth arrived promptly. Hickman cradled Jimmy's head in his arms; Roth took photographs, not because he wanted to exploit the situation but because it was all he could do. Jimmy's body was released from the wreckage and raced via ambulance to the emergency room of the Paso Robles War Memorial Hospital, where he was pronounced dead on arrival.

THE LAST JAMES DEAN BOOK
Artist: Dante Volpe
Publisher: William Morrow & Company
Year: 1984

Curiously (and incorrectly, it turned out) titled book of illustrations of James Dean by artist Dante Volpe. Many of the works are rather bizarre and include Volpe's interpretation of what Dean looked like nude.

LAST WORDS
"That guy's gotta see us. He's gotta stop."

THE LATE JAMES DEAN
One-shot cover-to-cover magazine about Dean that was published in Great Britain in 1983.

THE LAUGH

James Dean had, undeniably, a unique and distinctive laugh, on and off the screen. As described by *Giant* screenwriter Ivan Moffat:

> "He had a funny laugh. A most improbable laugh, like a goat. It was always unexpected. It wasn't necessarily at a joke. It was perhaps afterward, or whenever. But he'd let forth that funny laugh."
>
> *New York*, November 8, 1976

ROD LAUREN

RCA recording artist born in 1940 who was touted as a major new teen idol and "the next James Dean" circa 1959–1960. The hype, however, went unfulfilled. Lauren scored only a minor hit, "If I Had a Girl," which made it to number 31 on the *Billboard* charts.

LAW

In September 1950 James Dean registered to major in prelaw at UCLA. He soon abandoned that aspiration, however, in favor of acting. Over the years there has been speculation that Jimmy entertained the idea of a legal career only to appease his father; however, that interest seems to have been more sincere. In 1949 his friend Jim McCarthy asked him if he planned to take up acting as a profession. Jimmy responded:

> "No! No, sir! Not an actor. Never. . . . I'm a normal, sane type. I'm going to be a lawyer."
>
> *Modern Screen*

And in 1954, during production of *East of Eden*, Jimmy told a reporter:

> "I still planned on studying law [after he became an actor], particularly criminal law after reading about William J. Fallon, Clarence Darrow and Earl Rogers. I don't know how good a lawyer I might have become but I'm still young and if I flop as an actor I'll certainly return to law study."

How good a lawyer might he have become? After the release of *East of Eden* a reporter from United Press International interviewed Jimmy's former law professor, who opined:

> "What a waste of talent! James was a fine student. I always thought he'd be a good attorney, but now I can visualize him pleading a case, combining his knowledge of law with all that dramatic ability."

JEFF LAWENDA

Executive producer of the 1988 cable documentary "Forever James Dean."

PETER LAWFORD

Peter Lawford hosted the 1974 ABC television documentary "James Dean Remembered."

The films of Peter Lawford include *Easter Parade* (1948), *Little Women*

(1949), *Exodus* (1960), and *Harlow* (1965). He also appeared as a regular in the television programs "Dear Phoebe" (1954–1956) and "The Thin Man" (1957–1959).

JACK LAWRENCE
Co-producer of *Come Back to the Five and Dime, Jimmy Dean, Jimmy Dean,* a 1982 Broadway play.

BARBARA LEACH
Jim Dean's 1949 debate partner at Fairmount (Indiana) High School.

CLORIS LEACHMAN
Co-star of "Forgotten Children," a 1952 television presentation of the "Hallmark Hall of Fame" that also featured struggling young actor James Dean.

　　Born in 1926, Cloris Leachman has appeared in several films including *Kiss Me Deadly* (1955), *The Last Picture Show* (Best Supporting Actress Oscar, 1971), and *Young Frankenstein* (1974). On television she has appeared as a regular in such programs as "Lassie" (1957–1958), "The Mary Tyler Moore Show" (1970–1975), "Phyllis" (1975–1977), and "The Facts of Life" (1986–1987).

JOE LEAHY
Recorded the Unique Records tribute album *Music James Dean Lived By.* Leahy also composed some of the songs on the album, including "The Story of James Dean."

WILLIAM LEE
Actor who appeared in "Prologue to Glory," a 1952 episode of the NBC television program "Kraft Television Theatre" in which James Dean also appeared.

THE LEFT-HANDED GUN
The Left-Handed Gun was a movie biography about Billy the Kid that James Dean planned, but didn't live, to make. In 1958 Warner Brothers made the film with Paul Newman as its star. The film was produced by Fred Coe, directed by Arthur Penn, and written by Leslie Stevens (from a television play by Gore Vidal). The cast also included John Dehner, Lita Milan, and Hurd Hatfield.

"THE LEGEND THAT WON'T DIE"
See "ENTERTAINMENT TONIGHT."

PATRICIA LEONE
Playwright and producer of *James Dean: A Dress Rehearsal,* which was first produced in Denver, Colorado, in 1984.

JOAN LESLIE

Actress who co-starred in "Hill Number One," a 1951 Easter television special presented by "Family Theatre" in which James Dean made his official television debut.

Joan Leslie, born Joan Brodell in 1925, is a former child star in vaudeville and pictures. Her film credits include *Sergeant York* (1941), *Yankee Doodle Dandy* (1942), and *Rhapsody in Blue* (1945).

"LET ME BE LOVED"

Theme song of the 1957 documentary *The James Dean Story*. The song was written by Jay Livingston and Ray Evans and was sung by Tommy Sands. It was subsequently recorded by others but never made the pop charts.

OSCAR LEVANT

> Jimmy Dean once spent a night until five in the morning talking to me about himself and his world. At that time he was working on his biggest picture, *Giant*. Arthur Loew brought him to our house, along with Elizabeth Taylor, Michael Wilding, Joan Collins, and the producer of *Giant*, Henry Ginsberg. Arthur knew that one of my daughters was an ardent Jimmy Dean fan. It was a strange thing, but seeing my daughter's room, filled with dozens of pictures of him in various poses did not seem to please Dean. On the contrary, it depressed him. He said he felt crushed under the weight of such adulation. He turned out to be a fascinating and intelligent young man who talked fluently about artists in music. And he was surprisingly knowledgeable about such recondite composers as Schönberg and Bartók.
>
> Oscar Levant, *The Unimportance of Being Oscar*

An eccentric pianist known for his sharp tongue, Levant once said of himself, "I'm a controversial figure. My friends either dislike me or hate me." James Dean was one of his friends and a frequent guest at his house in Hollywood. According to Joan Collins, "Although [they were] total opposites, [they] got along famously. Each relished the other's unusualness."

In addition to being a pianist, Levant (1906–1972) was an actor who appeared in films including *Rhapsody in Blue* (1945), *Humoresque* (1946), *An American in Paris* (1951), and *The Band Wagon* (1953). He also authored the autobiographical (and gloriously titled) books, *A Smattering of Ignorance* (1944), *Memoirs of an Amnesiac* (1965), and *The Unimportance of Being Oscar* (1968). On television Levant hosted the "G.E. Guest House" game show (1951).

BORIS LEVEN

Russian-born (1900) art director of *Giant*, for which he received an Oscar nomination.

Leven's other film credits include *Alexander's Ragtime Band* (1938), *The Shanghai Gesture* (1942), *The Sound of Music* (1965), *The Sand Pebbles*

(1966), *Star!* (1968), *The Andromeda Strain* (1971), and *The Color of Money* (1986), all of which earned him Oscar nominations. He won an Oscar for *West Side Story* (1961).

LEVI STRAUSS AND COMPANY
In the 1980s and up until the present day James Dean's image has been used to sell blue jeans by Levi Strauss and Company in the United States and Japan.

RALPH LEVY
Hollywood television director who, in 1951, was a friend of Rogers Brackett. Although Levy never directed James Dean, he, presumably at Brackett's behest, made a series of phone calls to New York to help pave his way. James Sheldon recently recalled, "Ralph was at CBS doing, at that time, 'The Jack Benny Show' and 'Burns and Allen,' and Ralph was the one who sent Jimmy to me. And, strangely enough, it was Ralph who called me the day after Jimmy was killed to tell me that he was dead."

Ralph Levy, born in 1919, won a 1959–1960 Emmy award for directing "The Jack Benny Hour Specials." He later directed the films *Bedtime Story* (1964) and *Do Not Disturb* (1965).

BILL LEWIS
Indiana resident and ardent James Dean fan who, along with Sylvia Bongiovanni, founded the We Remember Dean International fan club in 1978. In 1980 Lewis resigned from WRDI and founded the James Dean Fan Club. He died in 1986 at the age of 40.

JEANETTA LEWIS
In 1950 Jeanetta Lewis was a theater arts student at UCLA who worked as a wardrobe girl on the university production of *Macbeth*. It was during production of the play that she met and began dating James Dean. Their relationship ended with a scene of high drama in July 1951 when Lewis learned that Jimmy was also dating Beverly Wills. A confrontation ensued. In retaliation against Jeanetta's verbal taunting, Jimmy slapped her hard across the face, and then again. According to Dean biographer Venable Herndon, "blood [then] spurted out of her lips. That stopped him cold."

RUSSEL LEWIS
In 1950, Dr. Russel L. Lewis served as one of the advisors of the Opheleos Men's Honor Service Organization at Santa Monica City College, of which Jim Dean was a member.

LEWIS' RETREAT
Fairmount, Indiana, restaurant where Jimmy used to hang out while growing up. Lewis' Retreat no longer exists.

SANDY LIEBERSON
Co-producer of the 1976 documentary *James Dean: The First American Teenager.*

***LIFE* MAGAZINE**
James Dean never made the cover of *Life*, but the magazine has published a couple of articles about him:

☆ March 7, 1955   "Moody New Star"
☆ September 24, 1956   "Delirium over Dead Star"

"THE LIFE OF EMILE ZOLA"
Previous publications have reported erroneously that James Dean appeared in "The Life of Emile Zola," a March 10, 1955, episode of the NBC television program "Lux Video Theatre." The reason for the confusion is that Dean did appear in an *interview* preceding (not following, as reported in still other reports) the show, and clips of *East of Eden* were shown following it.

"The Life of Emile Zola" *did* star Lee J. Cobb, Joy Page, Gloria Holden, Robert Warwick, Paul Richards, Dayton Lummis, Booth Colman, Shepard Menken, Edgar Barrier, and Lawrence Nyle. It was directed by Buzz Kulik.

"LIFE SENTENCE"
James Dean starred in "Life Sentence," an October 16, 1953, episode of the NBC television series "Campbell Soundstage." The program co-starred Georgann Johnson and featured Dean in one of his best performances, as ex-convict Hank Bradon.

"LIFE WITH FATHER"
In 1953 James Dean auditioned for the role of Clarence Day, Jr., in "Life with Father," a CBS television series. The show was based on the autobiographical articles written by Clarence Day, Jr., for *The New Yorker* in the 1920s. The articles subsequently spawned a bestselling novel, a Broadway play, and a Hollywood movie before being adapted into a television series. "Life with Father" ran from November 1953 to July 1955.

James Dean did not get the part. He was beaten out by an actor by the name of Ralph Reed, who was eventually replaced by another actor, Steven Terrell.

LIMELIGHT
New York City nightclub (address: 660 Sixth Avenue) where a memorial tribute to James Dean was held on September 24, 1985, to commemorate the 30th anniversary of Dean's death.

CHARLES LINDBERGH
After the release of *East of Eden* James Dean was considered a leading contender to portray Charles Lindbergh in the film biopic *The Spirit of St.*

Louis (1957). However, Dean reportedly turned down the role, citing a conflict with Lindbergh over how the role should be played. The role went to Jimmy Stewart, despite the fact that Stewart was 47, 22 years older than Lindbergh was at the time of his famous flight.

Lindbergh (1902–1974) was an American airmail pilot who gained worldwide fame when he landed in Paris from New York on May 21, 1927. The historic 33½-hour flight was the first solo nonstop flight across the North Atlantic.

ROBERT M. LINDNER

Rebel Without a Cause was originally the title of a book about juvenile delinquency by Dr. Robert M. Lindner. In 1946 the book was purchased by Warner Brothers, which planned to produce it as a movie. When the film finally went into production eight years later, Lindner volunteered his services as a consultant. However, Nick Ray, the film's director, had other ideas. Ray rejected Lindner's offer, and by the time the film had completed shooting in May 1955, virtually everything from Lindner's book had also been rejected—except, of course, for the title.

RAY LINN

It wasn't Raymond Massey humming in *East of Eden*; it was Ray Linn. For his professional and expert humming services Warner Brothers paid Linn $70.

PEGGY LIPTON

"The Mod Squad" Madonna of primetime television, Peggy Lipton had been linked romantically with Paul McCartney, Lou Adler, and Sammy Davis, Jr., but it was, according to a 1969 article in *TV-Movie Parade* ("Peggy Lipton's Dilemma: She's in Love with a Dead Man!"), James Dean with whom she was most in love.

According to the article Peggy had rebelled against her parents and the Beverly Hills community in which she was being raised and moved into a "hippie-type retreat" in Topanga Canyon. During that period "she came under the post-mortem spell of the Jimmy Dean mystique." The article proceeded to chronicle her alleged infatuation:

> One night, after an evening spent with a close friend of Jimmy's, Peggy went to bed and had what seemed like an extraordinarily vivid dream in which Jimmy came and made love to her. But it was not exactly a dream, because when she "woke up" Jimmy was still there, sitting in her bedroom speaking to her.
> This was the first of a long series of nocturnal visits in which Jimmy came to her bedroom, made love to her, and conversed with her as a friend and as a lover.

Prior to starring as Julie in the popular ABC series "The Mod Squad" (1968–1973), Peggy Lipton appeared in "The John Forsythe Show"

(1965–1966). In 1974 she married music producer and occasional movie producer (*The Color Purple*) Quincy Jones, whom she has since divorced. Recently, she returned to television as the sexually repressed diner owner in David Lynch's evening soap, "Twin Peaks."

"In David's work, everyone is sexually repressed."

Peggy Lipton

"LITTLE BASTARD"

The week of his death James Dean christened his new Porsche Spyder "Little Bastard" after his own nickname and commissioned car customizer George Barris to paint the name on the back end of the Porsche.

THE LITTLE PRINCE

For James Dean Antoine de Saint-Exupéry's classic, *The Little Prince*, was more than a favorite book; it was a philosophy. He read it repeatedly and often quoted passages to his friends. Jimmy was so enamored of the book that he wanted to direct a film version of it. The movie was eventually made, but not until 1974, as a musical directed by Stanley Donen, with songs by Frederick Loewe and Alan Jay Lerner. The cast included Richard Kiley, Steven Warner, Bob Fosse (in a dazzling turn), and Gene Wilder.

LITTLE RIVER INN

Hotel in Little River, California, three miles north of Mendocino, where the cast and crew of *East of Eden* resided during the late May and early June 1954 location shooting. Connie Reynolds, the inn owner's daughter who was in the third grade at the time, recently recalled, "Julie Harris was really nice. They were regular people. Jimmy slept in my bed. He had a case of poison oak and was laid up for a period. My mom cooked him some of his meals and did some of his ironing because he was so miserable."

What did she remember most about James Dean? "He blew his nose like a lumberjack."

Today the Little River Inn, built in 1853, is a California landmark. During his visit there James Dean stayed in Room 8.

"THE LITTLE WOMAN"

"The Little Woman" was a March 30, 1954, episode of the CBS television program "Danger" that starred Lydia Reed, Lee Bergere, and James Dean. The program was produced and directed by Andrew McCullough and featured Dean as Augie, a delinquent on the run who is provided shelter in a little girl's playhouse. According to McCullough, during rehearsals Jimmy developed a rapport with Lydia Reed, the eight-year-old playing the part of the little girl. "Wherever she went with the performance," McCullough marveled, "he was there supporting her. [His] was one of the most generous performances I've ever seen. Not an ounce of ego in it."

JAY LIVINGSTON
Co-writer of "Let Me Be Loved," the theme song of the 1957 documentary *The James Dean Story.* An Oscar-winning songwriter, Livingston was born in 1915 and usually collaborated with Ray Evans. For more biographical information, *see* RAY EVANS.

ROBERT LIVINGSTON
Director of *Dean,* an unsuccessful 1977 British stage musical.

RUSS LLEWELLYN
One of the assistant directors on *Giant.*

LLOYDS OF LONDON
The week of his death James Dean took out an insurance policy on his life with Lloyds of London. The policy was worth $100,000 and was subsequently awarded to Jimmy's father, Winton Dean.

GENE LOCKHART
Gene Lockhart co-starred in "Hill Number One," a 1951 Easter television special presented by "Family Theatre." "Hill Number One" featured James Dean in his official television debut. Lockhart later starred in "The Bells of Cockaigne," a 1953 episode of the NBC television program "Armstrong Circle Theatre" in which James Dean had a co-starring role.

　　Lockhart and Dean didn't get along. According to James Sheldon, who directed "The Bells of Cockaigne," "Gene Lockhart complained to me. I remember him coming to me and saying—and he was a very lovely man and a real pro—'You've got to talk to *that boy.* He's very difficult to work with, and I never know what he's doing. He's very rude.' "

　　In addition to his television appearances, Canadian-born Gene Lockhart (1891–1957) appeared in a multitude of films including *Blondie* (1938), *Algiers* (Best Supporting Actor Oscar nomination, 1938), *His Girl Friday* (1940), *Going My Way* (1944), *Leave Her to Heaven* (1945), and *The Man in the Grey Flannel Suit* (1956).

LOCKHEED AIRPORT
Burbank, California, airport that served as a location for *Giant.* In the film the airport was portrayed as Jett Rink's personal landing strip. Lockheed Airport is located at 2627 Hollywood Way.

DAVID LOEHR
　　"I'm obsessed. I don't think there is anything wrong with it. I'm
　　hoping to keep his memory going. It's a tribute."
　　　　　　　　　　　　　　　　David Loehr, *Gotham,* August 1989

New Yorker David Loehr is the undisputed "dean of Deanabilia." His

David Loehr (left) and friends Damien Chapa and Lenny.

collection of James Dean photographs, personal belongings, costumes, and memorabilia is without peer among Dean aficionados.

Loehr, born in Pittsfield, Massachusetts, was introduced to James Dean in 1974 via David Dalton's biography *James Dean: The Mutant King*. After reading the book, he saw a screening of *East of Eden* on a big screen at a Los Angeles film festival. He has been mesmerized (and collecting) ever since. According to Loehr, "I began searching memorabilia shops, bookstores, and flea markets for anything concerning James Dean. I found photos, books, magazines, and posters. Items seemed scarce since Dean had been gone for 20 years. Gradually I found things, and before long my collection filled an entire cardboard box."

Today the number of items in that cardboard box has grown to such enormity that the collection is stored at Loehr's James Dean Gallery, a 12-room house in Fairmount, Indiana. The gallery opened in September 1988 and represents the fulfillment of Loehr's longtime dream—a monument of memorabilia. It also signifies, in a way, Jimmy's return to his hometown.

David Loehr has funded his passion for James Dean by working as a clothing manufacturer in New York. He has also served as an archivist and/or photo researcher on several Dean-related projects, including the superb 1984 David Dalton/Ron Cayen biography *James Dean: American Icon*, the 1989 British photo book *James Dean: Shooting Star*, and the 1988 cable documentary "Forever James Dean." Loehr is also the founder of Jade Productions, which produces and organizes events related to Dean, such as the annual James Dean Walking Tour of New York Hangouts.

David Loehr has devoted his life to the memory of James Dean. While some might question his obsession, no one can question his success. Loehr is the quintessential Dean disciple.

ARTHUR LOEW, JR.

Circa 1954–1955 Arthur Loew, Jr., was a rich, young Hollywood playboy who dabbled in producing films (including *The Rack* with Paul Newman) and romancing women (Eartha Kitt, Joan Collins, et al.). He was also the cousin of *Rebel Without a Cause* screenwriter Stewart Stern, the grandson of both Marcus Loew (who founded MGM Studios), and Adolph Zukor (producer and pioneer of Paramount Studios), and a good friend of James Dean's. In 1956 Loew founded the James Dean Memorial Fund in honor of his friend at the Actors Studio in New York.

ELLA LOGAN

One of James Dean's dates. Jimmy had been introduced to Ella Logan by Elia Kazan on the set of *East of Eden*. Subsequently he was a frequent party guest at her Hollywood home. Later Logan appeared on Broadway in *Finian's Rainbow*.

BEVERLY LONG

Beverly Long first met James Dean in December 1950, when they were both cast, along with another young actor, Nick Adams, in a Pepsi commercial shot at Griffith Park in Hollywood. Each was fresh-faced, under 20, and virtually bursting with plans for the future. Beverly Long recently recalled, "Nick Adams was dating my roommate, and he had the [Pepsi] job and got the job for my roommate and for me. [Jimmy and I] talked about the fact that I thought it was so brave that he was gonna go to New York and seek his fortune and become an *actor*. And of course that's just what he did. I remember reading about him when he got the part in *See the Jaguar* and a couple of other things that he did. I remember reading about him, 'The bright young star on the horizon,' and thinking, 'Gee, I did a commercial with him.' "

Four years later Beverly Long was just another pretty Hollywood blond struggling to get a part. She was in a stage play with Corey Allen at the time, and film director Nick Ray saw the play and invited them both to audition for his new movie about juvenile delinquency, *Rebel Without a Cause*. Long remembers, "The first auditions were real chaos. They were *nuts*. They had every teenager, no, every young person in Hollywood auditioning!"

After she was cast as one of the gang members in *Rebel* in March 1955, Long went over to the Egyptian Theater in Hollywood to see *East of Eden*, which had just opened, and was flabbergasted by and unprepared for what she saw. The boy who had worked with her in the Pepsi commercial was going to be a star.

Back on the set Long found herself intimidated by Dean, but not only because of his sudden stature. Long recalls, "He seemed to be able to get my number. I was very easy prey for him. It seemed like no matter what I said, he would always kind of twist it and turn it into an off-color joke. I never knew quite how to deal with him, because he would do little things, play tricks on you, mind tricks. [With Jimmy] I was never quite sure that I wasn't gonna be the brunt of some joke. He was weird that way."

After giving up acting, Beverly Long became an entertainment agent. Today she owns and operates her own successful casting agency in Hollywood.

"A LONG TIME TILL DAWN"
"A Long Time Till Dawn" was a November 11, 1953, episode of the NBC television program "Kraft Television Theatre" that co-starred James Dean. The program was produced and directed by Dick Dunlap and written by Rod Serling. It co-starred Naomi Riordan, Robert Simon, Ted Osborn, and Rudolph Weiss.

"A Long Time Till Dawn" featured Dean as Joe Harris, a convicted felon just released from prison who attempts to straighten out his life. As described in the script by Serling, Harris was a poet and a gangster—"violence with big blue eyes." Although relatively obscure, "A Long Time Till Dawn" contains one of the finest performances by James Dean—in any medium.

LONGMONT, COLORADO
Fairmount (Indiana) High School senior Jim Dean competed in a national speech competition in Longmont, Colorado, on April 29–30, 1949. He placed sixth. On the night of April 29 Jimmy evaded coach and chaperon Adeline Nall and spent the evening scouting the town of Longmont.

LOOK MAGAZINE
One of the first, if not the first, periodicals to recognize the star potential in James Dean. *Look* has published the following articles about Dean:

☆ January 11, 1955   "These Will Be the Brightest Stars of 1955"
☆ October 16, 1956   "James Dean, The Legend and the Facts"*

Look cover that Dean appeared on.

PERRY LOPEZ
Circa 1954–55 Perry Lopez was a Warner Brothers contract player who met and befriended James Dean. The weekend of September 30, 1955, Lopez was at a Hollywood party when he learned of Jimmy's death. When told the news, Lopez, according to *The Hollywood Reporter*, "upended his drink and poured it on the bar."

Perry Lopez, born (believe it or not) Christian Julius Caesar Lopez in New York in 1931, was discovered by Joshua Logan for a touring company of

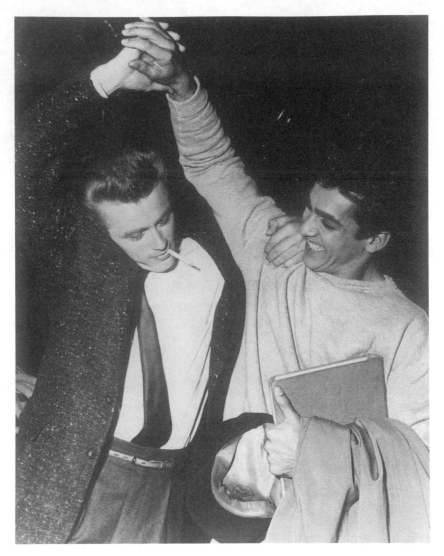

Dean cavorting with friend Perry Lopez.

South Pacific. Soon after he left the show in 1953, Lopez was the victim of an automobile accident in New York. While recuperating in Los Angeles, he screen-tested at Warner Brothers. Subsequent films included *Drum Beat* (1954), *Battle Cry* (1955), *Mister Roberts* (1955), *Hell on Frisco Bay* (1955), and *Chinatown* (1974).

LOS ANGELES, CALIFORNIA
James Dean first moved to Los Angeles with his parents in 1936, at the age of five, when his father was transferred to the Veterans Administration Hospital in Sawtelle, which is located between Santa Monica, Brentwood, and Westwood. In 1940, following his mother's death, Jimmy returned to

Indiana to be raised by his aunt and uncle.

Upon his high school graduation in June 1949, however, and with aspirations of stardom, 18-year-old Jimmy moved back to Los Angeles. For a little over a year he lived with his father and stepmother in their Santa Monica home, during which time he attended Santa Monica City College. By September 1950, however, his father had moved to Reseda, California, so, newly enrolled at UCLA, Jimmy got accepted into a fraternity and lived at the frat house in Westwood, where he stayed until early 1951, when he moved into a nearby apartment with his friend, Bill Bast. In the late summer of that year, after a falling-out with Bast, Jimmy left the Westwood area and moved into various hotels, apartments, and the homes of friends in Hollywood and West Hollywood until October 1951, when, with hopes of becoming a "real actor," he moved to New York City.

James Dean was escorted back to Los Angeles in March 1954 by director Elia Kazan, who wanted him to star in the film version of John Steinbeck's *East of Eden*. During the making of the picture Jimmy lived and worked, when not on location, primarily in the Burbank area (he also lived in his father's house in West Los Angeles for a short period). After *Eden* was completed in August 1954, Jimmy returned to New York. When preparations for *Rebel Without a Cause* began in January 1955, Jimmy returned to Los Angeles and moved into a home in the hills above West Hollywood, where he stayed, when not on location, until late July 1955. At that time Jimmy moved into a house in Sherman Oaks, in what is commonly regarded with disdain as "The Valley." It was this house that he left on the morning of September 30, 1955.

James Dean's Los Angeles: A Selective List and Tour Guide

Location	Address	City
Baldwin Hills	5975 Citrus Ave.	BaH
Barney's Beanery	8447 Santa Monica Blvd.	WH
*Beachcomber Cafe	1727 N. McCadden Pl.	H
Brentwood Country Mart	26th St. and San Vicente Blvd.	Br
Brentwood Elementary	740 Gretna Green Way	Br
CBS Radio	6121 Sunset Blvd.	H
Chateau Marmont Hotel	8221 Sunset Blvd.	WH
*Competition Motors	1219 N. Vine St.	H
*Crescendo Club	8572 Sunset Blvd.	WH
*Dr. James Cogan's office	414 N. Camden Dr.	BH
*Dr. Ronald Sattler's office	9629 Brighton Way	BH
*The Egyptian Theater	6708 Hollywood Blvd.	H
*Famous Artists Corporation	9441 Wilshire Blvd.	BH
Farmer's Market	Fairfax Ave. and 3rd St.	WH
*Foote, Cone and Belding	6233 Hollywood Blvd.	H
*George Barris's garage	3457 S. LaBrea Ave.	LA
*Googie's	8100 Sunset Blvd.	WH
*Gower Plaza Hotel	1607 N. Gower St.	H
Grauman's Chinese Theater	6925 Hollywood Blvd.	H
Griffith Park and Observatory	Los Feliz Blvd. and Vermont Ave.	H

*Hamburger Hamlet	8929 Sunset Blvd.	WH
Hollywood Walk of Fame	1717 N. Vine St.	H
Home	1422 23rd St.	SM
Home	814-B 6th St.	SM
Home	601 Gayley Ave.	WW
Home	Comstock Ave.	WW
Home	1607 N. Gower Ave.	H
Home	1667 S. Bundy Dr.	Sa
Home	3908 W. Olive Ave.	Bur
Home	4000 W. Olive Ave.	Bur
Home	1541 Sunset Plaza Dr.	WH
*Home	14611 Sutton St.	SO
*The Isabelle Draesemer Agency	8272 Sunset Blvd.	WH
*Jerry Fairbanks Productions	6052 Sunset Blvd.	H
*Kenneth Kendall's studio	8110 Melrose Ave.	WH
Knickerbocker Hotel	1714 N. Ivar Ave.	H
La Reina Theater	14626 Ventura Blvd.	SO
*Lew Bracker's Insurance Co.	12040 Wilshire Blvd.	Sa
Lockheed Airport	2627 Hollywood Way	Bur
Mocambo	8588 Sunset Blvd.	WH
Mulholland Drive	Mulholland Drive	H
*Pegot Waring's studio	8362 Melrose Ave.	WH
St. Timothy's Catholic Church	10425 W. Pico Blvd.	RPk
*Sandy and Beulah Roth's home	1158 Hacienda Pl.	WH
*Santa Monica City College	601 Pico Blvd.	SM
Santa Monica High School	601 Pico Blvd.	SM
*Schwab's Pharmacy	8024 Sunset Blvd.	WH
*Sunset Boulevard mansion	641 Irving Blvd.	HPk
UCLA	405 Hilgard Ave.	WW
Veterans Administration	Sawtelle and Wilshire Blvd.	Sa
*Villa Capri	1735 N. McCadden Pl.	H
Warner Brothers	4000 W. Olive Ave.	Bur
Wattles Park	Gardner St. and Franklin Ave.	H
*Will Wright's ice cream parlor	8252 Santa Monica Blvd.	WH
*Winton and Ethel Dean's home	7235 Yolanda Ave.	Res
*Winton and Ethel Dean's home	1527½ S. Saltair Ave.	Sa

---

*No longer in existence, no longer operated and occupied by same company or individual(s), or still in business but not at same address

Key

BaH	Baldwin Hills		Res	Reseda
BH	Beverly Hills		RPk	Rancho Park
Br	Brentwood		Sa	Sawtelle
Bur	Burbank		SM	Santa Monica
H	Hollywood		SO	Sherman Oaks
HPk	Hancock Park		WH	West Hollywood
LA	Los Angeles mid-city		WW	Westwood

LOS ANGELES COUNTY MUSEUM OF ART
On July 1, 1978, the Los Angeles County Museum of Art presented a tribute

called "Three Rebel Heroes," dedicated to John Garfield, Montgomery Clift, and James Dean. The tribute included the screening of movies starring each of the actors.

THE *LOS ANGELES HERALD-EXAMINER*
Los Angeles newspaper that very possibly published the last article about James Dean while he was alive. The article was headlined "James Dean Planning to Go on a Racing Kick When *Giant* Ends." It was dated September 16, 1955.

Other *Herald-Examiner* articles about Dean include:

☆ September 28, 1985   "30 Years Later, James Dean Fans Remain Devoted"
☆ September 30, 1985   "A Cause Without a Rebel"
☆ March 20, 1986   "James Dean, A Giant on Television"
☆ December 4, 1987   "James Dean, A Rebel Who Kept Himself in the Fast Lane"

The *Herald-Examiner* went defunct in 1989.

THE *LOS ANGELES MIRROR*
Defunct Los Angeles newspaper that published a few articles about James Dean, including:

☆ September 30, 1960   "James Dean's Fans Still Write to Him"

THE *LOS ANGELES MIRROR-NEWS*
Defunct Los Angeles newspaper that published several articles about James Dean, including:

☆ March 29, 1955   "Dean Wants Isolation"
☆ August 6, 1956   "Continued Worship of Dean Assumes Macabre Aspect"
☆ October 24, 1956   "Jinx Trails Dean's Car"
☆ April 25, 1957   "Elia Kazan Decries the James Dean Myth"

THE *LOS ANGELES TIMES*
Los Angeles newspaper that has published numerous articles about James Dean, including one of the first (if not the first) to appear in a major city newspaper. The article appeared in the November 7, 1954 (four months before the release of *East of Eden*) issue of the *Times* and was headlined "Jimmy Dean Says He Isn't Flattered by Being Labeled 'Another Brando.' "

Other *Times* articles about James Dean include:

☆ February 16, 1976   "Recurring Myth of Dean"
☆ December 18, 1977   "Jimmy Dean, Giant Legend, Cult Rebel" by Leonard Rosenman
☆ December 18, 1977   "Town Where James Dean Died Gets Memorial"
☆ February 8, 1981   "The Man Who Would Be 50" by Gene Owen
☆ September 29, 1983   "Driving in the Shadow of James Dean"
☆ July 7, 1985   "From the James Dean Archives"
☆ September 29, 1985   "Rebel with an Agent"
☆ September 30, 1985   "Elia Kazan Ponders the Dean Image"

LOUIE'S TAVERN
One of James Dean's New York hangouts, Louie's Tavern, was located in Greenwich Village at Seventh Avenue and West Fourth Street.

THE LOUIS SCHURR AGENCY
In 1952 James Dean was represented by the Louis Schurr Agency in New York City (address: 1501 Broadway). His agent was Jane Deacy, an enterprising woman who had worked her way up at Schurr from a secretarial position. When Deacy left Schurr to form her own agency later that year, James Dean went with her and Schurr, although he probably wasn't cognizant of it at the time, lost a major star client.

LOVERS
Over the years an innumerable number of women—and men—have been reported to have had a sexual relationship with James Dean. So many have been named, in fact, that no attempt to list them all will be made on these pages. Besides, James Dean was basically dispassionate in bed—more of a cuddler than a pounce and pump type—so some of his "partners" might have taken a pat on the head as foreplay or an open-mouthed kiss construed as oral sex.

Because of the still-controversial subject of homosexuality, only those men who have themselves suggested they had sex with Dean are included here. The women included either made the claim themselves or were reported to have had sexual relations with Dean by individuals who knew Jimmy. Therefore the following list is representative of James Dean's lovers, actual and alleged, and makes no pretense of being complete:

Cathy Anderson	John Gilmore	Betsy Palmer
Ursula Andress	Barbara Glenn	Dizzy Sheridan
Pier Angeli	Lilli Kardell	Christine White
Rogers Brackett	Lori Nelson	Beverly Wills
Lynne Carter		

GEORGE LOWTHER
Writer of "The Bells of Cockaigne," a 1953 episode of the NBC television program "Armstrong Circle Theatre" that co-starred James Dean.

KARL LUCAS
Actor who appeared in "The Bells of Cockaigne," a 1953 episode of the NBC television program "Armstrong Circle Theatre" that co-starred James Dean.

JERRY LUCE
Owner of Jerry's Bar and Restaurant, one of James Dean's favorite hangouts in New York City. Jimmy and Jerry had a friendly relationship, and on the occasions when Jimmy, then a struggling actor, couldn't afford to pay for the meatballs on his spaghetti Jerry waived the check.

PAUL LUKAS
Actor who starred in "The Thief," a 1955 episode of the ABC television program "U.S. Steel Hour" that co-starred James Dean.

Paul Lukas (1887–1971), born Pal Lukacs in Hungary, was primarily a film actor. His credits include *Little Women* (1933), *The Three Musketeers* (1935), *Dodsworth* (1936), *Watch on the Rhine* (Best Actor Oscar winner over Humphrey Bogart in *Casablanca*, 1943), *20,000 Leagues Under the Sea* (1954), *55 Days at Peking* (1963), and *Lord Jim* (1965).

SIDNEY LUMET
Before he became a renowned motion picture director, Sidney Lumet directed episodes of the television programs "Danger" and "Studio One." He also directed unknown actor James Dean in "The Capture of Jesse James," an early 1953 episode of the CBS program "You Are There."

Sidney Lumet, born in 1924, has had an impressive career that includes the films *Twelve Angry Men* (Best Director Oscar nomination, 1957), *A View from the Bridge* (1961), *Long Day's Journey into Night* (1962), *Serpico* (1973), *Murder on the Orient Express* (1974), *Dog Day Afternoon* (Best Director Oscar nomination, 1975), *Network* (Best Director Oscar nomination, 1976), *The Wiz* (1978), *Prince of the City* (Best Adapted Screenplay Oscar nomination, shared credit, 1981), *The Verdict* (Best Director Oscar nomination, 1982), *The Morning After* (1986), *Running on Empty* (one of the decade's underrated films, 1988), and *Family Business* (1989).

"LUX VIDEO THEATRE"
Early in his career, on March 17, 1952, James Dean co-starred in "The Foggy, Foggy Dew," an episode of the CBS television program "Lux Video Theatre." Later, on March 10, 1955, he did a live interview on this show (which had by then moved to NBC), immediately preceding a presentation of "The Life of Emile Zola." The interview was to promote *East of Eden*, which officially opened in New York that day. After Dean's death, on February 9, 1956, "Lux Video Theatre" presented the *Photoplay* Gold Medal awards ceremony, during which James Dean was given a posthumous special achievement award.

DIANA LYNN
Actress who co-starred in "The Thief," a 1955 episode of the ABC television program "U.S. Steel Hour" that also co-starred James Dean.

Former child actress Diana Lynn (1926–1971), born Dolores Loehr, also appeared in many films including *The Miracle of Morgan's Creek* (1944), *Our Hearts Were Young and Gay* (1944), and *The Kentuckian* (1955).

RONALD LYON
One of the producers of the 1974 television documentary "James Dean Remembered."

GENE LYONS
Co-star of "Sentence of Death," a 1953 episode of the CBS television program "Studio One Summer Theatre" that also co-starred James Dean.

Gene Lyons later appeared as Commissioner Dennis Randall, a regular character on the hit television series "Ironside" (1967–1975).

M

MOSS MABRY

Costume designer of *Rebel Without a Cause*. Mabry also designed Elizabeth Taylor's costumes for *Giant*, for which he received a 1956 Oscar nomination. Mabry received additional Oscar nominations for *What a Way to Go* (shared credit with Edith Head, 1964), *Morituri* (1965), and *The Way We Were* (shared credit, 1973).

MACBETH

James Dean portrayed Malcolm in a UCLA production of Shakespeare's *Macbeth*. The play was presented on the university campus at Royce Hall from November 29, 1950, until December 2, 1950. Dean performed his role,

College sophomore James Dean (right) in the UCLA production of *Macbeth*, 1950.

according to Bill Bast (who was also involved in the production), with "the most dreadful Indiana accent, a terrible farm-boy twang. [He] couldn't pronounce the Shakespeare, couldn't get his tongue around it."

PERCY MacKAYE
Playwright of *The Scarecrow*, a 1910 play reproduced off Broadway in 1953 with James Dean in a small part.

MacKaye, born in 1875, wrote numerous other plays including *Jeanne d'Arc* (1906) and *George Washington* (1920).

"A MADMAN'S MANUSCRIPT"

"It's about this real gone cat who knocks off several people. It also begins with a scream. I really woke up those judges."

James Dean, *New York Times*, March 13, 1955

For the 1949 National Forensic League speech competition, Fairmount (Indiana) High School senior Jim Dean performed a dramatic interpretation of "A Madman's Manuscript" from *The Pickwick Papers* by Charles Dickens. He placed first on the state level and sixth on the national level.

MADONNA
Pop music's metamorphic dance diva, Madonna Louise Ciccone (born in Bay City, Michigan, 1958) recorded a song about James Dean, "Jimmy, Jimmy," which was included on her *True Blue* album, released in 1986.

MAGAZINES
Beginning in 1956 and up until the present date, enterprising publishers have been printing special-issue one-shot magazines that feature, from cover to cover (and from every conceivable angle), Dean, Dean, and more Dean.

The following is a chronological list of the one-shot magazines that have been published (English language only) about James Dean.

Jimmy Dean Returns!	Rave Publishing	1956
The Official James Dean Anniversary Book	Dell Publishing	1956
The James Dean Album	Ideal Publishing	1956
The Real James Dean Story	Fawcett Publishing	1956
James Dean: A Story in Words and Pictures	Anabas Publishing (Great Britain)	1985
Screen Greats Presents James Dean	Starlog Press	1988
Film Threat: September 30, 1955 Never Happened	Gore Publishing	1988
The Best of James Dean in the Scandal Magazines 1955–1958	Shake Books	1988
James Dean: The Man and the Legend	SM Distribution (Great Britain)	1988

The 10 Important Magazine Articles About James Dean
Over the years there have been hundreds, if not thousands, of magazine articles written and published about James Dean. Most of them simply recycled often erroneous biographical material or wasted words on trivial

concerns. There have, however, been a few dozen articles that offered readers original, informative research and interviews. The following is a selection of 10 of those articles. In some cases the articles were written by people who knew Dean; in all cases the articles were written by people who had something to say.

1. "Moody New Star" photographs by Dennis Stock, *Life*, March 7, 1955
2. "Keep Your Eye on James Dean" by Hedda Hopper, *Chicago Tribune Magazine*, March 27, 1955
3. "Lone Wolf" by Richard Moore, *Modern Screen*, August 1955
4. "The Boy I Loved" by Emma Dean, *Photoplay*, March 1956
5. "Delirium over Dead Star" by Ezra Goodman, *Life*, September 24, 1956
6. "Death Drive: The Last Story About Jimmy" by Rolf Wutherich, *Modern Screen*, October 1957
7. "In Memory of Jimmy" by Dizzy Sheridan, *Photoplay*, October 1957
8. "NBC to Air 'Portrait' of Dean" by Donald von Widenman, *The Advocate*, February 25, 1976
9. "Soliloquy on James Dean's 45th Birthday" by Derek Marlowe, *New York*, November 8, 1976
10. "Epitaph for a Rebel" by William Zavatsky, *Rolling Stone*, October 16, 1980

MAGNUM PHOTOS
New York–based photo agency for which Dennis Stock worked when he shot his legendary Fairmount and New York sessions with James Dean in 1955.

MAID
Susan Bray was James Dean's maid in 1955.

MAKEUP ARTISTS
Gordon Bau was the designer and supervisor of the makeup department at Warner Brothers during James Dean's tenure there. Bau oversaw the makeup for *East of Eden, Rebel Without a Cause,* and *Giant.* However, the makeup men who actually worked on Dean (and who were not credited on screen) are:

☆ Robert Ewing: *East of Eden*
☆ Henry Villardo: *Rebel Without a Cause*
☆ Henry Villardo: *Giant*
☆ George Bau: *Giant*
☆ George Lane: *Giant*
☆ Frank Prehoda: *Giant*
☆ Bill Woods: *Giant*

EMMA MALLAN
During the summer of 1955 Emma Mallan was the proprietor of the El Paisano Hotel in Marfa, Texas, and host for the cast and crew of *Giant* during its location shooting in and around Marfa.

"MAMA"
Hit CBS television series (1949–1956) that was based on the book *Mama's*

Bank Account by Kathryn Forbes and the subsequent and highly successful Broadway play *I Remember Mama*. "Mama" starred Peggy Wood, Judson Laire, Dick Van Patten, Rosemary Rice, and Robin Morgan. It also *almost* starred James Dean. James Sheldon recently recalled, "He [Dean] had just arrived in New York, and I knew that the producers of a big hit show that I was in charge of at the [advertising] agency, 'Mama,' were looking for a replacement because Dick Van Patten, who was playing the part [of Nels, the young brother], was going into the army. So, I sent Jimmy over—and he got the part."

However, as fate would have it, after James Dean got the part Dick Van Patten was classified 4-F, was exempted from military service, and returned to the show. As for Dean, he was back out on the streets. Temporarily.

DANIEL MANN

> "Jimmy could never be told anything. Our play [*The Immoralist*] was ensemble and the actors had responsibilities to each other. But Jimmy had no graciousness, or politeness, or concern on stage. And yet, at the same time, he had flashes of real brilliance."
>
> Daniel Mann, *Motion Picture*, September 1956

He also had flashes of real temper, aimed at his director. James Dean did not get along with Daniel Mann, and the feeling was mutual.

Mann's directing career includes the films *Come Back, Little Sheba* (1952), *The Rose Tattoo* (1955), *I'll Cry Tomorrow* (1955), *The Teahouse of the August Moon* (1956), and *Butterfield 8* (1960), and the television movie "Playing for Time" (1980). It's interesting to note that Mann had far more success with actresses than actors. The projects listed above netted Best Actress Oscars for Shirley Booth, Anna Magnani, and Elizabeth Taylor (along with another nomination for Susan Hayward), and a Best Actress Emmy for Vanessa Redgrave.

JAYNE MANSFIELD

If Marilyn Monroe was the blond bombshell of the 1950s, Jayne Mansfield was the blond bomb-in-waiting, a 40-24-36 superstructure who threatened to explode out of her costumes at the slightest provocation. In one of Hollywood's more outlandish casting contemplations Mansfield, before she became a name, was one of the actresses considered for the part of Judy in *Rebel Without a Cause*. After he gave the part to Natalie Wood, director Nick Ray planned to cast Mansfield in a bit part as a car hop—before the scene was excised from the script.

MANTOVANI

With his 40-piece orchestra, Mantovani, born Annunzio Paolo Mantovani in Venice, Italy, in 1905, scored several hit versions of movie themes, including the themes from *Around the World in 80 Days* (1956) and *Exodus* (1960). One of his nonhit recordings was "Let Me Be Loved," the theme song from *The James Dean Story*.

LINDA MANZ

"Everyone tells me I look just like him. He had the same split in the eyebrow that I do, and the same hairline too."
                                        Linda Manz, *Los Angeles Times*, 1982

In the late 1970s and early 1980s Linda Manz, an actress from New York, was being touted as "the next Dean" or "the reincarnation of Dean." At the time Manz dismissed the comparison, saying that she had never seen a Dean film. But she also added that she was writing a film script about a street kid who discovers that she's the reincarnation of James Dean. Naturally, explained Manz, no one believes her—until she dies in a car crash.

The film career of Linda Manz includes *Days of Heaven* (1978), *King of the Gypsies* (1978), and *Out of the Blue* (directed by Dennis Hopper, 1982).

DONALEE MARANS

Actress who portrayed the wife of the character played by James Dean in "The Bells of Cockaigne," a 1953 episode of the NBC television program "Armstrong Circle Theatre."

MARFA, TEXAS

It is located somewhere south and east of El Paso in a region of the damned. The Marfans or Marfites or whatever they call themselves may be terrific individuals, but if they are, why don't they move?
                                        Mercedes McCambridge, *The Quality of Mercy*

Marfa, Texas, the unremarkable town with the phenomenal phantom lights, served as the primary location for Warner Brothers' mammoth production, *Giant*. From May 31 until June 4, 1955, the cast and crew of *Giant* descended by train and plane on the town of Marfa with their Hollywood money and their fake Texan accents and, for the next five weeks, literally took over the town. Most of the company was housed at the El Paisano Hotel. The stars, however, were provided with houses, rented from the townspeople, to share. James Dean, Rock Hudson, and Chill Wills, unlikely roommates in any other situation, were housed together in a residence owned by a Mr. and Mrs. Jackson.

The locals, for the most part, didn't mind the inconvenience. Many were employed as extras, and many profited from the production in some other manner. Most were just content to ogle Elizabeth Taylor and Rock Hudson and the newcomer named Dean. Some were starstruck, some were curious, and some were merely bemused by what was, in their view, much ado about nothing. Approximately 1,000 spectators, gathered from all neighboring parts, watched the daily shooting. They went to the Worth Evans Ranch, used in the film as Reata, which was actually located 20 miles west of Marfa. They also went to the Ben Avant Ranch, a small portion of which was used as Jett Rink's Little Reata, and which was located seven miles west of Marfa.

For the cast and crew Marfa, after its initial novelty, was a dust bowl and a bore. There was virtually no nightlife, and the days were spent under a sweltering sun, while George Stevens, the slowest of directors, painstakingly shot and reshot his film.

On July 10, 1955, most of the *Giant* company bade farewell to Marfa. A few days later James Dean, along with members of the second-unit film crew, also departed. The parting was, understandably, only fairly amicable and eagerly anticipated. The company returned to Hollywood. The Marfans, or Marfites, or whatever they call themselves, returned to Marfa, with its hot and monotonous days and its miraculous lights.

THE *MARION CHRONICLE-TRIBUNE*

Indiana newspaper that has published many articles about James Dean, including:

☆ September 28, 1975	"He Wasn't Perfect"
☆ September 30, 1980	"The Mist of a Legend, 25 Years Later"
☆ October 1, 1980	"For Them, James Dean Won't Die"
☆ April 16, 1983	"Stone Is Missing, but Spirit Remains"
☆ September 29, 1985	"James Dean, Legend and Legacy After 30 Years"
☆ September 29, 1985	"A Place Where the Dean Legend Is at Home"
☆ September 29, 1985	"Fairmount and James Dean: Going in Search of a Legend"
☆ September 1, 1986	"Although the Life Is Over, the Legend Lives"
☆ September 29, 1990	"Fairmount, and the World, Honor Dean"

MARION, INDIANA

Although Fairmount, Indiana, is generally regarded as James Dean's home-town, it was in the nearby town of Marion where he was born in the home of his parents. Today a memorial sidewalk plaque in the shape of a star commemorates the site at Fourth and McClure streets. It reads: "James Dean, Movie Actor. 1931–1955. A Legend in His Lifetime." At the same location another plaque reads: "On this site stood the Seven Gables [apartment complex] where James Dean, one of the most charismatic and idolized actors of all time was born on February 8, 1931. Erected by the Marion Quarterback Club."

OWEN MARKS

Film editor of *East of Eden*.

Owen Marks's other films include *Casablanca* (Best Editing Oscar nomination, 1943) and *Janie* (another Oscar nomination, 1944).

ARTHUR MARSHALL

In 1951 Arthur Marshall was an aspiring actor working as a parking lot attendant at CBS Studios in Hollywood. One of his co-workers was another aspiring actor, James Dean, with whom he had appeared in the UCLA production of *Macbeth*.

E. G. MARSHALL

Actor who starred in "Sleeping Dogs," a 1952 episode of the CBS television program "The Web" in which unknown actor James Dean appeared.

Born Everett G. Marshall in 1910, Marshall has had a lengthy career on stage and in films. The latter includes *The Caine Mutiny* (1954), *The Silver Chalice* (1954), *Twelve Angry Men* (1957), and *Superman II* (1980). He has also starred in the television programs "The Defenders" (for which he won a 1961–1962 Best Actor Emmy, 1961–1965), and "The New Doctors," aka "The Bold Ones" (1969–1973).

VIOLET MART
Jimmy's art teacher at Fairmount (Indiana) High School.

TASHA MARTEL
One of Jimmy's Hollywood girlfriends.

MARTIAL ARTS
Shortly before his death James Dean signed up to take a martial arts class in kendo, "the way of the sword." Kendo, a form of kenjutsu, is a sword fight, with participants attempting to score blows on various parts of the opponent's body. In order for a score to be registered, the swordsman (kendoka) must deliver a kiai, a shout, along with the blow. Despite its potentially violent nature, many consider kendo an exercise in spiritual discipline.

DEWEY MARTIN
After his death James Dean was replaced in the television special "The Battler" by Dewey Martin.

Martin, born in 1923, also appeared in films including *Knock On Any Door* (1949), *Prisoner of War* (1954), and *The Desperate Hours* (1955). Later he abandoned acting and worked as a lumberjack, a fisherman, and a cannery worker. He was also once married to singer Peggy Lee.

EDWARD MARTIN
One of James Dean's photographers.

RONALD MARTINETTI
Author of the fine biography *The James Dean Story*, published by Pinnacle Books in 1975. Martinetti, born in 1945, has also written for *Newsday* and the *Wall Street Journal*.

CLAUDIO MASENZA
Writer and director of the excellent Italian documentary *Hollywood: The Rebel James Dean*.

RAYMOND MASSEY
> He approached everything with a chip on his shoulder. The Method had encouraged this truculent spirit. Jimmy never knew his lines before he walked on the set, rarely had command of them when the

camera rolled and even if he had was often inaudible. Simple
technicalities, such as moving on cue and finding his marks, were
beneath his consideration. Equally annoying was his insistence on
going away alone once a scene was rehearsed and everything ready
for a take. He would disappear and leave the rest of us to cool off in
our chairs while he communed with himself somewhere out of sight.

Raymond Massey, *A Hundred Different Lives*

Raymond Massey portrayed Adam Trask, the stoic, Bible verse–spewing
father in *East of Eden*. It was a difficult assignment for Massey, who had
already appeared in more than 40 films in 25 years, primarily because of the
intolerable behavior of a newcomer, a 23-year-old punk who was to be the
film's star, James Dean. Massey was from the old school. Dean cut class.
Massey resented Dean's blatant lack of respect for filmmaking's accepted code
of conduct. Dean regarded Massey's "professionalism" with contempt, something for lessor actors to cling to, and reveled in jarring him out of his
rigidity. And, instead of amending the situation, director Elia Kazan manip-
ulated it by aggravating the animosity and then capturing it on film.

The film career of Raymond Massey (1896–1983) includes *The Speckled
Band* (England, 1931), *The Scarlet Pimpernel* (England, 1935), *The Prisoner
of Zenda* (1937), *Abe Lincoln in Illinois* (Best Actor Oscar nomination, 1940),
Arsenic and Old Lace (1944), *The Fountainhead* (1949), *Battle Cry* (1955), and
How the West Was Won (1963). On television Massey starred as Dr. Leonard
Gillespie in "Dr. Kildare" (1961–1966).

Interestingly, Ray Massey was one of the leading contenders for the role
of Uncle Bawley in *Giant*, a role that fortunately went to Chill Wills. The
idea of James Dean, Rock Hudson, and Raymond Massey sharing quarters
on location in Marfa, Texas, conjures up a less than harmonious living
arrangement.

MATADOR
For his first scene performance before members of the Actors Studio James
Dean adapted a character from the novel *Matador* by Barnaby Conrad. In the
scene the matador, played of course by Dean, prepares for his final bullfight.
As reported by writer David Garfield in *A Player's Place*, his study on the
Actors Studio:

> Dean, who was passionately interested in bullfighting, worked hard
> on the matador's ritualistic preparations, using only a few props: a
> statue of the Virgin, a candle, and the matador's cape. . . .
> His work provoked a long and penetrating critique from Strasberg.
> Dean listened impassively, but the color drained from his face. When
> Strasberg had concluded his remarks, the young actor slung his
> matador's cape over his shoulder and silently walked out of the room.

VIVIAN MATALON
Stage manager, *The Immoralist* (1954).

WALTER MATTHAU

Walter Matthau was one of the actors up for the part of Frank Stark, the emasculated father of the character portrayed by James Dean in *Rebel Without a Cause*. The role eventually went to another comedic actor, Jim Backus.

MATTSON'S

Now-defunct Hollywood clothing store where the Warner Brothers costume department reportedly obtained the red nylon jacket that James Dean made famous in *Rebel Without a Cause*. Following Dean's death and burgeoning posthumous popularity, there was an overwhelming public demand for replicas of the jacket, which Mattson's sold at the then-high price of $22.95 each.

MAXELL TAPES

Maxell Tapes featured the Dean image in a 1988 print advertisement that read:

> He was inarticulate and eloquent. A generation of adolescent rebellion expressed in surly manners and sensitive speech. He left behind a small but remarkable legacy of work. . . . So long as there are rebels without causes there will be the movies of James Dean to reflect their struggles and light their ways. Maxell. The tape that lasts as long as the legend.

FRANK MAZZOLA

Frank Mazzola played Crunch, one of the gang members in *Rebel Without a Cause*. Off screen, Mazzola had been involved with gangs at Hollywood High School. As such he was recruited by director Nick Ray to lend his particular expertise before and during the shooting of *Rebel*. In addition to participating in several discussions with Ray and screenwriter Stewart Stern, Mazzola, on March 8, 1955, took James Dean on a tour of Los Angeles locations frequented by juvenile delinquents. He also later helped to stage the pivotal knife-fight sequence in the film. For his services as consultant, Mazzola charged $200, a sum the front office at Warner Brothers begrudgingly paid.

Following his work on *Rebel*, Frank Mazzola was touted as a contender for the Rocky Graziano role in *Somebody Up There Likes Me*, a role that was later awarded to James Dean. Later Mazzola gave up acting and became a film editor.

DAVID McCALLUM

Actor, born in 1933, who was hyped as "The James Dean of England" in the 1950s. McCallum's films include *The Secret Place* (1956), *Billy Budd* (1962), *The Great Escape* (1963), and *The Greatest Story Ever Told* (1965). He is best known to American audiences, however, for his work in the hit television series "The Man from U.N.C.L.E." (1964–1968).

MERCEDES McCAMBRIDGE

It is somewhat surprising that Mercedes McCambridge was given co-star billing and was nominated for a Best Supporting Actress Oscar for her work in *Giant*. The issue is not the quality of her performance but the size of her role. *Giant* barely begins when McCambridge's character, the crusty Luz Benedict, is mangled to death by a mean horse.

During the location shooting in Marfa, Texas, McCambridge, true to her character in the film, was one of the few cast members to befriend James Dean. A few months later, in early October 1955, she learned of Dean's death, strangely enough, when she stopped at a gas station in Paso Robles, California, and spotted his shiny silver Porsche—rumpled and maimed and confined to a corner.

McCambridge, born in 1918, won a Best Supporting Actress Oscar in 1949 for her debut film performance, *All the King's Men*. Subsequent films include *Johnny Guitar* (1954), *Suddenly Last Summer* (1959), and *The Concorde: Airport 79* (1979). Her television credits include the early soap opera "One Man's Family" (1949–1950) and "Wire Service" (1956–1959).

Mercedes McCambridge was one of Dean's few friends in the *Giant* cast. During shooting, on July 31, 1955, she fell off a horse and suffered lacerations of the face.

In the 1970s McCambridge became president of an alcoholics' rehabilitation center, won a Best Supporting Actress Tony nomination for *The Love Suicide at Schofield Barracks* in 1972, and achieved a rather dubious (and controversially uncredited) distinction as the demonic voice of Linda Blair's tortured Regan in the 1973 neck-spinning classic, *The Exorcist*.

In 1981, McCambridge's autobiography, *The Quality of Mercy*, was published. She was quoted at the time:

> "I wanted to call the book *Life Is a Bitch* but my publisher wouldn't let me. People say I'm an angry person, but what they really mean is that if you say what you think, you're angry. And now people say I've written an angry book because it disagrees with other people."
>
> *Los Angeles*, June 1981

GLENN McCARTHY

Glenn McCarthy was the real-life rags-to-riches Texan who at least partially inspired Edna Ferber's Jett Rink in *Giant*. Warner Brothers was certainly aware of this fact and worked to draw distinctions between McCarthy and the film version of Rink (to be portrayed by James Dean). Warners was particularly concerned because its portrayal of Rink was unsympathetic and, according to the studio, "a thoroughly obnoxious character, one who is licentious, habitually drunk, and dedicated to the false principles of racial discrimination."

Nevertheless, upon the film's release in 1956 McCarthy, apparently satisfied with the differentiations between himself and Jett Rink, did not object. Glenn McCarthy died in January 1989 at the age of 81.

JIM McCARTHY

In 1949 Jim McCarthy was a 16-year-old student at the LaSalle Academy in New York City. That year he won a state speech competition and advanced to the national contest in Longmont, Colorado, where he met and befriended another contestant, Jimmy Dean.

When James Dean made his Broadway debut in *See the Jaguar* a little over three years later, he contacted his old friend Jim McCarthy, whom he called "Mac," and invited him to the show. Then, in early 1954, Dean again contacted McCarthy and invited him to the following day's opening performance of *The Immoralist*. As they parted company, McCarthy jokingly chastised Jimmy, "Try to be a good actor tomorrow." To which Dean replied in earnest, "I don't want to be a good actor. I want to be the best actor there is. Told you I'd get to the big town some day."

FLOYD McCARTY

Floyd McCarty was the still photographer on *Giant*. Unlike many other Dean photographers, McCarty has been generally unheralded over the years. Nevertheless, he is responsible for several of Dean's best and most famous photographs, including the legendary crucifixion shot.

TED McCORD

Ted McCord was the cinematographer on *East of Eden*. He also worked as a cameraman during the Virginia location shooting (which didn't involve Dean) on *Giant*.

McCord (1898–1976) also shot films including *Treasure of the Sierra Madre* (1948), *Johnny Belinda* (Best Cinematography Oscar nomination, 1948), *The Helen Morgan Story* (1957), *Two for the Seesaw* (Oscar nomination, 1962), and *The Sound of Music* (Oscar nomination, 1965).

PAT McCORMICK

In 1955, during breaks from shooting *Rebel Without a Cause*, James Dean took lessons in bullfighting from Pat McCormick, who was considered at the time to be America's leading matador.

ANDREW McCULLOUGH

Director of "Glory in Flower," a 1953 episode of the CBS television program "Omnibus" in which James Dean co-starred. McCullough later directed Dean again in "The Little Woman," a 1954 episode of the CBS program "Danger," which McCullough also produced.

CLYDE McCULLOUGH

Catcher for the Pittsburgh Pirates from 1948 to 1952 who, in October 1952, gave young hitchhikers James Dean, Bill Bast, and Dizzy Sheridan a ride to Indiana in his Nash Rambler. McCullough had been on an all-night driving trip to make an exhibition game in Des Moines, Iowa, the following day. During the ride McCullough befriended the struggling (and hungry) artists and even stopped at a roadside diner and bought them dinner. His unconditional generosity left an indelible impression on all three of them.

Interestingly, it was on December 3, 1952, that McCullough was traded by the Pirates to the Chicago Cubs—the same day that James Dean had his first major success, the Broadway opening of *See the Jaguar*.

McDONALD'S

There is a McDonald's franchise in Chicago, Illinois (address: 600 North Clark Street), that has a James Dean room filled with photographs and memorabilia. It's a decorative tribute, but what Dean has to do with Big Macs and Chicken McNuggets is beyond comprehension.

RODDY McDOWALL

Actor who co-starred in "Hill Number One," a 1951 Easter television special presented by "Family Theatre" in which James Dean made his official television debut. Later, in the summer of 1952, McDowall became acquainted with Dean in New York City.

McDowall, a slight and likable though often nervous-looking actor, was born in England in 1928. His film career has spanned over 50 years and includes *How Green Was My Valley* (1941), *Lassie Come Home* (1943), *Cleopatra* (1963), and *Planet of the Apes* (1968).

JOHN McENROE

The biggest-selling item at the 1989 U.S. Open tennis tournament in New York was a Nike poster of John McEnroe, tennis's bigmouthed bad boy, impersonating James Dean. The poster features McEnroe wearing a dark overcoat, walking through a misty Times Square, à la Dennis Stock's famous 1955 photo of Dean doing the same.

STEPHEN McHATTIE

Stephen McHattie gave a surprisingly effective performance as James Dean in the 1976 television movie "James Dean."

Canadian-born McHattie's other screen work includes the films *The People Next Door* (1970), *Moving Violation* (with Dean's friend Lonny Chapman and Dean's co-star Eddie Albert, 1976), *Gray Lady Down* (1978), *Death Valley* (1982), and *Belizaire the Cajun* (1986). His television films include "Search for the Gods" (1975), "Look What Happened to Rosemary's Baby" (1976), "Centennial" (miniseries, 1978–1979), and "Roughnecks" (1980). He also co-starred in the short-lived comedy series "Highcliffe Manor" (1979) and has made numerous stage appearances, including the Broadway plays *The Iceman Cometh* and *Mourning Becomes Electra*.

DON McHENRY

Co-star of "Forgotten Children," a 1952 television presentation of the "Hallmark Hall of Fame" in which James Dean also appeared.

The McDonald's James Dean room.

TROY McHENRY

Dr. Troy McHenry was a car racing enthusiast who, in 1956, obtained parts of James Dean's Porsche Spyder and had them installed in his own car. Later that year, in October, McHenry was killed in a car race in Pomona, California. The *Los Angeles Mirror-News* reported:

JINX TRAILS DEAN'S CAR

Several pieces of equipment from the powerful sports car in which actor James Dean crashed and died thirteen months ago were in a car in which a Beverly Hills physician was killed during a race Sunday. The physician, Dr. Troy McHenry, was killed when his sports car smashed into a tree during a race at the Pomona Fairgrounds.

McHenry had obtained the transmission, along with other parts, of Dean's Porsche from his friend Dr. William Eschrich. At the time Eschrich was quoted as saying "I don't believe he [McHenry] was using the transmission when he crashed, but he was using the hack swinging arms which hold the rear end."

FRANK McHUGH

Co-star of William Inge's "Glory in Flower," a 1953 episode of the CBS television program "Omnibus" in which James Dean was featured.

McHugh (1899–1981) appeared in more than 150 films, including *Going My Way* (1944), *State Fair* (1945), *There's No Business Like Show Business* (1954), and *Easy Come Easy Go* (1967). He also made numerous television guest appearances and was a regular on "The Bing Crosby Show" (1964–1965).

DONALD McKEE

Character actor who appeared in the September 11, 1953, episode of the NBC television program "The Big Story," which starred James Dean.

McKee made numerous other television appearances. He also appeared in the films *The Whistle at Eaton Falls* (1951) and *The Goddess* (1958). He died in 1968 at the age of 69.

McKINLEY ELEMENTARY SCHOOL

Contrary to the many previously published reports that have cited other California schools, James Dean attended McKinley Elementary School in Santa Monica from February 8, 1938 (first grade), until June 21, 1940 (third grade). McKinley Elementary still exists at 2401 Santa Monica Boulevard.

McKINLEY HOME FOR BOYS

Sherman Oaks, California, institution that was used as a location for *East of Eden*.

ROD McKUEN

Poet/singer/composer Rod McKuen was born in 1933. It's a little known fact that he was also once considered a promising young actor at Universal Studios who was hyped as "the next James Dean." McKuen's films include *Rock, Pretty Baby* (1956), *Summer Love* (1958), and *Wild Heritage* (1958).

CATHERINE McLEOD

Actress who co-starred in "Ten Thousand Horses Singing," a 1952 episode of the CBS television series "Studio One" in which unknown actor James Dean had a bit part.

McLeod, born in 1924, appeared in several films, including *I've Always Loved You* (1946), *So Young, So Bad* (1950), and *Ride the Wild Surf* (1964).

MAGGIE McNAMARA

New York actress friend of James Dean's who was considered for the part of Luz Benedict II in *Giant*, which eventually went to Carroll Baker.

McNamara, born in New York in 1928, was acclaimed for her Broadway and film performances in *The Moon Is Blue* (for which she was nominated for a Best Actress Oscar in 1953). She subsequently appeared in the films *Three Coins in the Fountain* (1954) and *Prince of Players* (1955). In 1978 she died from an overdose of sleeping pills.

BETTY McPHERSON

In 1949 Betty McPherson was the physical education teacher for girls at Fairmount (Indiana) High School. She was also the co-adviser of the senior class, of which James Dean was a member. Dean and McPherson befriended one another, and when she visited California during the summer of 1949, she went to see Dean at his father's house in Santa Monica. Today Betty McPherson reportedly resides in Florida.

STEVE McQUEEN

In the early 1950s Steve McQueen was an ex-Marine who had spent time in prison and just another struggling young actor scuffing the New York sidewalks, scouring for a job. He and James Dean were acquaintances and competitors, with Dean having a decided edge. After Dean's death McQueen was touted by many as "the next James Dean." A writer for *Movie World* magazine observed in 1964:

> He's the logical successor to Jimmy Dean. The clique that worshipped Dean . . . has a new Messiah in McQueen. Luckily, he is living longer than Dean did, so the cult will have a long, long time to thrive.

Longer, yes, but not long enough. Steve McQueen died of a heart attack in 1980 at the age of 50. But not before he became a top box-office star of the 1960s and 1970s. His films include *Somebody Up There Likes Me* (which was to have starred Dean, 1956), *The Blob* (1958), *The Magnificent Seven* (1960), *The Great Escape* (1963), *Love with the Proper Stranger* (with Natalie Wood,

Ex-marine
McQueen:
the man who
would be Dean?

1963), *The Cincinnati Kid* (1965), *The Sand Pebbles* (Best Actor Oscar nomination, 1966), *Bullitt* (1968), *Papillon* (1973), *The Towering Inferno* (1974), and *Tom Horn* (1980).

THE MEASUREMENTS

According to the Studio	*Actual*
Height: 5'10"	Height: 5'8"
Weight: 155 lbs.	Weight: 135 lbs.
Waist: 30"	Waist: 30"

MECHANICS
Competition Motors, Hollywood
Jay Chamberlain's garage, Burbank

DON MEDFORD
Don Medford is the television director who worked with James Dean more often than any other director. Medford first directed Dean in "The Evil Within," a 1953 episode of the ABC televison program "Tales of Tomorrow." A few months later he directed Dean in "Something for an Empty Briefcase," a 1953 episode of the NBC series "Campbell Soundstage." At the end of 1954, after Dean had completed *East of Eden*, Medford directed him in "I'm a Fool" and "The Dark, Dark Hour," two episodes of the CBS program "General Electric Theater," the former of which co-starred Natalie Wood and the latter Ronald Reagan.

Medford, born in 1917, directed films including *To Trap a Spy* (1966), *The Hunting Party* (1971), and *The Organization* (1971).

KAY MEDFORD
Actress who was seriously considered for the role of Kate, Cal Trask's prostitute mother in *East of Eden*. The role eventually went to Jo Van Fleet, who won a Best Supporting Actress Oscar for her performance.

RALPH MEEKER
Actor who was considered for the role of Jett Rink in *Giant*. Meeker, born Ralph Rathgeber, was 35 years old at the time *Giant* was shot.

JOHN COUGAR MELLENCAMP
> "The truth is, I didn't even know who James Dean was until I was out of high school. Everybody talked about how great this movie *Rebel Without a Cause* was, but I thought it was the worst movie I ever saw."
>
> John Cougar Mellencamp, *Los Angeles Times*, May 11, 1986

Reluctant James Dean fan, born in 1951 in Seymour, Indiana. John Cougar Mellencamp, fka John Cougar, mockingly refers to himself as the "Little Bastard," a sobriquet borrowed from Dean, has photos of Dean plastered across the walls of his studio, and included a reference to Dean in his song "Jack & Diane," which was number one on the *Billboard* charts for four weeks in 1982.

> "As I sit here every day, I just become at total odds with my generation, too. I hate to say this, but I feel like what John Lennon must have felt: I don't want to be in this race anymore, because it leads to nowhere."
>
> *Rolling Stone*, June 29, 1989

WILLIAM C. MELLOR
William C. Mellor was the cinematographer for *Giant*. After James Dean's death Mellor penned an article for *Picturegoer* magazine entitled "The Dean I Knew." It read, in part:

> In front of the camera he had an instinct that was nearly uncanny. I don't recall ever working with anyone who had such a gift. I recall one scene where he was in a shadow and had to lift his head to the light. We explained how it should go and he played it exactly right, to the half inch, the first time. He just seemed to know how it should be, without rehearsal or anything.

Mellor (1904–1963) also shot the films *A Place in the Sun* (with Elizabeth Taylor and Montgomery Clift, for which he won a Best Cinematography Oscar, 1951), *Bad Day at Black Rock* (1955), *The Diary of Anne Frank* (another Best Cinematography Oscar, 1959), and *State Fair* (1962), among others.

MENDOCINO, CALIFORNIA

In late May 1954 the cast and crew of *East of Eden* went to Mendocino, California, to shoot scenes that were supposed to be set in Monterey, California. Although there were no stars in the production, the people of Mendocino (1954 population: 803) responded warmly to the Hollywood film company. The women of the town cooked the meals for the cast and crew. In return Warner Brothers donated the money budgeted for food to the Mendocino Presbyterian Church. Friday, May 28, 1954, was officially declared "*East of Eden* Day" in Mendocino. All town businesses closed down for the day so that the townspeople could watch the filming. The single exception was the local bank, which remained open so that the company could film the scene in which Kate (Jo Van Fleet), the town madam, deposits her earnings.

PAUL MERRICK

Paso Robles, California, coroner and sheriff who examined James Dean's body and conducted the investigation into the circumstances surrounding his death.

THE METAMORPHOSIS

James Dean was one of the actors who participated in an August 1952 off-Broadway dramatic reading of Franz Kafka's *The Metamorphosis*. The reading was staged at the Village Theatre.

METHOD ACTING

James Dean was first introduced to the Method style of acting in a series of workshops conducted by actor James Whitmore in Brentwood, California, in 1951. The Method was employed by Lee Strasberg and the Actors Studio of New York, where Dean became a member in 1952. The style itself, dubbed by some as "the total immersion system," requires an actor to draw from his or her own personal experience. Strasberg defined the Method as:

> The sum total of the experience of the great actors throughout all ages and countries. The best things in it come from Stanislavsky. The rest comes from me. It sets no rules. It points a path that leads to control rather than hit or miss inspiration. It fosters fusion of the actor with his character. It is now represented in universities, and with workshops, dramatic schools, and little theater groups in every corner of every hamlet.

METRO-GOLDWYN-MAYER

Although Warner Brothers signed him, Metro-Goldwyn-Mayer was the first to express an interest in James Dean. It was after his December 1952 performance on Broadway in *See the Jaguar* that Dean was approached by a representative from MGM, who offered him a Hollywood screen test. Dean, guided by his agent, Jane Deacy, declined.

Less than three years later MGM negotiated with Warner Brothers to obtain Dean's services for MGM's picture *Somebody Up There Likes Me*.

Warner Brothers consented, with the condition that MGM lend Warners Elizabeth Taylor (MGM had already refused to loan out Grace Kelly) for its picture, *Giant*.

MEXICAN TOREADOR ASSOCIATION
Shortly prior to his death James Dean reportedly applied for membership in the Mexican Toreador Association.

MEXICO
With his passion for bullfighting, James Dean made several visits, via automobile, to Tijuana, Mexico.

PETER MEYERSON
Editor of the one-shot, cover-to-cover magazine *The Official James Dean Anniversary Book*, which was published by Dell in 1956.

SANDRA MICHAEL
Writer of "Harvest," a 1953 episode of the NBC television show "Robert Montgomery Presents the Johnson's Wax Program" that co-starred James Dean.

BETTE MIDLER
Bette Midler composed and recorded a song, "Come Back Jimmy Dean, Jimmy Dean" on her 1983 album *No Frills*.

Midler, born in Paterson, New Jersey, in 1945, received a Best Actress Oscar nomination for *The Rose* (1979), has won several Grammy awards, and had a number one record with "The Wind Beneath My Wings" (1989).

GJON MILI
Photographer friend of Elia Kazan's who, in early 1954, shot a series of black-and-white photo studies of Julie Harris with James Dean. The purpose of the test was to determine whether or not the pair made a believable romantic couple. Kazan had been concerned that Harris might appear too old for Dean, who was six years her junior.

MILITARY
See ARMED SERVICES.

VICTOR MILLAN
Victor Millan was a classmate of James Dean's at UCLA circa 1950–1951. While there Millan and Dean performed together in a school production of *Macbeth*. Five years later Millan was cast in a small part in *Giant*, which, of course, co-starred James Dean.

Millan also appeared in films including *A Touch of Evil* (an Orson Welles classic, 1958), *The FBI Story* (which co-starred Nick Adams, 1959), and *The Pink Jungle* (1968).

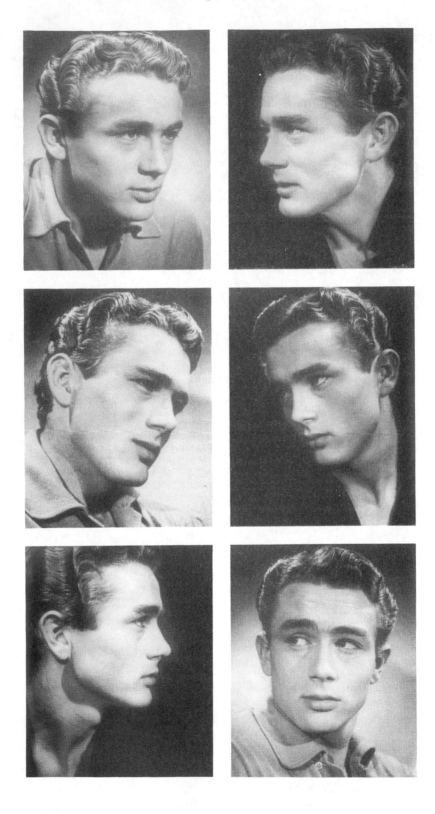

WILSON MILLAR

Los Angeles photographer who took some of the first, if not the first, professional photographs of James Dean in Los Angeles, circa 1951. Millar's studio at the time was located at 2060 North Highland Avenue.

JEANETTE MILLE

One of James Dean's Hollywood girlfriends, circa 1955. A few days before his death Jimmy presented Mille with a present, the Siamese cat that had been given to him by Elizabeth Taylor.

DICK MILLER

One of James Dean's photographers.

KEN MILLER

Actor who appeared with James Dean in a wardrobe test for *Rebel Without a Cause*. In the test Miller postured as one of the film's gang members.

MILLER PLAYHOUSE THEATRE GUILD

James Dean, using the name Byron James, was a member of the Miller Playhouse Theatre Guild, a Los Angeles drama troupe, in the summer of 1949.

MILLERTOWN BLUFF

Fictional location where the famous chickie-run sequence in *Rebel Without a Cause* was staged. Actually the shooting took place at the Warner Ranch in Calabasas, California.

SAL MINEO

> "I was in incredible awe of him. I was fascinated by him. I think it was sexual to an extent, but I had no idea or any understanding of affection between men. I really gave him hero worship, and I recognized later what it was, but the feeling then was that I couldn't wait to just get near him. . . . It was only years later that I understood I was incredibly in love with him."
>
> Sal Mineo on James Dean, *New York*, November 8, 1976

When he got the part of the puppy-eyed Plato in *Rebel Without a Cause*, Sal Mineo, born Salvatore Mineo, Jr., was 15 years old and a veteran of two major Broadway shows, *The Rose Tattoo* and *The King and I*, and two films, *Six Bridges to Cross* (1955) and *The Private War of Major Benson* (1955). At first Mineo wasn't even considered for the part in *Rebel*. James Dean wanted his friend Jack Simmons to get the role, and director Nick Ray had explicit instructions from the Warner Brothers front office *not* to cast any minors in the film. But after Simmons was tested and rejected and, more importantly, after Ray had set his sights on another minor, Natalie Wood, for the female lead, Sal Mineo was called in to test for the part.

Mineo: "We never became lovers. We could have like *that*."

Mineo: "It was only years later that I understood I was incredibly in love with him." After Dean's death Mineo tried to make spiritual contact with him.

> When I first met Jimmy, I was to read for Nick Ray, and I went to Nick's hotel and he introduced me to Jimmy. It was on a Sunday afternoon, and he said, "I'd just like you to go over a couple of scenes." But he hadn't told me ahead of time what role he wanted me to read.
>
> Sal Mineo, *James Dean: The First American Teenager*

The role, of course, was Plato, the fatherless birthday boy who has a photo of Alan Ladd pinned up in his school locker and a pistol hidden under his pillow, the boy who hangs out alone in a deserted mansion and is dragged into the police station for shooting a few puppies, and, above all, the boy who idolizes an older, stronger boy, Jim Stark.

Contrary to reports over the years that during the filming of *Rebel* James Dean and Sal Mineo became close friends, and contrary to speculation that they became lovers, they were essentially co-workers with a friendly relationship. Period. Mineo was nine years younger than Dean. He was also intimidated by and somewhat afraid of Dean, with his dramatically extreme mood swings. Further, Mineo was a minor. Natalie Wood played at being grown up and was able to become assimilated into the rest of the cast. Mineo was just a boy. As recalled by Beverly Long, "Sal was so little, so much younger than the rest of us, and he always had his social worker there. The social worker kept Sal apart from us a lot. His name was Tom, and he once went to the director and told him to reprimand us, the gang, because we smoked cigarettes and swore and were bad influences on Natalie and Sal. So we were given a lecture by Don Page, the assistant director. So Tom kept them, particularly Sal, away from us."

On the night of September 30, 1955, Sal Mineo was in New York City having dinner with Natalie Wood, Nick Adams, and Dick Davalos. Eventually they got around to their favorite subject and common interest—Jimmy Dean. Young, wide-eyed, and enthusiastic over the promise of their own futures, they mused on their friend Jimmy and his peculiar romance with danger and death. Together they prophesied that, within a year, he would be seriously injured in a car accident. They had no idea that, back in California and earlier that evening, Jimmy had died behind the wheel of his Porsche.

On an evening in February 1976, Sal Mineo was stabbed to death in the garage of his West Hollywood apartment (8563 Holloway Drive). Rumors ran rampant, and continue today, that Mineo had been engaged in the leather-and-chains gay underworld and that one of his tricks had taken his swordplay a little too seriously. Nonetheless the official records show that Sal Mineo was murdered without an apparent motive. He was 37 years old. His killer has never been found.

For his performance in *Rebel Without a Cause* Sal Mineo was nominated for a 1955 Best Supporting Actor Oscar. He was also cited by *The Film Daily* as having given one of the Best Performances by Juvenile Actors.

Mineo's other films include *Giant*, in which he had the surprisingly small role of Angel, *Crime in the Streets* (1956), *Somebody Up There Likes Me* (1956), *Tonka* (1958), *A Private's Affair* (1959), *The Gene Krupa Story* (1959), *Exodus* (Best Supporting Actor Oscar nomination, for which he was a favorite to win but lost to Peter Ustinov, 1960), *Escape from Zahrain* (1962), *Cheyenne Autumn* (1964), *The Greatest Story Ever Told* (1965), *Who Killed Teddy Bear?* (1965), *Krakatoa, East of Java* (1969), *80 Steps to Jonah* (1969), and *Escape from the Planet of the Apes* (1971).

At the height of his teen hearthrob status circa 1957–1958, Mineo also embarked on a short-lived recording career that spawned a few minor hits, including "Start Movin' " and "Lasting Love." Toward the end of his life he produced and starred in a revival of the gay-themed stage play *Fortune and Men's Eyes* and, at the time of his death, was in rehearsal for another play, *P.S. Your Cat Is Dead.*

MINETTA TAVERN
New York restaurant/bar frequented by James Dean. Still located in Greenwich Village (address: 113 MacDougal Street), the Minetta Tavern has been in existence since 1937.

VINCENTE MINNELLI
One of the finest directors in Hollywood history, Vincente Minnelli wanted

Dean to star in his 1955 MGM film *The Cobweb*. Warner Brothers, however, blocked the deal.

WORTHINGTON MINOR
Worthington Minor produced and adapted "Ten Thousand Horses Singing," a 1952 episode of the CBS television program "Studio One" in which James Dean had a bit part.

MR. MAGOO
> PLATO: Children? Well, we don't really encourage them. They're noisy and troublesome. Don't you agree?
> JUDY: Yes. And so terribly annoying when they cry. I just don't know what to do whey they cry. Do you, dear?
> JIM: Of course. Drown them like puppies.

During the shooting of the scene in *Rebel Without a Cause* in which Plato, Judy, and Jim "play house" in the deserted mansion and ponder what to do with crying children, James Dean spontaneously affected his finest Mr. Magoo impersonation, which he had learned from the master himself, Jim Backus, and delivered the line "Drown them like puppies."

However, when word got around Warner Brothers that Jimmy had impersonated Mr. Magoo and that Nick Ray planned to incorporate it into the film, a controversy erupted. Memos were passed. Finally a studio executive limousined to the set, approached Jimmy, and reportedly said, "Jimmy Dean, I understand you're doing an imitation of Mr. Magoo in this picture." Perplexed, Dean replied, "Yes, I am. What about it?" The executive then pleaded, "Well, this is *Warner Brothers*. Couldn't you switch it to Bugs Bunny?"

YASUO MIZUI
Renowned sculptor who was commissioned in 1985 by Seita Ohnishi to create a monument in honor of James Dean. Ever since, Mizui has been working on the 14-foot-high, 40-foot-long, 130-ton, $200,000 sculpture named the "Wall of Hope" near his home in Lacoste, France. Ohnishi reportedly plans to transport the limestone monument, upon its completion, to an undisclosed location in California.

DICK MODER
One of the assistant directors on *Giant*.

MODERN SCREEN MAGAZINE
After his death the editors of *Modern Screen* fan magazine paid tribute to James Dean with their Special Achievement Silver Cup Award for 1955. The presentation was made on "The Colgate Variety Hour" television program on November 27, 1955. *Modern Screen* rhapsodized:

A gifted young actor was taken from us this year, but not before you recognized his genius and exciting potential. His name was Jimmy Dean and to him—in your name—we present the *Modern Screen* Special Achievement Award for 1955. No star deserved it more.

Modern Screen published numerous articles about James Dean, including:

☆ March 1955   "I Nominate for Stardom" by Louella Parsons
☆ June 1955   "Smoldering Dynamite"
☆ August 1955   "Lone Wolf"
☆ October 1955   "The Secret Love That Haunts Jimmy Dean"
☆ October 1955   "The Last Story about Jimmy"
☆ December 1955   "Appointment with Death"
☆ December 1955   "This Was My Friend Jimmy Dean" by Mike Connolly
☆ January 1956   "A Tenderness Lost" by George Stevens
☆ January 1956   "Jim Dean's Funeral" by Louella Parsons
☆ March 1956   "Goodbye, Jimmy"
☆ October 1956   "Jimmy's Happiest Moments" by Nick Adams
☆ October 1956   "Your James Dean Memorial Medallion"
☆ December 1956   "It's Me, Jimmy" by Jim McCarthy
☆ January 1957   "Jimmy Dean's Last Message"
☆ February 1957   "His Love Destroyed Him"
☆ February 1957   "Was Jimmy Dean's Sports Car Jinxed?"
☆ March 1957   "I Almost Married Jimmy Dean. Who Am I?" by Beverly Wills
☆ October 1957   "James Dean's Last Passenger Recovers—Tells Complete Story of Fateful . . . Death Drive" by Rolf Wutherich
☆ October 1957   "What Jimmy Dean Believed"
☆ October 1957   "The Last Story about Jimmy"

IVAN MOFFAT

Co-writer of the screenplay of *Giant*, which had been adapted from the novel by Edna Ferber. For his work Ivan Moffat received a 1956 Best Adapted Screenplay Oscar nomination.

Moffat, who made headlines in 1961 when he married the daughter of the lady-in-waiting to the Queen mother of England, also adapted "The Thorn Birds" (1983) for television.

MONEY

Over the years an unfortunate rumor has persisted that, between the time he died and the time he was buried, James Dean's body was ransacked for money by an unscrupulous thief. In fact, at the time of his death James Dean had $33.03 in the pockets of his light blue trousers. The money was subsequently turned over to, and later accounted for by, the James Dean estate.

THE MONKEY'S PAW

In his sophomore year at Fairmount (Indiana) High School Jim Dean portrayed Herbert White in the school production of *The Monkey's Paw*.

MARILYN MONROE

What happens when two icons meet face to face? In the case of Marilyn Monroe and James Dean they practically had to be restrained from spitting. The brush occurred in Hollywood in 1954 at a screening of the new Brando picture, *On the Waterfront*. They attended separately—she was with Shelley Winters, he was with Nick Ray. Dean had made *East of Eden*, which had yet to be released, and was being courted by Ray to star in *Rebel Without a Cause*. He was still a nobody, albeit an unorthodox one, and the buzz in Hollywood was that he was a moody creep who had stars in his future. She, on the other hand, was the queen of the land, goddess of the silver screen. Still the conventional wisdom at the time pegged her as a breathy blond with a box-office bosom. Neither Dean nor Monroe was much impressed with the other. After the screening and perhaps inspired by Brando's on-screen antics, Dean was at his most audacious. Shelley Winters recalled in her 1989 autobiography *Shelley II: The Middle of My Century*:

> Jimmy came roaring down the mountain [on his motorcycle]. He started the deadly game of circling us. I was so angry, I was ready to run him over. I kept honking at him, and he kept putting his brakes on right in front of me. He was laughing and enjoying the game. . . . When we got to the Chateau Marmont, I quickly drove to the underground garage. Jimmy followed. Marilyn was rigid with fear, and I was ready to punch his lights out.

The evening continued, but failed to improve, at an intimate postscreening get-together in Nick Ray's bungalow at the Chateau Marmont. Marilyn Monroe was everything James Dean didn't like in a woman. She was an American blond, obsessed with her own looks, she was the movie star personified, and (at least at that time) she was decidedly *not* an actress of depth or conviction. As for James Dean, he was everything Marilyn Monroe didn't like in a man. He was a pretty boy and a punk, and she had no use for either; he was younger, when she preferred them older; he was, despite his earnest aspirations, hardly an intellectual giant; and he was considered at the time to be an imitation of Brando—why did she need an imitation when she could (and *did*) have the real thing? According to Shelley Winters, although Dean and Monroe remained in their separate corners, they "treated each other like resentful siblings . . . they ignored each other, and this attitude continued throughout a long night of conversation."

Several months later, on March 9, 1955, Marilyn Monroe served as a celebrity usher for the *East of Eden* benefit premiere in New York City. James Dean did not attend.

Marilyn Monroe, born Norma Jeane Mörtenson in 1926, appeared in 30 films, including *All About Eve* (1950), *Niagara* (1953), *Gentlemen Prefer Blondes* (1953), *How to Marry a Millionaire* (1953), *The Seven Year Itch* (1955), *Bus Stop* (1956), and *Some Like It Hot* (1959).

She died from a drug overdose in 1962, a death that has been shrouded in controversy ever since. What is no longer debated is her brilliance and talent as a movie comedienne.

MONTEREY, CALIFORNIA

East of Eden was set circa 1917 in Monterey and Salinas (approximately 17 miles apart), California. The scenes involving Kate, including the brothel scenes, were supposed to be set in Monterey but were shot in Mendocino.

ROBERT MONTGOMERY

Producer of "Harvest," a 1953 episode of the NBC television program "Robert Montgomery Presents the Johnson's Wax Program," in which James Dean co-starred.

    Robert Montgomery (1904–1981), born Henry Montgomery, appeared as an actor in numerous films, including *So This Is College* (1929), *Night Must Fall* (Best Actor Oscar nomination, 1937), and *Here Comes Mr. Jordan* (Best Actor Oscar nomination, 1941). On television, Montgomery hosted and produced the NBC show "Robert Montgomery Presents" (1952 Best Dramatic Program Emmy, 1950–1957) and produced another, less successful NBC show, "Eye Witness" (1953).

ELIZABETH MONTGOMERY

Robert Montgomery's daughter, Elizabeth Montgomery was one of the primary candidates for the role of Luz Benedict II in *Giant*, a role that eventually went to Carroll Baker. She was also considered for the lesser role of Luz's sister, Judy Benedict. Years later Montgomery attained fame as the witch with a twitch (and a wiggle) in the hit television series "Bewitched" (1964–1972).

MOONCALF MUGFORD

Fairmount High School play in which Jim Dean starred during his sophomore year. He portrayed the slightly insane, vision-seeing title character.

TERRY MOORE

James Dean attended the 1954 Los Angeles premiere of *Sabrina* with starlet Terry Moore. It was a minor disaster of a date (the film had chemistry; Dean and Moore did not), reportedly arranged by Dean's Hollywood agent, Dick Clayton.

    Terry Moore, born in 1929, has appeared in movies using four different names: Helen Koford (her real name), Judy Ford, Jan Ford, and Terry Moore. Her films include *The Murder in Thornton Square* (1943), *Mighty Joe Young* (1949), and *Come Back, Little Sheba* (Best Supporting Actress Oscar nomination, 1952). She also co-starred in the television western series "Empire" (1962–1964).

AGNES MOOREHEAD

Agnes Moorehead was one of the actresses considered for the part of Luz Benedict in *Giant*, a role that eventually went to Mercedes McCambridge. Moorehead (1906–1974) was best known as Endora, the not-so-wicked witch of a mother-in-law in television's "Bewitched" (1964–1972).

JOE MORASS
Actor who appeared in "Ten Thousand Horses Singing," a 1952 episode of the CBS television program "Studio One" in which unknown actor James Dean had a bit part.

PAUL MORENO
In 1955 Paul Moreno was a burly Cholame, California, entrepreneur. He owned the town's garage, towing service, service station, grocery store, and ambulance. And on the early evening of September 30, 1955, Moreno served as one of the ambulance attendants who futilely rushed James Dean's body to the Paso Robles hospital.

At the subsequent October 11, 1955, inquest Paul Moreno was called in for questioning. His testimony is recounted in part below.

> MORENO: The other fellow [Dean] was lying over the right-hand door of the Porsche, face down, one foot tangled in the pedals of the car, the brake or clutch. . . .
> DISTRICT ATTORNEY: He was lying over the right-hand door?
> MORENO: The right-hand door.
> DISTRICT ATTORNEY: He wasn't in the driver's position?
> MORENO: The foot was still in the pedals—it is not very wide.
> DISTRICT ATTORNEY: He was lying over the right-hand side, but his foot was caught in the pedals on the driver's side?
> MORENO: That is right.

Before he was dismissed, Paul Moreno further testified that, en route to the hospital, the ambulance carrying James Dean (who was either dead or dying) was involved in an accident. It seems that the ambulance was sideswiped by another car, the impact of which left a dent in its left side.

RITA MORENO
Actress who was up for the part of Juana, Dennis Hopper's Latin wife in *Giant*. However, that should come as no surprise. In the 1950s and throughout the 1960s Rita Moreno was offered virtually every ethnic female role in Hollywood. Nonetheless the part was eventually awarded to Elsa Cardenas.

EDGAR MORIN
Author of the book *The Stars* (Grove Press, 1961; originally published in France as *Les Stars*, 1957), which contains a chapter entitled "The Case of James Dean." The work was also published as an article about Dean in *The Evergreen Review* in 1958.

Morin, born in Paris in 1921, is a sociologist and journalist. His other works include *The Red and the White* (1970) and *Rumour in Orleans* (1971).

CLIFFORD MORRIS
Cast member, *Rebel Without a Cause*.

STEPHEN MORRISSEY
Author of the book *James Dean Is Not Dead*, published by Babylon Books in Great Britain in 1983. Morrissey, an unabashed Dean fan, is also the former lead singer of the rock band the Smiths, which disbanded in 1987 amid a riff between Morrissey and guitarist Johnny Marr. In 1988 Morrissey released a solo album, *Viva Hate*, which included the single "Suedehead," the music video of which was shot entirely in Dean's hometown of Fairmount, Indiana. With the Smiths, Morrissey had several hits on the British charts, including "The Boy with the Thorn in His Side," a Dean tribute (1985).

MARILYN MORRISON
Described in press reports as one of James Dean's Hollywood girlfriends. Morrison was the ex-wife of singer Johnnie Ray.

MARY MORTON
Following his death, James Dean's car racing helmet was sold to Mary Morton of Pasadena, California. The purchase price? $30.

ALINE MOSBY
Hollywood writer who reported in April 1955:

> James Dean is at times moody and/or shy. He is also intelligent, and his conversation, compared to most Hollywood actors, is positively brilliant.

MOTHER
Natural mother: Mildred Marie Wilson Dean
Foster mother: Ortense Winslow
Stepmother: Ethel Case Dean

MOTION PICTURE MAGAZINE
In May 1955 *Motion Picture* fan magazine named James Dean the fourth most popular movie actor in America. Who were numbers one through three?

1. Marlon Brando
2. Tony Curtis
3. Rock Hudson

   Motion Picture published several articles about James Dean, including:

☆ September 1955	"The Dean I've Dated" by Lori Nelson
☆ May 1956	"Jimmy Dean Is Not Dead"
☆ September 1956	"James Dean, His Life and Loves"
☆ November 1956	"You Can Make Jimmy Dean Live Forever" by Marcus Winslow
☆ February 1959	"The Ghost Who Wrecked Pier Angeli's Marriage"
☆ May 1961	"Where Is Jimmy Dean?"

MOTLEY
Costume designer of *The Immoralist* (1954).

Motley also designed the costumes for *The First Gentleman* and *Beckett*, both of which won Tony awards for costume design in 1958 and 1961, respectively. Motley received an additional Tony nomination in 1965 for the costumes in *Baker Street*.

MOTORCYCLES

"I've been riding since I was sixteen. . . . I don't tear around on it, but intelligently motivate myself through the quagmire and entanglement of your streets. . . ."
James Dean to Hedda Hopper, Chicago Tribune Magazine,
March 27, 1955

Back in Fairmount, Jimmy Dean obtained his first motorcycle from Carter Motors when he was 15 or 16 years old. He owned at least one until his death. His last motorcycle, a Triumph, had "Dean's Dilemma" painted on its side.

Jimmy on his first motorcycle, in Fairmount.

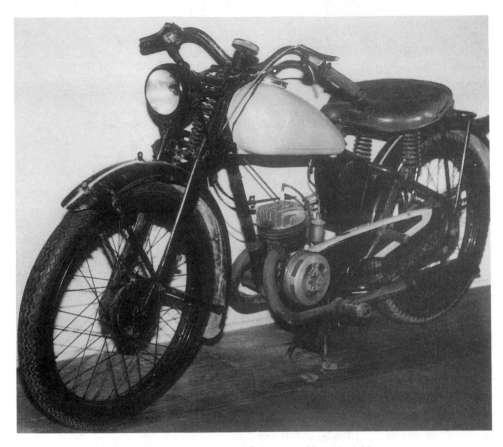

Jimmy's first motorcycle, on display at the Fairmount Historical Museum.

James Dean's collection of motorcycles included:

☆ a 1947 Czech Whizzer
☆ an English cycle
☆ a Harley
☆ a 500cc Norton
☆ an Indian 500
☆ an Italian Lancia scooter
☆ a British Triumph T-110

MOTT THE HOOPLE
British glitter rock band led by vocalist Ian Hunter that dedicated an album to James Dean in the early 1970s. In America Mott the Hoople charted only one minor hit, "All the Young Dudes" (produced by David Bowie, 1972).

MOVIE LIFE MAGAZINE
Movie Life fan magazine published numerous articles about James Dean, including:

☆ November 1955   "Daffy About Dean"
☆ December 1955   "The Untold Story of James Dean's Last Days"
☆ January 1956   "The Movie Life of James Dean"
☆ June 1956   "Jimmy Dean Fights Back from the Grave"
☆ July 1956   "James Dean's Strange Legacy"
☆ July 1956   "Secrets from Jimmy Dean's Past"
☆ August 1956   "The Secret Happiness of Jimmy Dean"
☆ September 1956   "Jimmy Dean, Why We Loved Him" by Nick Adams
☆ October 1956   Continuation of above article
☆ December 1956   "I Can't Forget Jimmy" by Natalie Wood
☆ January 1957   "The Untold Story of the Love Jimmy Lost"
☆ January 1957   "Should Elvis Presley Play Jimmy Dean?"
☆ February 1957   "Will They Cheat Jimmy Again?"
☆ May 1957   "What You Owe Jimmy Dean"
☆ July 1957   "Why They Want You to Forget Jimmy"
☆ September 1957   "In Loving Memory: James Dean"
☆ October 1957   "News from Dean Foundation"
☆ October 1957   "Did Jimmy Dean's Spirit Haunt the Studio?"
☆ October 1958   "James Dean: Three Years of Sorrow, Never Forgotten, Never
                                Replaced"
☆ April 1962   "James Dean—Pier Angeli"

"THE MOVIE STAR"

June 10, 1962, episode of the NBC television series "The DuPont Show of the Week" that was inspired by the death of James Dean. Written by Dean's friend Bill Bast and adapted by Robert Crean, the plot revolved around a character named Billy Allen, "the greatest movie idol since Valentino," who died an accidental death. His body is returned to his hometown in the Midwest for his funeral. "The Movie Star" starred Kathleen Widdoes (as the widow), Dane Clark, Norma Crane, and Harry Townes.

MOVIE STARS PARADE MAGAZINE

Movie Stars Parade fan magazine published numerous articles about James Dean, including:

☆ September 1955   "What Jimmy Dean Did to Hollywood"
☆ October 1955   "The Strange Lovemaking of Jimmy Dean"
☆ April 1956   "The Deepening Mystery of James Dean"
☆ May 1956   "The Boy Who Didn't Die"
☆ May 1956   "His Living Legacy, His Searching Heart"
☆ May 1956   "What Made Jimmy Run?"
☆ May 1956   "The Real Jimmy Dean"
☆ May 1956   "Those Who Loved Him"
☆ June 1956   "As You Remember Him"
☆ July 1956   "Secrets from Jimmy Dean's Past"
☆ August 1956   "What Jimmy Dean's Hometown Can Now Reveal"
☆ October 1956   "Should Elvis Presley Play Jimmy Dean?"
☆ December 1956   "Must We Stop Writing About Jimmy Dean?"
☆ February 1957   "Jimmy Dean's Fight to Live"
☆ April 1957   "James Dean's Memorial Page"

☆ May 1957   "James Dean's Memorial Page"
☆ June 1957   "Is Natalie Wood Betraying Jimmy Dean?"
☆ August 1957   "James Dean, the Tragedy Lives On"
☆ November 1957   "Goodbye, Jimmy Dean" by Steve Rowland
☆ October 1958   "Six Unsolved Mysteries of Jimmy Dean's Death"
☆ March 1962   "The Truth about Liz Taylor, Jimmy Dean and Me" by Rock
                          Hudson

MOVIELAND MAGAZINE

Movieland fan magazine published several articles about James Dean, including:

☆ November 1955   "Dean's Big Balk"
☆ November 1955   "Man of Many Moods"
☆ October 1956   "The Star Who Never Died"
☆ December 1956   "How Jimmy Dean Still Works Miracles for Others"
☆ February 1957   "An Unforgettable Day with Jimmy Dean" by Gene Owen
☆ December 1962   "Jean-Paul Belmondo, He's the French James Dean"
☆ August 1963   "Elvis Hears from James Dean"

THE MOVIES

"When he'd be drying dishes for me, Jimmy used to dream out loud about getting into the movies. 'Course, I didn't pay any attention. I figured that'd be impossible for an Indiana farm boy."

Ortense Winslow, James Dean's aunt,
Los Angeles Times, July 22, 1973

The Movies That James Dean Had a Bit Part In
Fixed Bayonets (1951)
Sailor Beware (1952)
Has Anybody Seen My Gal? (1952)

The Movies That Dean Starred In
East of Eden (1955)
Rebel Without a Cause (1955)
Giant (1956)

The (Theatrically Released) Movies About or Inspired by Dean
The James Dean Story (1957)
James Dean: The First American Teenager (1976)
September 30, 1955 (1977)
Come Back to the Five and Dime, Jimmy Dean, Jimmy Dean (1982)

Also see THE TELEVISION MOVIES ABOUT OR INSPIRED BY DEAN and THE VIDEO MOVIES ABOUT OR INSPIRED BY DEAN

The Movies That Dean Wanted to Do But Didn't
The Cobweb (1955)
Damn Yankees (1958)

Dr. Jekyll and Mr. Hyde (remake of 1932, 1941, etc., versions)
Fear Strikes Out (1957)
Gun for a Coward (never made)
The Left-Handed Gun (1958)
The Little Prince (1974)
Somebody Up There Likes Me (1956)

Also, film biographies of Harry Greb, Woody Guthrie, and Charles Lindbergh and a western with actor/director/writer Lonny Chapman

The Movies That Dean Turned Down
The Egyptian (1954)
The Silver Chalice (1954)
The Spirit of St. Louis (1957)

The Movies That Dean Was Turned Down For
Battle Cry (1955)
End as a Man (released as *The Strange One*, 1957)
Oklahoma! (1955)

The Movies Not About Dean That Have Featured His Image as Atmospheric Background (a Selective List)
The Accused (1988)
Back to the Future (1985)
Cousins (1989)
Earth Girls Are Easy (1989)
Good Morning, Vietnam (1987)
Mischief (1985)
Moscow on the Hudson (1984)
Running on Empty (1988)
Shirley Valentine (1989)

The Most Memorable Dean Movie Moments
There are certain moments in cinema history, whether the delivery of a certain line of dialogue (Bette Davis's show-stopping proclamation in *All About Eve*, "Fasten your seat belts. It's gonna be a bumpy night"; Gloria Swanson's tragi-comic signature, "Mr. DeMille, I'm ready for my close-up" in *Sunset Boulevard*) or an indelible image (Marilyn Monroe's skirt-raising ballet atop a sidewalk grating in *The Seven Year Itch*; Ann-Margret, singing and sizzling atop an unseen treadmill at the beginning and ending of *Bye Bye Birdie*), that transcend mere moviemaking. They are familiar yet startling upon every viewing. They are ingrained into our consciousness. They are unforgettable. They are *movie magic*.

James Dean may have starred in only three movies, but he left a number of memorable movie moments:

East of Eden: the scene in which he sits atop the train, wrapped in a sweater
East of Eden: the scene in which he holds on to the door frame as he is carried, screaming, out of his mother's house of ill repute

East of Eden: the scene of the birthday party and rejection by his father
Rebel Without a Cause: the opening monkey-fondling scene
Rebel Without a Cause: the scene in which he punches the desk at the police station
Rebel Without a Cause: the planetarium knife-fight scene
Rebel Without a Cause: the chickie-run scene
Rebel Without a Cause: the "Dad, stand up for me!" scene
Giant: the inheritance with rope tricks scene
Giant: the tea with Leslie scene
Giant: the oil explosion and confrontation with Bick scene

MULHOLLAND DRIVE

Famous strip of Hollywood asphalt, portions of which offer spectacular views of Los Angeles, especially popular among informed tourists and young lovers. James Dean found particular pleasure in racing his various motorcycles and sports cars up and down Mulholland.

HARRY MURPHY

The Paso Robles, California, assistant district attorney who participated in the October 1955 investigation into the death of James Dean.

THE MUSEUM OF BROADCASTING

New York City museum (address: 1 East 53rd Street) that has several of James Dean's television appearances on file for public inspection. In February and March 1986 the museum produced tributes to Dean in New York and Los Angeles that featured screenings of some of his television performances. In New York the tribute included a seminar with a panel consisting of David Dalton, Roy Schatt, and David Loehr. In Los Angeles the tribute was hosted by Martin Landau and held at the Los Angeles County Museum of Art's Leo S. Bing Theater.

MUSEUM OF MODERN ART

One of James Dean's New York hangouts (address: 11 West 53rd Street).

MUSIC

As a child Jimmy Dean played the violin, clarinet, and drums. In the Fairmount (Indiana) High School band he played drums during his freshman and senior years.

Contrary to popular misconception, Dean was not introduced to jazz by his Hollywood and New York friends. In fact, as early as 1950, he was a member of the Jazz Appreciation Club at Santa Monica City College. The club operated under the auspices of Dr. Clive Warner, "with the purpose of increasing knowledge and appreciation of great jazz from Dixieland to now."

In New York, circa 1952–1954, Dean became adept on the bongo drums, which, typically, he carried with him wherever he went. Later he learned to play the recorder, which he subsequently demonstrated in *East of Eden*. During the filming of *Giant* in 1955 he became interested in country music and learned to play the guitar.

As far as his musical tastes were concerned, Dean was an avid record collector, with eclectic interests that he worked to expand. It almost seemed as if he was attempting to distance himself from his Hoosier roots with his worldly interest in and knowledge of music ("Look, Ma, Schönberg!"). Like almost everyone else of the period, he liked Sinatra and Garland. However, he also liked the plaintive yodelings of Jimmie Rodgers, "the singing brakeman"; during the filming of *Rebel Without a Cause* he began collecting Israeli music; according to Nick Ray, Dean liked African tribal music, Afro-Cuban songs and dances, classical jazz, Jack Teagarden, Dave Brubeck, Haydn, and Berlioz; according to Beulah Roth and others, he liked Béla Bartók and Arnold Schönberg. Said Beulah, "He loved their music. He had all their recordings. It was very highbrow stuff. It was even beyond me. I couldn't imagine Jimmy liking this kind of thing." Jimmy also liked Renata Tebaldi of Milan's La Scala opera company; his favorite aria was "One Fine Day" from *Madame Butterfly*; and, in his own words, he liked "everything from 12th- and 13th-century music to the extreme moderns—you know, Schönberg, Berg, Stravinsky. I also like Sinatra's *Songs for Young Lovers* album."

Whatever he liked, he liked it *loud*. In March 1955 Jimmy bought a $400 hi-fi set. As he explained to a reporter, "Every time I tried to explain what I wanted, the salesman would interrupt with all sorts of technical terms about hi-fi. I got so disgusted I gave him a check so that I could get out of the store." As for his penchant for pumping up the volume, Beulah Roth was only one of many who contended, "It was so loud you could hear the stuff half a mile away!"

MUSICAL SELECTIONS FROM REBEL
Subtitled "The James Dean Musical," *Musical Selections from Rebel* was a theatrical presentation at Eighty-Eights Theater (address: 228 West 10th Street) in New York City. The show ran from May 15 to June 16, 1989.

"MY CASE STUDY"
In 1948, while a student at Fairmount (Indiana) High School, Jim Dean wrote an autobiographical essay titled "My Case Study." The report revealed, among other things, that the young Dean liked "to mold and create things." For the full report, *see* QUOTING DEAN.

MYOPIA
James Dean was seriously myopic and could barely see without his prescription eyeglasses.

N

ADELINE NALL

Over the years the James Dean legend has spawned many things, some of it macabre, some of it maudlin. One of the most pleasant things to evolve from it has been the celebrity of a diminutive but dynamic retired high school drama teacher by the name of Adeline Nall.

When Adeline Nall started teaching Jimmy Dean "Beginning Speech," she was Adeline Brookshire, and he was a sophomore at Fairmount (Indiana) High School. It wasn't their first encounter. Previously she had coached him in a dramatic reading competition for the Women's Christian Temperance Union. He lost on a technicality and blamed his teacher. It was to be a common pattern in their relationship. Back at Fairmount High (Room 21), from 1946 to 1949, Nall taught Dean Spanish, speech, and drama—Jimmy excelling at the last two and nearly flunking the former. Nall also advised and oversaw the production of the school plays, several of which Dean starred in. And, perhaps foremost, she instilled in her prize student the thespian motto "Act well your part for there all honor lies." He listened, he learned, and he paid heed to the creed. Said Nall, "Even then I recognized the talent of this gifted boy."

In 1949, senior Jim Dean won the Indiana speech tournament and advanced to the national competition in Longmont, Colorado. Adeline Nall was his coach and chaperon. When he placed a disappointing sixth, he once again faulted his teacher. Years later Mrs. Nall commented, "He lost a big speech contest and blamed me. He never could take criticism too well." Certainly, like many student-teacher relationships, this one held traces of both love and hate. Six years later, when explaining to a reporter how he became interested in acting, Dean credited Nall, albeit flippantly:

> "One of my teachers was a frustrated actress. Of course, this chick
> only provided the incident. A neurotic person has the necessity to
> express himself and my neuroticism manifests itself in the dramatic."
> *Photoplay*, July 1955

Eighteen years later she would tell reporters, "We used to squabble when he was my student. We'd always get back together somehow. Once, he offered me a cigarette in class just to be smart. I almost popped him. He was just that kind of a maverick kid."

The teacher last saw the student in February 1955, when *East of Eden* was about to be released and it appeared that James Dean was about to become a movie star. Jimmy virtually ignored his former teacher on that

Adeline Nall.

trip, but Adeline Nall did leave him with one final instruction: "Well, Jim, don't forget to be kind."

If Mrs. Nall was pained by her protégé's neglect on that visit to Fairmount, she has been consoled by the memory of Jimmy's late 1953 invitation to a rehearsal of *The Immoralist*, whose opening would later win him recognition. And she also has the fond remembrance of the time that he presented her with his painting of an orchid—because he knew that her real-life orchid would one day wither and he wanted to preserve its beauty for her.

A few months after Dean's trip home, shortly before his death, Adeline Nall took a leave of absence from teaching. Inspired, perhaps, by the success of her student, she boldly moved to New York to practice what she had been preaching for so many years. But Broadway barely batted an eye at the spectacled and then middle-aged schoolteacher, so she returned to Fairmount, where she has since become enshrined as a living reminder of her former pupil.

Since the death of James Dean, Adeline Nall has been thrust into the spotlight as a Dean spokesperson. Fans and interviewers from all over the world have clamored at her doorstep to worship at the temple of Nall. She has made numerous media appearances, including interviews in *The James Dean Story* (1957), the Italian documentary *Hollywood: The Rebel James Dean*, *James Dean: The First American Teenager* (1976), "Entertainment Tonight" (1985), "Show Biz Today" (1985), and "Forever James Dean" (1988). Biographer Venable Herndon dedicated his biography *James Dean: A Short Life* (1974) to her. In 1980 she delivered a stage recitation of the 25-year-old eulogy that had been read at Dean's 1955 funeral. And she made a video, *Adeline Nall's Memories at Fairmount High*, that sells via mail order. She is also said to be penning her autobiography with a Washington, D.C., collaborator.

Today, Adeline Mart Nall is in her mid-80s and still in the spotlight. In 1990 she went on a mini-tour around the country in which she met with friends and fans and doled out her anecdotes and remembrances of James Dean. It is a role that she enjoys playing. "Act well your part for there all honor lies." Mrs. Nall has certainly acted her part well. She is, arguably, the most famous former high school teacher of a movie star in recent history.

NAMES
Born: James Byron Dean
Early stage name: Byron James

Nicknames

Jim	Deaner	One-Speed Dean
Jimmy	Hamlet	Rack
Deanie	The Mickey Mouse Brando	Rock (while filming *Giant*)

Names He Sometimes Used to Refer to Himself

Jim (Brando/Clift) Dean	Hayseed Jim	The Little Bastard

Movie Character Names

Cal Trask	Jim Stark	Jett Rink

Jim Stark's Nicknames

Jamie	Jimbo	Toreador

N. RICHARD NASH
Playwright of *See the Jaguar*, which opened on Broadway at the Cort Theatre on December 3, 1952, with unknown actor James Dean in a featured role.

Nash, born Nathaniel Richard Nusbaum in 1913, also wrote the plays *The Second Best Bed* (1946), *The Young and the Fair* (1948), and *The Rainmaker* (1954), in addition to scripting the screenplay of *Porgy and Bess* (1959). Nash was also married, for a brief period, to actress Janice Rule.

NATIONAL SAFETY COUNCIL
On September 17, 1955, less than two weeks before his death, James Dean taped a public safety commercial for the National Safety Council. Unaware of the irony of his words, Dean told viewers: ". . . and remember, drive safely. The life you might save might be mine." *Also see* COMMERCIALS.

NATIONAL WESTMINSTER BANK
National Westminster Bank (Natwest) of England used the image of James Dean in its 1987 advertising campaign.

PATRICIA NEAL
The only time I ever worked with James Dean was in a 1953 off-Broadway production called *The Scarecrow*. He played the

Scarecrow's reflection in the mirror. He was an unknown then, but he was jolly good in every way. I knew then that he was born to become an actor.

Actress who co-starred in *The Scarecrow*, a 1953 off-Broadway production in which James Dean had a bit part.

Patricia Neal, born in 1926, has had an impressive career on stage and screen. For her stage work, Neal was awarded with a 1947 Best Debut Tony for *Another Part of the Forest*. Her films include *The Fountainhead* (1949), *A Face in the Crowd* (1957), *Hud* (Best Actress Oscar, 1963), and *The Subject Was Roses* (Best Actress Oscar nomination, 1968).

NECK
James Dean had a 15½-inch neck.

LORI NELSON
One of James Dean's Hollywood dates, Lori Nelson met him through his agent, Dick Clayton. Of her famous squire Nelson publicly gushed, "He was thoughtful about the little things that count to a girl. You never had to open the car door—he did it for you. And you could count on other attentions which mean a lot." She of course did not elaborate on what those "other attentions" were.

Interestingly, and perhaps as a result of Dean's recommendation, Nelson was up for the part of Judy in *Rebel Without a Cause*. Director Nick Ray received 400 letters (from a Lori Nelson fan club) demanding that she be cast in the part. Nevertheless, the part went to Natalie Wood. Later Nelson was also up for the part of Luz Benedict II in *Giant*, a part that was eventually awarded to Carroll Baker.

Nelson, born in 1933, appeared in films including *Ma and Pa Kettle at the Fair* (1952), *Bend of the River* (1952), *Walking My Baby Back Home* (1953), *Destry* (1954), *Mohawk* (1956), *Hot Rod Girl* (1956), and *The Day the World Ended* (1956). She also co-starred in the Betty Grable role in the television version of "How to Marry a Millionaire" (1957–1958).

Lori Nelson penned the article "The Jimmy Dean I've Dated" for *Motion Picture* magazine (September 1955).

RALPH NELSON
The unit manager on *Giant*.

RONALD NELSON
One of the California Highway Patrol officers who arrived at the scene following the James Dean collision in the late afternoon of September 30, 1955. In his accident report Ronald Nelson noted the following:

I received a call at 5:59 P.M. It occurred on U.S. 466 at the intersection of [Highway] 41, September 30, 1955. It was a side-swipe, head-on collision. There were two persons injured and one killed.

Number one injured was Donald Gene Turnupseed, driver of Vehicle #1. Number two injured was Rolf Wütherich, a passenger in the Dean car. The dead was James Byron Dean, dead-on-arrival at the hospital.

Nelson later testified at the coroner's inquest.

NEW HAVEN, CONNECTICUT

See the Jaguar, co-starring James Dean, had its out-of-town tryouts at the Parsons Theater in New Haven, Connecticut, November 13–15, 1952.

THE NEW YORK ACTORS MOTORCYCLE CLUB

A press release issued by Warner Brothers in 1955 read:

> James Dean has been elected president of The New York Actors Motorcycle Club. Other members are Marlon Brando and Wally Cox.

THE NEW YORK FILM CRITICS

The nominees for the 1956 New York Film Critics award for Best Actor were:

Yul Brynner, *The King and I*
James Dean, *Giant*
Kirk Douglas, *Lust for Life*

Laurence Olivier, *Richard III*
Gregory Peck, *Moby Dick*
Eli Wallach, *Baby Doll*

The winner was Douglas, with Brynner and Olivier in the runner-up spots.

NEW YORK, NEW YORK

> "It's a fertile, wonderful, generous city, if you accept its violence. It offers so many things to do. I go to dancing school, take percussion lessons, acting lessons, attend concerts, operas . . ."
> James Dean to Hedda Hopper, *Chicago Tribune Magazine*,
> March 27, 1955

James Dean entertained aspirations of moving to New York as early as April 1949. At the Longmont, Colorado, national speech tournament he befriended Jim McCarthy, the New York representative in the competition, and told him to expect, in the not-so-distant future, a knock on the door in the middle of the night.

Two-and-a-half years later, disillusioned by the artifice (not to mention his lack of success) in Hollywood, Dean moved to New York. His intent: to become a *real* actor. He later recalled his introduction to the city:

> "New York overwhelmed me. For the first few weeks I only strayed a couple of blocks from my hotel off Times Square. I would see three movies a day in an attempt to escape from my loneliness and depression. I spent a hundred and fifty dollars of my limited funds just on seeing movies."

After he overcame his initial intimidation, however, James Dean embraced the eccentricity of the city and soon came to personify its manic energy. He loved to experiment. New York was his laboratory, his classroom. He loved music. New York had rhythm. He was hungry and cold, and doors slammed in his face with a force like the backhand of a scorned lover, with the regularity of his morning cup of coffee. But at least he could *feel* it. In Hollywood doors slammed in his face and he didn't even know it.

He couldn't sleep. Neither could the city. He loved that. And when he finally did slumber and awoke pale-faced and with bags under his eyes, no one told him to go out to the desert to get some color. He loved that too. He loved the acting classes and thrived on the competition of the auditions. He walked everywhere. He studied everyone, absorbed everything. Always the outsider looking in. But in New York at least there was something to see. In New York people talked about ideas; in Hollywood they talked about concepts. New York was fertile, he would frequently say like the son of a farmer from Fairmount, Indiana. People could grow in New York. James Dean grew up in New York. His backyard was Times Square, and he found a particular fascination with its seediness. Culturally, morally, it was as far away from Indiana as he could get. Fairmount was his hometown, and Hollywood was his history (and his future), but New York was his home.

James Dean left New York in March 1954, lured away by the promise of fame in Hollywood. But with every break in his schedule he returned to his little apartment on West 68th Street, as if to cleanse his soul and rejuvenate his spirit. While he was in Hollywood making *East of Eden*, he wrote a letter to his girlfriend back in New York. The girl was Barbara Glenn, and the letter was printed in *James Dean: The Mutant King* by David Dalton. It is reprinted, in part, below:

> I don't like it here. I like it home and I like you and I want to see you. . . . I haven't been to bed with nobody and won't until after the picture and I am home safe in N.Y.C. (snuggly little town that it is). Sounds unbelievable, but it's the truth I swear. So hold everything, stop breathing, stop the town, all of N.Y.C. until (should have trumpets here) James Dean returns.

He had planned to return to New York a week after the car race in Salinas. He had planned to take a break from the movies for most of 1956. He had planned to return to the Broadway stage, where at least three plays were being offered to him. But, of course, James Dean never made it back to New York—or to Salinas for that matter. And today his face is plastered along the streets of Hollywood. But the odds are that his spirit is safe, back home in New York City.

James Dean's New York City: A Selective List and Tour Guide

*The Actors Studio   245 West 52nd St. (top floor)
*The Actors Studio   1545 Broadway at W. 46th St. (room 610)
(Note: Contrary to most other reports, Dean did not attend classes at the Actors Studio's present location, 432 W. 44th St.)

The Algonquin Hotel	59 W. 44th St.
*The Astor Theater	45th St. and Broadway
Central Park	
The Cherry Lane Theatre	38 Commerce St.
The Cort Theatre	138 W. 48th St.
*Cromwell's Pharmacy	30 Rockefeller Plaza
Dumont Barber Shop	49 W. 44th St.
*Foote, Cone and Belding	247 Park Ave.
Grand Central Station	Park Ave. and 42nd St.
(rehearsals of "Death Is My Neighbor")	
Hargrave Hotel	112 W. 72nd St.
Home	49 W. 44th St.
Home	W. 38th St.
Home	W. 46th St.
Home	13 W. 89th St.
Home	W. 56th St.
Home	19 W. 68th St. (fifth floor)
The Iroquois Hotel	49 W. 44th St. (Room 82)
*The Jane Deacy Agency	60 E. 42nd St.
*Jerry's Bar and Restaurant	1335 Sixth Ave.
*Jimmy Ryan's Bar	154 W. 54th St.
*The Louis Schurr Agency	1501 Broadway
*Louie's Tavern	564 11th Ave.
Minetta Tavern	113 MacDougal St.
Museum of Modern Art	11 W. 53rd St.
The Paris Theater	4 W. 58th St.
*The Rehearsal Club	47 W. 53rd St.
*The Roxy Theatre	Seventh Ave. and 50th St.
The Royale Theatre	242 W. 45th St.
The Royalton Hotel	44 W. 44th St.
Sardi's	234 W. 44th St.
Roy Schatt's Photo Studio	149 E. 33rd St.
*Theatre De Lys	121 Christopher St.
Times Square	Broadway from W. 42nd to W. 47th St.
YMCA	5 W. 63rd St.
Ziegfeld Theatre	141 W. 54th St.

*No longer in existence, no longer operated and occupied by same company or individual(s), or still in business but not at this address

THE *NEW YORK POST*

Newspaper that has published several articles about James Dean, including:

☆ August 19, 1956   "The Legend of Jimmy Dean"
☆ October 1, 1956   "3000 at Graveside for Anniversary of James Dean's Death"
☆ September 30, 1957   "Knock James Dean and You'll Find That He Still Has Fans"
☆ October 1, 1980   "Giant Tribute for the Rebel James"
☆ September 22, 1982   "Cult Gathering at Grave of Movie Idol"
☆ September 23, 1985   "James Dean's Still a Giant"

THE *NEW YORK TIMES*

The *New York Times* named *Giant* one of the 10 best pictures of 1956. The newspaper has also published several articles about James Dean, including:

☆ March 6, 1954   "Of Local Origin"
☆ March 13, 1954   "Another Dean Hits the Big League"
☆ March 17, 1955   "James Dean Confirmed for *Giant*"
☆ October 9, 1955   "Services for Dean"
☆ October 4, 1956   "Tribute to Actor Starts TV 'War' "
☆ October 31, 1956   "Reruns Scheduled for TV Plays Featuring the Late James Dean"
☆ July 26, 1957   "Two James Dean Grants Given to Young Actors"
☆ October 7, 1957   "Portrait of a Funeral"
☆ October 1, 1980   "Young Drawn to James Dean 25 Years After"

THE *NEW YORK WORLD-TELEGRAM AND SUN*

Defunct New York newspaper that published several articles about James Dean, including:

☆ March 31, 1955   "Drama Dean's Dish, Not Law"
☆ April 9, 1955   "Not a Brando, Claims Dean"
☆ May 3, 1956   "James Dean Still Gets Mail"
☆ May 21, 1956   "Actor Has Become Legend"
☆ November 3, 1956   "The James Dean Myth Blows Up"

PAUL NEWMAN

> "Bill, so help me God, every time I went to read for a part in New York, this son-of-a-bitch would be there. Every place I went, *he* went. . . ."

> Paul Newman to Bill Bast about James Dean,
> *James Dean* by Bill Bast

If Donald Turnupseed hadn't turned left on September 30, 1955, James Dean would have grown older and become Paul Newman—with a bit more of an edge and perhaps more passion. Likewise, if Dean had lived, Paul Newman might not have become the Newman we know today. He might not have had the opportunity.

James Dean and Paul Newman looked alike. Not identical, but close enough that Elia Kazan seriously considered them as the twins in *East of Eden*. In fact Newman came so close to getting the role opposite Dean that at least one newspaper reported he had been signed for it. The part, nonetheless, went to Dick Davalos. Newman later told Dean when they ran into each other on the Warner Brothers lot, "You know, you're a lucky bastard. I wanted that part in *Eden* so bad I could taste it."

Dean and Newman not only looked alike but were both members of the Actors Studio and were both emerging as actors at the same time and the same place. Consequently they were frequently pitted as rivals for the same role. It was a head-to-head, blue-eyes-to-blue-eyes competition that Dean invariably won. Paul Newman got his first film role, *The Silver Chalice* (1954), only after Dean turned it down.

In early March 1955, when Paul Newman was up for the part of James Dean's brother in *East of Eden*, the actors appeared together in a screen test. Elia Kazan, the film's director, wanted to see how the two actors looked together. He was also concerned (as he was with Julie Harris) that Newman not look too much older than Dean. In their careers Newman always seemed to be a half step behind Dean, but he was six years older. The screen test was improvised and basically featured the actors in a series of side-by-side poses. One amusing bit of business transpired as follows:

> DIRECTOR: Paul, do you think Jimmy will appeal to the bobby-soxers?
> PAUL NEWMAN: I don't know. Is he going to be a sex symbol? I don't usually go out with boys. But, with his looks, sure, sure, I think they'll flip over him.
> DIRECTOR: What about you, Jimmy, do you think the girls will like you?
> JAMES DEAN: Sure. All depends on whether I like them.

After James Dean's death a rumor reportedly circulated around New York City that, on the night of September 30, 1955, Paul Newman walked into a bar and said, "The son-of-a-bitch is dead. Now maybe I can get some of the good roles." True or not, Newman certainly did get some of the good roles. At the time of his death Dean had been set for several projects, including "The Battler" for television, in which his co-star was to be Paul Newman, and *Somebody Up There Likes Me*, as Rocky Graziano. After his death MGM conducted a series of auditions to replace him. Robert Wise, the film's director, reportedly saw "The Battler," which aired in October 1955, and decided to cast Newman. The film was released in 1956, and it made Paul Newman a star.

> "It wasn't so much a matter of whom I was acting with, it was whom I was *watching* . . . Marlon Brando, Maureen Stapleton, Geraldine Page, Jimmy Dean . . . a pretty hotshot group."
> Paul Newman on his apprenticeship at the Actors Studio,
> January 31, 1987

Elia Kazan once commented that he thought James Dean, if he had lived, would have had a film career similar to that of Steve McQueen. Not true. If James Dean had lived, he would have had a career similar to, if anyone's, Paul Newman's. Reviewing the filmography of Paul Newman, it is interesting to speculate as to which movies would have been appropriate for Dean.

In addition to those already mentioned, the films of Paul Newman include *The Rack* (1956), *Until They Sail* (1957), *The Helen Morgan Story* (1957), *The Long, Hot Summer* (1958), *The Left-Handed Gun* (another role that had been intended for Dean, 1958), *Rally 'Round the Flag, Boys!* (1958), *Cat on a Hot Tin Roof* (Best Actor Oscar nomination, 1958), *The Young Philadelphians* (1959), *From the Terrace* (1960), *Exodus* (1960), *The Hustler* (second Best Actor Oscar nomination, 1961), *Paris Blues* (1961), *Sweet Bird of Youth* (1962), *Hemingway's Adventures of a Young Man* (1962), *Hud* (third

Pier Angeli and Paul Newman in a publicity still from *Somebody Up There Likes Me*, the film James Dean had planned to make after completing *Giant*.

Best Actor Oscar nomination, 1963), *A New Kind of Love* (1963), *The Prize* (1963), *What a Way to Go!* (1964), *The Outrage* (1964), *Lady L* (England, 1966), *Torn Curtain* (1966), *Harper* (1966), *Hombre* (1967), *Cool Hand Luke* (fourth Best Actor Oscar nomination, 1967), *The Secret War of Harry Frigg* (1967), *Rachel, Rachel* (as director and producer, Best Picture Oscar nomination, 1968), *Winning* (1969), *Butch Cassidy and the Sundance Kid* (1969), *WUSA* (1970), *Sometimes a Great Notion* (also directed, 1971), *The Effect of Gamma Rays on Man-in-the-Moon Marigolds* (as director, 1972), *The Life and Times of Judge Roy Bean* (1972), *The Mackintosh Man* (1973), *The Sting* (1973), *The Towering Inferno* (1974), *The Drowning Pool* (1975), *Silent Movie* (1976), *Buffalo Bill and the Indians, or Sitting Bull's History Lesson* (1976), *Slap Shot* (1977), *Quintet* (1979), *When Time Ran Out . . .* (1980), *Fort Apache, The Bronx* (1981), *Absence of Malice* (fifth Best Actor Oscar nomination, 1981), *The Verdict* (sixth Best Actor Oscar nomination, 1982), *Harry and Son* (as director, writer, producer, and star, 1984), *The Color of Money* (seventh Best Actor Oscar nomination, first win, 1986; he had received an additional, honorary Oscar the year before), *The Glass Menagerie* (as director, 1987), *Fat Man and Little Boy* (1989), *Blaze* (for which his salary was $5 million, 1989), and *Mr. and Mrs. Bridge* (1990).

> "I think he would have surpassed both Marlon and me. I think he really would have gone into the classics."
> Paul Newman on James Dean, *Off Camera* by Leonard Probst

> "After a while, you simply have to keep an instrument oiled. You can't just throw it into the garbage and pick it up every four or five years and expect it to work."
> Paul Newman on acting, *Los Angeles Times Magazine*, March 15, 1987

In addition to his phenomenal film career Newman is a successful businessman, humanitarian, and champion of liberal causes. His Newman's Own food company, which makes spaghetti sauce, lemonade, popcorn, and salad dressing, has given over $26 million to various charities since its inception in 1982. His marriage to actress Joanne Woodward has spanned over 30 years and has survived the fatal 1978 drug overdose of Scott Newman, Newman's son from a previous marriage. His marriage, like his career, is one of Hollywood's best.

> "Someone once asked me what it was like to be married to the sexiest, most beautiful man in the world. I thought a minute and replied, 'Sexiness wears thin after a while and beauty fades, but to be married to a man who makes you laugh every day, ah, now that's a real treat!' "
> Joanne Woodward, *Good Housekeeping*, November 1989

REX NEWMAN
Reporter who served as the on-air investigator in the September 11, 1953, episode of the NBC television program "The Big Story" that starred James Dean.

THE NEWSPAPERS
The 10 Most Important Newspaper Articles about Dean
1. "James Dean First Place Winner in Dramatic Speaking," *Fairmount News*, April 14, 1949
2. "Jimmy Dean Says He Isn't Flattered by Being Labeled 'Another Brando,' " *Los Angeles Times*, November 7, 1954
3. "Another Dean Hits the Big League" by Howard Thompson, *New York Times*, March 13, 1955
4. "James Dean Planning to Go on a Racing Kick When *Giant* Ends" by Carroll Harrison, *Los Angeles Herald-Examiner*, September 16, 1955
5. Special Edition, "In Memory of James Dean," *Fairmount News*, October 1955
6. "Are Dean Fans 'Buying' Phony Idol?" by Maurice Zolotow, *Detroit Free Press*, October 28, 1956
7. "Remembering James Dean Back Home in Indiana" by Paul Hendrickson, *Los Angeles Times*, July 22, 1973

8. "Jimmy Dean, Giant Legend, Cult Rebel" by Leonard Rosenman, *Los Angeles Times*, December 18, 1977
9. "The Man Who Would be 50: A Memory of James Dean" by Gene Nielson Owen, *Los Angeles Times*, February 8, 1981
10. "Rebel with an Agent" by Debra Zahn, *Los Angeles Times*, September 29, 1985

NEWSWEEK MAGAZINE
Newsweek has published a few articles about James Dean, including:

☆ June 18, 1956   "Star That Won't Die"
☆ January 27, 1964   "Undying Voice"

"THE NEXT DEAN"

For 35 years there has been a steady and insistent lineup of brooding actors who have been proclaimed, boldly, as "the next Dean." However, hype aside, and as time has illustrated, no one has been able to fill the Dean denim, wear the Dean attitude, or project the same broken vulnerability or explosive outbursts of emotion with the impact achieved by the original.

Nevertheless, the following is a selective compilation of the actors who struck the pose and were compared with Dean or touted as "the next Dean." Some succeeded—to a degree—while others did not. Others are still trying.

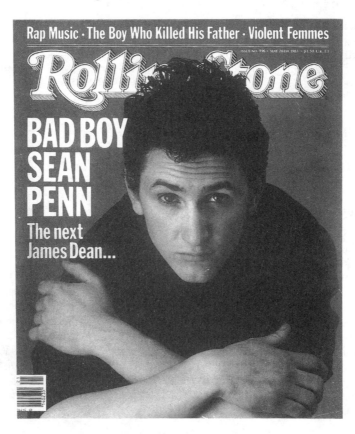

The 1950s: Stand-Ins

Nick Adams	Rod Lauren	Anthony Perkins
Harry Belafonte	Dewey Martin	Phillip Pine
Edd Byrnes	Rod McKuen	Elvis Presley
Joe Gersh	Sal Mineo	Cliff Robertson
Dennis Hopper	Don Murray	Steve Rowland
John Kerr	Paul Newman	Dean Stockwell

The 1960s: Hip Hippies

Warren Beatty	Adam Faith	Jack Nicholson
Jean-Paul Belmondo	Albert Finney	Rudolf Nureyev
Horst Buchholz	Stathis Giallelis	Michael Parks
Jack Chaplain	Laurence Harvey	Martin Sheen
Brandon de Wilde	Christopher Jones	Terence Stamp
Alain Delon	Steve McQueen	

The 1970s: New Generation—The Disco Deans

Brad Davis	Don Johnson	Al Pacino
Robert De Niro	Paul le Mat	John Travolta
Richard Gere	Linda Manz	

The 1980s: Still Brooding

Maxwell Caulfield	Corey Haim	River Phoenix
Johnny Depp	Alex MacArthur	Aidan Quinn
Matt Dillon	Judd Nelson	Charlie Sheen
Robert Downey, Jr.	Gary Oldman	Christian Slater
Richard Grieco	Sean Penn	

ANNA NICHOLAS

Actress who co-starred in *Dean*, a 1977 British stage musical. Nicholas portrayed three roles: Natalie Wood, Elizabeth Taylor, and Pier Angeli.

BOBBY NICK

Actor who appeared in the September 11, 1953, episode of the NBC television program "The Big Story," which starred James Dean.

PAUL NICKELL

Director of "Ten Thousand Horses Singing," a 1952 episode of the CBS television program "Studio One" in which unknown actor James Dean had a bit part. Nickell later directed Dean in a co-starring role in "Sentence of Death," a 1953 episode of "Studio One Summer Theatre."

"NO ROOM"

James Dean appeared in "No Room," an episode of the CBS television series "Danger" that aired on April 14, 1953 (not on March 14, 1953, as reported elsewhere). Dean portrayed a safecracker. The program starred Martin Kingsley and Irene Vernon.

JOHN NOBLE
One of the wardrobe men on *Giant*.

INDIA NOSE
India Nose was Jimmy Dean's teacher at Fairmount (Indiana) West Ward elementary school, where he attended grades four through six.

RAMON NOVARRO
Ramon Novarro, "Ben Hur" of the silent screen, was up for the part of Old Polo in *Giant*, which would have signified something of a comeback for him. However, the role eventually went to Alexander Scourby, and Novarro settled back into obscurity.

NUDITY
There is a famous photograph of a naked young man sitting, legs flung, in a tree. The man bears a resemblance to James Dean. However, the photo has been reproduced so often over the years that its image is fuzzy, and it is difficult to discern the identity of its subject. It *could* be James Dean. Or it could be Christopher Jones. Or it could simply be an anonymous tree climber with his hand on his hard-on. The photo, purported to be a still from a gay porno film that Dean allegedly made during his struggling years, was published, among other places, in *Screw* and *The Advocate*. As described by the writer from *The Advocate* (who obviously delighted in his wordplay):

> It is difficult to say who is attached to that mammoth, erect cock, but it sure looks like Dean, a giant in more ways than one.

Certainly James Dean had no qualms about appearing naked in public. In fact his friend Roy Schatt once related an incident in which Jimmy made an impromptu appearance at the front door of his New York apartment—naked. Other reports contend that once, during the making of *East of Eden*, Jimmy paraded naked from his dressing room to the set with the simple purpose of providing a jolt for the cast and crew. Additional reports claim that there is—somewhere—a series of photographs, taken in New York, of James Dean, naked and posed in various positions as a matador.

On a less sensationalistic note Dean appeared shirtless and very skinny in "The Bells of Cockaigne," a 1953 episode of the NBC television program "Armstrong Circle Theatre." Later, with a few more dollars in his pants pocket and a few more pounds in his belly, he again appeared sans shirt in *Rebel Without a Cause*.

NUMBERS
Birth date: 2-8-31
Death date: 9-30-55
Basketball jersey: 3 (Fairmount High School)
Basketball jersey: 10 (Santa Monica City College)
Porsche racing numbers: 75, 23 (Speedster)

Porsche racing number: 130 (Spyder)
Porsche license plate: 2Z77767
Ford station wagon license plate: 2Z27081
California driver's license: B854267
First home address: 320 East Fourth Street
Last home address: 14611 Sutton Street

RUDOLF NUREYEV

"If no dogs are barking at you, it means that you aren't worth anything."

Rudolf Nureyev, *Los Angeles Times*, March 22, 1987

In the 1960s Rudolf Nureyev (born in Russia, 1938) was hyped as "ballet's James Dean." *Time* magazine reported in November 1962:

Nureyev radiates a kind of savage excitement that he describes as "a mixture of tenderness and brutality." It has prompted comparisons with Nijinsky and even with the late actor James Dean, hero of the beatniks. Nureyev is like Dean in another respect; he is a complex and difficult animal offstage as he is on.

MAILA NURMI

Television's original gal ghoul, aka Vampira, the foremother of Morticia, Lily Munster, and Elvira. Nurmi gained further infamy after James Dean's death when a scandal magazine, *Whisper*, accused her of concocting a brew of black magic to punish Dean after he had rejected her amorous advances. The basis for the accusation, among other things, was a postcard photo of Nurmi as Vampira sitting beside an open grave, with the inscription "Darling, Come and Join Me!" which Nurmi had sent to Dean only days before his death. The article in *Whisper* provoked a rash of hate mail and public ill will targeted at Nurmi. Her career has never recovered.

James Dean first met Maila Nurmi at Googie's restaurant in West Hollywood in 1954. Beneath her black ghoul and gloom act, she was blond and beautiful and with eyebrows that invariably arched up to her hairline. Press reports at the time contended she was a self-styled witch and an acquaintance of Brando's. For Dean the combination was irresistible. He was intrigued. So was she. Although Dean wasn't yet a star, in Hollywood, where such things are important, he was the flavor of the month, and everyone wanted a taste. Nonetheless, despite numerous reports to the contrary, it is unlikely that they became lovers. Nurmi, eight years older than Dean, was married at the time. Further, their relationship involved a third and always present partner, a mutual friend, Jack Simmons.

Several months later the relationship soured. There was speculation that Dean resented Nurmi's exploitation of their acquaintance for publicity. Other reports contend that Dean merely tired of what he considered to be Nurmi's otherworldly pretensions. To Hedda Hopper he lashed out:

"I don't go out with witches, and I dig dating cartoons even less. I have never taken Vampira *out*, and I should like to clear this up. I have a fairly adequate knowledge of satanic forces, and I was interested to find out if this girl was obsessed by such a force. She was a subject about which I wanted to learn. I met her and engaged her in conversation. She knew absolutely nothing! She uses her inane characterization as an excuse for the most infantile expression you can imagine."

When Nurmi read Hopper's column, she countered in print with "I'll challenge him to an intelligence contest any time." Their relationship, whether it transpired in Nurmi's black-sheeted bed or merely over late-night coffee at Googie's pharmacy, was over.

Today Maila Nurmi is something of a recluse. Some reports contend that she has been working as a waitress in Hollywood. In 1976 she agreed to be interviewed in the documentary *James Dean: The First American Teenager*. In 1989 she made another appearance on "A Current Affair," in which she provided commentary on Dean's alleged death wish. When she was last heard from, the former Vampira was planning to go to court to sue Elvira (Cassandra Peterson) for allegedly infringing on her dark domain.

O

OBITUARIES

JAMES DEAN FILM STAR, DIES IN AUTO CRASH

James Dean, 24, one of Hollywood's brightest new motion picture stars, was killed early last night in a head-on collision at the rural town of Cholame, about 19 miles east of Paso Robles, the California Highway Patrol reported.

The young actor met death in his German-built Porsche sports car while en route to road races at Salinas. Patrolmen said Dean was dead on arrival at the Paso Robles War Memorial Hospital following the crash at the intersection of State Highway 41 and U.S. 466. . . .

Los Angeles Times, October 1, 1955

JAMES DEAN IS VICTIM AS CARS HIT HEAD ON

Paso Robles, Oct. 1 (AP):

Actor James Dean, the surly, brooding Caleb of the movie *East of Eden* was killed last night in the head-on highway crash of his brand new sports car near here.

The 24-year-old actor, often compared to Marlon Brando, was driving to a road race in Salinas, the location site for the movie which catapulted him to stardom.

The California Highway Patrol said a car driven by Donald Turnupseed, 23, of 1001 Academy St., Tulare, turned left off Highway 466 onto Highway 41 and collided almost head-on with Dean's Porsche Spyder. Turnupseed, a student at California Polytechnic College at San Luis Obispo, suffered minor injuries.

The collision occurred near the rural community of Cholame, 18 miles east of here. Dean was headed west in his $7000 car and the student turned off 466 onto 41 which leads to Tulare.

Ambulance driver Paul Moreno said the Indiana-born actor was still alive when taken from the wreckage but died en route to the War Memorial Hospital in Paso Robles. Dean suffered multiple fractures of both arms and internal injuries. . . .

Los Angeles Mirror, October 1, 1955

ACTOR WON FAME IN FIRST PICTURE

Death overtook speed-loving James Dean, 24-year-old film star and newest idol of the bobby soxers, at a highway intersection 28 miles east of Paso Robles last night.

A 150-mile-per-hour Porsche sport car for which Dean paid $7000 a few days ago collided with a college student's automobile at the junction of Highways 41 and 466 near Cholame.

When he reached Paso Robles' War Memorial Hospital, the boyish, thin-faced Dean was dead. His passenger, Rolf Wütherich, 28, mechanic, of 1219 North Vine Street was gravely injured.

But California Highway Patrolmen said that the driver of the other car, Donald D. Turnupseed, 23, of 1001 Academy Street, Tulare, escaped with minor injuries. . . .

Los Angeles Examiner, October 1, 1955

JAMES DEAN, FILM ACTOR, KILLED IN CRASH OF AUTO

Paso Robles, Calif. Sept. 30 (AP):

James Dean, 24-year-old motion picture actor, was killed tonight in an automobile accident near here.

A spokesman for Warner Brothers, for whom Mr. Dean had just completed *The Giant*, said he had no details of the accident except that the actor was en route to a sports car meeting at Salinas. He was driving a small German speedster.

The actor had appeared in *East of Eden*, released last April, and in *Rebel Without a Cause*, still unreleased. . . .

New York Times, October 1, 1955

Died: James Dean, 24, one time law student turned actor whose portrayal of a brooding, inarticulate adolescent in the movie, *East of Eden*, rocketed him to stardom after his souped-up, $7000 German sports car crashed head-on into another automobile near Paso Robles, Calif., Sept. 30.

Newsweek, October 10, 1955

Died: James Dean, 24, most promising young cinema actor of 1955 (*East of Eden*); in a collision as he sped along a darkening highway in his silver Porsche Spyder sports car to enter a road race one week after he completed work in a new film, *Giant*, near Paso Robles, Calif.

Time, October 10, 1955

MARGARET O'BRIEN

For a period Margaret O'Brien was the leading contender for the role of Judy in *Rebel Without a Cause*, a role that eventually went to Natalie Wood.

UNA O'CONNOR

Actress who was featured in "Prologue to Glory," a 1952 episode of the NBC television program "Kraft Television Theatre" in which unknown actor James Dean appeared.

Una O'Connor (1880–1959) also appeared in numerous films including *Cavalcade* (1933), *Bride of Frankenstein* (1935), *The Adventures of Robin Hood* (1938), and *Witness for the Prosecution* (1957).

CLIFFORD ODETS

Nicholas Ray's original choice to write *Rebel Without a Cause*.

Clifford Odets (1903–1963) was a playwright, several of whose works were adapted into films, including *Golden Boy* (which introduced William Holden, 1939), *Clash by Night* (which gave Marilyn Monroe an early dramatic role as a cannery worker, 1952), and *The Country Girl* (which won a Best Actress Oscar for Grace Kelly, 1954). Odets also authored several films directly for the screen, including *The General Died at Dawn* (1936), *Humoresque* (1946), and *Sweet Smell of Success* (1957).

THE OFFICIAL JAMES DEAN ANNIVERSARY BOOK
One-shot cover-to-cover magazine about James Dean, edited by Peter Meyerson and published in 1956 by Dell.

FRANK O'HARA
Poet who wrote the poem "For James Dean." O'Hara's other poems include "An Abortion," "Homosexuality," "Ode to Lust," "Lana Turner Has Collapsed!" and many others.

SEITA OHNISHI
Arguably Seita Ohnishi is James Dean's biggest fan in the world. Certainly no one has spent more money eulogizing his memory. In 1977 Ohnishi, a Japanese businessman, erected a monument to Dean outside a post office in Cholame, California, not far from the site where he was killed. The monument cost Ohnishi $50,000.

Additionally, Ohnishi has one of the world's largest collections of James Dean artifacts and memorabilia, including the negatives (and the rights to use them) of Sanford Roth's entire portfolio of James Dean photographs. He is, in the words of Roth's widow, Beulah, "the world's greatest James Dean fan. He is absolutely taken in by the material. He made me sell him a chair that Jimmy used to sit in. Anything that Jimmy touched, he wants in his collection."

Ohnishi's latest project in development is another, more massive (14 feet high, 40 feet long, 130 tons), $200,000 monument to Dean, which he commissioned sculptor Yasuo Mizui to create in the south of France in 1985. Upon its completion Ohnishi plans to ship the monster monument to an undisclosed location in California. Of his idol, Ohnishi, who does not speak English, said:

> "There are some things, like the hatred that accompanies war, that are best forgotten. There are others, like the love inspired by this young actor, that should be preserved for all time."

OKLAHOMA!

Remarkably James Dean was considered for the role of Curly in the film version of this smash Rodgers and Hammerstein Broadway musical hit. The role eventually went to Gordon MacRae, and considering Dean's voice, it was a good thing for the film (and for Dean) that it did. The image of James Dean belting out "Oh, What a Beautiful Morning" strikes a resoundingly false note.

Oklahoma! (1955) was directed by Fred Zinnemann, and, in addition to MacRae, starred Shirley Jones, Rod Steiger, Gloria Grahame (in a glorious turn as Ado Annie), Charlotte Greenwood, Gene Nelson, and Eddie Albert.

JERRY OLKEN

Actor, born in 1940, who appeared with Dean in a wardrobe test for *Rebel Without a Cause*. In the test Olken postured as one of the film's gang members. Later Olken changed his name (to Jud Taylor) and, eventually, his profession (to director for television). His telefilms include "Weekend of Terror" (1970), "Say Goodbye, Maggie Cole" (Susan Hayward's last role, 1972), and "Flesh and Blood" (1979).

"OMNIBUS"

Critically acclaimed cultural variety television series that ran on Sunday afternoon on CBS in 1952, on Sunday evening on CBS from October 1953 to April 1956, and on Sunday night on ABC from October 1956 to March 1957. The program was hosted by Alistair Cooke.

James Dean appeared in William Inge's "Glory in Flower," which was presented as the premier episode of the second season of "Omnibus."

ON THE WATERFRONT

Late in 1954 James Dean attended a screening of *On the Waterfront* at Columbia Studios. His companion was Nick Ray. Also at the screening were Marilyn Monroe and Shelley Winters.

On the Waterfront was directed by Elia Kazan and starred Marlon Brando. The film later won the Oscar as the Best Picture of 1954. It won additional Oscars for Kazan, Brando, and Eva Marie Saint.

BARBARA O'NEIL

Actress who was featured in "Run Like a Thief," a 1954 episode of the NBC television program "Philco TV Playhouse" that co-starred James Dean.

Barbara O'Neil is best remembered as Scarlett O'Hara's doomed mother in *Gone with the Wind* (1939). Her other films include *Stella Dallas* (1937), *All This and Heaven Too* (Best Supporting Actress Oscar nomination, 1940), and *The Nun's Story* (1959). O'Neil, who was born into a wealthy family, was married, very briefly, to director Joshua Logan in the 1940s. It was, according to Logan, a "loveless" marriage.

WILL O'NEILL

Before his death in 1987 Will O'Neill founded and organized the James Dean Memorial Run, which is held annually in Los Angeles on the last weekend of September.

OPHELEOS MEN'S HONOR SERVICE ORGANIZATION

In 1950 Jim Dean was elected into the prestigious Opheleos Men's Honor Service Organization of Santa Monica City College. The club was composed of the 21 most outstanding male students at the school. The members wore royal blue jackets and operated under the selfless motto "Service Without Hope of Conspicuous Reward."

D. H. ORCUTT

The foreman of the jury at the October 11, 1955, coroner's inquest into the death of James Dean.

ORPHAN?

Early publicity on James Dean contended that he had been orphaned as a baby. The idea may have been initiated to capitalize on public sympathy, as Marilyn Monroe had done with much success only a couple of years before. Or it might have been perpetrated in an effort to spare Dean's father, Winton, from the public spotlight. Either way, of course, it was a fabrication.

BILL ORR

Bill Orr, Warner Brothers vice president and executive in charge of talent, was responsible for screen-testing James Dean for *Battle Cry*. Orr, at the time, was married to studio honcho Jack Warner's daughter.

PAUL OSBORN

Upon reading Paul Osborn's screenplay of John Steinbeck's novel *East of Eden*, director Elia Kazan was so impressed that he rushed a letter to studio head Jack Warner, enthusing "It is one of the best [scripts] I ever had." Warner concurred and sent a letter to Osborn, dated November 17, 1953, congratulating him on his "fine dramatization." The letter concluded with Warner saying, "In these days, we more than ever welcome good writing."

The Academy of Motion Picture Arts and Sciences agreed with Kazan and Warner, bestowing on Osborn a 1955 Best Screenplay Oscar nomination. Interestingly, it had been Paul Osborn who initially cajoled Elia Kazan into considering James Dean for the leading role in *Eden*.

Osborn (1901–1988) was born in Evansville, Indiana. His other films include *The Young in Heart* (1938), *Madame Curie* (1943), *The Yearling* (1946), *Sayonara* (Best Adapted Screenplay Oscar nomination, 1957), *South Pacific* (1958), and *Wild River* (1960). He also wrote the plays *Hotbed* (1926), *The Vinegar Tree* (1930), *On Borrowed Time* (1938), *Point of No Return* (1951), and *The World of Suzie Wong* (1958).

TED OSBORN
Actor who appeared in "A Long Time Till Dawn," a 1953 episode of the NBC television program "Kraft Television Theatre," which starred James Dean.

THE OSCARS
> It's never happened that a posthumous Academy Award has been given an actor but Hollywood insiders expect the precedent to be set in the case of James Dean, killed in that wild auto crash. They believe his performance in *Rebel Without a Cause* will win him an Oscar, even though he's dead.
>
> Dorothy Kilgallen, October 1955

> The late James Dean is a favorite, with James Cagney and William Holden close seconds in one of the most entry-packed Oscar fights in many years.
>
> Aline Mosby, December 1955

In February 1956 James Dean was indeed nominated for an Oscar, posthumously, as the Best Actor of 1955. But it was not for his performance in *Rebel Without a Cause*, as suggested by Dorothy Kilgallen; it was for *East of Eden*. At the televised ceremony at which the nominations were read, actress June Haver read the name "James Dean" and added, "May God rest his soul. I would love to have the honor of writing his name on the [nominations black] board." The other names on the nominations blackboard were:

Ernest Borgnine, *Marty*
James Cagney, *Love Me or Leave Me*
Frank Sinatra, *The Man with the Golden Arm*
Spencer Tracy, *Bad Day at Black Rock*

No outlandish upsets were among the nominations, although Henry Fonda had been considered a strong contender that year for *Mister Roberts*, William Holden for *Love Is a Many Splendored Thing* and/or *Picnic*, and Burt Lancaster for *The Rose Tattoo*. Dean's nomination was the first posthumous nomination in the Best Actor category in the history of the Academy of Motion Picture Arts and Sciences. The distinction was later duplicated by Spencer Tracy in 1967 for *Guess Who's Coming to Dinner* and by Peter Finch in 1976, who was nominated (and won) for his "mad as hell" performance in *Network*.

James Dean received his nomination, and *East of Eden* received its other three nominations—Best Supporting Actress (Jo Van Fleet), Best Director (Elia Kazan), and Best Screenplay (Paul Osborn)—despite the fact that Warner Brothers had chosen not to support the film. Instead Warners put its money and clout behind its other big picture that year, *Mister Roberts*, which was nominated as Best Picture. The other 1955 nominees as Best Picture were *Love Is a Many Splendored Thing*, *Marty*, *Picnic*, and *The Rose Tattoo*.

Also competing in several categories that year was *Rebel Without a Cause*, which received nominations for Best Supporting Actor (Sal Mineo),

Best Supporting Actress (Natalie Wood), and Best Story (Nicholas Ray).

The winners were announced on March 21, 1956, at the Pantages Theatre in Hollywood. Jerry Lewis was the host. The projected heavy favorite was the small, low-budget *Marty*. Its star, Ernest Borgnine, was also expected to take home the Best Actor Oscar. Sensing this, days before the big event influential columnist Hedda Hopper launched a campaign to force the academy to present Dean with a special, honorary Oscar. She wrote in her column:

> I wonder if members of the Academy of Motion Picture Arts and Sciences will give him the Oscar as the Best Actor of the year. Knowing how fickle some of our people are, I'm asking the committee of the Academy to grant a special award in memory of one of the most sensitive, talented boys it's ever been my privilege to know.

The academy, however, pointed at its rule book, which dictated that nominees were not allowed to win honorary awards. The only honorary award presented that year was for *Samurai, The Legend of Musashi*, a Japanese picture deemed the year's Best Foreign Language Film (this was before the academy had established a separate category for foreign films). The other winners included:

Best Picture: *Marty*
Best Actor: Ernest Borgnine, *Marty* (the award was presented by Grace Kelly)
Best Actress: Anna Magnani, *The Rose Tattoo*
Best Supporting Actor: Jack Lemmon, *Mister Roberts*
Best Supporting Actress: Jo Van Fleet, *East of Eden*
Best Director: Delbert Mann, *Marty*
Best Story: Daniel Fuchs, *Love Me or Leave Me*
Best Screenplay: *Marty* by Paddy Chayefsky
Best Story and Screenplay: *Interrupted Melody* by William Ludwig and Sonya Levien

The following year Dean was again considered a candidate for his work in *Giant*. There was, however, some debate as to whether his work should have been designated in the Best Actor or Best Supporting Actor category. Actually his work in *Giant* was a supporting performance. But because he received star billing, and because Warner Brothers was determined to make the most of his posthumous popularity, he was positioned in the Best Actor category. When the nominations were announced on February 18, 1957, they included:

Yul Brynner, *The King and I*
James Dean, *Giant*
Kirk Douglas, *Lust for Life*
Rock Hudson, *Giant*
Laurence Olivier, *Richard III*

This time Dean didn't have a chance. The competition was between Yul Brynner and Kirk Douglas. Further, there wasn't much excitement over his

James Dean off the set of *Giant*: he didn't get an Oscar, but he did get an armadillo (and an artificially receding hairline).

nomination, although Hedda Hopper continued her campaign to coerce the academy into presenting him an honorary Oscar. The excitement of the 1956 Oscars revolved around the return from scandal of Ingrid Bergman, who was nominated (and later won) for *Anastasia*. Upsets in the nominations were few and mild. Marilyn Monroe was touted (and should have received a nomination) for *Bus Stop*; Elizabeth Taylor was expected to receive a nomination (which wasn't deserved or received) for *Giant*.

Nonetheless *Giant* was a major contender with a whopping 10 nominations and was considered a front-runner, along with Mike Todd's *Around the*

World in 80 Days, for the Best Picture Oscar. The other films competing as Best Picture were *Friendly Persuasion, The King and I,* and *The Ten Commandments.* Other *Giant* nominations included:

Best Supporting Actress: Mercedes McCambridge
Best Director: George Stevens
Best Adapted Screenplay: Fred Guiol and Ivan Moffat
Best Editing: William Hornbeck, Philip W. Anderson, and Fred Bohanan
Best Art Direction: Boris Leven, art direction; Ralph S. Hurst, set decoration
Best Costume Design: Moss Mabry and Marjorie Best
Best Music Scoring: Dimitri Tiomkin

The winners were announced on March 27, 1957, at the Pantages Theatre. Jerry Lewis was the host. The evening provided virtually no major surprises, with the possible exception of Anthony Quinn's nod as Best Supporting Actor for his very brief performance in *Lust for Life.* Had Dean been nominated in this category, he would have had his Oscar. The winners were:

Best Picture: *Around the World in 80 Days*
Best Actor: Yul Brynner, *The King and I*
Best Actress: Ingrid Bergman, *Anastasia*
Best Supporting Actor: Anthony Quinn, *Lust for Life*
Best Supporting Actress: Dorothy Malone, *Written on the Wind*
Best Director: George Stevens, *Giant* (the film's only winner)
Best Story: *The Brave One* by Robert Rich (aka Dalton Trumbo)
Best Adapted Screenplay: *Around the World in 80 Days* by James Poe, John Farrow, and
    S. J. Perelman
Best Original Screenplay: *The Red Balloon* by Albert Lamorisse

OUR HEARTS WERE YOUNG AND GAY
Jimmy Dean starred in a Fairmount (Indiana) High School production of *Our Hearts Were Young and Gay,* which was presented during his junior year in October 1947.

"OUR TOWN"
A few weeks before his death Jimmy attended a rehearsal of a television production of Thornton Wilder's *Our Town* at NBC Studios. James Sheldon, who attended the rehearsal with Jimmy, recently recalled, "We went to a dress rehearsal of 'Our Town' [which was being presented as a musical]— Frank Sinatra in 'Our Town' with Paul Newman and Eva Marie Saint. It was an hour television thing. And we sat in the control room. Jimmy was curious about the cast and crew and studio, and so forth. . . ."

OUR TOWN
In the summer of 1956 the James Dean Memorial Foundation staged a production of Thornton Wilder's *Our Town.* Featured in the cast was Jimmy's cousin Marcus Winslow, Jr.

GENE NIELSEN OWEN

Gene Owen, incorrectly identified elsewhere as Jean Owen, was James Dean's drama teacher and drama club adviser at Santa Monica City College circa 1949–1950. According to Owen, her student, Dean, had a problem with articulation, which she helped him to alleviate. "I told him that if anything would clear up fuzzy speech it would be the demanding soliloquies of Shakespeare." She proceeded to prove her point by coaching Dean on *Hamlet*

> "One day in class, Jimmy read some scenes from Edgar Allan Poe's *Telltale Heart*. He was magnificent—but then he always had a spectacular emotion for any scene he played. Later, during that same class, I asked Jimmy to read some scenes from *Hamlet*. That night, when I returned home, I informed my husband that I had finally found the right student to play Hamlet as I felt it should be played."
> Gene Owen, *Movieland*, February 1957

With her husband, Harold (who died in 1987 at age 78), Gene Owen established the Family Theater in Santa Monica in 1953. According to Mrs. Owen they also took Jimmy under their wing and made him a welcome guest in their home. It was a scene that Dean would later play with other older couples, including Sanford and Beulah Roth.

Years later Gene Owen penned articles about her former student that were published in *Movieland* magazine (February 1957) and the *Los Angeles Times* (February 8, 1981). She also appeared with her husband in the 1976 documentary *James Dean: The First American Teenager*.

P

PACIFIC INDEMNITY

The California insurance company that, in September 1955, had the unfortunate lack of foresight to insure James Dean's Porsche Spyder. Following Dean's death Pacific Indemnity paid the sum of $6,750 to his estate.

AL PACINO

> "I was in a play and they said, 'Hey, Marlon Brando! This guy acts like Marlon Brando!' I was about twelve. I guess it was because I was supposed to get sick onstage and I really did get sick every time we did this play. Actually, the person I related to was James Dean. I grew up with the Dean *thing*. *Rebel Without a Cause* had a very powerful effect on me."
>
> Al Pacino, *Playboy*

James Dean not only was Al Pacino's acting inspiration but also his benefactor—in a way. In the 1950s, after Dean's death, Pacino was the recipient of a $50 scholarship from the James Dean Memorial Foundation.

Former fruit farm worker, janitor, mail boy, shoe salesman, and furniture mover, Al Pacino, born Alfredo Pacino in 1939, made his film debut in *Me Natalie* (1968). He burst into stardom in the early 1970s with a string of exceptional pictures, and with his intense, Method-actor style was branded by some as "the next Dean." But in the latter part of the decade, and through the 1980s, Pacino went askew with a succession of mediocre films. In 1989 he made something of a resurgence with *Sea of Love*, and in the following year with *The Godfather Part III*. His other work includes *The Godfather* (1972), *Serpico* (1973), *The Godfather Part II* (1974), *Dog Day Afternoon* (1975), and *And Justice For All* (1979), all of which earned him Oscar nominations.

> "Pacino is a schmuck. His career went into the toilet."
>
> Oliver Stone, embittered that Pacino walked out on
> *Born on the Fourth of July*, *Vanity Fair*, October 1989

> "That's probably the reason I got into acting. So I don't have to think. I think the reason I act is for a relief from thinking."
>
> Al Pacino, *Los Angeles Times*, September 17, 1989

"PADLOCKS"

James Dean co-starred in "Padlocks," an episode of the CBS television series "Danger" that aired on November 9, 1954. The progam was directed by John Frankenheimer and co-starred Mildred Dunnock.

DON PAGE

Unit manager and an assistant director on *East of Eden*; also the first assistant director on *Rebel Without a Cause*.

GERALDINE PAGE

"I thought she was a bag lady. Then I looked up and saw she was a legend."

Cher on Geraldine Page, *People*

One of the great actresses of our time. In 1952 Geraldine Page was heralded for her off-Broadway performance in Tennessee Williams's *Summer and Smoke*. She then made her Broadway debut in *Mid-Summer*. And then, in early 1954, she starred as Marcelline, the sexually frustrated wife of a handsome but homosexual husband (played by Louis Jourdan) in *The Immoralist*. The play also featured James Dean in a supporting role as the seductive houseboy who taunts and tempts the husband.

For Dean the production of *The Immoralist* was tempestuous, laced with antagonism from the producer, director, writers, and certain cast members. His one solace was the friendship he found with Geraldine Page. Hers was the one voice he listened to, the one talent he respected.

Jimmy once drove his motorcycle into his friend Geraldine Page's backstage dressing room and asked her if she wanted a ride.

A doctor's daughter from Missouri, Geraldine Page, born in 1924, made her film debut in 1953 in *Taxi*. Her subsequent pictures include *Hondo* (Best Supporting Actress Oscar nomination, 1953), *Summer and Smoke* (Best Actress Oscar nomination, 1961), *Sweet Bird of Youth* (Best Actress Oscar nomination, 1962; she lost to Anne Bancroft, *The Miracle Worker*), *Toys in the Attic* (1963), *Dear Heart* (1965), *The Happiest Millionaire* (1967), *You're a Big Boy Now* (1967), *Monday's Child* (1967), *Whatever Happened to Aunt Alice?* (1969), *The Beguiled* (1971), *Pete 'n' Tillie* (fourth Oscar nomination, Best Supporting Actress, 1972), *J. W. Coop* (1972), *The Day of the Locust* (1975), *Nasty Habits* (1977), *Interiors* (fifth Oscar nomination, Best Actress, 1978), *Honky Tonk Freeway* (1981), *Harry's War* (1981), *I'm Dancing as Fast as I Can* (1982), *The Pope of Greenwich Village* (sixth Oscar nomination, Best Supporting Actress, 1984), and *The Trip to Bountiful* (seventh Oscar nomination, first win, Best Actress, 1985; this time, she beat Anne Bancroft, up for *Agnes of God*, in a role Page had originated on Broadway).

On television, Page won Emmys as Best Actress in a Drama for her performances in Truman Capote's "A Christmas Memory," a 1966–1967 presentation of "ABC Stage 67," and "The Thanksgiving Visitor," a 1968–1969 special presentation.

Still, despite her screen successes, it was on stage where Geraldine Page was most comfortable, and on stage where she was a star. Her stage credits include her Tony-nominated performances in *Sweet Bird of Youth* (1960), *Absurd Person Singular* (1975), *Agnes of God* (1982), and *Blithe Spirit* (1987).

In June 1987 Geraldine Page finished a Friday night performance of Noel Coward's *Blithe Spirit*, in which she co-starred with Richard Chamberlain and Blythe Danner. The following day, after she missed a matinee performance, she was found dead from a heart attack in her Manhattan apartment.

Geraldine Page was survived by her husband, actor Rip Torn, two sons, a daughter, and the superb work of an actress who obviously loved her job. As she once confided to a reporter, "I love *parts* and I love food."

EL PAISANO HOTEL

Marfa, Texas, hotel (address: 207 North Highland) that served as the company headquarters for 118 members of the cast and crew of *Giant* during the summer of 1955. The owner of the hotel was Mrs. Emma Mallan. Although James Dean, Elizabeth Taylor, Rock Hudson, and some of the other prominent members of the cast were indulged with rented homes in downtown Marfa, they generally ate their meals and congregated at the El Paisano.

Today the hotel has been converted into condominiums, but the historic building, built in the 1920s, remains intact.

PALM SPRINGS, CALIFORNIA

Upon his arrival in Los Angeles in March 1954 for the preproduction of *East of Eden*, James Dean was instructed by Elia Kazan to get some color in his face. Accordingly Dean rented a car and drove to Palm Springs with the sole mission of obtaining a tan.

The following year, on March 26, 1955, Dean returned to the desert to enter the Palm Springs Road Races. He won the preliminary race and placed second in the finals.

BETSY PALMER

> We had sort of an *intimate* relationship. We had a physical relationship. We dated very regularly. Then he went to California. I always had the sensation that he wouldn't live past 30—that he was going to burn himself out.

Betsy Palmer co-starred with James Dean in two 1953 television dramas, "Sentence of Death," an episode of the series "Studio One Summer Theatre," and "Death Is My Neighbor," an episode of the series "Danger." They were also, for a period, friends and lovers. Palmer recently recalled the attraction:

"We both came from the same school, Stanislavsky. We were both from Indiana. We were two Hoosiers. We dated. He would come by my apartment. I used to live on the West Side in the 60s, on 66th or 67th Street. It was a one-room apartment. I remember that Jimmy didn't have an apartment of his own at that time. We would eat mostly in, because we didn't have a lot of money then. I used to cook for him.

"I remember Jimmy got an apartment on the top floor of some brownstone. I remember the half window. My mother gave me a quilt, and I gave it to Jimmy. I also gave him sheets and bedding.

"We used to share music together and would exchange records. We both liked classical music. I had one of his records for years. I just gave it up a couple of years ago. I think it was called *The Spider Ceased*. We used to talk about books and movies. We walked the streets of New York together. We went to movies. . . .

"We rehearsed our play way up in Grand Central Station. I was a girl who rented a room, a girl who posed for those detective magazine covers. And Jimmy was the boy who worked and did the cleaning. But I don't remember if he killed me or what. My career was just starting to take off then. . . ."

Betsy Palmer was born Patricia Brumek in 1929. She has made numerous guest appearances on episodic television shows. She was also a regular on the quiz shows "Masquerade Party" (1956–1957), "What's It For?" (1957–1958), and "I've Got a Secret" (1957–1967) and on the short-lived drama series "Number 96" (1980–1981).

Palmer's film appearances include *The Long Gray Line* (1955), *Queen Bee* (1955), *The Tin Star* (1957), *The Last Angry Man* (1959), and *It Happened to Jane* (1959).

In 1989–1990 she was frequently seen on the best and most durable of the nighttime soaps, "Knots Landing." She portrayed Valene's slightly ditzy but dependable aunt, nicely filling a void in the show created when Julie Harris, who portrayed Valene's mother, departed in 1987.

Betsy Palmer, 1990.

Over the years Betsy Palmer has been extremely reticent about her relationship with James Dean and only now has chosen to publicly acknowledge it.

"He could become very angry over nothing," she said recently. "There was a great amount of moodiness. He was an unhappy person, I found. I think he always felt sad about not being raised by his parents. He carried that with him. He brooded about that. I enjoyed being with him, though, because I'm an introspective person too. We were lovers, but in a different way. It wasn't passionate; it was different. We were sympathetic towards one another."

EDITH PALMER
The person responsible for the body makeup (i.e., Dean as Jett Rink drenched in oil) on *Giant*.

PARAMOUNT PICTURES
James Dean had a bit part in the 1952 Paramount film *Sailor Beware*, another in a series of Dean Martin/Jerry Lewis comic vehicles. Three years later Paramount was negotiating with Warner Brothers to obtain James Dean to star in *Fear Strikes Out*.

THE PARAMOUNT THEATER
Los Angeles movie theater where *Rebel Without a Cause* was previewed on October 11, 1955. During the screening the audience broke into applause.

THE PARAMOUNT THEATER
Marion, Indiana, theater where *The James Dean Story* had its world premiere on August 13, 1957.

PARIS, FRANCE

James Dean planned to go to Paris in the spring of 1956 with Sanford and Beulah Roth. According to Beulah, "We had planned this trip to Europe. I had made this big map of Paris that I got at the Paris Metro, and we put it on the floor and traced our steps. We were going to introduce Jimmy to Picasso. We had already told Picasso this. I had written to Picasso's secretary saying that we were coming and we were gonna bring James Dean. We were gonna introduce him to Cocteau and all the great people that we had told him about. And he would've seen Paris. Jimmy once said to us, 'Can you walk up to the top of the Eiffel Tower?' And I said, 'I guess you can. But who would do it?' "

The Roths made their trip to Paris in the spring of 1956—without the company of James Dean.

THE PARIS THEATER

New York movie theater located across from the Plaza Hotel at 4 West 58th Street where Jimmy Dean used to hang out and raid popcorn during the fall of 1952, when visiting his girlfriend, Dizzy Sheridan. Sheridan was a Paris Theater usherette.

PARK CEMETERY

Fairmount, Indiana, cemetery where James Dean is buried. In 1983 the original pink granite gravestone that marked Dean's burial site was stolen

from the cemetery. The Dean bust that stood at the cemetery's entrance had been stolen years earlier. Today, every September, thousands of Dean fans still make the pilgrimage to Park Cemetery to visit the grave site. Some leave flowers and letters. Some leave cigarettes. Some chip away at the gravestone, which was eventually retrieved.

CAROLYN PARKS

In April 1949, Carolyn Parks was a Santa Rosa, California, high school junior. She was also the first-place winner in the National Forensic League's annual speech tournament held in Longmont, Colorado. Parks triumphed over Fairmount High School senior James Dean, who placed sixth.

MICHAEL PARKS

Of all the would-be Deans, Michael Parks is the actor who most blatantly *attempted* to emulate him. Parks had the brooding looks and posture but not the depth. He was a cardboard version of James Dean. In his defense, Parks wrote a 1965 "Letter to the Editor" of *Time* magazine that read:

> Sir: I appreciate the kind things that you said about me in your review of *Bus Riley's Back in Town* [April 23]. It is difficult for an actor today to bring in any kind of contemporary feeling and not be compared with either Marlon Brando or James Dean. I would like to thank you for pointing out that I may have some entity of my own.

The films of Michael Parks include *Wild Seed* (1964), *Bus Riley's Back in Town* (in which he was out-smoldered by Ann-Margret, 1965), *The Bible* (Italy, 1966), *The Happening* (1967), *The Private Files of J. Edgar Hoover* (1978), *Savannah Smiles* (1982), *Club Life* (1987), *The Return of Josey Wales* (1987), and *Arizona Heat* (1988). He also starred in the television series "Then Came Bronson" (1969–1970).

LOUELLA PARSONS

What I remember most about him was the little boy quality, shining forth at you from behind those thick glasses of his, tearing at your heart. He had that extreme and touching idealism of youth which made you wish that he would never have to be disillusioned. Now he won't be. He leaves behind his two films in which he proved that this distinctive magical performance in *East of Eden* was not merely a flash. In both *Rebel Without a Cause* and *Giants* [sic] I understand he far surpasses his first movie performance which made him an overnight star. In fact, it isn't hard to find many people in Hollywood who feel, given the years, Jimmy would have surpassed Marlon Brando, with whom he was so often compared.

Louella Parsons, *Chicago's American*, October 3, 1955

Famed Hollywood columnist Louella Parsons was one of the first to recognize the potential in James Dean. In a March 1955 article for *Modern Screen* magazine Parsons prophesied, "I nominate for Stardom: James Dean." Similarly, she proclaimed in a March 1955 issue of *Cosmopolitan*, "James Dean: New Face with Future."

Parsons was born Louella Oettinger on August 6, 1881, in Freeport, Illinois. Along with her rival, Hedda Hopper, Parsons became the most powerful movie columnist/observer in the history of the industry. When she died in 1972, a Hollywood era died along with her.

PARSONS THEATER

See the Jaguar had its out-of-town pre-Broadway tryout at the Parsons Theater in New Haven, Connecticut, from November 13 to November 15, 1952.

PASO ROBLES, CALIFORNIA

California city approximately 20 miles east of the site where James Dean was fatally injured on September 30, 1955.

PASO ROBLES WAR MEMORIAL HOSPITAL

Hospital about 28 miles from the crash site, where James Dean was rushed via ambulance on September 30, 1955. The ambulance arrived at the hospital at approximately 6:20 P.M. At that time Dean was pronounced dead on arrival.

ROBERT PASTENE

Actor who portrayed the title character in "Abraham Lincoln," a 1952 episode of the CBS television program "Studio One" in which James Dean had a brief part.

The Brooklyn-born Pastene also starred on television opposite Helen Hayes in "The Barretts of Wimpole Street" and in the Warner Brothers feature film *Jamboree* (1957).

PATRIOT BANKS

Patriot Banks of Boston used the Dean image in one of its advertising campaigns.

MARK PATTON

Actor who portrayed Joe, the Dean-inspired character in *Come Back to the Five and Dime, Jimmy Dean, Jimmy Dean*, a 1982 Broadway play and subsequent film.

Three years later, Patton had a leading role in *Nightmare on Elm Street Part Two: Freddy's Revenge*.

JOSEPH PAYNE

Fairmount (Indiana) artist who tutored Jimmy Dean.

JOAN PEACOCK

See JOAN WINSLOW.

PEBBLE BEACH ROAD RACE

James Dean had planned to enter his Porsche Speedster in the 1955 Pebble Beach Road Race, but mechanical complications emerged, and the Porsche was forced to spend the weekend of the race in the repair shop.

SEAN PENN

In the 1980s Sean Penn was lumped into an ever-increasing list of actors hyped as "the next James Dean." Unlike most of his cohorts, however, Penn has more than a pout and a pair of blue jeans to sustain his career. He has focus and concentration and intensity and talent—Dean trademarks. What he doesn't have, what he doesn't come close to having, is Dean's screen presence and vulnerability. Dean had a need to be loved, and he projected that onto the screen. Penn doesn't project warmth but exudes arrogance and bravado, and is inherently difficult to empathize with, regardless of the role he is playing.

"I like to drink and I like to brawl."
Sean Penn, *USA Today*, July 3, 1987

"When I saw him coming, I shut the windows and locked the doors."
Paul Adao, a photographer for the *New York Post*
whose car was mauled by Penn's kicking foot,
Los Angeles Times, July 5, 1988

Despite obvious talent, Penn's film career is in dire need of a hit. He has received a deluge of press coverage regarding his 1987 jail term and his volatile marriage to and divorce from metamorphic camera magnet Madonna, but no one's really discussing his films—or going to see them.

Sean Penn, born in 1960, is the son of director Leo Penn and actress

Eileen Ryan. Like James Dean, Penn left Los Angeles to be discovered in a Broadway play (*Heartland*) and was sent back to Hollywood to make movies. He made his film debut in *Taps* (which featured other young actors Timothy Hutton and Tom Cruise, 1981). Subsequent pictures have included *Fast Times at Ridgemont High* (1982), *Bad Boys* (which launched the comparisons with Dean, 1983), *Crackers* (1984), *Racing with the Moon* (1984), *The Falcon and the Snowman* (1985), *At Close Range* (which cost $7 million and made only $1 million, 1986), *Shanghai Surprise* (with Madonna, cost $11 million, made $1 million, 1986), *Colors* (a modest hit, cost $10 million, made $20 million, 1988), *Judgment in Berlin* (cost $6 million, made $250,000, 1988), *We're No Angels* (even with Robet De Niro the film flopped, 1989), and *State of Grace* (another flop, 1990).

PEOPLE MAGAZINE

People, with its circulation of nearly 3.5 million copies a week, has published only a few articles about James Dean. They include:

☆ October 13, 1980   "Dead 25 Years, James Dean Is Given Touching Hometown Tribute by Nostalgic Fans"
☆ March 18, 1985   "Rebel Without a Nose"
☆ August 7, 1989   "Obsessed by James Dean, Japan's Seita Ohnishi Makes a Monument to Fallen Rebel His Cause"

PEPSI-COLA

Three decades before Michael Jackson, Michael J. Fox, and Madonna did it, James Dean did it . . .

James Dean's first professional acting job was in a television commercial for Pepsi-Cola that was shot at Griffith Park in Los Angeles on December 13, 1950. The commercial took all day to shoot, and Jimmy, then 19, was paid $10 and provided with a boxed lunch. Also in the cast were Nick Adams and Beverly Long. According to Long, "We were all supposed to be drinking Pepsi-Cola, going round and round on the merry-go-round, having a wonderful time. And then they had a jukebox set up, and we were dancing and being silly. . . ." The latter scene, shamelessly directed at adolescent insecurities, played as follows:

ANNOUNCER: Say, y'wanna have more fun? Then come on along and let's join the Pepsi Crowd!
GROUP: (including Dean, singing) Pepsi-Cola hits the spot. A big, big bottle and it's got, bounce, bounce, bounce, bounce, go get Pepsi for the Pepsi bounce!
ANNOUNCER: Popularity, that's what Pepsi's got most of. Pepsi gives more fun, more bounce to the ounce. And more for your money, too. Wherever the crowd gathers, you're sure to find Pepsi. So why take less than Pepsi's best? Buy Pepsi by the carton!

ENRICO PEREGO

James Dean's number one fan in Italy. Enrico Perego is an active (albeit long-distance) member of the We Remember Dean International fan club based in Fullerton, California.

ANTHONY PERKINS

Yet another solemn-faced actor who was heralded as "the next Dean." As one fan publication put it in 1956:

> He gives off the same air of troubled loneliness that goads bobbysoxers to premature rampages of maternalism. He is of the same school of acting [as Dean]; his shy retiring manner and his habit of lowering his head and scuffing his feet as he speaks also calls Jimmy Dean to mind.

Anthony Perkins, born in 1932, has had a long and fairly successful career, but he will forever be typed as Alfred Hitchcock's knife-wielding mother-son act in *Psycho* (1960). Perkins's other films include *Friendly Persuasion* (Best Supporting Actor Oscar nomination, 1956), *Fear Strikes Out* (in a role intended for Dean, 1957), *Tall Story* (Jane Fonda's film debut, 1960), *Catch 22* (1970), *Play It As It Lays* (1972), *Murder on the Orient Express* (England, 1974), *Psycho II* (1983), *Crimes of Passion* (which contained a brilliant, unheralded performance by Kathleen Turner, 1985), and *Psycho III* (which he also directed, 1986).

RON PERKINS

The Culver City, California, police sergeant who consulted on the making of *Rebel Without a Cause*.

VOLTAIRE PERKINS

Character actor who appeared in "The Unlighted Road," a 1955 episode of the CBS television series "Schlitz Playhouse of Stars" that starred James Dean.

Perkins also appeared in the film *The Far Horizons* (1955).

GIGI PERREAU

Recorded the song "We'll Never Forget You," which was included on the Coral Records tribute album *The James Dean Story*.

Perreau, born Ghislaine Perreau-Saussine in 1941, was a child actress in the 1940s. Her films include *Madame Curie* (1943), *My Foolish Heart* (1949), and *Has Anybody Seen My Gal?* (in which Dean had a bit part, 1952).

PERU, INDIANA

In April 1949 James Dean competed in the statewide National Forensic League speech tournament held at Peru High School in Peru, Indiana. Representing Fairmount High School, Jimmy placed first.

PETS

☆ Like the hog-loving Suzanne Sugarbaker of the hit television comedy "Designing Women," James Dean had a pet pig. He kept the pig, which he bottle-fed, on the Winslow family farm in Fairmount, Indiana.

☆ a dog named Tuck, also on the Winslow farm

☆ a dachshund he named Strudel, circa March 1955, in Hollywood

☆ Jimmy was particularly fond of Louis XIV, a cat owned by Sandy and Beulah Roth. Noticing this, Elizabeth Taylor presented Jimmy with a Siamese kitten in September 1955. Jimmy named the kitten Marcus, after his cousin and uncle back in Fairmount. He joked with the Roths, "I've always hated to get up early. Now I'm up at 7:00 just to give Marcus breakfast." A few days before his death, however, Jimmy gave Marcus to a girlfriend, Jeanette Mille, later sparking rumors that his death was a planned suicide. In all likelihood he had merely given Mille the cat for safekeeping until his return from an extended trip. After Salinas he had planned to go to San Francisco and then to New York.

JOHN PEYSER
Director of "Death Is My Neighbor," a 1953 episode of the CBS television program "Danger" that co-starred James Dean.

FATHER PATRICK PEYTON
Producer of "Family Theatre," aka "Father Peyton's Family Theatre," a series of Los Angeles television specials. James Dean made his official television acting debut in the "Family Theatre" production of "Hill Number One" in 1951.

PHILADELPHIA, PENNSYLVANIA
On January 9, 1954, the cast and crew of *The Immoralist* traveled from New York to Philadelphia for a week of out-of-town tryouts at the Forrest Theatre (address: 1114 Walnut Street). While in Philadelphia James Dean stayed at the St. James Hotel (address: Walnut and 13th streets) and frequently ate at the Hickory House.

"PHILCO TV PLAYHOUSE"
Television drama series that aired on Sunday nights on NBC from October 1948 to October 1955. James Dean appeared in the "Run Like a Thief" episode, which aired on September 5, 1954.

MARGARET PHILLIPS
Actress who co-starred in "The Evil Within," a 1953 episode of the ABC television program "Tales of Tomorrow" in which James Dean also co-starred.

Phillips (1923–1984), from south Wales, had an extensive stage career. Her film credits include *A Life of Her Own* (1950) and *The Nun's Story* (1959).

THE PHOTOGRAPHERS
In front of a camera, he was a genius.   Sid Avery

The following is a selective list of James Dean's photographers.

Joseph Abeles	Mac Julian	Roy Schatt
Jack Allen	Gene Kornmann	Bert Six
Sid Avery	Bert Longworth	Phil Stern
Curtis Bernard	Edward Martin	Dennis Stock
Pat Clark	Floyd McCarty	Talbot
Nat Dallinger	Gjon Mili	Weegee
Frank Donato	Wilson Millar	Bob Willoughby
Earl Forbes	Dick Miller	Jack Woods
Jean Howard	Sanford Roth	Frank Worth

The Great Dean Photographs

☆ The first head shots—Wilson Millar
☆ The "torn sweater" series—Roy Schatt
☆ *Tintype with sow*—Dennis Stock
☆ *Times Square*—Dennis Stock
☆ Framed eyeglasses—Phil Stern
☆ The *Rebel Without a Cause* blue jeans series—Warner Brothers still photographer
☆ Crucifixion—Floyd McCarty
☆ Jett Rink and Reata—Floyd McCarty
☆ Rebel cowboy—Sid Avery
☆ Dean Texas—Sanford Roth

PHOTOGRAPHY

In May 1955 James Dean purchased a $600 Bolex 16mm motion picture camera with three lenses. His total cash outlay, including other photographic equipment, was $2,000. Dean purchased the camera because he

wanted to shoot his own short films before he progressed to directing big-budget motion pictures.

In addition, Dean was an avid and accomplished student of still photography who frequently subjected his friends and associates to the lens of his camera. He learned photography from his friend Roy Schatt and picked up additional instruction from the many other photographers with whom he worked. He had a particular penchant for shooting stills of the casts and crews on each of his films. During the shooting of *Rebel Without a Cause* Dean rode atop a 50-foot camera crane and snapped a series of panoramic shots of the *Rebel* set. He had planned to enter the photos in a photography magazine's annual contest for amateurs.

PHOTOPLAY MAGAZINE

In 1955 the editors of *Photoplay* fan magazine presented James Dean with a posthumous Gold Medal Special Achievement award for, in the words of *Photoplay*:

> His outstanding dramatic performances in *East of Eden* and *Rebel Without a Cause*. His brilliant and tragically brief career can serve as his own monument. There it stands, to show other young actors how much can be accomplished in a short time if genuine ability is combined with intensity of purpose and a sincere feeling of dedication.

In January 1957 *Photoplay*, after having published a series of Dean articles, printed a letter from one of its readers in St. Louis, Missouri. It read:

> I too think Jimmy Dean was a wonderful actor and I know many other people agree with me. But I think it is utterly ridiculous to keep on writing stories about him and selling metal charms of him. For heaven's sake, let the poor boy rest in peace. . . . After all, he has been dead over a year now, and nothing is going to bring him back.

Immediately following the letter the editors of *Photoplay* responded with a commentary of their own:

> The above letter reflects the thinking of thousands of Jimmy Dean's fans and of your editors. We heartily agree that the many promising young stars coming along should be given this space and attention. And we also feel that, were Jimmy alive to cast his vote, he would feel the same way. Therefore, *Photoplay* says its final farewell to Jimmy Dean with the publication of this letter.

Later that year, in its October issue, *Photoplay* published not one but two articles related to James Dean: a review of *The James Dean Story* by Natalie Wood and "In Memory of Jimmy" by Dizzy Sheridan.

In its time *Photoplay* was the best of the movie magazines. In addition to those already mentioned, *Photoplay* has published numerous articles about James Dean, including:

☆ July 1955   "Demon Dean" by Sidney Skolsky
☆ November 1955   "You Haven't Heard the Half About Jimmy" by Natalie Wood

☆ January 1956   "To James Dean"
☆ March 1956   "James Dean, the Boy I Loved" by Emma Dean
☆ September 1956   "There Was a Boy" by Bill Bast (excerpt from Bast's book, *James Dean*)
☆ October 1956   Continuation of "There Was a Boy"
☆ November 1956   Continuation of "There Was a Boy"
☆ November 1956   "Why the Rebel Craze Is Here to Stay"
☆ November 1956   "Dean Suicide Rumors!"
☆ January 1957   "The Rebel"
☆ November 1958   "Can Dean Stockwell Shake Off the Jimmy Dean Jinx?"
☆ June 1972   "The Legend of James Dean"

PICTUREGOER MAGAZINE

British fan magazine *Picturegoer* named James Dean the Best Actor of 1955 for his performance in *East of Eden*. *Picturegoer* also published several articles about Dean, including "The James Dean I Knew" by *Giant* cinematographer William C. Mellor in its December 29, 1956, issue.

ARTHUR PIERSON

Director of "Hill Number One," a 1951 Easter presentation of "Family Theatre" in which James Dean made his official television debut.

PHILLIP PINE

Phillip Pine portrayed Hilltop in the 1952 Broadway production of *See the Jaguar*. Later he replaced James Dean in the role of Bachir in *The Immoralist*.

Just prior to appearing in *The Immoralist*, Pine, a California native, appeared on Broadway in *One Bright Day*. His films include *The Set-Up* (1949), *My Foolish Heart* (1949), *Battleground* (1949), *The Red Light* (1949), *The Flame and the Arrow* (1950), *Dead Heat on a Merry-Go-Round* (1966), and *Hook, Line and Sinker* (1968). On television Pine made numerous guest appearances on shows like "Bonanza," "The Untouchables," "Police Story," and "Mannix." He was also a regular on the police drama "The Blue Knight" (1975–1976). In addition, Pine was the executive producer of the Fred Astaire film *The Amazing Dobermans* (1976).

TOM PITTMAN

Young actor who was killed in a car crash in November 1958. Newspapers reported at the time that Pittman had died "like Dean."

EDWARD PLATT

Actor who portrayed Ray Framek, the sympathetic juvenile officer whom Jim Stark tries to slug and then befriends in *Rebel Without a Cause*.

Years later Platt attained a degree of fame for his deadpan portrayal of "Chief" to Don Adams's "Get Smart" (1965–1970). Platt (1916–1974) also appeared in many films including *The Shrike* (1955), *North by Northwest* (1959), *Pollyanna* (1960), and *A Ticklish Affair* (1963).

MARION PLAYAN
Race car driver who won the May 1, 1955, race at Bakersfield, California, in
which James Dean placed third.

"PLAYHOUSE OF THE STARS"
See "SCHLITZ PLAYHOUSE OF STARS."

THE PLAYS
The Plays That Dean Appeared in on Broadway
See the Jaguar (1952)
The Immoralist (1954)

The Plays That Dean Wanted to Appear in but Didn't
Blood Wedding
Hamlet

The Plays That Dean Appeared in off Broadway
The Metamorphosis (1952)
The Scarecrow (1953)
Women of Trachis (1954)

The Plays That Dean Appeared in at the Actors Studio
Aria da Capo
End as a Man
The Sea Gull

The Play That Dean Appeared in at UCLA
Macbeth

The Play That Dean Appeared in at Santa Monica City College
She Was Only a Farmer's Daughter

The Play That Dean Appeared in in Summer Stock
The Romance of Scarlet Gulch

The Play That Dean Appeared in at Church
To Them That Sleep in Darkness

The Plays That Dean Appeared in at Fairmount High School
An Apple from Coles County
Goon with the Wind
The Monkey's Paw
Mooncalf Mugford
Our Hearts Were Young and Gay
You Can't Take It with You

The Plays About or Inspired by Dean
Dean (Great Britain, 1977)

Come Back to the Five and Dime, Jimmy Dean, Jimmy Dean (Broadway, 1982)
James Dean: A Dress Rehearsal (Denver, 1984)
Musical Selections from Rebel: The James Dean Musical (off Broadway, 1989)

POETRY

In addition to being an amateur musician, amateur painter and caricaturist, and amateur photographer, James Dean was an amateur poet and a student of poetry. His favorite poets? Federico García Lorca and James Whitcomb Riley.

S. LEE POGOSTIN

Telewriter of "Something for an Empty Briefcase," a 1953 episode of the NBC television series "Campbell Soundstage" in which James Dean co-starred.

Pogostin, born in 1926, also scripted various episodic television dramas including "People Kill Sometimes," the 1959 premiere telecast of the NBC show "Sunday Showcase," and the feature film *Synanon* (1965). In addition, he directed the films *Hard Contract* (1969) and *Golden Needles* (shared credit, 1974).

POLITICS

James Dean was basically apolitical. Still, despite his conservative upbringing, his leanings were liberal. Director Nicholas Ray, who knew him well, once stated that, had he lived, Dean would have been one of the demonstrators at the 1968 Democratic Convention in Chicago. He also claimed that the Chicago Seven had "all seen *Rebel Without a Cause* at least fifteen or twenty times."

THE PORSCHE AND JAMES DEAN: BUILT FOR SPEED

He called his car "The Little Bastard," having named it after himself. They were both small, slouched to the ground, and lightweight but with deceptive and explosive power. They were both obnoxious and audacious and utterly thrilling to watch. They were both built for adventure. They were both built for speed.

James Dean purchased his first Porsche, a white 356 1,500cc Super Speedster convertible, in March 1955. *East of Eden* was just being released, and its newfound star was in need of a new vehicle. The car was fast—fast enough to place in several major racing events but not fast ⁀nough to win. As early as May, speed demon Dean was looking for something stronger, something faster. On May 3 he attended the opening of Precision Motors Company, a Beverly Hills auto dealer specializing in the fast and the foreign. He mingled with the other auto aficionados, always studying, always absorbing, but walked away without a fix.

Then, on September 19, 1955, he ran into Porsche mechanic Rolf Wütherich walking down Hollywood Boulevard. Wütherich told Dean about the arrival of a new Porsche. At the time Dean was completing his work on the slow and lumbering *Giant* and again was in need of a new vehicle and a quick fix of speed. Two days and one test drive later James Dean walked into

Jimmy washing his Porsche Speedster.

The new Porsche Spyder.

Taking the Spyder out for a spin.

The Porsche Spyder, crumpled at the side of the road.

Competition Motors, not far from Hollywood and Vine, signed over his white Speedster (and, fatefully, his life) and a check in the amount of $3,700, and walked out with a sleek silver Porsche 550 Spyder. It had been a case of that old cliché about love at first sight.

He was enthralled. He had never been so proud of any*thing* in his life. He paraded it down the streets and zipped it through the Hollywood hills and parked it outside the homes of friends. As Ursula Andress recalled, "He was so thrilled with it. He wanted everybody to admire it." If they didn't notice or feigned disinterest, it only made him more determined to command their attention. His first order of business was to give the Porsche an identity. Accordingly he called on George Barris, customizer for the stars, and commissioned him to paint on its hood the racing number 130 and on its tail the flamboyant moniker "Little Bastard." The Porsche, after all, was a symbol not only of his newfound stardom but also of his newfound freedom and defiance.

In death he got their attention. The crippled remains of the once beautiful Porsche were carted off to pasture in nearby San Luis Obispo. The wreckage was later purchased by George Barris, who subsequently parceled out, for profit, its undamaged parts. The engine was purchased by racing enthusiast Dr. William Eschrich, who transplanted it into his own car. A year later, driving the car powered by Dean's engine, Eschrich was involved in a car crash that killed his friend, Dr. Troy McHenry. McHenry had been driving a car that was also equipped with parts from Dean's Porsche.

The rest of the wreckage, including the chassis, was kept by Barris. When the Porsche arrived from Los Angeles, it slipped from a tow truck and reportedly broke both legs of a bystander. Barris then donated the wreckage to the Greater Los Angeles Safety Council, which in turn sent the wreckage on a national tour to discourage young Dean followers from imitating his example. Fans paid 50¢ to sit behind its wheel.

The macabre exhibit endured a four-year run until the wreckage was stolen in 1960. Predictably the curious case of the Dean Porsche has prompted speculation on its being the Black Widow Spyder. As recently as 1989 the television program "A Current Affair" produced a segment about the curse of Dean and his Porsche. According to the show the Spyder "became a sinister tragedy of death for him and [for the] people that were associated with him."

Today the engine of Dean's Porsche is still in existence, as are various other of its parts. However, its chassis has not been seen in 30 years. Like its owner, its body is gone but its spirit remains.

Details on Dean's Porsche:

Chassis number: 550-0055   Engine number: 90059
License plate number: 2Z77767   Gearbox number: 10046

One final ironic note: James Dean's certificate of ownership was mailed to his house in Sherman Oaks in October 1955, weeks after his death.

THE PORSCHE: DRIVING WITH DEAN

The interior was cramped and smelled of new leather. . . . Jimmy threw the shift into first gear and with the gearbox protesting violently we screeched into the Hollywood Boulevard traffic. During the ten minutes it took us to get to Beverly Hills, I sobered up rapidly. He certainly did drive fast, even recklessly, but with the summer wind blowing through the open windows and the radio blaring, it was exhilarating.

Past Imperfect by Joan Collins

He took me to the market one day—Arrow Market on Santa Monica Boulevard. He took me there and I said, "Jimmy, okay thank you, but I'll walk home." *I couldn't be in that car!*

Beulah Roth

I felt like I was getting into a tomb. I had never ridden in a Porsche before. And when you get in and sit down, you sit *down*. And you feel like you're on the ground. I had the feeling like I was sitting in a coffin. It was scary. It was very scary. And Jimmy drove way too fast. He was a real show-off.

Beverly Long

He had the gleaming new Porsche delivered to the studio. I had the first ride. He drove back to my dressing room on the lot, over the "Slow" bumps on the studio streets. We bounced like a yo-yo, Jimmy gunning the motor like he was riding a Texas bull!

The Quality of Mercy by Mercedes McCambridge

BUZZ: You know, I like you.
 JIM: Why do we do this, then?
BUZZ: You've got to do something, now, don't you?

[From the chickie-run scene in *Rebel Without a Cause*, written by Stewart Stern]

PORTLAND PACIFIC COAST LEAGUE

During the shooting of *Giant* former Fairmount (Indiana) High School shortstop James Dean hosted six members of the Portland Pacific Coast League baseball team by showing them around the Warner Brothers lot.

POSTERS

Starting in the 1980s and up until the present, James Dean has become one of the biggest-selling poster boys on the market. His face can be found in stores everywhere, boyish and brooding and positioned right beside the bulging bodies of the men from Chippendales. The following is a sample list of the companies that are marketing Dean posters:

Advanced Graphics, 982 Howe Rd., Martinez, CA 94553
Art One Images, 990 Monterey Rd., Monterey Park, CA 91754
Arti Grafiche Ricordi, Via Cortina d'Ampezzo, 10, Milan, Italy 20139
The Gem Group, PO Box 8492, Kentwood, MI 49508

Gottried Helnwein Co., Neubaugasse 2, 070 Vienna, Austria
Graphics International (neon posters), 19755 Bahama St., Northridge, CA 91324
Hollywood Headlines, 535 Younge St., Toronto, ON M4Y 1Y5, Canada
Ideal Decor, Seefeld Str. 88, 8008 Zurich, Switzerland
Mirage Edition, Inc., 1658 10th St., Santa Monica, CA 90404
Statics, Unit 3, 49 Gorst Rd., London NW10 6LS, England

JOAN POTTER
Actress who appeared in "Keep Our Honor Bright," a 1953 episode of the NBC television program "Kraft Television Theatre" that co-starred James Dean.

JOHN POTTER
John Potter was one of the principals at Fairmount (Indiana) High School when Jim Dean was a student there.

FRANK PREHODA
One of the makeup artists on *Giant*.

THE PREMIERES
James Dean never attended the premiere screening of any of his films. Actually he had the opportunity to attend only one of them, *East of Eden*.

East of Eden
The premiere of *East of Eden* was held at the Astor Theatre in New York City on March 9, 1955, and served as a $50-per-seat benefit for the Actors Studio. Although Dean didn't attend, many others did. *The Hollywood Reporter* raved the following day:

FESTIVE 'EDEN' PREEM NETS $34,000 FOR ACTORS STUDIO
Brilliant Opening Dazzles Broadway

New York—The most brilliant world premiere in recent Broadway history, with the biggest turnout of celebrities and the most extensive press, radio and TV coverage, was staged by Warners last night at the Astor Theatre for Elia Kazan's *East of Eden*, in a $50 per seat performance that brought in an estimated minimum of $34,000 for the Actors Studio.

The formal opening included a private after-theatre supper and all-star entertainment at the Sheraton Astor Roof for the $50 stub holders, with Abe Burrows, Marilyn Monroe, Jule Styne and others doing their stuff for the guests.

Serving as "ushers" for the first nighters was a glamorous array including Marlene Dietrich, Margaret Truman, Celeste Holm, Marilyn Monroe, Mrs. Alfred Gwynne Vanderbilt, Mrs. William Rhinelander Stewart, Terry Moore, Eva Marie Saint, Arlene Francis, Marjorie Steele, Fleur Cowles, Ethel Linder Reiner, Anita Loos, Beatrice Straight, Maggi McNellis and Meg Mundy, all volunteering their services for the benefit performance.

Warners productions chief Jack L. Warner planed in from the

coast for the premiere. Producer-director Elia Kazan was also on hand, along with author John Steinbeck; Raymond Massey, who co-stars in the film with Julie Harris and James Dean; and Richard Davalos and Jo Van Fleet, featured in the cast.

TV, newsreel and radio coverage started as the stream of notables crossed the red-carpeted sidewalks between crowds of onlookers and were greeted under the marquee by Martin Block in a special live telecast over WPIX. Inside the lobby, Robert Frank, French reporter and Voice of America commentator, did a French-dialogue recording for later rebroadcast to Paris. Simultaneously, WRCA cameras both inside and outside the theatre filmed the event for showing on this morning's Dave Garroway program. On-the-spot interviews also were taped for today's luncheon at Sardi's radio show.

Steve Allen's "Tonight" program on WRCA-TV was telecast direct from the Astor Roof, while Tex and Jinx McCrary aired their regular WRCA radio show from the unique party.

The event received a tremendous advance campaign and the street-crowd turnout was one of the biggest that ever jammed around the front of a Times Square theatre.

East of Eden, which has aroused more advance interest than any picture in a long time, marks the screen debut of some brilliant newcomers headed by James Dean, Jo Van Fleet and Richard Davalos. Miss Van Fleet, Dean, Miss Harris and several other members of the film cast are members of the Actors Studio.

Interestingly, most of the press reports made little or nothing of Dean's no-show. Instead the press bemoaned that, at the postscreening party, Marilyn Monroe refused to sing "Diamonds Are a Girl's Best Friend," as she had purportedly promised to do.

Rebel Without a Cause
Probably because it was released so soon after the death of its star (October 26, 1955), the premiere of *Rebel Without a Cause* was low-key and unballyhooed.

Giant
What Warner Brothers lost in not hyping the premiere of *Rebel* it made up for a year later (October 10, 1956) with the lavish kickoff for *Giant*. It was labeled the premiere of the decade (just as *Eden* had been called the year before and *A Star Is Born* the year before that). Gable was there. So was Brando. Also on hand were Rock Hudson, Natalie Wood, Jayne Mansfield, and others.

Other Films
One of the premieres that James Dean *did* attend was the opening of *A Star Is Born*, which heralded Judy Garland's bravura comeback performance. The premiere was held on September 29, 1954, at the Pantages Theater in Hollywood. Also in attendance were Elizabeth Taylor, Joan Crawford, Clark Gable, Lucille Ball and Desi Arnaz, Lauren Bacall, Sophie Tucker, Kim

Novak, Shelley Winters, Hedda Hopper and Louella Parsons, Jack Warner, Debbie Reynolds, Tony Curtis and Janet Leigh, Liberace, et al. Dean, still virtually unknown (*Eden* hadn't been released yet), was ignored by the paparazzi.

He also attended the September 22, 1954, premiere of *Sabrina*, starring Audrey Hepburn, William Holden, and Humphrey Bogart, at the Paramount Theater in Hollywood. Dean's date, Terry Moore, clung to his arm for the cameras. Dean, meanwhile, obviously uncomfortable in a tuxedo, merely glowered.

Attending the premiere of *Sabrina* with Terry Moore.

ELVIS PRESLEY

Contrary to previous reports, and tempting though it may be to imagine, James Dean was not an obsessive Elvis Presley fan, nor was he even aware of the impact Presley was about to make. Rumor has it that Dean entertained Warners Brothers studio personnel with his pelvis-thrust impersonation of Presley performing "Hound Dog." However, the fact is that, although Elvis made an appearance on the "Louisiana Hayride" television show on March 5, 1955, the program was a regional one, shown only in the South. Presley did not make his national television debut until four months after Dean's death, on "Stage Show" (January 28, 1956). He made even more impact on "The Steve Allen Show" (July 1, 1956) and on "The Ed Sullivan Show" (September 9, 1956). As for "Hound Dog," Presley performed it on a June 5, 1956, episode of "The Milton Berle Show" and did not record it until July 2, 1956. If anything, Jimmy was aware of the song not through Presley but through its earlier versions recorded by Big Mama Thornton (1953) and Freddie Bell and the Bellboys (1955). As for Presley's first number one song, "Heartbreak Hotel," it wasn't even recorded until January 1956.

Elvis Presley, on the other hand, most certainly was aware of James Dean. He idolized him.

> "When Elvis Presley first came to Hollywood to make a movie, he came to see me. He was twenty-one and a millionaire. He had seen James Dean in *Rebel Without a Cause* and he wanted to know more about Jimmy . . . ."
> Dennis Hopper, *Dennis Hopper: A Madness to His Method,*
> by Elena Rodriguez

> When Elvis came to town, he looked up Nick, because he knew that he was Jimmy's friend.
>
> Bill Dakota

Dennis Hopper and Nick Adams were not the only Dean friends whom Elvis sought out. He also romanced Natalie Wood and Ursula Andress, attracted by their links to Dean. He also took Adams out on tour with him and entertained the idea of portraying Dean in a proposed motion picture biography. Presley's favorite film was *Rebel Without a Cause.* He memorized every line of dialogue from its script and occasionally entertained friends with his recitation of Jim Stark. Somehow, however, the idea of Presley as Dean—guitar in one hand, toy monkey in the other—doesn't quite gel.

When Dean died, his popularity soared, and posthumously he competed with Presley for the covers of fan magazines. One enterprising publisher even plastered both of their photos on the cover of a one-shot magazine entitled *Elvis and Jimmy.*

It was, in large part, the furor over Elvis Presley that prompted millions of teenage fans finally to stop mourning James Dean, who had died over a year before. As for Presley, he never fulfilled his early hype as "the musical James Dean," but he did carve out his own niche in the rare and pantheon ranks of legendary performers.

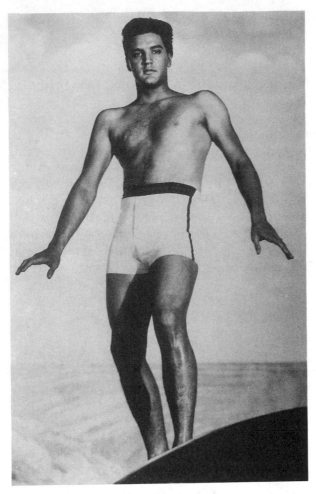

Elvis: publicity pose or identity crisis?

Elvis Presley was born in 1935 in Tupelo, Mississippi. A former usher and truck driver, he was signed to Sun Records in 1954, but it was not until after signing with RCA Records in November 1955 that he made a national impact. Presley's film career began in 1956 with *Love Me Tender*, extended through a slew of ridiculously bad (with a few exceptions) films during the 1960s, and ended with the documentary *Elvis On Tour* (1972). Presley died of drug-induced heart failure in Memphis on August 16, 1977. He was 42.

Elvis Presley's Number One Singles
1. "Heartbreak Hotel" (1956)
2. "I Want You, I Need You, I Love You" (1956)
3. "Don't Be Cruel" and "Hound Dog" (the biggest selling two-sided hit in history, 1956)
5. "Love Me Tender" (1956)
6. "Too Much" (1957)
7. "All Shook Up" (1957)

8. "Teddy Bear" (1957)
9. "Jailhouse Rock" (1957)
10. "Don't" (1958)
11. "Hard Headed Woman" (1958)
12. "A Big Hunk o' Love" (1959)
13. "Stuck on You" (1960)
14. "It's Now or Never" (1960)
15. "Are You Lonesome Tonight?" (1960)
16. "Surrender" (1961)
17. "Good Luck Charm" (1962)
18. "Suspicious Minds" (1969)

ROBERT PRESTON

The Mendocino, California, home of Dr. Robert Preston was used as a location (Kate's house) for the shooting of *East of Eden*. On June 2, 1954, with the production crew in his home, Preston, age 77, died of a heart attack. The shooting, nonetheless, continued.

PRINCETON UNIVERSITY

In 1956 *The Hollywood Reporter* reported:

> Ranking the late James Dean among the immortals of art, Princeton University has placed in its Lawrence Hutton Hall of Fame the life mask of the young Warners star whose career was cut short by his traffic death last year. It will share space with similar memorials of Edwin Booth, David Garrick, Beethoven, Thackeray and Keats. Dean is the youngest artist ever so honored.

PRIVATE LIVES MAGAZINE

The June 1957 edition of *Private Lives* magazine pronounced "Jimmy Dean's Alive!" The accompanying story contended, citing "authoritative sources," that Dean was alive and secretly hiding his hideously scarred face in New York City. The rag mag, disposing with any semblance of good taste, further trumpeted, "He didn't die! He lives on, maybe right next door to You! And someday soon, perhaps Jimmy, in his own way and in his own good time, will once more come back and face the world that waits for him." In the meantime the *Private Lives* editors offered a reward of $50,000 for anyone who could produce a still-breathing Jimmy Dean.

THE PRODUCERS
Producers Who Produced TV Programs in Which Dean Appeared

Mort Abrahams	"The Evil Within"	1953
Mort Abrahams	"I'm a Fool"	1954
Gordon Duff	"Run Like a Thief"	1954
Dick Dunlap	"A Long Time Till Dawn"	1953
Hudson Faussett	"The Bells of Cockaigne"	1953
Franklin Heller	"Sleeping Dogs"	1952
Franklin Heller	"Death Is My Neighbor"	1953
Maury Holland	"Keep Our Honor Bright"	1953

Martin Horrell	"Something for an Empty Briefcase"	1953
Cal Kuhl	"The Foggy, Foggy Dew"	1952
Andrew McCullough	"The Little Woman"	1954
Worthington Minor	"Ten Thousand Horses Singing"	1952
Robert Montgomery	"Harvest"	1953
Father Patrick Peyton	"Hill Number One"	1951
Fred Rickey	"Glory in Flower"	1953
William Self	"The Unlighted Road"	1955

Producers Who Produced Plays in Which Dean Appeared

Lemuel Ayers	*See the Jaguar*	1952
Terese Hayden	*The Scarecrow*	1953
Billy Rose	*The Immoralist*	1954

Producers Who Produced Movies in Which Dean Starred

Henry Ginsberg	*Giant*	1956
Elia Kazan	*East of Eden*	1955
George Stevens	*Giant*	1956
David Weisbart	*Rebel Without a Cause*	1955

Producers Who Produced Plays About or Inspired by Dean

Steven Bentinck	*Dean*	1977
Joel Brykman	*Come Back to the Five and Dime, Jimmy Dean, Jimmy Dean*	1982
Joseph Clapsaddle	*Come Back to the Five and Dime, Jimmy Dean, Jimmy Dean*	1982
Dan Fisher	*Come Back to the Five and Dime, Jimmy Dean, Jimmy Dean*	1982
Jack Lawrence	*Come Back to the Five and Dime, Jimmy Dean, Jimmy Dean*	1982
Patricia Leone	*James Dean: A Dress Rehearsal*	1984

Producers Who Produced TV Movies/Specials About or Inspired by Dean

William Bast	"James Dean"	1976
Ara Chekmayan	"Forever James Dean"	1988
Arthur Drooker	"James Dean: An American Original"	1983
John Forbes	"James Dean"	1976
Lewis Freedman	"The Movie Star"	1962
Ronald Lyon	"James Dean Remembered"	1974
Al Ramrus	"James Dean Remembered"	1974

Producers Who Produced Movies/Videos About or Inspired by Dean

Robert Altman	*The James Dean Story*	1957
Donatella Baglivo	*Hollywood: The Rebel James Dean*	*
Scott Bushnell	*Come Back to the Five and Dime, Jimmy Dean, Jimmy Dean*	1982
George W. George	*The James Dean Story*	1957
Sandy Lieberson	*James Dean: The First American Teenager*	1976
David Puttnam	*James Dean: The First American Teenager*	1976
Nick Taylor	*Bye Bye Jimmy*	*
Paul Watson	*Bye Bye Jimmy*	*
Jerry Weintraub	*September 30, 1955*	1977

*Made for the video market. No theatrical release date.

"PROLOGUE TO GLORY"

James Dean appeared in "Prologue to Glory," an episode of the NBC television program "Kraft Television Theatre." The episode, about the young Abraham Lincoln, starred Thomas Coley, Pat Breslin, Una O'Connor, William Lee, and Butch Clavell. It was written by E. P. Conkle and aired on May 21, 1952.

PROSTITUTION

Over the years there has been speculation that, during his struggling years, Dean resorted to peddling his physical wares on the streets of Hollywood and New York City. According to one story he once crashed a party at the home of actor Judson Laire and demanded of one of Laire's astonished guests, "Where is the money?!" According to Bill Dakota, who worked for Nick Adams, Dean and Adams lived together for a brief period, and "they used to argue over who was gonna wear the one pair of Levi's to hustle in." Further, Bill Bast once quoted his friend Jimmy as confessing "They [Hollywood's powerful] get these poor kids, saps like me, and make them perform. I did a little dancing myself. I was dumb. I thought it might pay off."

CAMERON PRUD'HOMME

Co-star of *See the Jaguar*, which opened on Broadway at the Cort Theatre on December 3, 1952, and featured unknown actor James Dean. Prud'homme portrayed Brad. Later Prud'homme hosted "The Evil Within," a 1953 episode of the ABC television program "Tales of Tomorrow" that co-starred Dean.

Cameron Prud'homme (1892–1967) also appeared in films including *Abraham Lincoln* (1930), *The Rainmaker* (1956), and *The Cardinal* (1963) and appeared as a regular on the television show "Young Mr. Bobbin" (1951–1952). Onstage he won a Best Supporting Actor Tony nomination for *New Girl in Town* (1958).

PSYCHOANALYSIS

Shortly before his death and with the frequent prodding of his friends and acquaintances, James Dean entered psychoanalysis. Marlon Brando, Stanley Meyer, and Shelley Winters, among others, all cajoled Dean to see a psychiatrist. Winters even contends that she paid for Dean to see Dr. Judd Marmor for a single session. Brando reportedly encouraged Dean to see his doctor, Dr. Mittleman. Dean's friend Oscar Levant claimed in 1968 that "I was told by Nick Ray that he had set up a date for Dean with a psychoanalyst, but he was killed in his motorcycle [sic] accident three days before the appointment." But according to another Dean friend, Leonard Rosenman, Dean did see a psychiatrist shortly before his death.

PUBLICISTS

Bill Hendricks was the director of publicity at Warner Brothers during James Dean's tenure there. Other studio publicists who worked with Dean included Ted Ashton, Steve Brooks, and Carl Combs.

BOB PULLEY

Bob Pulley was one of Jimmy's friends in Fairmount, Indiana. When Jimmy returned to Fairmount in February 1955, one of the people he visited with was Bob Pulley. In 1989 Pulley was elected president of the Fairmount Historical Museum, which among other things, preserves the name and memory of James Dean.

DAVID PUTTNAM

Co-producer of the excellent 1976 documentary *James Dean: The First American Teenager*.

Puttnam also co-produced the films *Midnight Express* (Best Picture Oscar nomination, 1978), *Chariots of Fire* (Best Picture Oscar winner, 1981), *The Killing Fields* (Best Picture Oscar nomination, 1984), and *The Mission* (Best Picture Oscar nomination, 1986). Puttnam also served a brief stint in 1987 as the head of production at Columbia Studios.

Q

AIDAN QUINN

People magazine dubbed him the "Rebel Without a Pause." Aidan Quinn, in the opinion of numerous Dean fans, is the actor who has come closest to recapturing the Dean essence with an appealing combination of intensity and vulnerability. Certainly he is among the most talented actors of his generation.

A former hot-tar roofer, Quinn, born in 1959 and raised in Dublin, Ireland, and Chicago, Illinois, made his film debut in *Reckless* (1984). His subsequent films have included *Desperately Seeking Susan* (1985), *The Mission* (England, 1986), *Stakeout* (1987), *Robinson Crusoe* (1989), and *Avalon* (1990). He also starred in the superlative television movies "An Early Frost" (1986) and "All My Sons" (1987).

QUOTING DEAN

Thirty-five years of legend have transformed James Dean into an icon that he himself would dismiss or fail to recognize. Perhaps the only way to define Dean purely is to evaluate him through his own words. It was Wim Wenders who once said, "Life is in color. But black and white is more realistic." The following, then, is James Dean—in black and white.

> I, James Byron Dean, was born February 8, 1931, Marion, Indiana. My parents, Winton Dean and Mildred Dean, formerly Mildred Wilson, and myself existed in the state of Indiana until I was six years of age.
>
> Dad's work with the government caused a change so Dad as a dental mechanic was transferred to California. There we lived until the fourth year. Mom became ill and passed out of my life at the age of nine. I never knew the reason for Mom's death, in fact it still preys on my mind.
>
> I had always lived such a talented life. I studied violin, played in concerts, tap-danced on theatre stages but most of all I like art, to mold and create things with my hands.
>
> I came back to Indiana to live with my uncle. I lost the dancing and violin but not the art. I think my life will be devoted to art and dramatics. And there are so many different fields of art it would be hard to foul-up, and if I did, there are so many different things to do—farm, sports, science, geology, coaching, teaching music. I got it and I know if I better myself that there will be no match. A fellow must have confidence.
>
> When living in California my young eyes experienced many

things. It was also my luck to make three visiting trips to Indiana, going and coming a different route each time. I have been in almost every state west of Indiana. I remember all.

My hobby, or what I do in my spare time, is motorcycle. I know a lot about them mechanically and I love to ride. I have been in a few races and have done well. I own a small cycle myself. When I'm not doing that I'm usually engaged in athletics, the heart beat of every American boy. As one strives to make a goal in a game there should be a goal in this crazy world for each of us. I hope I know where mine is, anyway, I'm after it.

I don't mind telling you, Mr. Dubois, this is the hardest subject to write about considering the information one knows of himself, I ever attempted.

> "My Case Study" to Roland Dubois,
> Fairmount High School principal, 1948

"My mother died on me when I was nine years old. What did she expect me to do? Do it all by myself?"

> to interviewer Wally Atkinson

I have to get *there* fast, Mrs. Nall.

> to teacher Adeline Nall

"I think there's only one true form of greatness for man. If a man can bridge the gap between life and death. I mean, if he can live on after he's died, then maybe he was a great man. To me, the only success, the only greatness, is immortality."

> to Reverend James DeWeerd

"At about twelve or thirteen, I found out what I was really useful for—to *live*. Why did God put all these things here for us to be interested in?"

"My father was a farmer, but he did have this remarkable adeptness with his hands. Whatever abilities I may have, crystallized there in high school, when I was trying to prove something to myself—that I could do it, I suppose."

> to reporter Howard Thompson

"My mother died when I was a kid. I used to cry on her grave and say, 'Why did you leave me? Why did you leave me?' And that changed into, 'I'm gonna show you! I'm gonna show you! I'm gonna be great!' "

> to Dennis Hopper

I wanna talk to you! Talk to me! Talk to me! Please!
> as Cal Trask, to his mother, played by Jo Van Fleet, *East of Eden*

"Studying cows, pigs and chickens can help an actor develop his character. There are a lot of things I learned from animals. One was that they couldn't hiss or boo me. I also became close to nature and am now able to appreciate the beauty with which this world is endowed."

"To grasp the full significance of life is the actor's duty; to interpret it his problem; and to express it his dedication. Being an actor is the loneliest thing in the world. You're all alone with your concentration and imagination, and that's all you have. Being a good actor isn't easy. Being a man is even harder. I want to be both before I'm done."

"The Studio makes you develop motivation. It makes you work from the inside out. [Hollywood will] permit you to be a good actor, but you really have to *want* to be one. And that desire I get from the Studio."

"How can I lose? In one hand I've got Marlon Brando yelling, 'Screw you,' and in the other, Montgomery Clift asking, 'Please help me.' "

to Dennis Hopper

"When a new actor comes along, he's always compared to someone else. Brando was compared to Clift, Clift to someone else. They can compare me to W. C. Fields if they want to."

to reporter Bob Thomas

"In a certain sense, I am a [fatalist]. I don't exactly know how to explain it, but I have a hunch there are some things in life we just can't avoid. They'll happen to us, probably because we're built that way—we simply attract our own fate, make our own destiny."

to reporter Jack Shafer, 1952

"How can you measure acting in inches?!"

when told he was too short to be an actor

"An actor must interpret life, and in order to do so must be willing to accept all the experiences life has to offer. In fact he must seek out more of life than life puts at his feet. In the short span of his lifetime, an actor must learn all there is to know, experience all there is to experience, or approach that state as closely as possible. He must be superhuman in his efforts to store away in the core of his subconscious everything that he might be called upon to use in the expression of his art."

"When an actor plays a scene exactly the way a director orders, it isn't acting. It's following instructions. Anyone with the physical qualifications can do that. So the director's task is just that—to direct, to point the way. Then the actor takes over. And he must be allowed the space, the freedom to express himself in the role. Without that space, an actor is no more than an unthinking robot with a chestful of push buttons."

"It was an accident, although I've been involved in some kind of theatrical function or other since I was a child—in school, music, athletics. To me, acting is the most logical way for people's neuroses to manifest themselves, in this great need we all have to express ourselves. To my way of thinking, an actor's course is set even before he's out of the cradle."

to reporter Howard Thompson

"I was raised in a simple way. We learn that the church and the theater are not just structures of brick and mortar. Hollywood is brick and mortar. So is New York. But within the confines of that brick and mortar, you find perceptive, receptive people which compensate for the exterior."

to Hedda Hopper

"I want to grow away from all this crap. You know, the petty little world we exist in. There's a level somewhere, where everything is solid and important. I'm going to try to reach up there and find a place I know is close to perfect, a place where this whole messy world should be, could be, if it would just take the time to learn."

"If I had one day when I didn't have to be all confused and I didn't have to feel that I was ashamed of everything. If I felt that I belonged someplace, you know?"

as Jim Stark, *Rebel Without a Cause*

"This [tree] is the largest and oldest living on earth. The secret of its size and longevity, despite thousands and thousands of years of storms and bad weather, is its thick bark. And it is the same thing with the human body. It can also have a thick bark with which to protect itself."

"This cat doesn't buy that. I came to Hollywood to act, not to charm society."

"No, I didn't read the novel. The way I work, I'd much rather justify myself with the adaptation rather than the source. I felt I wouldn't have any trouble—too much, anyway—with this characterization once we started because I think I understood the part. I knew, too, that if I had any problems over the boy's background, I could straighten it out with Kazan."

on *East of Eden*, to reporter Howard Thompson

"I'm a serious-minded and intense little devil, terribly gauche and so tense that I don't see how people stay in the same room with me. I know I wouldn't tolerate myself."

"This gift astonishes me. An actor must observe. He must feel the need to become involved in many things; he must have a cardinal interest in all things. Aristotle said, 'A gentleman should play the flute—but not too well.' At the time of youth when all your interests and dreams are coming into focus, you find a craft, acting, to help you untangle your natural resources, everything you've been interested in. Trust and belief are two prime considerations. You must not allow yourself to be opinionated. You must say, 'Wait. Let me see.' And above all, you must be honest with yourself."

to Hedda Hopper

Must I always be so miserable? I try so hard to make people reject me. Why? I don't want to write this letter. It would be better to remain silent. Wow! Am I fucked up.

in a letter to Barbara Glenn

Reporter: "Why don't you give the guy [a photographer] a break? After all, he's got a job to do."
Dean: "I didn't mean to be rude. It's just that I've got bags under my eyes, and I need a shave."

Things get mixed up all the time. I see a person I would like to get close to (everybody) then I think it would just be the same as before and they don't give a shit about me. Then I say something nasty or nothing at all and walk away. The poor person doesn't know what happened. He doesn't realize that I have decided I don't like him. What's wrong with people. Idiots. (I won't fail please.)

in a letter to Barbara Glenn

"Sure, I saw it. Not bad."

to a reporter on *East of Eden*

"Since I'm only 24 I guess I have as good an insight into this rising generation as any other young man at my age. And I've discovered that most young men do not stand like ramrods or talk like Demosthenes. Therefore, when I do play a youth, such as in *Rebel Without a Cause*, I try to imitate life. The picture deals with the problems of modern youth. It is the romanticized conception of the juvenile that causes much of our trouble with misguided youth nowadays. I think one thing the picture shows that's new is the psychological disproportion of the kid's demands on the parents. Parents are often at fault, but the kids have some work to do, too. But you can't show some far-off idyllic conception of behavior if you want the kids to come and see the picture. You've got to show what it's really like, and try and reach them on their own grounds. You know, a lot of times an older boy, one of the fellows the young ones idolize, can go back to the high school kids and tell them, 'Look what happened to me! Why be a punk and get in trouble with the law? Why do these senseless things just for a thrill?' I hope *Rebel Without a Cause* will do something like that. I hope it will remind them that other people have feelings. Perhaps they will say 'What do we need all that for?' If a picture is psychologically motivated, if there is truth in the relationships in it, then I think that picture will do good. I firmly believe that *Rebel Without a Cause* is such a picture."

"Maybe publicity *is* important. But I just can't make it, can't get with it. I've been told by a lot of guys the way it works. The newspapers give you a big build-up. Something happens, they tear you down. Who needs it? What counts to the artist is performance not publicity. Guys who don't know me, already they've typed me as an odd ball."

"If a choice is in order—I'd rather have people hiss than yawn. Any public figure sets himself up as a target and that is the chance he takes. Most of us have more than one choice and I chose to be what I am, rather than remain a farm boy back in Indiana. Despite the endless odds and issues along the way, I've never regretted it."

"Naturally, I shall always consider the role of Cal in *East of Eden* as a highlight in my career. It marked my debut in motion pictures. But best? Never! I consider my present role in *Rebel Without a Cause* better than the part of Cal. In each succeeding picture, I shall think of the part as better than the one before. I always must do better. I must improve. I must grow with each year. There is no point in an actor's life when he must feel that he has done his best. I always think that my best is yet to come. When it does arrive, I know that I shall not feel satisfied."

Reporter: "Isn't this pushing realism a bit?"
    Dean: "In motion pictures, you can't fool the camera. If we were doing this on stage we'd probably be able to gimmick it up—but not in a picture. Film fans are too critical these days. Anyway, I figure the only way to make a scene look realistic is to do it the way you know it would really happen. Don't pull any punches."
    on the set of the knife-fight sequence in *Rebel Without a Cause*

"The thing that interested me in *Rebel* was doing something that would counteract *The Wild One*. I went out and hung around with kids in Los Angeles before making the movie. Some of them even call themselves 'wild ones.' They wear leather jackets, go out looking for somebody to rough up a little. These aren't poor kids, you know. Lots of them have money, grow up and become pillars of the community! Boy, they scared me! But it's a constructive movie, it gives some of these kids, the ones who aren't out to be tough guys, something to identify with."

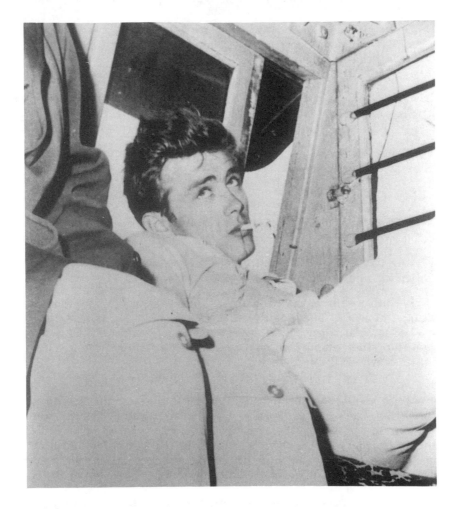

"Some day I would like to follow in the footsteps of my great idol, Elia Kazan. You know, Kazan was an actor at Warner Brothers a number of years ago. Then he began to direct Broadway productions and subsequently went on to direct exceptional motion pictures."

"I hate anything that limits progress and growth."

"[Today I'm shooting] the final scene. The death of Plato, the rediscovery of my father, which I seem to be doing quite frequently. The character that you usually see [after first reading a script] is, uh, sporadic. Too fantastic for reality. He does many things that a character shouldn't do and you [as an actor] have to select, constantly reevaluate your images, what you envision as the character. It continues, constant simplification, constant learning down to the specific point in hand, the line in the story, what the character is trying to do at this moment. Constantly trying to find the core, so to speak, to go ahead, to develop, and to attempt and to try. For instance, today, my emotional apparatus is, I don't know, plugged up or something. It's not coming easy for me."

to interviewer Shirley Thomas on the set of *Rebel Without a Cause*

"Since juvenile delinquency is based on violence, it is justified violence. We picture a very real situation that exists in this country—something that should be stamped out."

on columnist Erskine Johnson

"It was well worth it. I guess you have to work real hard and suffer a little if you're going to accomplish anything worthwhile."

at the completion of *Rebel Without a Cause*

"I felt very honored. I guess I'll just have to show my appreciation by doing my best in every acting job I get."

on learning that he had placed as one of the five favorite actors in a fan magazine poll

"With so many outside pursuits, I had to drop some of them so my acting wouldn't suffer."

"My fun days are over. I want to have my own company, my own properties, and someday my own theater."

"The trouble with me is I'm just dog tired. Everybody hates me and thinks I'm a heel. They say I've gone Hollywood. But, honest, I'm just the same as when I didn't have a dime. As I said I'm just tired. I went into *Giant* after a long, hard schedule on *Rebel Without a Cause*. Maybe I'll just go away."

to columnist Dorothy Manners

"An actor should thoroughly understand the character he is portraying and there is no better way than trying to be that person in the hours away from the camera. I developed a program of understanding Jett [Rink] and of doing the things he'd be likely to do. I didn't want any jarring notes in my characterization. Jett was a victim of his position in life. I want to play him sympathetically."

"A director's notebook is just an ordinary pad, but it has a very definite purpose in the acting profession. I use it to take notes on how a director works, how he uses lights, how he gets interesting and intricate camera angles, and just about every technique he employs in the shooting of a motion picture.

"I hope to use the notes as research material and background data when I make that big move into the field of directing. I know it won't come for a long while, but I'm preparing.

"I hope to have a collection of notes on the techniques of all of Hollywood's great motion picture directors."

"It took me a while to accustom myself to the Texas way of life, but I regard the weeks as particularly well spent. In my desire to learn more about the character of Jett Rink, I learned much about Texas and Texans. I've gotten to like the state and the people so much I'm apt to talk like a proud Texan even after *Giant* is completed."

after returning to Hollywood from Marfa

All this business about New York being more emotionally suited for an actor than Hollywood is so much hogwash. When an actor has to depend on what city he's in to perform, he might as well give up the profession. I figure that an actor should be able to perform in any city in the world—whether it be New York, Hollywood, or Podunk, U.S.A. In fact, the actor should be very happy to be working wherever he can.

When Elia Kazan first brought me out to Hollywood to star in *East of Eden*, I had the same misconception about Hollywood which so many New York people do; that the glamour city was just a false, hard-hearted mass of concrete in which talent was only something to buy and sell like vegetables at a grocery store.

However, I was never so wrong in all my life. Hollywood is a great place to work and relax at the same time. After a hard day's work you can always head for some quiet beach house away from all the high-pressure movie moguls.

While I was making my second picture, *Rebel Without a Cause*, I used to spend my weekends at Malibu Beach, playing volleyball, swimming, reading, and forgetting about the preceding week. I find that any actor who is so dedicated to his work that he can't find time to relax will not last long in this business. After a weekend at the beach, Monday morning found me fresh and raring to go to work. It proved to be a wonderful bit of self-imposed medication to get away from the hustle and bustle of Hollywood for the serenity of a tranquil beach resort.

Not that I will give up New York entirely. The city is a great metropolis with everything that an actor can ask for. It's a fertile, wonderful, generous place to live, if one can accept the violence and cadence, which I have become used to. There are so many things to do.

For instance, when I'm in New York, I go to dancing school, take percussion lessons, acting lessons, attend concerts, the opera, baseball and basketball games, and sometimes drive up to the Catskills for some fishing and camping.

But as an actor I have learned that it matters not in what city you may be in, you still must give out with a top performance if you wish to remain in this business for a good many years.

As a young man who was raised on an Indiana farm, near Fairmount, I am completely enthralled with the "big city." I don't think it's the place for anyone to live, but for working, you just can't beat it.

Such cities as New York, Hollywood, Chicago, Detroit and so on provide the right amount of cultural and spiritual atmosphere for young people during their growing up process. The tempo, drive, verve and pulse of a big city can do more for the ambitious soul than anything I can think of. When I first arrived in New York, fresh off the farm and with hayseed still in my hair, I admit I was frightened, terribly frightened. The tall buildings of the city seemed to be closing in on me and although I tried to break down the doors to every theatrical agency, nothing seemed to happen. For a while, I was discouraged. But then I decided that a challenge had been hurled my way—a challenge to beat this thing they called "big city fear." So I just kept plugging away, confident that in a short while I would be given the break I had been looking for.

Then, it seemed like only a period of a few days, I got myself a part in a play called *See the Jaguar*. My next Broadway show was in *The Immoralist*, in which I played an Arab boy, and for which I won the David Blum Award [sic] as the 'best young actor of the year.' That award, by the way, is one of my proudest possessions.

Next came Mr. Kazan, *East of Eden*, *Rebel Without a Cause*, and now I am in George Stevens' production of *Giant*. In *Giant* I play Jett Rink, the man who battles Rock Hudson for control of a huge Texas ranch and for the power which that ranch transposes throughout the whole of the Lone Star state.

In 1956, I head back to New York for some Broadway work. My contract with Warners gives me that year off for anything I want to do. But whether I am in Hollywood or New York, or back at Fairmount, Indiana, I will maintain and will continue to maintain, that all this business of one city being more emotionally suited for an actor than another city is just so much bunk.

> Dean attempting to make amends with Hollywood, in an official press release by Warner Brothers. The release carried Dean's byline, but it was obviously tampered with by a studio publicity rep. Nonetheless, much of Dean remained unequivocally intact.

Reporter: "Mr. Dean, I've come all the way from New York to see you."

Dean: "Madam, I've come all the way from New York to make a picture."

> on the set of *Giant*

"An actor should know a little about many things. He must do more than project his own personality on the screen. He should represent a cross section of many phases of life. The best way to succeed in this is to learn as much as possible about people and their pursuits. Any person stagnates if he does not add to his knowledge. I know I feel more alive when I am trying to master something new. Some day I want to direct. A director must be a perfectionist and a man of wide knowledge. That is why I sometimes feel there are too few hours in the day to even begin to learn what I need to know."

"The gratification comes in the *doing*, not in the results."

> to Bill Bast

"I don't think people should be subservient to movie idols. And I do not idolize Marlon Brando. Brando! If I imitate him subconsciously, I don't know about it. If I do it consciously, I'd be a fool to admit it. I would like to be a star in my own sense. I mean to be a very consummate actor, to have more difficult roles and fill them to my satisfaction. But not to be a star on the basis of gold plating. A real star carries its own illumination, an inward brightness."

> to reporter Aline Mosby

"Some of the things that have been printed about me are fantastic. One night I was supposed to have been at Ciro's and I was also reported in two other places. How could I be in three places at once?

I probably should have a press agent. But I don't care what people write about me. I'll talk to the ones I like; the others can print what they please."

to reporter Bob Thomas

"I want to enter at Salinas, Willow Springs, all the other places. Of course, I'll miss some of them because I have to do a TV spectacular in New York on October 18. But maybe I can catch a race back there. . . . I'll be very hard to catch."

to a reporter, September 1955

"Live fast, die young, and have a good-looking corpse."

quoting from Nick Ray's *Knock on Any Door*

Reporter: "What is the thing you respect above all else?"
  Dean: "That's easy. Death. It's the only thing left to respect. It's
        the one inevitable, undeniable truth. Everything else can
        be questioned. But death is truth. In it lies the only
        nobility for man, and beyond it, the only hope."

"One of the deepest drives of human nature is the desire to be
appreciated, the longing to be liked, to be held in esteem, to be a
sought-after person. There are six needs in life: love, security, self-
esteem, recognition, new experiences, and last, but not least, the need
for creative expression."

"What is essential is invisible to the eye."

quoting from *The Little Prince*

"What better way to die? It's fast and clean and you go out in a blaze
of glory."

on car racing

God gave James Dean so many gifts to share with the world, has he
the right to throw them away in the bullring?

inscribed in his copy of Hemingway's *Death in the Afternoon*

"Take a good look at me. You may not get the chance again."

to *Giant* cinematographer William C. Mellor, September 1955

"So long, I think I'll let the Spyder out."

to *Giant* director George Stevens, September 1955

R

ALAN RACHINS

Co-star of the hit television series "L.A. Law" (1986–) who said of James Dean:

> "I knew I wanted to be an actor when I was in the seventh grade and saw *Rebel Without a Cause*. There was this guy, James Dean, yelling at his father. And I thought, that's great. I thought that was absolutely stunning because I had a lot of anger toward my father and no way to express it."
>
> TV Guide, July 23, 1988

RADIO

In 1949 Jimmy Dean and his partner, Barbara Leach, represented Fairmount High School in a radio debate against rival school Marion High. The topic was the election process of the United States. Jimmy and Barbara argued that the U.S. president should be elected by a direct vote of the people, as opposed to the consensus of the electoral college. The debate was broadcast on WBAT-Radio in Marion, Indiana.

Over the years it has been repeatedly published that, during his struggling years circa 1951–1952, James Dean appeared on several radio programs, including "CBS Radio Workshop." However, since "CBS Radio Workshop" did not premiere until January 27, 1956, it can easily be deduced that his participation in it was nil. The radio programs that Dean *did* appear on include "Alias Jane Doe," "Hallmark Playhouse," "Stars over Hollywood," and "The Theatre Guild on the Air."

GENA RAMSEL

Actress who was featured in *Come Back to the Five and Dime, Jimmy Dean, Jimmy Dean*, a 1982 Broadway play.

AL RAMRUS

Writer and co-producer of the 1974 television documentary "James Dean Remembered."

DEBORAH RANCE

Former president of the now-defunct Dean Downunder fan club in Australia. Of her attraction to Dean, Deborah Rance relates: "I've been a Dean fan for roughly 10 years, which began simply by watching *East of Eden* one night on television. Jim seemed to reach out and stir my soul as I watched this young man absolutely torn apart by his own emotions. And he told me that I was no longer alone with mine.

"From my own experience Dean fans are the most genuine, honest, understanding people around. And why? Well, because Jim has taught us right from the start to be true to ourselves, that in the end it all comes down to how we look at ourselves. And if we are open and honest with ourselves, we can also be this way with others."

BILL RANDLE
Disc jockey who co-narrated the record album *The James Dean Story* for Coral Records in 1956.

LEON RASKIN
Born in 1945, Lee Raskin is a vice president of an investment management company in Baltimore, Maryland. He has been a car-racing enthusiast since the age of 13. He is a Porsche historian and a member of the Porsche Club of America and is generally regarded as an authority on James Dean's car-racing history, about which he has written several magazine articles.

RAVE MAGAZINE
Hollywood fan magazine that published several articles about James Dean, including:

☆ May 1956	"Did James Dean Really Die?"
☆ November 1956	"In His Own Words"
☆ January 1957	"I Was a Friend of Jimmy Dean" by Lynne Carter
☆ April 1957	"I Learned About Love from Jimmy Dean" by Lynne Carter
☆ April 1957	"Hot Rebel with a Cause"
☆ April 1957	"Why Jimmy Won't Win Any Oscars"
☆ September 1957	"Why Jimmy Dean Is a Living Lie"

NICHOLAS RAY
"Jim had a year away from Warner Brothers. We had planned to use that time to get our company started. We would have done both feature pictures and a television series, which would have allowed Jim to break in as a director. I think he would have been a great director."

> Nick Ray to Bob Thomas, *Los Angeles Mirror-News*,
> November 18, 1955

Of all the directors with whom he worked, James Dean's most significant relationship was with Nicholas Ray. Ray not only won Dean's confidence and trust, as Elia Kazan initially had, he also had the insight to allow Dean creative space in which to work. If Kazan's relationship with Dean was one of father-son, mentor-protégé, Ray's relationship with him was one of collaboration and mutual respect.

In fact Ray allowed his young actor so much territory (an unusual tactic in Hollywood, where directors often regard their actors with disdain) that

Will the real Jim Stark
please stand up?

"... a nice collaboration."

speculation abounded that Dean, with his newfound stardom, had wrested control of the picture from Ray. Jim Backus, one of the film's featured actors, publicly contended that Dean had actually co-directed *Rebel Without a Cause*. Others, however, dispute this. According to Beverly Long, "None of us knew about it if he did. I think maybe it was that Nick Ray was an extremely receptive director. He even took ideas from *us* [actors portraying the film's gang members]." Steffi Sidney concurs: "I saw only that Jimmy and Nick had a nice collaboration, a flow of ideas. I didn't see Jimmy direct anybody. I didn't see Jimmy get behind the camera and tell anybody where to move. He certainly didn't *physically* direct it. What I saw was a lead actor who had a nice collaboration with his director. He offered a lot of suggestions for his character and suggestions for a scene that involved his mother or father or Corey or Sal or Natalie. But I never saw him really direct. I think Nick Ray handled him very well because, at this point, he was becoming a big star. And I think he had a sense of his own worth. Nick had a very strong personality and a very strong visual sense of the overall picture. From what I understand, Nick handled Jimmy better than Elia Kazan did."

Ironically, years before, Ray had appeared as an actor in Elia Kazan's first play, *The Young Go First* (1935). And in 1945 he served as Kazan's assistant director on the acclaimed film *A Tree Grows in Brooklyn*. Two years later Ray made his own successful debut as a director with *They Live by Night*. His subsequent, sporadic career includes *A Woman's Secret* (1949), *Knock on Any Door* (1949), *Born to Be Bad* (1950), *In a Lonely Place* (which starred Ray's second wife, Gloria Grahame, 1950), *Flying Leathernecks* (1951), *On Dangerous Ground* (1951), *The Lusty Men* (1952), *Johnny Guitar* (1954), *Run for Cover* (1955), *Hot Blood* (1956), *Bigger Than Life* (1956), *The True Story of Jesse James* (1957), *Bitter Victory* (made in France, 1957), *Wind Across the Everglades* (1958), *Party Girl* (which featured Corey Allen, 1958), *Savage Innocents* (France and Italy, 1959), *King of Kings* (1961), *55 Days at Peking* (Spain, 1962), and *Dreams of Thirteen* (1976). He also appeared in the 1977 film *The American Friend*, which co-starred ex-*Rebel* gang member Dennis Hopper.

During his career Nick Ray was always considered something of an oddity, a Hollywood outsider. During the postproduction of *Rebel* Ray sent a memo to his boss, Jack Warner, that began:

> My name is Nick Ray and I just finished making a picture for you called *Rebel Without a Cause*. I thought maybe you'd forgotten my name because the last time we met any closer than bowing distance was in your office late at night and you'd wished you'd never met me and I thought you should have felt just the opposite. . . .

Even after the success of *Rebel* Ray was relegated by the studios to making grade-B pictures. He found some favor with European critics, but in Hollywood he was generally dismissed as the maker of turgid and boring, albeit well-photographed, melodramas.

Had James Dean lived, and had he formed a production company with Ray as he had contemplated, Nick Ray's career certainly would have benefited. Dean's box-office clout would have forced Hollywood's acceptance, however begrudged, of Ray, and he would have had far better material to work with. As it turned out, however, *Rebel*, for which he was nominated for a Best Story Oscar, was the pinnacle of his career.

Nick Ray was born Raymond Kienzle in 1911. He died of cancer in 1979, leaving behind a crowded shelf of unfinished films and unrealized dreams.

> "There were probably very few directors with whom Jimmy could ever have worked. To work with him meant exploring his nature, trying to understand it; without this, his powers of expression were frozen. He retreated, he sulked. He always wanted to make a film in

which he could personally believe, but it was never easy for him. Between belief and action lay the obstacle of his own deep, obscure uncertainty."

Nick Ray, *Variety*, December 1956

"The last time I saw James Dean was when he arrived without warning at my Hollywood home about three in the morning. That evening we had met for dinner. We had talked for several hours of many things, of future plans, including a story called 'Heroic Love' that we were going to do."

Nick Ray, *Nicholas Ray* by John Francis Kreidl

RONALD REAGAN

"I do recall very clearly that I was struck by how very much James Dean off camera resembled the James Dean you saw on camera. He worked very hard at his craft, rehearsed with very much the same intensity that he gave the part on camera.

"Most of us, after awhile in pictures, hold back somewhat in rehearsal and save our punch for the take. As I say, Jimmy Dean did not do this. He seemed to go almost all-out anytime that he read the lines. . . ."

Ronald Reagan, then governor of California (1973), in *The James Dean Story* by Ron Martinetti

Ronald Reagan starred opposite James Dean in "The Dark, Dark Hour," a 1954 episode of the CBS television series "General Electric Theater," which Reagan hosted for eight years (1954–1962). In the episode Reagan portrayed a doctor confronted by a gun-brandishing delinquent played by Dean. The program aired live from Hollywood on December 12, 1954, after the completion of *East of Eden* but before its release.

Following Dean's death CBS executives opted to rerun "I'm a Fool," another episode of "General Electric Theater" that had starred Dean. As the host and "program supervisor" of the show, Reagan introduced the episode in his typically amiable manner:

Good evening. We are pleased to present James Dean and Natalie Wood in a repeat performance of Sherwood Anderson's "I'm a Fool," starring Eddie Albert as the narrator, on "The General Electric Theater."

In a moment, in answer to a great many requests, we will present a film of a fine performance by James Dean in a "General Electric Theater" play. It was a performance that helped attract nationwide attention to his talent. And we present it as one of the landmarks, and his progress toward, the great roles of his brief career.

Those of us who worked with Jimmy Dean carry an image of his intense struggle for a goal beyond himself. And curiously enough, that's the story of the boy he portrays tonight. Eddie Albert is the narrator, Natalie Wood is the girl, in Sherwood Anderson's "I'm a Fool."

Reagan, born in 1911, a former baseball game announcer, appeared on television in "The Orchid Award," a 1953–1954 musical variety series that he hosted; and "Death Valley Days (1965–1966), which he dropped out of when elected governor of California. He also appeared as a guest in numerous episodic programs, including "Ford Theatre," in which he and Nancy Davis made their professional debut as a team in a February 5, 1953, episode entitled "First Born."

Reagan's numerous films include *Love Is on the Air* (1937), *Brother Rat* (1938), *Dark Victory* (1939), *An Angel from Texas* (which co-starred the newly married Reagan and Jane Wyman, 1940), *Knute Rockne—All American* (as George Gipp, 1940), *King's Row* (the closest he came to an Oscar nomination, 1942), *This Is the Army* (1943), *John Loves Mary* (during the making of which he split from Wyman, 1949), *The Hasty Heart* (1950), *Bedtime for Bonzo* (1951), *Hong Kong* (by the time of its release, Reagan was newly married to Nancy Davis, 1952), *Hellcats of the Navy* (with Nancy, 1957), and *The Killers* (1964).

THE REAL JAMES DEAN
Author: John Gilmore
Publisher: Pyramid Books
Year: 1975

Standard biography that flirts with sensationalism. The cover copy oozes with promises of revelation: "James Dean—as he actually was—a lover of men as well as women." But author Gilmore went only as far as stating that he knew Dean and *suggesting* that they had been lovers. He offered far more detail in subsequent interviews with the *Los Angeles Free Press* and *The Hollywood Star*.

THE REAL JAMES DEAN STORY
One-shot cover-to-cover magazine about Dean printed by Fawcett Publications in 1956. *The Real James Dean Story* was edited by Mary Callahan and includes articles by Bob Hinkle, Lori Nelson, Hedda Hopper, and Sal Mineo, among others.

REATA
Name of the sprawling Benedict ranch in *Giant*. What Tara was to *Gone with the Wind*, Reata was to *Giant*. The set of the Reata mansion was actually constructed in Hollywood, disassembled, and sent to Marfa, Texas, by train, where it was reassembled for the location shooting, then disassembled and freighted back to Hollywood.

The Worth Evans ranch, located 20 miles west of Marfa, was used as the location for Reata. Little Reata, Jett Rink's inherited property, was actually the Ben Avant ranch, located approximately seven miles west of Marfa.

REBEL
A line of men's cologne that was advertised using the Dean image and the

accompanying copy "Rebel: With or Without a Cause. The man's fragrance, when a woman has her choice!"

THE REBEL
Author: Royston Ellis
Publisher: Consul Books, Great Britain
Year: 1962

One of the earliest biographies about Dean.

REBEL WITHOUT A CAUSE
Book by Dr. Robert Lindner, subtitled *The Hypnoanalysis of a Criminal Psychopath*, that was published by Grove Press in 1944. The protagonist in Lindner's book, an actual case study, was an imprisoned psychopath by the name of Harold. The title aside, the book bears virtually no resemblance to the Warner Brothers film made in 1955.

REBEL WITHOUT A CAUSE ★★★
1955   111 minutes   WarnerColor   CinemaScope
Warner Brothers
Directed by: Nicholas Ray
Produced by: David Weisbart
Screenplay by: Stewart Stern
Adaptation by: Irving Shulman
Story by: Nicholas Ray
Photographed by: Ernest Haller
Edited by: William Ziegler
Music by: Leonard Rosenman
Cast: James Dean, Natalie Wood, Sal Mineo, Jim Backus, Ann Doran, Corey Allen, William Hopper, Rochelle Hudson, Dennis Hopper, Edward Platt, Steffi Sidney, Marietta Canty, Virginia Brissac, Beverly Long, Ian Wolfe, Frank Mazzola, Robert Foulk, Jack Simmons, Tom Bernard, Nick Adams, Jack Grinnage, Clifford Morris, Jimmy Baird, Dick Wessel, Nelson Leigh, Dorothy Abbot, Louise Lane, House Peters, Gus Schilling, Bruce Noonan, Almira Sessions, Peter Miller, Paul Bryar, Paul Birch, Robert Williams, David McMahon

Rebel Without a Cause, a 1944 book by Dr. Robert Lindner, was purchased by Warner Brothers for $5,000 in 1946. At that time Warners intended it as a vehicle for rising stage star Marlon Brando, who subsequently nixed the project. For the next eight years *Rebel* sat on a studio shelf, a movie without a director, a star, or a script.

In 1954 Columbia had *The Wild One* with Brando, MGM had *The Blackboard Jungle*, and Warner Brothers was primed for a juvenile delinquency movie of its own. As the studio began to dust off the jacket of Lindner's book, director Nicholas Ray entered the picture. As he later explained, "I thought the material [the book] was good, but I did not

---

want to do a story about a boy who had been caught. I also did not want to do a picture which inferred that delinquency breeds in low income groups [as *The Blackboard Jungle* was doing] or in slum areas." Subsequently Ray called his secretary into his office and dictated to her for the next eight hours. According to Ray, "By seven o'clock in the morning my ideas were on paper, and by nine o'clock, I had put them before the studio officials. That evening the deal was closed."

Ray titled his 17-page treatment *The Blind Run*. It was dated September 18, 1954, and featured a trio of teenagers—Eve, Jimmy, and Demo—as its primary characters. Jimmy was the leader of a gang, but

Down for the count. James Dean, pinned by Corey Allen, smolders for the camera.

most of the drama revolved around Demo, a young criminal who is sentenced to death by a court of law.

Warners bought Ray's story but not his title. For a while the project was dubbed *The Juvenile Story*. Then it became *Rebel Without a Cause*. *Rebel* went into preproduction on September 27, 1954. Much to Robert Lindner's chagrin, everything but his title was scrapped. Initially Ray wanted Clifford Odets to adapt *The Blind Run* into a screenplay. When he learned that Odets was unavailable, Ray opted for Leon Uris. From the outset Ray wanted his picture to depict reality, not some contrived Hollywood pontification of knife-wielding, chain-wailing delinquents. He enlisted the support and consultation of criminologists, psychiatrists, juvenile court judges, and the California Youth Authority. Further, he sent Uris on evening excursions, riding shotgun with members of the Culver City Police Department. Also from the outset he developed his project with the idea of casting James Dean as his star. Ray had seen an early screening of *East of Eden* and had been struck by the young actor's intensity and authenticity.

Early in preproduction it was obvious to Ray that he had made a mistake in hiring Uris, who was promptly replaced by Irving Shulman. It was Shulman, in large part, who transformed *The Blind Run* into some semblance of *Rebel Without a Cause*. Shulman was still involved with the project when James Dean was enlisted into the film's fold in December 1954. There has been some speculation that Shulman and Dean clashed, or at least suffered a lack of communication, which resulted in Shulman's eventual replacement. In January Stewart Stern, screenwriter cousin of Dean's friend Arthur Loew, Jr., and a friend of *Rebel*'s composer, Leonard Rosenman, was hired for the project.

Certainly there were problems with the script. In one version of the ending Jim Stark vented his anger over Plato's death toward his own father. In another version Plato didn't die at all. In another the ending called for either Jim or Plato to climb atop the dome of the planetarium. There were also innumerable changes prompted by the studio censor. Originally Judy was hauled into the police station on charges of solicitation. Also excised from the script was any implication that Judy was cheap or even sexually *active*. Even her "love scene" with Jim Stark was trimmed so that it would not appear that any actual sex had transpired. Also problematic in the script and with the censor was the relationship between Jim and Plato. One letter from the censor to the studio read "It is of course vital that there be no inference of a questionable or homosexual relationship between Plato and Jim." For that reason a kiss between the two was omitted from the script. The censor also suggested cutting the word *punk*, which in those primitive times was, for some, slang for homosexual. Nevertheless, despite the cuts the

Rebel Without a Cause: a little bit of *Romeo and Juliet*, a lot of rebellion.

Steffi Sidney: "I think it's pure rumor
that Jimmy directed this film."

scenes with Jim and Plato bristled with latent homosexuality.

Because of problems with the script and the censor, and for personal reasons of his own, James Dean almost did not make *Rebel Without a Cause*. In retrospect his qualms were certainly understandable. Both *East of Eden* and *Giant*, the latter of which he was all but set for, were undisputably grade-A pictures, quality pictures with the full support of the studio. In contrast *Rebel* was a relatively minor project, a grade-B picture with an outcast director and an unproven story. Both *Eden* and *Giant* had been bestselling novels by important writers with a proven audience. For Dean, *Rebel* presented a considerable risk. *Eden* hadn't yet been released, but the conventional wisdom in Hollywood was that his performance was going to make him a star. He needed to follow it up with something of better, or at least comparable, quality.

Twice during preproduction Dean fled Hollywood for New York, leaving Nick Ray and producer David Weisbart in limbo. The first time was in December 1954. Determined, Ray got on a plane and went after him. In New York the two men became friends. A couple of weeks later, back in Hollywood, Nick Ray held the first reading of *Rebel* at his Chateau Marmont bungalow—James Dean was one of the participants.

The second time Dean fled the production was in February, just weeks before the film was scheduled to start shooting. It was on that trip to Fairmount, Indiana, and then to New York, that Jimmy was accompanied by photographer Dennis Stock, who captured the period on film for posterity. Meanwhile, back in Hollywood, Nick Ray frantically began looking for another actor to portray Jim Stark, while also reserving hope that Dean would return. The character, as prescribed by Ray, was "seventeen or eighteen, a senior in high school, new to the community, normal in every respect but one—his exaggerated need for attention. His courage, charisma, and drive all stem from it. He has arrived at the point where he will do anything in order to be accepted for what he is, as he is. For he has come to realize that in his family, he is the receptacle for his mother's anger against his father and vice versa. This is a boy with a rage within who is at the stage of rebellion which can lead him to disaster. At the same time, he exhibits a potential for development into a better than average human being." Among others, Ray tested Dennis Hopper for the part.

On March 6, three days prior to the New York premiere of *East of Eden*, Dean returned to Hollywood. For the next several days he laid low, kept to himself. *Eden* opened to mostly rave reviews, and Dean was heralded in some quarters as a major new star. On March 10 he was ready to come out of hiding and appeared in a live television interview. He was also ready to commit to Ray and to *Rebel*. With one successful film behind him, Dean hungered for a second. He was attracted to the social consciousness of the picture, to the idea of working on a film he believed in. He was also lured by Ray's promise to involve him in every phase of the creative process.

Nick Ray was savvy enough to sense that having Dean in his picture elevated it to another level. The rest of the *Rebel* casting process became a mammoth undertaking. Even the casting of the film's gang members became an epic exercise. Beverly Long recently recalled, "The first auditions were real chaos. They were nuts. They had every teenager, every young person in Hollywood, auditioning. And you would go in on cattle calls. They had literally hundreds of kids. I must have gone on three or four auditions. It seemed like they were making a big deal about it. Every time we'd go in for these interviews, Nick would just talk to us about our background, about our family life, what kind of kids we were. I don't know, he was so strange; he was a very iconoclastic kind of director. He was not like anybody I had ever, ever worked for before."

In addition, there were the primary roles of Judy and Plato, and due to various child welfare regulations Ray was under explicit instructions from the Warner Brothers front office *not* to cast any minors in the part. For Judy, Ray was looking for a young actress to play a girl "who has found no satisfaction in any of her promiscuous relations with boys her own age." A girl who was in love with her father, whom she considered an "Adonis" (Judy's promiscuity, as noted previously, was later excised from the script). Plato, according to Ray, "should look a little like Wally Cox at the age of fifteen." At this stage there was also a fourth primary character, a girl by the name of Helen, described by Ray as a conniving friend of Judy's.

Initially the leading contenders for the role of Judy were Margaret O'Brien, 18, and Debbie Reynolds, 23, both established names. Then something happened. According to several sources, Nick Ray, 44, had an affair with Natalie Wood, 17. Wood, at the time, was known only as a child actress and was anxious to graduate to adult roles. Nick Ray became her champion. Publicly he touted her as "the most talented young actress since Helen Hayes first stepped onto a stage. I believe she will be one of Hollywood's biggest stars within two years." Eventually Ray coerced the Warner Brothers front office into casting Wood in the part.

With one minor cast in a major role the door was opened for Ray to cast 15-year-old Sal Mineo in the part of Plato. Having two minors in the film certainly complicated the shooting schedule and risked Ray's reputation with the studio. Steffi Sidney, one of the film's gang members, recently recalled, "We were working with two minors, Sal and Natalie, which meant that you had only four hours a day with them.

They were on the set eight hours—four hours in school and four hours working. I think Nick felt, well, if he had Natalie, he might as well go with Sal too. I guess he felt there was so much he could shoot around, with Jimmy and the parents and the gang and all those scenes. In those days I never even thought of that. Of course, as I got older and got into production myself, I always wondered, *"Why* did he take on the burden of an extra minor?' "

For the next two weeks James Dean went into training. He went out on night prowls, hanging out in neighborhoods frequented by Los Angeles–area gangs. He hung out with Frank Mazzola, a former real-life gang member who had been hired to act as a consultant as well as to play one of the film's gang members. He spent three days with one particular gang, assimilating their every nuance. He read as did the other young actors in the cast, under orders from Nick Ray, the chapter "Creation of a Delinquent Character" from a book entitled *Delinquents in the Making.* With Stewart Stern and Nick Ray he worked on drafting a final script. He learned his lines by tape-recording them, and then replaying them. And he amazed everyone at Warner Brothers with his good spirits and amicable temperament. Upon receiving a freezer full of ham from his Uncle Marcus's farm back in Fairmount, Dean announced that he was going to host a barbecue and invite everyone at the studio. It was behavior hardly befitting a rebel.

> "It looks as though we will have the first important movie to be made about kids of this generation."
> Nicholas Ray to David Weisbart, prior to the start of *Rebel*

On March 23, 1955, James Dean and others assembled for wardrobe tests. On Monday, March 28, *Rebel* went before the cameras. Then, within four days, everything changed.

Rebel Without a Cause was a B picture, shooting in black-and-white. In fact, some of the exterior sequences at Griffith Park had already been shot when Jack Warner stepped in and halted the action. Suddenly, after six months of preproduction, Warner decided that *Rebel* should be shot in color. There were a few reasons for the conversion. First *The Blackboard Jungle* was being shot over the hill in Culver City, and Warner probably wanted to distinguish his picture from the MGM project. Second, and more important, was timing. By the time *Rebel* was beginning to go before the cameras, James Dean had emerged as a major star discovery with the release of *East of Eden*, which opened in Los Angeles on March 16. Over the years it has been reported that Warner almost canceled *Rebel* in mid-shooting amid fears about the film's revolutionary theme of middle-class juvenile delinquency and that he was convinced to proceed with the project only after viewing the

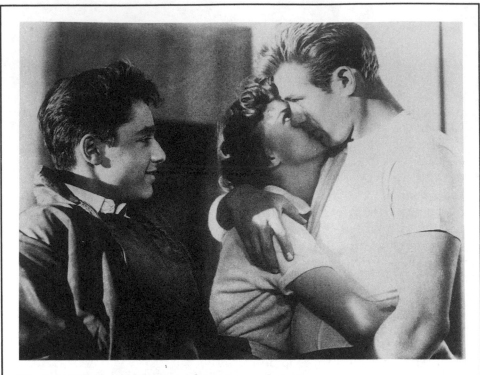

The *Rebel* trio: I only have eyes for you.

The first sign that *Rebel* was a box-office hit came from New York, which reported that it was doing 25 percent better business than the high-grossing *East of Eden*.

To direct or not to direct—that is the question. James Dean, directing Ann Doran in a rehearsal of *Rebel*. That's Jim Backus on the right, looking dazed, like he didn't know what hit him.

Early rebelling. Nick Ray conducts a test. Note the script under Dean's arm.

footage of Dean in *Rebel* that had already been shot. This is absurd or at least highly improbable. In the motion picture industry the bottom line is money. So, when Jack Warner and the executives at Warner Brothers read the reviews of *East of Eden*, gleefully counted its box-office receipts, and sat back in their projection room and saw the early black-and-white footage from *Rebel*, pulling the plug on the film was the last thing on their minds. They were thinking color. And the color was green.

> We started out making a routine program picture, black-and-white. A picture about teenage kids. I thought sort of an Ozzie and Harriet—with venom. They started shooting, then, all of a sudden, the picture shut down. And I thought, 'What's this?' Well, it seems that the reports had come back from *East of Eden*. They had a star on their hands, so they took it from the top. No budget, no schedule. [We could] take all the time we wanted. They made it real big time.
>
> Jim Backus, CNN

> "Nick Ray should lose very little time in picking up in color the scenes he has already shot as he knows what has to be done. In the future, do not leave the studio until you have checked with [Steve] Trilling or me as THIS IS A VERY IMPORTANT PICTURE and we must see the dailies together. . . . The black and white dailies Friday night looked excellent. . . . Did you go out to the location to check everything?"
>
> Jack Warner to *Rebel* producer Dave Weisbart, April 2, 1955

In a matter of days *Rebel* was promoted to grade-A picture status. Nick Ray was allotted more money and time. Some of the costumes were revised to conform to Warnercolor. For instance, Jimmy's black leather jacket was exchanged for a red nylon windbreaker. With the additional time some of the scenes were shot lavishly. The staircase scene, in which Jim Stark batters his father in anguish and frustration, was shot *17* times, much to the dismay of a beaten and bruised Jim Backus.

The time also allowed Dean the luxury of his infamous scene preparations, which typically involved jumping up and down, shadow boxing, or climbing up and down a 50-foot ladder. Backus recalled in his autobiography, *Rocks on the Roof*:

> The scene called for him to have an intensely dramatic argument with the [police] officer in charge, and end up by hysterically banging on the desk in frustration and rage.
>
> He kept the cast and crew waiting for one whole hour. Keeping an entire company waiting for an hour sent the production department in a panic.
>
> Jimmy spent the hour . . . sitting in his darkened dressing room with a record player blasting out the "Ride of the

Valkyrie," and drinking a quart of cheap red wine. When he felt ready, he stormed out, strode onto the set, did the scene, which was practically a seven-minute monologue, *in one take,* so brilliantly, that even the hard-boiled crew cheered and applauded.

The date was April 22, and during the shooting of the scene to which Backus referred, Jimmy slammed his fist into the police officer's desk with such force that he had to be rushed to a nearby hospital. Fortunately no bones were broken and shooting was not delayed. Nonetheless, for the next week Jimmy's hand was wrapped with an elastic bandage, and Ray had to shoot around it.

Dean was also injured during the shooting of the knife-fight sequence with Corey Allen. As was made much of at the time, real switchblades were used. Inadvertently Allen nicked Dean in the neck, and blood started to trickle beneath Jimmy's right ear. A first-aid man rushed over to Jimmy and applied a compress. Nick Ray called a break. It was not an isolated injury. According to Beverly Long, "[The scene] was a bitch to do. I remember it was very hot, really miserable and hot. It was so intricate. Jimmy had so many different shirts he had to take on and off. The shirt that would get blood on it, and then another shirt. It seemed like he was constantly changing shirts."

Essentially, during *Rebel* James Dean was given carte blanche by Nick Ray. Consequently Dean improvised huge stretches of film, and a lot of what he didn't improvise he rewrote. Nowhere was this more evident than in the film's unforgettable opening sequence, in which Jimmy rolled around on a residential street, fondling a stuffed monkey. Beverly Long recently recalled, "I remember it vividly because it was about four in the morning and it was freezing cold. We were up here on Hollywood Boulevard. We were sitting on the curb, and we all had blankets around us. And I'm sitting on the curb, not more than seven or eight feet away from Jimmy, watching him do the scene. And Ernie Haller, the cameraman, was lying on his stomach, camera on the ground. And Jimmy said to Nick, 'I have an idea. Let me try something.' And Nick said, 'Fine.' So, when Jimmy did that [with the monkey], all of it, he just shot it. It wasn't even rehearsed. And I remember sitting there and just being blown away. I remember thinking 'Oh, my God. I'm working with a genius. He's crazy, but he's really, really talented.' "

It was midway through the production of *Rebel* that Dean began to comprehend the impact of *East of Eden.* He was a movie star. On location in Griffith Park he was besieged by 25 teenage girls. For 20 minutes he sat on a trash can and signed autographs. As he told reporters, "Least I can do for their courtesy in asking for my name is to provide paper and pen." More meaningful to Dean was when he received, on the set on May 12, a seven-foot-long, six-foot-wide scroll signed by 3,000 residents of his hometown in Grant County, Indiana, congratulating him on his performance in *Eden*.

Off the set *Rebel* resembled something of a romantic merry-go-round. Prior to shooting, Natalie Wood was involved with Nick Ray. During filming she fell for James Dean. Meanwhile, Dennis Hopper was madly in love with Natalie, who was also receiving flowers on the set every day from 20th Century–Fox sound man Sonny Belcher. Steffi Sidney had a crush on Hopper, while Beverly Long dated both Corey Allen and Jack Grinnage. As for Dean, he seemed to spend most of his time with *Rebel* gang member Jack Simmons.

Still, despite the considerable amount of amorous action, boredom was prevalent, as it is on most Hollywood productions. Particularly dull was the lengthy shooting at Griffith Park. Often Jimmy took his co-stars for a spin around the planetarium parking lot in his new white Porsche Speedster. Sometimes, between shots, the cast members would play charades or improvise scenes. As for Dean, he fraternized with the crew and absorbed as much as he could. He also spent time reading a book titled *How to Build Character* as well as Edna Ferber's *Giant*, despite claims to the press that he preferred to concern himself with the script and not the source. Also with *Giant* in mind, he spent as much time as he could in the sun, much to Nick Ray's chagrin, to obtain the weather-beaten look of Jett Rink. Natalie Wood once attempted to join Jimmy in the sun but became faint from overexposure, which delayed shooting. Occasionally Dean also entertained the company with his impersonations. His repertoire included an impersonation of Elia Kazan directing Marlon Brando, one of Charlie Chaplin, and one of Brando in a scene from *On the Waterfront*.

Because several scenes had to be reshot in color, and because several scenes were shot excessively, *Rebel* was running perilously behind schedule. Money wasn't the factor as much as time. Dean was committed to start work on *Giant*, in Texas, at the beginning of June. To Warner Brothers, *Rebel* had become an important picture, but *Giant* was *the* picture, and Nick Ray and Dave Weisbart were constantly reminded of that fact. On May 23 *Giant* started shooting at the studio. On May 26 *Rebel Without a Cause* completed shooting at the studio.

After the death of James Dean, Warner Brothers went ahead with the scheduled release of *Rebel*. There was some concern that fans wouldn't turn out for a dead star, but nevertheless, in its marketing campaign the studio urged theater owners to "play up James Dean." Advertisements for the film proclaimed, "This kid has a chip on both shoulders! He's Jim Stark, teenager who thinks he has to be bad to make

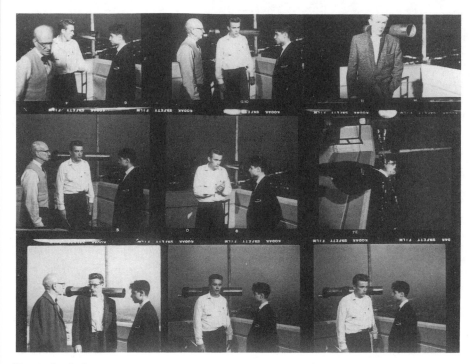

Framed rebel.

good!" And "This kid has a date you'll remember all the way down your spine!" And "J.D. James Dean! Juvenile Delinquent! Just Dynamite!" The film, obviously aimed at the youth market, was marketed like an exploitation picture and did unexpectedly enormous business. It premiered on October 26, 1955, at New York's Astor Theater. It was four weeks after Dean's death.

The impact of *Rebel*, upon its release and over the years, has been phenomenal. *East of Eden* is James Dean's best film, but *Rebel Without a Cause* is the film that he is most associated with and best remembered for. It's a good, though flawed, film. Particularly problematic is the superficial, simplified development of the film's gang. It is unfortunate that three sequences actually shot for the film were excised from its final print. All three involved the gang: a crucial opening sequence in which the gang members are introduced as they stomp on an innocent passerby, an establishing scene at the police station in which Jim Stark is first introduced to the gang, and a dance sequence in the Griffith Observatory in which the actors/gang members were allowed to develop their individual characters. These scenes would have been instrumental in providing character and depth to the gang and would have helped the film better address its theme of middle-class juvenile delinquency.

However, such scenes involving the gang took camera time away from James Dean, and by the time *Rebel* started shooting it had become primarily a vehicle for Dean, the biggest new sensation in Hollywood. Also disturbing about the film is its outlandishly cardboard caricatures of all four parental figures, particularly Jim Backus's apron-stringed father of Jim Stark. Further, it attempts to titillate its audience with suggestions of incest, homosexuality, and teenage sexuality, and yet it does nothing to address any of these issues. Nick Ray wanted realism; he got a softened, censored, recycled version of it.

Still, *Rebel* has considerable visual style and contains remarkable performances by both James Dean and Natalie Wood. Sal Mineo also won acclaim, and an Oscar nomination, upon the film's release, but in retrospect he is overawed and overwhelmed by Dean's presence throughout the film.

> In all honesty, I thought the film was going to be a good film, but I didn't think it was going to be a piece of history. And I don't think any of us did. Little did I know that *Rebel* would really be my niche in history, as well as a lot of these other people. To this day I don't think it's that great a film. I'm still bewildered that after 35 years kids who were born in 1955 or 1959 or 1960 can associate with it, identify with it.
>
> Steffi Sidney

> I just thought I was doing another "Blondie." Irascible father with long-suffering wife and crazy teenage kid. . . . I kept looking for the dog!
>
> Jim Backus, Academy of Motion Picture Arts
> and Sciences tribute, 1983

REBEL WITHOUT A CAUSE
A 1958 stage play adapted by James Fuller from the movie of the same name.

REBELS: THE REBEL HERO IN FILMS
Standard book by Joe Morella and Edward Epstein, published by Citadel Press in 1971, that includes a chapter on James Dean entitled "Dean: The Ultimate Rebel." The text is a rehash of old material.

REBELS UNITED: THE ENDURING REALITY OF JAMES DEAN
Author: Joel Brean
Publisher: Brean-Jones Publishing
Year: 1984

Rebels United is many things, but it is *not* a rehash of old material. It is, perhaps, the strangest book ever published about James Dean. The basic premise has Jimmy making half a dozen afterlife visits (materializations) to earthling author Joel Brean, commencing in 1976 and ending in 1982. Their discussions, or "conversation transcripts" as they are referred to by Brean, are the basis for the book. Dean, through Brean, espouses his beliefs on the nuclear arms race, karma, philosophy, the Kent State tragedy, and more.

In one of the book's most bizarre passages Brean quotes Dean as saying "Universal selves, take off all of your clothes. . . . If you have followed my directions, you, your universal self, are totally naked. I am totally naked. . . . We press our universal selves into each other, deeper than the skin, muscles merging with muscles, bones blending with bones. We feel our hearts united, beating in unison. . . Your lips are united with my lips. Your eyes, nose, ears and face are united with my eyes, nose, ears and face. Your tongue and my tongue are united. Your brain and my brain are one. . . ."

It's that kind of a book. Readers, of course, will have to decide for themselves how much of this is universal fact and how much is one man's fantasy. Many will be offended; some will be amused; some will be amazed that this paperback book ever got published in the first place—until they realize that it was self-published.

THE RECORDS: A DEAN DISCOGRAPHY
The Albums by Dean
☆ *James Dean on the Air*
  Label: Sandy Hook Records
  Broadcasts of two of James Dean's television dramas, "The Unlighted Road" and "I'm a Fool"

The Movie and Television Soundtrack Albums
☆ *Giant*
  Artist: Dimitri Tiomkin
  Label: Capitol Records
  Music from *Giant*
☆ *James Dean: Soundtrack Excerpts, Dialogue and Music from James Dean's Three Greatest Performances*
  Label: Warner Brothers Records
  Original soundtrack excerpts, dialogue, and music from *East of Eden*, *Rebel Without a Cause*, and *Giant*
☆ *The James Dean Story*
  Artist: Leith Stevens
  Label: Capitol Records
  Music from *The James Dean Story*
☆ *September 30, 1955*
  Artist: Leonard Rosenman
  Label: MCA Records
  Music from *September 30, 1955*

The Tribute Albums
☆ *James Dean: He Never Said Goodbye*
  Artist: Rod Wimmer
  Label: Caprice Records

Songs include "He Never Said Goodbye," "Go Back with Me," "The Gift," "Momma's Hope, Momma's Dream," "Love I Believed Your Lie," "Because of My Dreams," "That Tree upon the Hill," "Where I'll Never Say Goodbye to You," "I'd Like to Be Alone with You," "I'm Just the Singer of This Song"

☆ *The James Dean Story*
Artist: Narrated by Steve Allen and Bill Randle with vocals by Dick Jacobs, Jimmy Wakely, and George Cates
Label: Coral Records
Music and dialogue from *East of Eden* and *Rebel Without a Cause* and songs including "Jimmy, Jimmy," "His Name Was Dean," "We'll Never Forget You," "James Dean (Just a Boy from Indiana)," "There's Never Been Anyone Else But You," "The Ballad of James Dean"

☆ *Music James Dean Lived By*
Artist: Joe Leahy's Orchestra and Chorus with vocals by Jack Carroll and Bob Graybo
Label: Unique Records
Songs include "The Story of James Dean," "*East of Eden* theme," "I'll Close My Eyes," "Misunderstood," "Give Me a Moment Please," "Dream Lover," "*Giant* theme," "There's Never Been Anyone Else But You," "*Rebel Without a Cause* theme," "Masquerade," "Love Story," "We Could Make Such Beautiful Music Together"

☆ *Theme Music from the James Dean Story*
Artist: Chet Baker and Bud Shank
Label: World Pacific Records
Jazz version of music from the 1957 motion picture *The James Dean Story*

☆ *A Tribute to James Dean*
Artist: Ray Heindorf and the Warner Brothers Orchestra
Label: Columbia Records
Music from *East of Eden*, *Rebel Without a Cause*, and *Giant*

☆ *A Tribute to James Dean*
Artist: Art Mooney
Label: MGM Records
Music from *East of Eden* and *Rebel Without a Cause*

☆ *A Tribute to James Dean*
Artist: Leonard Rosenman
Label: Imperial Records
Music from *East of Eden*, *Rebel Without a Cause*, and *Giant*

RECREATION
See HOBBIES, SPORTS.

RED RIVER DAVE
Singer who recorded several songs about Dean, including "James Dean," "James Dean, Deck of Cards," "Jimmy Dean Is Not Dead," "Hymn for James Dean," and "Home in Indiana, James Dean."

REDBOOK MAGAZINE
Redbook published a September 1956 article, "James Dean," by Joe Hyams.

LYDIA REED
Actress who starred in "The Little Woman," a 1954 episode of the CBS television series "Danger" that co-starred James Dean.

Reed later co-starred as Aunt Hassie in the popular television series "The Real McCoys" (1957–1963). Her Broadway stage credits include *The Number* (1951) and *Mrs. McThing* (1952).

RALPH REED
Actor who beat out James Dean for the role of Clarence Day, Jr., in the 1953 television series "Life with Father."

BOB AND CHERRY REES
Bob and Cherry Rees, husband and wife, are Texas-based Dean collectors and members of the We Remember Dean International fan club. The couple's collection includes videos, posters, photos, and a chunk of plaster and a fence post from the Reata set of *Giant*. Says Bob, "I don't think that there has been an actor before or since then who has so personified the struggle of youth in establishing an identity and maturity in life." He also stated, "We are fans, but we aren't fanatical." The Reeses also collect material on Judy Garland and Marilyn Monroe and are particularly fascinated by anything to do with the 1950s.

GEORGE REEVES
Actor who was considered for the part of Ray Framek, the sympathetic police officer in *Rebel Without a Cause*. The role eventually went to Edward Platt.

THE REHEARSAL CLUB
In the early 1950s the Rehearsal Club was a hotel for struggling female artists, not unlike the Studio Club in Hollywood. One of its frequent visitors was James Dean, who used to date one of the hotel's residents, Dizzy Sheridan. The Rehearsal Club, no longer in existence, was located at 47 West 53rd Street.

RELIGION
James Dean was brought up in a Quaker family (as were most residents of Fairmount, Indiana), although his mother, Mildred, was a Methodist. Quakers, known as "The Religious Society of Friends," are known for their virtues of family, simplicity of life, nonviolence, and justice.

Reportedly, at the height of his romance with Pier Angeli, Dean considered converting to the Catholic religion to appease Angeli's mother. He even wore a medal of St. Christopher, presented to him by Pier, affixed to his belt.

RESEDA, CALIFORNIA
Circa 1950–1951 Winton and Ethel Dean lived at 7235 Yolanda Avenue in Reseda, California. James Dean was a visitor, albeit an infrequent one, at their home.

RESTAURANTS
James Dean's favorite restaurants in Hollywood were Googie's and the Villa

Capri; his favorite restaurant in New York was Jerry's Bar and Restaurant. He was also spotted, on occasion, at the following:

☆ Barney's Beanery, West Hollywood
☆ Beachcomber Cafe, Hollywood
☆ Brown Derby, Los Feliz
☆ Ciro's, Hollywood
☆ Cromwell's, New York City
☆ Frascati's, Los Angeles
☆ The Garden of Allah, Hollywood
☆ Hamburger Hamlet, West Hollywood
☆ Huff's, Hollywood
☆ La Rue, Los Angeles
☆ Lewis' Retreat, Fairmount
☆ Louie's Tavern, New York City

☆ The Luau, Los Angeles
☆ Margaritas, New York City
☆ Minetta Tavern, New York City
☆ The Mocambo, West Hollywood
☆ Patsey's Pizza, West Hollywood
☆ Riker's Coffee Shop, New York City
☆ Romanoff's, Beverly Hills
☆ Sardi's, New York City
☆ Schwab's, West Hollywood
☆ Tam O'Shanter, Los Angeles
☆ Villa Nova, West Hollywood

LANCE REVENTLOW

In 1955 Lance Reventlow, son of Woolworth heiress Barbara Hutton, was a 21-year-old car-racing enthusiast. On the late afternoon of September 30 Reventlow was en route to Salinas, California, where he was registered to compete in a race. At about 5:00 P.M. Reventlow pulled his Mercedes into the parking lot at Blackwell's Corner, a gas station/grocery store. While there, he stopped and talked to another Salinas-bound speedster, James Dean. Reportedly the two men made plans to have dinner that evening in Paso Robles.

In 1972 Lance Reventlow was killed in an airplane crash.

THE REVIEWS
Macbeth

> Malcolm [played by sophomore James Dean] failed to show any growth, and would have made a hollow king.
>
> *Spotlight*, UCLA, December 1950

"Hill Number One"

HILL NUMBER ONE (FAMILY THEATRE)

As with two previous religious subjects filmed by Father Patrick Peyton for television, the biblical story of the first Easter was shown on every station in the U.S. and will be repeated for many years to come. As a pictorial record of the Resurrection, it is a moving spectacle with strong appeal for old and young alike. Performed by seasoned actors and of high technical quality, "Hill Number One," to be accorded its rightful place in Hollywood TV production, need admit of no superior.

. . . Players both in the war and biblical sequences gave inspired performances and the direction of Arthur Pierson was imaginative and compelling.

Such an ambitious undertaking by Father Peyton is worthy of viewing beyond the confines of TV set owners. It can stand its own ground on theatre screens and in years to come will be an Easter special in picture houses around the world. Father Peyton and Jerry Fairbanks again have proved that film is mightier than books or Bibles in penetrating the consciousness of Christian people.

Daily Variety, March 26, 1951

☆ ☆ ☆

See the Jaguar
ARTHUR KENNEDY HEADS THE CAST IN RICHARD NASH'S SYMBOLIC WESTERN DRAMA, 'SEE THE JAGUAR'
By Brooks Atkinson

Since every one concerned with the production has worked very hard, one should no doubt be full of respect for the effort. . . . Michael Gordon has directed it as though he were preparing the company for battle. And the actors run, jump and shout until the audience is exhausted.

But work is not admirable unless something is accomplished. And in the opinion of one theatregoer, "See the Jaguar" accomplishes nothing but noise and confusion. . . . When the final curtain came down, this theatregoer felt especially grateful to the makers of a movie Western that is eloquent without losing its simplicity. "High Noon," terse in style, makes a clear and devastating statement. "See the Jaguar" is verbose and says nothing.

New York Times, December 4, 1952

PLAY IS BAFFLING AND CONFUSING
By John McClain

The surging emotions of a segment of Southern American hill folk were given a pretentious and bewildering going-over in something called "See the Jaguar," which opened at the Cort Theatre last night.

Arthur Kennedy and a group of capable actors took part in the strident hoe-down but when the dust had lifted from the floor it was difficult to determine what, if anything, had been happening.

. . . The gimmick employed to create [the] crisis is a strange young man, James Dean, who has been locked in an ice house for about 20 years. The gentle people want to protect him, the mob wants to grab him and get the money his mother is supposed to have left him.

. . . Forgetting the befuddling details, there are excellent performances by Arthur Kennedy, Cameron Prud'homme, Roy Fant, Phillip Pine and several others in the large cast. I never believed that Constance Ford was part of this squalid group, but that was not particularly the fault of her acting.

. . . But if you want to see "See the Jaguar"—you had better hurry.

New York Journal American, December 4, 1952

'SEE THE JAGUAR'
By Walter F. Kerr

In "SEE THE JAGUAR," which opened at the Cort Wednesday, author N. Richard Nash has come within inches of working a theatrical miracle. He has taken one of the most venerable and most stereotyped formulas of our time . . . and very nearly made it all seem fresh, vivid and believable.

. . . James Dean adds an extraordinary performance in an almost impossible role: that of a bewildered lad who has been completely shut off from a vicious world by an overzealous mother and who is coming upon both the beauty and the brutality of the mountain for the first time.

It is the author's bad luck—and ours, too—that so much that is striking finally goes down the drain of an over-insistent symbolism. . . . Michael Gordon's wonderfully vigorous stage direction continues to pound away at us; the actors drive on with almost compulsive conviction, but the story we have been following has descended to obvious mechanics. . . . What started out as a surprisingly convincing evening ends as a disappointingly contrived one.

New York Herald Tribune, December 4, 1952

'JAGUAR' HAS OBSCURE SPOTS
By William Hawkins

"See the Jaguar" is a play of poetic quality that takes place in a world of barbaric viciousness. Its strange story is symbolic and striking, but it suffers from the tragic inconvenience of being very obscure.

. . . Arthur Kennedy dominates the work as the school teacher, making him vivid and masculine and desperate.

. . . Constance Ford, as his beloved, is an extremely talented young actress, who is never at a loss with a character whose opinions and devotions are mercurial. She gives every separate scene a substantial value, and it is a pity that there is not a more logical progress to her story.

Roy Fant is humorous and sympathetic as a cheery old man who loses his life in the big hunt, and Margaret Barker is wistful and dignified as the unbalanced mother. Cameron Prud'homme is the ruthless bullying father, and Philip Pine is forceful as his younger counterpart. James Dean is gently awkward as the ignorant boy.

New York World-Telegram and Sun, December 4, 1952

"SEE THE JAGUAR" OPENS AT THE CORT
By Lee Mortimer

I have no idea who N. Richard Nash is, nor do I care, but I am sure he must be a young man who is lovingly spoken of by his doting relatives as "a genius." Furthermore, he is a man with a message, though I think Western Union could have delivered it better.

. . . You can tell when actors are really great, when they sell themselves despite lines that would gag a Y.M.C.A. social director playing the unsullied hero in the annual theatrical and strawberry festival. Arthur Kennedy takes plenty of abuse from Nash but comes out a winner, and Miss Ford is altogether too pretty and talented to be made to look so silly. No show is complete without a character actor who thefts the show. This has two, namely Roy Fant as Grandpa Ricks and James Dean who impersonates a weird young man locked up in an ice house since childhood by a weird old mother who wants to isolate him from the wicked world.

New York Daily Mirror, December 4, 1952

'SEE THE JAGUAR' LOVELY TO SEE AND HEAR, BUT IT MAKES NO SENSE
By John Chapman

So much of the best theatre has gone into "See the Jaguar," which Lemuel Ayers and Helen Jacobson presented last evening at the Cort Theatre, that it is a pity that one small ingredient was left out. The ingredient I mention is a play, and a play is no more than a believable story. If "See the Jaguar" had a reasonably credible story, it would be the best new piece on Broadway—but it hasn't, so it isn't.
. . . Arthur Kennedy is a rugged fellow as the teacher, Cameron Prud'homme is a mean old man as the storekeeper, and Constance Ford is an attractive expectant parent of an already half-orphaned child. There is also a nice character part played by Roy Fant, who is a harmless old coot engaged in the business of tattooing mountaineers. Before last night I never heard of a mountaineer getting tattooed, but Fant makes a good job of it. As the boy, James Dean is very good. With all those good actors . . . it's a pity everybody didn't come out with a play. Because we need a play, badly.

New York Daily News, December 4, 1952

DEATH AND IDEAS IN THE MOUNTAINS
By Richard Watts Jr.

If N. Richard Nash, author of "See the Jaguar," which opened at the Cort Theater last night, will forgive me for describing his new play in the words of another dramatist, I would say that it is full of sound and fury, signifying nothing.
. . . According to the playwright, there is in this mountain community a great bully of a man who has bad dreams and a pretty daughter and keeps wild animals in cages. There is also a young schoolmaster, who loves the daughter and is scorned by the father, and he tries to save from the old man's sadistic wrath a youthful innocent who had been locked up in his mother's ice house. Through a moment of moral weakness on the part of the teacher, the boy is captured and imprisoned in a cage meant for a jaguar, and the idealistic pedagogue is killed trying to rescue him. . . . Whatever he is saying, he is not skillful about it, however fine his motives.
It assuredly isn't the fault of the actors. . . . James Dean achieves the feat of making the childish young fugitive believable and unembarrassing.

New York Post, December 4, 1952

☆ ☆ ☆

"Something for an Empty Briefcase"

There's little wrong with the new Friday night NBC-TV "Campbell Sound Stage" series that a good, believable script can't cure. . . . This one by S. Lee Pogostin, with Susan Douglas and James Dean in the leads, was out of the Dead End Kids school of literature and concerned a kid just finished with a four-month rap as a first offender deciding on one last petty larceny job to get enough bucks to buy a briefcase. To him that's the symbol of respectability and going straight, even though an empty briefcase.

. . . With such unbelievable story content and a casting choice for the male lead that was confusing it would have taken more than an elaborate street setting and the other scene switches to bring forth a telling production. Neither the dialog nor the thinking was the end result of a 22-year-older who had previously made no attempt to leave the life of petty gangdom. His mugging and repetitive hard gesturing were on the ludicrous side, if their intent was to show the sensitivity and groping of the suddenly awakened thief.

Variety, July 22, 1953

"Death Is My Neighbor"

CBS-TV exec producer William Dozier brought in two top stars, Sir Cedric Hardwicke and Walter Hampden, for his Tuesday night crime block, "Suspense" and "Danger," last week, but a comparative newcomer, James Dean, stole the spotlight from both of them. Dean, cast with Hampden on "Danger" in the role of a psychotic young janitor, delivered a magnetic performance that brought a routine meller alive.

. . . Dean's performance was in many ways reminiscent of Marlon Brando's in "Streetcar," but he gave his role the individuality and nuances of its own which it required. He's got quite a future ahead of him. Hampden's part called for less in the way of histrionics, but gave him an opportunity to emit that quality of gentleness that's become a trademark with him in past years. Miss Palmer was good, as were minor characters. John Peyser's direction permitted no lapses, and Franklin Heller gave the show its usual good production values.

Variety, September 2, 1953

"Glory in Flower"

"Omnibus" was back on the air Sunday for its second year, with one of its better shows for the premiere. It made for a highclass, varied hour-and-half of entertainment, with just an occasional bit of pretentiousness or archness creeping in.

. . . Session's most ambitious offering, the preem of a William Inge play written for TV, "Glory in Flower," didn't come off completely despite some excellent performances. A good mood piece in the main about a sensitive small-town piano teacher's longtime crush on a miner's son who went off to become a prizefighter but remained a boor, show was a little too disjointed and confused, as well as too editorial and preachy. But Jessica Tandy gave a poignant portrayal of the teacher, and got good support from Ed Binns, as the pug; Hume Cronyn, as a barkeep, and Frank McHugh, as a traveling salesman.

Variety, October 7, 1953

☆ ✪ ☆

The Immoralist

'THE IMMORALIST,' BY RUTH AND AUGUSTUS GOETZ, MADE FROM ANDRE GIDE'S NOVEL
By Brooks Atkinson

Having made "The Heiress" from a Henry James novel, Ruth and Augustus Goetz have now dramatized André Gide's "The Immoralist," which was acted at the Royale last evening.

. . . Under Daniel Mann's direction, the performance is extraordinarily honest and skillful. In the part of the distraught wife Miss Page fulfills the hopes that theatregoers have had for her since she appeared in "Summer and Smoke" downtown. She gives a deeply felt portrait of a broken heart and a wounded spirit.

. . . Mr. Jourdan's husband is evenly matched. . . . [His] interpretation of the part helps to give the play stature and sincerity. The other parts are well played, too—Charles Dingle as the compassionate, redoubtable manager of the estate; David J. Stewart as an educated native of the African village; John Heldabrand as a scornful French physician; Paul Huber as a provincial army doctor; Adelaide Klein and James Dean as African villagers.

Mr. Mann's direction does seem to be too deliberately paced in the last act, and perhaps the tempo is too uniform all the way through. But he has gotten under the surface of the play by recognizing the spiritual torment of the characters. "The Immoralist" is an admirable piece of work. The tragedy is austere, crushing and genuine.

New York Times, February 9, 1954

By Brooks Atkinson

"The Immoralist" comes as close to Greek tragedy as you are likely to get in a modern drama. It is detached, impersonal, grim, pitiless. . . . Written less scrupulously, the story of "The Immoralist" might have turned out to be morbid or rancid. But Mr. and Mrs. Goetz have avoided the cheap approaches to a repellent theme. They have written sparingly. They are objective and unemotional. The play is cold and reticent.

. . . Under Daniel Mann's direction, "The Immoralist" is extremely well acted.

. . . As Marcelline, Miss Page gives a poignant performance of great insight and resourcefulness. . . . It is a superb piece of acting in the precise tone of the play.

As Michel, Louis Jourdan gives an attractive performance. . . . In the part of a paternal bailiff, Charles Dingle gives another one of his forceful and lucid performances. . . . Note the silent probity of Adelaide Klein, playing the part of a native housekeeper who despises the languid vices. Note the self-respect and intellectual agility of David J. Stewart as one of the damned; and the insidious charm of James Dean as an idle native houseboy.

New York Times, February 14, 1954

'THE IMMORALIST'
By Walter F. Kerr

In adapting Andre Gide's "The Immoralist" for the stage, Ruth and Augustus Goetz have brought a quiet, patient candor to the subject of homosexuality. But a quiet, patient candor is not precisely an exhilarating theatrical vein.

. . . The evening finds its strongest images in Geraldine Page's second-act torment. The actress is something of a technical virtuoso, able to make a sinking inflection, or a defeated gesture, shimmer with meaning. She has also, at this writing, mastered her earlier tendency to splatter her effects too generously over the stage. For nearly all of "The Immoralist" she is giving a reserved, economical, beautifully shaded performance.

Louis Jourdan handles the difficult central role with great simplicity. He is plausible and persuasive at every turn—direct, open-eyed, effortless. Charles Dingle is briefly ingratiating as a warm-hearted family retainer, James Dean makes a colorfully insinuating scapegrace.

New York Herald Tribune, February 9, 1954

A GRAVE DRAMA ABOUT ABNORMALITY
By Richard Watts Jr.

Let it be said for "The Immoralist" that it is a serious attempt to treat a difficult dramatic subject with dignity, and that it doesn't try for easy sensationalism. It is also well acted. But after these compliments have been paid the play by Ruth and Augustus Goetz, which had its official opening at the Royale Theater last night, I'm afraid there is little I can add on behalf of their dramatization of Andre Gide's at least semi-autobiographical novel about the complex marital problem of a homosexual archeologist at the turn of the century.

. . . The difficult role of the archeologist is played with admirable tact and sympathy by Louis Jordan, and Geraldine Page, with her woebegone voice, is believable and touching as the unhappy wife. David J. Stewart is quietly effective as the philosophical homosexual, and James Dean is realistically unpleasant as the slimy one. . . . "The Immoralist" seemed to me pretty dull theatergoing.

New York Post, February 9, 1954

FAILS TO STIR SERIOUS EMOTIONAL REACTION
By John McClain

Taking a highly charitable view of "The Immoralist," which was revealed to the critics last night at the Royale after a week of paid previews, one is obliged to report that it is a strangely unfulfilling effort.

The elements of good drama are there, the quality of Andre Gide's novel appears to have been faithfully translated to the stage yet it somehow fails to inspire any serious emotional reaction.

Why? I should say the fault lies half with the original conception of M. Gide's, half with the current conception of M. Billy Rose, who produced.

The situation involved is that of a congenital homosexual who marries and then discovers that he is hopelessly incapable of leading a normal marital life.

. . . This is certainly a provocative consideration of an ageless dilemma, but at the Royale it is given merely a surface reading. . . .

The writing seems to skirt the fringes of the issue, rather than facing up to facts that have become fairly pedestrian in our present world.

. . . Bill Rose will beat the drum for this one and may get away with it. But in my considered opinion it is fare, only fair, for a small and specialized audience.

New York Journal American, February 9, 1954

'IMMORALIST' TREATS HARD SUBJECT WITH SYMPATHY
By Robert Coleman

Daniel Mann has directed "The Immoralist" at a deliberate pace, deliberately avoiding a showy display of the sensational. Louis Jourdan acts the young scientist with a sincerity and honesty that compel respect. Geraldine Page, as the disillusioned wife, is quite touching.

Charles Dingle is good as a humane friend and retainer. James Dean and David J. Stewart, two excellent actors, are rightly realistic—the one as a venal panderer and the other as a tragic figure who accepts his fate with courage and no false pretenses.

. . . Frankly, "The Immoralist" is not much of a play. It is too reticent in its statements, too subdued in mood to be theatrically absorbing. Its appeal is likely to be limited—limited to those interested in sociology. The emotion is implied in the script, though seldom realized on stage. It is like sitting on a dynamite charge that never explodes.

New York Daily Mirror, February 9, 1954

'THE IMMORALIST' SURE ENOUGH IS
By John Chapman

"The Immoralist," which was presented before reviewers last evening at the Royale Theatre, is a clinical drama about a sex deviate who manages one husbandly gesture. As a result the mixed-up gent and his generally frustrated frau decide that they had better go on living together in the hope that their child will turn out normal. I suppose another title for the piece could be "From Here to Maternity."

. . . The principal roles are played by Louis Jourdan and Geraldine Page. They are good actors. I was embarrassed for them last evening. And for me, too.

New York Daily News, February 9, 1954

'IMMORALIST' MARKED BY TENDER TRAGEDY
By William Hawkins

"The Immoralist," playing at the Royale Theater, is a delicate, tender tragedy which is beautifully acted and exquisitely directed.

In spite of all this, it may well leave you cold. It simply is not moving, not even touching, owing to the fact that the leading characters have so little life outside the immediate snare of their personal tragedy.

. . . "The Immoralist" is beautifully produced.

Louis Jourdan is fine as the husband, playing with an inner languor and great pace that make the man believable.

Geraldine Page shows great new assurance as the wife. She plays the rising tragedy and the drunken climax with discipline and fine selectiveness.

Charles Dingle is a warm and reassuring family retainer, and David J. Stewart underplays the shepherd most effectively. It is James Dean as the houseboy who clearly and originally underlines the sleazy impertinence and the amoral opportunism which the husband must combat.

New York World-Telegram and Sun, February 9, 1954

THE IMMORALIST

The plight of the homosexual in contemporary society, which in the theatre seldom rises above the level of a burlesque emporium . . . provides the sturdy substance of this adaptation of André Gide's autobiographical novel. The Ruth and Augustus Goetz work is an honest, forthright, almost clinically introspective study of the difficulties of a young French archaeologist (Louis Jourdan) and his wife (Geraldine Page), whose attempt to escape the consequences of his nature proves utterly frustrating.

. . . A middle way is the course scrupulously hewn by the Goetzes and director Daniel Mann—one which borders on the reportorial and suggests an austere air of detachment. But there is drama enough in their story, and it is played for precisely all it is worth, and no more, by the skilled leading actors. In his Broadway debut, Jourdan uses understatement to register the dilemma of the archaeologist. The nature of the script makes it inevitable that he is overshadowed by Miss Page, who gives a beautifully controlled, virtuoso performance. The supporting parts are all well cast—Charles Dingle and Dean are especially good.

Theatre Arts, April 1954

"The Little Woman"

Andrew McCullough apparently intends to stress characterization and mood rather than ultra-violence on the CBS-TV "Danger" series if last Tuesday's is any criterion.

. . . Last week's play was "The Little Woman," by Joe Scully, with title role taken by moppet Lydia Reed, a young charmer if ever there was one. Lydia has built herself a dream world in a slum alley—a habitat with all the props and knickknacks—and her best friends are Lee Bergere, the cop on the beat, and James Dean, who gets himself involved as transmission belt for a couple of yeggs intent on snatching plates used for counterfeiting.

It wasn't much of a yarn but the thesping was good, particularly that of Lydia. . . . A neat first try for McCullough in bringing "Danger" out of the rut.

Variety, April 7, 1954

"Run Like a Thief"

An offbeat theme provided a touch of the unusual on the Philco TV Playhouse over NBC-TV Sunday but unfortunately lacked the strength to bring its characters to life and it didn't provide them with sufficient motivation to make the story ring true.

This was the first Playhouse under the Gordon Duff production banner and it offered proof that prior high standards of the program would be preserved. Sunday's show, "Run Like a Thief," had much of the quality that makes for good TV; it had good performances and created a good deal of suspense.

. . . Kurt Kasznar played the waiter with warmth and intelligence. Gusti Huber registered as the wife, giving a performance that seemed to almost put more into the part than there was to it. . . . James Dean as the boy, Kasznar's protege, emerged as a rather unclear figure even though his thesping was beyond reproach. He was the man the script forgot to explain, and the void made a difference.

. . . Jeffrey Hayden directed with a fine sense for movement even though in spots the show definitely lagged.

Variety, September 8, 1954

☆ ☆ ☆

"I'm a Fool"

I'M A FOOL (GENERAL ELECTRIC THEATRE)

There must have been universal appeal in the General Electric Theatre's showcasing last night of Sherwood Anderson's classic short story of a foolish, youthful lie. Over the years, the story's greatest appeal has been that it struck home, touching the general human failing of wanting to impress people—particularly the girl. . . . The sets and process work (which didn't always work properly) had a tendency to weaken the sincerity of Don Medford's direction and some excellent thespic work, particularly by James Dean.

. . . Eddie Albert narrated the story in the role of the protagonist, aged and wiser, recounting an adventure that befell him in his youth. It was a fine job of handling the chore and it was matched by a sensitive and moving performance by Dean as the boy. Natalie Wood impressed as the girl and there was good support from Roy Glenn as Burt, a trainer who befriends the boy.

Daily Variety, November 11, 1954

☆ ☆ ☆

"The Dark, Dark Hour"

THE DARK, DARK HOUR (G. E. THEATRE)

Ronald Reagan, host of General Electric Theatre, elects to take on the added duty of star in this latest entry, but the choice of subject isn't a happy one. Not much interest or sympathy accrues to any of the characters, and as plotted in Arthur Steuer's teleplay the unfoldment lacks dramatic highlights that might have been reached.

. . . Reagan's part is negatively enacted and Constance Ford as his wife is called upon for illogical action as she fails to understand why her husband, though covered by a gun, doesn't immediately attack the delinquent. This role is played by James Dean, but he has been called upon to overact. Jack Simmons is the pal who dies on the operating table.

Don Medford's direction is hindered by script weakness, but he keeps his characters moving through employment of a fluid camera.

Daily Variety, December 14, 1954

☆ ☆ ☆

East of Eden

The picture is a brilliant entertainment and more than that, it announces a new star, James Dean, whose prospects look as bright as any young actor's since Marlon Brando. . . . Dean, a young man from Indiana, is unquestionably the biggest news Hollywood has made in 1955. Dean, like Julie Harris, Marlon Brando, Eva Marie Saint, and most of the people Kazan uses, is a product of the Actors Studio, something known as "the tilted-pelvis" school of naturalistic acting. Like so many Studio students who have been brought up on "The Stanislavsky Method," Dean tries so hard to find the part in himself that he often forgets to put himself into the part. But no matter what he is doing, he has the presence of a young lion and the same sense of danger about him. His eye is as empty as an animal's, and he lolls and gallops with the innocence and grace of an animal. Then, occasionally, he flicks a sly little look that seems to say: "Well, all this is human, too—or had you forgotten?"

Time, March 1955

East of Eden is a somber mood piece that may break no box-office records. But it will be received gratefully by anyone with more than an escapist interest in the screen.

Newsweek, March 1955

[James Dean is] destined for a blazing career.

Frank Quinn, *New York Daily Mirror*, March 1955

[James Dean is] a young actor aping Mr. Brando.

Whitney Bolton, *New York World-Telegram and Sun*, March 1955

[James Dean is] a new star.

Kate Cameron, *New York Daily News*, March 1955

KAZAN PRODUCTION LOADED WITH ASSETS
By Jack Meffitt

There can be no doubt as to the artistic merits of this picture. Beautifully acted, and superbly directed by Elia Kazan, it is bound to be one of the year's important contributions to screen literature. . . . The boxoffice asset that is most important is the debut, in the leading role, of a handsome and dynamic young actor named James Dean. This is the boy who is apt to captivate the typical movie fans. . . . He is that rare thing, a young actor who is a great actor and the troubled eloquence with which he puts over the problems of misunderstood youth may lead to his being accepted by young audiences as a sort of symbol of their generation. He's the only player I've ever seen who'd be completely right for Romeo. It is inevitable that he will be compared to Marlon Brando, though he is no carbon copy of that capable player. He has a completely individual screen personality. If this film is to reap the profits it deserves, no time should be lost in giving him a big fan magazine buildup.

The Hollywood Reporter, February 16, 1955

EAST OF EDEN

Powerfully somber dramatics from the pages of John Steinbeck's "East of Eden" have been captured and put on film by Elia Kazan in this class screen treatment. It is a tour de force for the director's penchant for hard-hitting forays with life, and as such undoubtedly will be counted among his best screen efforts.

. . . Much pro and con probably will develop about James Dean, unknown to whom Kazan gives a fullscale introduction. It is no credit to Kazan that Dean plays his lead character as though he were straight out of a Marlon Brando mold. Just how flexible his talent is will have to be judged on future screen roles, although he has a basic appeal that manages to get through to the viewers despite the carboning another's acting style.

. . . Miss Harris gives her particular style to an effective portrayal of the girl torn between the love offered by the good brother and the sex attraction of the neurotic. Davalos wins sympathy with an excellent performance for his film debut. Massey is fine as the religious father who finds it difficult to understand the need his neurotic son has for affection.

Daily Variety, February 16, 1955

By Bosley Crowther

Only a small part of John Steinbeck's "East of Eden" has been used in the motion picture version of it that Elia Kazan has done, and it is questionable whether that part contains the best of the book.

. . . In one respect, it is brilliant. The use that Mr. Kazan has made of CinemaScope and color in capturing expanse and mood in his California settings is almost beyond compare.

. . . [James Dean] who is here doing his first big screen stint, is a mass of histrionic gingerbread.

He scuffs his feet, he whirls, he pouts, he sputters, he leans against walls, he rolls his eyes, he swallows his words, he ambles slack-kneed—all like Marlon Brando used to do. Never have we seen a performer so clearly follow another's style. Mr. Kazan should be spanked for permitting him to do such a sophomoric thing. Whatever there might be of reasonable torment in this youngster is buried beneath the clumsy display.

. . . In short, there is energy and intensity but little clarity and emotion in this film. It is like a great, green iceberg: mammoth and imposing but very cold.

New York Times, March 10, 1955

☆ ☆ ☆

"The Unlighted Road"
THE UNLIGHTED ROAD (SCHLITZ PLAYHOUSE OF STARS)

Warner pactee James Dean hit the "Road" before swinging to
stardom in WB's "East of Eden," and the result was an exploitation
boon to Meridian producer Bill Self. This, Dean's first vidfilm,
occasioned a good deal of interest.

Walter C. Brown's original yarn and teleplay deals with an ex-GI
(Dean) who wanders into a roadside diner one night, gets a job, and
finds himself inadvertently involved in a hijacking racket. He's
framed on a murder rap, but eventually his innocence is proved.

Dean projects an interesting, offbeat personality, but underplays so
much his performance loses some of its effectiveness.

Murvyn Vye, Edgar Stehli, Pat Hardy and Charles Wagenheim are
good in support, and Jus Addiss' direction is ditto. Brown's teleplay
has suspense.

Daily Variety, May 10, 1955

☆ ☆ ☆

Rebel Without a Cause

The late James Dean reveals completely the talent latent in his *East
of Eden* performance. As a new and unwilling member of the gang,
a boy who recognized more clearly than any of the others his need
for help, he projects the wildness, the torment and the crude
tenderness of a restless generation. Gone are the Brando mannerisms,
gone too the obvious Kazan touch. He stands as a remarkable talent;
and he was cut down, it would seem, by the very passions he exposes
so tellingly in this strange and forceful picture.

Arthur Knight, *Saturday Review*, October 1955

The performance of the star, James Dean, will excite discussion,
especially in connection with the irony of his own recent crash. . . .
In *East of Eden* under Elia Kazan's direction, the twenty-four-year-
old actor was wildly thought to be doing a Marlon Brando. But freed
from Kazan's evaluations of character this resemblance vanishes.
Almost free of mannerisms under Ray's pacing, Dean is very effective
as a boy groping for adjustment to people. As a farewell performance
he leaves behind, with this film, genuine artistic regret, for here was
a talent which might have touched the heights.

Variety, October 1955

The movie is written and acted so ineptly, directed so sluggishly, that
all names but one will be omitted here. The exception is Dean, the
gifted young actor who was killed last month. His rare talent and
appealing personality even shine through this turgid melodrama.

William Zinsser, *New York Herald Tribune*, October 1955

Again one is impressed by the effect of powerful emotion so
harnessed and controlled that if it were not carefully rationed it
would explode.

Milton Schulman, *Sunday Express*

As a starring vehicle for Dean, *Rebel Without a Cause* is satisfactory, giving the late, lamented young actor a role similar to the one he had in his first picture, *East of Eden*. And with complete control of the character, he gives a fine, sensitive performance of an unhappy, lonely teenager, tormented by the knowledge of his emotional instability. [But] as an honest, purposeful drama of juvenile hardness and violence, the film just doesn't measure up.

Wanda Hale, *New York Daily News*, October 1955

'REBEL WITHOUT A CAUSE' REAL MONEY ATTRACTION

The exhibitor can expect this story of juvenile delinquency to capture the "Blackboard Jungle" type of audience and be a real money picture. It contains some extraordinarily good acting by the late James Dean, Natalie Wood and Sal Mineo (who is coming up fast and reveals to be a real trouper in this one). The direction by Nicholas Ray is outstanding. Ray stages police station scenes with true realism and he catches the mood of the sub-world of teen-age savagery in an attention-holding manner. There is a reckless, silly and (from an adult point of view) thoroughly unnecessary duel with switch blades that is chilling and a frenzied contest, in which two punks vie with each other to see who will be the last to throw himself out of a car that is racing toward a cliff, that is hair raising. The dialogue of Stewart Stern's screenplay and Irving Shulman's adaptation catches the stumbling inarticulate voice of youth with singular accuracy. . . . In my opinion, this is a superficial treatment of a vital problem that has been staged brilliantly.

Jack Moffitt, *The Hollywood Reporter*, October 21, 1955

REBEL WITHOUT A CAUSE (C'SCOPE MELODRAMA-WARNERCOLOR)

"Rebel Without a Cause" is a tense, exciting melodrama, camera-probing the particular problems of a small group of the young, rather than an overall looksee at juvenile delinquency.

. . . There seems little question, particularly on the basis of his performance here, that the late James Dean would have matured into stellar importance had not his talent been lost to pix recently in a fatal highway auto accident. In this topnotch David Weisbart production, Dean's second major film outing, the young actor had a much more promising showcasing than in his first, "East of Eden." Under Nicholas Ray's sock direction, the Marlon Brando mannerisms displayed in the initialer are gone and the role here carries much greater audience sympathy and response as a result.

. . . Miss Wood, fast maturing as a young lady, and a constantly improving actress, is splendid. Exceptionally fine is Mineo's sensitive study of lonely youth. Story smartly does not go into detail about the other teenage characters, leaving development uncluttered in concentrating on the lead trio.

There is some quality thesping by several adult players, notably Jim Backus' portrait of Dean's father, a weak, bumbling do-gooder who does little that is right.

Daily Variety, October 21, 1955

By Bosley Crowther

It is a violent, brutal and disturbing picture of modern teen-agers that Warner Brothers presents in its new melodrama at the Astor, "Rebel Without a Cause." . . . Like "Blackboard Jungle" before it, it is a picture to make the hair stand on end.

Screenwriter Stewart Stern's proposal that these youngsters would be the way they are for the skimpy reasons he shows us may be a little hard to believe.

. . . But convincing or not in motivations, this tale of tempestuous kids and their weird ways of conducting their social relations is tense with explosive incidents.

. . . However, we do wish the young actors, including Mr. Dean, had not been so intent on imitating Marlon Brando in varying degrees. The tendency, possibly typical of the behavior of certain youths, may therefore be a subtle commentary but it grows monotonous. And we'd be more convinced by Jim Backus and Ann Doran as parents of Mr. Dean if they weren't so obviously silly and ineffectual in treating with the boy.

There is, too, a pictorial slickness about the whole thing in color and CinemaScope that battles at times with the realism in the direction of Nicholas Ray.

New York Times, October 27, 1955

Giant

It is James Dean who gives the most striking performance and creates in Jett Rink the most memorable character in *Giant*. Devotees of the cult which has grown up around him since he was killed in an auto crash just after *Giant* was filmed may be somewhat surprised to see him slouching around in dark glasses and a pencil-thin mustache as the dissipated hotel and oil tycoon in the latter stages of the film. But his earlier depiction of the amoral, reckless, animal-like young ranch hand will not only excite his admirers into frenzy, it will make the most sedate onlooker understand why a James Dean cult ever came into existence.

Herbert Kupferberg, *New York Herald Tribune*, October 1956

In the light of the current death cult starring the late James Dean, it's probably safe to assume that he'll be the strongest draw on the *Giant* marquee. No one should be disappointed, and the film only proves what a promising talent has been lost. . . . Dean delivers an outstanding portrayal . . . it's a sock performance.

Variety, October 1956

It's Dean, Dean, Dean. It is the late James Dean as Jett Rink that the audience will be watching—and there are many who will be watching with fascination and love. For as everyone knows, this young man who died in an auto smash-up has caused a mass hysteria at least equal to that caused by Valentino.

Hollis Alpert, *Saturday Review*, October 1956

[Elizabeth Taylor's] scenes with an off-hand ranch hand were rendered pointless by James Dean's one and only successful acting style—the loutish and malicious petulance which present-day teenagers profess to admire. Dean made the young Jett Rink such a boor not even a wife more neurotic than the one Miss Taylor was portraying could have thought him attractive. Since Dean is dead I shall say nothing about his attempt to portray the mature Jett Rink, except to say it is embarrassing to see.

Courtland Phipps, *Films in Review*, October 1956

James Dean's talent glows like an oilfield flare.

George Christian, *Houston Post*, October 1956

James Dean, who was killed in a sports car crash two weeks after his last scene in *Giant* was shot, in this film clearly shows for the first (and fatefully the last) time what his admirers always said he had: a streak of genius. He has caught the Texas accent to nasal perfection, and mastered that lock-hipped, high-heeled, stagger of the wrangler, and the wry little jerks and smirks, tics and twitches, grunts and giggles that make up most of the language of a man who talks to himself a good deal more than he talks to anyone else. In one scene, indeed, in a long drunken mumble with actress Carroll Baker, Dean is able to press an amazing array of subtleties into the mood of the movement, to achieve what is certainly the finest piece of atmospheric acting seen on the screen since Marlon Brando and Rod Steiger did their "brother" scene in *On the Waterfront*.

Time, October 1956

He may well have been the most promising young actor of this generation.

Walter O'Hearn, *Montreal Star*, October 1956

Dean was in the championship class.

Edwin Schallert, *Los Angeles Times*, October 1956

GEORGE STEVENS' 'GIANT' AN EPIC FILM IN A CLASS WITH THE ALL-TIME GREATS
GIANT-SIZE DRAMA OF TEXAS IS BIG IN SCOPE, TREATMENT

The George Stevens Production of "Giant" for Warners, which Stevens also directed, is a monumental drama as big and inspiring as the locale for which it is named, Texas. . . . "Giant" stands shoulder-to-shoulder with the great ones. . . .

Miss Taylor gives a fine performance. . . . Rock Hudson is powerful in perhaps the best portrayal of his career. . . . Carroll Baker is very good as their daughter and manifests a real screen personality.

. . . As for James Dean, there is no doubt that his death has added poignancy to his every appearance. But there is nothing macabre about it, he is too vital; it is easy to see why the fact of his passing is so hard to accept by so many. Stevens has directed him beautifully, taking full advantage of Dean's unusual ability to act with his whole body as much as with his voice or face. A single scene, where Dean paces out the first land he has ever owned, is unforgettable. Shot from below, with only Dean's expressive silhouette seen against the sky, it has rhythm and beauty and says more than a thousand words could.

The Hollywood Reporter, October 10, 1956

By Bosley Crowther

Apparently the subject of Texas is so large and provocative that no one can get going on it without taking a large amount of time. Producer-director George Stevens demonstrates the point. In his much-touted color film version of Edna Ferber's big Texas novel, "Giant," . . . he takes three hours and seventeen minutes to put his story across. That's a heap of time to go on about Texas, but Mr. Stevens has made a heap of film.

. . . Under Mr. Stevens' direction, an exceptionally well-chosen cast does some exciting performing. Elizabeth Taylor . . . makes a woman of spirit and sensitivity who acquires tolerance and grows old gracefully. And Rock Hudson is handsome, stubborn and perverse but oddly humble as her spouse.

However, it is the late James Dean who makes the malignant role of the surly ranch hand who becomes an oil baron the most tangy and corrosive in the film. Mr. Dean plays this curious villain with a stylized spookiness—a sly sort of off-beat languor and slur of language—that concentrates spite. This is a haunting capstone to the brief career of Mr. Dean.

. . . "Giant," for all its complexity, is a strong contender for the year's top-film award.

New York Times, October 11, 1956

BURT REYNOLDS

When Bill Dakota of the now-defunct James Dean Memorial Foundation of Hollywood was struggling to raise funds to have a statue of James Dean erected, one of his principal financial supporters was actor Burt Reynolds. Reynolds reportedly donated $1,000 to the cause.

DEBBIE REYNOLDS

For a period Debbie Reynolds was Warner Brothers' top choice for the role of Judy in *Rebel Without a Cause*. The role eventually went to Natalie Wood.

ADDISON RICHARDS

Actor who appeared in "Keep Our Honor Bright," a 1953 episode of the NBC television program "Kraft Television Theatre" that co-starred James Dean.

Addison Richards (1887–1964) had extensive stage and film experience. The latter includes *Riot Squad* (1934), *Colleen* (1936), *Since You Went Away* (1944), and *The Oregon Trail* (1959). On television Richards co-starred as a regular in the programs "Cimarron City" (1958–1960), "Fibber McGee and Molly" (1959–1960), and "Pentagon U.S.A." (1953).

PAUL RICHARDS

Actor who appeared in a 1953 Actors Studio production of *End as a Man*, in which James Dean also appeared.

Paul Richards (1924–1974) appeared in the films *The Black Whip* (1955), *Tall Man Riding* (1955), and *Battle for the Planet of the Apes* (1973). He also starred in the television series "Breaking Point" (1963–1964).

FRED RICKEY

Producer of "Glory in Flower," a play by William Inge that featured James Dean and was presented in a 1953 episode of the CBS television program "Omnibus."

NAOMI RIORDAN

Actress who co-starred as the unfortunate wife of the character portrayed by

James Dean in "A Long Time Till Dawn," a 1953 episode of the NBC television program "Kraft Television Theatre." Earlier, Riordan had appeared in the Broadway play *The Velvet Glove* (1949).

RIPPING OFF LAYERS TO FIND ROOTS
Original scene, aka *Waiting on the Beach*, penned by Christine White that was used as an audition scene by White and her partner, James Dean, to gain entrée into the Actors Studio in 1952. The scene dramatized an evening encounter at the beach between an intellectual beachcomber named Sam (Dean) and a southern aristocrat named Clayton (White). In it Dean had lines like "You can toss your whole life away and nobody will care! Don't you hear me? It is me, we, all of us . . . are alone!"

JOHN RITTER
Actor who hosted a television special entitled "Teenage America" in which he donned a jacket out of *Rebel Without a Cause* and attempted a James Dean impersonation.

John Ritter, born in 1948, is the son of actress Dorothy Fay and singing star Tex Ritter. He has appeared in several films but has had far more success on television as a regular on "The Waltons" (as Reverend Matthew Fordwick, 1972–1977), and as the star of "Hooperman" (1987–1989). He is best known, however, as Jack Tripper on the mega-successful series "Three's Company" (for which he won a Best Actor Emmy in 1984, 1977–1984).

"I don't want to go down in history as Jack Tripper."

John Ritter

RIVERSIDE DRIVE EMERGENCY HOSPITAL
After pounding his fist into a desk in a fit of Method acting realism during the April 1955 shooting of *Rebel Without a Cause*, James Dean was rushed to the Riverside Drive Emergency Hospital for x-rays.

TERRANCE ROBAY
Actor who was slated to star as James Dean in the 1977 British stage musical *Dean*. However, shortly before opening night Robay walked out on the project and was replaced by Glenn Conway.

"ROBERT MONTGOMERY PRESENTS"
Acclaimed NBC television drama series (Best Dramatic Program Emmy winner, 1952) that aired on Monday nights from January 1950 to June 1957. The actual title of the show varied from week to week, depending on the sponsor; for example, "Robert Montgomery Presents the American Tobacco Theatre," "Robert Montgomery Presents the Johnson's Wax Program," and "Robert Montgomery Presents Your Lucky Strike Theater."

James Dean co-starred in "Harvest," a 1953 Thanksgiving episode of

"Robert Montgomery Presents the Johnson's Wax Program." Typical of his industrious career at the time, Dean spent most of the holiday week in rehearsals. And typical of television production in general, he and the rest of the "Harvest" company were hindered by a time constraint. According to the show's director, James Sheldon, "We had a reading on Sunday; blocked on Monday; rehearsed Monday, Tuesday, Wednesday, and Thursday; and had a run-through for Mr. Montgomery on Friday. Saturday we were off, Sunday we were rehearsing on-camera, and Monday we blocked, had a dress rehearsal, and went on the air."

LEON ROBERTS
The wardrobe man on *East of Eden* and *Rebel Without a Cause*.

CLIFF ROBERTSON
After Dean's death Cliff Robertson was one of several actors hyped as "the next James Dean." Robertson, perhaps taking his publicity too seriously, rented Dean's old Hollywood apartment.

Born in 1925, Robertson made his film debut in *Picnic* (1955). His subsequent pictures include *PT 109* (as President Kennedy, 1963), *Charly* (Best Actor Oscar, 1968), and *Star 80* (1983).

ROCK AND ROLL
James Dean arguably was one of the forefathers of rock and roll music. Certainly, as the genre pays perpetual homage to Chuck Berry, Fats Domino, Elvis Presley, and others, it also owes a debt of gratitude to James Dean. Not only did Dean influence the way in which a generation of teenagers expressed themselves; he also impacted what they listened to and left profound influences on, among other musicians, Presley and the Beatles.

In 1985 the industry trade publication *Music Connection* was the first to finally acknowledge the role James Dean played in the emergence of rock and roll:

> The world was shaky and just getting ready to rock and roll. James Dean held the bullets in his hand and searched for the electric gun that would liberate us with its sound. The gun went "a-wap-bop-a-loo-mop-a-lop-bam-boom!"
> John Lennon said "Before Elvis there was nothing." But Elvis knew that he owed a debt to James Dean. Dean was the first to represent onscreen the member of a generation that had not yet come of age. . . . James Dean was the first rock star and he had to sing and dance without music.

ROCKS ON THE ROOF
Autobiography, written by Jim Backus and published in 1958 by G. P. Putnam's Sons, that contained an entire chapter about James Dean and Backus's working relationship with him.

RODEO

Dean made tentative plans to use the roping and riding skills he learned while making *Giant* by competing in a November 1955 rodeo at San Francisco's Cow Palace. Dean planned to enter the rodeo with Bob Hinkle.

MARK ROESLER

Indiana attorney who, in 1984, obtained the lucrative licensing rights to the James Dean image. Today Roesler continues to represent the James Dean estate as president of the Curtis Management Group.

> "I'm a business agent. I have a lot of clients . . . most of them are dead."
>
> Mark Roesler, *The Illustrated London News*

> "In a homogenous society like Japan, they admire rebels. In England his appeal is from nostalgia. And the French think he's sexy."
>
> Mark Roesler on the Dean appeal, *Adweek*, June 27, 1988

THE ROLES
The Television Shows

PROGRAM	ROLE	DESCRIPTION
"Abraham Lincoln"	William Scott	court-martialed soldier
"The Bells of Cockaigne"	Joey Frazier	blue-collar worker
"The Big Story"	Todd	——
"The Capture of Jesse James"	Bob Ford	man who shot Jesse James
"The Case of the Sawed-Off Shotgun"	Arbie Ferris	reform school grad
"The Case of the Watchful Dog"	Randy Meeker	son of a moonshiner
"The Dark, Dark Hour"	——	gun-toting delinquent
"Death Is My Neighbor"	——	psychotic janitor
"The Evil Within"	Ralph	lab assistant
"The Foggy, Foggy Dew"	Kyle McCallum	teenage boy who meets a stranger
"Glory in Flower"	Bronco	troubled adolescent
"Harvest"	Paul Zalenka	farm boy who enters the navy
"Hill Number One"	John the Apostle	——
"Hound of Heaven"	Young Angel	a young angel
"I'm a Fool"	The Boy	teenage boy who lies about his identity to impress a girl
"Keep Our Honor Bright"	Jim	college student who attempts suicide
"Life Sentence"	Hank Bradon	convict
"The Little Woman"	Augie	delinquent
"A Long Time Till Dawn"	Joe Harris	ex-convict who tries to go straight
"No Room"	——	safecracker
"Prologue to Glory"	Denny	——
"Run Like a Thief"	Rob	disillusioned youth
"Sleeping Dogs"	——	bellhop who helps solve a murder

"Something for an Empty Briefcase"	Joe Adams	juvenile delinquent
"Ten Thousand Horses Singing"	——	bellhop
"The Thief"	——	rich son suspected of stealing
"The Unlighted Road"	Jeff Latham	teenage drifter/coffee shop worker, in trouble with the law

The Plays

PLAY	ROLE	DESCRIPTION
The Immoralist	Bachir	sleazy homosexual houseboy
See the Jaguar	Wally Wilkins	emotionally disturbed 16-year-old boy

The Movies

MOVIE	ROLE	DESCRIPTION
East of Eden	Cal Trask	teenage boy in search of his father's love
Giant	Jett Rink	renegade rags-to-riches ranch hand
Rebel Without a Cause	Jim Stark	teenage boy who fights to become a man

The Roles That Dean Wanted to Play But Didn't

Nick Adams, "The Battler"
Billy the Kid, *The Left-Handed Gun*
Dr. Jekyll and Mr. Hyde
Morgan Evans, "The Corn Is Green"
Rocky Graziano, *Somebody Up There Likes Me*
Harry Greb
Woody Guthrie
Hamlet
Charles Lindbergh, *The Spirit of St. Louis*
Jim Piersall, *Fear Strikes Out*
Romeo

ROLLING STONE MAGAZINE

Rolling Stone has published a few articles about James Dean, including:

☆ June 20, 1974	"The Making of a Celluloid Rebel" by David Dalton*
☆ October 16, 1980	"Epitaph for a Rebel" by William Zavatsky

---

*cover story

THE ROMANCE OF SCARLET GULCH

When James Dean moved to Los Angeles in 1949, he appeared in a summer stock theater production of *The Romance of Scarlet Gulch*. At that time the 18-year-old Dean was using the name Byron James.

ROMANOFF'S
In the 1950s Romanoff's was *the* restaurant favored by the Hollywood elite.
James Dean, not one for show business snobbery, dined there just once. It
was in January 1955, and his dinner companions included Humphrey Bogart, Nicholas Ray, and Margaret O'Brien. At the time O'Brien was the
leading contender for the role of Judy in *Rebel Without a Cause.*

Romanoff's, no longer in existence, was owned by Gloria and Mike
Romanoff and was located at 326 North Rodeo Drive in Beverly Hills.

NICHOLAS ROMANOS
Known to some as Nikko, Nicholas Romanos was the maître d' at James
Dean's favorite Hollywood restaurant, the Villa Capri.

BOB ROMEO
Musician who accompanied Dean on flute in a jam session that was taped
and subsequently marketed on record as "James Dean on Conga Drums in an
Ad-Lib Session."

BILLY ROSE
Producer of *The Immoralist,* which opened on Broadway on February 8,
1954, and featured James Dean.

Born William Samuel Rosenberg in New York, Rose (1899–1966) was
also the husband of comedienne Fanny Brice (his first of five marriages), a
showman, a nightclub and theater owner, and a lyricist of repute with songs
including "It's Only a Paper Moon," "More Than You Know," and "Me and
My Shadow." He also had his own television show, "The Billy Rose Show"
(1950–1951). On Broadway, he produced, among other plays, *Clash by Night*
(1943) and *Carmen Jones* (1943).

STUART ROSENBERG
Stuart Rosenberg directed James Dean in a 1953 episode of "The Big Story."

Born in 1925, Rosenberg went on to direct films including *Murder, Inc.*
(1960), *Cool Hand Luke* (1967), *The Drowning Pool* (1975), *The Amityville
Horror* (1979), and *The Pope of Greenwich Village* (1984). Rosenberg also
directed a few television movies, and won a 1962–1963 Best Director Emmy
for "The Madman," an episode of the dramatic series "The Defenders."

LEONARD ROSENMAN
I first met Jimmy in the beginning of 1953 when he was appearing
in a play called *Women of Trachis.* I was writing music to that
production at the time. And I was introduced to him by the director,
Howard Sackler, who referred to him as "a tough kid who sleeps on
nails." And I didn't see him again for about a week. And suddenly,
one night, he came to my house. I didn't recognize him. He rang the
doorbell and appeared in a motorcycle outfit, black leather. He
looked like a member of the Gestapo. He introduced himself and
asked if I would teach him piano. And I said I certainly would.

Initially composer Rosenman was also going to make his acting debut in *East of Eden*. The plan, however, was scrapped.

> He had a tremendous desire to be an intellectual. He wanted to be different than he was. I think he had a pathological desire for attention, but I don't really fault him for that, because that's an occupational disease of an actor anyway.
> Leonard Rosenman, *James Dean: The First American Teenager*, 1976

James Dean was drawn to Leonard Rosenman as he was drawn to most of the people who became his friends. Rosenman had something that Dean wanted, knew something that Dean wanted to know: James Dean wanted to learn how to play the piano. With that simple, initial impetus their relationship developed much deeper, certainly much deeper than what Dean was accustomed to. Leonard Rosenman became his closest friend, his confidant, his older brother—if not his father, his intellectual adviser, and, in a sense, his conscience.

In turn Dean was largely responsible for orchestrating Rosenman's career as a major motion picture composer. He took a more active interest in Rosenman's career than he did in the careers of any of his other friends.

Likely this was because Rosenman worked in an entirely separate field from Dean, unlike Bill Bast, whose aspirations to write were shared by Dean. Between Rosenman and Dean there was no divisive jealousy or competition. Further, Dean sincerely believed in Rosenman's talent. It was through James Dean that Rosenman got his agent, Jane Deacy, and his first movie job, *East of Eden*. It was also through Dean that Rosenman was hired to score *Rebel Without a Cause*.

Leonard Rosenman, born (1924) and raised in Brooklyn, studied under Schönberg and received his bachelor of arts degree from the University of California, Berkeley, in 1950. In addition to *Eden* and *Rebel* his credits include *The Cobweb* (1955), *Lafayette Escadrille* (1958), *The Chapman Report* (1962), *Fantastic Voyage* (1966), *Hellfighters* (1969), *Beneath the Planet of the Apes* (1970), *Race with the Devil* (1975), *Barry Lyndon* (England, Best Adapted Score Oscar, 1975), *Bound for Glory* (Best Adapted Score Oscar, 1976), *The Car* (1977), *The Lord of the Rings* (1978), *Promises in the Dark* (1979), *Hide in Plain Sight* (1980), *Cross Creek* (Best Original Score Oscar nomination, 1983) and *Star Trek IV: The Voyage Home* (Best Original Score Oscar nomination, 1986). Rosenman also composed the scores for the television miniseries "Murder in Texas" (1981) and "Celebrity" (1984) and the score of the 1956 Broadway play *A Hatful of Rain*, which was directed by Dean's friend, Frank Corsaro, and co-starred another Dean friend, Christine White.

Shortly before his death James Dean had a falling out with Leonard Rosenman, and over the years the latter has been somewhat reticent about the breakup except to say, "[Jimmy] was in a period in his life where he drank a good deal. And he was kind of drunk and disorderly, and I had just outgrown that kind of thing."

Rosenman, who was in New York at the time, learned about Dean's death from Jane Deacy. In the succeeding years he recorded an album for Imperial Records, *A Tribute to James Dean*, scored the Dean-inspired film *September 30, 1955* (1977), and appeared in interviews on "James Dean Remembered" (1974), *Hollywood: The Rebel James Dean, James Dean: The First American Teenager* (1976), and "A Current Affair" (1989).

> "He never was able to figure out why he couldn't simply play the Beethoven sonatas without learning something about music."
> Leonard Rosenman on James Dean, *Los Angeles Times*,
> December 18, 1977

> He was terribly insecure about his lack of knowledge in general.
> Leonard Rosenman on James Dean,
> Academy of Motion Picture Arts and Sciences tribute, 1983

> "I loved Jimmy, but would have preferred that society had listened to Mozart instead."
> Leonard Rosenman on James Dean, *Los Angeles Times*,
> December 18, 1977

WALTER S. ROSS
Author of *The Immortal*, a fictional biography of James Dean published by Simon and Schuster in 1958.

GABRIEL ROTELLO
Co-host of a memorial tribute to James Dean held at the Limelight nightclub in New York on September 24, 1985, to commemorate the 30th anniversary of his death.

BEULAH ROTH
> Sandy called me up and said, "What are you having for dinner? I want to bring a young actor home with me." I said, "I'm making chicken curry and chutney. I don't know if he's gonna like it. Where's he from?" Sandy said, "I don't know. He's a country boy." Anyway, he brought Jimmy home, and it was love at first sight. He loved me and I loved him, and he *hated* the chicken curry.
>
> Beulah Roth

Although his familial roots were safe and secure back home with Marcus and Ortense Winslow in Fairmount, Indiana, James Dean always seemed to be seeking some semblance of family. In addition, he always seemed to be seeking out individuals from whom he could learn, and Sandy and Beulah Roth, an intelligent, cultured, and well-traveled couple, had a lot to teach him. They also opened their home to him in West Hollywood (1158 Hacienda Place), where he was a frequent guest during the summer of 1955.

> There was something about him. I never met a country boy before. I'm a city girl. He was not the kind of person I usually meet.
>
> Beulah Roth on James Dean

> We had a lot of fun. He was with us constantly. We talked about Europe; we talked about everything. And it was not a mother and father and son relationship, believe me. We were contemporaries. We were old enough to be mother and father, but we were his contemporaries. He treated us as such, and we treated him the same. We took him everywhere we went.
>
> Beulah Roth on James Dean

> We bought a house in 1955, and we couldn't wait for Jimmy to see it. The escrow was over on November 5, and Jimmy never did see it.
>
> Beulah Roth on James Dean

Beulah Roth died in Los Angeles of cancer in October 1990 at the age of 83.

BOB ROTH
Fairmount, Indiana, friend of Jimmy's who was interviewed in the 1988 documentary "Forever James Dean."

SANFORD ROTH

Renowned photographer Sandy Roth first met James Dean on the lot at Warner Brothers. The studio had hired Roth to photograph either of its two rising stars, Jack Lemmon or James Dean; Roth opted for Dean. The two men became immediate friends, drawn together by Dean's insatiable quest for knowledge. Roth's widow, Beulah, recently recalled their introduction: "We were living in Europe, and Sandy was called back by Warner Brothers telling him that there was a young actor in *Giant* and they'd like him to do offstage material on him. Jimmy had just come back from Texas. This was when they were back at Warners. They came back to do interiors. Sandy didn't know what Jimmy Dean looked like. He was walking through one of the alleys at Warner Brothers, and a young man came over to him and saw Sandy's camera around his neck, and he said, 'What kind of a camera is that?' And Sandy said, 'It's a Nikon.' And the guy said, 'Can I try it? Can I look through it?' Sandy said, 'Sure. I'm Sandy Roth.' And the guy said, 'I'm James Dean.' And Sandy said, 'Oh, you're the fellow I'm gonna work on. What are you doing tonight?' "

On the afternoon of September 30, 1955, Roth, traveling in Dean's station wagon, trailed Dean and his Porsche on the road to Salinas with the intent of capturing the race on film for *Colliers* magazine. Roth, accompanied by Bill Hickman, another Dean friend, arrived at the crash site 10 minutes after the accident. According to Beulah, Roth accompanied Jimmy in the ambulance and was at the Paso Robles hospital when he was pronounced dead. Roth later told a reporter for the *Chicago Tribune*, "I saw Jimmy. He was thrown back behind the wheel and I knew he was dead. His neck was broken."

Later Sandy Roth penned two articles about his friend, "The Late James Dean" for *Colliers* (November 25, 1955) and "Jimmy Dean: The Assignment I'll Never Forget" for *Popular Photography* (July 1962).

In 1962 Roth died of a heart attack while in Rome. Over the years his photographs of James Dean have been kept in circulation by his widow, Beulah, and have been published and republished in books and magazines all over the world. One book, *Jimmy*, composed entirely of Roth's photographs, was published in Japan in 1983. A similar book, *James Dean*, was published in the United States the same year. Today the catalog of Roth's Dean photos is owned by Dean mega-fan Seita Ohnishi, a Japanese businessman.

For years after the crash rumors abounded that, on the afternoon of September 30, 1955, Sanford Roth had taken two final shots of James Dean as his body was pinned and next to lifeless inside the Porsche. The rumors stemmed from a 1956 article in *Life* magazine that read: "Photographer Sanford Roth, an old friend of Dean's who was trailing him in another car the day he died, has been offered large sums for the two shots he got of the dead actor in the smashed Porsche." The article then quotes Roth as saying "They will never be released. And nobody will ever see them. It was a ghoulish, horrible sight. I took them for one reason—if there was a question by the insurance companies or police as to who was driving."

The existence of the photographs was reasserted in Warren Newton Beath's 1986 book *The Death of James Dean*. However, according to Beulah Roth, "This business in Warren Beath's book that [Bill] Hickman claimed that Sandy photographed Jimmy's body in the car—that is the lie of all time. And I wrote to Warren Beath and said, 'I demand an apology! How dare you scar my husband's character as a man!' And he did send me a letter of apology. *There was never such a picture!* Sandy photographed the wreck of the car for the insurance company. And I never published those until long after it happened."

> "Jimmy, who had never been [to Europe], was coming with us. He wanted to walk down the Boulevard Montparnasse in Paris, to study sculpture there, to buy crazy sweaters in Capri and to meet Cocteau and Miro."
>
> Sanford Roth, *Colliers*, November 25, 1955

MAXINE ROWLAND

Maxine Rowland, an Ohio seamstress, has been a Dean devotee for many years. An active member of the We Remember Dean International fan club since its inception in 1978, Maxine has an extensive collection of Dean memorabilia and has made numerous visits to Fairmount, Indiana. Every February and September she designs baskets of flowers to place on Jimmy's grave in behalf of WRDI. Says Maxine, "My love and devotion for Jimmy has taken on a whole new meaning because of the many new friends I have made in We Remember Dean International."

STEVE ROWLAND

Friend of Dean's who almost accompanied him on the road to Salinas. At the time Rowland was a fan magazine writer and a sometime actor, said by some to physically resemble Dean. Rowland was also considered for the role of Pinky Snythe in *Giant*, which eventually went to Bob Nichols. When he learned of Jimmy's death, Rowland promptly sold his motorcycle in protest. As reported in the October 3, 1955, edition of *Daily Variety*, "Steve Rowland, who had been invited to accompany Dean on the ride north, is curbing his reckless side." Later Rowland penned the article "Goodbye, Jimmy Dean" for *Movie Stars Parade* (November 1957).

Rowland's films include *Two Weeks with Love* (1950) and *Excuse My Dust* (1951), both of which were directed by his father, Roy Rowland. As a singer he charted several songs on the Spanish hit parade, including "I've Got a Woman," "Linda Lou," "She's Gone," and "Dancing Shoes."

ROXY THEATRE

New York City theater where *Giant* had its much ballyhooed premiere on October 10, 1956. The Roxy Theatre, no longer in existence, was located at Seventh Avenue and 50th Street.

THE ROYALE THEATRE
Broadway theater, located at 242 West 45th Street, where André Gide's *The Immoralist* ran from February 8, 1954, until May 1, 1954.

THE ROYALTON HOTEL
In 1952 struggling actor Jimmy Dean attempted to rent an apartment at the Royalton (address: 44 West 44th Street), but found that it was too expensive. Nonetheless the hotel served as one of his hangouts, and it was here that he spent the night of December 3, 1952, the opening night of his Broadway debut in *See the Jaguar*.

In 1988, after a $40 million renovation, the Royalton reopened at the same location.

ROYCE HALL
UCLA theater in which Shakespeare's *Macbeth* was staged from November 29, 1950, until December 2, 1950. The play featured sophomore Jim Dean.

E. T. RUENITZ
In 1950 E. T. Ruenitz was an adviser to the Opheleos Men's Honor Service Organization of Santa Monica City College, of which Jim Dean was a member.

PETE RUGGULO

One night, during the production of *Rebel Without a Cause*, a group of musicians got together at Nick Ray's bungalow in the Chateau Marmont and had an impromptu jam session. Ruggulo was on trumpet, Leonard Rosenman was on piano, Tony Mazzola was on guitar, Nick Ray was on harmonica, and Jimmy Dean was on—what else?—the bongos.

"RUN LIKE A THIEF"

Episode of the NBC television series "Philco TV Playhouse" that starred Kurt Kasznar, Gusti Huber, James Dean, and Barbara O'Neil. The episode was produced by Gordon Duff, directed by Jeffrey Hayden, and written by Sam Hall. It aired on September 5, 1954.

"Run Like a Thief" revolved around a waiter (Kasznar) who finds a bracelet belonging to his boss. After some deliberation the waiter opts to keep the bracelet and present it to his wife. James Dean portrayed Rob, the waiter's young protégé, who is disillusioned by the entire scenario.

NATHAN RUSSELL

Recorded the song "His Name Was Dean" for Forest Records.

WHITEY RUST

Fairmount, Indiana, friend of Jimmy's who served as one of the pallbearers at his funeral.

S

ARLENE SACHS
One of James Dean's New York girlfriends, aka Arlene Lorca, who was interviewed in the 1957 documentary *The James Dean Story*.

HOWARD SACKLER
Howard Sackler directed James Dean in *Women of Trachis*, a 1954 off-Broadway reading. Also a playwright, Sackler wrote *The Great White Hope*, for which he won the 1969 Best Play Tony award. He later adapted the play into a 1970 movie.

ALAN AND ART SACKS
Along with fighter Mushy Callahan, Alan and Art Sacks, identical twins, alternated as James Dean's stand-in on *Rebel Without a Cause*.

SAILOR BEWARE
Sailor Beware, or "Dean Martin and Jerry Lewis Enlist in the Navy," is notable for one reason and one reason only: in its cast of sailor-suited young actors was Jimmy Dean, barely noticeable, in a bit part.
  Sailor Beware, released by Paramount in 1952, was produced by Hal Wallis, directed by Hal Walker, written by James Allardice and Martin Rackin, and starred Dean Martin, Jerry Lewis, Corinne Calvet, Marion Marshall, Robert Strauss, and Leif Erickson.

ST. JAMES HOTEL
Philadelphia hotel where James Dean resided during the January 1954 out-of-town tryouts of *The Immoralist*. The hotel was located at the corner of Walnut and 13th Streets.

MICK ST. MICHAEL
Compiled the 1989 book *James Dean: In His Own Words*, published by Omnibus Books in Great Britain.

ROGER ST. PIERRE
Writer of *James Dean: A Story in Words and Pictures*, a one-shot magazine published by Anabas Books (Great Britain) in 1985.

ST. TIMOTHY'S CATHOLIC CHURCH
Legend has it that, on the afternoon of November 24, 1954, James Dean sat on his motorcycle across the street from St. Timothy's Catholic Church in

Los Angeles. When the newly married Pier Angeli and Vic Damone emerged, beaming, from their wedding ceremony, Dean is said to have gunned his engine in protest.

St. Timothy's Catholic Church is still located at 10452 West Pico Boulevard.

SALARY

Pepsi commercial (1950)	$10 flat fee
"Hill Number One" (1951)	$150 flat fee
See the Jaguar (1952)	$75 per week (the show lasted four days)
Miscellaneous TV shows (1953)	$200–$300 flat fee
"Harvest" (November 1953)	$500 flat fee
The Immoralist (1954)	$300 per week
East of Eden (made in 1954)	$1,000 per week (minimum 10 weeks guaranteed)
"The Unlighted Road" (1955)	$2,500 flat fee
Rebel Without a Cause (1955)	$1,250 per week (minimum 10 weeks guaranteed)
Giant (made in 1955)	$1,500 per week* (minimum 10 weeks guaranteed)
TV rerun fee for "Harvest"	$7,500 flat fee
"The Corn Is Green" (what he would have made)	$20,000 flat fee
Warner Brothers contract (would have been in effect after *Giant*; included nine films over six years)	$900,000 total fee

*It's interesting to note that for the same picture Mercedes McCambridge made nearly $3,000 a week, Chill Wills $2,000, Paul Fix $1,500, Jane Withers $1,000, Sal Mineo (who had next to a walk-on part) $1,000.

SALINAS, CALIFORNIA

It's sadly ironic that James Dean was killed en route to, of all places, Salinas, California, about 350 miles northwest of Hollywood, where he had shot portions of *East of Eden* just 15 months before. His name and image will forever be linked with the town of Salinas, the birthplace of *Eden*'s author, John Steinbeck.

People Invited to Join Jimmy (and People Who *Claimed* to Have Been Invited to Join Jimmy) on His Last Ride to Salinas

Nick Adams	Charlie Nolan Dean	Steve Rowland
Ursula Andress	Winton Dean	Bill Stevens
Bill Bast	Bill Hickman*	Rolf Wutherich*
Lew Bracker	Mercedes McCambridge	
Jane Deacy	Sanford Roth*	

*Those who actually did go with him

ALBERT SALMI

Actor who starred in a 1953 Actors Studio production of *End as a Man*, which co-starred James Dean. The same year, Salmi was featured in the off-Broadway production of *The Scarecrow*, in which Dean also appeared.

Salmi, born in 1928, appeared in several films including *The Brothers*

Karamazov (1958), *Wild River* (1960), and *Brubaker* (1980). He also co-starred as a regular in the television programs "Daniel Boone" (1964–1965) and "Petrocelli" (1974–1976). In April 1990 Salmi was shot to death.

SAN FRANCISCO, CALIFORNIA
Following his scheduled car race in Salinas, James Dean planned to spend the first week of October 1955 vacationing in San Francisco, California, before returning east to New York.

RAYMOND SANDS
Raymond Sands was the Los Angeles physician who treated fatally ill Mildred Dean, Jimmy's mother, from September 1939 to July 1940.

TOMMY SANDS
Singer who recorded "Let Me Be Loved," theme song of the 1957 documentary *The James Dean Story*.

Sands, born in Chicago in 1937, enjoyed teen heartthrob status, briefly, circa 1957–1958. His song hits included "Teen-Age Crush" (1957), "Goin' Steady" (1957), and "Sing Boy Sing" (1958). His films include *Sing Boy Sing* (1958), *Babes in Toyland* (1960), *The Longest Day* (1962), and *None But the Brave* (1965). Sands was also married to singer Nancy Sinatra (1960–1965).

SANTA BARBARA, CALIFORNIA
On Memorial Day 1955 James Dean entered a car race in Santa Barbara, California. He was in fourth place when his Porsche Speedster burned a piston. It was his final professional race. He also occasionally visited Santa Barbara to see Cisco, his horse, which was boarded on a local ranch.

SANTA MONICA, CALIFORNIA
During his short life James Dean was a frequent resident of the beach community of Santa Monica, California. From the time he was five until his mother's death when he was nine, Jimmy lived with his parents at 1422 23rd Street in Santa Monica. He was then sent back to Fairmont, Indiana, to be raised by relatives. Following his high school graduation in 1949, however, Jimmy returned to Santa Monica and lived with his father and stepmother in their home at 814-B Sixth Street.

During the last years of his life Jimmy lived mainly in New York City, West Hollywood, and the San Fernando Valley, but during breaks from shooting he frequently visited Santa Monica and its neighbor, Malibu.

SANTA MONICA CITY COLLEGE
Jimmy Dean was enrolled in Santa Monica City College the fall semester of 1949 and the spring semester of 1950. At that time the school was in the process of moving to its new campus, so a temporary facility was set up on the Santa Monica High School campus.

At the college Jimmy was on the school basketball team, in the drama club, and in a jazz appreciation club and was elected as a member of the Opheleos Men's Honor Service Organization, which was composed of the school's 21 most outstanding male students. At that time the school's official nickname was Corsairville, although it was referred to by its students, presumably because of the shabby condition of its buildings, as "Splinterville."

Today the school, age 60, is one of the oldest junior colleges in the country. It is now known as Santa Monica College and is located at 1900 Pico Boulevard, where it has been since 1952.

Santa Monica College's Celebrity Alumni
James Dean
Dustin Hoffman
Sean Penn
Arnold Schwarzenegger

SANTA MONICA HIGH SCHOOL
Santa Monica High School not only served as the location of Santa Monica City College circa 1949–1950; it also served as the location of the fictional Dawson High School in *Rebel Without a Cause* (1955). For allowing the *Rebel* company to invade its campus Warner Brothers paid the Santa Monica High student body the sum of $150. Santa Monica High is still located at 601 Pico Boulevard.

SARDI'S
James Dean celebrated the opening nights of both of his Broadway plays, *See the Jaguar* (December 3, 1952) and *The Immoralist* (February 8, 1954), at Sardi's, the legendary New York City restaurant. On the first occasion Jimmy was accompanied by Dizzy Sheridan; on the second it was Barbara Glenn, along with his Uncle Marcus and Aunt Ortense Winslow, who had traveled from Fairmount, Indiana. Sardi's is still located at 234 West 44th Street.

DON SARGENT
Recorded the song "His Name Was Dean" for Mecca Records.

RONALD E. SATTLER
Beverly Hills dentist who treated James Dean in 1955. After Jimmy's death Dr. Sattler billed the Dean estate for an unpaid bill in the amount of $15. At the time Dean was a patient, Dr. Sattler's offices were located at 9629 Brighton Way.

SATURDAY REVIEW MAGAZINE
Saturday Review has published several articles about James Dean, including:

☆ October 13, 1956   "It's Dean, Dean, Dean" by Hollis Alpert
☆ August 27, 1961   "Rebel with a Cause"

☆ August 1982   "James Dean Collecting Is Now Worldwide"
☆ August 1982   "James Dean's Memorial in Cholame"

ROBERT SAUDEK
Executive producer of "Glory in Flower," a 1953 episode of the CBS television program "Omnibus" that featured James Dean.

SAWTELLE, CALIFORNIA
In 1936 dental technician Winton Dean was transferred from the Marion Veterans Administration Hospital in Indiana to the Sawtelle Veterans Administration Hospital in Sawtelle, a California neighborhood adjacent to Santa Monica and Westwood. Consequently Winton moved his wife, Mildred, and his five-year-old son, Jimmy, into a residence close to the hospital. Interestingly, during the same period 11-year-old Norma Jeane Baker, later known as Marilyn Monroe, was released from a Los Angeles orphanage and sent to live at her Aunt Ana Lower's home, also in Sawtelle.

Years later, when he was flown to Los Angeles from New York to make *East of Eden*, Jimmy lived for a short period with his father and stepmother at their home at 1667 South Bundy Drive in Sawtelle. In 1955 Winton and his wife moved to another house in Sawtelle, located at 1527½ Saltair Avenue, where Winton's then-famous son was an occasional visitor.

JOHN SAXON
Actor who was tested for the role of Buzz in *Rebel Without a Cause*. The role eventually went to Corey Allen. After the death of James Dean, Saxon tested for Dean's role in the television production of "The Battler." The role, however, was given to Dewey Martin.

THE SCARECROW
Off-Broadway play that James Dean appeared in at the Theatre de Lys. The cast included Patricia Neal, Eli Wallach, Douglas Watson, Anne Jackson, Milton Carney, Bradford Dillman, Milton Selzer, Mary Bell, Albert Salmi, Alan MacAteer, Zita Rieth, Harold Preston, Sybil Baker, Eavan O'Connor, Ed Williams, and Stefan Gierasch. Jimmy had a small role without dialogue. The play was directed by Frank Corsaro, written by Percy MacKaye, and produced by Terese Hayden. It opened on June 16, 1953 (not on March 16, 1953, as repeatedly published elsewhere), and ran until June 21, 1953.

Based on a story by Nathaniel Hawthorne, *The Scarecrow*, originally staged on Broadway in 1911, was set in 17th-century Massachusetts and revolved around a scarecrow (played in the revival by Douglas Watson) who is brought to life by a devil.

TOBY SCARSTED
One of the body makeup artists on *Giant*.

NATALIE SCHAFER

Actress who was considered for the role of Jim Stark's mother in *Rebel Without a Cause*. Ironically, if she had gotten the part (it eventually went to Ann Doran), Natalie Schafer would have been paired with Jim Backus, who 10 years later, played Thurston Howell III to her Lovey Howell in the television camp classic "Gilligan's Island" (1964–1967).

DORE SCHARY

Writer-producer Dore Schary (1905–1980) was the vice president in charge of production at MGM Studios between 1948 and 1956. Shortly before his death James Dean went to MGM and met with Schary to discuss starring in the film *Somebody Up There Likes Me*. Dean reportedly strolled into Schary's office, spotted what appeared to be a gold telephone, and without muttering "Hello," or some other form of polite introduction, queried, "Hey, is that *gold*?" To which Schary replied, "Yes, Mr. Dean, it is." Years later Schary described the encounter in his autobiography, *Heyday*:

> I broke the silence. "I wish you'd tell me what role I should play. Should I be in the back of the desk with a fat cigar? Or should I swing a golf club or polo mallet?" Dean looked at me and smiled, walked over, thrust out his hand to me, and over our hand shake sat down and said, "How are you?" Apparently, I'd passed a test of sorts.

In addition to his role as MGM mogul, he was ultimately responsible for such films as *Battleground* (which he also produced and which was nominated for a Best Picture Oscar, 1949) *On the Town* (1949), *Adam's Rib* (1949), *Father of the Bride* (Best Picture Oscar nomination, 1950), *King Solomon's Mines* (Best Picture Oscar nomination, 1950), *The Asphalt Jungle* (1950), *An American in Paris* (Best Picture Oscar winner, 1951), *Quo Vadis* (Best Picture Oscar nomination, 1951), *Singin' in the Rain* (1952), *Ivanhoe* (Best Picture Oscar nomination, 1952), *The Band Wagon* (1953), *Julius Caesar* (Best Picture Oscar nomination, 1953), and *Seven Brides for Seven Brothers* (Best Picture Oscar nomination, 1954).

Schary was also a screenwriter who won a 1938 Best Original Story Oscar (shared credit) for *Boys Town*. Following his dismissal from MGM, Schary turned to Broadway, where he wrote and produced the hit play *Sunrise at Campobello*, which he later adapted into a successful 1960 motion picture.

ROY SCHATT

> During our first meeting Jim asked me if I would shoot him, not as a regular session, but to document his activities. It soon developed that he wanted to shoot me as well, so we began classes. I immediately found out that his concentration was not to be counted on, which meant that our classes were somewhat unpredictable and by necessity changeable in form.

However, when he was interested and participating, his energy was powerful. He had that greatest of intellectual qualities—curiosity about everything.

Roy Schatt, James Dean: A Portrait

Formidable photographer Roy Schatt befriended James Dean in New York in 1954. He became, simultaneously, Dean's teacher in photography and Dean's photographer (not unlike the way Leonard Rosenman became Dean's teacher in piano and the composer of *East of Eden* and *Rebel Without a Cause*).

Jimmy became a frequent visitor at Schatt's studio (149 East 33rd Street) and a frequent subject of Schatt's camera. Schatt's *Torn Sweater* session with James Dean includes some of the finest photos ever taken of him. These and other photos were included in *James Dean: A Portrait* by Roy Schatt, published in 1982 by Delilah Books.

"He was always on . . . Mr. Theater."

Roy Schatt on James Dean, We Remember Dean
International memorial tribute, 1985

"SCHLITZ PLAYHOUSE OF STARS"

CBS television dramatic anthology series that aired on Friday nights from October 1951 to March 1959. James Dean appeared in "The Unlighted Road," a May 6, 1955, episode of the "Schlitz Playhouse of Stars." It was his final television performance.

THE SCHOOLS

The following is a chronological list of the schools that Jimmy Dean attended.

SCHOOL	YEARS	GRADE	AGE
Brentwood Elementary	Sept. 1936–May 1937	kind.	5–6

SANTA MONICA CITY SCHOOLS
ELEMENTARY PERMANENT RECORD CARD

DATE OF BIRTH February 8, 1930   PARENT'S NAME W. A. Dean

PLACE OF BIRTH Marion, Indiana   NAME Dean, Byron James (Jimmy)

Date of Entrance	SCHOOL	GRADE	TEACHER	Days Present	Days Absent	Date of Leaving OR Term Ending
2-7-38	McKinley	A1	Wilson	72⅞	14½	6-17-38
9-12-38	"	B2		68	18	1-27-39
1/30/39	"	A2	Powell	76	17	6/14/39
9/11/39	"	B3	"	77.2	14.3	3/3/40
2-5-40	"	A3	Garretson	80.10	12.90	6-21-40

Jimmy's record at McKinley Elementary School, 1938–1940.

Brentwood Elementary	Sept. 1937–Feb. 1938	1	6–7
McKinley Elementary	Feb. 1938–May 1938	1	7
McKinley Elementary	Sept. 1938–May 1939	2	7–8
McKinley Elementary	Sept. 1939–May 1940	3	8–9
Fairmount West Ward	Sept. 1940–May 1941	4	9–10
Fairmount West Ward	Sept. 1941–May 1942	5	10–11
Fairmount West Ward	Sept. 1942–May 1943	6	11–12
Fairmount High School	Sept. 1943–May 1944	7	12–13
Fairmount High School	Sept. 1944–May 1945	8	13–14
Fairmount High School	Sept. 1945–May 1946	9	14–15
Fairmount High School	Sept. 1946–May 1947	10	15–16
Fairmount High School	Sept. 1947–May 1948	11	16–17
Fairmount High School	Sept. 1948–May 1949	12	17–18
Santa Monica City College	Sept. 1949–May 1950	Fr.	18–19
UCLA	Sept. 1950–Feb. 1951	So.	19–20

SCHOTT BROTHERS

New Jersey–based outerwear company (address: 358 Lehigh Avenue, Perth Amboy, New Jersey 08861) that markets a line of James Dean jackets.

AARON SCHROEDER

Co-wrote the song "Jimmy, Jimmy" for the motion picture *The James Dean Story* (1957).

ARNOLD SCHULMAN

Arnold Schulman wrote the television adaptation of Sherwood Anderson's "I'm a Fool," a 1954 episode of the CBS television program "General Electric Theater" that co-starred James Dean.

Schulman later wrote the Broadway plays *A Hole in the Head* (1957), *Jennie* (1963), and *Golden Rainbow* (1968).

SCHWAB'S

In the 1950s Schwab's was a famed West Hollywood coffee shop and pharmacy (address: 8024 Sunset Boulevard) where aspiring actors and actresses used to sip coffee, swap conversation, and generally loiter in hopes of being discovered. James Dean was one of those struggling young actors. Schwab's closed its doors in 1985, ending an era.

SCREEN GREATS PRESENTS JAMES DEAN

One-shot cover-to-cover magazine about Dean published by Starlog Press in 1988.

SCREEN LEGENDS: JAMES DEAN (HIS LIFE AND LEGEND)

One-shot magazine, half of which was devoted to James Dean; the other half was devoted to Dean's *Giant* co-star Carroll Baker. *Screen Legends* was edited by Gene Ringgold and published in 1965 by Associated Professional Services.

SCREEN STARS MAGAZINE

Hollywood fan magazine that published several articles about James Dean, including:

☆ September 1956   "The James Dean I Knew" by Nick Adams
☆ November 1956   "The Immortal Dean"
☆ March 1957   "Leave Him to Heaven"
☆ May 1957   "Hollywood's Mixed-Up Blabber-Mouths" by Nick Adams

SCREEN STORIES MAGAZINE

Hollywood fan magazine that published several articles about James Dean, including:

☆ September 1956   "The Unlighted Road: The Jimmy Dean Festival"
☆ November 1956   "Jimmy Dean, Two Memories"
☆ November 1956   "The Actor Jimmy Dean" by George Stevens

THE SCREEN TESTS

James Dean's first screen test was for Warner Brothers' *Battle Cry* in 1954. He didn't get the part; Tab Hunter did.

In Hollywood screen tests are produced for a variety of reasons. Most obviously an actor appears in a screen test to audition for a role. Often, however, an actor who has already obtained a role appears in a test to pair himself with actors who are being considered for other roles in the same picture.

Elia Kazan *knew* almost immediately, instinctively that he wanted James Dean for the part of Cal Trask. He confirmed his instinct with a test of Dean conducted in New York on February 16, 1954. What he was less certain of was with whom he should be cast. Consequently Kazan and his assistant, Guy Thomajan, conducted a series of additional screen tests of Dean with Dick Davalos and Paul Newman, who were the leading contenders for the role of Aron, Cal's brother. Dean was also paired in tests with Julie Harris and Joanne Woodward, who were the leading contenders for the role of Abra.

> "I remember staying at his apartment the night before [the test] and really assimilating these characters and developing the relationship as best we could. I remember we were extremely tired when we went in."
>
> Dick Davalos on his screen test with James Dean

THE SCREENWRITERS
See THE WRITERS.

JOE SCULLY

Telewriter of "The Little Woman," a 1954 episode of the CBS television program "Danger" that co-starred James Dean.

THE SEA GULL

James Dean appeared in an Actors Studio production of Chekhov's *The Sea*

Gull. He portrayed Konstantin Treplev, an outcast writer. The presentation also featured actor Joseph Anthony.

SEE THE JAGUAR

The Cort Theatre   December 3,1952   Five performances
Written by: N. Richard Nash
Directed by: Michael Gordon
Produced by: Lemuel Ayers in association with Helen Jacobson
Settings by: Lemuel Ayers
Costumes by: Lemuel Ayers
Cast: Arthur Kennedy, Constance Ford, Cameron Prud'homme, Roy Fant, James Dean,
    Margaret Barker, Phillip Pine, David Clarke, George Tyne, Arthur Batanides, Ted
    Jacques, Florence Sundstrom, Dane Knell, Harrison Dowd, Harry Bergman, Tony Kraber

During the summer of 1952 21-year-old James Dean secretly campaigned for a role in Lemuel Ayers's forthcoming Broadway play, *See the Jaguar*. Jimmy was introduced to Ayers through Rogers Brackett, but instead of articulating his intentions Jimmy calculatingly charmed his way into Ayers's life and won a position as a crewman aboard Ayers's yacht. Then, when *Jaguar* went into production a month or so later, Jimmy was able to request and obtain a reading.

Still, director Michael Gordon claims to have auditioned 100 young actors for the part and says that Dean's selection had more to do with his projection of naïveté than with his personal liaison with producer Ayers. Likely it was a combination of the two. Dean's agent Jane Deacy attributed his success to another factor:

> "Dean walked into the producer's office for an interview. The producer told Dean he was too short. Dean walked over to the producer and told him to stand up. The producer came up to Dean's shoulders. That brash attitude landed him the job."

"The job" was the role of 17-year-old Wally Wilkins, a tortured and captive innocent, defenseless in the face of a brutal society—literally. Wally has spent his entire life overprotected by his neurotic, albeit noble-minded mother (Margaret Barker), whose maternal instincts included locking her son in an icehouse locker to keep him from the outside world. Prior to her death she releases her son (without informing him of her fate), gives him a gun, and sends him off to venture into the world she so feared. Wally, with the body of a young man and the mentality of a newborn chick, roams the mountainside, inhales the air, and stares up at the sky with a wonder forgotten by most.

Meanwhile Brad (Cameron Prud'homme), the town landlord, storekeeper, and resident bully, who captures and cages wild animals and displays them like zoo trophies to be ogled by customers at his store (signs proclaim "See the Ocelot," "See the Weasel," etc.), sets out with a dual mission: to capture a jaguar (he already has a cage and a sign that reads, of course, "See the Jaguar") and to find the simpleminded boy, who, according to rumor, has a monetary inheritance in his pocket.

While Brad leads a town search for him, Wally stumbles upon a young couple who subsequently attempt to shelter him. The couple, an honorable schoolteacher by the name of Dave Ricks (Arthur Kennedy) and Janna (Constance Ford), Brad's daughter, are in love, unmarried, and expecting a baby (a radical development by 1952 standards). Their introduction to Wally transpired in the following scene written by N. Richard Nash:

(Narrowly, Wally Wilkins enters. He is perhaps seventeen, a guileless, innocent face and a world of wonder in his eyes. He wears worn work clothes, spotlessly clean and newly mended. He carries his mother's rifle loosely, not at all like a weapon.)

JANNA: What are you doing—prowling around the cages?

WALLY: Just lookin' at the animals . . . (as if cataloguing them for himself) That's birds—and other critters—

JANNA: What do you want?

WALLY: I come to find my Ma. Is she about somewheres?

DAVE: Your Ma—who's that? What's your name?

WALLY: (uncertainly) I—my name—it's Wally . . . Wilkins.

GRAMFA RICKS: Christamighty! (With a whoop—to the others) You see! I told you there's a boy! (Quickly, to Wally) But you ain't got no beard! They said you got a beard!

WALLY: My Ma she took it off—she took a razor and cut the hair away. (then, proudly) She give me these clean overalls. And two new shoes—they twinge a little. Did you see my Ma?

JANNA: (Quietly) Your Ma's not here.

WALLY: (Puzzled) She opened up the locker door and said, "In a little while—when I ha'd gone—you walk the hill—and ask for Davie Ricks," she said. "It'll all be strange—so don't git lost—" (To Gramfa) Are you Davie Ricks? Or am I lost?

DAVE: I'm Davie Ricks. (He makes a movement toward Wally who quickly steps back, raising his gun a little.) Don't be afraid.

WALLY: (Lowering gun) I ain't afraid. But everything is big. I remember it from when I was a kid, but not so big.

DAVE: (Raptly) I'd think it would seem smaller now. (Eagerly) What does it look like, boy? I've always wondered—if I could see it new—what would it look like?

WALLY: (Stretching out one hand to the bigness) You can't touch nothin' . . .

DAVE: That's right—you can't!

WALLY: (Encouraged) It's got a fancy lot of colors to it— and everything is like my Ma explained—except no stars. (Disappointed) Did she make them up?

DAVE: No. At night. The stars come out at night.

WALLY: That's so. I'm clean mixed up . . . The stars at night . . .

James Dean as Wally Wilkins in *See the Jaguar* by Kenneth Kendall.

DAVE: You wanted me for something? What?

WALLY: (Reaching into his shirt, he brings out a folded sheet of paper.) My Ma—she said to give you this. (Handing Dave the paper) She writ it out herself.

GRAMFA: What's in it? Read it out.

DAVE: (As Dave reads it, Wally is quite still, studying his surroundings.) "Dear Davie Ricks. This is my son Walter that I hid from all the meanness of the world. (Dave looks a moment at Wally.) Maybe I was wrong to hidden him this way—maybe I was

right. But I loved him dear and didn't want him for
hurt to come his way. So I couldn't figger to do
different. When he's alone he bound to git in trouble and be in pain. So I choose a man who got a
good in him. I choose you, Davie Ricks, to start
him off in a gently way. He got an aunt in Wendle
City. I writ her that my boy is comin' and she'll be
watchin' for the trains. All you gotta do is walk
him across the hill to the depot and get his ticket
for him. He'll be all right if you just say a word or
two to take the scare out of him. And prepare him
a little. He thinks the world is all me and the songs
I sung him. You see, I didn't have no heart to tell
him that all men won't be good like you—and all
women won't love him like me. So tell him a little.
And say I won't be back. I won't never be back and
he ain't to hope I'll be back. And tell him for me
that I say goodbye, Walter, goodbye, son."

As the play progresses, however, Wally shoots and kills the jaguar in defense, and in revenge the brutish Brad imprisons Wally in the cage intended for the jaguar.

Rehearsals went well, with Dean agreeable for the most part. In particular he got along well with Arthur Kennedy, a member of the Actors Studio, who had already won a Tony award for *Death of a Salesman* and had been nominated for a few Academy awards as well.

Out-of-town tryouts were held in November 1952 at the Parsons Theater in New Haven, Connecticut. Opening night on Broadway came two weeks later, on December 3, at the Cort Theatre. In the audience that night were Bill Bast, Dizzy Sheridan, Jane Deacy, and James Sheldon, among others.

The night was a tremendous success for James Dean. *See the Jaguar* heralded, at the age of 21, his Broadway debut. It was a showcase role in an important play. It didn't matter that the show itself received, at best, mixed reviews; it didn't even matter that the show, after a mere five performances, shut down with an astounding abruptness. *See the Jaguar* changed his life, as he had sensed it would. It made him a *name*, it separated him from the overcrowded pack of Broadway's Brando-wannabes, and for the next year it put him in demand by television producers (not exactly known for their casting originality) seeking to hire an actor to play an emotionally pent-up, disturbed youth. And perhaps most importantly, it validated for James Dean what he had previously only suspected: that he was, at the very least, of Broadway caliber.

WILLIAM SELF
Producer of "The Unlighted Road," a 1955 episode of the CBS television program "Schlitz Playhouse of Stars" in which James Dean made his final television appearance.

"SENTENCE OF DEATH"

> I called him James, because I preferred to call people by their full name. We had worked on another show together in addition to "Danger"; it was sponsored by Westinghouse—I remember that. Maybe it was "Westinghouse Summer Theater," 1951 or 1952. No, it was right before "Danger."
>
> Betsy Palmer

Right before they did "Danger" together (August 25, 1953), James Dean and Betsy Palmer appeared in "Sentence of Death," an episode of the CBS television program "Studio One Summer Theatre." The episode co-starred Gene Lyons and Ralph Dunn, was directed by Paul Nickell and written by Adrian Spies and Thomas Walsh, and aired on August 17, 1953.

SEPTEMBER 30, 1955

Hyped in its print advertisements as "The Day That Shook a Generation," *September 30, 1955* told writer/director James Bridges's autobiographical story of a young man's idolization of James Dean and how Dean's death impacted the young man's life.

The genesis of *September 30, 1955* was a play written by Bridges entitled, tellingly, *How Many Times Did You See "East of Eden"?* With the success of his 1973 film *The Paper Chase*, Bridges became empowered to turn *How Many Times . . . ?*, his pet project, into a film. He chose Richard Thomas to play Jimmy J., the character based on himself; Jerry Weintraub to produce it; and Leonard Rosenman to score it. He incorporated footage of James Dean, from *East of Eden*, into its intensely personal framework.

Still, upon its release in December 1977 *September 30, 1955* not only failed to shake a generation; it barely managed a ripple at the box office.

ROD SERLING

Telewriter of "A Long Time Till Dawn," a 1953 episode of the NBC television program "Kraft Television Theatre" that provided James Dean with one of his best vehicles, a substantial role as a young criminal torn between the love of his family and his violent psychotic tendencies.

Rod Serling (1924–1975) was one of the finest writers ever to work in television. His Emmys include those for "Patterns" ("Kraft Television Theatre," 1955), "Requiem for a Heavyweight" (a television landmark, 1956), "The Comedian" ("Playhouse 90," 1957), "The Twilight Zone" (which he created and won two Emmys for in the 1959–1960 and 1960–1961 seasons, and which ran from 1959 to 1965 and from 1985 to 1987), and "It's Mental Work" ("Bob Hope Presents the Chrysler Theatre," 1963–1964). Serling also created the shows "The New People" (1969–1970) and "Night Gallery" (1970–1973, the latter in which Steven Spielberg made his directorial debut).

In 1975, Serling was slated to host a summer variety television series entitled "Keep on Truckin'," but he died two weeks before the show's premiere.

SEVENTEEN MAGAZINE
Teen magazine that published "An Actor in Search of Himself," an October 1955 article about James Dean.

IVAN SEWARD
One of Jimmy Dean's grade school teachers at Fairmount (Indiana) West Ward elementary school.

SEX
Also see HOMOSEXUALITY.

> It's probably hearsay to say this, but I felt he was asexual. I didn't *ever* get any sexual things from him at all. I never got any sexual vibes. And I don't think anybody else did. I never knew anybody who knew him who got any sexual vibes from him.
>
> Beverly Long

> "I've known many actors who have been twisted up in their sex lives, but never anybody as, as, I guess, *unhealthy* is the word, as sick and unhealthy as Dean was."
>
> Elia Kazan, *Omaha Sunday World Herald*, October 28, 1956

> Jimmy had gained considerable experience with women in his less than twenty-one years [sic]. He had learned, for example, that he scored most successfully with older women and he told me one story of how he had managed to get a pass mark in one of his school classes only after having an affair with the teacher.
>
> Joe Hyams, *Mislaid in Hollywood*

> "It wasn't that he was particularly sexual in his relationships. In fact, most of the time he was asexual, if that makes sense."
>
> John Gilmore, *The Hollywood Star*

> Like many others in the entertainment world, he had a strong sex drive. There were times when his days were so filled with activity that there was no time left for sleep or rest.
>
> *Exposed* magazine

SHADY CHARACTER, UNLIMITED
New York City company (address: 160 Madison Avenue, 10016) that markets a line of James Dean eye wear.

THE SHAMROCK HOTEL
Houston, Texas, hotel (address: 6900 South Main Street) that served as the model for Jett Rink's Emperador Hotel in *Giant*. According to Dean aficionado Cherry Rees, who worked as an administrative assistant at the Shamrock from 1979 to 1984, the hotel was built by Glenn McCarthy (the inspiration for Ferber's Jett Rink) in 1949 and opened in a lavish ceremony on St. Patrick's Day that year. In the early 1950s McCarthy sold the Shamrock to the Hilton Corporation, which changed the hotel's name to the Shamrock-Hilton, the name that was used until the hotel's demise in 1986.

BUD SHANK

Recorded (with Chet Baker) the tribute album *Theme Music from 'The James Dean Story'* for World Pacific Records, from which the single "Let Me Be Loved" (with "Jimmy, Jimmy" as its B side) was released.

Born Clifford Shank, Jr., in Dayton, Ohio, in 1926, Shank was a recording artist (alto sax and flute), and a studio musician for television and movies. He was considered an important figure on the West Coast jazz scene in the 1950s. Later, he composed the scores of several films, including *War Hunt* (1961). In the mid-1980s Shank abandoned work as a studio musician to concentrate on performing at beebop revival concerts.

SHE WAS ONLY A FARMER'S DAUGHTER

A Santa Monica City College drama department production in which Jim Dean appeared. His co-stars included other SMCC students: Dick Mangan, Nancy McGrath, Rosemary Cicco, Allan Light, Betty Youst, Ellen Sidman, and Ann McCormack. *She Was Only a Farmer's Daughter* was presented as a part of the school's 1950 May Day festivities.

CHARLIE SHEEN

One of the many young actors touted as "the next James Dean" during the 1980s. However, Dean was one big, explosive nerve; his emotion seemed drawn from deep within. Sheen, on the other hand, is of the "grit your teeth, clench your jaw, and stare hard" school of acting.

Born Carlos Irwin Estevez in New York City in 1966, Sheen's film credits include *Grizzly II* (1984), *Red Dawn* (1984), *Lucas* (1986), *The Boys Next Door* (1986), *Platoon* (in a role originally intended for his brother, Emilio Estevez; 1986), *The Wraith* (1987), *Three for the Road* (1987), *No Man's Land* (1987), *Wall Street* (1987), *Eight Men Out* (1988), *Major League* (1989), *Men at Work* (directed by and co-starring Emilio, 1990), and *Navy SEALS* (1990).

MARTIN SHEEN

The patriarch and most talented of the acting Sheens (or the acting Estevezes for that matter), Martin Sheen was obviously affected profoundly by James Dean. During the 1960s and 1970s Sheen was frequently compared to Dean, and nowhere were the similarities more apparent than in Sheen's performance in Terrence Malick's exemplary film, *Badlands* (1973).

Born Ramon Estevez in 1940, Martin Sheen made his stage debut in 1959 in the off-Broadway play *The Connection*, which he followed with his Broadway debut in *Never Live Over a Pretzel Factory*. But it was Frank Gilroy's *The Subject Was Roses*, a 1965 Broadway hit, for which he received a Best Supporting Actor Tony nomination, and its film adaptation three years later, in which Sheen garnered national acclaim. His other films include *The Incident* (1967), *Catch 22* (1970), *Apocalypse Now* (1979), *Gandhi* (England, 1982), *That Championship Season* (1982), *The Dead Zone* (1983), *The Believers* (1987), *Wall Street* (1987), *Da* (1988), and *Beverly Hills Brats* (1989). He also made his directorial debut in 1990 with *Cadence*. In addition, he has had considerable success in made-for-television movies, including "That Certain Summer" (a genre landmark, 1973) and "The Execution of Private Slovik" (1974).

In September 1980 Sheen traveled to Fairmount, Indiana, to attend the 25th anniversary memorial services for James Dean. At the ceremonies he dedicated several plaques in acknowledgment of the impact James Dean has had, not only on Martin Sheen but on two generations of actors.

> "Jim Dean and Elvis were the spokesmen for an entire generation. When I was in acting school in New York, years ago, there was a saying that if Marlon Brando changed the way people acted, then James Dean changed the way people *lived*. He was the greatest actor who ever lived. He was simply a genius."
>
> Martin Sheen on James Dean, *People*

> "No one came before him, and there hasn't been anyone since."
>
> Martin Sheen on James Dean, *James Dean: American Icon*
> by David Dalton

JAMES SHELDON

When James Dean moved to New York in 1951, one of his first orders of business was to contact advertising executive James Sheldon. Contrary to previously published reports, it was not Rogers Brackett who introduced the pair (at least not directly; Sheldon didn't even know Brackett). James Sheldon recently recalled, "A director friend of mine, Ralph Levy, was working out here [in Los Angeles], and he asked me to see this boy that was a friend of a friend of his [Brackett]—and would I see him when he came to New York?

"I wasn't directing at that time; I was supervising commercials on different shows. And Jimmy came up to the office. He had just arrived in town. He was living at the YMCA on 63rd Street. . . . And I asked him to read a scene—just to see, you know, what he was like. And he read very well."

So well, in fact, that Sheldon sent Dean to audition for a regular co-starring role on a television show he handled. The show was "Mama," based on the Broadway hit *I Remember Mama*, and the part was the one played by Dick Van Patten, who was being replaced because he had been drafted into the military. As fate would have it, Jimmy got the part, but Van Patten was excused from service and returned to the show.

James Sheldon's role in discovering James Dean, or at least in nurturing his early career, has never really been explored. Previous books have stated that the two became roommates and have even implied that their relationship extended beyond the realm of friendship. However, the facts are that the two men never became roommates and that their friendship was strictly platonic. As Sheldon states matter-of-factly and without design, "We were friends. We palled around. I was married at the time. Jimmy attached himself to me, and I would lend him money. Or I would call people up and say, 'Did you see so-and-so?' It became a little bit annoying after a while, but we got along very well. I liked him, and so I sent him over to directors he didn't know." At least one of them, Bob Stevens, gave him a job, a part in an episode of the television program "Suspense."

Further, and perhaps more importantly, James Sheldon introduced James Dean to another friend of his—his agent. Her name was Jane Deacy. And not only did Deacy sign Dean as a client; she, perhaps more than anyone other than Dean himself, was also responsible for his eventual success.

Meanwhile James Sheldon (who also had a part in the discovery of Troy Donahue) turned to directing. He was given *his* break by Fred Coe. According to Sheldon, "Fred had worked in New York, and he gave me a job on 'Philco Playhouse,' which he produced. And I did a pilot of a series for him called 'Mr. Peepers.' " The show, with Wally Cox and Tony Randall, became a substantial hit. Sheldon later directed James Dean twice. The first occasion was on "Armstrong Circle Theatre" in an episode entitled "The Bells of Cockaigne"; the second was on "Harvest," an episode of "Robert Montgomery Presents the Johnson's Wax Program."

In early 1955 Sheldon moved to Los Angeles as the entire television industry gradually gravitated west. He last saw Jimmy Dean on September 25, 1955, at a party in Dean's honor at the Chateau Marmont hotel. Years later, he wistfully recalled, "It was the Sunday before the Friday that he died." Sheldon also dismissed theories attributing Dean's death to suicide or some sort of death wish. "He was all excited about what he was doing. He was excited about his [new] car. We were gonna do this [television] thing together. He was gonna do 'The Battler.' I don't believe the death wish theory. I have no reason to believe it at all."

James Sheldon's durable, successful career as a director has included numerous episodic television programs, including multiple episodes of "McMillan and Wife," which starred Rock Hudson.

ELIZABETH "DIZZY" SHERIDAN

Years before she was the co-star of television's "Alf" (as neighbor Rachel Ochmonek), Liz Sheridan was "Dizzy" Sheridan, a New York City dancer with a flair for the dramatic, a sometime singer with a salty tongue and an easy laugh. She was also one of the loves in the life of James Dean. Of their introduction in early 1952 Sheridan recalled:

> He was wet. And he was blond. And his glasses were all wet. And he was a tiny bit shorter than I was. So he looked small and blond and wet. And lovely. I just remember that he was terribly intense. And we intensely spoke about intense things.
>
> *Hollywood: The Rebel James Dean*

They were drawn together, of all things, by bullfighting—also by the peculiar desperation that comes with being young and hungry and living in the big city. To describe their relationship as an affair is to trivialize it. It was more of a friendship between two creative people who nurtured each other's courage and reaffirmed each other's existence at a time when few others seemed to notice. They held hands in Central Park. They played records for one another over the telephone. And they shared their dreams over a candle-light dinner in which a bowl of Shredded Wheat was the main course. "We would sit and talk for hours and hours, and it was a desperate kind of feeling he had toward seeing me anytime that he had a spare moment and talking to me anytime that he had a spare moment," Dizzy wrote of Dean in *Photoplay*, "almost like he didn't have anybody else either. He just sort of hung on, and, I guess, I must have been particularly lonely at the time, too, because we got to be inseparable."

For a short period, for economic as well as emotional reasons, Dizzy and Dean lived together at a time when such arrangements were regarded with disdain, if not contempt. But nothing, it is written, lasts forever—particularly when one is young. It was inevitable that with success the nature of their relationship would deteriorate, but not before Jimmy proposed marriage. And although Dizzy didn't marry him, she did hitchhike with him from New York to Fairmount, Indiana, to meet his folks. It wasn't a honeymoon; it was the culmination of their friendship.

And then came *See the Jaguar*, and for Jimmy the struggle, or at least one form of it, ended. A series of television shows followed. And then *The Immoralist*. And then *East of Eden*. And then stardom and death and immortality in rapid, dizzying succession. Dizzy wasn't so much left out in the cold as she was left scratching her head, wondering why he had changed and, worse, why *she* had changed. She later acknowledged, "After he got established, then *I* was afraid and I started to hang on to him. And he didn't seem to want the responsibility of having anybody hang on to him, because he was going up too fast. That was just extra weight."

So Dizzy packed her bags and moved to the Virgin Islands. Later she moved to Puerto Rico, where she worked as a dancer until she was shot in the left foot by a gunman during a robbery. So she turned to singing and then acting. She appeared in two New York plays, *Ballad for a Firing Squad* (1968) and *The American Hamburger League* (1969).

The last time she saw Jimmy Dean was during one of her visits back to New York. They were in a cab. He grabbed her hand as she exited and said, "Now that I am more or less established and can help you, I wish you would come out to Hollywood, and I'll see if I can get you some dancing." She learned about his death while in Puerto Rico. She was in a movie theater. A paperboy shouted the news from the street. It was a cold jolt of an ending to what was once a warm, intense, and loving friendship.

> "I want to be placed on a piano in some cafe and just sing my ass off until I die."
>
> Liz Sheridan, 1989 *TV Guide*, September 30, 1989

NANCY SHERIDAN

Actress who appeared in "Harvest," a 1953 episode of the NBC television series "Robert Montgomery Presents the Johnson's Wax Program" that co-starred James Dean.

Sheridan also appeared in the plays *Sure Fire!* (1926), *Jupiter Laughs* (1940), and *The Dragon's Mouth* (1955), among others.

SHERMAN OAKS, CALIFORNIA

At the time of his death James Dean was living in a rented house at 14611 Sutton Street in the city of Sherman Oaks in the San Fernando Valley. The house has since burned down.

SHOES

In his footwear James Dean had a penchant for black motorcycle boots. He also wore sneakers and penny loafers. His shoe size? A reported 9E.

"SHOW BIZ TODAY"

Entertainment information series on the Cable News Network that produced a segment about James Dean in 1985 to commemorate the 30th anniversary of his death. The segment was hosted by Sandy Kenyon and featured footage, photographs, and interviews with Ortense Winslow, Marcus Winslow, Jr., Adeline Nall, Dick Davalos, Dennis Hopper, Eartha Kitt, Martin Landau, Corey Allen, Jim Backus, Ernie Tripke, Bill Dakota, and others.

IRVING SHULMAN

One of the screenwriters of *Rebel Without a Cause*. During preproduction Shulman was replaced by Stewart Stern. On screen Shulman received an "adaptation by" credit, with Stern getting the actual screenplay credit. Shulman also penned a book, *Children of the Dark*, which was based on *Rebel Without a Cause*. The book was published by Henry Holt in 1956.

Irving Shulman, born in 1913, wrote several other books, including the biography *Harlow* (which caused a legal furor upon its release, 1964) and the novel *Upbeat* (1965).

HERMAN SHUMLIN

One of the backers of the Actors Studio and a Broadway producer and director of considerable repute. Herman Shumlin, of Atwood, Colorado, was the original director of the 1954 staging of André Gide's *The Immoralist*. However, his reputation notwithstanding, he was fired from the production by its producer, Billy Rose, and was replaced by Daniel Mann.

The following year, Shumlin (1898–1979) scored a revenge of sorts by receiving a Tony nomination as Best Director for *Inherit the Wind*. He later won the Tony for producing *The Deputy* (1964), which he also directed. His first Broadway success was the smash hit *Grand Hotel*, which was produced in 1930. However, he is probably best known as the man who discovered Lillian Hellman, who was a reader in his office when she wrote her first play, *The Children's Hour*, which Shumlin produced in 1934. He later produced other Hellman plays including *The Little Foxes* (1938).

In addition to his work in the theater, Shumlin directed the superlative 1943 Bette Davis film *Watch on the Rhine* (adapted from yet another Hellman play, which Shumlin had also produced on Broadway), as well as the 1945 picture *Confidential Agent*.

Dean, drunk and disorderly at the Villa Capri. He's got Steffi Sidney in one arm, his stomach in the other. When Sidney was seven years old, Orson Welles used her in his magician's act. He sawed her in half.

STEFFI SIDNEY

The first time I met Jimmy was when we were testing, or getting our wardrobe looked at. He came up to me, and he just sort of swaggered, and then he *hit* me real hard. And I thought, "What the hell did he do that for?" The next time he wandered over I said, "What, you're not going to hit me again?" And he said, "No, no. My name is Jimmy Dean.' "

Steffi Sidney

According to Warner Brothers casting sheets, Steffi Sidney, daughter of noted Hollywood columnist Sidney Skolsky, was one of the actresses considered for the role of Judy, the female lead in *Rebel Without a Cause*, before it was awarded to Natalie Wood. The part that she *did* get was the one of Millie, one of the film's gang members. It wasn't much of a part, but Steffi was determined to make the most of it. She recently recalled with bemusement, "Stewart Stern decided that my character of Millie was insecure. So, I thought, well gee, what does an insecure girl do? I decided she'd comb her hair all the time. So I carried a brush throughout the picture, not that you ever saw it." Like the other actors who portrayed members of the gang, Steffi supplemented her acting salary by wearing her own clothes in the picture.

Wanting to be alone on the set of *Rebel*, while Steffi
Sidney makes a point.

"We got a wardrobe fee," said Steffi. "I think it was three dollars a day for the shoes and three dollars a day for the jacket. So that's an extra six dollars. We were all trying to make as much money as we could." And like the other actors who portrayed members of the gang, most of Sidney's part was excised out of the final print. She was left with, in her own succinct words, "one line and a sneeze."

Still, her part in the film has endeared her to Dean fans throughout the world and has made more of a lasting impression than her other film appearances, which include *The Life of Riley* (1948), *The Eddie Cantor Story* (produced by Skolsky, 1953), and *Teacher's Pet* (1958).

The last time Sidney saw Jimmy Dean was a few weeks before his death at a party for Frank Sinatra held at the Villa Capri restaurant in Hollywood. As she recalled recently, the evening left a vivid impression on her: "I don't know whether he was drunk when he came, but he sure was drunk by the time he left. He came wandering over to me. His fly was open. He had just finished *Giant*, I think. His hair was cut back where they aged him. And he said, 'You know, Steffi, we've never had our picture taken together. Let's have a picture taken together.' And I said, 'Sure, Jimmy.' So he put his arm around me, and they took a picture. The irony was that the eight-by-tens arrived at my house the morning of September 30, 1955."

SYLVIA SIDNEY
Actress who was considered for the part of Judy's mother in *Rebel Without a Cause*, a role that eventually went to Rochelle Hudson.

SIGMA NU
UCLA fraternity (then located at 601 Gayley Avenue in Westwood) that James Dean belonged to for a short period, circa 1950–1951. He was eventually ejected from the group for breaking various rules and regulations. His violations included engaging in a fistfight with one of his "brothers."

THE SILVER CHALICE
Nineteen fifty-four Warner Brothers movie that James Dean turned down. His instincts were good; the film wasn't.
   The Silver Chalice was produced and directed by Victor Saville and written by Lesser Samuels from a novel by Thomas Costain. It starred a toga-clad Paul Newman (one of the film's few entertaining diversions) in the role turned down by Dean. It was Newman's film debut. Years later, he reportedly took out an ad in the Hollywood trade papers to formally apologize for the film. It co-starred, ironically, Pier Angeli. In fact, it was while visiting the set of *Chalice* that Dean first met Angeli. The rest of the cast included Jack Palance, Virginia Mayo, Walter Hampden, Joseph Wiseman, Alexander Scourby, Lorne Greene, Michael Pate, E. G. Marshall, and in a small role, disguised by a bad bleached-blond dye job, 16-year-old Natalie Wood.

BETTY LOU SIMMONS
The death of James Dean prompted innumerable oddities, including an article that appeared in *Lowdown* magazine entitled "The Girl James Dean Was Going to Marry!" The article, penned by Joel Raleigh, contended that on November 2, 1954, James Dean was driving "his German Porsche" through the backwoods of Baton Rouge, Louisiana, when he stumbled upon a native lass by the name of Betty Lou Simmons. Naturally, as the article would have it, the former farm boy and the farm girl fell instantly in love and made urgent plans to marry after Jimmy completed work on *Giant*.
   As proof of the scenario the article reprinted a Western Union telegram that Dean purportedly wired to Betty Lou. It read: "BOUGHT YOU A DIAMOND RING AND HAVE PLACED ORDER FOR TEN COUNT THEM TEN CHILDREN. MISS YOU TERRIBLY AND PRAY FOR YOU EVERY NIGHT. PRAY FOR ME AND LOVE ME, JIMMY." The telegram was dated March 7, 1955. According to Raleigh, who apparently failed to do his research, "Jimmy needed Betty Lou's prayers, for the following day he was killed."
   As anyone remotely interested in James Dean knows, he was killed on September 30, 1955, not on March 8, 1955. Further, Jimmy didn't even own a Porsche in November 1954. He bought his first Porsche the following March. And what was James Dean doing driving the backwoods of Baton Rouge, Louisiana, in the first place? The real lowdown is that he wasn't.

JACK SIMMONS

Certainly one of the most mysterious, and therefore interesting, characters involved in the James Dean story. Unfortunately little is known about Jack Simmons or his relationship with Dean. What *is* known is that Simmons was also a friend of television's Vampira, Maila Nurmi, and that the three of them (along with other friends Binky Doyle, Jack Kramer, and Brad Jackson) were a common late-night attraction at Googie's coffee shop on Sunset Boulevard. What is also known is that Simmons hailed from Philadelphia, was 20 years old, and was practically handed his first acting job by James Dean. It was in the December 1954 "General Electric Theater" episode "The Dark, Dark Hour," in which Jimmy co-starred with Ronald Reagan.

Jimmy also campaigned intently to coerce Nicholas Ray into casting Simmons as Plato, the second male lead in *Rebel Without a Cause*. He got as

The character of Plato was reportedly modeled after Jack Simmons, James Dean's close and mysterious friend.

far as getting Simmons an audition with Ray. However, according to the film's screenwriter, Stewart Stern, "I wanted the role to have homosexual overtones—but he [Simmons] was too much. Plato was young, yes, and searching for warmth, but he would have been too much." Instead Simmons was cast in the much smaller role of Moose, one of the gang members. In the film he is the one who gives Dean's character, Jim Stark, the knife in the Griffith Observatory fight scene.

What is also known is that practically every day during the shooting of *Rebel* Jack Simmons arrived and departed with James Dean. As Beverly Long recently recalled, "I just knew that Jimmy had this really strange little friend who he insisted be on the movie. And Jack was on the movie. Jimmy used to bring him to the set. I remember that they would show up, a lot of times, together. He would bring him and take him home. I don't know *how* he knew him. Nobody ever explained it to me.

"He was the strangest little person you saw in your life. He was like a little bird, flitting about. Most of us didn't have too much to do with Jack Simmons. We would all kind of look at each other and kind of say, 'Who is this guy?' "

Reportedly Jack Simmons was living with Jimmy during the making of *Rebel* and, according to some sources, even up until the time of Jimmy's death. An interesting, telling item appeared in a Sidney Skolsky column in the July 1955 issue of *Photoplay*. It read, "Jack is always around [Jimmy's] house and set. He gets Jimmy coffee or a sandwich or whatever Jimmy wants. Jack also runs interference for Dean when there are people Jimmy doesn't want to see. There are many people trying to contact a nobody who has just become a star."

The truth about Simmons and his role in the life of James Dean will likely remain ambiguous until Simmons himself decides it should be otherwise. Over the years he has maintained an extremely low profile in matters regarding his old friend, and that is one of the few incontestable truths about Jack Simmons. He was, at least for a period, a very close friend of James Dean's.

"He had this strange little friend. . . ." That's Jack Simmons centered between Corey Allen and James Dean.

ROBERT SIMON

Actor who appeared in "Sleeping Dogs," a 1952 episode of the CBS television program "The Web" in which James Dean also appeared. Simon later appeared in "A Long Time Till Dawn," a 1953 episode of the NBC series "Kraft Television Theatre" in which Dean also appeared. By the time of the latter show, however, Dean's roles had been upgraded to co-starring status.

Simon also appeared in the Broadway plays *No for an Answer* (1941), *Truckline Cafe* (1946), and *Sundown Beach* (1948).

FRANK SINATRA

A few weeks before his death Jimmy attended a party hosted by Frank Sinatra at the Villa Capri restaurant in Hollywood. That evening Sinatra entertained Dean and his other guests, who included Lauren Bacall and Walter Winchell, with songs from his *Wee Small Hours of the Morning* album.

Interestingly, during the casting of *Giant* George Stevens received a letter from an executive at Rogers and Cowan, a major entertainment public relations firm, imploring him to consider casting Frank Sinatra—as Jett Rink! The letter read, in part:

> I have a serious thought about your *Giant* casting, and despite the fact that it's wild, I'll pass it on. Unfortunately, he is *not* a client of mine: Frank Sinatra. I think he'd make a helluva Jett Rink, and he could probably learn to talk Texas if he had to. I saw him the other night in a Warner musical, *Young at Heart*, and he turns in a completely different characterization from the one in *Suddenly*. I think he's a good actor. . . .

SIXTEEN MAGAZINE

In its November 1957 issue *Sixteen* magazine published a cover tribute to James Dean entitled "Jimmy Dean: How Great Is He? (2 Years Later)." The inside article proceeded to compare Dean with Elvis Presley, Pat Boone, Ricky Nelson, Tommy Sands, Sal Mineo, and the other teen idols of the day.

Other *Sixteen* articles about James Dean include:

☆ November 1957   "Jimmy Told Me: 'Don't Print That Photo!' " by Frank Worth
☆ March 1959   "Jimmy the Kid"
☆ September 1959   "A Tribute to Jimmy"

SIDNEY SKOLSKY

Sidney Skolsky (1905–1983) was a Hollywood columnist/reporter for more than 50 years. He is best known for his columns in the *New York News* and the *New York Post*, the latter of which was published daily. Skolsky was also syndicated by United Features, and his column appeared in Los Angeles in the *Hollywood Citizen-News*.

Unlike most of his peers, Sidney Skolsky took a particular interest in struggling unknown actors and actresses, many of whom used to frequent Schwab's drugstore in the hope of being discovered. Accordingly Skolsky maintained his office on the mezzanine floor of Schwab's, where he had a view of the soda fountain patrons.

Jimmy showing off his shaved hairline to Sidney Skolsky.

Skolsky wrote an article on James Dean that appeared in *Photoplay*. The setting was Googie's, Schwab's next-door rival and a notorious Dean hangout:

> Then a young fellow approaches. He is wearing a black leather
> jacket, a pair of old-fashioned steel-framed glasses. [It's] Jimmy Dean.
> I can tell by the way they greet him that they respect him. The talk
> continues. Jimmy slumps in the booth, seldom opens his mouth.
> When he does join in, all listen, and he says something like this:
> "All neurotic people have the necessity to express themselves. For me,
> acting is the most logical."

In addition to being a columnist, Skolsky was also a part-time movie producer. He produced two pictures, *The Jolson Story* (1946), which was a major, Oscar-nominated hit, and *The Eddie Cantor Story* (1953). For years, Skolsky developed *The Jean Harlow Story*, which he planned to produce as a starring vehicle for Marilyn Monroe. However, according to Skolsky, "On the Sunday they found Marilyn dead, I had an appointment with her for that afternoon at four to work on *The Jean Harlow Story*."

"SLEEPING DOGS"

Episode of the CBS television program "The Web" that featured James Dean in one of his earliest television appearances. The show aired on February 20, 1952.

LOIS SMITH

Actress who had a small but significant part in *East of Eden*, the role of Kate's sympathetic bar slave. For the role Smith starved herself on a diet of black coffee, lettuce, carrots, and bread. Not surprisingly, she was a member of the Actors Studio at the time. Like James Dean, she was discovered on Broadway (in a play called *Time Out for Ginger*) by Elia Kazan. She was subsequently hailed for her performance in *Eden* and was named one of *The Film Daily*'s selections as having given one of the best performances by a juvenile actress during 1955.

Following *Eden*, Warner Brothers had understandably high hopes for the career of Lois Smith. She was one of several young actresses considered for the role of Luz Benedict II in *Giant*. However, the role went to Carroll Baker, and for Lois Smith (born in 1930) stardom never came. Her films include *Strange Lady in Town* (1955), *Five Easy Pieces* (1970), and *Resurrection* (1980).

WILLIAM SMITHERS

Another Actors Studio member, William Smithers appeared with James Dean in a 1953 Studio production of *End as a Man*. During breaks from rehearsals Smithers and Dean entertained themselves by performing duets (with Jimmy on the recorder) of baroque music.

Smithers later appeared as a regular on the television programs "The Witness" (1960–1961), "Peyton Place" (1965–1966), and "Executive Suite" (1976–1977). Since 1981 he has also been popping in and out of "Dallas" as Jeremy Wendell.

THE SMITHS

See STEPHEN MORRISSEY.

LOUIS SOBOL

In his newspaper column "On the Beat" dated March 2, 1955, Louis Sobol was one of the first to forecast stardom for James Dean. In his review of *East of Eden* Sobol wrote, "Out of it emerges a brand new young star—Jimmy Dean."

SOCIAL SECURITY NUMBER

James Dean's social security number was 310-28-1959.

SOMEBODY UP THERE LIKES ME

Shortly before his death James Dean agreed to appear in the Rocky Graziano biopic for MGM, *Somebody Up There Likes Me*. The film was to be produced by Charles Schnee, directed by Robert Wise, and written by Ernest Lehman.

It's easy to see what appealed to Dean about the role. Graziano was a kid from the Lower East Side of New York City who overcame a record of reformatories and prisons to become the middleweight boxing champion of the world. The drama was inherent, and Dean, who had learned how to fight for *East of Eden*, was eager to display his newfound skills. MGM certainly was eager—and lucky—to have him. The only way that MGM could obtain his services was by exercising a contract option that stemmed from MGM's loaning of Elizabeth Taylor to Warner Brothers for *Giant*. The option gave MGM its pick of Warner Brothers stars, and after the release of *East of Eden* MGM decided on Dean.

After Dean's death MGM scurried about in search of a replacement. After he reportedly saw "The Battler" (which was also to have starred Dean) on television, Robert Wise chose Paul Newman. *Somebody Up There Likes Me*, released in 1956, made Newman a star.

The film, ironically, co-starred Pier Angeli and Sal Mineo. The cast also included Everett Sloane, Eileen Heckart, Joseph Buloff, Harold J. Stone, and Robert Loggia. Joseph Ruttenberg won an Oscar for his cinematography. The film received an additional Oscar for its art direction.

"SOMETHING FOR AN EMPTY BRIEFCASE"

Episode of the NBC television series "Campbell Soundstage" that starred James Dean. The program was directed by Don Medford, produced by Martin Horrell, and written by S. Lee Pogostin. It co-starred Susan Douglas and aired on July 17, 1953.

Dean portrayed Joe Adams, yet another juvenile delinquent who strives to go straight. But before he does, he decides to commit one last petty larceny job to purchase a briefcase, albeit an empty one, which would symbolize his new life of respectability.

THE SONGS BY DEAN

"Dean's Lament" and "Jungle Rhythm" are two songs that James Dean performed on the conga drums. The songs were audiotaped and released after his death on the 45rpm *James Dean on Conga Drums in an Ad-Lib Jam Session*. The songs featured Bob Romeo on flute and were released by Romeo Records.

THE SONGS ABOUT DEAN

The following is a selective alphabetical list of the songs that have been recorded about or in tribute to James Dean.

SONG	ARTIST
"American Rebel"	Chris Busone
"Ballad of James Dean"	Dick Jacobs
"Ballad of James Dean"	Dylan Todd with the Joe Reisman Orchestra
"Ballad of James Dean"	The Four Tunes
"A Boy Named Jimmy Dean"	Dick Jacobs
"Come Back Jimmy Dean, Jimmy Dean"	Bette Midler
"Deanie Boy"	Tommy Deans Orchestra
"Dean's 11th Dream"	James Dean Driving Experience
"He's My Jim"	Joanna Dean
"His Name Was Dean"	Jimmy Wakely and the George Cates Orchestra
"His Name Was Dean"	Nathan Russell Orchestra and vocal under the direction of Ray Ellis
"His Name Was Dean"	Don Sargeant
"Home in Indiana, James Dean"	Red River Dave
"Hymn for James Dean"	Red River Dave
"I Miss You Jimmy"	Veretta Dillard
"James Dean"	The Eagles
"James Dean"	The Goo Goo Dolls
"James Dean"	The Jets
"James Dean"	The Kevin Brown Band
"James Dean"	Larry John McNally
"James Dean"	Red River Dave
"James Dean, Deck of Cards"	Red River Dave
"James Dean, the Greatest of All"	Red River Dave
"James Dean (Just a Boy from Indiana)"	Jimmy Wakely and the George Cates Orchestra
"The James Dean Love Song"	Red River Dave
"James Dean's First Christmas in Heaven"	Red River Dave
"James Dean's Message to Teenagers"	Richard Buckley
"James, 1955"	Gary Hardier
"Jamie Boy"	Kay Starr
"Jim Dean of Indiana"	Phil Ochs
"Jimmy Dean"	Troll
"Jimmy Dean Is Not Dead"	Red River Dave
"Jimmy, Jimmy"	Chet Baker and Bud Shank
"Jimmy, Jimmy"	Madonna
"Jimmy, Jimmy"	Jimmy Wakely and the George Cates Orchestra
"Let Me Be Loved"	Chet Baker and Bud Shank
"Let Me Be Loved"	Eydie Gorme
"Let Me Be Loved"	Mantovani
"Let Me Be Loved"	Tommy Sands
"The Memory of You"	The Three Jays
"Message from James Dean"	Billy Hayes Orchestra conducted by Archie Bleyer
"Ridin' with James Dean"	Joan Jett
"A Young Man Is Gone"	The Beach Boys

SONGS THAT REFER TO DEAN

The following is a selective alphabetical list.

SONG	ARTIST
"American Pie"	Don McLean
"Cadillac Ranch"	Bruce Springsteen
"Fade Away and Radiate"	Blondie
"He's a Rebel"	The Crystals
"Hound Dog Man"	Roy Orbison
"Jack and Diane"	John Cougar Mellencamp
"The Kid's a Punk"	Slik
"Movie Star"	Harpo
"The Punk"	Cherry Vanilla
"Rebel"	Carol Jarvis
"Rebel"	John Miles
"Rebel, Rebel"	David Bowie
"Rebel Rouser"	Bob Welch
"Rebels Without a Clue"	The Bellamy Brothers
"Rock On"	David Essex
"Rock On"	Michael Damian
"School Days"	Loudon Wainwright III
"Stars"	Janis Ian
"Texas in My Rear View Mirror"	Mac Davis
"Vogue"	Madonna
"Walk on the Wild Side"	Lou Reed
"We Didn't Start the Fire"	Billy Joel
"Wild Children"	Van Morrison

SOPHOCLES

In 1954 James Dean appeared in an off-Broadway reading of *Women of Trachis*, an adaptation by Ezra Pound of a one-act play by Greek dramatist Sophocles (496–406 B.C.).

J. D. SOUTHER

Singer/songwriter John David Souther co-wrote the song "James Dean," recorded by the Eagles in 1974.

JAMES SPADA

In the mid-1960s New York–born and –raised James Spada was a member of the James Dean Memory Fan Club and president of the Marilyn Monroe Memorial Fan Club. Today Spada is a bestselling biographer whose subjects include Monroe, Barbra Streisand, Bette Midler, Katharine Hepburn, Grace Kelly, and Peter Lawford.

SPEECH

With the release of *East of Eden* James Dean was lambasted by some critics for slurring his words and mumbling, à la Marlon Brando. According to

Gene Nielsen Owen, Jimmy's college drama teacher, his speech was difficult to discern because he wore an upper plate in his mouth, the result of a dental problem. However, his high school drama teacher (who also taught him speech and coached him on the debate team), Adeline Nall, contends that Dean had no problem whatsoever with articulation and that his movie mumbling was pure contrivance.

AARON SPELLING
Before he became a primetime producer of such television mega-hits as "The Love Boat," "Fantasy Island," "Charlie's Angels," and "Dynasty," Aaron Spelling was an actor. He was up for the role of Pinky Snythe in *Giant*, which eventually went to Bob Nichols.

ADRIAN SPIES
Co-writer of "Sentence of Death," a 1953 episode of the CBS television program "Studio One Summer Theatre" that co-starred James Dean. Spies wrote for several other programs in the 1950s including "Playhouse 90," "The Walter Winchell File," "Wagon Train," and "Schlitz Playhouse of Stars." His numerous credits in subsequent years include episodes of "T. J. Hooker" and "In the Heat of the Night."

THE SPIRIT OF ST. LOUIS
Warner Brothers movie about Charles Lindbergh that James Dean reportedly turned down. The picture was made anyway and was released in 1957 with James Stewart as Lindbergh. The film was produced by Leland Hayward, directed by Billy Wilder, and written by Wilder and Wendell Mayes.

SPORTS
In his senior year at Fairmount High School, James Dean was named the school's top athlete. While at Fairmount he excelled at basketball and pole-vaulting. He also played baseball. As a child he was a prodigious figure skater. Later his interests turned to bullfighting and, of course, car racing.

THE SPORTS CAR CLUB OF AMERICA
In 1955 Dean was a member of the Sports Car Club of America (SCCA), a car-racing organization.

BRUCE SPRINGSTEEN
Like Elvis Presley, with whom he has been compared, Bruce Springsteen is a major James Dean fan. He paid homage to Dean in his song "Cadillac Ranch" and is said to have carried David Dalton's book *James Dean: The Mutant King* on the road with him for a year.

THE STAGE
See THE PLAYS.

JOHN STANDER

In 1955 John Stander was the assistant mortician at the Kuehl Funeral Home in Paso Robles, California, where the body of James Dean was taken on the evening of September 30. It was John Stander who signed Dean's death certificate.

STAND-INS

Mushy Callahan, *East of Eden*	Bill Gunn, *The Immoralist*
Mushy Callahan, *Rebel Without a Cause*	Alan Sacks, *Rebel Without a Cause*
Joe D'Angelo, *Giant*	Art Sacks, *Rebel Without a Cause*

MAUREEN STAPLETON

Despite her young age (she was only 30 at the time), Maureen Stapleton was one of the actresses considered to play the role of Judy's mother in *Rebel Without a Cause*. The role eventually went to Rochelle Hudson.

CHARLIE STARKWEATHER

Teenaged murderer who bore a slight physical resemblance to his idol, James Dean. As described by Starkweather's sister, "He used to pose like James Dean. He'd stand there with a cigarette hanging from out of the front of his mouth. You know, with the lips apart so that his teeth would show." Years later Starkweather provided the inspiration for *Badlands*, a 1973 motion picture that starred Martin Sheen, who was also inspired by Dean.

MANYA STARR

Telewriter of "The Evil Within," a 1953 episode of the ABC television program "Tales of Tomorrow" that co-starred James Dean.

Starr also produced the 1960 Broadway play *Whisper to Me*.

TILLIE STARRIET

The hairstylist on *East of Eden* and *Rebel Without a Cause*.

THE STARS

Book by Edgar Morin that contains a chapter called "The Case of James Dean." Originally the book was published as *Les Stars* in France in 1957. The chapter on Dean was subsequently published in *The Evergreen Review* the following year. In 1961 Grove Press published the entire book in English under the title *The Stars*.

"STARS OF TOMORROW"

In 1955 the Motion Picture Exhibitors honored 10 performers in its annual "Stars of Tomorrow" poll. They were named, presumably, in order of preference:

1. Jack Lemmon	5. Ernest Borgnine	8. Richard Egan
2. Tab Hunter	6. James Dean	9. Eva Marie Saint
3. Dorothy Malone	7. Anne Francis	10. Russ Tamblyn
4. Kim Novak		

"STARS OVER HOLLYWOOD"
CBS Radio program on which James Dean appeared in 1951. It was through Dean's connection with the advertising agency of Foote, Cone and Belding, which handled the show, that he got the job.

"Stars over Hollywood" aired on Saturday mornings from 1941 to 1954. The show usually featured light comedies with a regular cast consisting of Basil Rathbone, Alan Hale, Sr., and Ann Rutherford.

THE STATLER HOTEL
Los Angeles hotel that was used as one of the locations for *Giant*. Shooting took place at the Statler in early August 1955. In the film the hotel served as Jett Rink's Emperador Hotel. Today the hotel is known as the Hilton Center and is still located at 930 Wilshire Boulevard.

EDGAR STEHLI
Actor who appeared in "The Unlighted Road," a 1955 episode of the CBS television program "Schlitz Playhouse of Stars" that starred James Dean in his final television performance. Previously Stehli had also appeared with Dean in "Hound of Heaven," a 1953 episode of the NBC program "The Kate Smith Show."

Onstage, Stehli made his Broadway debut in 1920 with *The Treasure*. His many other plays include *Hamlet* (1922), *Arsenic and Old Lace* (1941), and *The Devils* (1965). He also wrote the 1927 play *The Ladder*, which he also starred in.

ROD STEIGER
Rod Steiger starred in "The Evil Within," a 1953 episode of the ABC television program "Tales of Tomorrow" that co-starred James Dean.

Steiger, born in 1925, made his film debut in the Pier Angeli vehicle *Teresa* (1951). He attained stardom of his own with *On the Waterfront* (Best Supporting Actor Oscar nomination, 1954). His subsequent film credits include *Oklahoma!* (1955), *The Court-Martial of Billy Mitchell* (1955), *The Pawnbroker* (Best Actor Oscar nomination, 1965), *Doctor Zhivago* (1965), and *In the Heat of the Night* (Best Actor Oscar winner, 1967).

JOHN STEINBECK
> The picture is not like the book, but in a larger sense the picture *is* the book. I am more than glad that my book has contributed, among all the other considerations, to what is probably the best motion picture I have ever seen. Isn't it odd to be able to say this in humility!
>
> John Steinbeck to audience at the New York
> premiere of *Eden*, March 9, 1955

Salinas-born John Steinbeck (1902–1968) is the author whose 25th novel, *East of Eden*, was adapted into a star-making motion picture for James Dean.

Other films adapted from Steinbeck works include *Of Mice and Men* (1939), *The Grapes of Wrath* (1940), *Tortilla Flat* (1942), *The Moon Is Down*

(1943), *The Red Pony* (1949), *Viva Zapata!* (1952), and *The Wayward Bus* (1957).

For the movie rights to *East of Eden*, copyrighted in 1952, Warner Brothers paid Steinbeck the then-huge sum of $125,000 plus 25 percent of the film's net receipts.

> "Jesus Christ, he *is* Cal!"
> John Steinbeck to Elia Kazan upon meeting James Dean

PHIL STERN

Phil Stern's introduction to James Dean was not unlike Phil Stern's photographs: disarming, unusual, and intensely spontaneous. Stern was driving his car down Sunset Boulevard in West Hollywood. Speed demon Dean, on his motorcycle, was darting in and out of traffic in the same neighborhood. A collision almost occurred. Instead an acquaintance, both personal and professional, developed, and today, more than 35 years later, Phil Stern's photographs of James Dean stand among the finest ever taken of him.

In addition to his shots of Dean, Phil Stern's outstanding portfolio includes photos of the Hollywood A-list alumni: Marlon Brando, Frank Sinatra, Judy Garland, Marilyn Monroe, etc.

> "One of the things that justify the motion picture industry."
> Phil Stern after seeing an early screening of James Dean's
> performance in *East of Eden* in January 1955

STEWART STERN

At the time he was hired to script *Rebel Without a Cause* after Leon Uris and Irving Shulman had been fired from the same job, Stewart Stern was only 30 years old. His connections to the project were considerable. He had already established a relationship with James Dean through his cousin, Arthur Loew, Jr., and through his friend, *Rebel* composer Leonard Rosenman. About his introduction to Dean at Loew's house, Stern later said, "I arrived at his house to find somebody in the living room whom I had never seen before, an odd young man with no front teeth. He had lost them in a fall out of a barn when he was a kid in Indiana. Now he had broken his upper plate, and it was away being fixed. He said he was James Dean."

Prior to *Rebel*, Stewart Stern had one screenwriting credit. He wrote *Teresa*, which launched Pier Angeli to stardom and won Stern a Best Story Oscar nomination. His subsequent credits have included *The Rack* (produced by Loew; it starred Paul Newman, with whom Stern has had a lifelong personal and professional relationship, 1956), *Thunder in the Sun* (adaptation credit, 1958), *The Outsider* (1962), *The Ugly American* (which starred Brando, 1963), *Rachel, Rachel* (Best Screenplay Adaptation Oscar nomination, 1968), *The Last Movie* (Dennis Hopper's follow-up to *Easy Rider*, 1971), and *Summer Wishes, Winter Dreams* (1973). In addition, Stern scripted the telefilms "Sybil" (Emmy winner, Best Writing in a Special, 1976–1977) and "A Christmas to Remember" (1978). He also wrote the 1989 book *No Tricks in My Pocket: Paul Newman Directs*.

Rebel Without a Cause garnered Stewart Stern his second Oscar nomination. During the making of the picture he worked closely with James Dean, with whom he developed a friendly relationship. After Dean's death Stern reluctantly scripted the documentary *The James Dean Story* (1957). He agreed to do the project despite qualms about participating in the then-rampant exploitation of Dean.

> "Marlon is a manipulator and so was Jimmy. I mean, I think there was, along with all the other qualities, a metal-hard core, submerged, which allowed him to operate very consciously and never be the victim. That's why I say I didn't know him. I think I *sensed* him, but I didn't *know* him."
>
> Stewart Stern, *New York*, November 8, 1976

STETSON

The Stetson Company of New York (350 Fifth Avenue, 10118) is marketing a line of James Dean hats. More than 35 years ago Stetson provided the hats worn in the film *Giant*.

ARTHUR STEUER

Telewriter of "The Dark, Dark Hour," a 1954 episode of the CBS television program "General Electric Theater" that starred Ronald Reagan and James Dean.

Steuer also wrote the 1955 stage play, *The Terrible Swift Sword*.

"THE STEVE ALLEN SHOW"

NBC comedy variety series that aired a tribute to Dean on October 14, 1956. *Also see* STEVE ALLEN.

BILL STEVENS

Race car driver/mechanic who was a friend of James Dean's circa 1955.

GEORGE STEVENS

Of the three film directors with whom he worked, James Dean was least compatible with George Stevens. At the time Stevens was considered one of the finest filmmakers in America. It was a sentiment shared by Dean—*before* he started work on *Giant*.

> "... Then there's George Stevens, the greatest [director] of them all. I'm supposed to do *Giant* for him. This guy was born with the movies. So real, unassuming. You'll be talking to him, thinking he missed your point, and then—bang—he has it."
>
> James Dean, *New York Times*, March 13, 1955

Dean's ardent, early enthusiasm was reciprocated by Stevens, who told a reporter, "Long before the movies or anyone else in Hollywood had heard of Dean, I saw him in a half-hour television play ["A Long Time Till Dawn"]. It was the first time that I ever watched anxiously for the credits so I could find out who this brilliant, sensitive actor was."

James Dean grimaces at his director, George Stevens.

With *Giant* touted as the moviemaking event of the year, practically every name actor in Hollywood showed up at Stevens's doorstep on bended knee. James Dean was no exception. He openly, unabashedly campaigned for the role of Jett Rink and eventually captured Stevens's favor. One of the factors leading to Stevens's decision was a performance Dean gave in a television program entitled "You Are There." Stevens sent a memo to CBS on September 1, 1954, requesting a copy of the show. The episode was "The Capture of Jesse James," and it featured Dean as Bob Ford, the man who shot Jesse James. Stevens saw the show on September 28 and apparently liked the way Dean looked in western duds.

However, almost immediately into the Marfa, Texas, location shooting, it became apparent that the two men had different visions of Ferber's story. Stevens, who had been preparing the project for nearly three years, envisioned an epic story told on a vast landscape. Dean, directly out of his highly collaborative project with Nick Ray, saw it as a small story, a triangular character study, with epic implications. It is also significant to note that by the outset of *Giant* Dean was seriously entertaining aspirations of becoming a film director himself and was certainly aggressive in his stance that Stevens's approach to the film was full of artifice.

Stevens, on the other hand, dismissed Dean's protests as an actor's vanity. As he later contended, "Jimmy never understood that Jett Rink was only part of the film. . . . Edna Ferber in the book never intended Jett Rink to be the central figure." He, of course, had a point. Stevens may have been used to being the sole visionary on all of his films, but James Dean was also accustomed to being the sole primary figure in all of *his* films. Working in an ensemble that had to battle for screen time with landscape and cattle was something Dean never quite adjusted to.

During the first week on the Marfa set Dean was soundly reprimanded by Stevens in front of the entire *Giant* company. From that point their relationship was irreparably damaged, no matter how cordial it sometimes appeared later. As Rock Hudson related to *The Hollywood Reporter*: "He hated George Stevens, didn't think he was a good director, and he was always angry and full of contempt."

Dean vented his anger at Stevens with schoolboy impertinence. Once, on the set, he called him "fatso." More often he held up production by showing up late. His most drastic strike took place when the company returned to Los Angeles. It was July 23, and Dean simply decided not to show up for work on a day that he was scheduled to be in front of the cameras. Later, almost immediately after he completed work on *Giant*, Dean showed up at the Warner Brothers lot in his new Porsche. He drove over to the *Giant* set and asked Stevens if he wanted to go for a short ride. It wasn't so much a question as it was a dare. Stevens got in, and Dean tore off. It was Dean's adolescent way of regaining control, of telling his director "You no longer own me."

> "All in all it was a hell of a headache to work with him. He was always pulling and hauling, and he had developed this cultivated, designed, irresponsibility. 'It's tough on you,' he'd seem to imply, 'but I've just got to do it this way.' From the director's angle, that isn't the most delightful sort of fellow to work with."
> George Stevens, *Saturday Review*, October 13, 1956

On the evening of September 30, 1955, George Stevens received a phone call. According to Beulah Roth, it was she who made the call: "Sandy [Roth] called me at a quarter to six to tell me. He was crying. He told me to get on the phone to Warner Brothers and to find George Stevens and break the news. And I did. I called the projection room, and I got George Stevens. I never heard a response on the other end. He just hung up."

The following day Stevens told the *Los Angeles Mirror-News* that Dean's death was "a great tragedy. He had extraordinary talent." Still, during the following year leading to the release of *Giant*, Stevens seemed to harbor reservations about Dean and his overwhelming posthumous popularity. *Giant*, after all, was a George Stevens production in much the same way that *East of Eden* had been an Elia Kazan production. But as he had with Kazan to a lesser extent, Dean stole Stevens's thunder and his picture, but, alas, not his Oscar. Among *Giant's* 10 nominations, only Stevens went home with a statuette.

The career of George Stevens (1904–1975) began in 1933 with *The Cohens and Kellys in Trouble*. His subsequent credits include *Bachelor Bait* (1934), *Kentucky Kernels* (1934), *Laddie* (1934), *The Nitwits* (1935), *Alice Adams* (his first important picture, 1935), *Annie Oakley* (1935), *Swing Time* (one of the all-time great musicals, 1936), *A Damsel in Distress* (1937), *Quality Street* (1937), *Vivacious Lady* (1938), *Gunga Din* (1939), *Vigil in the Night* (1940), *Penny Serenade* (1941), *Woman of the Year* (1942), *The Talk of the Town* (1942), *The More the Merrier* (Best Director Oscar nomination, 1943), *I Remember Mama* (1948), *A Place in the Sun* (Best Director Oscar winner, 1951), *Something to Live For* (1952), *Shane* (Best Director Oscar nomination, 1953), *The Diary of Anne Frank* (Best Director Oscar nomination, 1959), *The Greatest Story Ever Told* (1965), and *The Only Game in Town* (in which he directed Elizabeth Taylor a third time, 1970).

> "He had it coming to him. The way he drove, he had it coming."
> George Stevens to Elizabeth Taylor,
> *Elizabeth Taylor: An Informal Memoir*

LEITH STEVENS
Leith Stevens composed the score of the 1957 motion picture documentary *The James Dean Story*.

Stevens (1909–1970) also composed the scores of *The Wild One* (1954), *The Five Pennies* (Best Scoring of a Musical Oscar nomination, 1959), *A New Kind of Love* (Best Adapted Musical Score Oscar nomination, 1963), among other films.

ROBERT STEVENS
Director of a "Suspense" episode that James Dean appeared in early in his television career.

Stevens, born in 1925, directed several films, including *The Big Caper* (1957), *Never Love a Stranger* (in which he directed Steve McQueen, early in *his* career, 1958), *I Thank a Fool* (England, 1962), *In the Cool of the Day* (early Jane Fonda, 1963), and *Change of Mind* (1969). On television, Stevens won a 1957 Best Director Emmy for "The Glass Eye," a presentation of "Alfred Hitchcock Presents."

DAVID J. STEWART
Co-star of *The Immoralist*, which opened on Broadway on February 8, 1954, and featured James Dean.

The season prior to the opening of *The Immoralist* Stewart, an Actors Studio member from Omaha, Nebraska, won the Clarence Derwent award as "The Outstanding Young Actor of the Year" for his performance in *Camino Real*. He also appeared on Broadway in *The Rose Tattoo* (1951), *Anastasia* (1954), and *After the Fall* (1964).

FRED STEWART

A founding member of the Actors Studio who directed James Dean in a studio production of Edna St. Vincent Millay's *Aria da Capo*.

In addition to directing, Stewart was an actor and made numerous Broadway appearances. His stage credits include *The Crucible* (1953) and *Cat on a Hot Tin Roof* (1955). He died in 1970 at the age of 63.

JAMES STEWART

Even though he was 47 years old at the time it was made, Jimmy Stewart reportedly campaigned for the role of Jett Rink in *Giant,* which of course went to 24-year-old James Dean. Interestingly, Stewart was also one of Elia Kazan's primary choices for the role of Dean's father in *East of Eden,* a role that eventually went to Raymond Massey. A picture that Stewart *did* make that Dean turned down was *The Spirit of St. Louis* (1957).

DENNIS STOCK

In 1955 New York–born Dennis Stock was a 27-year-old photographer with the Magnum Agency who obtained an assignment from *Life* magazine. His job? To shoot a photo essay on rising and moody new star James Dean.

Stock initially met Dean at Nick Ray's bungalow at the Chateau Marmont in West Hollywood. After seeing an early screening of *East of Eden,* which overwhelmed him, Stock orchestrated the now-famous *Life* (March 7, 1955) shoot. His intent was to capture James Dean in those seemingly fleeting moments between hometown boy in Fairmount, Indiana, struggling hipster actor in New York, and emerging star in Hollywood.

The photos, all shot in black-and-white, are probably the most revealing photos ever taken of James Dean. They have been in circulation, in various forms, for more than 35 years (best displayed in Stock's book, *James Dean Revisited*) and have been studied and committed to memory by Dean aficionados all over the world.

As for Dennis Stock, he developed a friendship, albeit a brief one, with James Dean, and it was through Dean's efforts that Stock was hired as the dialogue director (a curious job for a photographer) on *Rebel Without a Cause*.

FRED STOCKER

Fred Stocker of Albany, Indiana, is the creator and organizer of the James Dean Memorial Rod Run, a Fairmount, Indiana, car show that has been held for more than 30 years.

DEAN STOCKWELL

Not since the late James Dean with whom he is often compared has a young man appeared who aroused the hot controversy that rages around Dean Stockwell. Like Jimmy Dean, he is accused of being filled with bitterness, unrest and conceit. . . .

Photoplay, June 1958

After Jimmy Dean's death actor Dean Stockwell, who was being touted by some as "the next Dean," was involved in an automobile accident in which he dented his Renault. Subsequent magazine articles pondered such preposterous dribble as "Can Dean Stockwell Shake the Jimmy Dean *Jinx*?" Stockwell balked at the comparison—so much so that he stopped wearing his eyeglasses in public because cynics contended that they were a prop in his alleged effort to emulate Dean.

The facts are that Dean Stockwell was working in movies when James Dean was in junior high school back in Fairmount, Indiana. Born in 1938, Stockwell was a child actor with credits including *Anchors Aweigh* (1945), *Abbott and Costello in Hollywood* (1945), and *Gentleman's Agreement* (1947). His subsequent career, one of Hollywood's most durable, includes the films *Compulsion* (1959), *Sons and Lovers* (England, 1960), *Long Day's Journey Into Night* (1962), *Dune* (1984), *Paris, Texas* (1984), *Blue Velvet* (1986), *Beverly Hills Cop II* (1987), and *Married to the Mob* (Best Supporting Actor Oscar nomination, 1988). Since 1989, Stockwell has been co-starring on the television series "Quantum Leap."

ARTHUR STORCH
Actor who appeared in a 1953 Actors Studio production of Calder Willingham's *End as a Man*, in which James Dean also appeared. Unlike Dean, Storch stayed with the show, in which he made his official New York debut when it opened at the Theatre de Lys in September 1953.

Storch, born in New York in 1925, also appeared on stage in *Look Homeward, Angel* (1957). His film credits include *The Strange One* (1957), *The Mugger* (1958), and *Girl of the Night* (1960). In 1961 Storch turned to directing stage productions.

LOUIS CLYDE STOUMEN
Erroneously credited elsewhere as the producer of the 1957 documentary *The James Dean Story*. Actually Stoumen was the film's production designer and was responsible for the creative filming of the innumerable still photos incorporated into the film.

Prior to his work on *The James Dean Story*, Louis Clyde Stoumen won an Oscar for directing the documentary short *The True Story of the Civil War* (1956) and was nominated for another one for directing the documentary feature *The Naked Eye* (1956).

HARRY STRADLING
Elia Kazan's first choice as cinematographer for *East of Eden*. When Stradling turned out to be unavailable, Kazan selected Ted McCord.

"STRAIGHTAWAY"
Nineteen sixty-two television series that featured a Dean-inspired episode

entitled "To Climb Steep Hills." "Straightway" starred Brian Kelly and John Ashley and aired on ABC for one season.

LEE STRASBERG

> Lee was drawn to anyone with a tic, perhaps because neurotics seem to have heightened sensitivities. He loved highly gifted freaks. He loved that negative-positive level of genius in the crazily desperately talented Kim Stanley and Geraldine Page and Jimmy Dean.
>
> Cindy Adams, *Lee Strasberg: The Imperfect Genius*

Lee Strasberg, born in Austria in 1901, is generally regarded as the most influential acting coach of our time.

In 1948 he became the artistic director of the Actors Studio in New York, and his name has been synonymous with that organization ever since. He gained worldwide recognition for his teaching of the Method as well as for his impressive celebrity-studded student body.

Initially James Dean worshiped the mention of Lee Strasberg's name. His devotion soured, however, after he was accepted into the Actors Studio and was severely reprimanded by Strasberg in front of the class. As he confided to Bill Bast, "I don't know what happens when I act—inside. But, if I let them dissect me, like a rabbit in a clinical research laboratory or something, I might not be able to produce again. They might sterilize me! That man had no right to tear me down like that." Dean stalked out of the studio. He eventually returned, lured back by another studio member, but he did so with a measure of caution and a wall of defenses. It was only with the security of stardom that Jimmy returned to the chorus of those singing Strasberg's virtues. To the *New York Times* Dean hailed Strasberg as "an incredible man, a walking encyclopedia with fantastic insight."

In October 1956 Lee Strasberg stood before his class at the Actors Studio and talked about his former student. The session was audiotaped and is reprinted in part below.

> I saw Jimmy Dean in *Giant* the other night, and I must say that . . . [Strasberg breaks down, crying] You see, that's what I was afraid of. [Long pause] When I got out of the cab, I cried. And it was funny, because, actually, I was crying out of two reasons. It was pleasure and enjoyment, which is odd, but I must say I cried from that, too. And the other thing was seeing Jimmy Dean on the screen.
>
> I hadn't cried when I heard of his death. Jack Garfein called me from Hollywood the night it happened, and I didn't cry. It somehow was what I expected. And I don't think I cried from that now. What I cried at was the waste, the waste.
>
> *Strasberg at the Actors Studio*, edited by Robert Hethmon

Since the 1960s the Actors Studio has lost its original prestige. Still, Lee Strasberg won acclaim for his own performances in the films *The Godfather*

Part II (his film debut, Best Supporting Actor Oscar nomination, 1974), *. . . And Justice for All* (1979), and *Going in Style* (1979).

Strasberg died in 1982, leaving behind a legacy of disputed brilliance and undeniable impact.

SUSAN STRASBERG

Born in 1938 to Lee and Paula Strasberg, actress Susan Strasberg was one of several actresses considered for the role of Luz Benedict II in *Giant*, which eventually went to Carroll Baker. Strasberg was also, according to press reports, one of James Dean's dates.

She later married and divorced Christopher Jones, touted by some as "the next Dean."

Strasberg made her film debut in 1955 in William Inge's *Picnic*. Her subsequent credits include *Stage Struck* (1958), *Hemingway's Adventures of a Young Man* (1962), *The Brotherhood* (1968), and *In Praise of Older Women* (1978). She also co-starred in the television programs "The Marriage" (with Hume Cronyn and Jessica Tandy, 1954) and "Toma" (1973–1974).

> James Dean courted Susan Strasberg in jeans, a dirty leather jacket and cowboy boots. Susan was as happy as if he had dressed in a tuxedo.
>
> *The Hollywood Reporter*, 1955

A STREETCAR NAMED DESIRE

Wardrobe tests for *Rebel Without a Cause* were held on the set of *A Streetcar Named Desire* on the Warner Brothers lot. This was ironic, of course, considering the Brando/Dean comparisons that were running rampant in Hollywood at the time. Making the most of the situation, Jimmy entertained those present by impersonating Brando's staircase wailing of "Stella!"

EDDIE STUART

Wrote the song "His Name Was Dean" from the motion picture soundtrack of *The James Dean Story*.

"STUDIO ONE"

Sponsored by Westinghouse, "Studio One" was an acclaimed CBS drama series that ran primarily on Monday nights from November 1948 to September 1958. During summer months the show ran under the altered title "Studio One Summer Theatre."

James Dean appeared in several episodes of "Studio One," including a bit part in "Ten Thousand Horses Singing" (March 30, 1952), a featured role in "Abraham Lincoln" (May 26, 1952), and a co-starring role in "Sentence of Death" (August 17, 1953).

SUICIDE

After his death speculation abounded that James Dean had committed suicide. Supporters of this theory pointed out that Dean had been obsessed with death, that he had taken out a life insurance policy the week of his death, that he had given away his cat days before his death, that he was still mourning the loss of Pier Angeli to Vic Damone, that he was mourning the more recent break-up with Ursula Andress, that he kept a noose hanging from the ceiling of his home, and on and on.

One magazine, *Anything Goes*, published an article entitled "Did Jimmy Dean Commit Suicide?" Another magazine, *Hush-Hush*, pondered the same question. According to the latter publication, "Jimmy killed himself as surely and as quickly as if he had used a gun or the noose-knotted rope he kept in his apartment."

Proponents of the suicide theory, however, failed to mention that, just prior to his death, Dean had signed a $100,000-per-film contract; that he was about to return to New York, where he had three Broadway producers groveling at his feet; that he was signed to star in two major television productions; that he had made a highly promising film that would be released within weeks; that he would likely be nominated for an Oscar for his film debut; and, perhaps most telling, that he had invited practically all of his friends to accompany him on the trip to Salinas. Suicide victims don't usually invite an audience to witness their death. Further, on the afternoon of September 30 James Dean had a passenger with him in his Porsche. Even if he *had* contemplated suicide, it is highly unlikely that he would have risked taking another life with him.

The suicide theory was simply propagated by a faction of the publishing industry that sold magazines by sensationalizing Dean's death. And it was paid for by a mostly young and gullible audience who refused to believe that their brooding idol had died a simple, accidental death.

ED SULLIVAN
In October 1956, television impresario Ed Sullivan (1901–1974) became embroiled with rival Steve Allen over, of all things, a tribute to James Dean. *Also see* "THE ED SULLIVAN SHOW."

JOSEPH SULLIVAN
Actor who appeared in *Women of Trachis* (1954), in which James Dean also appeared.

Sullivan, born in New York in 1918, appeared on Broadway in several plays, including *The Country Girl* (1950), *The Rainmaker* (1950), and *Fiddler on the Roof* (1964).

SUNDEX
In 1989 Sundex, a telephone credit card company, issued a James Dean telephone credit card.

FLORENCE SUNDSTROM
Cast member of *See the Jaguar* (1952), which featured James Dean.

Florence Sundstrom later appeared as a regular in the television series

"The Life of Riley" (1955–1956). Her film credits include *The Rose Tattoo* (1955), *The Vagabond King* (1956), *Spring Reunion* (1957), and *Bachelor in Paradise* (1961). Onstage she appeared in *Bright Honor* (1936), *The Rose Tattoo* (1951), and *Look Homeward, Angel* (1957).

SUNSET BOULEVARD

The deserted mansion sequences in *Rebel Without a Cause* were shot in the same house used in the classic motion picture *Sunset Boulevard*. Interestingly the 22-room mansion wasn't located on Sunset Boulevard (or even in Beverly Hills) at all. Instead it was located at 641 Irving Boulevard at the intersection with Wilshire Boulevard.

The house was owned by J. Paul Getty, who was paid $200 a day by Warner Brothers for its use in *Rebel Without a Cause*. It was built in 1922 and torn down in 1957. *Rebel* was its last hurrah.

LELA SWIFT

Director of "Sleeping Dogs," a 1952 episode of the CBS television program "The Web" in which James Dean appeared.

Dean as a glamour boy. Note the Method actor bruises.

T

TABLEHOPPERS
West Hollywood nightclub, located on Sunset Boulevard, that was one of James Dean's hangouts. It was at Tablehoppers where Dean's impromptu musical performance, later marketed as *James Dean on Conga Drums in an Ad-Lib Jam Session*, took place.

"TALES OF TOMORROW"
Science fiction television series, sponsored by Kreisler Watch Bands, that aired Friday nights on ABC from August 1951 to June 1953. On May 1, 1953, James Dean co-starred in "The Evil Within" episode of "Tales of Tomorrow." The show starred Rod Steiger and Margaret Phillips.

JESSICA TANDY
Jessica Tandy starred in "Glory in Flower," a 1953 episode of the CBS television program "Omnibus" in which James Dean was featured. Later Tandy was one of several actresses considered for the part of Luz Benedict, which eventually went to Mercedes McCambridge.

Born in Great Britain in 1909, Jessica Tandy is, undisputably, one of the first ladies of the American stage. Her Broadway credits include three Tony Awards as Best Actress for her performances in *A Streetcar Named Desire* (1948), *The Gin Game* (1978), and *Foxfire* (1983). She received additional nominations for *Rose* (1981) and *The Petition* (1986).

Tandy's surprisingly limited film career includes *The Seventh Cross* (1944), *A Woman's Vengeance* (1948), *The Birds* (1963), *The World According to Garp* (1982), *Best Friends* (1982), *Cocoon* (1985), *Batteries Not Included* (1987), *Cocoon: The Return* (1988), and *Driving Miss Daisy* (Best Actress Oscar, 1989).

Tandy has been appearing on television since 1939, and has made numerous guest appearances on episodic programs. She also starred, along with her husband Hume Cronyn, in the short-lived NBC situation comedy "The Marriage" (1954), the first network series to be broadcast in color. In 1987 she again starred with Cronyn in a "Hallmark Hall of Fame" production of "Foxfire," for which she won a Best Actress Emmy.

REBA TASSELL
Actress who portrayed the love interest of the character portrayed by James Dean in "Harvest," a 1953 episode of the NBC television program "Robert Montgomery Presents the Johnson's Wax Program." Tassell later changed her

name to Rebecca Wells, married director Don Weis, and is now known as Rebecca Weis.

ELIZABETH TAYLOR

> You are an odd one, aren't you, Jett?
>
> Elizabeth Taylor to James Dean in *Giant*

At the time she made *Giant* Elizabeth Taylor was 23 and had the kind of beauty that made even the most seasoned set technicians spin around and stop in their cables, drop their chins, open their mouths, and *stare*. She was so beautiful that even heterosexual women dropped at her feet. In an industry of hype and illusion Elizabeth Taylor was (and remains, to a large extent) the genuine article: a movie star who looks like a movie star, off the screen, in person, up close. As Richard Burton wrote in his diary, she was beautiful "beyond the dreams of pornography."

Taylor's beauty was not only disarming but unsettling, and upon their introduction James Dean was among the intimidated—shy, awkward, fumbling. The meeting took place in the Warner Brothers green room. Dean was making *Rebel Without a Cause* at the time. Taylor, a contract star for MGM, for whom she had been making films since the age of 11, was visiting the lot. She was taken on a tour and given Doris Day's old dressing room. She was also taken on a ride around the Warner Brothers lot—by Dean—in his Porsche.

Giant represented to her not only a furlough of sorts but also a considerable challenge. As the film progressed, she was to age into a 55-year-old, graying grandmother, the mother of Carroll Baker, who in real life was actually one year her senior. George Stevens had initially wanted Grace Kelly for the part. When she turned out to be unavailable, Stevens selected Taylor, which prompted speculation in Hollywood over whether or not she could handle the role. After all, at the time and despite the acclaim she had received four years earlier in another George Stevens film, *A Place in the Sun*, Elizabeth Taylor was known primarily as an extraordinary beauty, *not* an extraordinary talent.

Still, as *Giant* commenced shooting in Marfa, Texas, in June 1955, she quickly captivated the entire company, and practically everyone fought for morsels of her attention. Initially she spent most of her free time with Rock Hudson, much to the dismay and envy of James Dean. Dean didn't like Hudson, and the feeling was more than reciprocated. At one point Hudson aligned with Taylor and Carroll Baker, united in frustration by what they perceived (and were correct in perceiving) to be Dean's shameless inclination to steal scenes, no holds barred, without regard for his fellow actors.

But then something happened. Dean befriended Taylor and whisked her away from the group. Carroll Baker recalled in her autobiography, *Baby Doll*:

> She went off mysteriously each evening with Jimmy, and none of us could figure out where they went. They would arrive for dinner

together, she would sit in the balcony next to him during the rushes, and then they would slip away for what seemed like most of the night.

It is much to her credit that Elizabeth Taylor has always been attracted to the underdog, the less fortunate. In her relationships with men she has been extremely giving emotionally, nurturing, maternal. As for Dean, it seemed no matter where he went, he was always in search of a man who would father him and a woman who would mother him. He loved to be cuddled, to be held, to be comforted. On the set of *Giant* he was akin to a stray dog that nobody wants, guarded, sullen, wounded. Elizabeth Taylor became his adoptive protector.

We had an extraordinary friendship. We would sometimes sit up until three in the morning, and he would tell me about his past, his mother, minister [Reverend DeWeerd], his loves, and the next day he would just look straight through me as if he'd given or revealed too

Elizabeth Taylor on James Dean: "The memories I have of him are very happy. I loved him a lot. He was a great talent."

much of himself, given too much of a part of himself away, and it would maybe take, after one of these sessions, a couple of days before we'd be back on friendship terms. He was very afraid to give of himself.

Elizabeth Taylor on James Dean

He was very afraid of being hurt. He was afraid of opening up in case it was turned around and used against him.

Elizabeth Taylor on James Dean

Another element bonding Taylor and Dean was the difficulty they had with their director. At one point George Stevens admonished Taylor before the cast and crew (just as he had done earlier with Dean), saying that all she cared about was looking glamorous and that she would never become "a real actress." To compound the tension Elizabeth had back problems, which Stevens insisted were either imagined or contrived.

In fact, during the film's production, an entire file was maintained solely to document Taylor's illnesses, hospitalizations, late arrivals, and the numerous shooting delays they caused. In addition to her back problems, she suffered a leg infection, exhaustion, and laryngitis.

According to Carroll Baker, among others, James Dean worshipped Elizabeth Taylor. Typical of his nature, however, he pushed her away and put a wedge in their friendship. He did it with a prank that seemed innocent enough. One day, a photographer showed up on the set to take publicity shots of Taylor. While the photographer was at work, Jimmy snuck up behind Elizabeth, picked her up, and held her upside down, revealing her undergarments. Taylor, known to have a wicked sense of humor, but also a consummate professional, was livid and their relationship cooled down.

Nonetheless, shortly before he completed his work on *Giant*, Jimmy was presented with a kitten by Elizabeth. He named it Marcus, after his uncle and cousin back home in Fairmount, Indiana. Taylor later remarked "I think he loved that kitten and was as close to that kitten as anything in life."

Suddenly, the phone rang. I heard him [Stevens] say, 'No, my God. When? Are you sure?' And he kind of grunted a couple of times and hung up the phone. He stopped the film and turned on the lights, stood up and said to [those in] the room, 'I've just been given the news that Jimmy Dean has been killed.' There was an intake of breath. No one said anything. I couldn't believe it; none of us could. So several of us started calling newspapers, hospitals, police, the morgue. The news was not general at that time. After maybe two hours the word was confirmed.

Elizabeth Taylor: An Informal Memoir

The day after James Dean's death, a Saturday, George Stevens ordered the cast and crew to continue shooting—business as usual. Taylor balked. Kitty Kelley, in her biography *Elizabeth Taylor: The Last Star*, quotes Rock Hudson:

> "George was not very kind to her. Elizabeth is very extreme in her likes and dislikes. If she likes, she loves. If she doesn't like, she loathes. And she has a temper, an incredible temper which she loses at any injustice. George forced her to come to work after Dean's death . . . but she let him have it."

She also got sick to her stomach. According to a notation made on October 1, 1955, by a Warner Brothers executive, "she lost her breakfast in the makeup department." *Giant* cinematographer William C. Mellor recalled, "This was a moment I shall not forget. Elizabeth Taylor, highly strung, emotional, broke down and sobbed—she remained in a state of near-collapse for three days." She was subsequently hospitalized, and according to the October 4 edition of *The Hollywood Reporter*, "The real inside on why Liz went to the hospital: She worked herself into hysteria crying over the death of James Dean, her *Giant* co-star."

Elizabeth Taylor surprised many with her apparent depth of feeling for James Dean, and more, later, with the maturity of her performance in *Giant*. Her other films include *There's One Born Every Minute* (1942), *Lassie Come Home* (1943), *Jane Eyre* (1944), *The White Cliffs of Dover* (1944), *National Velvet* (1944), *Courage of Lassie* (1946), *Cynthia* (1947), *Life with Father* (1947), *A Date with Judy* (1948), *Julia Misbehaves* (1948), *Little Women* (1949), *Conspirator* (England, 1949), *The Big Hangover* (1950), *Father of the Bride* (1950), *Father's Little Dividend* (1951), *Quo Vadis?* (1951), *A Place in the Sun* (1951), *The Light Fantastic* (1951), *Love Is Better than Ever* (1952), *Ivanhoe* (1952), *The Girl Who Had Everything* (1953), *Rhapsody* (1954), *Elephant Walk* (in which she replaced Vivien Leigh, 1954), *Beau Brummell* (1954), *The Last Time I Saw Paris* (1954), *Raintree County* (Best Actress Oscar nomination, 1957), *Cat on a Hot Tin Roof* (Best Actress Oscar nomination, 1958), *Suddenly, Last Summer* (Best Actress Oscar nomination, 1959), *Butterfield 8* (Best Actress Oscar winner, 1960), *Scent of Mystery* (1960), *Cleopatra* (1963), *The V.I.P.s* (England, 1963), *The Sandpiper* (1965), *Who's Afraid of Virginia Woolf?* (Best Actress Oscar winner, 1966), *The Taming of the Shrew* (1967), *Doctor Faustus* (1967), *The Comedians* (1967), *Reflections in a Golden Eye* (1967), *Boom* (1968), *Secret Ceremony* (England, 1968), *The Only Game in Town* (1970), *X, Y and Zee* (England, 1972), *Hammersmith Is Out* (1972), *Under Milk Wood* (England, 1973), *Night Watch* (England, 1973), *Ash Wednesday* (1973), *The Driver's Seat* (Italy, 1973), *The Blue Bird* (1976), *A Little Night Music* (1977), *Winter Kills* (1979), *The Mirror Crack'd* (England, 1980), and *Young Toscanini* (1988).

After the death of her friend Rock Hudson, Elizabeth Taylor has devoted much of her time to AIDS awareness, education, and fundraising; she has married and divorced a seventh time; she has marketed a highly successful perfume; and she has managed to parlay her weight losses and gains into a national spectator sport. But, whatever she has done, she has continued to keep a nation enthralled for five decades.

NICK TAYLOR
Produced and directed the 1989 British documentary *Bye Bye Jimmy*.

VAUGHN TAYLOR
Actor who co-starred in "Ten Thousand Horses Singing," a 1952 episode of the CBS television program "Studio One" in which James Dean had a bit part. Taylor later co-starred in "Harvest," a 1953 episode of the NBC program "Robert Montgomery Presents the Johnson's Wax Program," and in "The Bells of Cockaigne," a 1953 episode of the NBC program "Armstrong Circle Theatre," both of which co-starred James Dean.

Vaughn Taylor (1910–1983) also appeared in numerous films including *Jailhouse Rock* (1957), *Cat on a Hot Tin Roof* (1958), *Psycho* (1960), *The Russians Are Coming, The Russians Are Coming* (1966), and *In Cold Blood* (1967).

TEACHERS
Grade School

India Nose	Ivan Seward

High School

Hugh Caughell, Biology	Adeline Nall, Drama, English, Spanish
Myrtle Gilbreath, Citizenship	Paul Weaver, Physical Education
Violet Mart, Art	

College

Sanger W. Crumpacker, Physical Education	Gene Owen, Drama

Drama

Lee Strasberg	James Whitmore

Other

Ted Avery, rope tricks	
Rogers Brackett, literature, fine art, etc.	Bob Hinkle, dialogue
Mary Carter, art	Cyril Jackson, drums
Mushy Callahan, boxing	Pat McCormick, bullfighting
James DeWeerd, fine art, philosophy, etc.	Joseph Payne, art
Katherine Dunham, dance	Leonard Rosenman, piano
Zina Glad, dance	Roy Schatt, photography
Monte Hale, guitar	Pegot Waring, sculpture
Tom Hennesy, skin diving	Dr. Clive Warner, jazz appreciation

THE TEAHOUSE OF THE AUGUST MOON
Broadway play for which James Dean auditioned and was rejected. The audition took place at the Martin Beck Theatre, and Dean was auditioning to replace David Wayne in the star role of Sakini. However, even Jimmy was not convinced that he could effectively portray a fey Oriental, and during his

audition he repeatedly broke down in laughter on stage. The part eventually went to Burgess Meredith. In the subsequent film version the role was played by Marlon Brando.

TEEN MAGAZINE

In 1957 *Teen* magazine sponsored two "James Dean Scholarships" to the Pasadena Playhouse College of Theater Arts. The celebrity judges enlisted to select the scholarship recipients included Tony Curtis, Janet Leigh, Stanley Donen, Van Johnson, Donna Reed, and Eva Marie Saint.

TEETH

James Dean had dental problems . . .

☆ As a child Jimmy broke two of his front teeth and the rest of his life had to wear a bridge, which he would pop in and out to amuse his friends.
☆ During the shooting of *Rebel Without a Cause* production had to be shut down for a day due to Dean's dental problems.
☆ During the shooting of *Giant* Jimmy had to be excused from an afternoon of shooting, again due to dental problems. The matter was serious enough to merit a Warner Brothers memo, dated August 12, 1955. It read:

> Dr. Pincus, dentist in Beverly Hills, called Henry Ginsberg [*Giant*'s producer] this morning to check whether it would be ok to pull a very bad wisdom tooth for James Dean. Mr. Ginsberg asked him, if possible, to wait until Saturday night. They are fixing the tooth so that he can work tomorrow at the airport. The tooth will be pulled Saturday night.

TELEPHONE

☆ In May 1954, during the shooting of *East of Eden*, Jimmy's phone numbers were TH 2-5752 (home) and Ariz 8-2018 (answering exchange).
☆ In 1955, during the shooting of *Rebel Without a Cause*, he used the same answering exchange that Rock Hudson did. The phone number of their service was HO 7-5191. Dean retained this service up until the time of his death.

THE TELEVISION SHOWS THAT JAMES DEAN APPEARED ON

> It was the beginning of television, and nobody *knew* anything. So we did the best we could. But into this background came this cute little boy from Indiana. . . .
>
> James Sheldon

The following is a chronological videography of James Dean's considerable, but relatively unexplored, career in television. It is the most comprehensive record of its kind.

SEGMENT TITLE	SHOW TITLE	NETWORK	DATE
"Hill Number One"	"Family Theatre"*	N/A	3-25-51
"Sleeping Dogs"	"The Web"	CBS	2-20-52
"Ten Thousand Horses Singing"	"Studio One"	CBS	3-3-52
"The Foggy, Foggy Dew"	"Lux Video Theatre"	CBS	3-17-52

"Prologue to Glory"	"Kraft Television Theatre"	NBC	5-21-52
"Abraham Lincoln"	"Studio One"	CBS	5-26-52
"Forgotten Children"	"Hallmark Hall of Fame"	NBC	6-2-52
"Hound of Heaven"	"The Kate Smith Show"	NBC	1-15-53
"The Case of the Watchful Dog"	"Treasury Men in Action"	NBC	1-29-53
"The Capture of Jesse James"	"You Are There"	CBS	2-8-53
"No Room"	"Danger"	CBS	4-14-53
"The Case of the Sawed-Off Shotgun"	"Treasury Men in Action"	NBC	4-16-53
"The Evil Within"	"Tales of Tomorrow"	ABC	5-1-53
"Something for an Empty Briefcase"	"Campbell Soundstage"	NBC	7-17-53
"Sentence of Death"	"Studio One Summer Theatre"	CBS	8-17-53
"Death Is My Neighbor"	"Danger"	CBS	8-25-53
N/A	"The Big Story"	NBC	9-11-53
"Glory in Flower"	"Omnibus"	CBS	10-4-53
"Keep Our Honor Bright"	"Kraft Television Theatre"	NBC	10-14-53
"Life Sentence"	"Campbell Soundstage"	NBC	10-16-53
"A Long Time Till Dawn"	"Kraft Television Theatre"	NBC	11-11-53
"The Bells of Cockaigne"	"Armstrong Circle Theatre"	NBC	11-17-53**
"Harvest"	"Robert Montgomery Presents the Johnson's Wax Program"	NBC	11-23-53
"The Little Woman"	"Danger"	CBS	3-30-54
"Run Like a Thief"	"Philco TV Playhouse"	NBC	9-5-54
"Padlocks"	"Danger"	CBS	11-9-54
"I'm a Fool"	"General Electric Theater"	CBS	11-14-54
"The Dark, Dark Hour"	"General Electric Theater"	CBS	12-12-54
"The Thief"	"The U.S. Steel Hour"	ABC	1-4-55
"The Life of Emile Zola"***	"Lux Video Theatre"	NBC	3-10-55
"The Unlighted Road"	"Schlitz Playhouse of Stars"	CBS	5-6-55

---

*"Family Theatre" was not a weekly television series; rather, it was a series of religious specials. "Hill Number One" was not televised via network; it aired on various local stations throughout the country.

**According to James Sheldon, who directed "The Bells of Cockaigne" and "Harvest," the two programs could not have aired only a week apart. Sheldon recalls that "Cockaigne" aired in early 1954. However, according to every available record on the subject, it aired as indicated here.

***Dean was *not* in "The Life of Emile Zola" as reported elsewhere. He did, however, appear in a live interview *preceding* the broadcast to promote *East of Eden*.

Note: There are indications that James Dean also appeared in an episode of "Suspense," directed by Robert Stevens. More specific information, however, is unavailable.

Television Shows That Dean Was Scheduled to Do But Didn't (Because of His Death)

"The Battler"
"The Corn Is Green"

Note: At the time of his death all three networks were negotiating with Dean to do a series of Shakespearean plays, which would have started airing in the fall of 1956.

Made-for-Television Movies and Documentaries About Dean
"James Dean Remembered" (1974)
"James Dean" (1976)
"Forever James Dean" (1988)

Television Programs That Have Featured Tributes to Dean
"The Colgate Variety Hour" (1955)
"The Ed Sullivan Show" (1956)
"The Steve Allen Show" (1956)
"Hollywood Close-Up" (1983)
"Entertainment Tonight" (1985)
"Show Biz Today" (1985)
"A Current Affair" (1989)
"Instant Recall" (1990)
"20/20" (1990)

Television Shows with Episodes Inspired by Dean
"The Movie Star," "The Dupont Show of the Week" (1962)
"To Climb Steep Hills," "Straightaway" (1962)

Television Shows That Have Featured Dean Posters and/or Photographs as Atmospheric Background
"AfterMash"
"Full House"
"General Hospital"
"Growing Pains"
"Happy Days"
"Head of the Class"
"Moonlighting"
"Perfect Strangers"
"Quantum Leap"
"21 Jump Street"

"TEN THOUSAND HORSES SINGING"
Episode of the CBS television program "Studio One" in which James Dean had a bit part, including a couple of words of dialogue, as a hotel bellboy. "Ten Thousand Horses Singing" starred John Forsythe, Catherine McLeod, Vaughn Taylor, and Joe Morass. It was directed by Paul Nickell and produced and adapted (from a story by Robert Carson) by Worthington Minor. It aired on March 3, 1952.

THEATRE DE LYS
In June 1953 James Dean appeared in *The Scarecrow* at the Theatre de Lys, an off-Broadway theater located in Greenwich Village (address: 121 Christopher Street).

During the summer of 1953 Terese Hayden produced four plays at the Theatre de Lys, employing many members of the Actors Studio, including Patricia Neal, Eli Wallach, Anne Jackson, Leo Penn, Bradford Dillman, Albert Salmi, and David J. Stewart. The plays were, in the order in which they were staged:

Maya, June 9–14
The Scarecrow, June 16–21
School for Scandal, June 23–28
The Little Clay Cart, June 30–July 5

"THE THEATRE GUILD ON THE AIR"

ABC radio program, sponsored by U.S. Steel, on which unknown actor James Dean appeared in 1951. "The Theatre Guild on the Air" was broadcast from 1945 to 1953. In 1953 it made the transition to television under the series title "The U.S. Steel Hour."

"THE THIEF"

After he made *East of Eden*, but before its release, James Dean co-starred in "The Thief," an episode of the ABC television program "The U.S. Steel Hour." Dean portrayed the young son of a rich family who is suspected of stealing money. The show was directed by Vincent J. Donehue and written by Arthur Arent, from a play by Henri Bernstein. It aired on January 4, 1955, and co-starred Paul Lukas, Mary Astor, Diana Lynn, and Patric Knowles.

In his scenes Dean reportedly conjured up every bit of business he could think of to steal the show from his far more experienced co-stars. At one point Paul Lukas, who was playing the father of Jimmy's character, exploded on the set. "This son of a bitch," he shouted to the director, in reference to Dean, "is absolutely crazy!"

GUY THOMAJAN

Guy Thomajan, an assistant to Elia Kazan, directed the 1954 screen test between James Dean and Dick Davalos. Later he served as the dialogue director on *East of Eden*.

A former Broadway actor, Thomajan, of Armenian descent, was signed by Warner Brothers to make his film debut in *The Breaking Point* (1950). More interested in work behind the camera, he became a protégé of Elia Kazan, assisting him on *A Streetcar Named Desire* (1951), *On the Waterfront* (1954), and other films. He also directed summer stock stage productions.

BOB THOMAS

Hollywood writer who was interviewed in the Italian documentary *Hollywood: The Rebel James Dean*.

GREG THOMAS

Indiana attorney who, in tandem with Mark Roesler in 1984, obtained the licensing rights to market the James Dean image.

RICHARD THOMAS

Actor who starred in *September 30, 1955* as a young man who was greatly affected by the death of James Dean. During production of the film Thomas suffered an ankle sprain from a motorcycle tumble, and shooting had to be suspended.

At the time, Richard Thomas, born in 1951, was known to audiences as John Boy Walton in "The Waltons" (1972–1977), a role (and an image) that he has yet to truly overcome despite some fine work and a few bold career choices.

T. T. THOMAS
Author of the fictitious autobiography *I, James Dean*, published in paperback by Popular Library in 1957.

HOWARD THOMPSON
Reporter for the *New York Times* who interviewed James Dean and wrote the subsequent (and significant) article "Another Dean Hits the Big League." The article was published in the March 13, 1955, edition of the *Times*.

THE TICKET
On September 30, 1955, at 3:30 P.M. James Dean was stopped on the highway by California highway patrolman O. V. Hunter. Hunter ticketed Dean for traveling 65 mph in a 55 mph zone. The ticket summoned Dean to appear in court in the town of Lamont, California, on October 17, 1955. According to the ticket, the weather conditions at the time were "clear," the traffic was "normal," and the road conditions were "good."

TIME CAPSULE
In 1985, in an effort to capitalize on the renewed interest in James Dean, Warner Brothers released a video package entitled "The Dean Legacy." To promote the video collection, which included Dean's three films, Warners sponsored a promotion in which a James Dean time capsule was initiated on September 27, 1985. Accompanying the time capsule presentation was a James Dean look-alike contest in which members of the *Rebel Without a Cause* gang served as judges.

The time capsule is presently stored at the University of Southern California and is scheduled to be opened in the year 2085.

TIME MAGAZINE
Time has published several articles about James Dean, including:

☆ September 3, 1956   "Dean of the One-Shotters"
☆ November 26, 1956   "Dean Cult"
☆ August 4, 1961   "The Teutonic James Dean"

TIMES SQUARE
One of James Dean's New York hangouts.

DIMITRI TIOMKIN
Composed the score of *Giant*, the soundtrack of which was released on Capitol Records. During the filming of *Giant* Tiomkin was a frequent presence on the set, an unusual opportunity for a film composer, hoping to be inspired as the action took place. For his work on *Giant* Tiomkin received an Oscar nomination. For Tiomkin it was one of literally dozens.

Russian-born Dimitri Tiomkin (1899–1979) composed a plethora of film scores in a phenomenal career that included *Alice in Wonderland* (1933), *Lost Horizon* (Oscar nomination, 1937), *Mr. Smith Goes to Washington* (Oscar nomination, 1939), *The Corsican Brother* (Oscar nomination, 1942), *The Moon and Sixpence* (Oscar nomination, 1943), *The Bridge of San Luis Rey* (Oscar nomination, 1944), *Champion* (Oscar nomination, 1949), *High Noon* (Best Song Oscar winner, Best Score Oscar winner, 1952), *The High and the Mighty* (Best Score Oscar winner, Best Song Oscar nomination, 1954), *Wild Is the Wind* (Best Song Oscar nomination, 1957), *The Old Man and the Sea* (Oscar winner, 1958), *The Young Land* (Best Song Oscar nomination, 1959), *The Alamo* (Best Song Oscar nomination, Best Score Oscar nomination, 1960), *Town Without Pity* (Best Song Oscar nomination, 1961), *The Guns of Navarone* (Best Score Oscar nomination, 1961), *55 Days at Peking* (Best Song Oscar nomination, Best Score Oscar nomination, 1963), *The Fall of the Roman Empire* (Best Score Oscar nomination, 1964), and *Tchaikovsky* (Best Score Adaptation Oscar nomination, 1971).

TIP'S RESTAURANT
James Dean's first stop en route to Salinas, California, on September 30, 1955, was at Tip's Restaurant (aka Tip's Diner) in Castaic Junction. Dean reportedly had a glass of milk.

"TO CLIMB STEEP HILLS"
Episode of the ABC television series "Straightaway" that starred Paul Carr as a young, car-racing movie star, a character inspired by James Dean. The episode aired on March 28, 1962, and also starred series regulars Brian Kelly and John Ashley.

TO THEM THAT SLEEP IN DARKNESS
Church play in which Jimmy Dean portrayed a blind boy. It was his performance in this play that convinced Jimmy's aunt and uncle, and others in Fairmount, Indiana, that he should become an actor.

DYLAN TODD
Recorded the song "The Ballad of James Dean" for RCA Records.

MICHAEL TODD
After seeing an early screening of *East of Eden*, producer Mike Todd sent a cable to Elia Kazan on February 10, 1955. It read, in part:

> This is a fan letter. I saw *East of Eden* last night and after I recovered from the impact and was walking away from the projection room, I attempted to analyze why I was so spellbound . . . *this is a very big, special star coming up.* I don't feel that anything could stop this guy Dean from being a star although such pre-labels have stopped other potentials.

Michael Todd, born Avrom Goldenborgen in 1907, won the 1956 Oscar for Best Picture for *Around the World in 80 Days*. Two years later, in March 1958, he was killed when his private plane, "The Lucky Liz," named after his wife, Elizabeth Taylor, crashed in New Mexico.

BILL TODMAN

Producer of the television game show "Beat the Clock," on which struggling actor James Dean was employed as a stunt tester in late 1951. It was through his "Beat the Clock" connection that Jimmy was cast in a February 20, 1952, episode of the CBS television program "The Web." "The Web," an acclaimed dramatic series of the period, was produced by Mark Goodson and Bill Todman.

THE TONY AWARDS

It has been published repeatedly that James Dean won a 1954 Tony award as the Best Supporting Actor in a Drama for his work in *The Immoralist*. In fact, however, the Tony that year went to John Kerr for *Tea and Sympathy*.

MEL TORMÉ

Singer Mel Tormé had a brief encounter with James Dean in September 1955. Tormé recalled the incident in his autobiography *It Wasn't All Velvet* (1988):

> One night, back in Hollywood, as I fulfilled a return engagement at the Crescendo on the Sunset strip, a young man invited me over to his table. . . . "I'm James Dean," he said, rising and offering me his hand. I shook it and sat. He was in a fit of passion for bongo drums. Having just seen me play drums in my act, he asked me if I played bongos. I told him I had been fooling with them a bit. "I'd sure like to play 'em, really play 'em, you know?" "Well, Jim, when you have some time, I'll be glad to show you what I know. It's not much, but . . ." "When?" he asked me. "When could you teach me?" "Well, I'm off to Australia next week. How about right after I get back?"

As fate would have it, Tormé returned to America on October 1, 1955, and learned that Jimmy had been killed the day before.

TRACK AND FIELD

At Fairmount (Indiana) High School Jim Dean was a pole-vaulting champion on the track and field team, of which he was a member for four years.

SPENCER TRACY

At the 1955 Cannes Film Festival, held between April 25 and May 11, the Best Male Performance prize was awarded to Spencer Tracy for his work in *Bad Day at Black Rock*. In the voting Tracy topped Ernest Borgnine for his performance in *Marty* and James Dean for his work in *East of Eden*.

TRAINS

☆ When nine-year-old Jimmy Dean returned to Fairmount, Indiana, from Los Angeles, he traveled aboard the same train that freighted his dead mother's body.

☆ When he went to Longmont, Colorado, to compete in a national speech competition in April 1949, Jimmy, accompanied by his teacher, Adeline Nall, traveled by train from Indiana.

☆ Following his graduation from high school in May 1949, Jimmy moved to Los Angeles. Again he traveled by train.

☆ Two years later he took a train from Chicago to his new home in New York City.

BING TRASTER
The owner of the Traster Nursery in Fairmount, Indiana, and a longtime friend of the Dean family, Bing Traster was interviewed in the 1957 documentary *The James Dean Story*. He recalled:

> "Jimmy had a little something up here [points to his head] that the other boys don't have. . . . When Jimmy would get down in the dumps and get the blues he'd get on his motorsickle and go out to the old homestead and meditate. He seemed to derive a lot of comfort from it. He had spiritual values that the other kids didn't have."

BETTE TREADVILLE
Actress who appeared in *East of Eden*.

"TREASURY MEN IN ACTION"
NBC television program in which James Dean appeared in two episodes, "The Case of the Watchful Dog," which aired on January 29, 1953, and "The Case of the Sawed-Off Shotgun," which aired on April 16, 1953.

TRIBUTES, MEMORIALS, AND MONUMENTS
In Marion
Birth site plaques

In Fairmount
Fairmount High School plaque
The Fairmount Historical Museum (James Dean Room)
The Fairmount Museum Days Festival
The James Dean Gallery
The James Dean Memorial Rod Run
The James Dean Memorial Scholarship Trust

In New York
The James Dean Walking Tour of New York Hangouts
The Museum of Broadcasting tribute, 1986

In Los Angeles
The Academy of Motion Picture Arts and Sciences tribute, 1983
The Griffith Park Monument
The James Dean Memorial Car Rally
The James Dean Memorial Run
James Dean Day, September 30, 1985
The Museum of Broadcasting tribute, 1986

In Cholame
The James Dean Memorial

Other
The Wall of Hope Monument (built in France)

STEVE TRILLING
Jack Warner's executive assistant at Warner Brothers, who oversaw the production of *East of Eden*, *Rebel Without a Cause*, and *Giant*.

ERNEST TRIPKE
On September 30, 1955, Ernest Tripke was one of the California Highway Patrol officers at the scene of the crash that killed James Dean. Tripke, who reported for work that day at 6:00 P.M., arrived at the scene at 6:20 P.M.

Years later he was interviewed on several television programs and in the documentary *James Dean: The First American Teenager* (1976). Of the accident that landed him a dubious niche in history, Tripke recalled:

> "There was considerable difficulty in removing Dean because his feet became entangled in the clutch and brake pedal assembly. Dean had very little blood on him. He did have a broken neck, and I think he had a crushed skull."

THE TRIUMPH AND TRAGEDY OF JAMES DEAN
A comic book biography of James Dean.

TROLL
Swedish recording group consisting of teenage girls who had a hit in 1989 with the song "Jimmy Dean."

TROUBLE ALONG THE WAY
According to previously published reports, James Dean had a bit part in the 1953 John Wayne picture *Trouble Along the Way*. However, Dean's appearance in the film has never been documented, and given the timing, it seems unlikely. The film was directed by Michael Curtiz, produced and written by Melville Shavelson, and co-starred Donna Reed and Charles Coburn.

FRANÇOIS TRUFFAUT
Former French film critic turned acclaimed film director, François Truffaut was one of James Dean's earliest and most ardent supporters. Of Dean he wrote in the film publication *Cahiers du Cinema*:

> The concern of the film journal must be with James Dean, who *is* the cinema, in the same sense as Lillian Gish, Chaplin, Ingrid Bergman, etc. James Dean has succeeded in giving commercial viability to a film [*East of Eden*] which would otherwise scarcely have qualified, in breathing life into an abstraction, in interesting a vast audience in moral problems treated in an unusual way.
>
> His short-sighted stare prevents him from smiling, and the smile drawn from him by dint of a patient effort constitutes a victory. His powers of seduction—one has only to hear an audience react when Raymond Massey refuses the money, which is his love—are such that he can kill his father and mother on the screen nightly with the full blessing of both art-house and popular audiences.

Truffaut also wrote about Dean, "His acting goes against fifty years of filmmaking. Each gesture, each attitude, each mime is a slap in the face of tradition."

T-SHIRTS

The following is a selective list of the numerous companies that are marketing James Dean T-shirts.

Amich, S.A., Floridablanca, 17, Mataro, Barcelona, Spain
Bowe Industries, 69-20 76th St., Middle Village, NY 11379
Camp Beverly Hills, 9615 Brighton Way, Beverly Hills, CA 90210
Koss Corporation, 4129 N. Port Washington Ave., Milwaukee, WI 53212
Lenny N.Y.C., GPO Box 7961, New York, NY 10116-4635
Magazine Zum Globus, Dept. 488, Eichstrasse 27, Zurich, Switzerland CH-8045
National Screenprint, 9749 Hamilton Rd., Eden Prairie, MN 55344
The Sassy Club, 8 E. 48th St., New York, NY 10017
Shirt Shed, 570 S. Miami St., Wabash, IN 46992
Top Heavy, C76 Wilford St., Newton, New South Wales 2042, Australia

JEANNINE TUDOR

Jeannine Tudor is a member of the We Remember Dean International fan club from Joliet, Illinois. Of her interest in Dean, Tudor says, "I guess, like most, I see myself in James Dean—wanting to belong yet being a loner."

LANA TURNER

James Dean and Lana Turner shared the same bed—but at different times. When told by prospective landlord Dave Gould, "That's the bed Lana Turner slept in when she rented this place," James Dean enthusiastically wrote out a check and moved into his new furnished home at 1541 Sunset Plaza Drive in West Hollywood.

DONALD TURNUPSEED

On Friday afternoon, September 30, 1955, Donald Gene Turnupseed, a freshman at the California Polytechnic Institute in San Luis Obispo, was driving his 1950 black-and-white Ford to his parents' home in Tulare. At the intersection of U.S. 466 and Highway 41 Turnupseed made a left turn and met James Dean—in a head-on collision that would alter the course of his life.

Immediately after the crash Turnupseed, dazed but barely injured, mumbled to a witness at the scene that he hadn't seen the Porsche until he was already into his turn. Dean was rushed via ambulance to the hospital. His passenger, Rolf Wütherich, was seriously injured and also rushed to the hospital. As for Turnupseed, he was left stranded on the highway. He had to hitchhike back home to Tulare.

At the subsequent coroner's inquest on October 11, Donald Turnupseed was cleared of any wrongdoing in the death of James Dean. Fate and one left turn had simply dealt him an unkind and devastating blow. Not only was he involved in an accident that resulted in one man's death, but it was a death that will never be forgotten, a death whose reverberations are still being felt all over the world. At the time Turnupseed reportedly reenlisted in the navy. Over the years he has kept an extremely low profile and, on the subject of James Dean, an adamant silence.

TV AND MOVIE SCREEN MAGAZINE

Entertainment publication that published several articles about James Dean, including:

☆ September 1956	"Jimmy Dean, The Story He Wanted to Tell"
☆ May 1957	"Jimmy Dean's Happiest Night"
☆ November 1959	"I Still Remember James Dean" by Sal Mineo

20TH CENTURY–FOX

Dean had a bit part in the 1951 20th Century–Fox film *Fixed Bayonets*.

THE 21 CLUB
In February 1955, months after completing *East of Eden*, James Dean and Dick Davalos reunited at New York's 21 Club (address: 21 West 52nd Street) at a party they hosted for friends.

GEORGE TYNE
Actor who appeared in *See the Jaguar* (1952), which featured James Dean in his Broadway debut.

On stage George Tyne also appeared in *A Sound of Hunting* (1945), *Threepenny Opera* (1954), and *The Country Wife* (1957). His films include *A Walk in the Sun* (1946), *Sands of Iwo Jima* (1949), *Not with My Wife You Don't!* (1966), and *I Will, I Will . . . for Now* (1976).

ROBERT WAYNE TYSL
Author of the exhaustive book *Continuity and Evolution in a Public Symbol: An Investigation into the Creation and Communication of the James Dean Image in Mid-Century America*, published in 1965 by Michigan State University.

U

UNCLES
Charlie Nolan Dean
Howard Wilson

UNDERSTUDIES
Bill Gunn, *The Immoralist* (1954)
Dane Knell, *See the Jaguar* (1952)

THE UNITED STATES ARMY
See ARMED SERVICES.

UNIVERSAL PICTURES
James Dean had a bit part in the 1952 Universal picture *Has Anybody Seen My Gal?* The film was produced by Ted Richmond, directed by Douglas Sirk, and written by Joseph Hoffman. It starred Charles Coburn, Piper Laurie, and Rock Hudson.

UNIVERSITY OF CALIFORNIA, LOS ANGELES
In September 1950 sophomore Jimmy Dean transferred from Santa Monica City College to the nearby and more prestigious University of California, Los Angeles (UCLA). While there Jimmy majored in prelaw and minored in theater arts. He also pledged to the Sigma Nu fraternity and, for a short period, lived at the Sigma Nu frat house on Gayley Avenue. In December he won a major role in the school's production of *Macbeth*, which was presented on the campus's Royce Hall stage.

Later he was turned down for a role in another school production, *The Dark of the Moon*, and after being booted out of his fraternity for various infractions he abruptly quit school to pursue a full-time acting career. It was February 1951. At the same time another future icon, Marilyn Monroe, was entering UCLA to enroll in art appreciation and "Backgrounds in Literature" courses.

> "When I graduated from high school [sic] I enrolled as a pre-law student at U.C.L.A. But I stayed only two years [sic]. I couldn't stand the tea-sipping, moss-walled academicians."
> James Dean to Hedda Hopper, *Chicago Tribune Magazine*,
> March 27, 1955

> "Just for the hell of it, I signed up for a pre-law course at U.C.L.A. That did call for a certain knowledge of histrionics."
> James Dean, *New York Times*, March 13, 1955

On February 8, 1981, UCLA (address: 405 Hilgard Avenue) commemorated the 50th anniversary of its former student's birth with "A Tribute to James Dean." The event included screenings of *James Dean: The First American Teenager, East of Eden, Rebel Without a Cause,* and *Giant* and took place at the campus's Melnitz Theater.

"THE UNLIGHTED ROAD"
James Dean's final venture into television drama was "The Unlighted Road," an episode of the CBS program "Schlitz Playhouse of Stars." The show was

James Dean, slouched and smoking on the set of "The Unlighted Road," with Pat Hardy, 1955.

produced by William Self, directed by Justus Addiss, and written by Walter C. Brown. It starred Dean, Murvyn Vye, Pat Hardy, Edgar Stehli, Charles Wagenheim, Voltaire Perkins, and Robert Williams and aired on May 6, 1955 (not June 1, as reported elsewhere).

Dean portrayed Jeff Latham, a teenage hitchhiker/drifter who wanders into a coffee shop, where he obtains a job and attempts to build a decent future for himself. Conflict arises, however, when he innocently becomes involved with criminal characters who lead him down "The Unlighted Road."

Following Dean's death, and provoked by what the producer defined as immense public demand, "The Unlighted Road" was rebroadcast. It was the first repeat in the history of the "Schlitz Playhouse of Stars." It was subsequently rebroadcast several more times.

LEON URIS
Leon Uris was the original writer signed to adapt Nicholas Ray's "The Blind Run" into a motion picture screenplay, which was eventually produced as *Rebel Without a Cause.* As his initiation into the project, Uris met with child psychiatrists and juvenile court judges and rode shotgun with the Culver City police. However, early into the production he was fired by Ray and replaced by Irving Shulman.

Uris, born in Baltimore in 1924, later gained fame as the author of the bestselling novel *Exodus* (1957), which was adapted into a 1960 film. He also penned the books *Battle Cry* (1953) and *Armageddon* (1964) and the screenplay of *Gunfight at the O.K. Corral* (1957).

"THE U.S. STEEL HOUR"
Long-running television drama series broadcast by ABC on Tuesday nights from October 1953 to June 1955 and by CBS on Wednesday nights from July 1955 to June 1963.

James Dean appeared in "The Thief," a January 1955 episode of "The U.S. Steel Hour." According to previous accounts, he also appeared in a 1952 episode entitled "Prologue to Glory." In fact, however, "Prologue to Glory" was an episode of the NBC show "Kraft Television Theatre" and not "The U.S. Steel Hour."

Prior to sponsoring a television program, U.S. Steel broadcast a radio show, "The Theatre Guild on the Air," on which James Dean also appeared.

V

RUDOLPH VALENTINO

> After thirty years of being the world's number one ghoul-magnet,
> Rudy was suddenly discovering that he has a real tough competitor
> in the late James Dean.
>
> a 1956 fan publication

The death of Rudolph Valentino in New York on August 23, 1926, provoked a rash of mass hysteria the likes of which were not seen in Hollywood until the death of James Dean nearly 30 years later. The print media contemplated whose death caused the greater sensation. While Valentino won points for inciting street riots and a slew of devotional suicides, one magazine surmised that Dean would eventually be crowned champion in the headstone-to-headstone competition because "The trouble with Rudy was that he didn't give much of a damn about girls. . . ."

The official cause of Valentino's death was peritonitis. Rumors attributed it to poison.

VICTOR VALLEJO

One of the wardrobe men on *Giant*.

MAMIE VAN DOREN

In her autobiography, *Playing the Field* (G. P. Putnam's Sons, 1987), 1950s bombshell Mamie Van Doren claimed to have once shared a titillating motorcycle ride with James Dean. Wrote Van Doren:

> He slipped off his jacket and put it around my shoulders. As he did,
> he brought his face close to mine. "You like motorcycles, Mamie?" I
> nodded and he kissed me. It was a soft, awkward, adolescent kiss,
> tasting of cigarette smoke and beer. Jimmy cupped my breasts with
> his hands and we kissed again, more deeply. "Jimmy," I breathed,
> "not here." He stopped and searched in my eyes as if looking for
> what I really meant. "Then where?"

However, the flirtation failed to culminate because, according to Mamie, of her devout loyalty to Ray Anthony, her husband to be.

Born Lucille Olander in Rowena, South Dakota, in 1933, Van Doren worked as a secretary and model before she became a star of mostly B-grade pictures. She usually played the blonde with the tight sweater, the tight skirt, and the loose morals. Her films include *Forbidden* (1954), *The Second Greatest Sex* (1955), *Teacher's Pet* (1958), *High School Confidential* (1958), *Sex Kittens Go to College* (1960), and *The Navy Versus the Night Monsters* (1966).

"The studios exploited everybody. They used you like a piece of meat. All of a sudden, you were part of an assembly line. At Universal, they gave us all the same bra to wear."

Mamie Van Doren, *Mandate*, August 1984

JO VAN FLEET

Actress who won an Academy Award as the Best Supporting Actress of 1955 for her superb performance in *East of Eden* (her film debut) as Kate, the successful businesswoman and embittered madam who is confronted by Cal Trask (James Dean), the son she had deserted many years before.

Van Fleet, born in 1919, was a member of the Actors Studio. Her stage credits include *Camino Real* (1953), *The Trip to Bountiful* (Best Supporting Actress Tony winner, 1954), and *Look Homeward, Angel* (Best Actress Tony nomination, 1958). Her film credits include *The Rose Tattoo* (1955), *I'll Cry Tomorrow* (1955), *The King and Four Queens* (1956), *Gunfight at the O.K. Corral* (1957), *This Angry Age* (Italy, 1958), *Wild River* (1960), *Cool Hand Luke* (1967), *I Love You, Alice B. Toklas* (1968), *80 Steps to Jonah* (1969), *The Gang That Couldn't Shoot Straight* (1972), and *The Tenant* (France, 1976). On television she appeared in the 1980 miniseries "Power."

Interestingly, Van Fleet was also considered for the role of Luz Benedict in *Giant*, which eventually went to Mercedes McCambridge.

VAN NUYS TRAFFIC COURT

In 1951 Jimmy was ordered to appear in Van Nuys Traffic Court after he had let $25 in traffic tickets go unpaid. Bill Bast, in his biography *James Dean*, recalled his friend pleading in self-defense:

"Your honor, I know I have done the wrong thing by not taking care of this ticket before now. But I was afraid. You see, I'm a student at U.C.L.A. I've been having a rough time of it. I mean, with money. I don't have much and what I have goes mostly for food and books. I know twenty-five dollars doesn't sound like much to you, Your Honor, but to me, it could mean food for a whole month, or books for a whole semester. . . ."

According to Bast the judge succumbed to Jimmy's performance and reduced the fine to $5.

DICK VAN PATTEN

Years before "Eight Is Enough," Dick Van Patten co-starred in a hit CBS television series entitled "Mama." In the show Van Patten portrayed Nels, the young brother. It was a name he later gave to one of his real-life tennis-playing sons. At any rate, during the run of the show, circa early 1952, Van Patten was drafted into the army. He was to be replaced in the show by a young, unknown actor by the name of James Dean. However, as fate would have it, Van Patten avoided the army with a 4-F classification and returned to the show. As for Dean, he went back to pounding the proverbial pavement.

Of course it is interesting to speculate about what would have transpired if James Dean *had* appeared as a regular on "Mama." Likely he would have been typecast in comedy and never would have become the brooding film star. Possibly he would have had a career not dissimilar to that of Dick Van Patten.

Van Patten's success has been primarily restricted to television, in which his credits include "Mama" (1949–1956), "The Partners" (1971–1972), "The New Dick Van Dyke Show" (1973–1974), "When Things Were Rotten" (created by Mel Brooks, 1975), "Eight Is Enough" (1977–1981), and "W.I.O.U." (1990–). Van Patten's film credits include *Joe Kidd* (1972), *Westworld* (1973), *The Strongest Man in the World* (1975), *Gus* (1976), *Freaky Friday* (1977), and *High Anxiety* (1977).

VIVIAN VANCE

Vivian Vance was up for the part of Mrs. Lynnton in *Giant*, which eventually went to Judith Evelyn.

At the time, Vance was a television star by virtue of her performance as Ethel Mertz in the smash hit series "I Love Lucy" (1951–1961), for which she won a 1953 Best Supporting Actress Emmy award.

VARIETY

Entertainment trade paper, aka *Daily Variety*, that has published several articles about James Dean, including:

☆ July 11, 1956   "In Death, James Dean a Hero to French"
☆ October 27, 1965   "Jimmy Mania: Dean and Bond"
☆ January 5, 1966   "James Dean"
☆ September 2, 1980   "James Dean's Death 25 Years Ago to Be Recalled"
☆ March 3, 1986   "James Dean's TV Apprenticeship Surveyed in Fest Screenings"

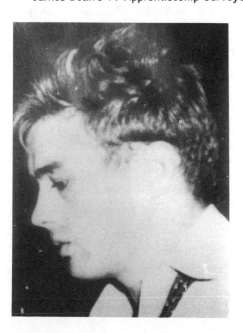

IRENE VERNON

Actress who co-starred in "No Room," a 1953 episode of the CBS television program "Danger" in which James Dean appeared.

Irene Vernon later appeared as Louise Tate (1964–1966) on the hit television series "Bewitched."

BYRON VICE

Despite romantic claims that he was named after Lord Byron, James Byron Dean was named for Byron Vice, a friend of Winton Dean's. Byron Vice was an Indiana florist.

LUCIA VICTOR

Stage manager, *The Immoralist* (1954).

VICTORIA VIDAL

Teacher of "James Dean: The Star Persona," a six-week course at the Art Center College of Design in Pasadena, California. The course included the reading of a novel, a quiz, a five-page report, and screenings of *East of Eden, Rebel Without a Cause, Giant,* and *Hollywood: The Rebel James Dean.* The purpose of the course, which was given during the summer of 1990, was to answer the question "What is the universal appeal of this young actor?"

VIDEO

With the emergence of home video in the 1980s the legend of James Dean experienced a revival that has been flourishing ever since.

Dean Movies Available on Home Video
(all on Warner Home Video; also available in a laser disc package released by Warners in 1990 under the title *The James Dean 35th Anniversary Collection*)
East of Eden
Giant
Rebel Without a Cause

Documentaries and Movies About or Inspired by Dean Available on Home Video
Bye Bye Jimmy (Great Britain)
Come Back to the Five and Dime, Jimmy Dean, Jimmy Dean (Forum Home Video)
Hollywood: The Rebel James Dean (Kartes Video)
James Dean (New World Video)
James Dean: The First American Teenager (Vid-America Video)
The James Dean Story (Pacific Arts Video)

Documentary Videos That Include Dean
All-Time Movie Greats (Goodtimes Video)
George Stevens: A Filmmaker's Journey (Continental Video)
Hollywood Bad Boys (AmWest Video)
Hollywood Scandals and Tragedies (MPI Home Video)
Those Crazy Ol' Commercials (Goodtimes Video)

VILLA CAPRI
The night before his death James Dean dined at his favorite Italian restaurant, the Villa Capri. Dean was a frequent, sometimes nightly, patron of the Villa Capri, which also attracted, among others, Bogart, Bacall, Sinatra, Garland, and Monroe. Sometimes his escort was Ursula Andress. Sometimes it was Lilli Kardell. At other times he dined alone. Occasionally, when the restaurant was overcrowded, he'd eat alone—in the kitchen.

The Villa Capri was owned by Patsy D'Amore and, in 1955, was located at 1735 North McCadden Place in Hollywood.

> Dean showed up with Lilli Kardell at the kleig-lighted Villa Capri "premiere" celebrating the addition of—two washrooms.
>
> *Variety*

VILLAGE THEATRE
Off-Broadway theater in which James Dean performed a reading from Franz Kafka's *The Metamorphosis* in August 1952.

HENRY VILLARDO
Henry Villardo was one of James Dean's makeup men at Warner Brothers. During the Marfa, Texas, location shooting of *Giant* Villardo entertained the cast and crew with his impersonation of James Dean. Dean reportedly laughed loudest.

Just prior to his death Jimmy took out an advertisement in the souvenir program of the Make Up Artists Ball. The ad featured a photograph of Jimmy's eyes and a note of appreciation that read "Thanks Hank."

VIOLIN
As a child Jimmy Dean became quite adept at playing the violin. He later told Hedda Hopper:

> "When I was four or five, my mother had me playing the violin—[I was a] blasted child prodigy. My mother died when I was eight [sic], and the violin was buried, too."

VOGUE MAGAZINE
One of the first national publications to recognize the star potential of James Dean. In its February 1955 issue *Vogue* declared:

> James Dean, thin, intense, with such strong projection that he is always noticed, has brought that projection fairly quickly to the public. In his first movie, *East of Eden*, still unreleased, he's a smash.

DANTE VOLPE
Artist whose illustrations comprise *The Last James Dean Book*, which was published by Morrow Books in 1984. The book includes Volpe's interpretation of James Dean—in the nude.

JOHNNY von **NEUMANN**
Owner of Competition Motors in Hollywood who, in September 1955, sold James Dean his ill-fated Porsche.

MURVYN VYE
Co-star of "The Unlighted Road," a 1955 episode of the CBS television program "Schlitz Playhouse of Stars" that featured James Dean in his final television role.

   Murvyn Vye (1913–1976) appeared in several films including *Golden Earrings* (1947), *A Connecticut Yankee in King Arthur's Court* (1949), *Al Capone* (1959), and *Andy* (1964). He also co-starred in the television comedy series "The Bob Cummings Show" (1961–1962).

W

CHARLES WAGENHEIM

Actor who appeared in "The Unlighted Road," a 1955 episode of the CBS television program "Schlitz Playhouse of Stars" that starred James Dean.

Charles Wagenheim later appeared as Halligan (1967–1975) on the landmark television western series "Gunsmoke."

ROBERT WAGNER

When James Dean walked out of *Rebel Without a Cause* shortly before the film was scheduled to start shooting, relatively unknown actor Robert Wagner was one of several actors considered to take over the role of Jim Stark. Of course, if he had gotten the part, Wagner would have been paired with his future wife, Natalie Wood.

WAIST

Depending on his weight, James Dean generally wore pants with a 30- or 32-inch waist.

WAITING ON THE BEACH

See RIPPING OFF LAYERS TO FIND ROOTS.

JIMMY WAKELY

Country music singer who recorded several songs, including "His Name Was Dean," "James Dean (Just a Boy from Indiana)," "James Dean," and "Jimmy, Jimmy" for the Coral Records tribute album *The James Dean Story*.

KEN WALKEN

Actor who appeared in the September 11, 1953, episode of "The Big Story," which starred James Dean.

Ken Walken also appeared in the New York stage plays *The Climate of Eden* (1952) and *The Visit* (1958).

WILLIAM WALLACE

Set decorator, *Rebel Without a Cause*.

ELI WALLACH

Eli Wallach starred in *The Scarecrow*, an off-Broadway play in which James Dean had a bit part. The play was presented at the Theatre de Lys in June 1953.

Eli Wallach, born in Brooklyn in 1915, was a member of the Actors Studio. His extensive stage credits include *Camino Real* (1953), *The Teahouse of the August Moon* (1954), and a 1951 Best Supporting Actor Tony award for his performance in *The Rose Tattoo*. On television, Wallach won a 1966–1967 Best Supporting Actor Emmy for his performance in "The Poppy Is Also a Flower." Somehow, he never attained film stardom. His credits include *Baby Doll* (his film debut, 1956), *The Misfits* (Clark Gable and Marilyn Monroe's final completed film, 1961), *How the West Was Won* (1963), *How to Steal a Million* (1966), *The Tiger Makes Out* (in which he co-starred with his wife, Anne Jackson, 1967), *Cinderella Liberty* (1973), *The Deep* (1977), and *Winter Kills* (1979).

THOMAS WALSH
Co-writer of "Sentence of Death," a 1953 episode of the CBS television program "Studio One Summer Theatre" that co-starred James Dean.

ANDY WARHOL
> He's not our hero because he was perfect, but because he perfectly represented the damaged but beautiful soul of his time.
>> Andy Warhol on James Dean, *Interview*

Dean fan Andy Warhol's portrait of James Dean (from the series ADS) was used as the cover of the 1984 photo book and biography *James Dean: American Icon*.

PEGOT WARING
Shortly before his death Jimmy took sculpting lessons from Pegot Waring at her studio in West Hollywood. Under Waring's tutelage Jimmy began sculpting his self-portrait in clay. It was never finished. After his death Waring bequeathed the sculpture to Sandy and Beulah Roth, who subsequently presented it to Jimmy's father. In 1955 Pegot Waring's studio was located at 8362 Melrose Avenue.

CLIVE WARNER
In 1950 Dr. Clive Warner was the adviser of Santa Monica City College's jazz appreciation club, of which Jim Dean was a member.

JACK WARNER
On December 14, 1954, studio honcho Jack L. Warner sent a note to *Giant* producer Henry Ginsberg suggesting that Sydney Chaplin, Charlie's son, be cast as Jett Rink. The suggestion, of course, went unheeded, and James Dean was cast in the part. Dean was not particularly fond of his boss, Warner. In fact he was sometimes openly contemptuous. On one occasion Warner was walking down the lot, having a discussion with an important motion picture exhibitor. When he saw his new star James Dean, Warner summoned him over so that he could introduce him to the visiting VIP. Jimmy approached

as instructed. However, when he reached Warner, he surveyed him up and down, motioned toward Warner's outfit, and in his best mogul impersonation ordered, "Have it cleaned and burned." And then he walked away.

The last and most prominent of the four founding Warner brothers, Jack L. Warner (1892–1978) was the quintessential movie mogul. He ruled with a clenched fist and a tight wallet, and during the studio's heyday he churned out his films with assembly-line speed and precision. Among the innumerable films he oversaw for his studio were *The Jazz Singer* (1927), *The Life of Emile Zola* (Best Picture Oscar, 1937), *The Maltese Falcon* (Best Picture Oscar nomination, 1941), *Yankee Doodle Dandy* (Best Picture Oscar nomination, 1942), *Casablanca* (Best Picture Oscar winner, 1943), *The Treasure of the Sierra Madre* (Best Picture Oscar nomination, 1948), the Bette Davis classics (*Jezebel*, Best Picture Oscar nomination, 1938; *Now, Voyager*, 1942; and *Watch on the Rhine*, Best Picture Oscar nomination, 1943; etc.), *A Streetcar Named Desire* (Best Picture Oscar nomination, 1951), *A Star Is Born* (1954), *Mister Roberts* (Best Picture Oscar nomination, 1955), the three James Dean pictures, *Sayonara* (Best Picture Oscar nomination, 1957), *Auntie Mame* (Best Picture Oscar nomination, 1958), and *The Nun's Story* (Best Picture Oscar nomination, 1959). In his latter years with the studio he founded, Warner personally produced *My Fair Lady*, for which he was publicly lambasted for casting Audrey Hepburn instead of Julie Andrews, who originated the role on Broadway. Nonetheless, the film won him the 1964 Best Picture Oscar. Warner also produced *Camelot* (1967), *1776* (1972), and *Dirty Little Billy* (1972).

WARNER BROTHERS

James Dean, believe it or not, is a very sensitive young man. So sensitive, in fact, that he just couldn't stand seeing his picture up with all the others that decorate the wall of Warner Bros. Green Room, the place where the stars and executives chow down. So the other day the Boy Wonder of the *Giant* set shuffled in and yanked down his fancy portrait.

It wasn't that Dean minded being on display along with other big stars like John Wayne and Alan Ladd, he explained. But he felt it was something akin to degrading to also share wall space with some of the mere starlets and glamour dolls who beam down on the diners. I wonder what Jimmy would say if he knew some of his co-workers are starting a fund to enroll him in some of Dale Carnegie's courses.

Kendis Rochlen, columnist, *Los Angeles Mirror-News*, September 2, 1955

Clive Hirschhorn wrote in his 1979 tome *The Warner Brothers Story*, "Qualitatively it [the 1950s] was the studio's least distinguished decade, despite several good films such as *A Streetcar Named Desire, A Star Is Born, Mister Roberts, Auntie Mame*, and *The Nun's Story*, and the huge impact made by James Dean and the three films in which he appeared."

The four Warner brothers, Harry (president), Jack (vice president),

Off the set of *Giant*: an unlikely trio share a laugh under the Warner banner.

Samuel, and Albert, had their first movie hit in 1917 with *My Four Years in Germany*. Subsequently they produced a series of Rin Tin Tin flicks and the first singing and talking feature, *The Jazz Singer* (1927). The overwhelming success of the latter signified the birth of the talkies. In the thirties and forties Warners flourished with a series of gangster pictures (*Little Caesar*, *Public Enemy*, etc.) and a star roster that included Bette Davis, James Cagney, Errol Flynn, Humphrey Bogart, and Joan Crawford.

In the 1960s Warners had success with the musicals *My Fair Lady* and *The Music Man*. It also had two of the best films of the decade with *Bonnie and Clyde* and *Who's Afraid of Virginia Woolf?* However, by 1967 Jack Warner was the only brother still associated with the family business. That year he sold his share to Seven Arts, which, two years later, sold the company to Kinney National Service.

In the 1970s Warners produced *A Clockwork Orange, Dog Day Afternoon, All the President's Men*, and *The Exorcist*, the last of which became the biggest box-office hit in the studio's history. In the 1980s Warners scored substantial commercial successes with *Private Benjamin, Beetlejuice, Lethal Weapon* and *Lethal Weapon II*, and, of course, *Batman*, which eclipsed *The Exorcist* as the studio's most successful picture. In 1989 Warners merged with Time, Inc., to become Time-Warner, Inc.

In March 1954 Warner Brothers flew James Dean first class from New York to Los Angeles and, on April 7, signed him to a studio contract with a starting salary of $1,000 a week. The studio also advanced him $700, which he agreed to pay back in weekly increments of $100. In the event that Dean was unable to complete his work on *Eden* due to "incapacity or default," Dean agreed to reimburse the studio for the cost of his transportation to Los Angeles. That, of course, proved to be unnecessary. On October 7, 1954, the studio renewed his six-month option, and renewed it again on April 2, 1955. Under that original contract and its subsequent extensions, Dean would have earned $3,000 a week by the time of his ninth film. However, in the weeks before his death his agent, Jane Deacy, successfully negotiated for him a new six-year, nine-picture contract that would have paid him $100,000 a film. As a Warner Brothers executive told the *Los Angeles Mirror-News* at the time of Dean's death, "He was the hottest property we had. We had big plans for him." The week after his death the flags at Warner Brothers were flown at half-mast in his honor.

Certainly for Warners, 1955 (along with 1956, for that matter) was the year of James Dean. *East of Eden* and *Rebel Without a Cause* were both unlikely commercial successes. The following year *Giant*, which was expected to do big business, did phenomenal business, becoming one of the biggest hits in the studio's history (up until that time).

Although he acted with open disdain toward the studio executives, James Dean found acceptance and validation and some semblance of a home at Warner Brothers. When actress Carroll Baker arrived at Warners in early 1955, she was amazed at the transformation that had come over him from his years in New York. In her autobiography, *Baby Doll*, she described a lunch she had with Jimmy in the Warner Brothers cafeteria:

> He certainly had changed. He had never been this outgoing before, at least not with me. Maybe his success had given him more confidence?
>
> I ordered a Betty Grable salad, but Jimmy didn't bother to order lunch and spent his time table-hopping. (Was this the same boy? Was this the Jimmy who normally appeared and disappeared without so much as a word?)

"WARNER BROTHERS PRESENTS"

"Warner Brothers Presents" was the umbrella title for three rotating television programs: "Casablanca," "Cheyenne," and "Kings Row," which were broadcast by ABC on Tuesday nights from September 1955 to September 1956. At the end of each week's presentation a 10- to 15-minute segment was devoted to promoting current Warner Brothers theatrical releases. The segments usually included film clips and interviews that were conducted by the show's host and narrator, Gig Young.

On the October 11, 1955, episode of "Warner Brothers Presents," a promotional piece for *Rebel Without a Cause* was aired. The segment included an interview with the film's producer, David Weisbart, and footage of Dean on the set.

A similar segment was shot during the Marfa, Texas, location shooting of *Giant*. However, by the time of that film's release in October 1956, "Warner Brothers Presents" had been canceled, and the piece was not aired.

WARNER RANCH

The chickie-run sequence in *Rebel Without a Cause* was shot on the Warner Ranch in Calabasas, California.

ANN WARR

Along with her husband, Harry, Ann Warr is generally regarded as the Fairmount, Indiana, town historian. Ann was the president of the Fairmount Historical Museum for 10 years, and during that period she presided over the annual Fairmount Museum Days Festival, with its many James Dean–related activities.

WASHINGTON, D.C.

On May 7 and 8, 1949, the senior class of Fairmount (Indiana) High School visited Washington D.C. Jim Dean, wearing his class of '49 sweater, toured the various monuments, including the Lincoln Memorial. He also visited the Smithsonian.

THE *WASHINGTON POST*

The *Washington Post* has published several articles about James Dean, including:

☆ September 30, 1985   "After 30 Years. . ."

PAUL WATSON

Producer and director of the 1989 British documentary *Bye Bye Jimmy*.

WATTLES PARK

The opening sequence of *Rebel Without a Cause*, much of which was excised from the final print of the picture, was shot outside of Wattles Park in Hollywood.

WAX
James Dean has been immortalized in wax at Madame Tussaud's Waxworks in London (address: Baker Street Station).

DAVID WAYNE
Actor with whom James Dean once visited Tijuana, Mexico.

WBAT RADIO
Marion, Indiana, radio station on which Jim Dean represented Fairmount High School in a 1949 debate.

WE REMEMBER DEAN INTERNATIONAL
The premiere James Dean fan club in existence. Founded in 1978 by Bill Lewis of Indiana and Sylvia Bongiovanni of New York (now of Fullerton, California), the club started out with 10 members and has since burgeoned into an impressive testament to Dean, with membership in South Africa, New Zealand, Australia, Japan, Italy, Holland, Yugoslavia, Switzerland, Denmark, Poland, Germany, France, Sweden, Austria, Belgium, England, and, of course, the United States.

Today the club continues to be run with remarkable efficiency and sincerity by Bongiovanni and operates "to preserve the memory of James Dean, while providing the members with a network to share both information and thoughts about Jimmy."

We Remember Dean International publishes a newsletter every other month. Membership information can be obtained by writing to Sylvia Bongiovanni at PO Box 5025, Fullerton, California 92635.

PAUL WEAVER
"Jimmy wasn't the kind of boy—well, in those days, a coach could put his arm around a boy, . . . partly in affection, but partly just to get near to talk. . . . But I'm sure that I felt at the time that Jimmy felt uncomfortable . . . with you being that close. Maybe he wouldn't have been if we'd been alone. I don't know."
Paul Weaver, *James Dean: A Short Life* by Venable Herndon

During his senior year in 1949 Jim Dean was the starting guard and top scorer on the Fairmount Quakers basketball team. His coach and physical education instructor was Paul Weaver. Jimmy compensated for his lack of height with considerable effort. Weaver later recalled:

"He was a normal, intelligent boy, very neat, with a fine personality. He participated in all school activities, was popular, and much better looking than in the movies. He worked very hard at everything he did."
Chicago Tribune, September 9, 1956

"THE WEB"
Television drama series that aired on CBS from July 1950 to September 1954

and on NBC from July 1957 to October 1957. Unknown actor James Dean appeared in "Sleeping Dogs," a February 20, 1952, episode of "The Web." The show was directed by Lela Swift, produced by Franklin Heller, and starred Anne Jackson, E. G. Marshall, and Robert Simon. It was hosted and narrated by Jonathan Blake. Dean was featured as a bellhop who helps solve a murder.

CLIFTON WEBB
Another Indiana boy who made good in Hollywood. Clifton Webb was instrumental in, among other things, persuading Hedda Hopper to see James Dean's performance in *East of Eden*, something she had previously refused to do. Actor William Redfield told a writer for *New York* magazine in 1976:

> "The rumors were rife that he [James Dean] was Clifton Webb's protege. Which always struck me as odd, because Jimmy in his manner in my presence didn't strike me as at all a homosexual. But of course that often happens. And I don't think he exclusively was. And what exactly went on between Webb and him I don't know, though I imagine it took a sexual form."

Clifton Webb, born Webb Hollenbeck in 1889, was a child singer and dancer, a Broadway star, a ballroom dancer, and then a movie star (after appearing in a slew of silent pictures) with *Laura*, for which he was nominated for a 1944 Best Supporting Actor Oscar. Webb's other films include *The Razor's Edge* (Best Supporting Actor Oscar nomination, 1946), *Sitting Pretty* (Best Actor nomination, 1948), *Mr. Belvedere Goes to College* (1949), *Cheaper By the Dozen* (1950), *Three Coins in the Fountain* (1954), *The Man Who Never Was* (England, 1956), and *Satan Never Sleeps* (1962). His most famous role was that of Mr. Belvedere, which he played in a series of pictures, and which inspired the 1985 television situation comedy of the same title.

It is generally accepted in Hollywood that Clifton Webb was homosexual. He never married, and his mother, Maybelle, was his constant companion. According to Martin Grief, author of *The Gay Book of Days*, "Once both he [Webb] and Tallulah Bankhead were smitten with the same handsome Austrian army officer and vied for the uniformed stud. . . ."

Clifton Webb died of a heart attack in his Beverly Hills home in 1966.

WEIGHT
☆ At birth: eight pounds, 10 ounces
☆ His usual adult weight: 140 pounds
☆ What his California driver's license claimed he weighed: 135 pounds
☆ What his studio biographies claimed he weighed: 155 pounds

JERRY WEINTRAUB
Producer of the 1977 Dean-inspired film *September 30, 1955*.

Jerry Weintraub, born in 1937, won a 1974–1975 Emmy for producing the television special "An Evening with John Denver." His film credits include *Nashville* (Best Picture Oscar nomination, 1975), *Oh, God!* (1977), *Cruising* (1980), *All Night Long* (1981), *Diner* (1982), and *The Karate Kid* (1984).

DAVID WEISBART
Producer of *Rebel Without a Cause*.

David Weisbart (1915–1967) was a former film editor (he was nominated for a 1948 Best Editing Oscar for *Johnny Belinda*) turned movie producer. In addition to *Rebel*, his producing credits include *Maru Maru* (1952), *Love Me Tender* (Elvis Presley's film debut, 1956), *Kid Galahad* (1962), *Goodbye Charlie* (1964), and *Valley of the Dolls* (1967).

BEN WEISMAN
Co-wrote the song "Jimmy, Jimmy," which was recorded on the Coral Records tribute album *The James Dean Story*.

RUDOLPH WEISS
Actor who appeared in "A Long Time Till Dawn," a 1953 episode of the NBC television program "Kraft Television Theatre" that starred James Dean.

Rudolph Weiss also appeared in the New York stage plays *Two on an Island* (1940), *The Three Sisters* (1959), and *The Deadly Game* (1966).

THE WESLEYAN TABERNACLE
Fairmount, Indiana, church where Jimmy Dean's 1949 high school graduation ceremonies were held. Thirty-one years later, on September 30, 1980, a memorial service was held at the Wesleyan Tabernacle to commemorate the 25th anniversary of Dean's death. Martin Sheen was the guest of honor.

WEST HOLLYWOOD, CALIFORNIA
Dubbed the first gay city in the country, the city of West Hollywood paid homage to its former resident James Dean by proclaiming September 30, 1985, "James Dean Day."

In 1954 Dean rented a house on Sunset Plaza Drive, above the Sunset strip in West Hollywood. Three years earlier he had lived in the same neighborhood with his benefactor, Rogers Brackett. In West Hollywood Jimmy hung out at various nightclubs on the strip, at Googie's, Barney's Beanery, and other local favorites. He was also a frequent guest in the home of Sandy and Beulah Roth, who lived on Hacienda Place, just north of Santa Monica Boulevard.

WESTINGHOUSE
Sponsor of the CBS television program "Studio One" in which James Dean made several appearances.

PATRICIA WESTMORE
The younger sister of the famous Westmore brothers, all of whom worked as

movie hairstylists and/or makeup artists, Patricia Westmore was one of the hairstylists on *Giant*. Her father, George Westmore (1879–1931), was the man who did Valentino's hair. Her brothers were Mont (1902–1940), Ern (1904–1968), Perc (1904–1970), Wally (1906–1973), Bud (1918–1973), and Frank (1923–).

WESTWOOD, CALIFORNIA
During his brief stint at UCLA from September 1950 until February 1951, Jimmy Dean lived at the Sigma Nu fraternity house at 601 Gayley Avenue in Westwood, California. From there he moved to an apartment on Comstock Avenue, also in Westwood, with his friend Bill Bast. Today Westwood is a mecca of movie theaters, restaurants, bars, shops, and high-rise office buildings.

WHISPER MAGAZINE
Hollywood fan magazine that published several articles about James Dean, including:

☆ February 1956   "James Dean's Black Madonna"
☆ April 1956   "James Dean's Fans Speak Their Mind"
☆ August 1956   "The Girl James Dean Left Behind"
☆ December 1956   "James Dean vs Elvis Presley"
☆ February 1957   "How James Dean Got an Oscar"
☆ December 1957   "James Dean, Ghost Rider of Polonio Pass"

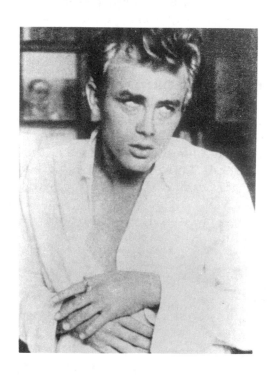

CHRISTINE WHITE

In the early 1950s Christine White was like thousands of other struggling, young New York actors and actresses. She was trying to obtain membership into the Actors Studio, the prestigious school that had propelled the career of Brando, among others. She was in her agent Jane Deacy's office, typing a script, when she first met Jimmy Dean. She looked up, saw a pair of glasses and a borrowed suit, and went back to typing as an act of dismissal. White later wrote, in the third person, about the introduction in an article for the *International Press Bulletin*:

> He walked slowly back to the doorway. She looked at his hunched shoulders, the pockets with hands in them. If he were an actor she might've talked to him, but ambition was too precious a power to waste on a funny-looking little guy with glasses who couldn't possibly be an actor. She watched him hesitate in the doorway then careen around the frame and disappear into the waiting room.

It was mid-1952. Dean eventually cajoled White into writing an original scene for the two of them to use as their Actors Studio audition scene. She did, and for the next two months they rehearsed in her apartment, in his hotel room at the Iroquois, in cabs, in bars, in restaurants, in Central Park. They became, as they kidded, "partners in crime." They also became accepted members into the Actors Studio.

James Dean's relationship with Christine White was very much like his other close relationships with women: more spiritual than physical, almost like a brother and sister kinship. As she defined it years later, "We were soul mates."

Reportedly, Dean attempted to have Chris White, whom he called "Face," considered for the role of Judy in *Rebel Without a Cause*. However, the role went to Natalie Wood, and White had to wait for the Broadway production of *A Hatful of Rain*, which opened in November 1955, a month after Dean's death, for any real success as an actress.

In addition to *A Hatful of Rain*, Chris White appeared in the New York stage play *The Long Watch* (1952). Years later she had a small part in Bill Bast's television movie "James Dean" (1976).

DAVID WHITE

Actor who appeared in "Keep Our Honor Bright," a 1953 episode of the NBC series "Kraft Television Theatre" that co-starred James Dean.

On the New York stage, White appeared in *Leaf and Bough* (1949), *The Earth Spirit* (1950), and *A Roomful of Roses* (1955). Later, he scored a success as Larry Tate in the hit comedy television series "Bewitched" (1964–1972).

JOHN ROBERT WHITE

One of the eyewitnesses of the September 30, 1955, car crash that killed James Dean.

MARK WHITMAN
Author of *The Films of James Dean*, published in Great Britain by BCW Publishing in 1974 and in the United States by Greenhaven Press in 1978.

JAMES WHITMORE

> "Whitmore saw me in a college play and told me I should forget about law and think more of acting as a career. I decided that if such a well-known actor as Whitmore had confidence in me, I should have a little confidence in myself. So I took the big step."
>
> James Dean

James Whitmore introduced James Dean to Method acting in 1951 in a series of classes that he taught to a group of 20 students in a room on the second floor of the Brentwood Country Mart in Brentwood, California. It was Whitmore who was primarily responsible for encouraging the 20-year-old Dean to move to New York to pursue a serious acting career. As Dean acknowledged in the *New York Times* (March 13, 1955), "I came here at the suggestion of Jimmy Whitmore, a fine actor, and a good boy, a real New York boy, who wasn't too happy out at Metro."

Born in 1921, Whitmore, an Actors Studio member, won acclaim on Broadway for his performance in *Command Decision* (1948). He made his subsequent film debut with *The Undercover Man* (1949). His other film credits include *The Asphalt Jungle* (1950), *Battle Cry* (1955), *Oklahoma!* (1955), *Planet of the Apes* (1968), and *Give 'Em Hell Harry* (Best Actor Oscar nomination, 1975). On television, Whitmore starred in the programs "The Law and Mr. Jones" (1960–1962), "My Friend Tony" (1969), and "Temperatures Rising" (1972–1974). He also won a 1989 Best Supporting Actor ACE (cable) award for his performance in "Glory! Glory!"

Interestingly, back in 1955 James Whitmore was considered for the role of Ray Frame, the sympathetic juvenile officer who points Jim Stark (the character portrayed by James Dean) in the right direction.

> "There is always somebody in your life who opens your eyes and makes you see your mistakes and stimulates you to the point of trying to find your way. Not of rectifying your mistakes, but of growing. In my life, that somebody was James Whitmore. He encouraged me to go to New York and with the fortification of his knowledge of theater and the right way of working, I went.
>
> "Whitmore was working at Warners when I came out [for *East of Eden*], and I wanted to thank him for his kindness and patience, but he said, 'It's not necessary. Elia Kazan did the same thing for me, and you will do the same for someone else.' I feel I have been of some benefit to young actors. It's the only way to repay Jimmy."
>
> James Dean to Hedda Hopper

OSCAR WILDE
Legendary author who was imprisoned for his homosexual relationship with Lord Alfred Douglas. Oscar Wilde (1854–1900) was one of James Dean's

favorite writers. Dean used to read aloud from Wilde's autobiographical *De Profundis*.

ALEC WILDER

Upon his arrival in New York in late 1951, one of the first people Jimmy Dean contacted was composer Alec Wilder. The introduction was made, indirectly, through Rogers Brackett. At the time Wilder lived at the Algonquin Hotel. Later Wilder composed the incidental score for *See the Jaguar*, a 1952 play in which Dean made his Broadway debut. In the play Jimmy sang a song, "Green Briar, Blue Fire," which had been written by Wilder.

Alec Wilder was born in Rochester, New York, in 1907. He composed the score for the plays *Thumbs Up* (1934), *Peter and the Wolves* (1941), *The Bird Cage* (1950), *Once Over Lightly* (1955), and *Kittiwake Island* (1960), among others. He also composed the score for the film *The Sand Castle* (1961).

WILL: THE LAST WILL AND TESTAMENT OF JAMES DEAN

James Dean didn't live long enough to draft a will. The week of his death, however, he did take out a $100,000 life insurance policy. Reportedly he planned to have it distributed as follows: $85,000 to Marcus and Ortense Winslow; $10,000 for the education of Marcus Winslow, Jr.; and $5,000 to his grandparents, Charlie and Emma Dean. However, because he did not live to finalize his intentions, the entire sum was awarded to his closest living relative, his father, Winton Dean.

WILL WRIGHT'S ICE CREAM PARLOR

In the 1950s Will Wright's Ice Cream Parlor was a West Hollywood hangout frequented by, among many others, James Dean. At the time there were several locations; most often Jimmy went to the shop located at 8252 Santa Monica Boulevard. According to Dean friend Beulah Roth: "We used to go there all the time. The best ice cream in the world. We were in there one night, and there was a girl sitting at the counter having a soda or something, and she said, 'Aren't you James Dean?' And he said, 'Yes.' When she walked out, he said, 'How the hell did she know who I am?' See, he never knew."

KENT WILLIAMS

New York actor friend of James Dean's. They met outside an agent's office. Said Williams, "I thought, 'There's one of the greatest faces I've ever seen.' " After Dean's death Kent Williams reportedly worked to establish the James Dean Memorial Foundation.

Years later, Kent Williams co-starred in the television series "Mickey Spillane's Mike Hammer" (1984–1987).

ROBERT WILLIAMS

Actor who appeared in "The Unlighted Road," a 1955 episode of the CBS television series "Schlitz Playhouse of Stars" in which James Dean starred.

WADE WILLIAMS

In 1985 Wade Williams discovered rare footage of James Dean appearing in a 1953 episode of the ABC television series "Tales of Tomorrow." The episode, entitled "The Evil Within," featured Dean as Rod Steiger's lab assistant. Williams owned the rights to the series.

BEVERLY WILLS

> We began to talk about acting and Jimmy lit up. He told me how interested he was in the Stanislavsky Method, where you not only act [as] people, but [as] things, too. "Look," said Jimmy, "I'm a pine tree in a storm." He held his arms out and waved wildly. To feel more free, he impatiently tossed off his cheap, tight blue jacket. He looked bigger as soon as he did, because you could see his broad shoulders and powerful build. Then he got wilder and pretended he was a monkey. He climbed a big tree and swung from a high branch. Dropping from the branch he landed on his hands like a little boy, chuckling uproariously at every little thing. Once in the spotlight, he ate it up and had us all in stitches all afternoon. The "creep" had turned into the hit of the party.
>
> Beverly Wills, *Modern Screen*, March 1957

Bill Bast met Beverly Wills at CBS Radio in the spring of 1951. At the time Beverly, daughter of comedienne Joan Davis, was an actress playing the role of Fluffy Adams on the weekly radio comedy "Junior Miss." Bill and Beverly double-dated with Jimmy and one of his girlfriends. A couple of months later Bill, Beverly, and Jimmy were sitting together in the front seat of a car when Beverly suddenly sprang the news: "Bill, there's something we have to tell you. It's *Jimmy* and me, now. I mean, we're in love." A couple of months later Jimmy and Beverly split up, and Jimmy moved to New York. Beverly rebounded by reconciling with Bill. The pair eventually became engaged before Bill followed his friend and moved to New York.

After Dean's death Wills penned the ludicrously titled "I Almost Married James Dean. Who Am I?" article for *Modern Screen* magazine. She also co-starred (1953–1955) in her mother's situation comedy television series "I Married Joan."

CHILL WILLS

Actor who co-starred as Uncle Bawley in *Giant*. During the five-week location shooting in Marfa, Texas, Chill Wills shared a house with (and undoubtedly worked to keep the peace between) Rock Hudson and James Dean. Back in Hollywood, during a weekend break from shooting, Wills chartered a boat and went fishing off Catalina Island. His companions were Monte Hale, Dennis Hopper, and James Dean.

Best known as the voice of Francis the Talking Mule, Chill Wills (1903–1978) appeared in films including *Boom Town* (1940), *The Harvey Girls* (1946), *The Alamo* (Best Supporting Actor Oscar nomination, 1960), and *Mr. Billion* (1977). On television Wills co-starred in the programs "Frontier Circus" (1961–1962) and "The Rounders" (1966–1967).

HOWARD WILSON
James Dean's uncle, Mildred Dean's brother, of Jonesboro, Indiana.

JOHN WILSON
James Dean's grandfather, Mildred Dean's father, John Wilson was a factory worker from Gas City, Indiana.

MINNIE SLAUGHTER WILSON
James Dean's grandmother, Minnie Slaughter Wilson, died when her daughter, Mildred, was still a child.

ROD WIMMER
Singer and songwriter from Indiana who wrote and recorded the tribute album *James Dean: He Never Said Goodbye.*

CHUCK WINSLOW
Son of Marylou and Marcus Winslow, Jr., Chuck Winslow inherited Jimmy's old bedroom in the Winslow farmhouse outside of Fairmount, Indiana.

JOAN WINSLOW
James Dean's cousin, Marcus and Ortense Winslow's daughter, Joan Winslow was born in 1926. She was 14 years old at the time that Jimmy moved in with her family.

Joan Winslow married Mayron Peacock during World War II. For weeks before the wedding Jimmy collected rice, which was hard to come by, to throw at his newlywed cousin. Also prior to the service, he tied a string of clanking cans to the back end of the couple's getaway car.

Today Joan Peacock, still married, is mother to Gerrell Reece and Jane Ann Peacock and lives in the Fairmount, Indiana, area.

MARCUS WINSLOW
"Both are wise and gentle and have a great gift for loving. Theirs is like a Quaker home should be. You never hear a harsh word. Best of all, they are happy as well as good—and that's what Jimmy needed most after the shock of losing his mother."
Emma Dean, Jimmy's grandmother, *Photoplay*

"You can't find a finer man than Marcus Winslow, and so far as choosing between the way my sister would mother Jimmy and how some housekeeper might take care of him, there's just no question."
Winton Dean to Emma Dean, *Photoplay*

After the death of his mother in July 1940 nine-year-old Jimmy Dean returned to Fairmount, Indiana, to be raised by his uncle and aunt, Marcus and Ortense Winslow.

Marcus Winslow was born in July 1900. The 15-room farmhouse in which he was raised and in which Jimmy was raised was built in 1904 and sits on 350 acres of land. Marcus, a slight, bespectacled man, was a skilled

The Winslow farm home in which Jimmy was raised.

farmer in whose fields grew corn, oats, and hay. As Jimmy later told a reporter, "My father was a farmer, but he did have this remarkable adeptness with his hands."

Unlike Jimmy's natural father, Winton Dean, Marcus Winslow was entirely supportive of Jimmy's decision to become an actor. When Jimmy moved to Los Angeles and later to New York, Marcus gave him a sole set of instructions. "Now Jimmy," he said, "I don't want you running up a board bill. Stay out of debt. If you get short, let me know." There were periods, of course, when Jimmy was short to the point of starvation. It was Marcus Winslow who always put money in the mail. Later, when Jimmy started getting work on television, Marcus bought a television set and invited friends, neighbors, and relatives over to watch.

The last time Marcus and Ortense Winslow saw Jimmy was in September 1955, days before his death. They had driven to California to visit with him and with his father, Winton. They didn't hear about his death until they arrived back in Fairmount on Monday, October 3. Later, in April 1957, they returned to Los Angeles and visited the Warner Brothers lot where Jimmy had worked.

For the next 20 years Marcus Winslow stood on the porch of his Fairmount farm and greeted the thousands of visitors who came from all over the world to see the house that James Dean had been raised in, to meet and talk to the people who had raised him. Understandably he grew tired of sharing his home with the world. As he told a reporter for the *Los Angeles Times* (July 22, 1973):

> "Hell, I've said it until I'm sick of sayin' it. Jim Dean was just like any other kid who grew up in this town. He played basketball, he

went to Sunday meeting at Back Creek Quaker Church, and he did his chores on the farm. He used to tag around after me, opening gates so I wouldn't have to get off the tractor. And he loved to ride that little black cycle of his through the meadow. . . ."

Marcus "penned" the article "You Can Make Jimmy Dean Live Forever" in the November 1956 issue of *Motion Picture* magazine. He also appeared, rather uncomfortably, in the 1957 documentary feature *The James Dean Story*. He died on April 6, 1976.

> "Maybe the honest way to tell you how Marcus and Jimmy got along would be to repeat what one of Jimmy's classmates said to me. 'Ma Dean,' he said, 'I always envied Jimmy. My dad never took time to play with me, but Marcus was forever out there shooting baskets with Jimmy, or passing a football, or taking him hunting, or showing him how to do stunts."
>
> Emma Dean, *Photoplay*, March 1956

MARCUS WINSLOW, JR.

Jimmy Dean was 12 years old and had been living with the Winslows for three years when Marcus Winslow, Jr., was born on November 2, 1943. "Markie," as Jimmy fondly referred to him, was more like Jimmy's little brother than his cousin. Although Jimmy moved to California in 1949, he made frequent return visits to Fairmount, during which he spent much of his time with Markie, playing with him, teaching him, trying to be a role model for him.

The summer after Jimmy's death 12-year-old Markie made his acting debut in the James Dean Memorial Foundation production of Thornton Wilder's *Our Town*. But if there was speculation in Fairmount that Markie would follow in his famous cousin's footsteps, it was eventually dispelled. Instead Marcus Junior opted for selling tractors for a living.

Over the years, and up through the present, Marcus Winslow, Jr., has continued to live in the family homestead, now with his wife and children. He has also continued his father's tradition of greeting the thousands of fans who continue to show up at the Winslow doorstep.

> What did Jimmy talk about? He talked about Markie. He loved that little boy. . . .
>
> Beulah Roth

MARYLOU WINSLOW
Wife of Marcus Winslow, Jr.

ORTENSE WINSLOW

> "He come in right away and wanted to know where his bedroom was. He wanted to see his bedroom. He just ran all over the house to see if anything had been changed. Everybody just bent over backward for him. They felt so sorry for him."
>
> Ortense Winslow on nine-year-old Jimmy Dean after he was picked up at the train station following his mother's death, *Hollywood: The Rebel James Dean*

Ortense Winslow (right) the aunt who raised Jimmy. She
is pictured here with a visiting Dean fan, Diane Hanville, in
1988.

"Some day, when I make it, I'm going to see to it that they sell this
place and move to a drier climate, like Arizona, where Mom's
arthritis won't bother her so much. Some day, they're going to have
the kind of life they deserve, without all the work and worry."
                    James Dean to Bill Bast, 1952, *James Dean* by Bill Bast

When Jimmy Dean moved in with them, Marcus and Ortense Winslow gave
him their bedroom. It wasn't that there wasn't enough room in the house for
him; it was, as Ortense told *Photoplay*, that "He liked our bedroom set better.
It was maple and that seemed right for a boy." Shortly after his arrival and up
until the time of his death, Jimmy referred to Ortense as "Mom." The
affection was mutual. In response to press reports that labeled him an

unwanted child, Ortense was compelled to object: "We have read where he was sort of pushed off onto us. But that is not true. We wanted him."

Ortense Winslow, Winton Dean's sister, was born April 1, 1901. A former secretary, Ortense was a member of the local Women's Christian Temperance Union and an active member of her church, for which she was the organist.

After her husband's death in 1976 Ortense moved out of the family house and into the town of Fairmount. Later she moved into a nursing home in Marion and is now reportedly living in Fairmount again.

> Of course, as soon as we found out he was on TV in New York, we ran right out and bought a television so we could watch him. Of course, we'd hardly move or breathe so we could see every bit of it. We thought he looked so thin. His face looked thin.
> Ortense Winslow, *Hollywood: The Rebel James Dean*

> He was just an interesting youngster. He would help me work, and he'd help Mark.
> Ortense Winslow, "Entertainment Tonight"

DANIEL WINTER

The death of James Dean had strange consequences for a young Parisian man by the name of Daniel Winter. *Variety* reported from France in 1956:

> There's a fellow here named Daniel Winter, who passes as a double for Dean, and who's had his life made miserable via his resemblance to the late actor. Papers say Winter is considering having his face changed to avoid being taken for Dean.

SHELLEY WINTERS

Shelley Winters was considered for the role of Vashti Snythe in *Giant*, which eventually went to Jane Withers. Winters, an Actors Studio member, attended classes with Jimmy. In her biography of Lee Strasberg, Cindy Adams reported an incident that involved Dean and Winters:

> Dean was using an affective memory. He had a knife and, deep into reliving something, he nicked himself. Lee never moved, but Shelley Winters jumped up. "Stop the scene," she cried. "I can't stand this." Lee wanted to kill her. "Shelley," he said, "he's an unstable boy. He was just now working something through and you may well have stopped the one thing that could have helped him forever."

Winters wrote about the same incident in her autobiography, *Shelley: Also Known as Shirley* (William Morrow & Co., 1980):

> [He] began to weep. I looked at Strasberg, who was watching Jimmy in an intellectual and dispassionate manner. Jimmy began playing with an unopened knife. He was smiling, but the tears were flowing down his face. I was terrified for him and kept looking at Strasberg, hoping he would stop the exercise. I thought I noticed a thin line of blood on Jimmy's wrist. . . .

We struggled for the knife, and he started laughing. . . . I noticed a white scar on Jimmy's right wrist, and . . . I saw that his left wrist also had a white scar on it. He was quite strong for such a slight boy, and all I could think of to say was "Stop, Jimmy! I've got a back brace on. I've been in an automobile accident!"

Shelley Winters, born Shirley Schrift in 1922, made her film debut in 1943 with *What a Woman!* Her subsequent film credits include *A Double Life* (1947), *Red River* (1948), *A Place in the Sun* (Best Actress Oscar nomination, 1951), *The Big Knife* (1955), *The Diary of Anne Frank* (Best Supporting Actress Oscar, 1959), *Lolita* (England, 1962), *A Patch of Blue* (Best Supporting Actress Oscar, 1965), *Harper* (1966), *Wild in the Streets* (1968), *The Poseidon Adventure* (Best Supporting Actress Oscar nomination, 1972), *Blume in Love* (1973), and *King of the Gypsies* (1978). On television, Winters won a 1963–1964 Best Actress Emmy for her performance in "Two Is the Number," an episode of "Bob Hope Presents the Chrysler Theatre."

ROBERT WISE

Oscar-winning director (*West Side Story*, 1961; *The Sound of Music*, 1965) and co-editor of the Orson Welles classics *Citizen Kane* (1941) and *The Magnificent Ambersons* (1942), Robert Wise was set to direct James Dean in *Somebody Up There Likes Me*, the biopic about boxing champion Rocky Graziano. Reportedly Wise initially had reservations about MGM's decision to cast Dean in the picture. He was concerned that Dean did not have the prerequisite physique, which he felt was essential to the role. After Dean's death Robert Wise directed *Somebody Up There Likes Me* (1956) with Paul Newman in the leading role.

WISH YOU WERE HERE, JIMMY DEAN
Author: Martin Dawber
Publisher: Columbus Books, Great Britain
Year: 1989

Yet another biography riddled with inaccuracies. Handsomely illustrated by Kenneth Kendall and others.

JANE WITHERS

"Sometimes, we'd just sit and talk, or we'd listen to music for a couple of hours at a time without saying a word. Sometimes he'd get up and dance. He used to do modern, interpretive things. Jimmy had a wonderful pantomimic gift—I couldn't compare him to anyone else. He had a quality and style all his own."

Jane Withers, *Cosmopolitan*, August 1956

Jane Withers was a child star of the 1930s who made her movie comeback as Vashti Snythe in *Giant*. During filming she got along well with Dean, and according to Withers Jimmy stopped by her house the morning of his death and asked her to accompany him to the races in Salinas.

Withers, born in 1926, made her film debut in 1934 with *Bright Eyes.* Her subsequent credits include *Ginger* (1935), *The Farmer Takes a Wife* (1935), *Affairs of Geraldine* (1946), and *Captain Newman, M.D.* (1963).

> "For three weeks that boy used to come into the hotel dining room for dinner wearing the same sport shirt. One night, I went up to him and said, 'Look, I'm getting tired of that shirt, aren't you?' And he said, 'No, I like this shirt.' I said, 'Then would you let me wash it for you?' And he said, 'No, I like this shirt the way it is.' "
>
> Jane Withers, *Cosmopolitan*, August 1956

THE WITNESSES TO THE ACCIDENT THAT KILLED JAMES DEAN

Donald Dooley	Ruth Hord	John Robert White
Clifford Hord	Thomas Frederick	

IAN WOLFE

Actor who portrayed the Griffith Observatory lecturer in *Rebel Without a Cause.*

Born in 1896, Ian Wolfe appeared in films including *The Barretts of Wimpole Street* (1934), *The Great Caruso* (1951), and *The Fortune* (1975). On television Wolfe co-starred in the short-lived series "Wizards and Warriors" (1983).

WOMEN OF TRACHIS

In early 1954 James Dean appeared in a dramatic reading of *Women of Trachis*, a one-act play by Sophocles adapted by Ezra Pound. The reading was presented by the New School for Social Research at the Cherry Lane Theatre. It was directed by Howard Sackler and, along with Dean, featured Eli Wallach and Joseph Sullivan and a score by Leonard Rosenman.

WOMEN'S CHRISTIAN TEMPERANCE UNION

Fairmount, Indiana, organization that sponsored various theatrical productions and competitions in which young Jimmy Dean participated and excelled.

NATALIE WOOD

> "The producer, Mort Abrahams, told him to sit with me since we were the young lovers in the piece. But he just grunted, and we'd got halfway through the reading before he did come and sit by me. He was introspective during the read-through and very indirect in his manner towards people. I remember when I went to lunch I noticed him soundlessly following me. We had lunch together every day while we were working. He always had a radio with him and played classical music."
>
> Natalie Wood, *James Dean: A Biography* by John Howlett

Natalie Wood first met James Dean on the set of *East of Eden*. The first time they worked together was in "I'm a Fool," a November 1954 episode of the

CBS television program "General Electric Theater." Nearly 20 years later Natalie reminisced in the *Los Angeles Times*:

> "I remember as if it were this morning the first time I met him. He arrived on a motorcycle in a pair of jeans held up by a safety pin. He didn't come through the door, but rather through a window loft. I thought he was totally weird . . . until I began working with him."

At the time she tested for *Rebel Without a Cause* Natalie Wood, 17, was perceived by many as a former child actress whose career was substantially behind, not in front of, her. Her chances for obtaining the role were tenuous at best. Both Debbie Reynolds and Margaret O'Brien were also up for the part, and at the time both were bigger marquee names than Natalie Wood.

Even at 17 Natalie was savvy enough to realize that *Rebel Without a Cause* was her passage to adult stardom. She didn't just audition for the part;

James Dean to Natalie Wood before shooting their *Rebel* love scene: "You look green. And you know how green photographs in color." After *Rebel*, Wood was up for the part of Lacey Lynnton, Elizabeth Taylor's character's sister in *Giant*.

she campaigned for it. As she confided to Hedda Hopper, "I wanted this picture more than anything. I was in Nick Ray's office daily for a month waiting to see what would happen after my test." She was also allegedly in director Nick Ray's bed. According to several sources, the two had something of an affair prior to the start of *Rebel*, and Ray became Natalie's champion at the studio. While Warner Brothers executives wanted Debbie Reynolds in the part, Ray adamantly petitioned for Wood. As late as March 1, 1955, Ray was still pleading his case. In a memo he issued to the studio front office Ray prophesied that the studio might develop a star of its own with Natalie Wood. At the time Ray also volunteered to work closely with her on voice, wardrobe, and hair.

When he saw Natalie Wood's screen test, Jack Warner groused that she was in need of a vocal coach. Ray subsequently enlisted the services of speech therapist Nina Moise. Warner eventually acquiesced, and Natalie Wood was cast in the picture.

Nick Ray was not the only one on the *Rebel* set who thought well of Natalie Wood. She was adored by practically everyone. Beverly Long recently recalled, "She was so sweet. I was extremely fond of Natalie. She was just a terrific girl, a really terrific person. We got to know each other quite well." And at least one cast member, Dennis Hopper, fell in love with her.

But it was James Dean with whom *she* fell in love, despite the fact that he generally regarded her with little more than brotherly affection. According to Sal Mineo, who also fell in love with Dean, "He was all she could talk about. Every night for weeks in a row, she went to see *East of Eden*—she must have seen it over fifty times. She even taught me to play the theme song from the picture on the piano." Hedda Hopper concurred: "Natalie Wood, who aged beautifully from a child star to a ripe old eighteen, fell hard for her co-star, James Dean." Natalie openly fawned in Dean's presence. She later commented that she constantly found herself hoping to grow older so that the two of them might start dating. Actually the two did date, casually, usually after a long day of shooting and usually at the Hamburger Hamlet on Sunset.

Still, Wood, like many other Dean co-stars, was unnerved by his penchant for stealing scenes and his wildly fluctuating temperament. Dick Davalos, who had worked with Dean earlier on *East of Eden*, recalled, "I remember Natalie Wood would come to me. We were very close at that time, and she was not happy with the way Jimmy would do this kind of—attention getting [in a scene]—let's put it that way. And I would counsel her, having been through it myself. Also, as was characteristic of him, Dean occasionally treated his young co-star as though she didn't exist. At other times he would toy with her emotions, testing the limits and boundaries of her affection for him. Natalie gently reprimanded Dean in public. "Jimmy," she said in a confused state of protest and rationalization, "is a very introspective actor. He lives his part with such verve that it sometimes spills over and seems to injure the feelings of other people. He doesn't mean to do this however."

Usually, however, Natalie Wood, like most of the actors in the cast, was thrilled simply to be working with Dean, who was being heralded at the time as Hollywood's new genius:

> "It's just pulsating. Jimmy generates theatrical electricity. Anyone playing with him can't help but feel his tempo and drive. Even if Jimmy doesn't have a line to speak, I feel he's talking to me. I can tell by the way he looks, the movement of his hands, the slight motion of his facial muscles. I've never felt so excited with an actor as I do with Jimmy."

At the time *Rebel Without a Cause* was shooting, Natalie Wood was a senior at Van Nuys High School. As she told reporters, "Dean is the current rage at school and my popularity has zoomed one thousand percent ever since the kids read that I would be working with him." Almost immediately after *Rebel* completed shooting in June 1955, Natalie graduated from high school. She marked the occasion by buying herself a new red convertible. She also had a swimming pool built in the backyard of her parents' house. Among the first to use the pool were Nick Adams, Sal Mineo, and James Dean.

She had reason to celebrate. The early word on *Rebel Without a Cause* was that Natalie Wood was going to be one of the few actresses to make a successful transition from child actress to adult star. As Natalie gushed, "In *Rebel* I wear an entirely new hairdo! No more pigtails, no more bobby socks, no more nice-little-girl-next-door parts." James Dean, in his evaluation of his co-star, was more thoughtful: "It was great working with her," he offered. "She has pep, vitality, and all the attributes of a powerful performer. I hope that I can work with her in the near future."

In the near future, however, Dean died. On the night of his death Natalie Wood was in New York, having dinner with Sal Mineo, Nick Adams, and Dick Davalos. As Natalie recalled years later:

> "We were talking about Jimmy's lifestyle and Nick ventured the opinion that Jimmy wouldn't live till thirty. We pooh-poohed the idea. Later, when we finished eating, Nick and Sal walked me to my hotel. I was still under age then with a studio chaperone, and it was she who heard the news. She told Nick and Sal and asked them not to say anything to me because I had an early call the next day and she wanted me to sleep. Next morning the chaperone had to tell me because down in the lobby the newspapers had it on all the headlines."

For her subsequent, highly successful career, Natalie Wood owed a great debt of gratitude to Nick Ray and James Dean. Ray went to great lengths to get Warner Brothers to take her. As for Dean, it was after his death and with the release of *Rebel Without a Cause* that Natalie garnered a substantial following. Teenage boys who idolized Dean wanted to date her; teenage girls wanted to *be* her so that they could have dated Dean. Natalie Wood became a star, in large part because of her association with James Dean.

Despite the fact that she was thoroughly overshadowed by Dean in *Rebel Without a Cause*, Natalie Wood displayed a remarkable presence in the film.

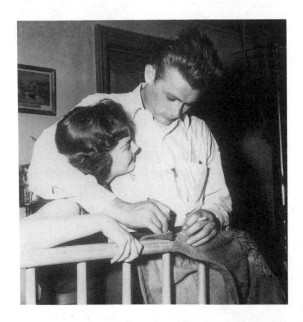

Dean, with blood on his shirt, signs Natalie Wood's suede autograph jacket. He was her 100th co-star to sign. Wood's mother later burned the signatures with a hot needle for posterity.

For her performance she was nominated for a Best Supporting Actress Oscar. She was also named as having given one of *The Film Daily*'s Best Performances by Juvenile Actresses and was presented with the National Association of Theatre Owners' award as the Star of Tomorrow.

Born Natasha Gurdin in 1938, Natalie Wood made her film debut in 1943 with *Happy Land*. Her subsequent film credits include *Tomorrow Is Forever* (1946), *The Bride Wore Boots* (1946), *Miracle on 34th Street* (for which she was chosen as "the most talented juvenile star of the year" by *Parents* magazine, 1947), *Driftwood* (1947), *Scudda Hoo! Scudda Hay!* (1948), *No Sad Songs for Me* (1950), *The Blue Veil* (1951), *The Star* (1952), *The Silver Chalice* (1954), *Cry in the Night* (1956), *The Searchers* (1956), *Marjorie Morningstar* (1958), *Kings Go Forth* (1958), *Cash McCall* (1960), *Splendor in the Grass* (Best Actress Oscar nomination, 1961), *West Side Story* (1961), *Gypsy* (1962), *Love with the Proper Stranger* (Best Actress Oscar nomination, 1963), *Sex and the Single Girl* (1964), *The Great Race* (1965), *Inside Daisy Clover* (1966), *This Property Is Condemned* (1966), *Penelope* (1966), *Bob & Carol & Ted & Alice* (1969), *Pepper* (1974), *Meteor* (1979), *The Last Married Couple in America* (1980), and *Brainstorm* (1983).

On television Natalie Wood appeared in the series "The Pride of the Family" (1953–1954) and in the telefilms "The Affair" (with her husband, Robert Wagner, 1973), "Cat on a Hot Tin Roof" (1979), and "From Here to Eternity" (1979).

On November 19, 1981, Natalie Wood drowned in a boating accident off Catalina Island. The circumstances surrounding her death have been shrouded in controversy ever since. She was the third of the three stars of *Rebel Without a Cause* to die a mysterious, premature death.

> "When Dean acts, he really throws everything into it. . . . I had bruises on my arms to prove it."
>
> Natalie Wood

BILL WOODS
One of the makeup men on *Giant*.

JOANNE WOODWARD
> "You kind of feel like a prizefighter trying to dodge the blows. And working with Jimmy was like that. I was fond of him, but he made me feel uncomfortable, as Marlon always did."
>
> Joanne Woodward, *New York*, November 8, 1976

Elia Kazan's second choice for the role of Abra, James Dean's love interest in *East of Eden*, was Joanne Woodward. Woodward was actually screen-tested for the part. Shot was the Ferris wheel scene, which, as played by James Dean and Joanne Woodward, was far more passionate than the one subsequently played by Dean and Julie Harris. Interestingly, Woodward's future husband, Paul Newman, was Kazan's second choice for the role of Aron Trask, Abra's other love interest in the picture. Also of interest, Woodward was considered for the role of Luz Benedict II in *Giant*, which eventually went to Carroll Baker.

FRANK WORTH
Photographer who once took a photo of Jimmy crouching down, from the back, in which the top of his underwear was exposed from underneath his blue jeans. According to Frank Worth, Jimmy objected to the shot. After Dean's death Worth penned an article for *Sixteen* magazine entitled "Jimmy Told Me: Don't Print That Photo!" Accompanying the article was a reproduction of the hardly controversial photograph.

JOHN WRIGHT
At the time of his death James Dean was planning to star in a screen biography of Billy the Kid. He was collaborating on the project with television writer John Wright.

THE WRITERS
The Writers of TV Shows That Dean Appeared In

TELEWRITER	TV SHOW	YEAR
Arthur Arent	"The Thief"	1955
Walter C. Brown	"The Unlighted Road"	1955
E. P. Conkle	"Prologue to Glory"	1952
John Drinkwater	"Abraham Lincoln"	1952
Frank Gregory	"Death Is My Neighbor"	1953
Sam Hall	"Run Like a Thief"	1954
Earl Hamner	"The Kate Smith Show"	1953
George Roy Hill	"Keep Our Honor Bright"	1953
J. Albert Hirsch	"The Foggy, Foggy Dew"	1952
William Inge	"Glory in Flower"	1953
George Lowther	"The Bells of Cockaigne"	1953
Sandra Michael	"Harvest"	1953
Worthington Minor	"Ten Thousand Horses Singing"	1952
S. Lee Pogostin	"Something for an Empty Briefcase"	1953
Arnold Schulman	"I'm a Fool"	1954
Joe Scully	"The Little Woman"	1954
Rod Serling	"A Long Time Till Dawn"	1953
Adrian Spies	"Sentence of Death"	1953
Manya Starr	"The Evil Within"	1953
Arthur Steuer	"The Dark, Dark Hour"	1954
Thomas Walsh	"Sentence of Death"	1953

The Writers of Plays That Dean Appeared In

PLAYWRIGHT	PLAY	YEAR
Ruth and Augustus Goetz	*The Immoralist*	1954
Percy MacKaye	*The Scarecrow*	1953
N. Richard Nash	*See the Jaguar*	1952
Ezra Pound	*Women of Trachis*	1954

The Writers of Movies That Dean Starred In

SCREENWRITER	MOVIE	YEAR
Fred Guiol	*Giant*	1956
Ivan Moffat	*Giant*	1956
Paul Osborn	*East of Eden*	1955
Stewart Stern	*Rebel Without a Cause*	1955

The Writers of Books, Plays, or Other Source Material That Became a TV Program, Play, or Movie That Dean Appeared In

WRITER	TV PROGRAM, PLAY, OR MOVIE	YEAR
Sherwood Anderson	"I'm a Fool"	1954
Henri Bernstein	"The Thief"	1955
Robert Carson	"Ten Thousand Horses Singing"	1952
Edna Ferber	*Giant*	1956
Andre Gide	*The Immoralist*	1954
Nicholas Ray	*Rebel Without a Cause*	1955
Sophocles	*Women of Trachis*	1954
John Steinbeck	*East of Eden*	1955

The Writers of TV Movies or Specials About Dean

TELEWRITER	TV MOVIE OR SPECIAL	YEAR
William Bast	"James Dean"	1976
Ara Chekmayan	"Forever James Dean"	1988
Al Ramrus	"James Dean Remembered"	1974

The Writers of Plays About or Inspired by Dean

PLAYWRIGHT	PLAY	YEAR
Ed Graczyk	*Come Back to the Five and Dime, Jimmy Dean, Jimmy Dean*	1982
John Howlett	*Dean*	1977
Patricia Leone	*James Dean: A Dress Rehearsal*	1984

The Writers of Movies About or Inspired by Dean

SCREENWRITER	MOVIE	YEAR
James Bridges	*September 30, 1955*	1977
Ray Connolly	*James Dean: The First American Teenager*	1976
Ed Gracyzk	*Come Back to the Five and Dime, Jimmy Dean, Jimmy Dean*	1982
Claudio Masenza	*Hollywood: The Rebel James Dean*	*
Stewart Stern	*The James Dean Story*	1957

---

*Not released theatrically

WRITING

James Dean's ultimate goal was to become a writer. As he related to Hedda Hopper:

"Acting is wonderful and immediately satisfying, but it is not the be-all end-all of my existence. My talents lie in directing and, beyond that, my great fear is writing. That's the God. I can't apply the seat of my pants right now. I'm too youthful and silly. I must have some age. I'm in great awe of writing and fearful of it . . . but some day."

ROLF WÜTHERICH

Contrary to legend, James Dean was *not* alone in his Porsche on the afternoon of September 30, 1955. He was accompanied by Rolf Wütherich, his 28-year-old German mechanic. Dean was killed; Wütherich was thrown from the car, seriously injured. He spent a year in the hospital; emotionally he was scarred for life.

It was Wütherich who, on September 19, 1955, introduced James Dean to the Porsche Spyder. Dean purchased the low-slung speed machine with the stipulation that Wütherich personally service it for each race and that he accompany him to Salinas.

Two years later Wütherich wrote an article for *Modern Screen* magazine entitled "Death Drive." It read, in part:

A 1950 model Ford was coming at us. Suddenly, the car swung out toward the center of the highway to turn onto Highway 41, its left wheels over the center line. Then we hit. My head slammed against the dashboard, and my body was thrown out of the car, yards down the highway. I passed out instantly.

Dimly I remember being lifted by the ambulance workers. I came to in the ambulance. Then I thought, "Jimmy! Where was Jimmy? What had happened to him?" I saw him as though I were looking through a leaden haze. There he was—my friend Jimmy—lying limp, covered with blood, bones fractured, neck broken. He was beyond help—anyone's help.

Again and again, during the months I lay in the hospital, I tormented my memory to recall those few seconds before Jimmy's death. Was there an instant before he died when he knew he was dying . . . Did he know pain . . . I do not know. The only thing I can remember is the soft cry that escaped from Jimmy . . . the little whimpering cry of a boy wanting his mother . . . or of a man facing his God.

Over the years there has been speculation that it was Wütherich who was driving the Porsche at the time of the accident and not Dean. In fact, at the coroner's hearing, two witnesses, Tom Frederick and Don Dooley, suggested that the man in the white T-shirt (Dean) had *not* been driving the car, that it had actually been the man in the red T-shirt (Wütherich). The matter got so complicated that one confused juror protested, "How are we supposed to know who had a white T-shirt on and who had a red one on?" Curiously, however, the entire matter was dismissed by the district attorney, who instructed the jurors, "You know as much as we do on it. This court is interested first in who is the deceased person and how he came to his death. It is not really material who had a white T-shirt on. . . ." So, a ruling was never actually made as to who was driving the Porsche. From his hospital bed Rolf Wütherich insisted that Dean had been driving the Porsche, and that, despite the controversy, is generally regarded as fact.

Wütherich later filed unsuccessful lawsuits against the Dean estate and against the driver of the other vehicle, Donald Turnupseed. In his court documents against the latter Wütherich charged "the Defendant has no good defense to this action; accident was proximately caused by his negligence." However, as was the case with his earlier suit, against the Dean estate, Wütherich's court action was dismissed because it had not been filed in the required span of time.

Wütherich later returned to West Germany and reportedly was committed to a psychiatric hospital. As fate would have it, he was killed in a traffic accident on July 28, 1981, at the age of 53.

KEENAN WYNN
On Thanksgiving Day 1954 Keenan Wynn and his wife hosted a dinner party in their Hollywood home. In attendance were Rod Steiger, Ralph Meeker, Arthur Loew, Jr., Jim Backus, and James Dean, among others. On another occasion Wynn instructed Jimmy Dean how to go hill climbing—on his motorcycle.

DIANE WYNTERS
In April 1955 James Dean dined at the Villa Capri with British actress (and Hollywood newcomer) Diane Wynters. They were seen, by at least one observant reporter, holding hands.

Y

STEVE YEAGER
Compiled the discography published in *James Dean: The Mutant King* (1974).

YMCA
When he first moved to New York City at the end of 1951, Jimmy Dean lived in a room at the YMCA (address: 5 West 63rd Street).

"YOU ARE THERE"
Television series that was broadcast on Sunday nights on CBS from February 1953 until October 1957. The show, hosted by Walter Cronkite, featured reenactments of historical events.

On his 22nd birthday, February 8, 1953, James Dean starred in an episode of "You Are There" entitled "The Capture of Jesse James." He portrayed Bob Ford, the man who shot Jesse James.

YOU CAN'T TAKE IT WITH YOU
George S. Kaufman play that was presented by Fairmount (Indiana) High School in April 1949. FHS senior Jimmy Dean had a starring role.

"YOU GOTTA STAY HAPPY"
Nineteen forty-eight story written by Robert Carson that was later adapted into "Ten Thousand Horses Singing," a 1952 episode of the CBS television program "Studio One" in which unknown actor James Dean had a bit part.

GIG YOUNG
Actor who interviewed James Dean in a September 1955 television commercial for the National Safety Council. Young also hosted the "Warner Brothers Presents" promotional episode for *Rebel Without a Cause*, which aired after Dean's death in October 1955.

Gig Young, born Byron Barr in Minnesota in 1913, appeared in numerous films including *Misbehaving Husbands* (1940), *The Gay Sisters* (in which he portrayed a character named Gig Young, hence his name change, 1942), *The Three Musketeers* (1948), *Teacher's Pet* (Best Supporting Actor Oscar nomination, 1958), *They Shoot Horses, Don't They?* (Best Supporting Actor Oscar winner, 1969), and *Lovers and Other Strangers* (1970). On television Young co-starred in the short-lived programs "The Rogues" (1964–1965) and "Gibbsville" (1976).

In 1978 Young, an alcoholic, married his fourth wife, Kim Schmidt (his earlier marriages included Elizabeth Montgomery, 1956–1963). A few weeks later he killed his new wife, and then himself, with a .38 revolver.

"YOU'RE TEARING ME APART"
Radio documentary about Dean produced in Great Britain.

MICHAEL YUDIN
Executive producer of the 1988 cable television documentary "Forever James Dean."

Z

EARL ZETSCHE

While driving to a *Giant* location in Marfa, Texas, during the summer of 1955, James Dean noticed a car that had skidded off the highway into a ditch. He pulled over, checked out the injured driver, and summoned an ambulance. The following Sunday, Reverend Earl Zetsche, the local pastor, said a prayer of thanks to James Dean for saving the life of the young driver.

The Warner Brothers publicity department later issued the following release:

> Nobody on the *Giant* company knew about James Dean's service to a negro boy until Dean was specially cited by the Reverend Earl Zetsche of the First Christian Church in Marfa, Texas during his Sunday sermon. Zetsche complimented Dean for his Christian brotherhood in standing over a negro boy, critically injured in an automobile accident, for a half hour to protect him from the hot sun until an ambulance arrived.

ZIEGFELD THEATRE

James Dean auditioned for a part in *The Immoralist* in producer Billy Rose's office, which was located on the top floor of the Ziegfeld Theatre in New York City (address: 141 West 54th Street). Later, rehearsals for the play were also held at the Ziegfeld, which was owned by Rose. Since then the Ziegfeld has been converted into a movie theater.

WILLIAM ZIEGLER
Editor of *Rebel Without a Cause*.

William Ziegler also edited *The Housekeeper's Daughter* (1939), *Strangers on a Train* (1951), *Auntie Mame* (Oscar nomination, 1958), *The Music Man* (Oscar nomination, 1962), *My Fair Lady* (Oscar nomination, 1964), and *The Omega Man* (1971).

ZINA GLAD'S MARION COLLEGE OF DANCE AND THEATRICAL ARTS
At the age of five Jimmy Dean was enrolled by his mother into Zina Glad's Marion College of Dance and Theatrical Arts. It was there that James Dean was given his introduction to the theater.

WILLIAM ZINSSER
Film critic for the New York *Herald Tribune* who, in his review of *East of Eden*, gave one of the earliest and best summations of James Dean and his screen appeal:

> Everything about Dean suggests the lonely misunderstood nineteen-year-old. Even from a distance you know a lot about him by the way he walks—with his hands in his pockets and his head down, slinking like a dog waiting for a bone. When he talks, he stammers and pauses, uncertain of what he is trying to say. When he listens, he is full of restless energy—he stretches, he rolls on the ground, he chins himself on the porch railing like a small boy impatient of his elders' chatter . . . occasionally he smiles unaccountably, as if at some dark joke known only to him. . . . You sense the badness in him. But you also like him.

MAURICE ZOLOTOW
Maurice Zolotow, an excellent writer, was one of James Dean's harshest and most vocal critics. In October 1956 Zolotow penned an article for the *Omaha Sunday World Herald* entitled "Jimmy Dean Should Be Nobody's Idol—Late Actor Was Sadistic, Uncouth, Arrogant, Cruel and a Filthy Slob." The article, which berated Dean as "emotionally immature," "sexually sadistic," and "a second-rate actor," read, in part:

> He was surly, ill-tempered, brutal, without any element of kindness, sensitivity, consideration for others, or romantic passion. He was physically dirty. He hated to bathe, have his hair cut, shave, or put on clean clothes. He smelled so rankly that actresses working in close contact with him found him unbearable.

Maurice Zolotow was born in New York City in 1913. He has authored such books as *Never Whistle in a Dressing Room* (1944), *The Great Balsamo* (1946), *No People Like Show People* (1951), *Marilyn Monroe* (1960), *Stagestruck: The Romance of Alfred Lunt and Lynn Fontanne* (1965), *Shooting Star: A Biography of John Wayne* (1974), and *Billy Wilder in Hollywood* (1977).

A SELECTED BIBLIOGRAPHY

BOOKS

Adams, Cindy. *Lee Strasberg: The Imperfect Genius of the Actor's Studio.* New York: Doubleday and Co., 1980.

Adams, Leith, and Keith Burns (eds.). *James Dean: Behind the Scene.* New York: Birch Lane Press, 1990.

Backus, Jim. *Rocks on the Roof.* New York: G. P. Putnam's Sons, 1958.

Baker, Carroll. *Baby Doll.* New York: Arbor House, 1983.

Bast, William. *James Dean.* New York: Ballantine, 1956.

Beath, Warren Newton. *The Death of James Dean.* New York: Grove Press, 1986.

Blum, Daniel. *Theatre World 1953–54, 1954–55.*

Collins, Joan. *Past Imperfect.* New York: Simon & Schuster, 1984.

Dalton, David. *James Dean: The Mutant King.* Coronado, California: Straight Arrow Books, 1974.

——, and Ron Cayen. *James Dean: American Icon.* New York: St. Martin's Press, 1984.

Garfield, David. *A Player's Place.* New York: Macmillan Publishing, 1980.

Herndon, Venable. *James Dean: A Short Life.* New York: Doubleday and Co., 1974.

Hopper, Hedda, with James Brough. *The Whole Truth and Nothing But.* New York: Doubleday and Co., 1963.

Howlett, John. *James Dean: A Biography.* London: Plexus Publishing, 1975.

Hyams, Joe. *Mislaid in Hollywood.* New York: Peter H. Wyden, 1973.

Kazan, Elia. *Kazan: A Life.* New York: Alfred A. Knopf, 1988.

Kreidl, John Francis. *Nicholas Ray.* Boston: Twayne, 1977.

Martinetti, Ronald. *The James Dean Story.* New York: Pinnacle, 1975.

McCambridge, Mercedes. *The Quality of Mercy.* New York: Times Books, 1981.

McNeil, Alex. *Total Television.* London: Penguin, 1980.

Parish, James Robert. *Actors Television Credits.* Toronto: Scarecrow Press, 1973.

Schatt, Roy. *James Dean: A Portrait.* New York: Delilah, 1982.

Steen, Mike. *Hollywood Speaks: An Oral History.* New York: G. P. Putnam's Sons, 1974.

Stock, Dennis. *James Dean Revisited.* New York: Viking Press, 1978.

ARTICLES

Adams, Val. "Tribute to Actor Starts TV 'War,' " *New York Times*, October 4, 1956.

Bluttman, Susan. "Rediscovering James Dean: The TV Legacy," *Emmy*, October 1990.

Breen, Ed. "James Dean's Indiana," *Traces*, fall 1989.

Capote, Truman. "The Duke in His Domain," *The New Yorker*, November 9, 1957.

Dean, Emma. "The Boy I Loved," *Photoplay*, March 1956.

Ferrell, David. "Car Customizer Shifts Gears to Personal Project," *Los Angeles Times*, October 30, 1989.

Goodman, Ezra. "Delirium Over Dead Star," *Life*, September 24, 1956.

Hendrickson, Paul. "Remembering James Dean Back Home in Indiana," *Los Angeles Times*, July 22, 1973.

Hopper, Hedda. "Keep Your Eye on James Dean," *Chicago Tribune Magazine*, March 27, 1955.

Marlowe, Derek. "Soliloquy on James Dean's 45th Birthday," *New York*, November 8, 1976.

Matthews, Lou. "Highway 46 Revisited," *LA Weekly*, September 27, 1985.

McCarthy, Jim. "It's Me, Jimmy . . . ," *Modern Screen*, December 1956.

Moore, Richard. "Lone Wolf," *Modern Screen*, August 1955.

Nall, Adeline (as told to Val Holley). "Grant County's Own," *Traces*, fall 1989.

Owen, Gene Nielson. "The Man Who Would Be 50: A Memory of James Dean," *Los Angeles Times*, February 8, 1981.

Pearlman, Cindy L. "James Dean: Alive on Campus," *Campus U.S.A.*, spring 1988.

Raskin, Lee. "Little Bastard: The Search for James Dean's Spyder," *Porsche Panorama*, July 1984.

Shaw, Bill. "Dead 25 Years, James Dean Is Given a Touching Hometown Tribute by Nostalgic Fans," *People*, October 13, 1980.

Sheridan, Dizzy. "In Memory of Jimmy," *Photoplay*, October 1957.

Taylor, Clarke. "Elia Kazan Ponders the Dean Image," *Los Angeles Times*, September 30, 1985.

Thompson, Howard. "Another Dean Hits the Big League," *New York Times*, March 13, 1955.

Von Wiedenman, Donald. "NBC to Air 'Portrait' of Dean," *The Advocate*, February 25, 1976.

Yates, Brock. "Far from Eden," *Car and Driver*, October 1985.

Zahn, Debra. "James Dean: Rebel with an Agent," *Los Angeles Times*, September 29, 1985.

Zavatsky, William. "Epitaph for a Rebel," *Rolling Stone*, October 16, 1980.

DOCUMENTARIES

"Forever James Dean," 1988.

Hollywood: The Rebel James Dean, no theatrical release date.

The James Dean Story, 1957.

"James Dean Remembered," 1974.

James Dean: The First American Teenager, 1976.

"Entertainment Tonight: The Legend That Won't Die," 1985.

"Show Biz Today," CNN, 1985.

SOURCES

A

"I have made great strides in my craft . . .": Reprinted in several books including *James Dean* by Bill Bast and *James Dean: A Short Life* by Venable Herndon.

"It seemed simple . . .": *A Player's Place* by David Garfield.

"[Dean sat] in a sort of poutish mess . . .": *A Player's Place* by David Garfield.

"I got cast in *Rebel* . . .": Raw footage from CNN interview for the television program "Show Biz Today."

"Jimmy come by my house . . .": *Mislaid in Hollywood* by Joe Hyams.

"[When] I was introduced . . .": *James Dean: The First American Teenager* (documentary, 1976).

"No one mourned his death . . .": *The Hollywood Reporter*, October 1955.

"I could hear what went on . . .": *Kazan: A Life* by Elia Kazan.

"I figure that when I went back . . .": Reprinted in *James Dean: The Mutant King* by David Dalton.

"Jimmy is the only man . . .": Reprinted in *James Dean: The Mutant King* by David Dalton.

B

"He wasn't too coachable . . .": *The James Dean Story* (documentary 1957).

"When I first met him . . .": "A Tribute to James Dean" sponsored by the Academy of Motion Picture Arts and Sciences, 1983.

"In real life, [Jimmy] was not . . .": *The Advocate*, February 25, 1976.

"[Jimmy] was cocky and arrogant . . .": "Entertainment Tonight," "The Legend That Won't Die," September 1985.

"[Stewart Sutcliffe] was really our leader . . .": Reprinted in *James Dean: The Way It Was* by Terry Cunningham.

"He would be at parties . . .": *James Dean: The First American Teenager* (documentary, 1976).

"I think reading was probably . . .": *James Dean: The First American Teenager* (documentary, 1976).

"He was dead and gross examination . . .": From the transcript of the coroner's inquest.

"He said, 'We have to get married.'. . .": "A Current Affair," May 1989.

"My primary interest in Jimmy . . .": *The James Dean Story* by Ron Martinetti.

"It was a question of marrying . . .": *Continuity and Evolution in a Public Symbol: An Investigation into the Creation and Communication of the James Dean Image in Mid-Century America* by Robert Wayne Tysl.

"When I finally met Dean . . .": *The New Yorker*, November 9, 1957.

"Acting has absolutely nothing to do . . .": *Los Angeles* magazine, March 1989.

"I have often thought . . .": *TV Guide*, April 19, 1986.

"He wrote me how he loved . . .": *Modern Screen*, December 1956.

C

"I didn't think very much of him . . .": *Conversations with Capote* by Lawrence Grobel.

"In those final days . . .": *Los Angeles Times*, July 22, 1973.

"I've been a joke . . .": *Interview* magazine, May 1982.

"I never liked myself . . .": *Parade*, May 19, 1985.

"He's a punk and a helluva talent . . .": *Montgomery Clift* by Patricia Bosworth.

"Jimmy used to call Monty Clift . . .": *James Dean: A Biography* by John Howlett.

"My theory is never stand . . .": *TV Guide*, January 25, 1986.

"Intense, moody, incredible charisma . . .": *Playboy* magazine, June 4, 1990.

"[Jimmy] had a collection of the worst jokes . . .": "A Tribute to James Dean," Academy of Motion Picture Arts and Sciences, 1983.

"[Dean's] death caused a loss . . .": *James Dean: The Way It Was* by Terry Cunningham.

"Jimmy fell completely . . .": *James Dean* by William Bast.

"As a human being . . .": *Lee Strasberg: The Imperfect Genius of the Actors Studio* by Cindy Adams.

"Jimmy Dean, he was a good boy . . .": *Santa Monica Outlook*, November 10, 1989.

D

"Jimmy was a cute . . .": *Hollywood: The Rebel James Dean* (documentary).

"I'd say that James Dean . . .": *Campus USA*, Spring 1988.

"He was nobody's . . .": *Campus USA*, Spring 1988.

"He had a lot of pep . . .": CNN interview, 1985.

"There was a genius quality . . .": CNN interview, 1985.

"I never knew him . . .": *Movieland*, February 1957.

"He was real upset . . .": *Santa Monica Outlook*, November 10, 1989.

"I thought he was pretty much . . .": *Modern Screen*, March 1957.

"He sapped the minds . . .": *James Dean* by William Bast.

"He looked hungry . . .": *Photoplay*, October 1957.

"We didn't wire Jimmy money . . .": *Chicago Tribune*, September 9, 1956.

"I was typing in an office . . .": *James Dean: The First American Teenager* (documentary, 1976).

"He was so unhappy . . .": *Photoplay*, October 1957.

"He could look in a delicatessen . . .": *Whisper*, August 1956.

"He was a boy . . .": *The James Dean Story* (documentary, 1957).

"**He was a sad-faced, introverted . . .**": *Lee Strasberg: The Imperfect Genius* by Cindy Adams.

"**His existence seemed so . . .**": *Shelley: Also Known as Shirley* by Shelley Winters.

"**He didn't comb his . . .**": *Wish You Were Here, Jimmy Dean* by Martin Dawber.

"**He was very beguiling . . .**": *Hollywood: The Rebel James Dean* (documentary).

"**The latest genius . . .**": *The Whole Truth and Nothing But* by Hedda Hopper.

"**Jim knew how to *play* . . .**": *James Dean: American Icon* by David Dalton and Ron Cayen.

"**He just reminded me . . .**": *Forever James Dean* (documentary, 1988).

"**He was so twisted . . .**": *James Dean: A Short Life* by Venable Herndon.

"**He would be bothered . . .**": *The James Dean Story* (documentary, 1957).

"**When I worked with . . .**": Reprinted in *James Dean: In His Own Words* by Mick St. Michael.

"**I have a great respect . . .**": Reprinted in *Wish You Were Here, Jimmy Dean* by Martin Dawber.

"**This boy's pretty smart . . .**": *Los Angeles Mirror-News*, March 11, 1955.

"**I was walking down the hallway . . .**": CNN interview, 1985.

"**There were mornings . . .**": "James Dean Remembered," (documentary, 1974).

"**He was so inspiring . . .**": *James Dean: A Biography* by John Howlett.

"**The most exciting young talent . . .**": Warner Brothers press release, 1955.

"**I used to tell people . . .**": Warner Brothers press release, 1955.

"**I was terrified . . .**": "James Dean Remembered," (documentary, 1974).

"**He didn't show you much . . .**": *Hollywood Speaks: An Oral History* by Mike Steen.

"**I think that he really . . .**": "James Dean Remembered," (documentary, 1974).

"**I hadn't seen the rushes . . .**": *James Dean: A Biography* by John Howlett.

"**Jimmy had, in my estimation . . .**": *James Dean: The First American Teenager* (documentary, 1976).

"**He would all of a sudden . . .**": *The James Dean Story* (documentary, 1957).

"**George Stevens, master editor . . .**": *The Quality of Mercy* by Mercedes McCambridge.

"**Dean wanted success badly . . .**": The *New York World-Telegram*, November 3, 1956.

"**He wasn't easy to know . . .**": *Collier's*, November 25, 1955.

"**He had the enthusiasm . . .**": We Remember Dean International memorial tribute, 1985.

"**He died at just the right . . .**": *Life*, September 24, 1956.

"**He seemed to come into . . .**": *Variety*, October 3, 1955.

"**There is no part of Jimmy . . .**": *Modern Screen*, January 1956.
"**James Dean's death . . .**": *Montgomery Clift* by Patricia Bosworth.
"**One felt that he was a boy . . .**": Reprinted in *Wish You Were Here, Jimmy Dean* by Martin Dawber.
"**I liken it to a kind of star . . .**": "Forever James Dean," (documentary, 1988).
"**He was the loneliest man . . .**": *Anything Goes.*
"**People were robbed . . .**": CNN interview, 1985.
"**Dean was withdrawn . . .**": *Hollywood Babylon II* by Kenneth Anger.
"**the damaged but beautiful soul . . .**": *Andy Warhol's Interview.*
"**James Dean was more . . .**": *Hollywood in a Suitcase* by Sammy Davis, Jr.
"**His film career was one . . .**": "A Tribute to James Dean," sponsored by the Academy of Motion Picture Arts and Sciences, 1983.
"**All of us were touched . . .**": "James Dean Remembered," (documentary, 1974).
"**We are as caught up . . .**": *The New Yorker.*
"**He seemed to capture . . .**": CNN interview, 1985.
"**Jimmy Dean started . . .**": *James Dean: The First American Teenager* (documentary, 1976).
"**I'll be damned . . .**": *Los Angeles Times*, September 30, 1985.
"**I wish everybody . . .**": *Photoplay*, October 1957.
"**You would have thought . . .**": *James Dean: The Way It Was* by Terry Cunningham.
"**I've often wondered . . .**": The *Marion Chronicle-Tribune*, September 1985.
"**Oh, God . . .**": *Los Angeles Times*, February 16, 1976.
"**I've directed eight pictures . . .**": Warner Brothers press release, 1955.
"**I heard her say . . .**": CNN interview, 1985.
"**Obviously, there was a strong tension . . .**": *Kazan: A Life* by Elia Kazan.
"**He had to think of it . . .**": "A Current Affair" interview, 1989.
"**I think he saw death . . .**": "A Current Affair" interview, 1989.
"**He had a death cloud . . .**": *Los Angeles Times*, October 30, 1989.

E
"**Jimmy's got to get . . .**": *A Hundred Different Lives* by Raymond Massey.
"**[Ray] simply couldn't stand the sight . . .**": *Kazan: A Life* by Elia Kazan.
"**We began to suspect . . .**": *James Dean: A Biography* by John Howlett.
"**the fact he had no . . .**": *Emmy*, October 1990.
"**He wore these thick glasses . . .**": *Campus USA*, Spring 1988.
"**[Off screen] he had these pale . . .**": *New York*, November 8, 1976.
"**What I remember most . . .**": *Chicago's American*, October 3, 1955.

F
"**After all the years . . .**": *James Dean* by William Bast.
"**Man, the minute I get . . .**": *Modern Screen*, December 1956.
"**Jimmy told none . . .**": *James Dean: The Way It Was* by Terry Cunningham.

G

"I can still remember . . .": Warner Brothers press release.

"George Stevens, for my money . . .": Warner Brothers press release.

"He blamed everything . . .": *James Dean: American Icon* by David Dalton and Ron Cayen.

"I don't know how . . .": CNN interview, 1985.

"was of the opinion that aging Jimmy . . .": The George Stevens Collection, the Academy of Motion Picture Arts and Sciences.

"It is imperative . . .": The George Stevens Collection, the Academy of Motion Picture Arts and Sciences.

"People simply cannot . . .": *New York World-Telegram and Sun.*

"The passing of James Dean . . .": The George Stevens Collection, the Academy of Motion Picture Arts and Sciences.

"He had a terrible attitude . . .": *Emmy,* October 1990.

"The little son-of-a-bitch . . .": *James Dean: A Short Life* by Venable Herndon.

H

"The great one in that picture . . .": *James Dean: A Biography* by John Howlett.

"I doubt that Jimmy . . .": *Kazan: A Life* by Elia Kazan.

"He was a very brilliant . . .": We Remember Dean International memorial tribute, 1985.

"You've got to treat . . .": *Baby Doll* by Carroll Baker.

I

"He was abominable . . .": Hollywood: *The Rebel James Dean* (documentary).

"He played that scene . . .": *Rocks on the Roof* by Jim Backus.

K

"Kazan asked me . . .": Warner Brothers press release.

"By the time the picture . . .": Warner Brothers press release.

"Dean is a wonderful . . .": *Los Angeles Times,* July 1954.

"The film was a success . . .": *Los Angeles Times,* September 30, 1985.

L

"It was a fairly humiliating experience . . .": "A Tribute to James Dean," the Academy of Motion Picture Arts and Sciences, 1983.

"No! No, sir! . . .": *Modern Screen,* December 1956.

"Although [they were] total opposites . . .": *Past Imperfect* by Joan Collins.

"Wherever she went . . .": *Emmy,* October, 1990.

M

"the most dreadful Indiana accent . . .": *Hollywood: The Rebel James Dean,* (documentary).

"Try to be a good actor . . .": *Modern Screen,* December 1956.

N

"We used to squabble . . .": *Los Angeles Times,* 1973.

"He was thoughtful about the little things . . .": *Motion Picture,* September 1955.

"You know, you're a lucky bastard . . .": *James Dean* by William Bast.

O

"It is one of the best . . .": Warner Brothers Archives, University of Southern California.

"I told him that . . .": *Movieland,* February 1957.

P

"all seen *Rebel* . . .": *The Real Paper.*

"They [Hollywood's powerful] get these poor young kids . . .": *James Dean* by William Bast.

"I was told by Nick Ray . . .": *The Unimportance of Being Oscar* by Oscar Levant.

Q

"My father was a farmer . . .": *New York Times,* March 13, 1955.

"My mother died . . .": *Rolling Stone,* October 16, 1980.

"Studying cows . . .": Warner Brothers press release.

"When a new actor . . .": Associated Press.

"In a certain sense . . .": *Modern Screen.*

"It was an accident . . .": *New York Times,* March 13, 1955.

"This [tree] is the largest . . .": *The Hollywood Reporter.*

"This cat doesn't . . .": *Photoplay,* July 1955.

"No, I didn't read . . .": *New York Times,* March 13, 1955.

"I'm a serious-minded . . .": *Los Angeles Times,* 1954.

"This gift astonishes me. . . .": *Chicago Tribune Magazine,* March 27, 1955.

"Why don't you give . . .": *Modern Screen,* August 1955.

"Since I'm only 24 . . .": Warner Brothers press release.

"Maybe publicity *is* . . .": *Modern Screen,* August 1955.

"Naturally, I shall always . . .": Warner Brothers press release.

"Isn't this pushing realism . . .": *Los Angeles Examiner,* May 22, 1955.

"The thing that interested . . .": *Rolling Stone,* June 20, 1974.

"Some day I would . . .": Warner Brothers press release.

"I hate anything . . .": *Los Angeles Times,* 1954.

"Since juvenile delinquency . . .": *Los Angeles Mirror-News,* June 1955.

"It was well worth . . .": Warner Brothers press release.

"I felt very honored . . .": Warner Brothers press release.

"With so many . . .": Warner Brothers press release.

"My fun days . . .": Warner Brothers press release.

"An actor should thoroughly . . .": Warner Brothers press release.

"A director's notebook . . .": Warner Brothers press release.

"It took me a while . . .": Warner Brothers press release.

"All this business . . .": Warner Brothers press release.

"An actor should know . . .": Warner Brothers press release.

"The gratification . . .": *James Dean* by William Bast.

"I don't think people . . .": United Press International.

"Some of the things . . .": The Valley *Times*, May 5, 1955.

"One of the deepest . . .": *The Hollywood Reporter*.

"Take a good look . . .": *Picturegoer*, December 29, 1956.

"So long, I think . . .": *Modern Screen*, January 1956.

R

"My name is Nick . . .": Warner Brothers Archives, University of Southern California.

"I thought the material . . .": Warner Brothers Archives, University of Southern California.

"By seven o'clock . . .": Warner Brothers Archives, University of Southern California.

"seventeen or eighteen . . .": Warner Brothers Archives, University of Southern California.

"should look a little . . .": Warner Brothers Archives, University of Southern California.

"the most talented young actress . . .": Warner Brothers press release.

"It looks as though . . .": Warner Brothers Archives, University of Southern California.

"Nick Ray should lose . . .": Warner Brothers Archives, University of Southern California.

"[Jimmy] was in a period . . .": *James Dean: The First American Teenager* (documentary, 1976).

"Dean walked into . . .": Warner Brothers press release.

"After he got established . . .": *Photoplay*, October 1957.

"Now that I am . . .": *Photoplay*, October 1957.

"I wanted the role . . .": *Continuity and Evolution in a Public Symbol: An Investigation into the Creation and Communication of the James Dean Image in Mid-Century America* by Robert Wayne Tysl.

"I have a serious thought . . .": The George Stevens Collection, the Academy of Motion Picture Arts and Sciences.

"He used to pose . . .": *Life*, February 10, 1958.

"I arrived at his house . . .": *Hollywood Speaks: An Oral History* by Mike Steen.

"I don't know what happens . . .": *James Dean* by William Bast.

T
"We had an extraordinary . . .": "Good Morning America."
"He was very afraid . . .": "The Today Show."
"I think he loved . . .": "Good Morning America."
"This was a moment . . .": *Picturegoer*, December 29, 1956.
"This son of a bitch . . .": *Emmy*, October 1990.
"This is a fan letter . . .": Warner Brothers Archives, University of Southern California.

W
"Whitmore saw me . . .": Warner Brothers press release.
"Bill, there's something . . .": *James Dean* by William Bast.
"My father was a farmer . . .": *New York Times*, March 13, 1955.
"Now Jimmy, I don't want . . .": *Photoplay*, March 1956.
"We have read where . . .": *The James Dean Story* (documentary, 1957).
"I remember Natalie Wood . . .": CNN interview.
"Jimmy is a very introspective . . .": Warner Brothers press release.
"It's just pulsating . . .": Warner Brothers press release.
"In *Rebel* I wear . . .": Warner Brothers press release.
"When Dean acts . . .": Warner Brothers press release.

PHOTOGRAPH CREDITS

Photograph by Sanford Roth, from the Seita Ohnishi Collection, © 1987 by S. Ohnishi
Pages: xii, 265 (bottom), 394 (top), 457

Photograph by Joseph Abeles
Page: 6

The Steffi Sidney Collection
Pages: 12, 241, 426, 492, 493

The Author's Collection
Pages: 22, 24, 31, 34, 49, 53, 100, 104, 121, 134, 145, 149, 150 (top and bottom), 151 (top and bottom), 153, 164, 173, 180, 204, 206 (right), 220, 233, 237, 249, 257, 259, 264 (top and bottom), 265 (top), 297, 308, 324, 369, 378, 382, 389, 395 (bottom), 400, 410, 417, 428 (top and bottom), 433 (bottom), 470, 478, 519, 541, 569 (bottom), 576, 577, 591

Courtesy of Kenneth Kendall
Pages: 27 (left and right), 483

Courtesy of Ed Lane
Pages: 28 (left and right), 131, 293

The Sylvia Bongiovanni Collection, © Fairmount Historical Museum
Pages: 35, 40, 174

Photograph by Ken Grant
Page: 54

The Sylvia Bongiovanni Collection
Pages: 59, 74, 75, 77 (top), 102, 128, 141, 148, 154, 156, 167 (top), 177, 195, 196, 197, 200 (top and bottom), 206 (left), 209, 215, 217 (left and right), 226, 247, 250, 253, 258, 336 (left and right), 394 (bottom), 413, 421 (top and bottom), 432 (top and bottom), 433 (top), 437, 465 (left and right), 495, 498, 508, 531, 544, 554, 566, 569 (top)

Collectors Book Store
Pages: 64, 87, 94, 96, 203, 315, 330, 360, 402, 516, 537

The Diane Hanville Collection
Pages: 77 (bottom), 352

Courtesy of Maxwell Caulfield
Page: 80

The Fairmount Historical Museum
Pages: 129, 133, 166, 345, 395 (top)

Photographs by Matt DeHaven
Pages: 167 (bottom), 168, 169 (top and bottom), 171, 236, 383, 560

The David Loehr Collection
Pages: 267, 305, 533

Photograph by Kara Knack
Page: 285

Photograph © by Sanofi Beauty Products
Page: 289

Courtesy of Jeannine Tudor
Page: 327

Photographs by Wilson Millar
Pages: 334 (all)

Photograph by Nelva Jean Thomas, Courtesy of the Fairmount Historical Museum
Page: 344

Photograph © 1990 by Straight Arrow Publishers, Inc. All rights reserved. Reprinted by permission.
Page: 362

The Academy of Motion Picture Arts & Sciences
Pages: 374, 548

Courtesy of Betsy Palmer
Page: 381

The Bill Dakota Collection
Page: 496

Photograph by Maxine Rowland
Page: 562

HEDDA HOPPER: "You've got a long and beautiful life ahead of you."
JAMES DEAN: "I hope the second adjective is the more abundant."
Hollywood, March 1955